A-Z DEVON

CW00506836

Key to Map Pages	2-5
Large Scale Exeter City Centre	6-7
Large Scale Plymouth City Centre	8-9
Map Pages	10-159
Large [...]	[...]4
Road [...]	[...]6
Index [...]	[...]8
Index [...]	[...]0

REFERENCE

Motorway	M5	Airport		✈
Primary Route	A30	Car Park (selected)		P
A Road	A3052	Church or Chapel		†
B Road	B3212	City Wall (Large Scale only)		⌂⌂⌂⌂⌂
Dual Carriageway		Cycleway (selected)		🚲
One-way Street		Fire Station		■
Traffic flow on A Roads is also indicated by a heavy line on the driver's left.		Hospital		Ⓗ
Road Under Construction		House Numbers (A & B Roads only)		136 / 87
Opening dates are correct at the time of publication.		Information Centre		𝒊
Proposed Road		National Grid Reference		³25
Restricted Access		Park and Ride		Honiton Road P+R
Pedestrianized Road		Police Station		▲
Track / Footpath		Post Office		★
Residential Walkway		Safety Camera with Speed Limit		㉚
Railway	Station / Heritage Station / Level Crossing / Tunnel	Fixed cameras and long term road works cameras. Symbols do not indicate camera direction.		
Tramway	Stop	Toilet		▽
		Viewpoint		☀ 🔆
Built-up Area	WESTERN WAY	Educational Establishment		▢
Beach		Hospital or Healthcare Building		▢
Local Authority Boundary		Industrial Building		▢
National Park Boundary		Leisure or Recreational Facility		▢
Post Town Boundary		Place of Interest		▷
Postcode Boundary (within Post Town)		Public Building		▢
		Shopping Centre or Market		▢
Map Continuation	20 / Large Scale Centres 8 / Road Map Pages 160	Other Selected Buildings		▢

SCALE

Map Pages 6-9 & 124 (inset)	Map Pages 10-159
1:8,448 7½ inches (19.05cm) to 1mile 11.8cm to 1km	1:16,896 3¾ inches (9.52cm) to 1mile 5.9cm to 1km
0 — ⅛ — ¼ Mile	0 — ¼ — ½ Mile
0 — 100 — 200 — 300 — 400 Metres	0 — 250 — 500 — 750 Metres

EDITION 4   2019
Copyright © Geographers' A-Z Map Co. Ltd.

© Crown copyright and database rights 2019 OS 100017302.

Safety camera information supplied by www.PocketGPSWorld.com
Speed Camera Location Database Copyright 2019 © PocketGPSWorld.com

A-Z AZ AtoZ
registered trade marks of
Geographers' A-Z Map Company Ltd

www./az.co.uk

KEY TO MAP PAGES

North Section

SCALE

```
0   1   2   3   4   5   6 Miles
0 1 2 3 4 5 6 7 8 9 10 Kms
```

Devon County Boundary — ·· — ·· —
National Park Boundary ————

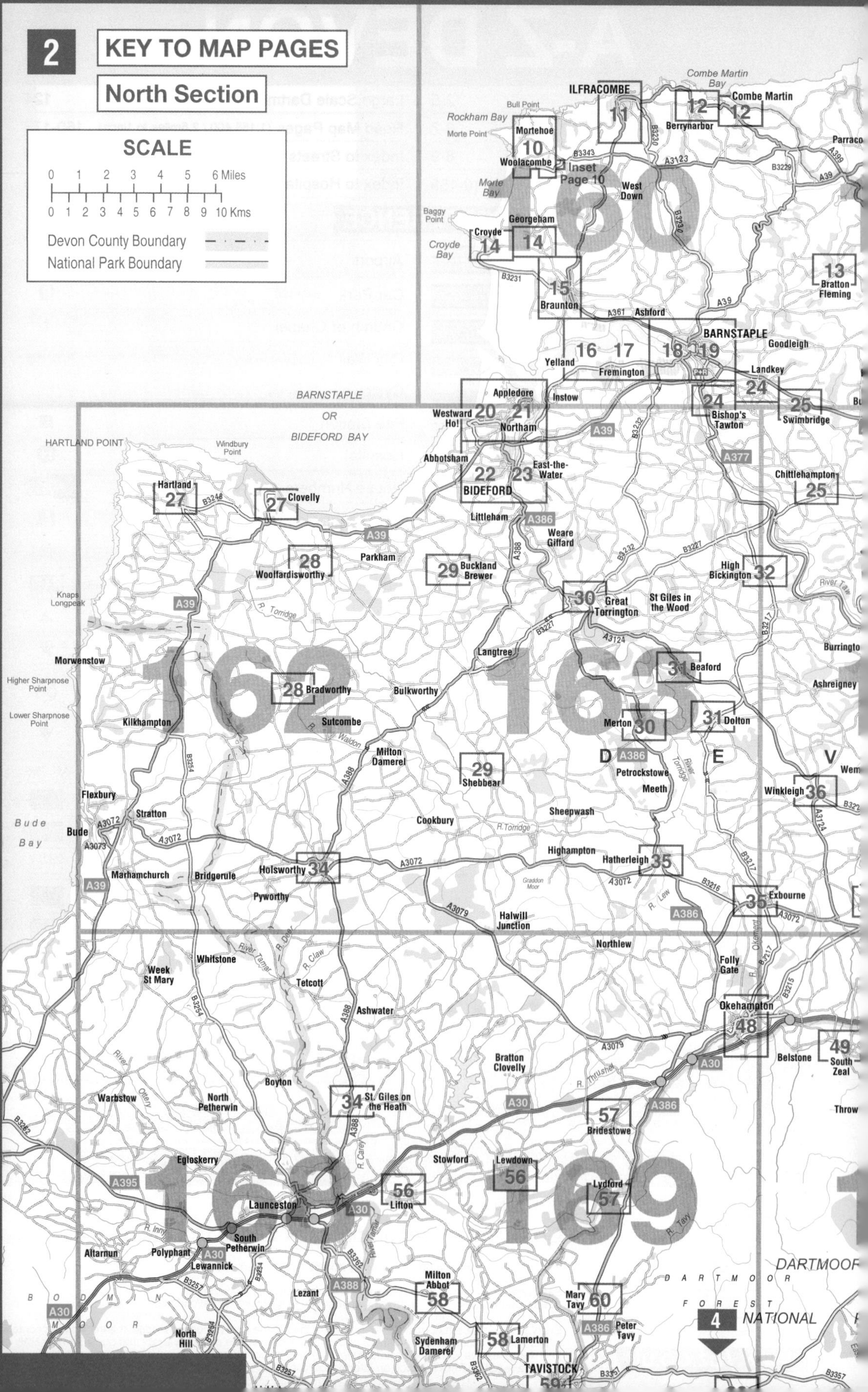

Combe Martin Bay

ILFRACOMBE **11**
Rockham Bay
Bull Point
Morte Point
12 — Combe Martin
12
Berrynarbor
Mortehoe **10**
Woolacombe
West Down
Parraco
60
A3123
Inset Page 10
Morte Bay
A361
Baggy Point
Georgeham
Croyde Bay
Croyde **14** **14**
13 Bratton Fleming
B3231
15
Braunton
Ashford
A361
BARNSTAPLE
Goodleigh
Yelland **16** **17** **18** **19**
Fremington
Landkey
24
Swimbridge
25

BARNSTAPLE
OR
BIDEFORD BAY

HARTLAND POINT
Windbury Point

Westward Ho! **20** **21** Northam
Appledore
Instow
Bishop's Tawton **24**
A39
25
Chittlehampton
A377

Hartland **27** B3248 **27** Clovelly
Abbotsham
22 **23** East-the-Water
BIDEFORD
Littleham
Weare Giffard
A386
High Bickington **32**
25

28 Woolfardisworthy
Parkham
29 Buckland Brewer
30 Great Torrington
St Giles in the Wood
River Tarr

Knaps Longpeak
A39
162
R. Torridge
30
163
Langtree
31 Beaford
Burringto

Morwenstow
Higher Sharpnose Point
28 Bradworthy
Bulkworthy
31 Dolton
Ashreigney

Lower Sharpnose Point
Kilkhampton
Sutcombe
Merton **30**
D A386 E
Winkleigh **36** V Wem
B3254
Milton Damerel
29 Shebbear
Petrockstowe
Meeth

Flexbury
A3072
Stratton
Cookbury
Sheepwash
B3217

Bude Bay
Bude A3073
Marhamchurch
Bridgerule
Holsworthy **34**
A3072
Highampton
Graddon Moor
R. Torridge
Hatherleigh **35**
A3072

Pyworthy
A3079
Halwill Junction
A386
35 Exbourne
A3072

Week St Mary
Whitstone
River Tamar
R. Claw
Northlew
Folly Gate
B3215

Tetcott
Ashwater
A30
Okehampton **48**
B3217

Warbstow
North Petherwin
Boyton
34 St. Giles on the Heath
A30
Bratton Clovelly
A3079
R. Thrushel
49 South Zeal
Belstone
Throw

Egloskerry
A395
56
Stowford
Lewdown **56**
57 Bridestowe
A386

Launceston
A30
56 Lifton
Lydford **57**
168
169
DARTMOOR

Altarnun
Polyphant A30
Lewannick
South Petherwin
Lezant
A388
Milton Abbot **58**
Mary Tavy **60**
FOREST
4 NATIONAL

North Hill
A30
Sydenham Damerel
58 Lamerton
Peter Tavy
A386

TAVISTOCK

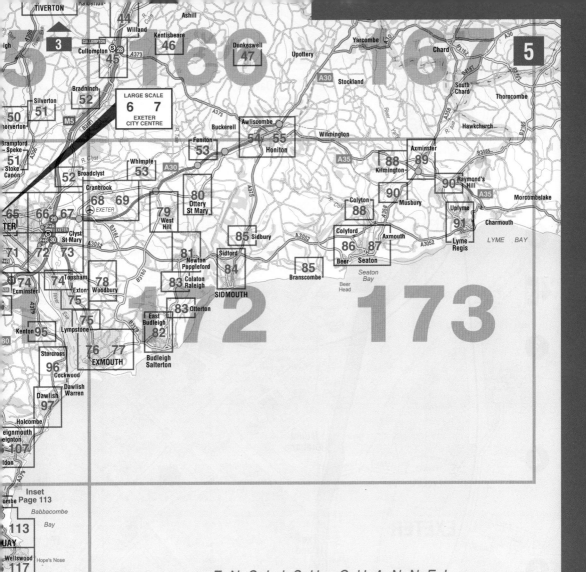

ENGLISH CHANNEL

KEY TO MAP PAGES

South Section

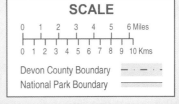

SCALE

0 1 2 3 4 5 6 Miles

0 1 2 3 4 5 6 7 8 9 10 Kms

Devon County Boundary — · — · —

National Park Boundary ————

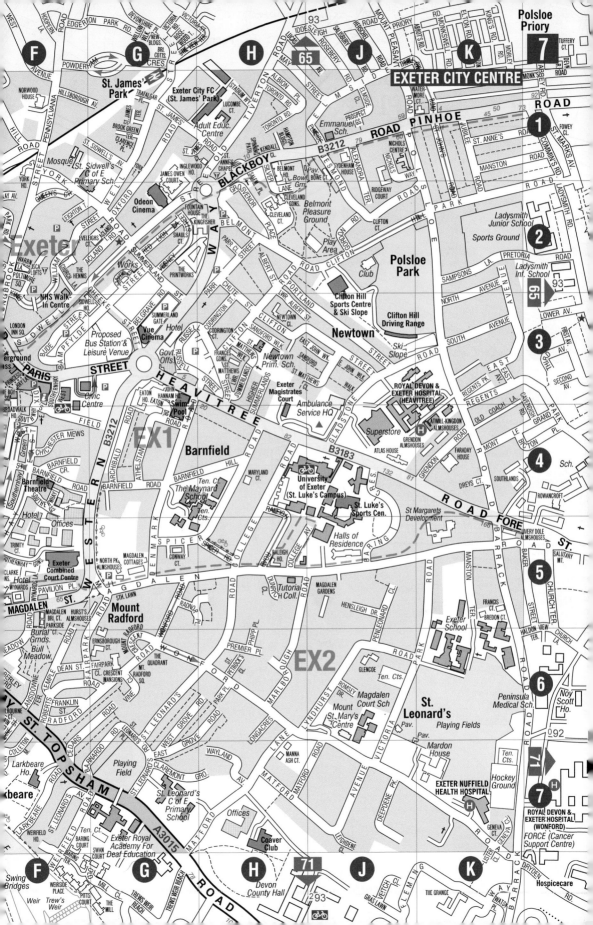

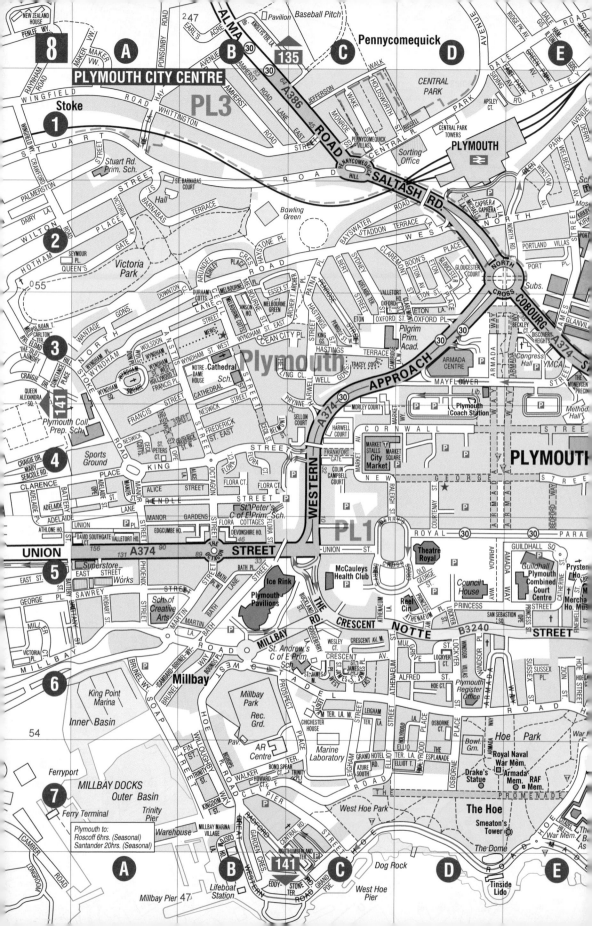

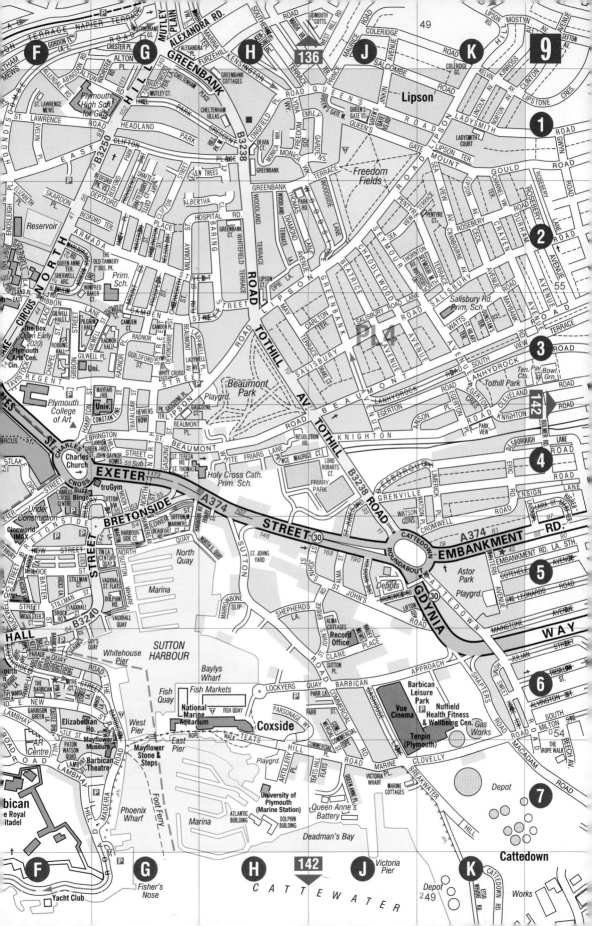

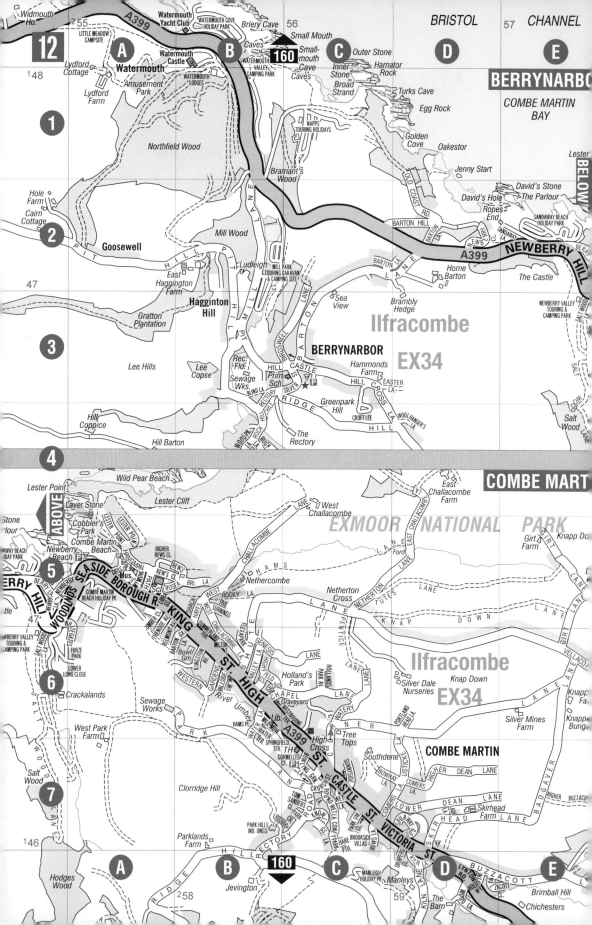

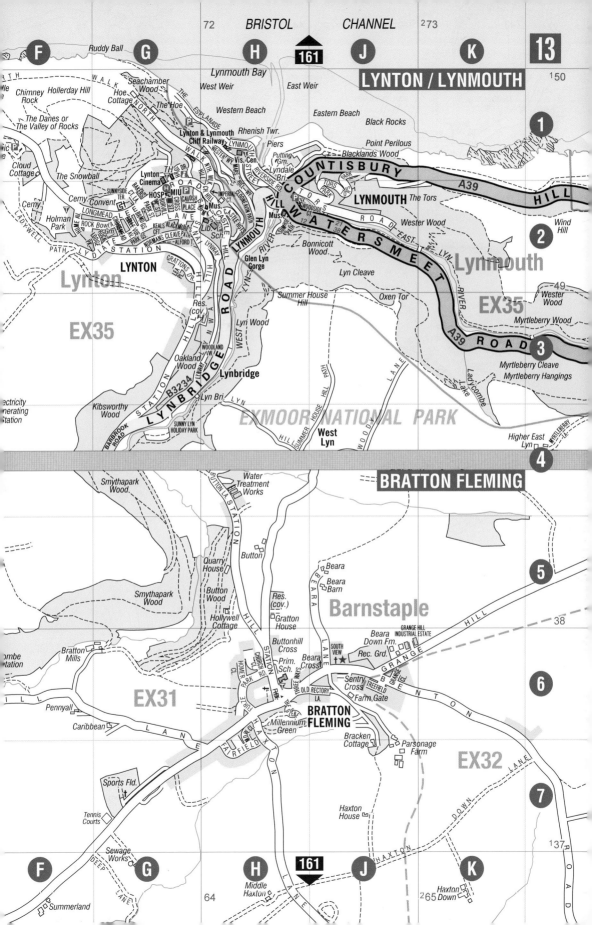

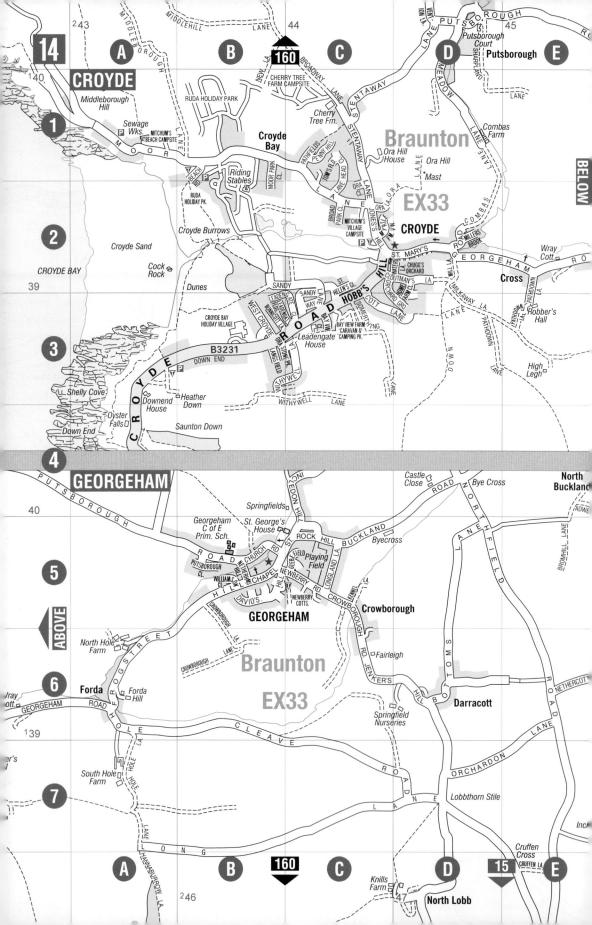

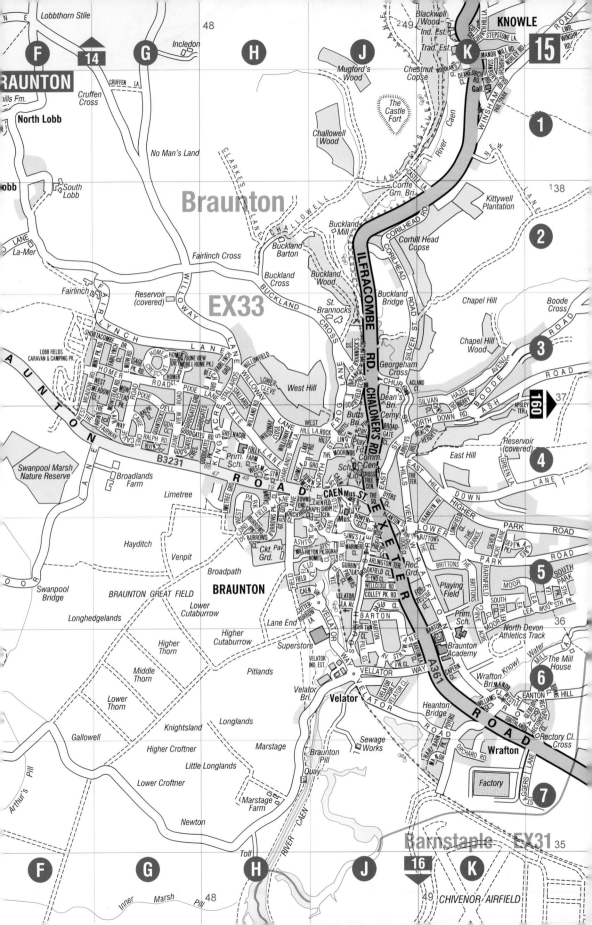

A B C D E

15

A361

49 50

CHIVENOR AIRFIELD

RMB CHIVENOR

TINEVER

HEANTON LA

CHIVENOR CARAVAN PARK

MEADOWLAND RD.
THISTLE BRI. RD.
A. NTONE QL.
FILMER CL.
COPSE
HEANTON LEA

Chivenor Cross

Chivenor

DUCKPOOL RD.
TAMAR RD.
CHIVENOR INDUSTRIAL ESTATE
ROAD TAW
EXE CL.
YEO RD.
TORRIDGE RD.
FOWEY RD.
TAMAR
HAWKRIDGE
DART CL.
TORRIDGE ROAD
TAMAR RD.
TAW CRES.
TAW

1

Marstage Farm

RIVER CAEN

135
Toll House Tolli

2

34

3

Pill's Mouth

160

R I V E R

Chivenor Ridge

Allen's Rock

Monkey

4

Coniger Ridge

Home Farm Marsh

Saltpill Duck Pond (Nature Reserve)

33

Isley Marsh

Chillparks

THE GREEN

ST. AND

RO

5

Isley Marsh Nature Reserve
Isley Marshes Bird Sanctuary

East Yelland Marsh

Lower Yelland Farm

CHILPARK

6

ESTUARY BUSINESS PARK

Yelland Cross

YELLAND YELLAND

B3233

BEECHFIELD
THORN
LEA KNO
TWO TREES
HOME
BARN
WOOD CL.
OLD
PARK RO
CROSS CL.
MERRYTHORN
PLANTATION
BLACKLAND
WHE
ASPEN

Depot

YELLAND DRIVE

ST. KATHERINE'S CL.
POTTERY
ALLENSTYLE
ALLENSTYLE WY.
ALLENSTYLE GS.
ALLENSTYLE CL.
ALLEN-STYLE RD.
ALLENSTYLE RD.
ROOKS FM. RD.
BRIMBLECOMBE
DRAKE
BRIMBLECOMBE WY.
GRENVILLE RD.
PAUL

Allenstyle Wood

THE WILLOWS
Gibb's Plantation

Sampson's Plantation

32

Sewage Works

LINSCOTT CL.
RDS. CR.
BALLARDS CRES.
POST CRES.
BALLARDS CRES.
BALLARDS GRO.
LITTLEMOOR CL.

YELLAND

Paul Steeple

Sloley's Plantation

Square Close

7

WEST B3233

LAGOON
WELCH'S LA.
Long Grove
VIEW
LANE

West Yelland

Long Grove

West Yelland Farm

Brake Plantations

Cle
Plan

OLD RECTORY
PECTORY
ESTUARY WL.

A B C D E

49 50

Broadmaid's Copse

Cross Head

Bickleton Wood

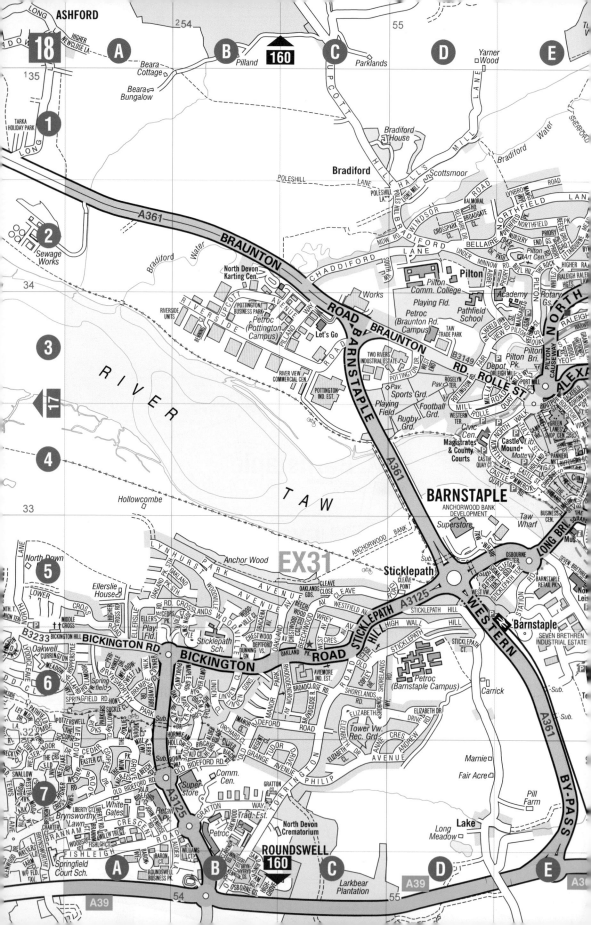

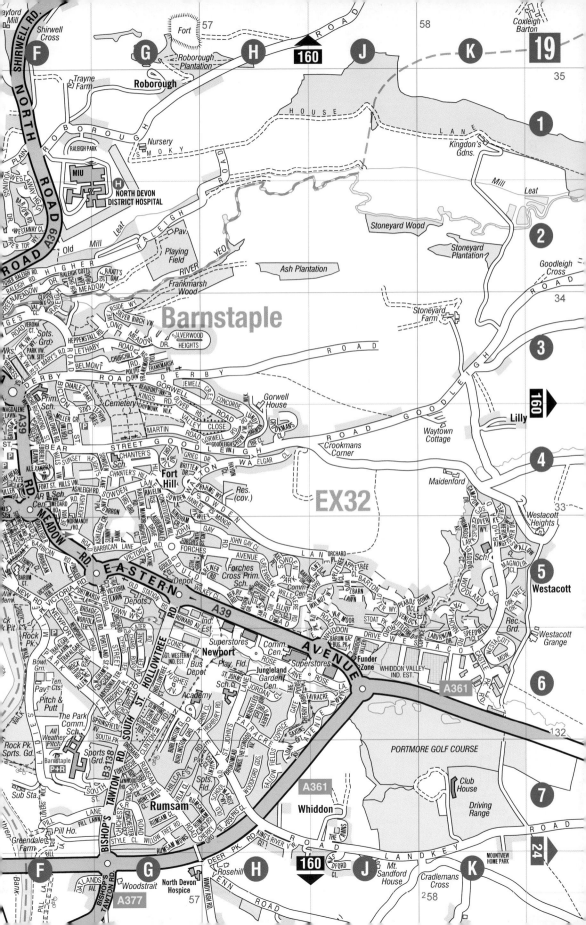

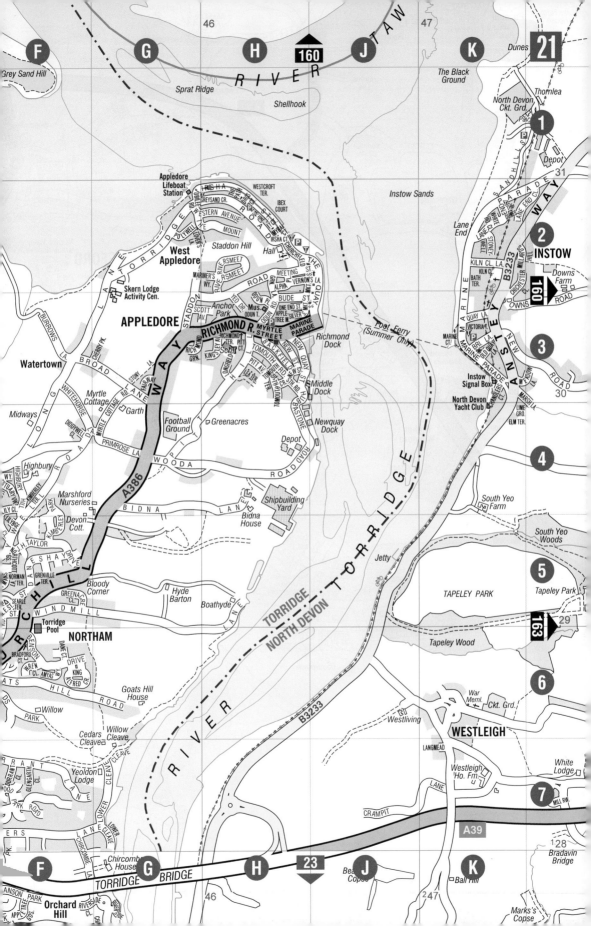

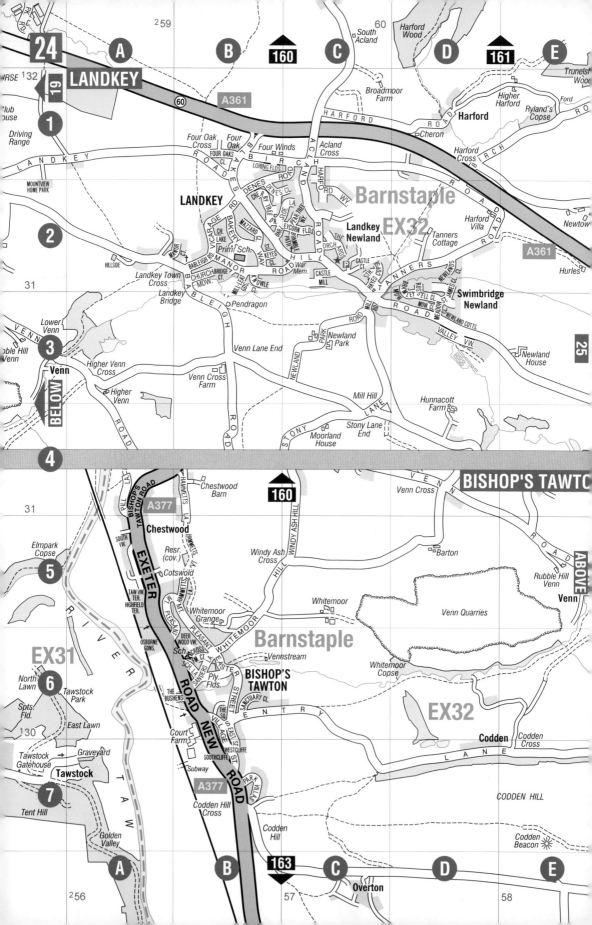

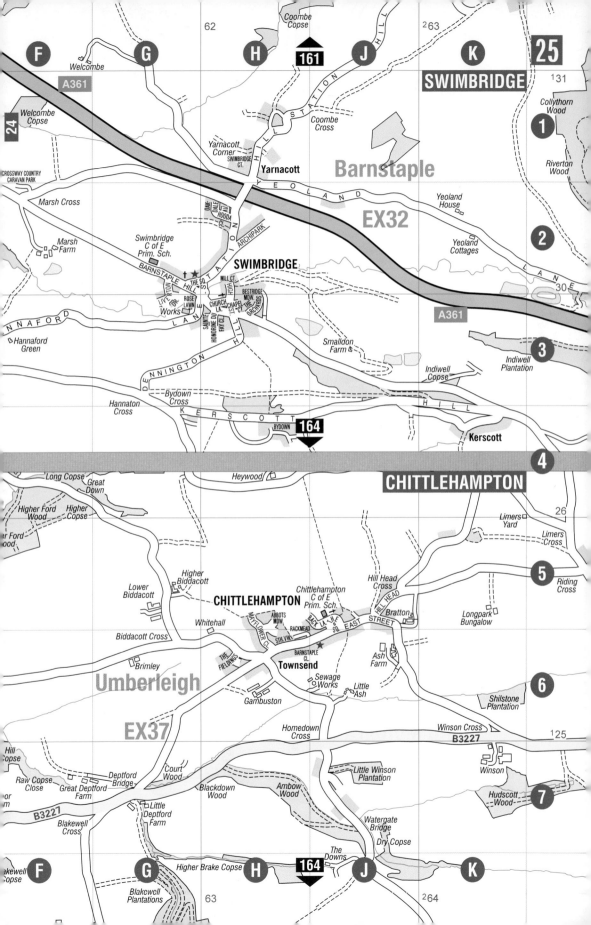

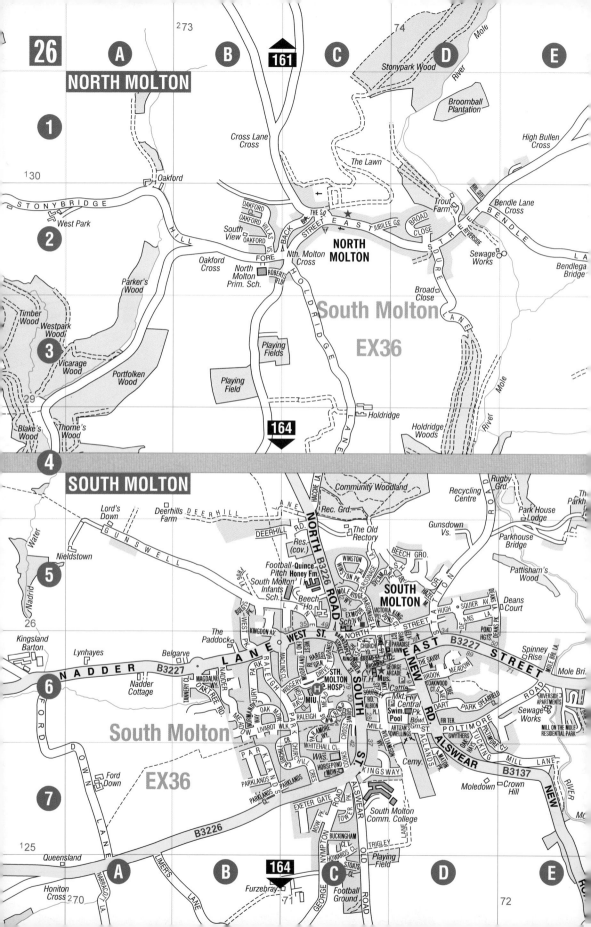

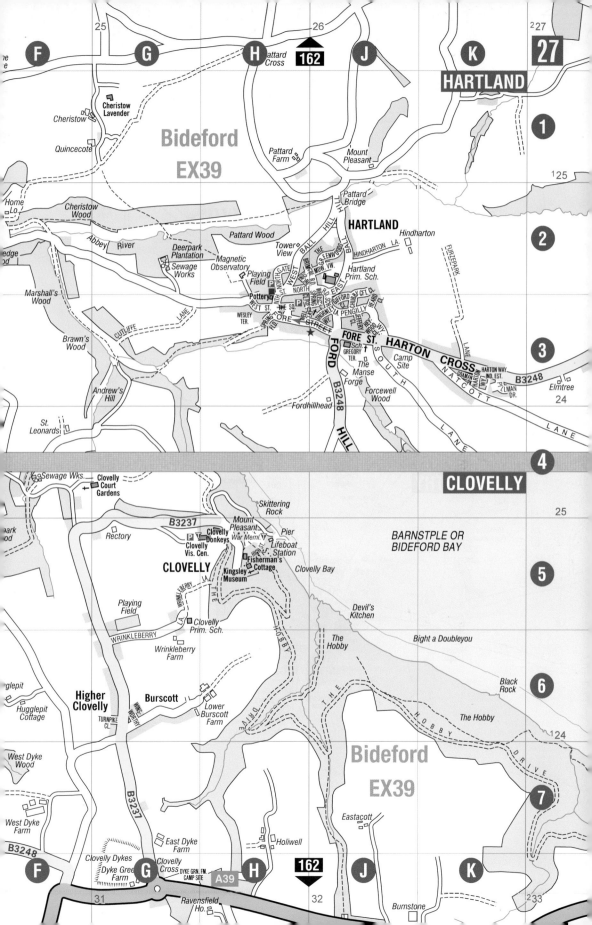

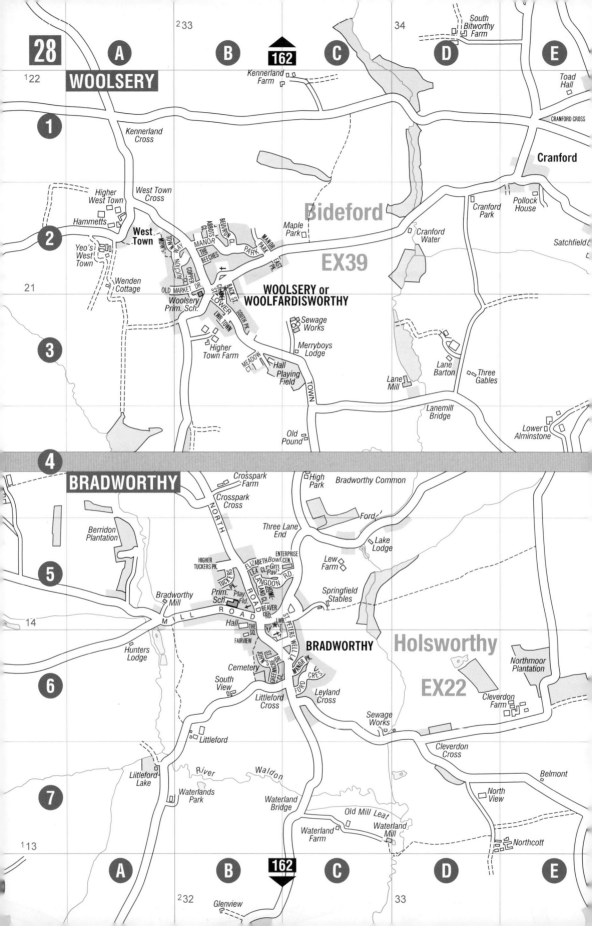

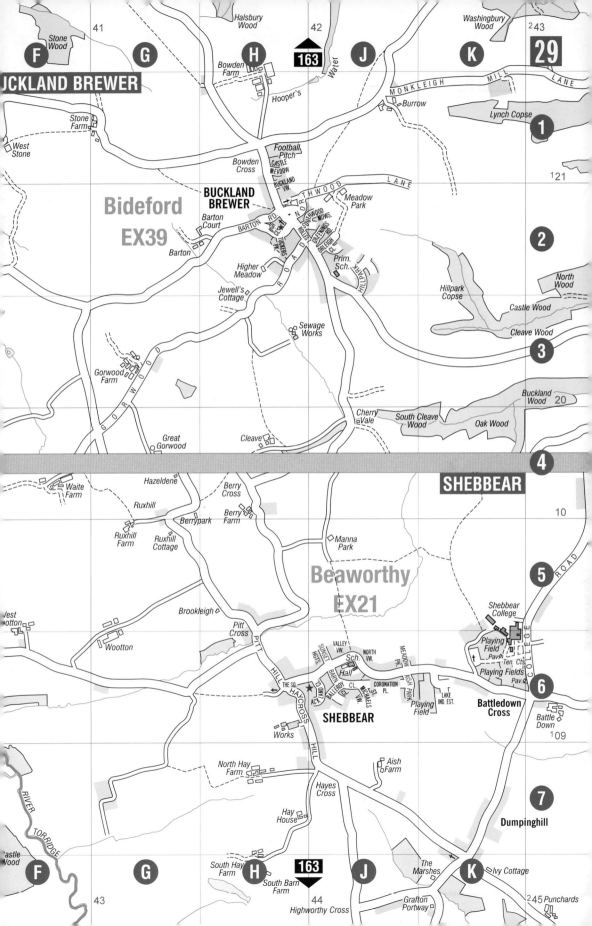

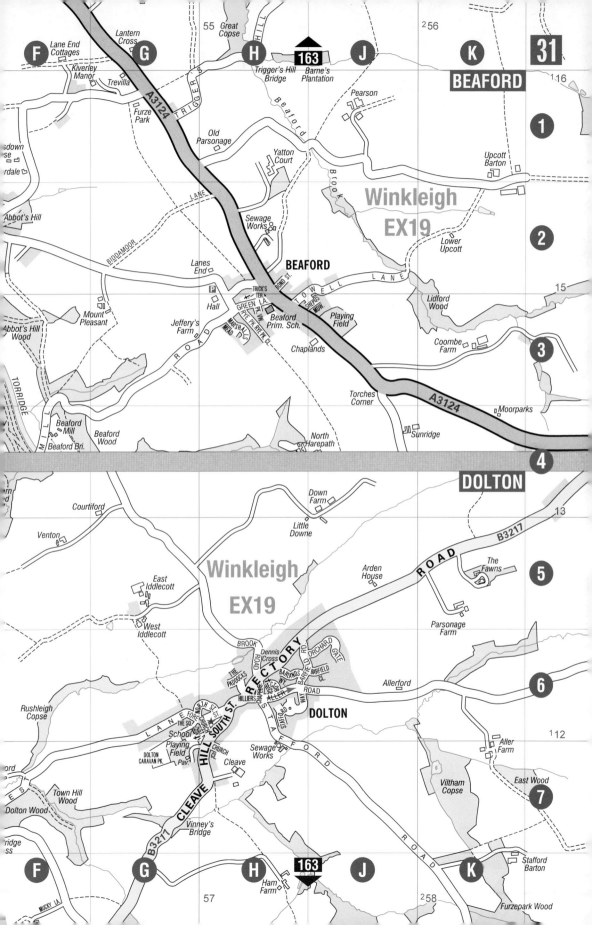

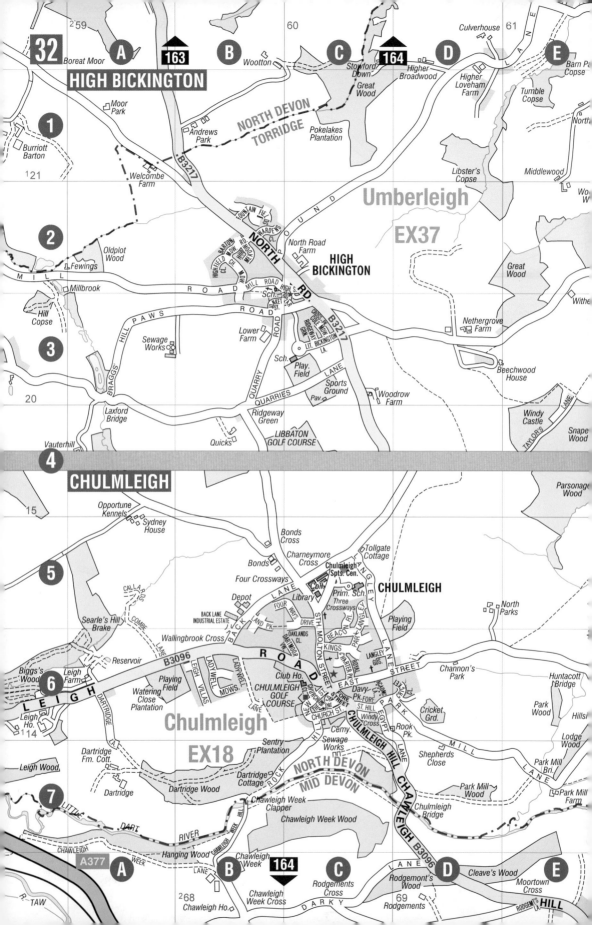

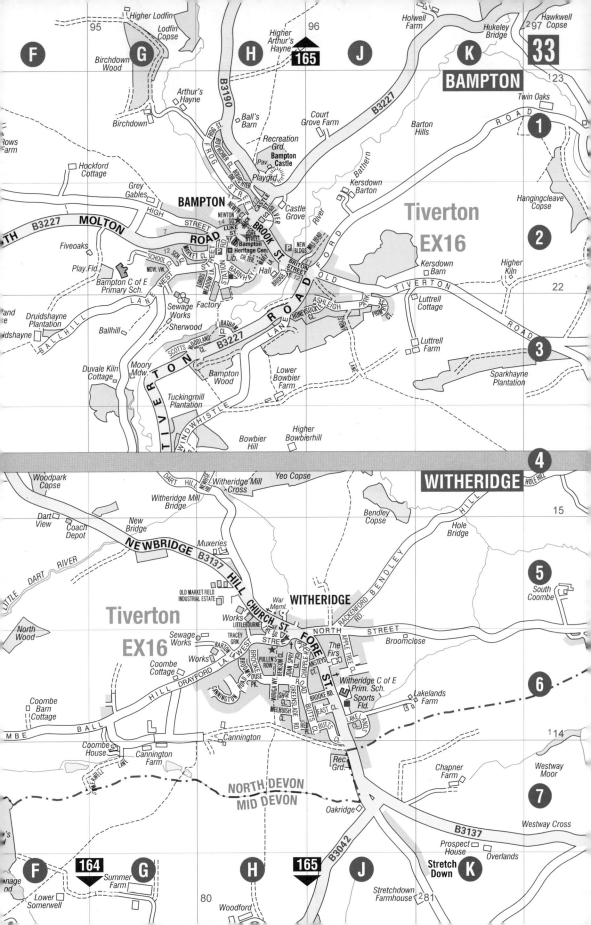

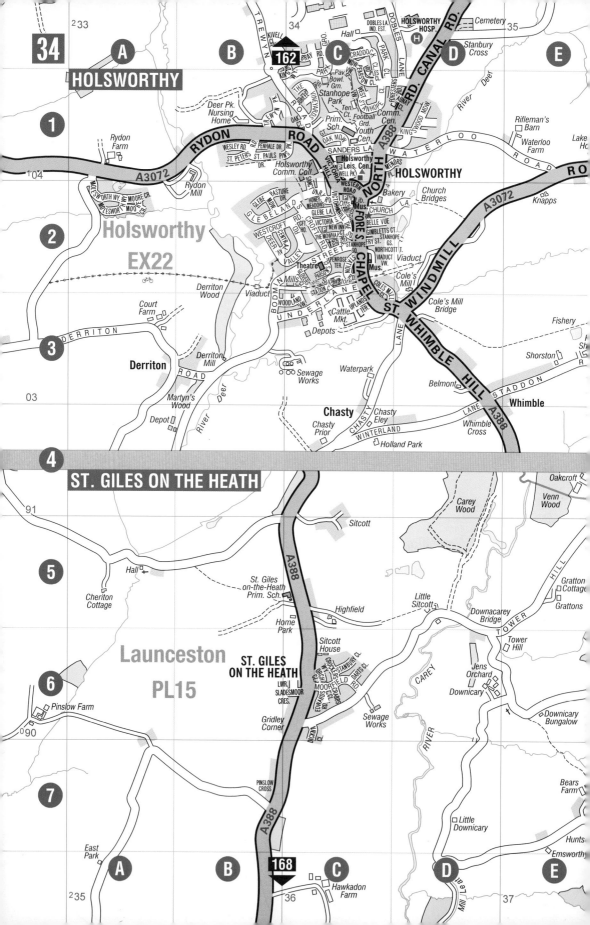

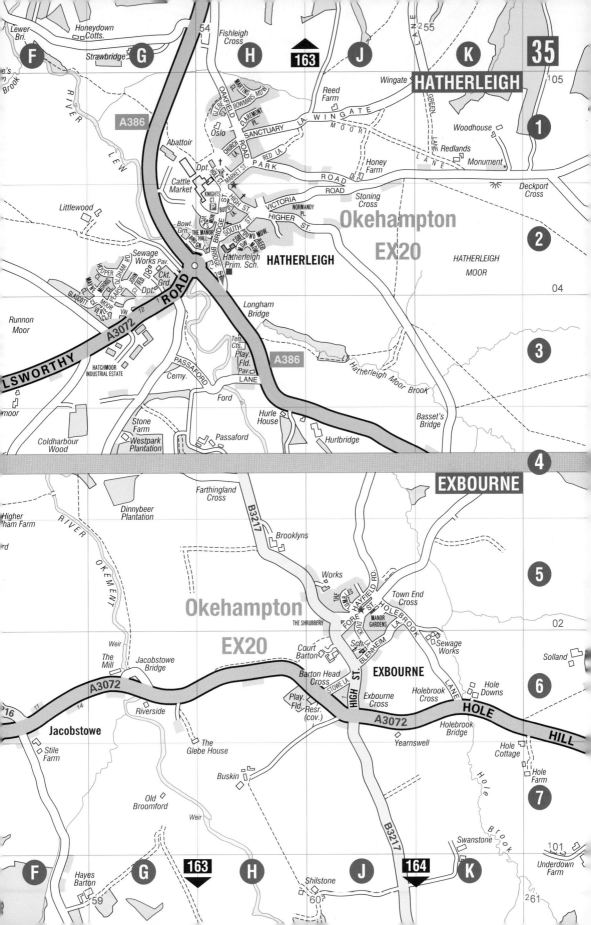

F **G** **H** **J** **K**

Lewer Bri.
Honeydown Cotts.
Strawbridge
Fishleigh Cross
▲ 163

Wingate
HATHERLEIGH
105

RIVER LEW
A386
Abattoir
Oslo
MARTINS MDN.
OAKFIELD
GLEBE
C.LAREMONT PL.
BOWMANS
SANCTUARY
CHURCH LA.
RED LA.
WINGATE
MOOR LA.
GREEN LANE
Reed Farm
Redlands
Woodhouse
Monument
1

Littlewood
Dpt.
†
Cattle Market
KNIGHTS CT.
P
HIGH ST.
MARKET ST.
VICTORIA
NORMANDY PL.
HIGHER ST.
ROAD
ROAD
Honey Farm
Stoning Cross
Okehampton EX20
Deckport Cross
2

Bowl. Grn.
THE MANOR HALL
SOUTH ST.
COMBOUND MDN.
BRIDGE ST.
HATHERLEIGH
HATHERLEIGH MOOR
04

Sewage Works
Pav.
HOOPER CL.
MOORE
PEARSE CL.
JOHN
OLD (DUHAM RD)
MOORES
Ckt. Grd.
Dpt.
Hatherleigh Prim. Sch.
Longham Bridge

Runnon Moor
GLASCOTT CL.
MAYNE
VW
A3072
HATCHMOOR INDUSTRIAL ESTATE
ROAD
PASSAFORD LANE
Cemy.
Teh. Cts.
Play. Fld.
Pav.
A386
Hatherleigh Moor Brook
3

LSWORTHY
moor
Coldharbour Wood
Stone Farm
Westpark Plantation
Passaford
Ford
Hurle House
Hurlbridge
Basset's Bridge

4 **EXBOURNE**

Higher ...ham Farm
RIVER OKEMENT
Dinnyeer Plantation
Farthingland Cross
B3217
Brooklyns

Okehampton

Works
THE TIMBERS
HAYFIELD RD.
Town End Cross
5
02

Weir
The Mill
Jacobstowe Bridge
EX20
THE SHRUBBERY
FORE ST.
MANOR GARDENS
BLENHEIM
Sch.
HOLEBROOK
Court Barton
Solland

A3072
Riverside
Jacobstowe Bridge
Barton Head Cross
STOWE LA.
HIGH ST.
LANE
EXBOURNE
Exbourne Cross
Holebrook Cross
Hole Downs
6

16
11
14
Stile Farm
The Glebe House
Play. Fld.
Resr. (cov.)
A3072
Yearnswell
Holebrook Bridge
HOLE HILL
Hole Cottage
Hole Farm
7

Buskin
Old Broomford
Weir
B3217
Swanstone
Underdown Farm
101
261

Hayes Barton
59
163 ▼
Shilstone
60?
164 ▼

F **G** **H** **J** **K**

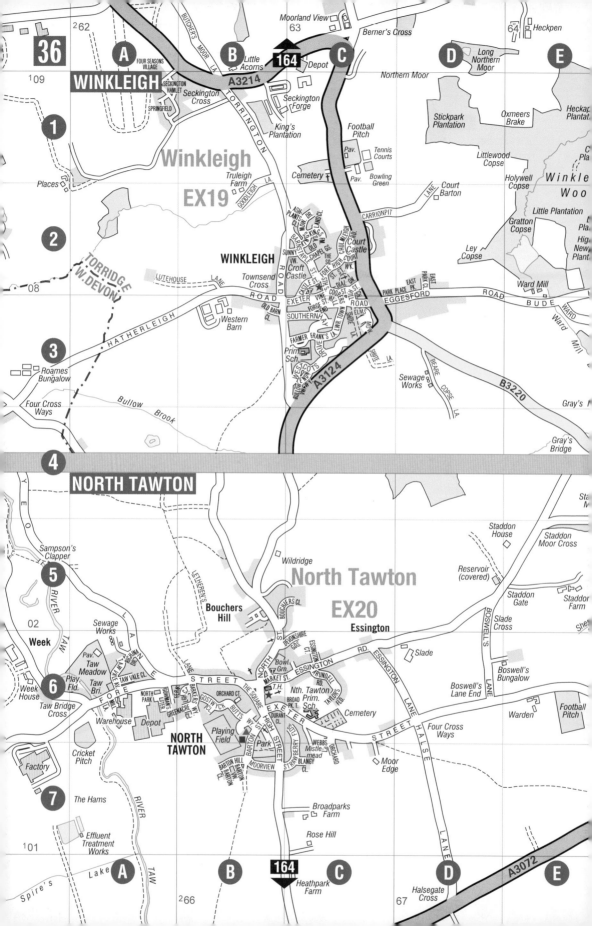

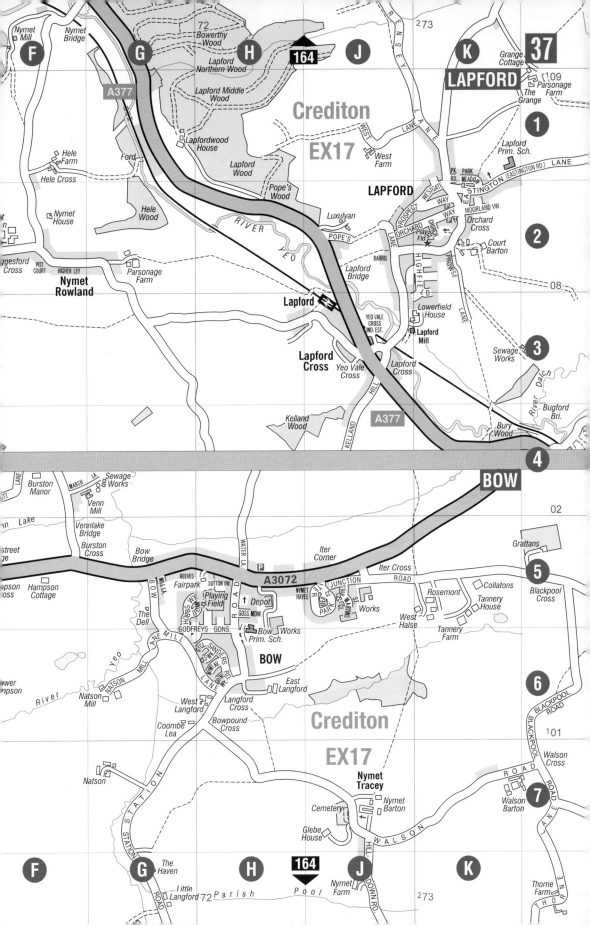

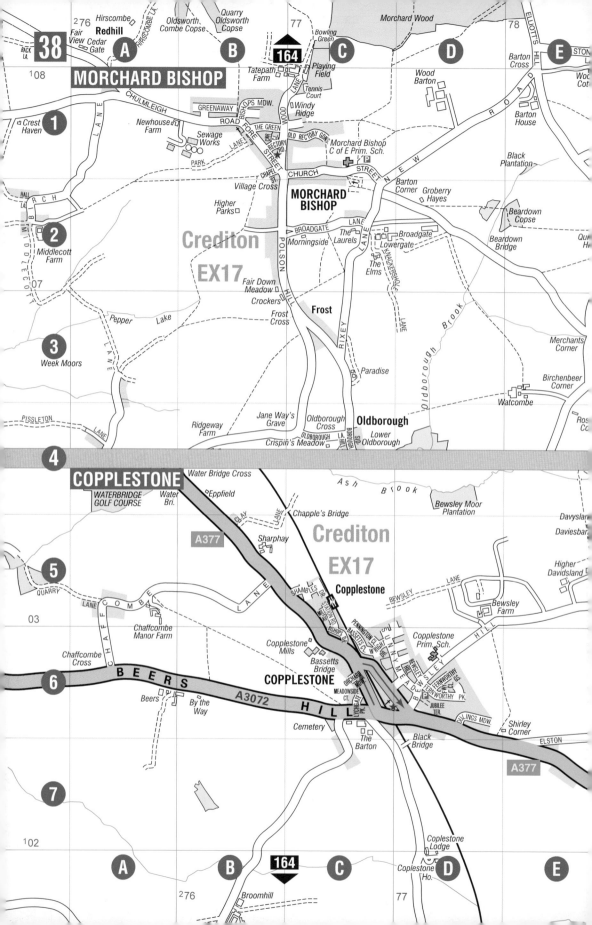

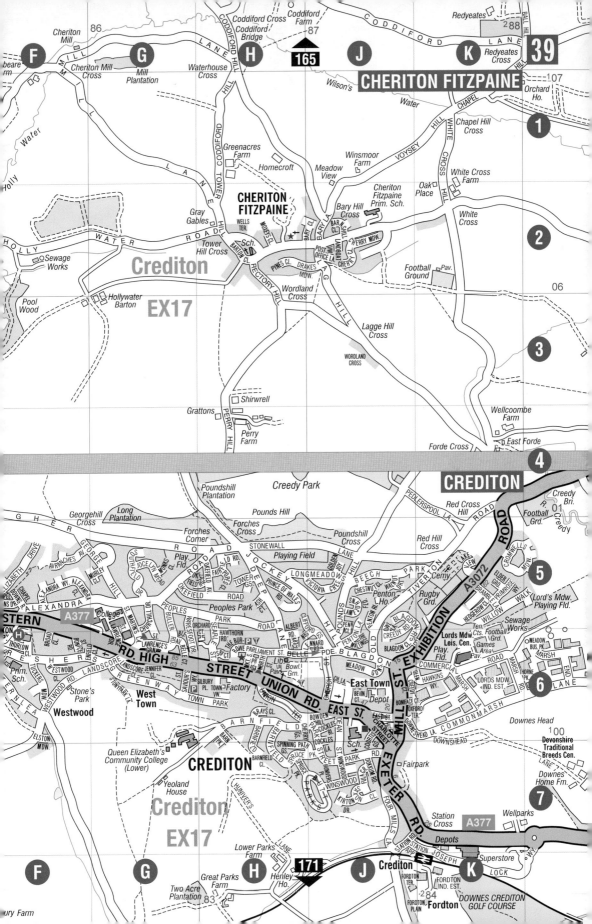

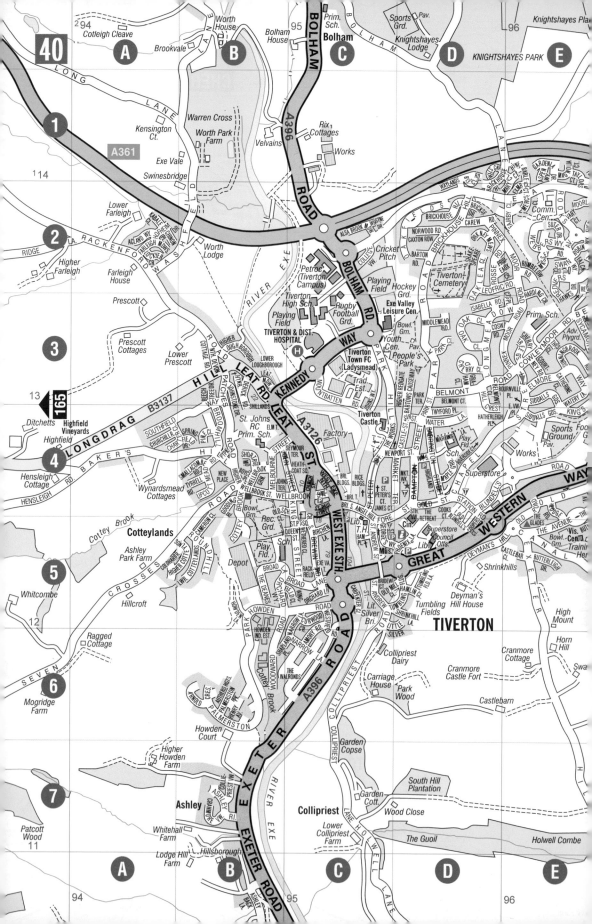

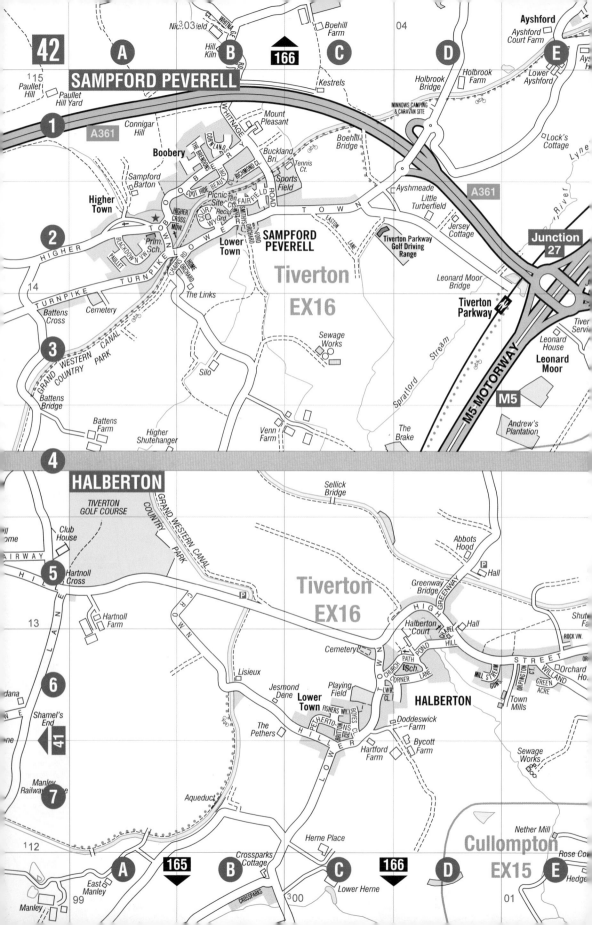

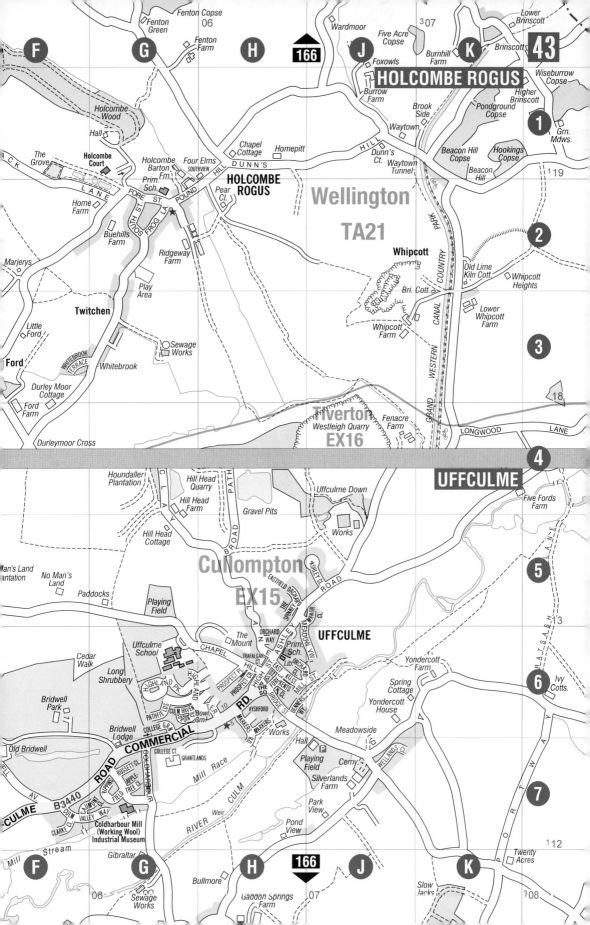

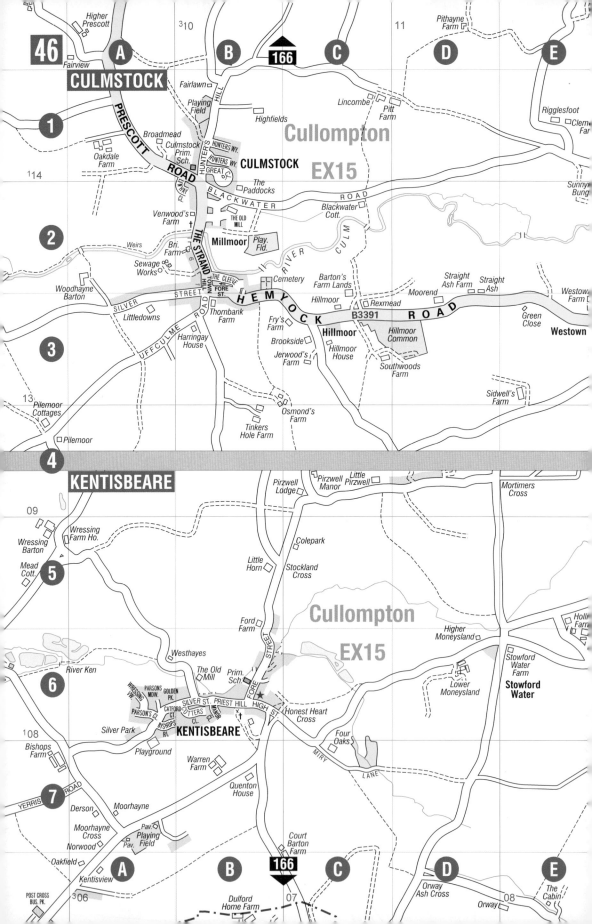

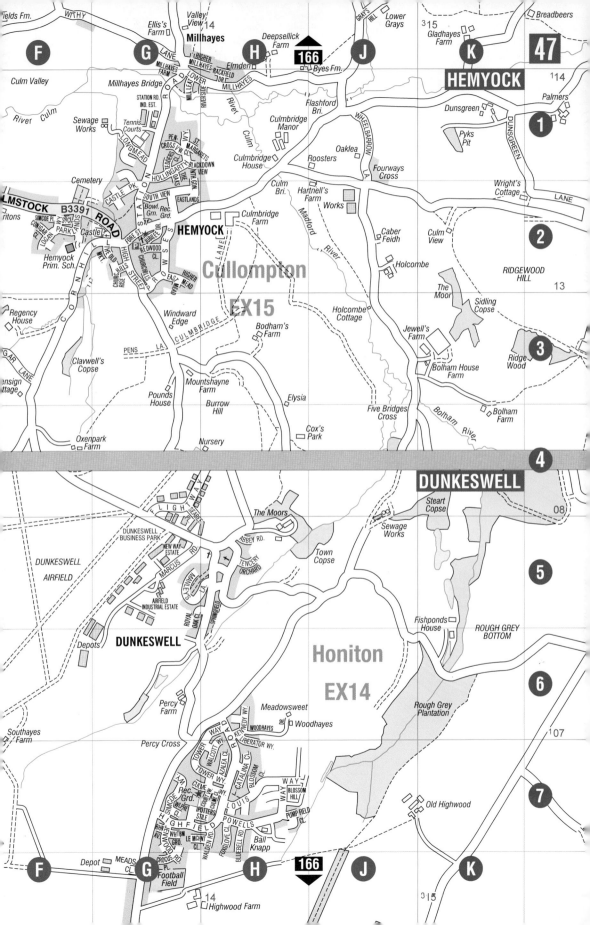

HEMYOCK

Cullompton
EX15

DUNKESWELL

Honiton
EX14

F G H 166 J K

Breadbeers
Lower Grays
315
Gladhayes Farm
114
Palmers
Dunsgreen
1
Pyks Pit
Wright's Cottage
2
Culm View
RIDGEWOOD HILL
13
The Moor
Sidling Copse
3
Ridge Wood
Bolham House Farm
Bolham Farm
4
08
Steart Copse
5
Fishponds House
ROUGH GREY BOTTOM
6
107
Rough Grey Plantation
Old Highwood
7

Valley View 14
Ellis's Farm
Millhayes
Deepsellick Farm
166
Gray's Hill
Higher Millhayes
Elmden
RACKFIELD DR
Byes Fm.
Millhayes Bridge
Lower Millhayes
RIVERSIDE
WHEELBARROW
Dunsgreen
Culm Valley
Millhayes Farm
STATION RD. IND. EST.
Flashford Bri.
Fourways Cross
River Culm
Sewage Works
Tennis Courts
Culmbridge Manor
Culmbridge House
Roosters
Oaklea
Caber Feidh
LONGMEAD
PEN. CROSS
ST. MARGARETS
BLACKDOWN VIEW
Cemetery
THE MEAD
Culm Bri.
Hartnell's Farm
Works
Holcombe
CASTLE PK.
SOUTH VIEW
EASTLANDS
Culmbridge Farm
LMSTOCK
B3391 ROAD
Bowl. Grn.
Rec. Grd.
Culmbridge Farm
Holcombe Cottage
Jewell's Farm
tritons
SIMCOE PL.
CASTLE
FORE ST.
JUBILEE DR.
HEMYOCK
HIGH STREET
REDWOOD CL.
CHURCHILLS
HIGHER MEAD
Madford River
Five Bridges Cross
Hemyock Prim. Sch.
CHURCHILL RISE
CORNHILL
Windward Edge
Bodham's Farm
Holcombe Cottage
Bolham River
Regency House
CULMBRIDGE LANE
PENS LA.
Elysia
GAR LANE
 nsion ttage
Clavwell's Copse
Mountshayne Farm
Burrow Hill
Cox's Park
Oxenpark Farm
Pounds House
Nursery

LIGHT WAY
SEABEE
Dunkeswell Business Park
The Moors
ABBEY RD.
Town Copse
Sewage Works
NEW WAY ESTATE
MARCUS
ROAD
TENCERY ORCHARD
DUNKESWELL AIRFIELD
MARTINS LA.
AIRFIELD INDUSTRIAL ESTATE
ROYAL OAK CL.
SPRINGFIELD
Depots
DUNKESWELL
Percy Farm
Meadowsweet
Woodhayes
KENNEDY WY.
Woodhayes
Southayes Farm
Percy Cross
TOWER WAY
WALLCOTT WY.
LIBERATOR WY.
TOWER WAY
AZALEA CL.
CATALINA CL.
BLOSSOM CL.
BLOSSOM HILL
WAY
Rec. Grd.
CULME WY.
LOUIS WAY
PUMP FIELD CL.
SIMCOE
SPOTTERS STILE
POWELLS
Ball Knapp
Depot
MEADS CL.
HIGHFIELD
WALDEN RD.
FONGLOE CL.
BLUEBELL RD.
Football Field
F G CROCUS PL. LE MCHNT CL. H 166 J K
14
Highwood Farm
315
Old Highwood

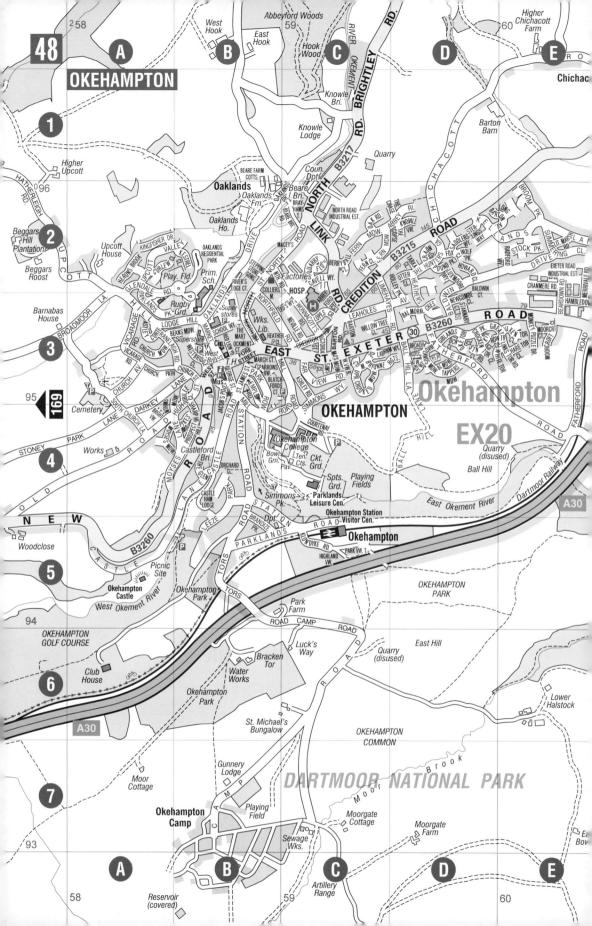

258

A B C D E

West Hook
East Hook
Abbeyford Woods
59
Hook Wood
Higher Chichacott Farm
60

Chichac

1

RIVER OKEMENT
BRIGHTLEY RD.
Knowle Bri.
Knowle Lodge
Quarry
Barton Barn

Higher Upcott

HATHERLEIGH RD.
96

2
Beggars Hill Plantation
Beggars Roost

Coun. Dpts.
NORTH RD.
B3217
Beare Farm Cotts.
Oaklands
Oaklands Fm
Beare Bri.
BRAY HAMS
North Road Industrial Est.

LINK ROAD
CHICHACOTT
ROAD
B3215
Knowle Vw.
SADDLERS WAY

3
Barnabas House
BROADMOOR LA.
UPCOTT HILL
Upcott House
Upcott
KINGFISHER DR.
VALLEY
HERONS BROOK
CURLEW
Play. Fld.
Prim. Sch.
Oaklands Residential Park
Oaklands Ho.
GLENDALE
VICARAGE RD.
CASTLE
Rugby Grd.
Super stores
Superstore
SCHOOL LN.
THE MART
OCKMENT FORE
West Bri.
Cin.
Mus.
CREDITON RD.
Factories
COLLIERS
HOSP.
H
CAVEL WY.
CREDITON ST.
EXETER RD.
EXETER ROAD INDUSTRIAL EST.
CRANMERE RD.
HAMBLEDON

95
◄ 169
Cemetery
CHURCH AV.
SOUTH CHURCH
STONEY PARK
Works
CHURCH PATH
EAST ST.
T.H. STREET
MARCH CT.
SPARROWS RW.
OKEHAMPTON
EXETER ROAD
B3260
Okehampton
EX20
Quarry (disused)
Ball Hill

4
OLD
NEW
CASTLE ROAD
Castleford Bri.
ORCHARD CL.
CASTLE HAM LODGE
Okehampton College
Bowl. Grn.
Ten. Cts.
Pav.
Ckt. Grd.
COURTENAY RD.
Spts. Grd.
Playing Fields
East Okement River
Dartmoor Railway

5
Woodclose
B3260
Picnic Site
Simmons Pk.
Parklands Leisure Cen.
STATION ROAD
PARKLANDS
KLONDYKE RD.
Okehampton Station - Visitor Cen.
Okehampton
HIGHLAND VW.
PARK VW. T.
A30

6
OKEHAMPTON GOLF COURSE
Club House
Okehampton Castle
Okehampton Park
West Okement River
TORS
Okehampton Park
ROAD CAMP ROAD
Park Farm
Luck's Way
Bracken Tor
Water Works
Quarry (disused)
East Hill
OKEHAMPTON PARK
Lower Halstock

94

7
Moor Cottage
Gunnery Lodge
CAMP ROAD
St. Michael's Bungalow
Playing Field
Okehampton Camp
Sewage Wks.
OKEHAMPTON COMMON
Moorgate Cottage
Moorgate Farm
Moor Brook
DARTMOOR NATIONAL PARK
Ea Bov

93

A B C D E

58
Reservoir (covered)
59
Artillery Range
60

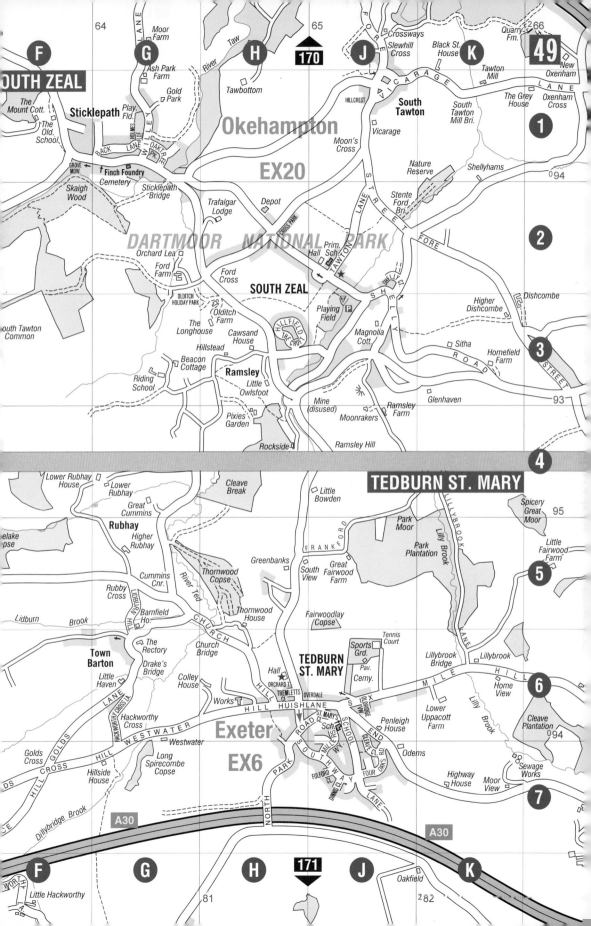

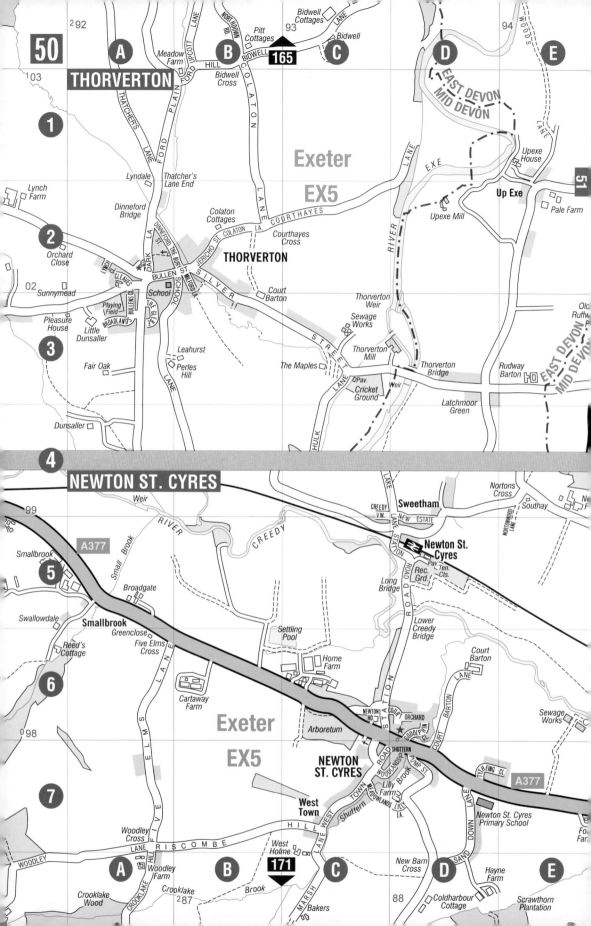

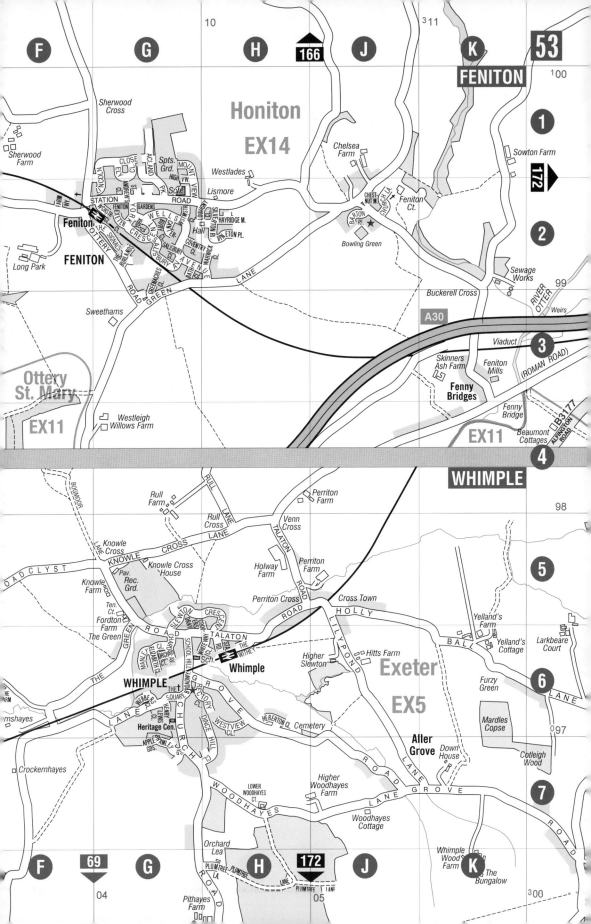

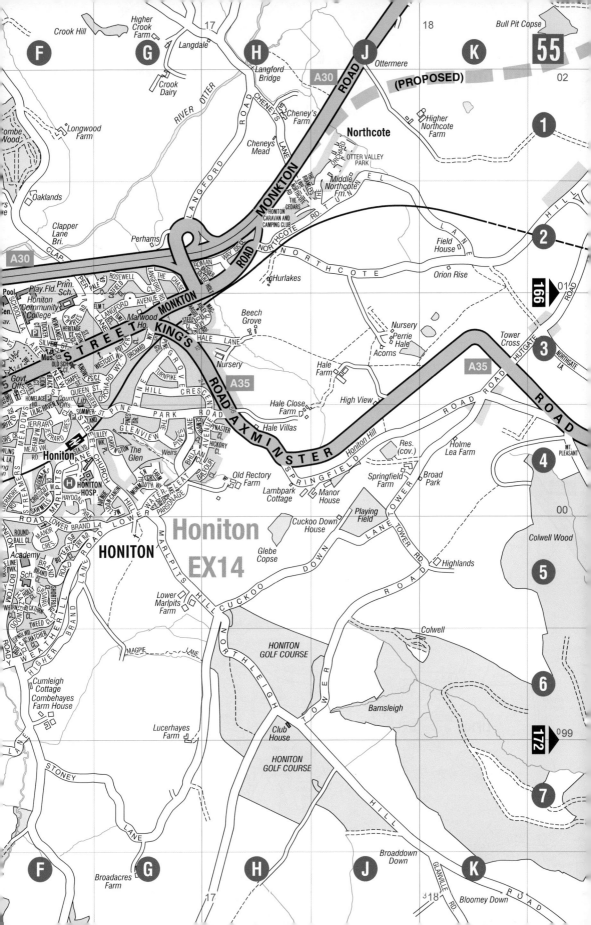

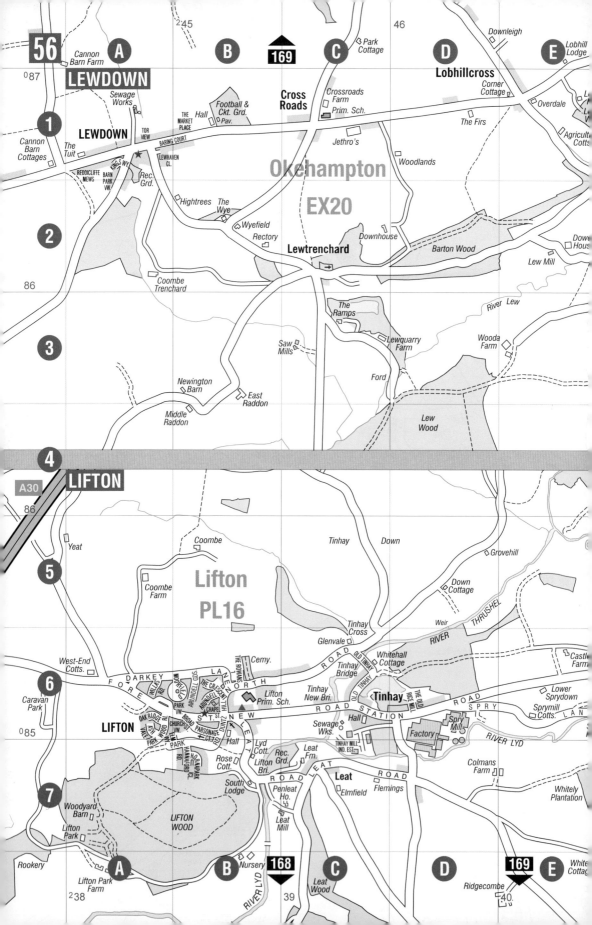

56

LEWDOWN

A   B   **▲ 169**   C   D   E

245   46

087

Cannon Barn Farm

Downleigh

Lobhill Lodge

Lobhillcross

Sewage Works

Corner Cottage

Park Cottage

1

THE MARKET PLACE

Hall

Football & Ckt. Grd. Pav.

Cross Roads

Crossroads Farm

Prim. Sch.

Overdale

The Firs

LEWDOWN

TOR VIEW

BARING COURT

Jethro's

Agricultural Cotts

Cannon Barn Cottages

The Tuit

KING'S WY.

LEWHAVEN CL.

Woodlands

REDDICLIFFE MEWS

BARN PARK VW.

Rec. Grd.

Hightrees

The Wye

Okehampton

EX20

2

Wyefield

Rectory

Downhouse

Barton Wood

Lew Mill

Lewtrenchard

Dow House

86

Coombe Trenchard

River Lew

The Ramps

Wooda Farm

3

Saw Mills

Lewquarry Farm

Newington Barn

East Raddon

Ford

Middle Raddon

Lew Wood

4

LIFTON

A30

86

LIFTON

Yeat

Coombe

Tinhay   Down

Grovehill

5

Coombe Farm

Lifton

PL16

Tinhay Cross

Down Cottage

Weir

THRUSHEL

West-End Cotts.

Cemy.

Glenvale

RIVER

Whitehall Cottage

Castle Farm

6

FORE

DARKEY

THE ROMANS

LANE NORTH

ROAD

Tinhay Bridge

OLD TINHAY

Lower Sprydown

Caravan Park

WORK RD.

WILLS RD.

ARUNDELL CL.

THE CRESCENT

ARUNDELL RD.

Lifton Prim. Sch.

Tinhay New Bri.

Tinhay

THE OLD RICE MILL

ROAD

SPRY

Sprymill Cotts.

LANE

085

LIFTON

OAK RIDGE RD.

ASH WD.

PARK VW.

CHAPEL

CHURCH VW.

PARSONAGE

BROAD

ST. DUNT

NEW

Hall

STATION

Spry Mill

Factory

RIVER LYD

PARK RD.

HANNIFORD RD.

HQ

RAMPARK

Rose Cott.

Lyd Cott.

Lifton Bri.

Rec. Grd.

Sewage Wks.

Hall

Leat Fm.

Tinhay Mill IND. EST.

ROAD

Colmans Farm

7

Woodyard Barn

South Lodge

Penleat Ho.

LEAT

ROAD

Leat

Flemings

Whitely Plantation

Lifton Park

LIFTON WOOD

Leat Mill

Elmfield

Rookery

A   B   Nursery   **▼ 168**   C   D   **▼ 169**   E

White Cottage

Lifton Park Farm

RIVER LYD

Leat Wood

Ridgecombe

238

39   40

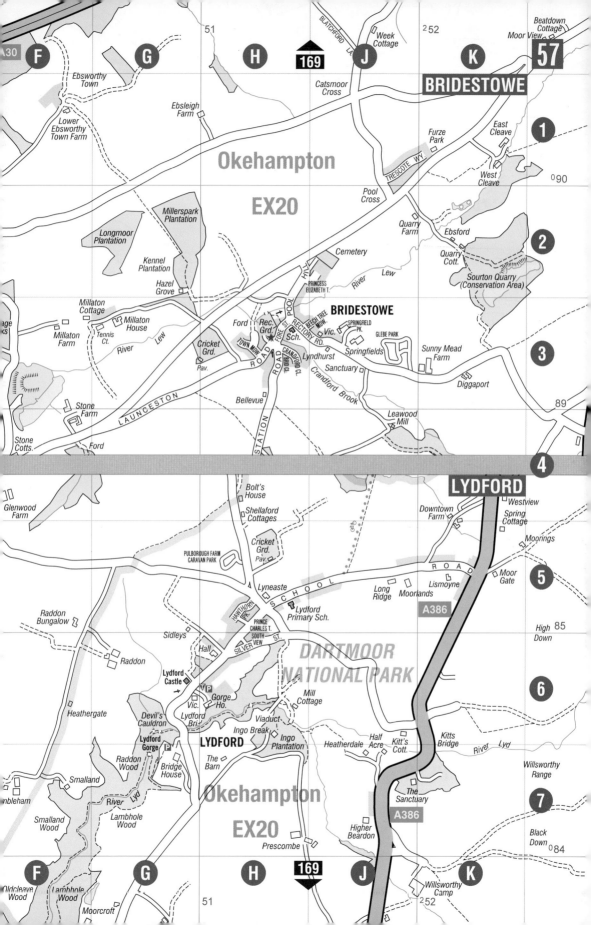

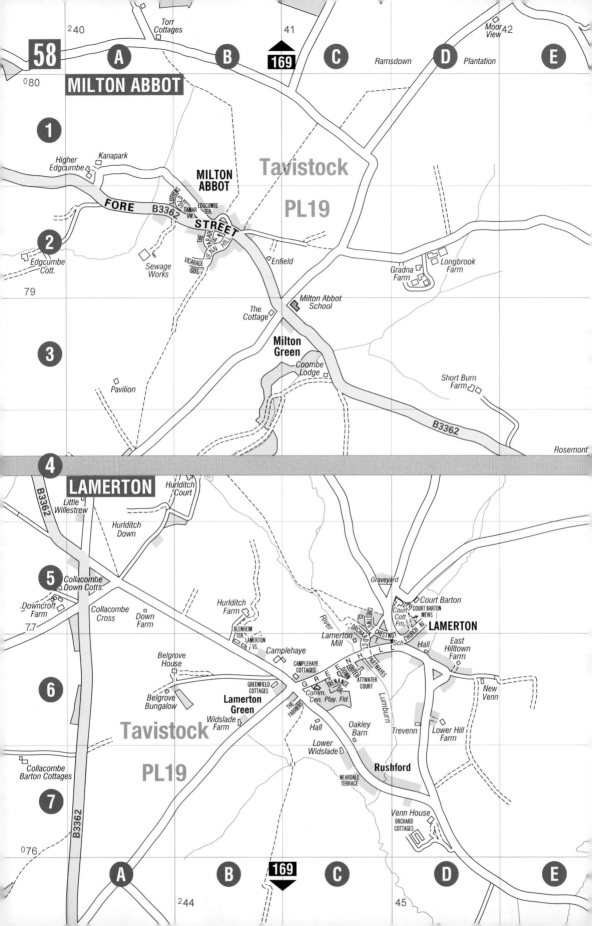

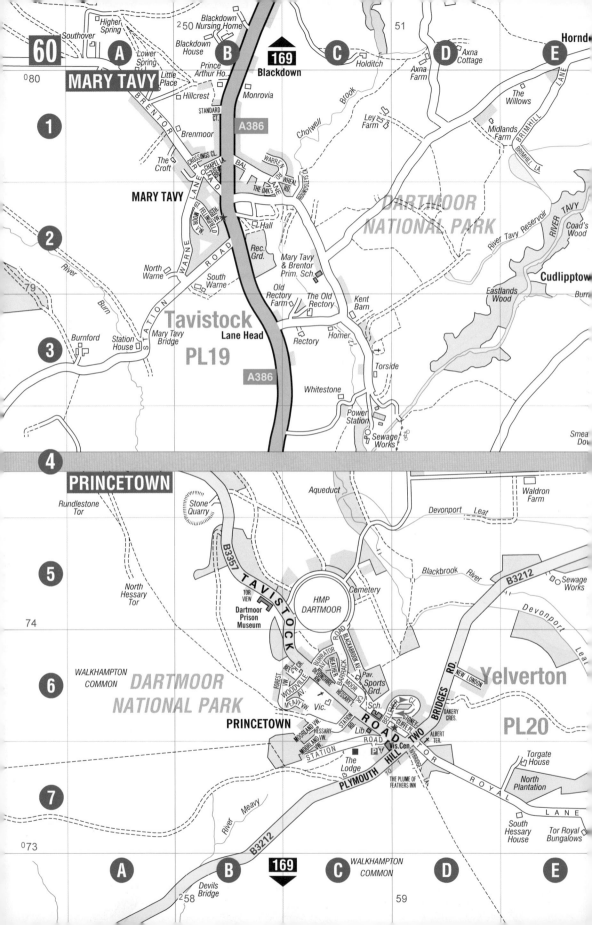

MARY TAVY

A   B   C   D   E

Hornd

1

Southover
Higher Spring
Lower Spring
Little Place
Hillcrest
Blackdown Nursing Home
250
Blackdown House
Prince Arthur Ho.
Monrovia
STANDARD CT.
▲ **169** Blackdown
51
Holditch
Axna Farm
Axna Cottage
The Willows
Midlands Farm
BRIMHILL
BRIMHILL LA.

A386
Brenmoor
The Croft
CROSSINGS CL.
CHAPEL LA.
BAL
WARREN RD.
WHEAL RD.
THE OAKS
BROOKSMEADOW

Cholwell
Brook
Ley Farm

DARTMOOR NATIONAL PARK

MARY TAVY

GT. FELLINGFIELD
M.T. WOOD
WARNE ROAD
Hall
Rec. Grd.
Mary Tavy & Brentor Prim. Sch.

River Tavy Reservoir
RIVER TAVY
Coad's Wood

2

North Warne
South Warne
Old Rectory Farm
The Old Rectory
Kent Barn

Eastlands Wood
Cudlipptow
Burn

79

River
Burn
STATION ROAD

Tavistock
Mary Tavy Bridge
Lane Head
Rectory
Homer
Torside

3

Burnford
Station House
PL19
A386
Whitestone

Power Station
Sewage Works
Smea
Dov

4

PRINCETOWN

A   B   C   D   E

Rundlestone Tor
Stone Quarry
Aqueduct
Waldron Farm
Devonport Leat

5

North Hessary Tor
B3357
TAVISTOCK ROAD
TOR VIEW
Dartmoor Prison Museum
HMP DARTMOOR
Cemetery
Blackbrook River
B3212
Sewage Works
Devonport Leat

74

6

WALKHAMPTON COMMON
DARTMOOR NATIONAL PARK
BURRATOR
BEECH PK.
DEVONSHIRE
HEATHER
BARRACK
Pav.
Sports Grd.
NEW LONDON
Yelverton
FOREST VW.
WOODVILLE
MEAVY VW.
BLACKABROOK AV.
MOOR CL.
HESSARY
Sch.
BRIDGES RD.
OAKERY CRES.
PL20

PRINCETOWN
MOORLAND VW.
MOORLAND VW.
MOORLAND VW.
HESSARY
STATION ROAD
Vic.
Lib
ROAD
Vis.Cen.
STATION
PH
BELLEVER
STONEY
CLIFF R.
ROAD TWO
TOR ROYAL
Torgate House
North Plantation
ALBERT TER.

7

River Meavy
The Lodge
PLYMOUTH HILL
THE PLUME OF FEATHERS INN
BRIDGES
LANE
South Hessary House
Tor Royal Bungalows

073

A   B   C   D   E

258
Devils Bridge
B3212
▼ **169**
WALKHAMPTON COMMON
59

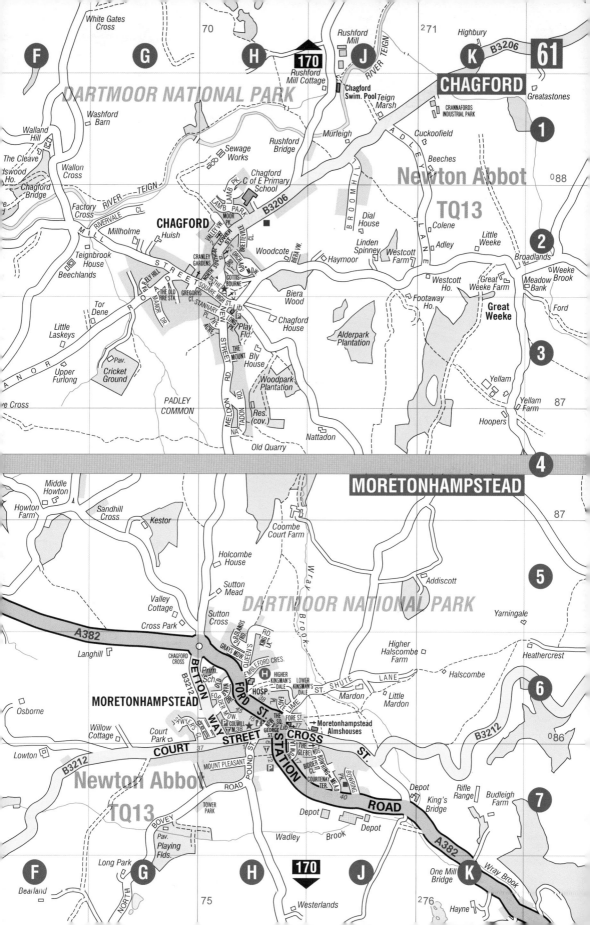

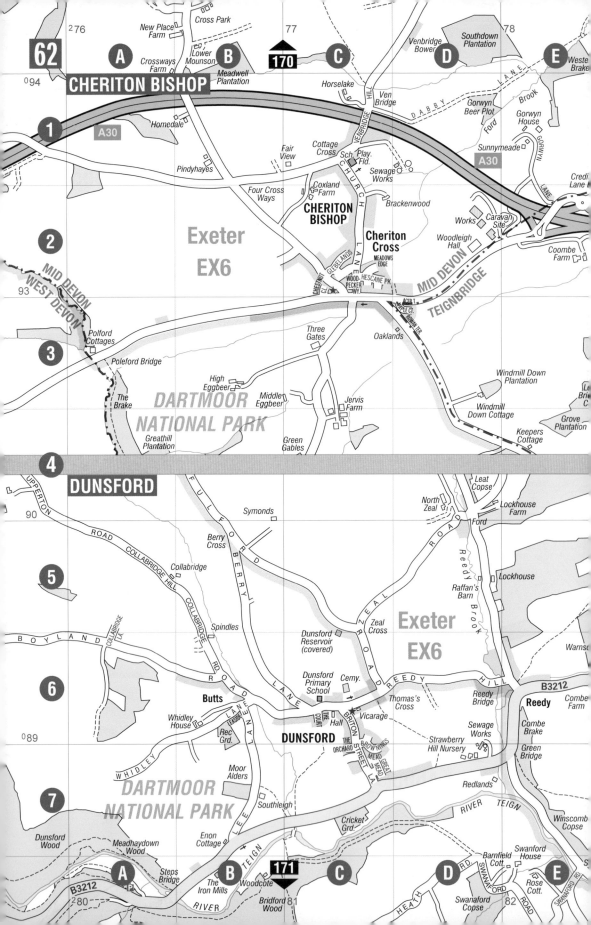

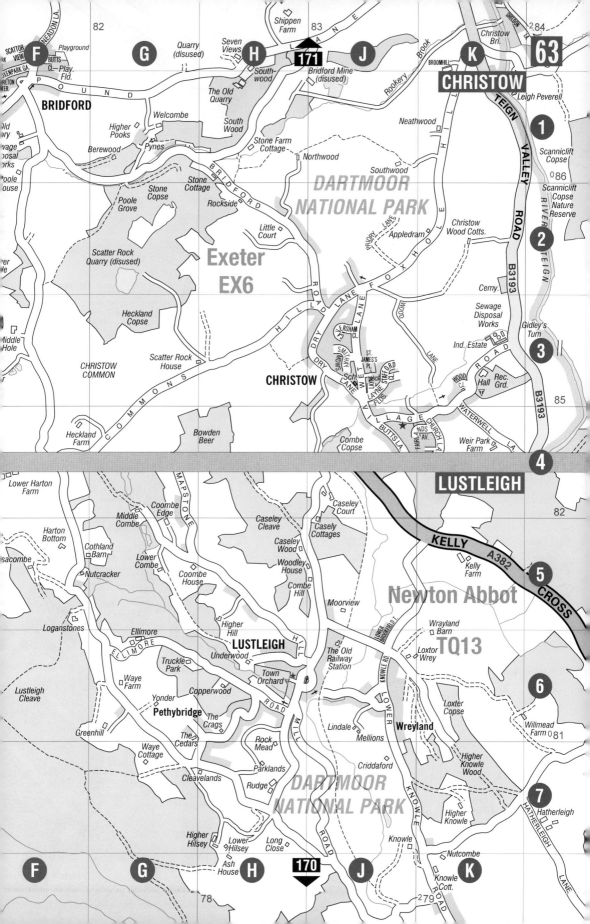

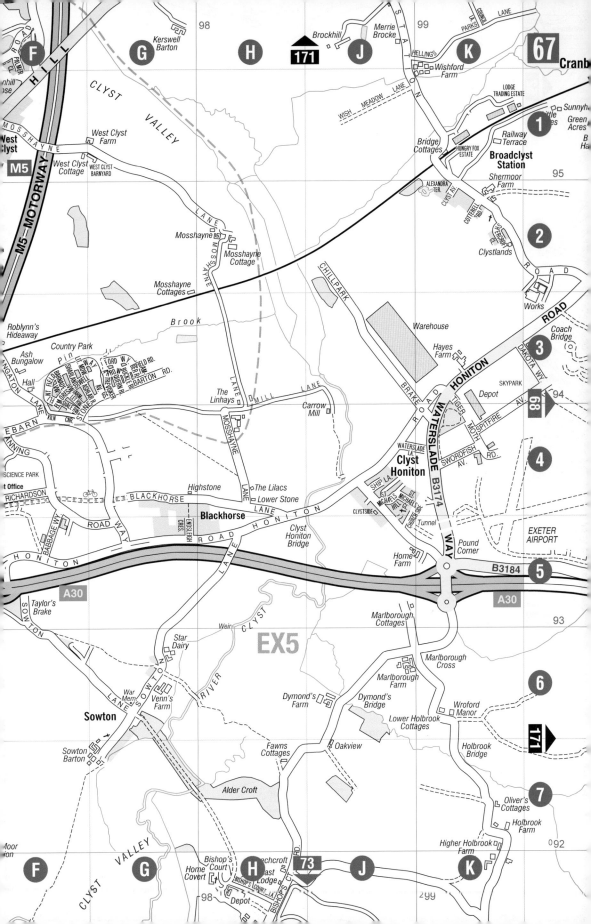

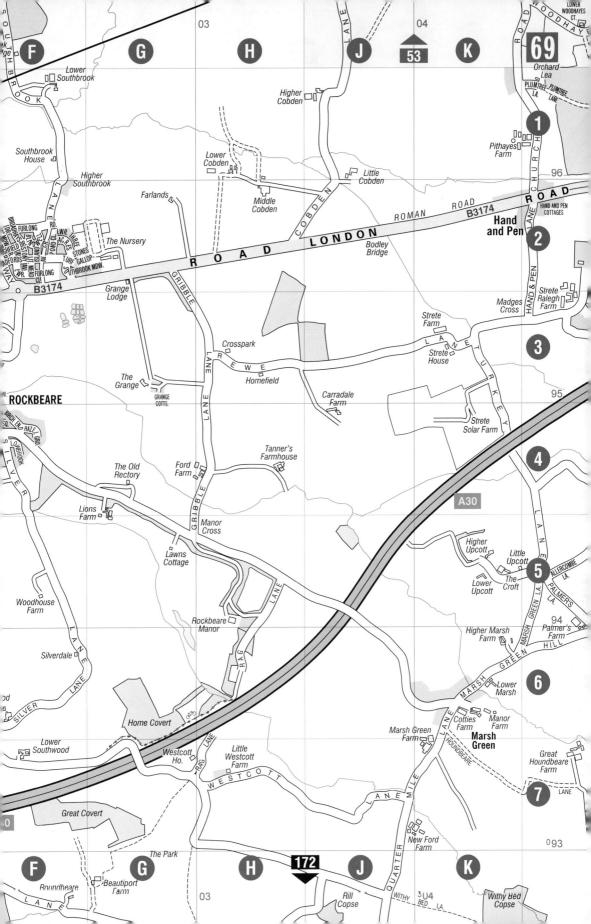

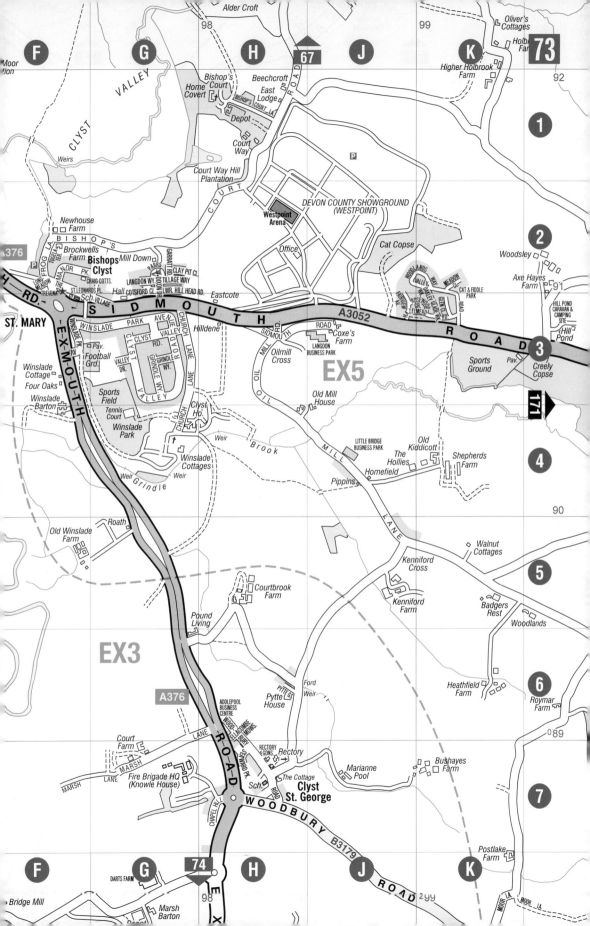

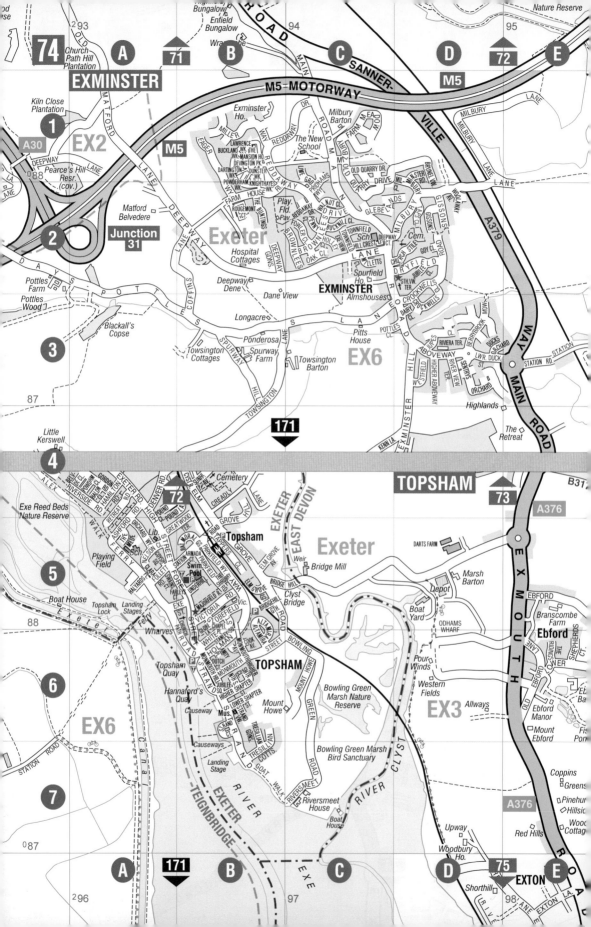

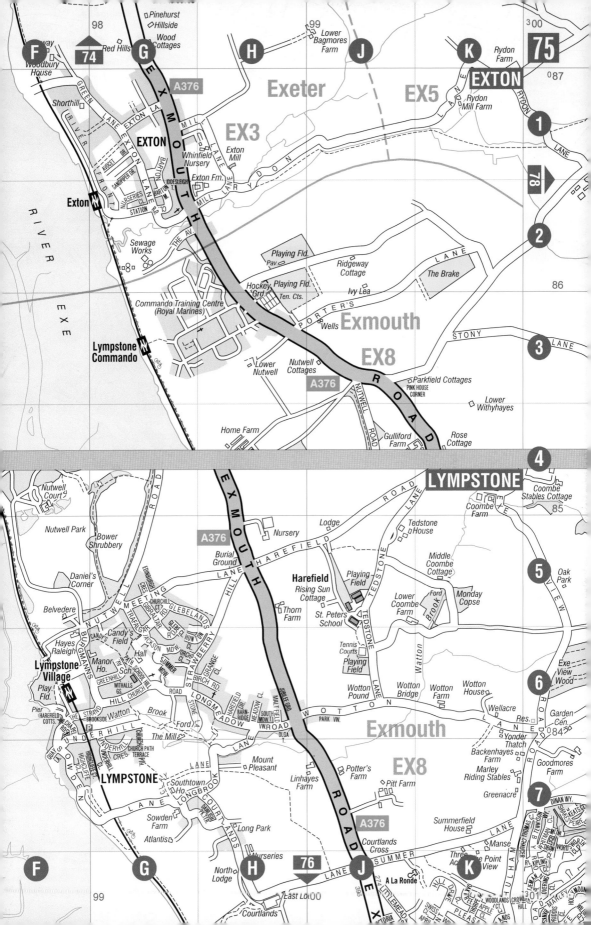

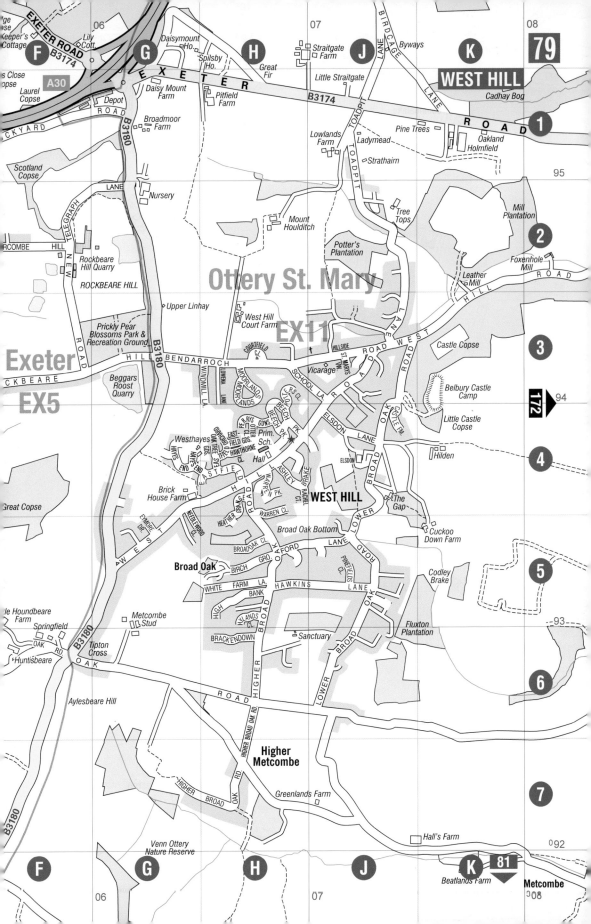

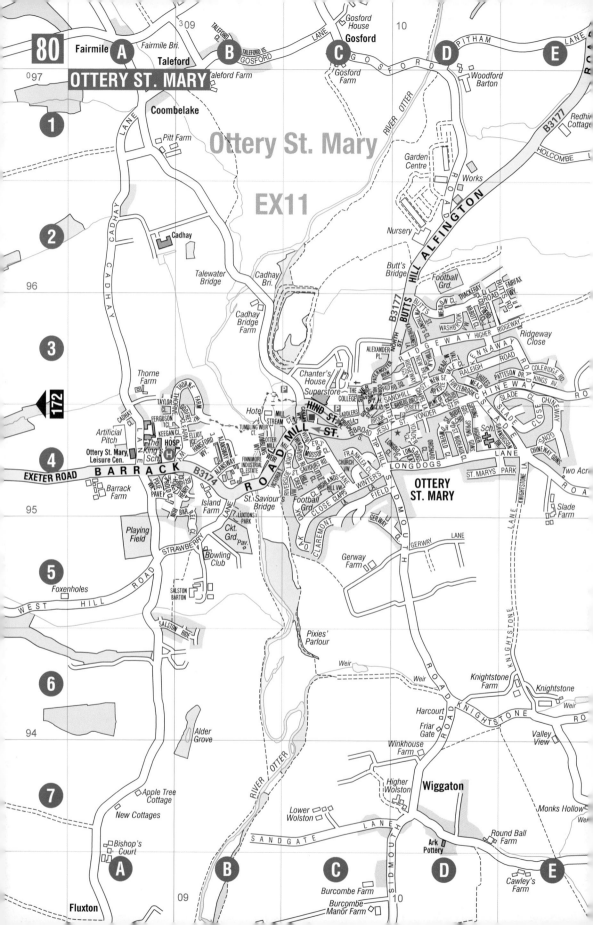

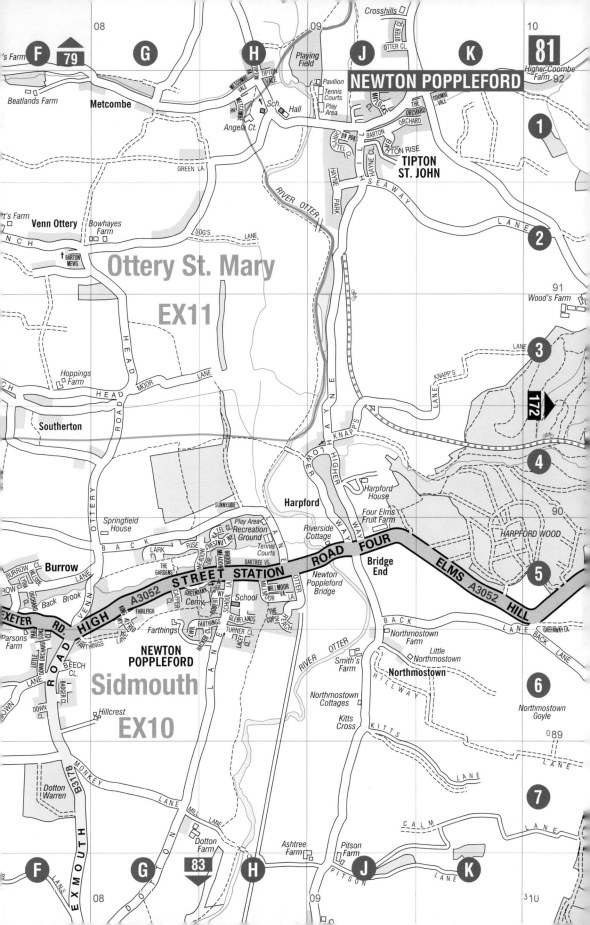

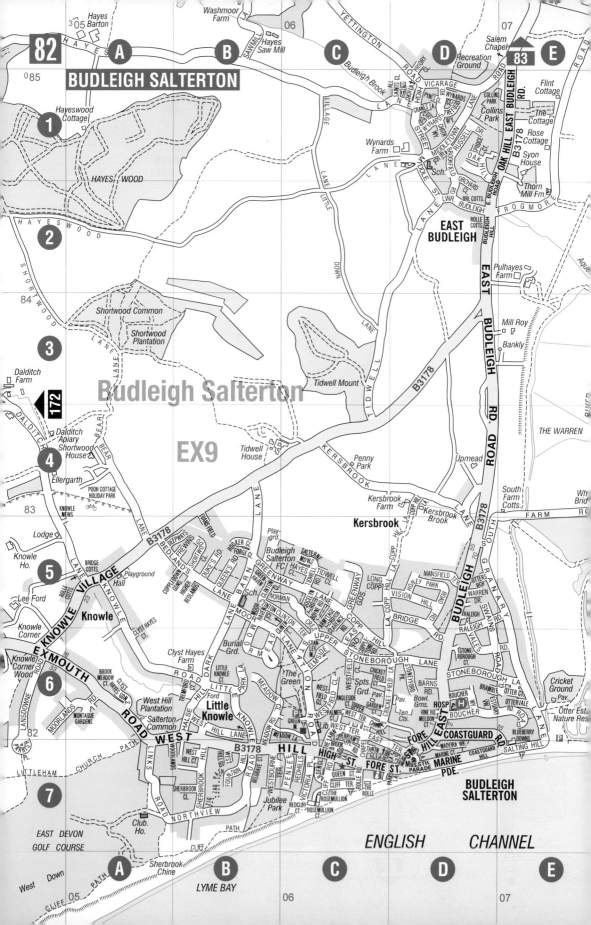

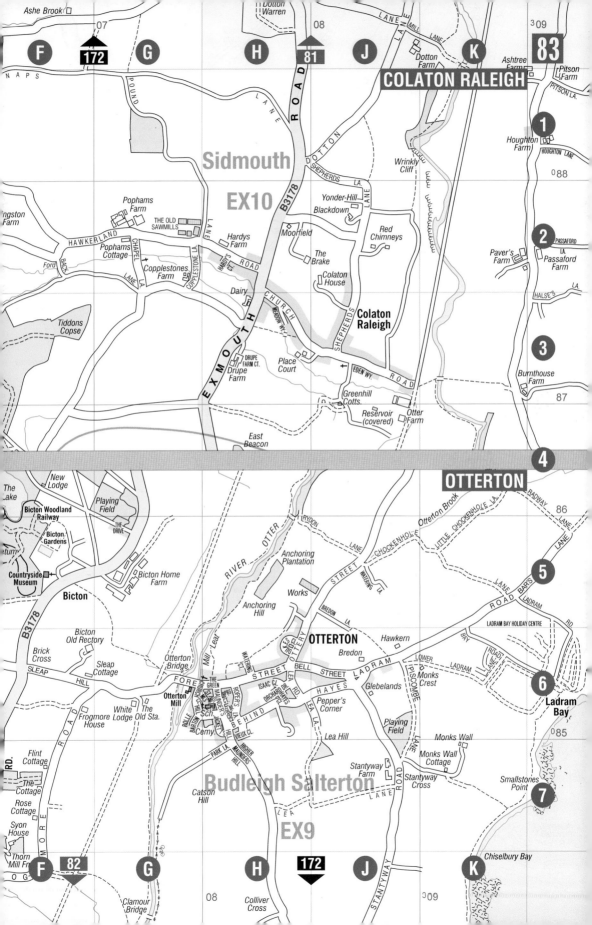

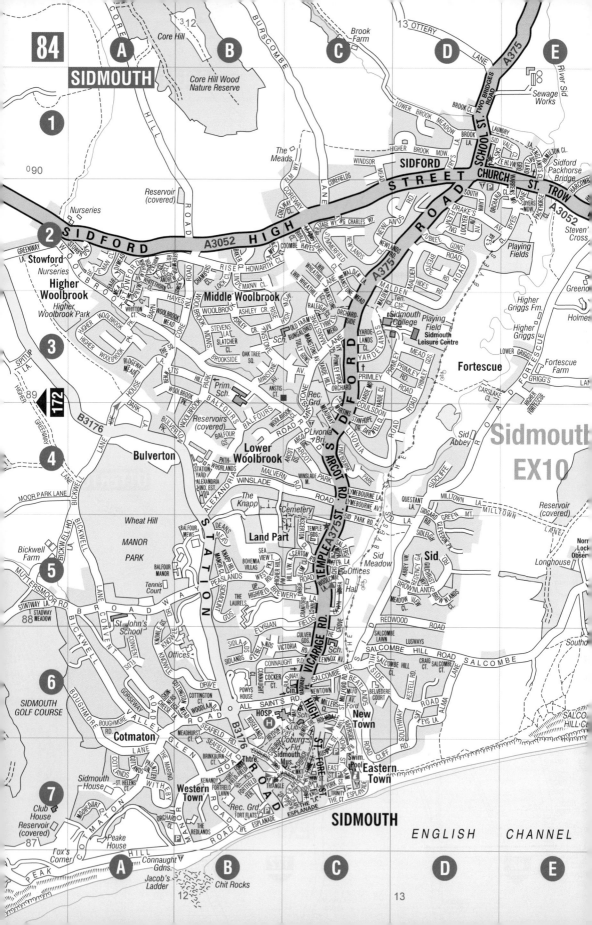

A   B   C   D   E

1

Core Hill
3.12
Core Hill Wood
Nature Reserve

Brook
Farm

13 OTTERY

A375

River Sid

Sewage
Works

Two Bridges

School St.

LAUNDRY

Sidford
Packhorse
Bridge

²90

Reservoir
(covered)

Nurseries

The
Meads

Higher Brook Mdw.

Lower Brook Meadow

Brook Cl.

Sid Vale

Hamilton Cl.

SIDFORD

2

SIDFORD   A3052   HIGH   STREET   CHURCH ST. TROW

ROAD

A3052

Steven's
Cross

Greenway La.

Stowford
Nurseries

Higher
Woolbrook

Higher
Woolbrook Park

Middle Woolbrook

Newlands
Road

Drake's Av.

Playing
Fields

Greeno

Higher
Griggs Fm.

Higher
Griggs

Holmes

3

172

B3176

89

SPITUP LA.

HIGHER GREENWAY LANE

Prim.
Sch.

Balfours
Road

Reservoirs
(covered)

Sidmouth
College

Sidmouth
Leisure Centre

Playing
Field

Primley

Fortescue

Fortescue
Farm

Grigg's La.

**Sidmouth
EX10**

4

Bulverton

Lower
Woolbrook

Livonia
Bri.

Winslade
M.

WINSLADE
ROAD

MALVERN RD.

Sid
Abbey

MOOR PARK LANE

Wheat Hill

The Knapp

Cemetery

Land Part

Lymebourne Av.

Sid Park Rd.

Sid
Meadow

MILLTOWN LA.

MILLTOWN
LANE

Reservoir
(covered)

Norr
Lock
Obser

5

Bickwell
Farm

MUTTERSMOOR RD.

MANOR
PARK

Balfour
Mews

Balfour
Manor

Tennis
Court

STATION ROAD

DEAN
MEAD

KNAPP HILL

Bohemia
Villas

The
Laurels

BREWERY

Offices

Sid La.

Sidlands

Sid
Hall

BROWNLANDS

Longhouse

Southe

88 STINTWAY LA.
STADWAY MEADOW

BICKWELL

St. John's
School

Knowle

Offices

Victoria
Rd.

Lennox Av.

SALCOMBE
LAWN

LUSWAYS

SALCOMBE   HILL   ROAD   SALCOMBE

Salcombe
Hill Cl.

6

SIDMOUTH
GOLF COURSE

BOUGHMORE ROAD

GLEN   ROAD

VALLEY

Cottington
Mead

WOODLAND

All Saint's
Rd.

Connaught

Cocker's
Ct.

Newtown

H HOSP.

SALCOMBE RD.

New
Town

Swim.
Pool

Eastern
Town

REDWOOD   ROAD

Belvedere
Court

SALCO
HILL C

7

Club
House

Reservoir
(covered)

87

Fox's
Corner

Sidmouth
House

ST. HELENS
CT.

Cotmaton

Western
Town

Coburg
Fld.

Sidmouth
Mus.

Rec. Grd.
Fort Flats

ESPLANADE

SIDMOUTH

ENGLISH   CHANNEL

PEAK HILL

12   Connaught
Gdns.

Jacob's
Ladder

Chit Rocks

A   B   C   D   E

13

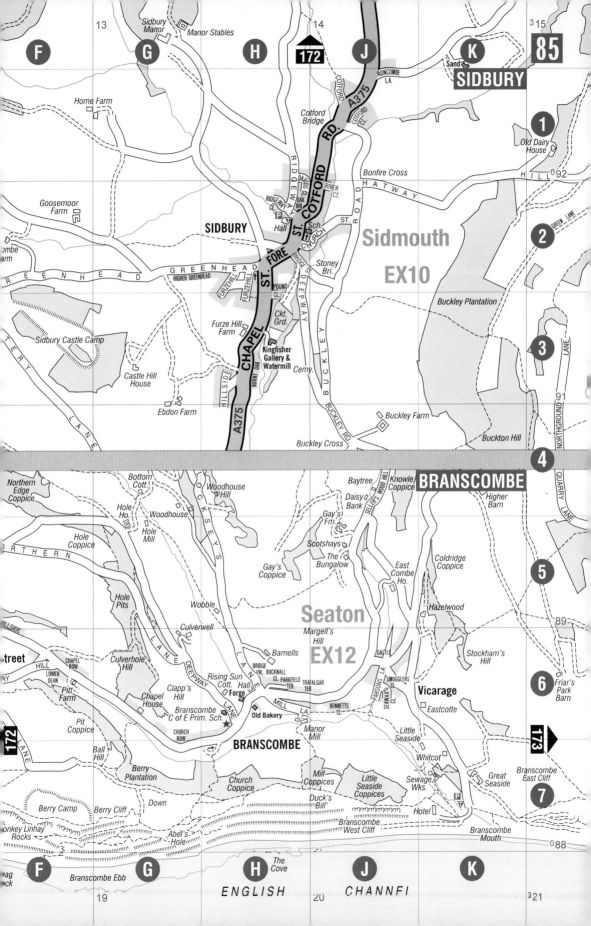

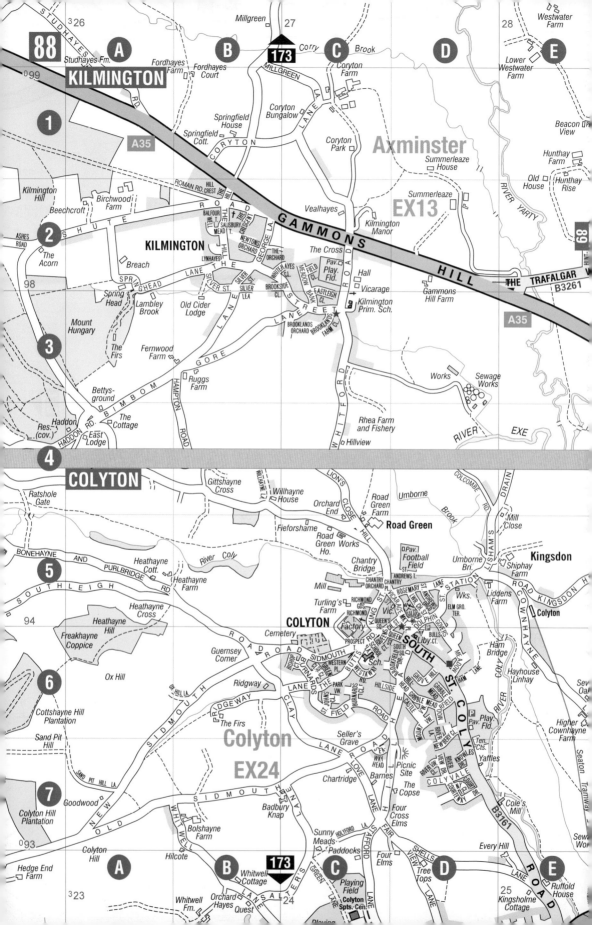

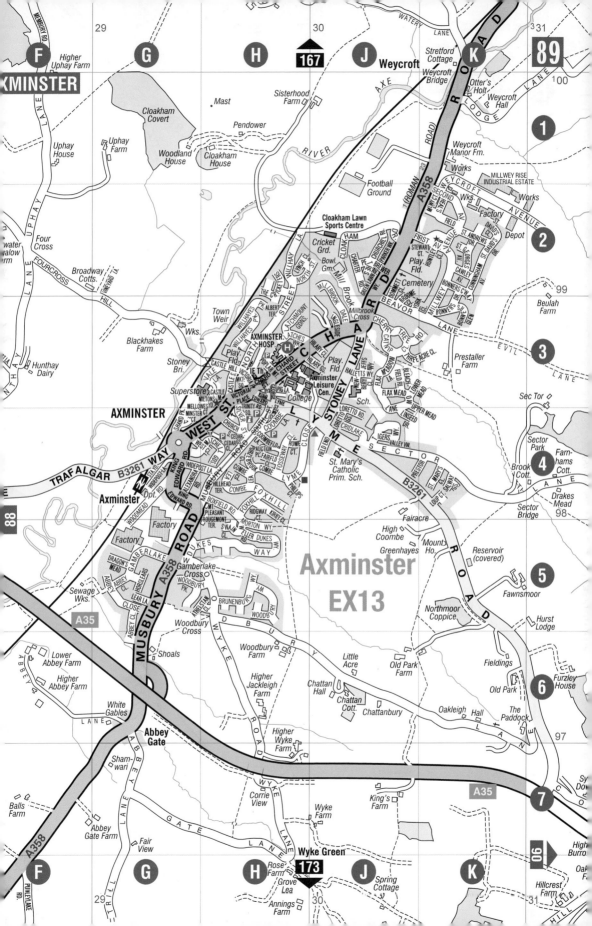

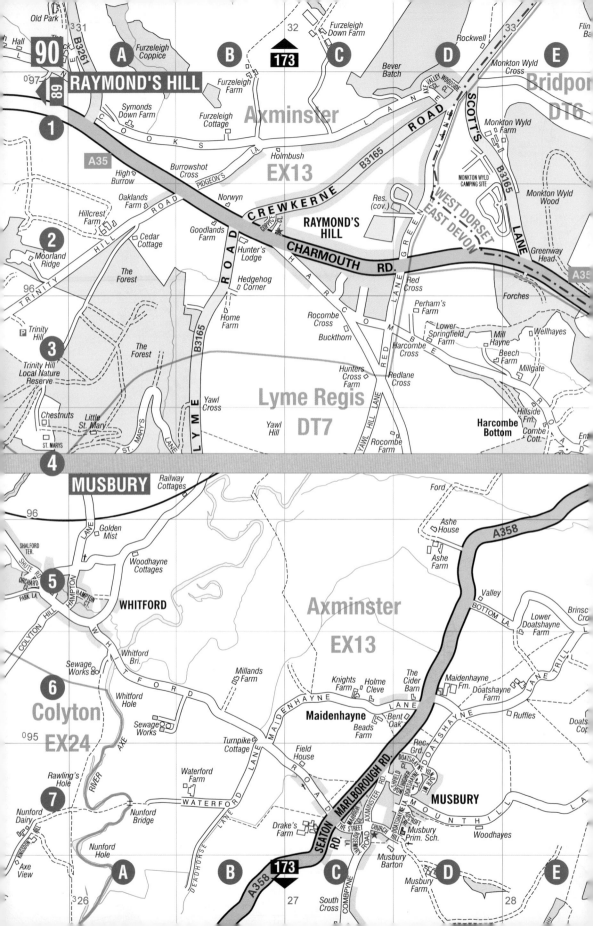

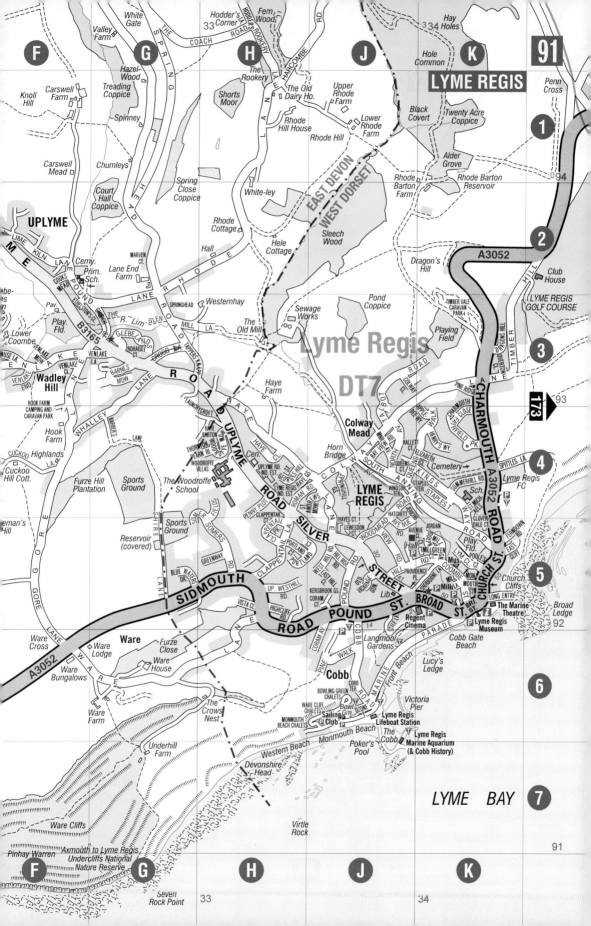

LYME REGIS

Lyme Regis
DT7

LYME BAY

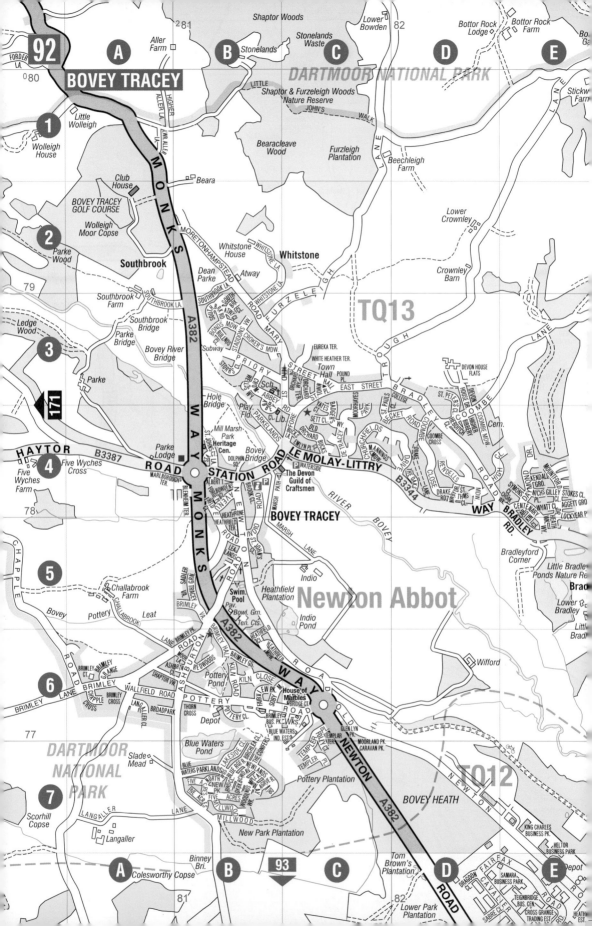

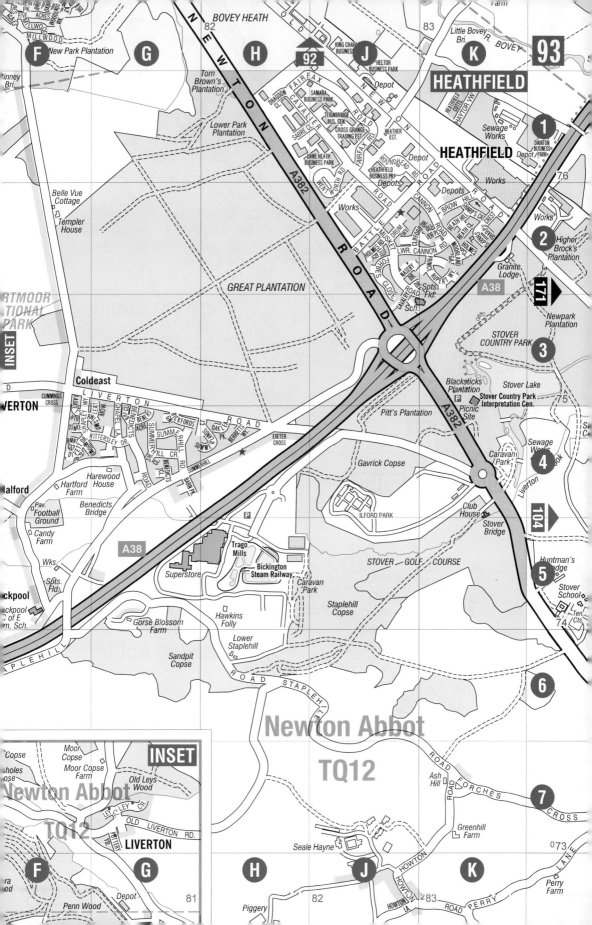

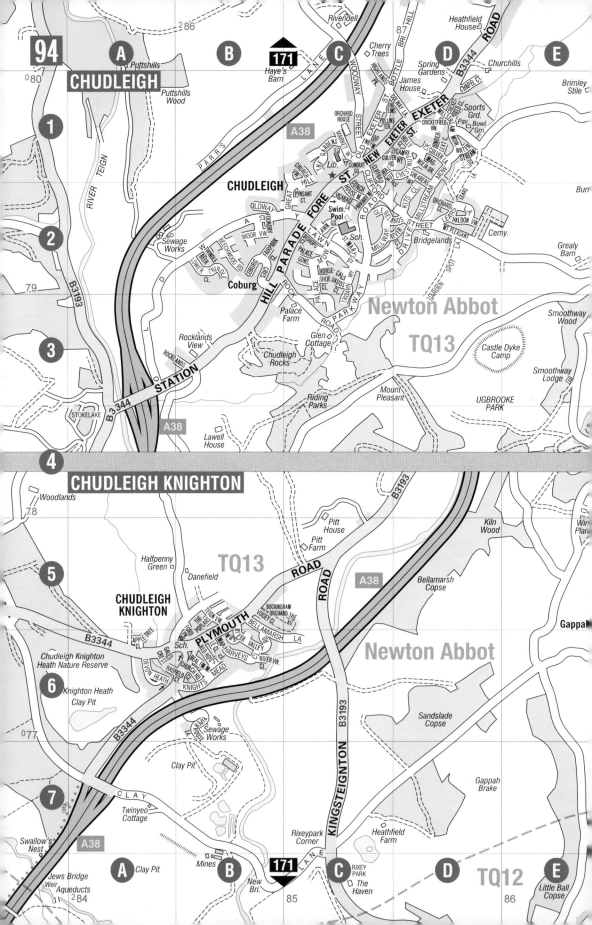

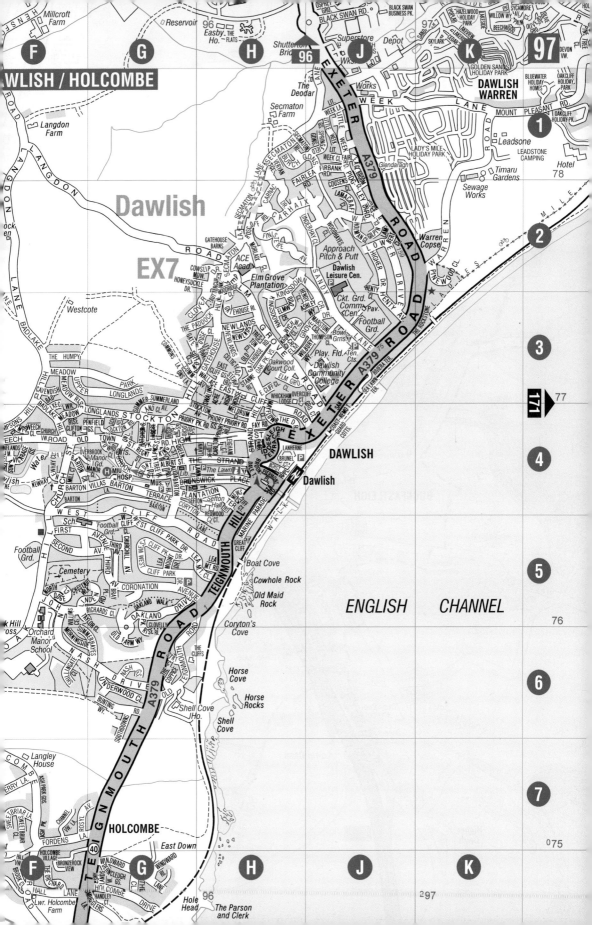

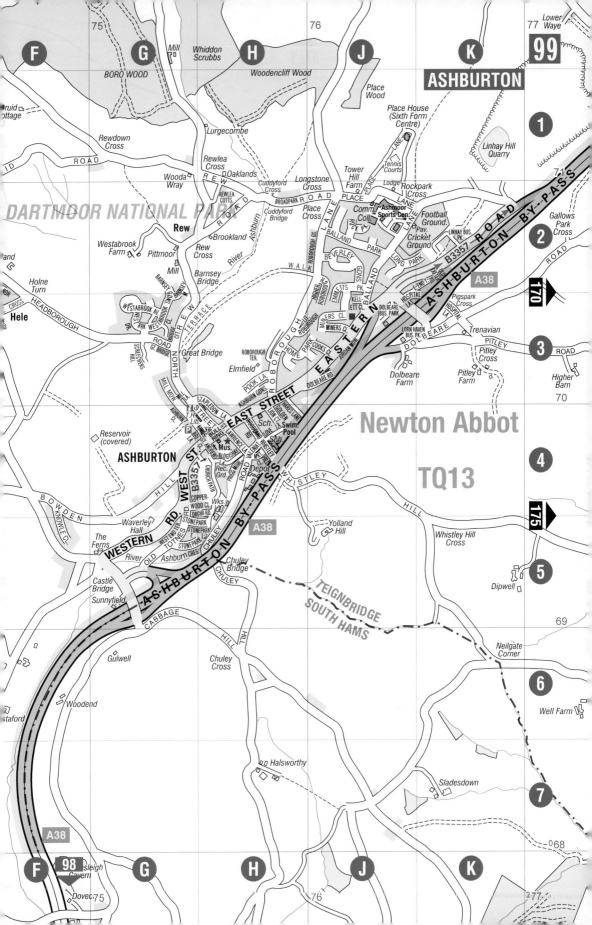

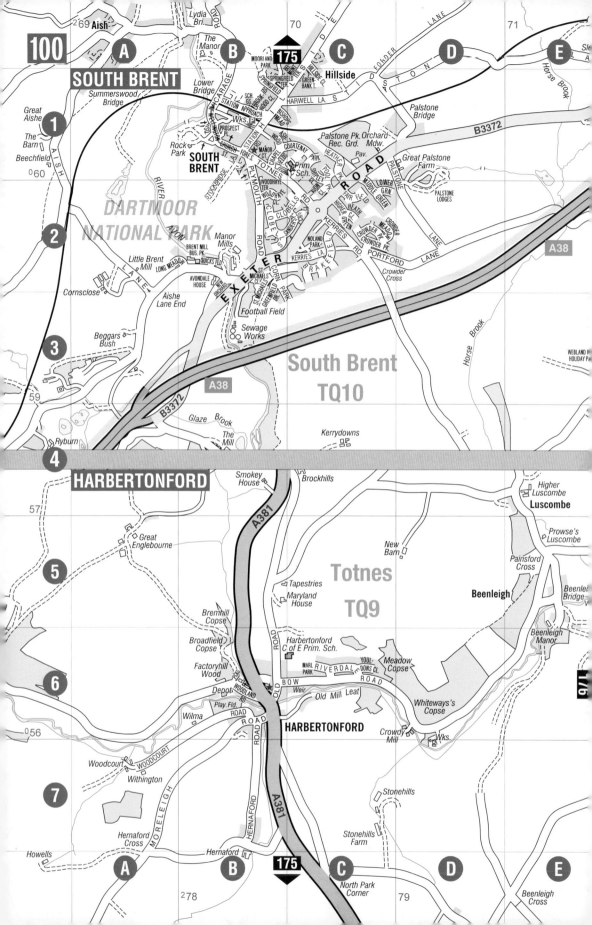

Map labels

DENBURY

IPPLEPEN

Newton Abbot TQ12

Dainton

Grid references (top margin)
F G H 176 J K

Grid references (bottom margin)
F G 176 H J K

Right margin numbers
1 069 2 108 3 68 4 5 67 110 6 7 66

Top section (Denbury area)
- Oxenham's Wood
- Sewage Works
- Rifle Range
- F'ball Ground
- Channing's Wood
- Playground
- Stubbins Cross
- HMP CHANNINGS WOOD
- Denburydown
- Heathfield
- Peartree Cross
- Start Cross
- Greenhill Plantation
- MOORLAND AV
- FAIRVIEW RD
- Horse Hill
- Norden Farm
- DENBURY DOWN LA
- HEATHFIELD RD
- WOODLAND CL
- WEST END TER.
- Prim. Sch.
- EAST ST.
- STREET
- GREENHILL
- Ryd Cross
- WOODLAND ROAD
- TOWNSEND
- WEST ST.
- WEST DOWN RD.
- ORCHARD CL.
- SOUTH ST.
- **DENBURY**
- Newton Cross
- IPPLEPEN CROSS
- Denbury Down Cross
- DETBURY
- DENBURY LA
- DENBURY GREEN
- COPSEY
- DENBURY LANE
- Denbury Down Plantation
- Halwell Cross
- Home Park
- DORNAFIELD CARAVAN PARK
- Wrenwell Cross
- Halwell Farm
- Tornewton

Bottom section (Ipplepen area)
- Clennon's Linhay
- Clennon
- Stallage
- Nursery & Garden Centre
- The Devon Bird of Prey Centre
- Driving Range
- Gote Linth
- MOOR
- BEECH
- Danes
- Football Ground
- Cricket Ground Pav.
- DORNAFIELD LANE
- Lidmore Copse
- Woodville
- Club House
- DAINTON PARK GOLF COURSE
- onpark od
- TREES
- Denbury Cross
- Dornafield Cross
- Reservoir (covered)
- ROSS PARK CARAVAN PARK
- Park Hill Farm
- ROAD
- Lyde's Linhay
- LANE
- TOWNSEND HILL
- ELLIOTT CT.
- Newton Abbot TQ12
- Park Hill
- LAPTHORNE INDUSTRIAL ESTATE
- OLMAN HILL
- The Priory
- TREMLETT GR.
- DORNAFIELD RD
- Dornafield
- DR. W.
- MEADOW PK.
- CAUSEWAY CROSS
- MARLDON
- PARK HILL
- Cross Park
- **IPPLEPEN**
- CAUNTER'S
- NORTH END CL.
- BROOKFIELD
- ORCHARD CL.
- DR.
- EAST STREET
- BARN PK
- Dainton
- Church Hills
- FORE ST.
- PATERNOSTER LANE
- POPLAR TER.
- BORN CL.
- Lane End Cross
- THORNE ORCHARD
- LANG WY
- ROSE GDS.
- BUTTLANDS IND. EST.
- Dainton Elms Cross
- ORLEY
- The Glebe
- SILVER ST.
- CHURCH PATH
- NEWHAYES
- Prim. Sch.
- CROFT RD.
- CROFT MDW.
- CROKERS WY.
- ORCHARD RD.
- CLARENDON RD.
- WENTWORTH CL.
- JUNIOR ROAD
- DR. JOHN CROKER RD
- LEDGS.
- A381
- ROAD
- Crosslands
- Orley House
- ROAD
- CLAMPIT
- BILTOR
- Rec Grd.
- Tennis Court
- Bowl. Grn.
- GATEHELANDS CT.
- COMBE CL.
- CLAMPIT CL.
- DINKS
- Blackstone Cross
- Wrigwell Cross
- Swallowfield
- Maitlands
- Dainton Tunnel
- Bulle
- Barton House
- Newhay Cross
- BLACKSTONE RD.
- Beltor Cross
- Croker's Farm
- WRIGWELL LANE
- Cockleford Bridge
- Ipplepen Quarry (dis.)
- Tors Barn
- CONNIFORD LANE
- BILTOR RD
- Hannafords
- TOTNES
- Wood's Barn
- Bilver Cottage
- Bilver Cross
- 176
- Wrigwell Bridge

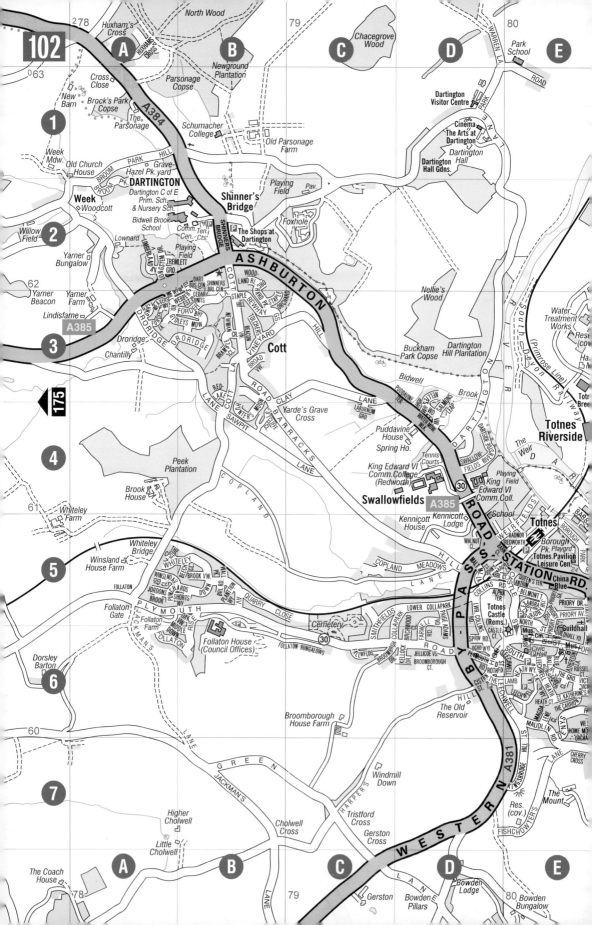

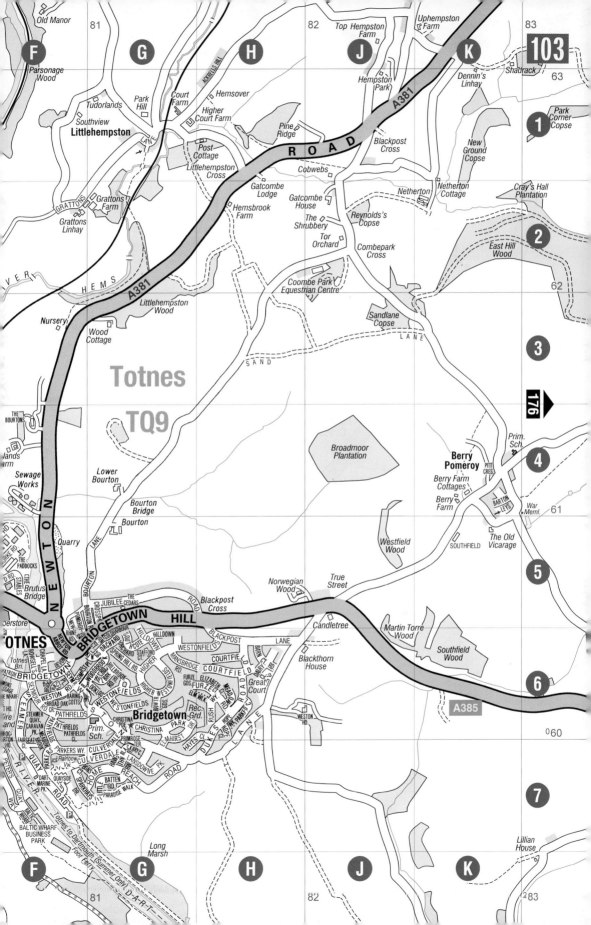

F Old Manor
Parsonage Wood

81

G Tudorlands
Southview
Littlehempston
Park Hill
Grattons
Grattons Farm
Grattons Linhay

H 82
Court Farm
Hemsover
Higher Court Farm
Post Cottage
Littlehempston Cross
Gatcombe Lodge
Hemsbrook Farm
Pine Ridge
Gatcombe House

J Top Hempston Farm
Hempston Park
Cobwebs
Blackpost Cross
The Shrubbery
Tor Orchard
Reynolds's Copse
Combepark Cross

K Uphempston Farm
Dennin's Linhay
Shadrack 63
Netherton
Netherton Cottage
New Ground Copse
Cray's Hall Plantation

1 Park Corner Copse

2 East Hill Wood
62

A381 ROAD

R I V E R   H E M S

A381

Totnes
TQ9

The Bourtons
lands arm
Sewage Works
Nursery
Wood Cottage
Littlehempstson Wood
Coombe Park Equestrian Centre
SAND
Sandlane Copse
LANE

3

Broadmoor Plantation

Berry Pomeroy
Berry Farm Cottages
Berry Farm
PITT CRES.
BARTON LEYS
Prim. Sch.
War Meml.
The Old Vicarage
SOUTHFIELD

4 61

176

5

Lower Bourton
Bourton Bridge
Bourton
Quarry
THE PADDOCKS
Brutus Bridge
NEWTON
BOURTON LANE

Norwegian Wood
True Street
Westfield Wood
Martin Torre Wood
Southfield Wood

6

TOTNES
BRIDGETOWN HILL
Blackpost Cross
Candletree
Blackthorn House
Bridgetown
Prim. Sch.
WESTON HO.
Great Court
A385
060

7

Baltic Wharf Business Park
Long Marsh
Totnes to Dartmouth (Summer Only) Foot Ferry
R I V E R   D A R T

F 81
G 82
H
J 82
K 83

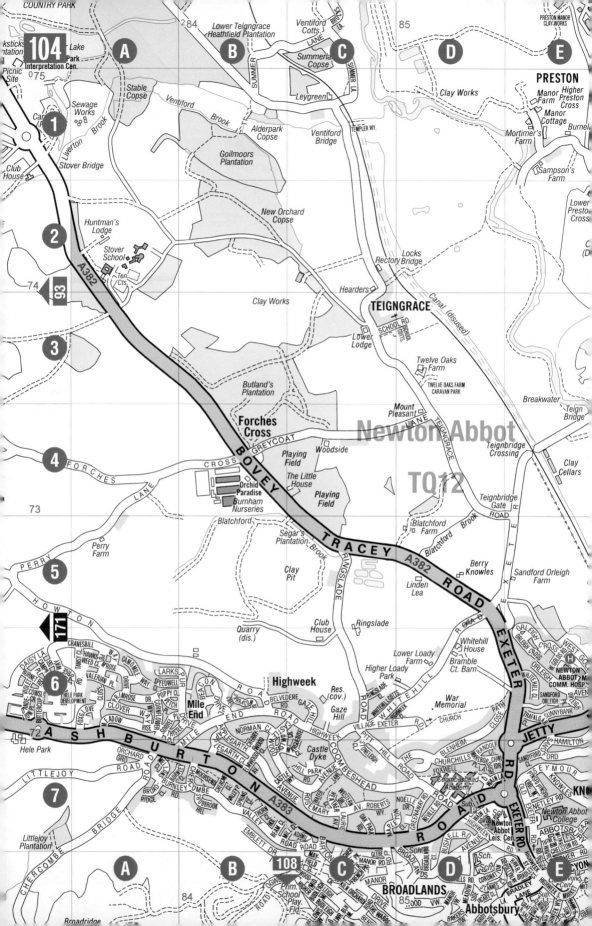

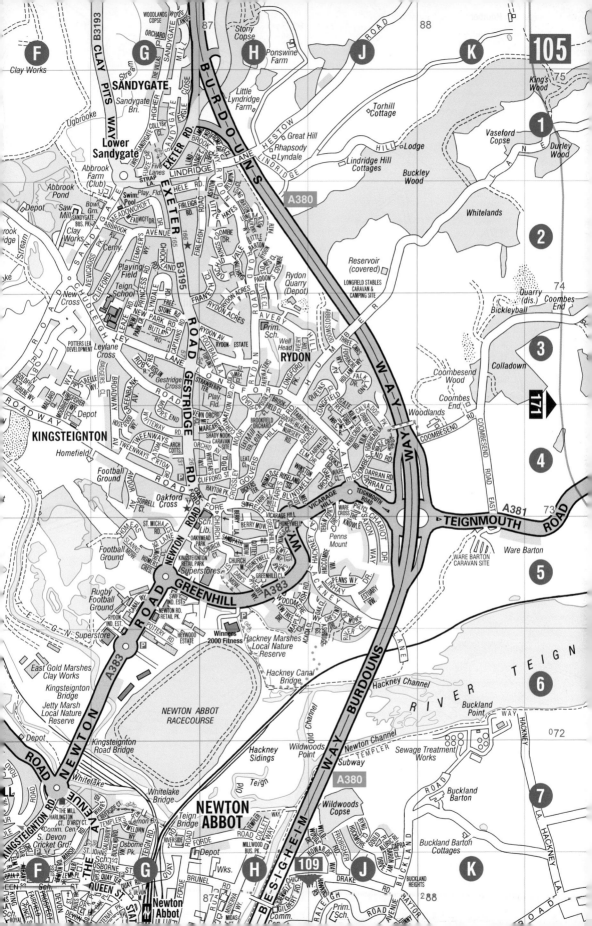

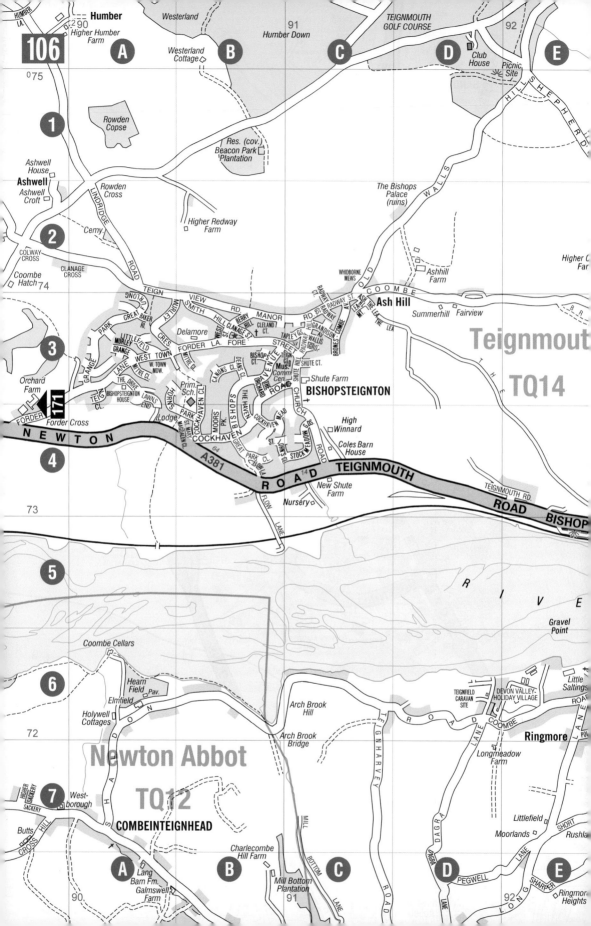

106

Humber

Higher Humber Farm

Westerland

Westerland Cottage

Humber Down

TEIGNMOUTH GOLF COURSE

Club House

Picnic Site

Rowden Copse

Res. (cov.) Beacon Park Plantation

Ashwell House
Ashwell
Ashwell Croft

Rowden Cross

Higher Redway Farm

The Bishops Palace (ruins)

Ashhill Farm

Higher C Far

Cemy.

COLWAY CROSS

Coombe Hatch

CLANAGE CROSS

Whidborne Mews

Ash Hill

Summerhill   Fairview

Radway   Radway

PARK
GREAT
BAKER RL.
MURLEY
SMITH
VIEW
TEIGN
FURLONG
HILL
MANOR
CLANAGE ST.
BERRY
RD.
GRANDISON
WALLS
CROFT

Delamore

LITTLEFIELD
GRANGE
WEST TOWN
MITRE CL.
LANE
FORDER LA.
FORE
STREET
TEIGN
BISHOPS CT.
Mus.
Comm Cen

Shute Farm

Orchard Farm

171

FORDER   Forder Cross

TEIGN CL.
BISHOPSTEIGNTON HOUSE
THE DRIVE
LAWNS END
Lodge
Prim. Sch.
PARK
COCKHAVEN CL.
BISHOPS
THE HAVEN
ORCHARD
CHURCH
AVENUE

BISHOPSTEIGNTON

High Winnard

Coles Barn House

N E W T O N

A381

R O A D   **TEIGNMOUTH**

New Shute Farm

Nursery

FLOW LANE

TEIGNMOUTH

TEIGNMOUTH RD.

ROAD   **BISHOP**

R   I   V   E

Gravel Point

Coombe Cellars

Hearn Field   Pav.

Elmfield

Holywell Cottages

Arch Brook Hill

Arch Brook Bridge

Teignfield Caravan Site

DEVON VALLEY HOLIDAY VILLAGE

Little Saltings

Ringmore

Longmeadow Farm

Newton Abbot

HIGHER SACKERY

Westborough

SACKERY

Butts

CROSS HILL

TQ12

COMBEINTEIGNHEAD

Charlecombe Hill Farm

MILL BOTTOM LANE

Mill Bottom Plantation

TEIGNHARVEY

COOMBE

DAGRA LANE

PEGWELL LANE

Littlefield

Moorlands

SHORT
Rushla

SHARPER

LONG

Lang Barn Fm. Galmswell Farm

Ringmore Heights

Teignmout

TQ14

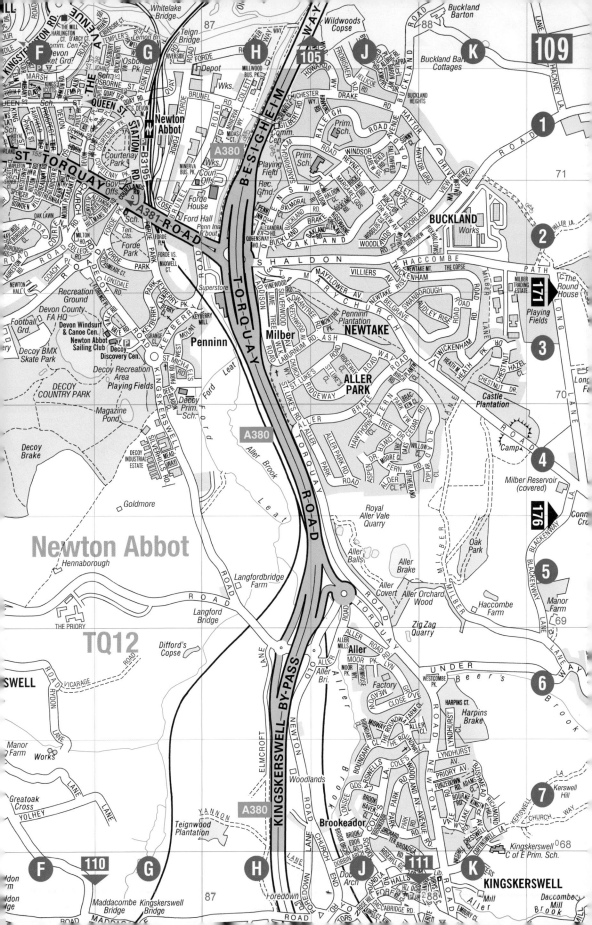

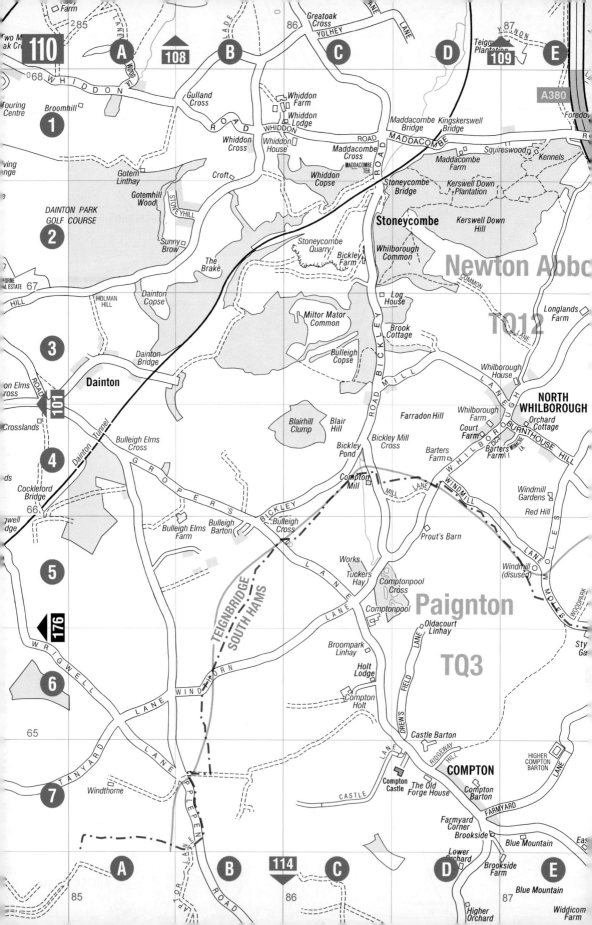

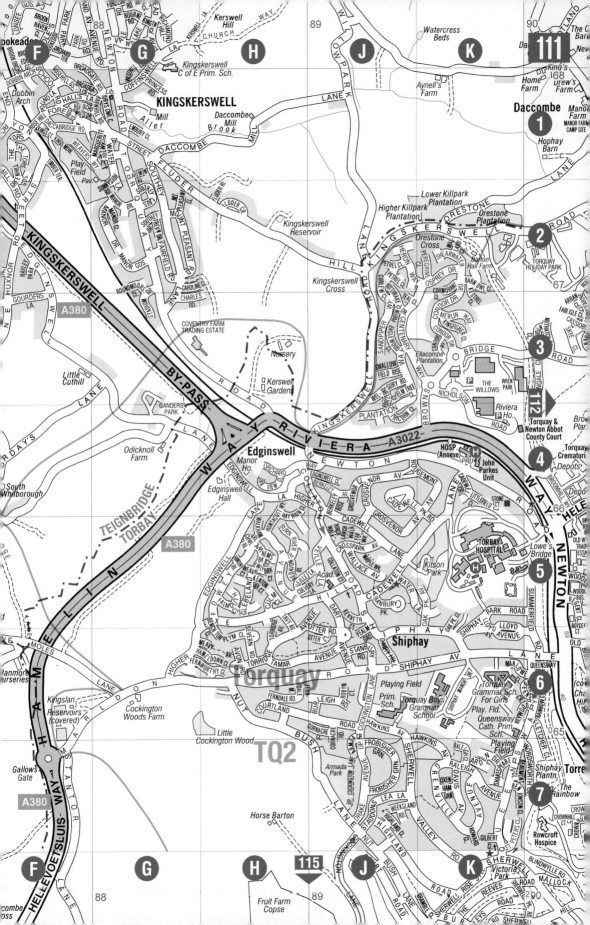

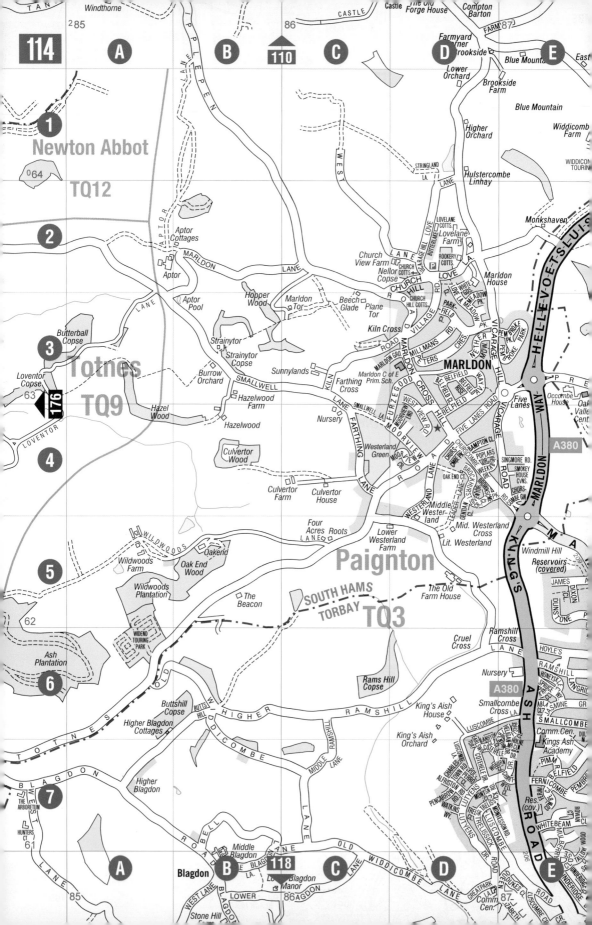

115
111
116
119
F
G
H
J
K
1
2
3
4
5
6
7
88
89
90
63
62
61
Horse Barton
Fruit Farm Copse
Rosery Grange
Meadow Farm
Almshouses
Stantor
Stantor Cottages
Stantor Barton
Stantor Linhay
A380
Cockington Court Craft Centre
Cockington Country Park
Church Wood
Cockington Forge
Torquay
Cockington
Lanscombe
Lodge
Warren Barn
Hellinghay Plantation
Manscombe Plantation
TQ2
Scadson Plantation
Petersfield
TOTNES ROAD
Occombe Cross
Radio Transmitting Sta.
Three Barrows
East Down
Burrow Down
East Down Plantation
Round Down Wood
Browse's Brake
Hollicombe Lake
Round Hill
Ten Acre Brake
Preston Prim. Sch.
Hollicombe
Livermead
Chelston
Victoria Park
Ridgefield
Thornhill Brake
Preston Park
Playing Field
Preston
Shorton
Shorton Manor
Shorton Woods
Shorton Farm
Oil Cove
Hollicombe Park
Hollicombe Beach
Chadwell Cen.
Resource Cen.
Hollicombe Head
TORBAY ROAD
A3022
B3201
B3060
Preston Sands
TOR BAY
Oldway Mansion
Tennis Courts
Oldway
Oldway Primary Sch.
Playing Field
The Brunel Acad.
Parkfield
Redcliffe Court
Comm. Cen.
Cemetery
Victoria Park
Paignton Pier
PAIGNTON
The Grn.
Sands
HOSP.
MARINE DRIVE
ESPLANADE RD.
MARINE PARADE
PROMENADE

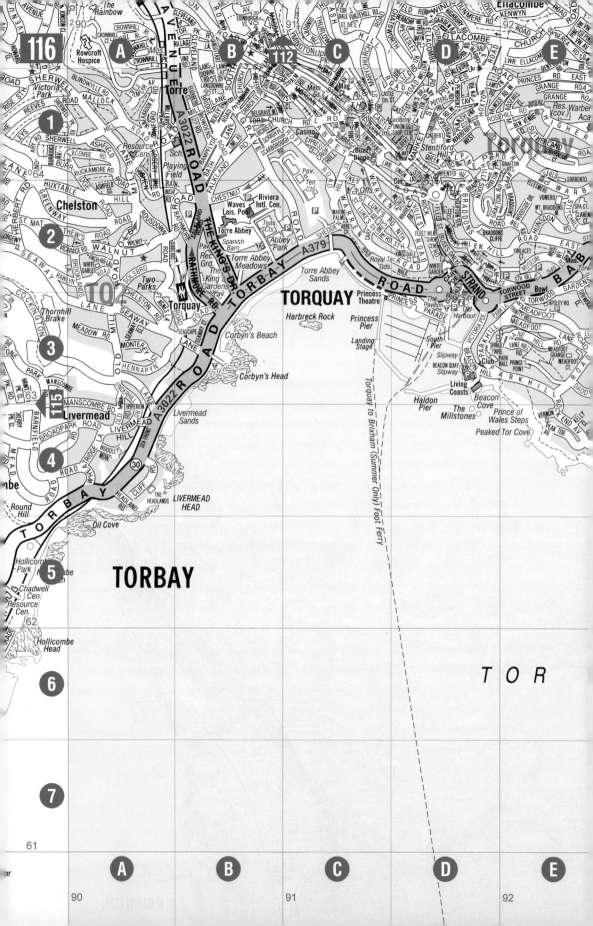

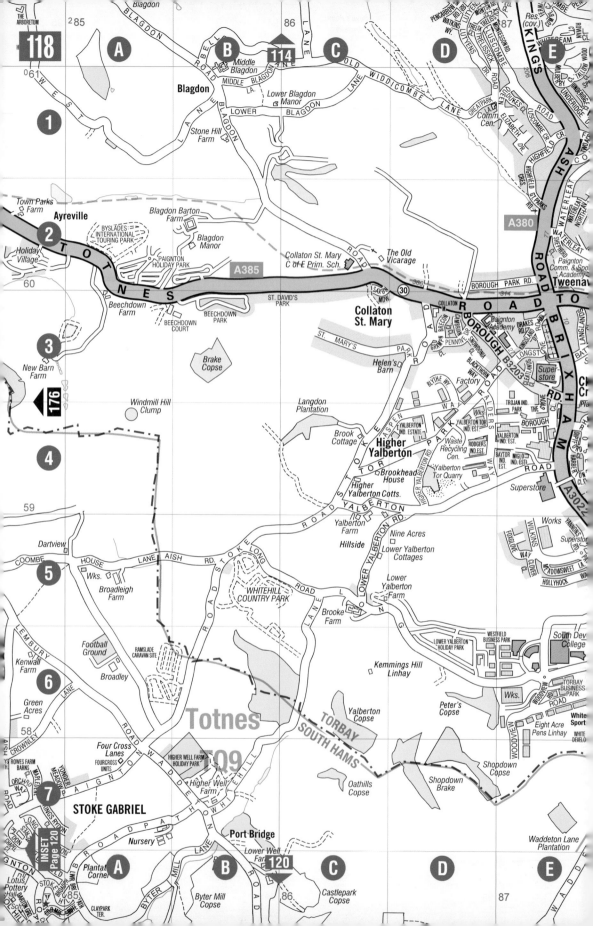

STOKE GABRIEL

2 85 86 87

A B C D E

INSET

1

Nursery

Plantation Corner

Lotus Pottery Hall

Byter Mill Copse

Pords Bridge

Lower Well Farm

ort Brid 118

Totnes

Castlepark Copse

TQ9

Quarry Wood

Water Lane Plantation

Waddeton Pool

Wadde Barto WADDETON COTTS

Water Lane Plantation

0 57

Mill Pool

South Downs Wood

Overcreek

Byter Downe House

WADDETON ROAD

Pool Plantation

East Farm

Waddeton Home farm

Kenly Wood

2

Sandridge Bottom

Toms Plantation

Slate Wood

INSET

58

STOKE GABRIEL

3

Totnes

Five-Knot Farm

Southlands Kennels

TQ9

Southlands Farm

HIGHER WELL MEADOW

CROWNLEY LA

ROWES FARM BARNS

MAPLEHNE ROAD

KINGS RYDON

LONG RYDON

HILLFIELD

ANDREWS LA

POUND FIELD

BARN PARK

MADDICKS ORCHD

NEW RD

Lotus Pottery Hall

STOK HILL

East Wood

The Cliffs

Sandridge Boat House

RIVER DART

Boat House

Higher Gurrow Point

Gurrow Point House

Lower Gurrow Point

4

River Dart

Totnes to Dartmouth Foot Ferry (Summer Only)

57

2 84

RIVERSIDE ROAD

Totnes to Greenway (Summer) Foot Ferry

Hunterswood

5

Rivendale

East Cornworthy

Seagull House

DITTISHAM MILL CREEK

Dittisham Mill

Dittisham Court

Football Pitch

HAM LA

Dittisham Sailing Club

GREENWAY

176

55

Bramble Torre

DITTISHAM

LOWER ST

HIGHER ST

RIVERSIDE

ORCHARD PK

Pier

THE QUAY ST

Greenway Quay

Ferry Cottage

Greenway

6

Dartmouth

TQ6

Meadow Cottages

THE LEVEL

MANOR

Lower Dittisham

The Old Rectory

The River Farm

Binhay Copse

Anchor Stone

Totnes to Dartmouth (Summer Only) Foot Ferry

Cott Farm

Bozomzeal Cross

Res. (cov.)

River Farm Cottage

River Farm House

Reservoir (covered)

Hamblyn's Coombe

7

Bullcombe Copse

Foxhole Copse

Downton Wood

Waterfields Cottage

LORD'S WOOD

54

Little Coombe

Little Coombe Plantation

Foxenhole

Fire Beacon Hill

124

85 86 87

A B C D E

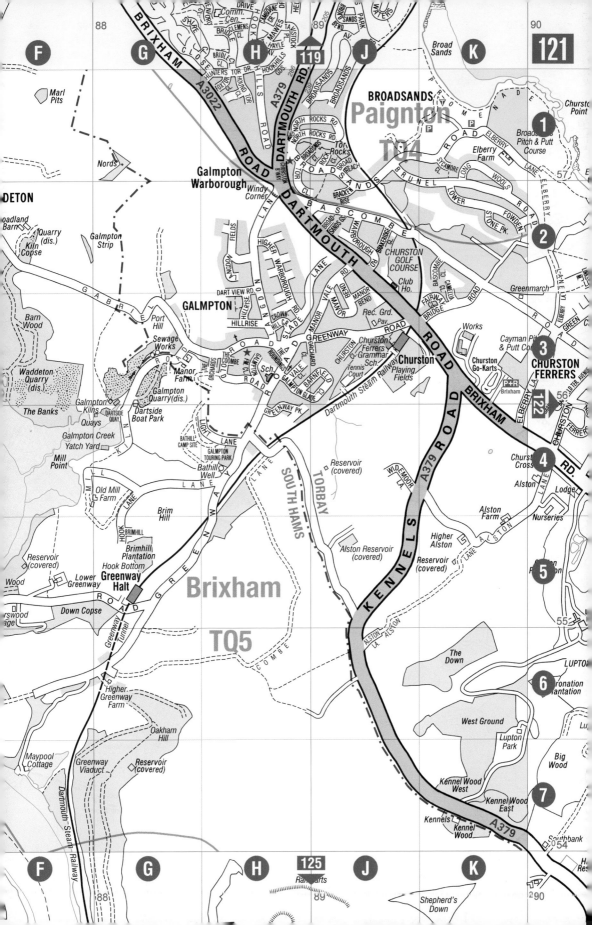

F **G** **H** **119** **J** **K** **121**

88 89 205 90

Marl Pits

Nords

DETON

Broadland Barn

Quarry (dis.)

Kiln Copse

Galmpton Strip

GABRIEL

Barn Wood

Port Hill

Sewage Works

Waddeton Quarry (dis.)

The Banks

Galmpton Kilns Quays

DARTSIDE QUAY

Manor Farm

Galmpton Quarry (dis.)

Dartside Boat Park

Galmpton Creek Yatch Yard

Mill Point

Old Mill Farm

HOOK

Brim Hill

BRIMHILL

Reservoir (covered)

Lower Greenway

Brimhill Plantation

Hook Bottom

Greenway Halt

Down Copse

rswood age

Wood

Higher Greenway Farm

Oakham Hill

Greenway Viaduct

Reservoir (covered)

Maypool Cottage

Dartmouth Steam Railway

BRIXHAM

BROADSANDS

Broad Sands

Paignton TO4

Galmpton Warborough

Windy Corner

Comm. Cen.

KINGDON FIELDS

HIGHER WARBOROUGH RD

CROWN HILL RISE

HILLRISE

Galmpton

HILLRISE

DART VIEW RD.

MANOR VALE LANE

LANGDON RD.

GREENWAY RD.

THE COOMBE

The ORCHARDS

Sch

GALMPTON GLADE

BARNFIELD

MANOR BEND

CROWN

VALE

The ROUNDINGS

ORCHARD

Churston Ferrers Grammar Sch.

Tennis Court

Dartmouth Steam Railway

Churston

Churston Go-Karts

North Rocks Rd.

NORTH ROCKS RD.

Tor Rocks

BROADSANDS RD.

Brack's Rise

BROAD RCH.

BRUNEL

WARBOROUGH RD.

CHURSTON GOLF COURSE

Club Ho.

MANOR RD.

Rec. Grd.

Pav.

Playing Fields

BASCOMBE

Works

Churston Sta.

Pitch & Putt Course

Elberry Farm

SYCAMORE

LOWER FOWDEN

STONE PK.

FAIRWAY

BRIDGE

CAMELIA

Greenmarch

ELBERRY LA.

GREEN

Cayman Pitch & Putt Cou

CHURSTON FERRERS

Churston Cross

CHURSTON FERRER

1

Churston Point

2

3

4

5

6

7

57

56

55

54

P+R Brixham

Alston

Lodge

Nurseries

WIDEMOOR LA.

ALSTON

Alston Farm

Higher Alston

Reservoir (covered)

Reservoir (covered)

KENNELS ROAD

A379 ROAD

TORBAY

SOUTH HAMS

COOMBE

GREENWAY ROAD

Brixham TO5

Reservoir (covered)

Reservoir (covered)

Alston Reservoir (covered)

The Down

LUPTON

ronation Plantation

West Ground

Lupton Park

Big Wood

Kennel Wood West

Kennel Wood East

Kennels

Kennel Wood

A379

Southbank

Shepherd's Down

F **G** **125** **H** **J** **K**

88 89 290

Rail arts

BRIXHAM A3022 ROAD

DARTMOUTH RD.

A379

DARTMOUTH ROAD

1

57

Brixham Breakwater Lighthouse

THE BREAKWATER

2

Shoalstone Beach
Shoalstone Pool
Shoalstone Point
Quay
Berry Head Quarry (dis.)
Berry Head Lighthouse

(Foot Only) Foot Ferry

Brixham Marina

Jetty
The Hard
Coastguard Station
BREAKWATER CT.
Ash Hole Cavern
Berry Head Fortifications

BREAKWATER ROAD
VICTORIA RD.

Club
New Fish Quay
Torbay Lifeboat Station
Breakwater Beach
DEVONCOURT CT.

New Pier
Outdoor Education Centre
HEATH CT.
WILLBOROUGH GDNS.
SANDS RD.
Berry Head Farm
Beacon
Old Redoubt
Visitor Cen.

BERRY HEAD

HARBOUR
HEATH
RISE
MARINA DRIVE
SCOTT CL.
WASHBOURNE CL.
ANCHORAGE CL.

Golden Hind
KINGS REACH
BERRY HEAD ROAD
HEATH PK.

3

KING ST.
NORTH VIEW RD.
ELKINS HILL
GREAT REA RD.
RANSCOMBE RD.
WALL CL.
WALL RD.
HERITAGE WAY
VIGILANCE WAY
The Bungalow
Beacon
BERRY HEAD COUNTRY PARK
Old Redoubt

56

LOWER REA RD.
RANSCOMBE CL.
GILLARD ROAD
Football Grd.
PROVIDENT CL.
HERITAGE
LOUVILLE CAMP
Picnic Site
Berry Head National Nature Reserve

Mew Stone
Cod Rock

MOUNT PLEASANT
Leisure Centre
Brixham College
Brixham C of E Prim. Sch.
Play. Fld.
Swim. Cen.
Playing Field
FOURVIEW CT.
CENTRY RD.
MARINA
LANDSCOVE HOLIDAY PARK

4

REA BARN CL.
Astley Park
HIGHER RANSCOMBE RD.
Pav.
HILL PK. RD.
SEA LANE
Kiln House
Durl Head
Durl Rock

BARN HILL
PENN MEADOWS
MOORSTONE
DOUGLAS AV.

QUEEN'S CRES.
EDINBURGH RD.
RADNOR CL.
RIVIERA BAY HOLIDAY PARK

ENGLISH

5

MEADOWS
WISHINGS RD.
ST. MARY'S BAY

CHANNEL

HIGHER PENN
ST. MARY'S
SHARKHAM
PENN CT.
ST. MARY'S DR.
Mussel Rock

EALING CT.
The Grove
MARGENT RD.
ST. MARY'S HO.
SHARKHAM DR.

54

INSET

A379
KINGSWEAR RD.
ROAD
RADDICOMBE DRIVE
Hillhead

Mine (dis.)
Berry Head National Nature Reserve
BRIDGE ROAD
HILLHEAD HILL
PENNHILL LA.
RADDICOMBE PARK
LINHAY CL.
Raddicombe
Raddicombe Farm

6

SOUTH BAY HOLIDAY PARK
Shaft (dis.)
Mag Rock
Sharkham Point
B3205
Pennhill Chase
Pennhill

Brixham TQ5

SLAPPERS HILL
HILLHEAD HOLIDAY PARK

7

Cliff

053

Dartmouth TQ6
Nethway Quarry (disused)

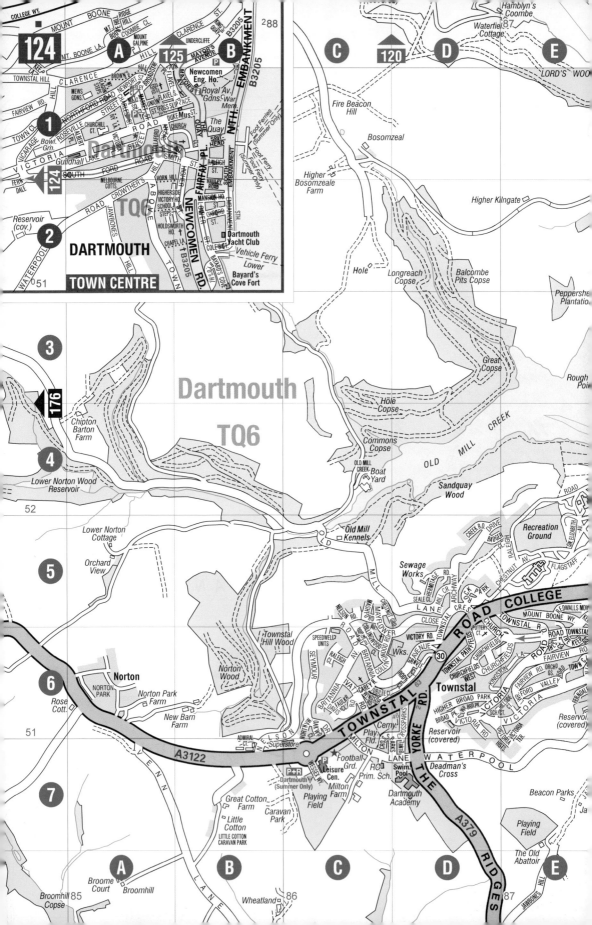

1

Kennel Wood West
Kennel Wood East
90
Kennels
Ken. W
54
Hi Res

Ramparts

Shepherd's Down

Fort

Brixham

Bridge Road Wood

LONG WOOD

A379 ROAD

TQ5

INSET Page 123

2

SLAPPER'S HILL

53

Higher Noss Point
Works
Noss Plantation
Noss Creek
Marina
Noss Ho.
Noss Plantation

BRIDGE

Croftland Farm
NETHWAY CROSS

3

Pontoons

RIVER

Slips

BRIDGE RD.

B3205

Hoodown Farm

ROAD BROAD

Dragon House

176

Pontoon
Quay
Pier
Pontoon

DART

Rocks

Golf House

Oversteps House
Oversteps Cottage

Cattery & Kennels

Boohay

ROAD PEPPER LA.

52

BROAD

Boohay Farm

4

Sandquay Wy.
ESPLANADE
SANDQUAY
Beatty Wy.
FLOATERS
DART MARINA
Higher
Vehicle Ferry
Dartmouth Steam Railway

Cemetery
Lodge
Waterhead Brake

HIGHER CONTOUR RD.

Res. (cov.)

5

PRINCE OF WALES RD.
Coronation
Cts.
COLLEGE WAY
8
Dittisham (Summer Only) Foot Ferry
Dartmouth Harbour
Dartmouth to Totnes

Hoodown Wood

HOODOWN LANE

WATERHEAD RD.

ROAD BROAD

RIDLEY

Reservoir (covered)

51

6

EMBANKMENT
THE COOMBE
COOMBE RD.
COMBE CL.
RIDGE
CLARENCE
VAVA
THE
CROWTHER'S
DARTMOUTH
Newcomen Eng. Ho.
Royal Av. Ho.
Lock
Darthaven Marina
Pontoon Berths
Waterhead Viaduct
Waterhead Creek
WATERHEAD TER.

BRIXHAM ROAD

CONTOUR
WESTERLAND
UPPER WOOD LA.
Playing Field
Kingswear Wood

Fountain Violet Farm

NEWCOMEN RD.
SMITH
DUKE
FOSS
ZION
Vehicle Ferry
Lower
Foot Ferry
Kingswear
Visitors' Cen.
FORE ST.
BELGRAVIA TER.
HIGHER ST.
WOODLAND HGTS.
MOUNT PLEASANT
Sch.
LOWER CONTOUR RD:
Kingswear

SOUTH TOWN
COLLEGE
BAYARD'S
ABOVE TOWN
Yacht Club
Bayard's Cove Fort
Bayard's Cove
Redoubt
BEACON
CHURCH HILL BEACON
CASTLE RD.
CHURCH HILL
LANE

The Grange
Home Farm

Crockers Cottage
Colt Cott.
BROWNSTONE RD.

Higher Brown-stone

7

Hyde Hill
Dyer's Hill
Stoke Cliff
WARFLEET RD.
SWANNATON
Dartmouth to Dartmouth Castle Foot Ferry (Summer Only)
Halftide Rock
One Gun Point
Landing Stage
Boat House
BROOKHILL
Gommerock (remains of)
Peach House
Higher Brownstone Farm

SWANNATON

Kingswear

A **B** **C** **D** **E**

Sticklepath Wood
249
RIVER WALKHAM
Furzeland Down Wood
Furzeland Down
Birchcleave Wood
50
Birchcleave
51

Sewage Works
Bedford House
SORTRIDGE PARK
WESTPARK VILLAS
HIGHERTOWN

1
169
070
Bedford Bridge
Dartmoor Country Holidays (MAGPIE LEISURE PK.)
Madeira Villas
WHITCHURCH
GREEN
WAY CL.
KNIGHTON TER.
WALKHAM
SPRYS TENEMS
WALK

A386

Viaduct

T A V I S T O C K (PLYMOUTH ROAD)

CHAPEL
COPPER FIELDS
RIVERSIDE CL.
CARADON CT.
CHICESTER RD
PINKREBER
TOWN FARM CL.
TORR RD
GRAYBRIDGE RD.
WEIR
SOUTH VW.
PLACE LA.
VILLAGE LA.

2
ROBOROUGH DOWN
Harwood Plantation
Harwood House
30
MANOR
MANOR 63
ESTATE
THE OLD STATION
TOR RD.
PHOENIX RD.
ST JOHN'S RD.
QUILLET

Alston Cottage
Down Lane Farm
Kilmantain
Harwood Farm

3
Alston
Coppicetown Lodge
Long-Ash
North Plantation
Football Pitch

69
174

4
Uppaton Farm
Home Plantation
Roborough Down Picnic Site

NETHERTON ESTATE
CROSS PK.
Cerny
Lovecombe
Lovecombe Cottage
The Garden House
KNIGHTONS UNITS
ROAD
South Plantation

5
CHAPEL MDW.
PRIM. SCH.
BUTT PK.
MODYFORD
Buckland Monachorum
Knighton
Little Wood
POUND
CUXTON MDWS.
HILLSIDE CL.
WALK
THE VICARAGE
OLD QUARRY RD.
The Vicarage
Roborough Downs

HILL
VIEW
68
Crapstone Cottage
THE
WOODCHURCH
CRESCENT

6
Quarry Pk. Ho!
Crapstone House
Crapstone
CRAPSTONE TER.
GRIMSTONE T. ★
THE GLADE
WOODSIDE TER.
BUCKLAND CT. WOODCROFT
YELVERTON BUS. PK.
WHISTLEY DOWN
Axtown
CRAPSTONE
AXTOWN LANE
Riding Sch.

Playing Field
FOXGLOVE END
MORLEY
DR.
SEATON
WY.
ABBEY
CL.
LANE
HILL
Whistleigh Farm
MOORLAND CT.

7
Gate Cottage
ABBEY MDW.
DARTMOOR CARAVAN PARK
Abbeymoor
Yelverton Golf Driving Range
STOKE
HILL
Sewage Works ∞
Axtown Farm

67
North Lodge Cotts.
Venton Farm
Stokehill
GREEN
51

Buckland Abbey
49
50

A **B** **C** **D** **E**

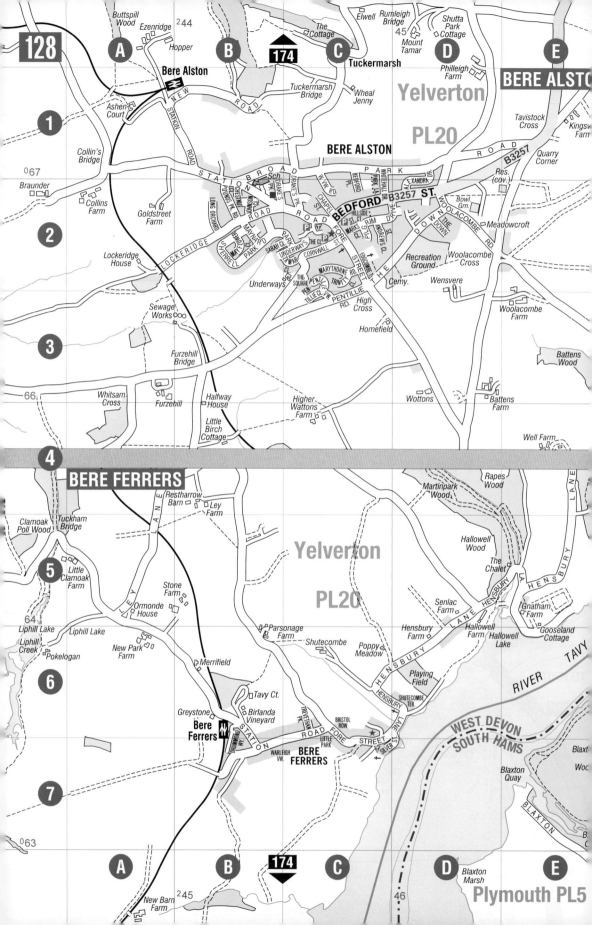

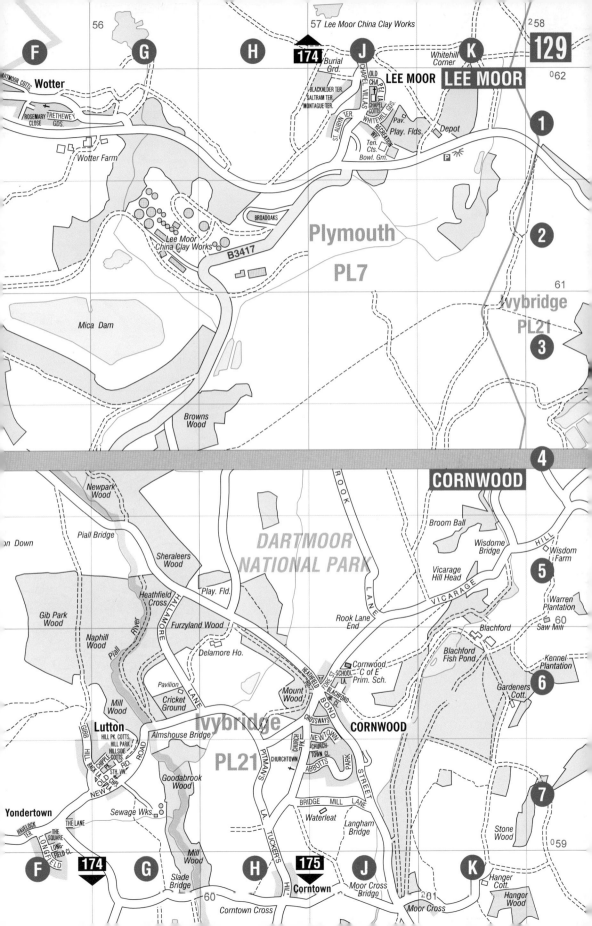

A **B** **C** **D** **E**

CARGREEN

Penyoke

1

Saltash

PL12

062

WEST DEVON
CORNWALL

Weir
Point

244

New Barn 45
Farm

Yelverton
PL20

2

3

Neal
Point

RIVER TAVY

Warleigh
Point

Pennylake
Pond

Warleigh Point
Nature Reserve

Warleigh Wood
Nature Reserve

Warleigh Quay

Warleigh
House

War

Park
Plantations

RIVER

WEST DEVON
SOUTH HAMS

61

◄ **174**

60

4

5

6

7

59

RIVER TAMAR
CORNWALL PLYMOUTH TAMAR

Warren
Point

Tamerton
Bridge

Works

Factories

Ernesettle

Lower
Ernesettle

Sewage
Works

RNAD ERNESETTLE

Sports
Ground

Club

Woodlands
House

Badgers
Park
Wood

Tamerton Lal

STATION

Playing
Field

Scout
HQ

Comm.
Cen

NTH
WEALD GS.

ST. AIDAN'S
CT.

TERICK
Lib.

MANSTON CL.
HORNCHURCH

TANGMERE
AV.

MALLING

Rec. Grd.

DIGBY GRO
MERE

ROCHFORD

LYMPNE

FOWE

RD.

BIGGIN

MANBY

STAPLE
FORD GDS.

WES.

LAKESIDE
AV.

UXBRIDGE

WEST HORNCHURCH RD.

ERNESETTLE

HILL

DRIVE

BIGGIN

KENLEY
GDS.

ROCHF
GD'S
HILL

NORTHOLT

DRAKE CT.

ROAD

MARTLESHAM
PL.

EVAL

Ernesettle
School

CHIVENOR
WLK.

MIDSTONE
WK.

CROYDON
GDS.

PEMBREY

REDHILL
WK.

Agaton Fort

GRAVESE END

DEBDEN
CT.

CROYDON
WK.

GDNS.

SNT.

PEMBREY
WK.

GARD.

ACKL
INGTON

KINGE

YELVERTON
CLOSE

CULDROSE
PL.

PERRANWORTH

Club

Depot

CLOSE

AGATON
FORT RD.

BIGGIN
HILL

MARINA

QUEENS

JUBILEE RD

KINGS

Ernesettle
Battery

THE
GREEN

KINSALE RD.

514

VICTORIA
ROAD

CROWNHI

Marriott

Ernesettle Wood

A38

134

MARETT

DUNSTONE
RD.

Playing
Field

CHATSWORTH
GDNS.

PARK

THE

A **B** **134** **C** **D** **E**

Ernesettle
Farm

45 iec.
Ten. Grd.

TAMAR
BRIDGE

Royal Albert Bridge

Toll Booths 44

TAMAR-BRIDGE-RD.

WAVERLEY RD.

BLOXHAM RD.

AGATON
BUCKINGHAM

VICTORIA

ROA

ROMAN

PLAISTOW

PRIESTLEY

St. Bude
Foundat
C of E Jun. Sch

Inf.
Sch.

ROW

TAMERTON
Comm.
Cen

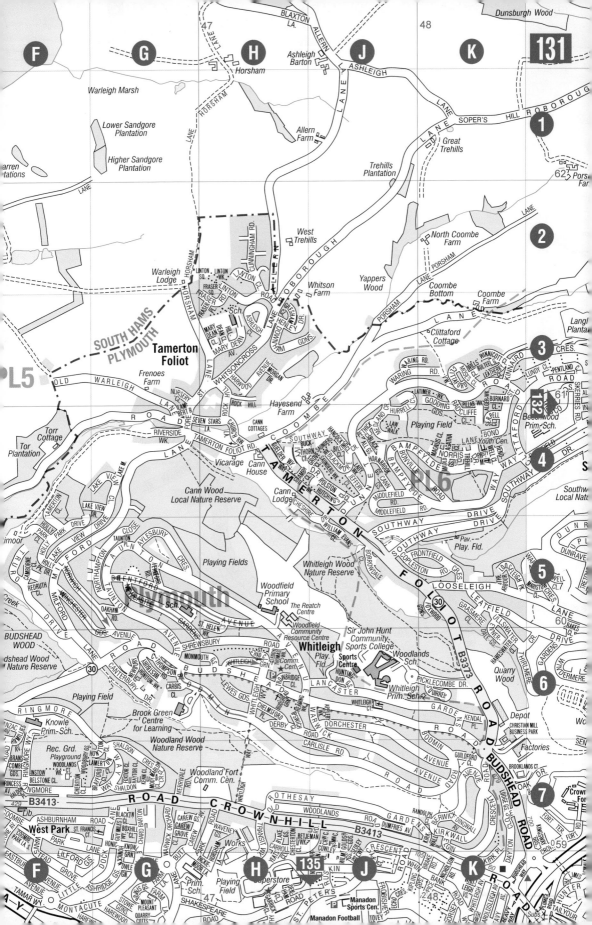

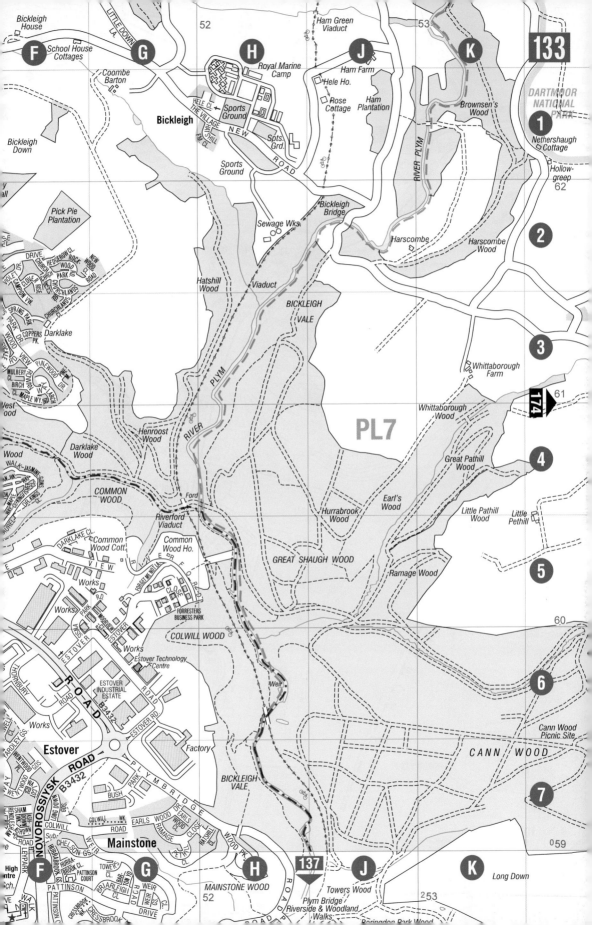

133

Bickleigh House
School House Cottages
F
Little Down La.
G
Coombe Barton
H
Royal Marine Camp
Ham Green Viaduct
53
J
Ham Farm
Hele Ho.
Rose Cottage
Ham Plantation
K
Brownsen's Wood
DARTMOOR NATIONAL PARK
1
Nethershaugh Cottage
Hollow-greep
62

Bickleigh Down
Bickleigh
Hele Cl.
The Village
New Mill Cl.
Sports Ground
Spts Grd.
Sports Ground
NEW ROAD
Sewage Wks.
Bickleigh Bridge
RIVER PLYM
Harscombe
Harscombe Wood
2

Pick Pie Plantation
Hederson Cl.
Rock Park
Chigh
Churchlands
Clove Rise
Spring Park
Coppers Pk.
Darklake
Mulbery Cl.
Birch
Rowan Cl.
Maple Wy.
Larch
Pinewood Dr.
View
West Wood
Hatshill Wood
Viaduct
BICKLEIGH VALE
Whittaborough Farm
174
61
Whittaborough Wood

RIVER PLYM
Henroost Wood
Darklake Wood
3

PL7
Great Pathill Wood
4

Wood
Walk
Jasmine Gdns.
Dr. Kings
Laurel
COMMON WOOD
Ford
RIVER
Hurrabrook Wood
Earl's Wood
Little Pathill Wood
Little Pethill
5

Riverford Viaduct
Common Wood Cott.
Common Wood Ho.
Darklake Cl.
View
RIVER FORD
Forget Me Not La.
Close
Works
Works
Park
Moorsom
Estover
Road
Forresters Business Park
GREAT SHAUGH WOOD
Ramage Wood
60

COLWILL WOOD
Estover Technology Centre
6

Estover Industrial Estate
Thornbury
ESTOVER ROAD
B3432
Estover Rd.
Works
Works
Factory
Weir
CANN WOOD
Cann Wood Picnic Site

Estover
NOVOROSSIYSK ROAD
B3432
ROAD
Park
BICKLEIGH VALE
7

Mainstone
High Centre
Sub.
Chelson Gdns.
Colwill Road
Colwill Wk.
Earls Road
Wood
Ramage Cl.
Pletn Cl.
Hatshill Cl.
Wood Pk.
7

59

F
Pattinson Court
Pattinson
Dressbrook
Tower Cl.
Briarcliff
Weir Cl.
G
Drake Dr.
H
MAINSTONE WOOD
137
Plym Bridge
Bickleigh Vale Riverside & Woodland Walks
J
Towers Wood
253
K
Long Down

52
53
60
61
62
59

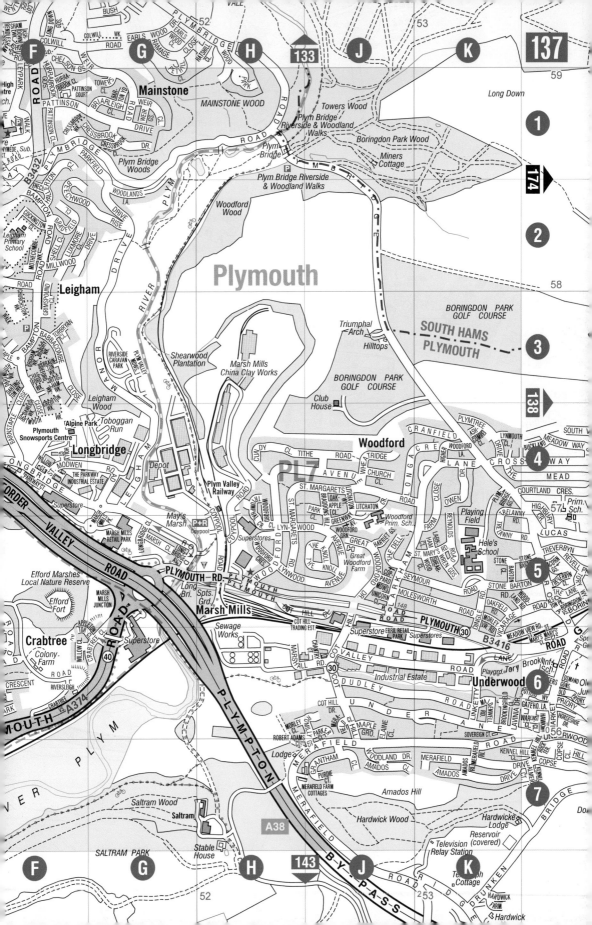

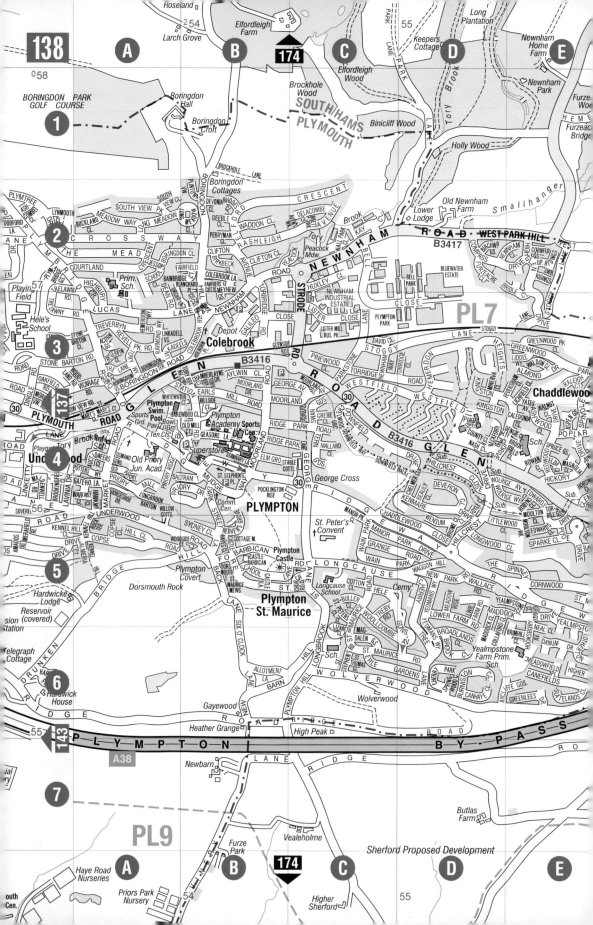

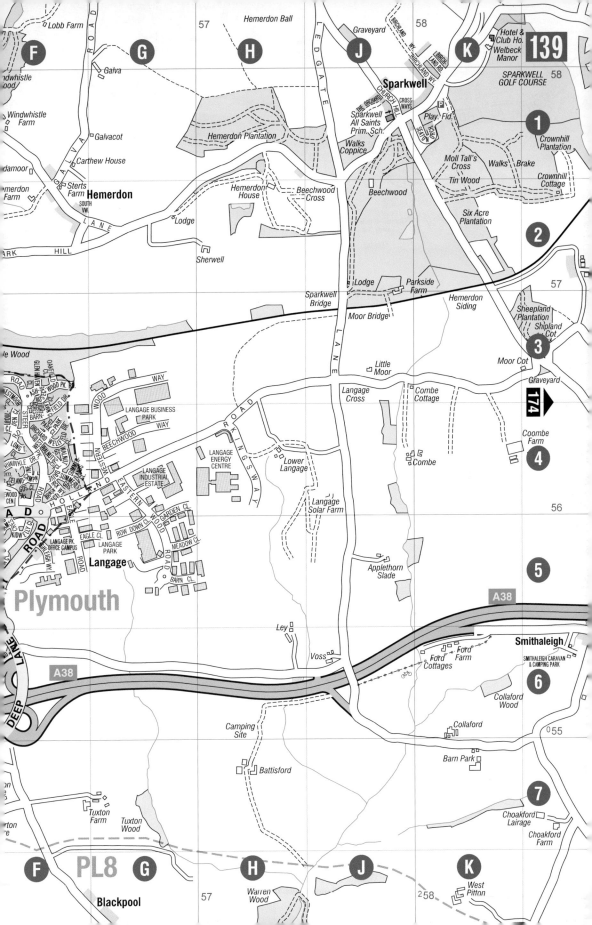

F **G** **H** **J** **K**

Lobb Farm
Galva
Windwhistle Wood
Windwhistle Farm
Galvacot
ndmoor
merdon Farm
Carthew House
Sterts Farm
Hemerdon
SOUTH VW.
GALVA
LANE
PARK HILL
K HILL

Hemerdon Plantation
Hemerdon House
Hemerdon Cross
Lodge
Sherwell
Beechwood Cross

Hemerdon Ball

57 58

Graveyard
BUCKLAND WK.
BUCKLAND WY.
BIRCH LANE RD.

Sparkwell
THE ORCHARDS
CHURCH HILL
CROSS-WAYS
Sparkwell All Saints Prim. Sch.
Walks Coppice
Play. Fld.
ROAD SEATS

Hotel & Club Ho. Welbeck Manor
SPARKWELL GOLF COURSE 58

Moll Tall's Cross
Beechwood
Six Acre Plantation
Tin Wood
Walks Brake

Crownhill Plantation **1**
Crownhill Cottage

2

Lodge
Parkside Farm
Sparkwell Bridge
Moor Bridge
Hemerdon Siding
57

Sheepland Plantation
Shipland Cot
Moor Cot **3**

le Wood
GLEN HAVEN
OAKFIELD RD.
WOOD PK.
ASH WOOD
WESTMOR
ROBB CL.
STEER
BARN
ORCHARD
WELLFIELD DR.
FIELD DR.
LONG T.
GDS. CL.
WOLMITE
SUMMER
CELAND RD.
HOLLAND ROAD
BEECHWOOD
WESTERN WOOD
EASTERN WOOD
GARDEN CL.
ROW DOWN CL.
MEADOW CL.
BARN CL.
EAGLE CL.
KINGSWAY
WOOD
KIDWELLY
HIGH WY.
LANGAGE PK.
OFFICE CAMPUS
Langage
WOOD CEN
WAY
WAY
LANGAGE BUSINESS PARK
LANGAGE ENERGY CENTRE
LANGAGE INDUSTRIAL ESTATE
LANGAGE PARK

Langage Cross
Combe Cottage
Little Moor
Combe

174 ▶
Graveyard
Coombe Farm **4**

Lower Langage
Langage Solar Farm
56

Applethorn Slade

5

Plymouth

Ley
Voss

A38
Ford Farm
Ford Cottages
Smithaleigh
SMITHALEIGH CARAVAN & CAMPING PARK

6
Collaford Wood
Collaford
55

DEEP LANE
A38

Camping Site
Battisford

Barn Park

7
Choakford Lairage
Choakford Farm

Tuxton Farm
Tuxton Wood
rton

F **PL8** **G** **H** **J** **K**

Blackpool
57
Warren Wood
258
West Pitton

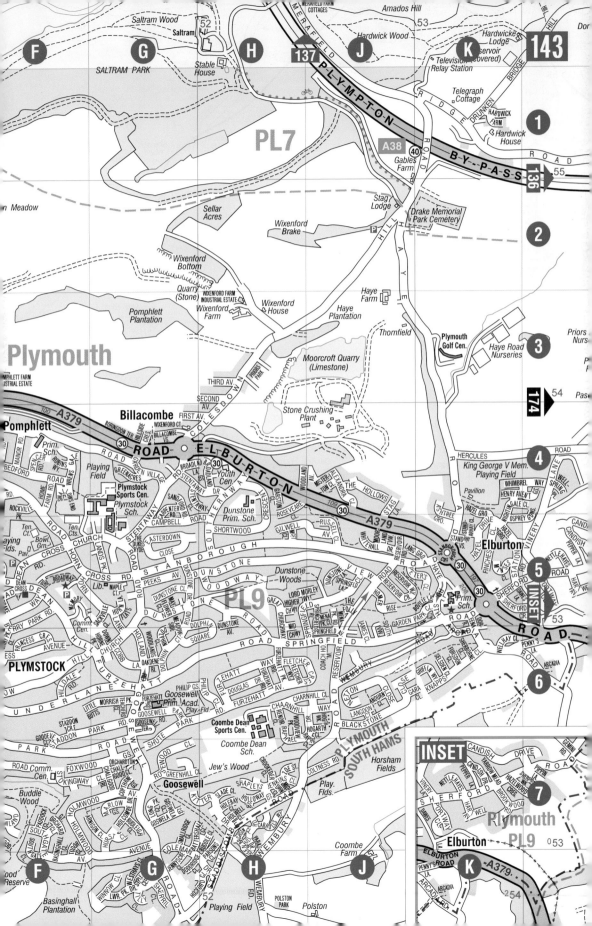

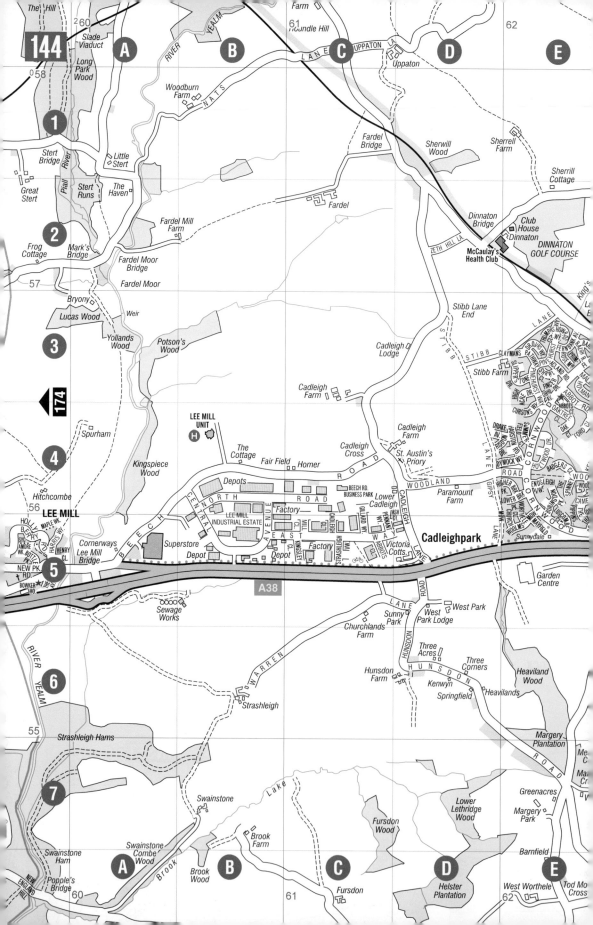

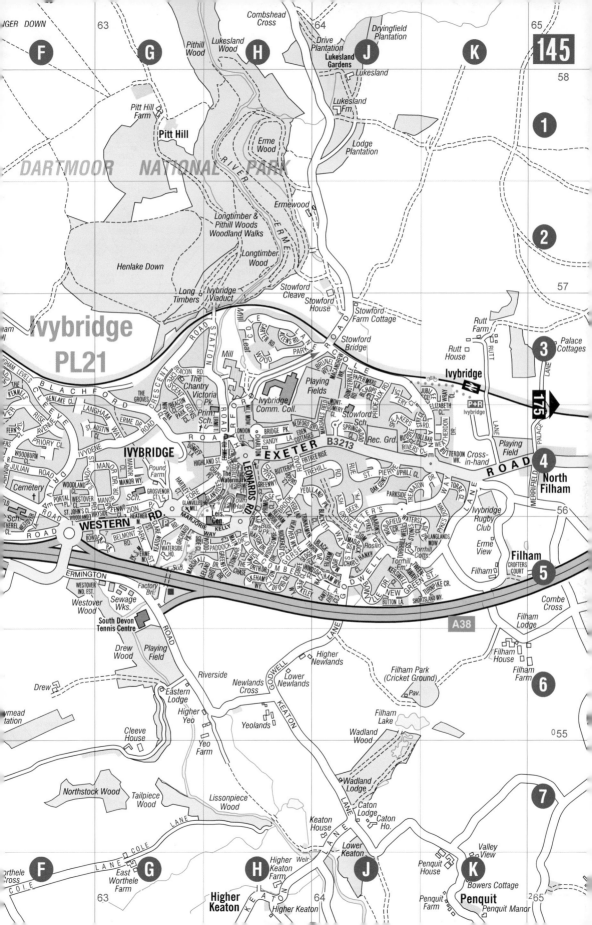

Combshead Cross

Dryingfield Plantation

Pithill Wood

Lukesland Wood

Drive Plantation

Lukesland Gardens

Lukesland

Lukesland Fm.

Pitt Hill Farm

Pitt Hill

Erme Wood

Lodge Plantation

DARTMOOR   NATIONAL PARK

Rutt Farm

Palace Cottages

Longtimber & Pithill Woods Woodland Walks

Rutt House

Henlake Down

Longtimber Wood

Stowford Cleave

Stowford House

Stowford Farm Cottage

Ermewood

Long Timbers

Ivybridge Viaduct

Stowford Bridge

Ivybridge PL21

Mill

The Chantry

Victoria Pk.

Prim. Sch.

Playing Fields

P+R

Ivybridge

175

Ivybridge Comm. Coll.

Stowford Sch.

Rec. Grd.

Playing Field

ROAD

IVYBRIDGE

EXETER B3213

Cross-in-hand

Cemetery

WESTERN

North Filham

Ivybridge Rugby Club

Erme View

Filham

CROFTERS COURT

South Devon Tennis Centre

Westover Ind. Est.

Westover Wood

Sewage Wks.

Drew Wood

Playing Field

A38

Combe Cross

Filham Lodge

Filham House

Filham Farm

Drew

Riverside

Higher Newlands

Filham Park (Cricket Ground)

Pav.

Eastern Lodge

Newlands Cross

Lower Newlands

Cleeve House

Higher Yeo

Yeo Farm

Yeolands

Filham Lake

Wadland Wood

Northstock Wood

Tailpiece Wood

Lissonpiece Wood

Wadland Lodge

Caton Lodge

Caton Ho.

Valley View

Keaton House

Lower Keaton

Penquit House

Bowers Cottage

East Worthele Farm

Higher Keaton Farm

Weir

Penquit Farm

Penquit

Penquit Manor

Higher Keaton

Higher Keaton

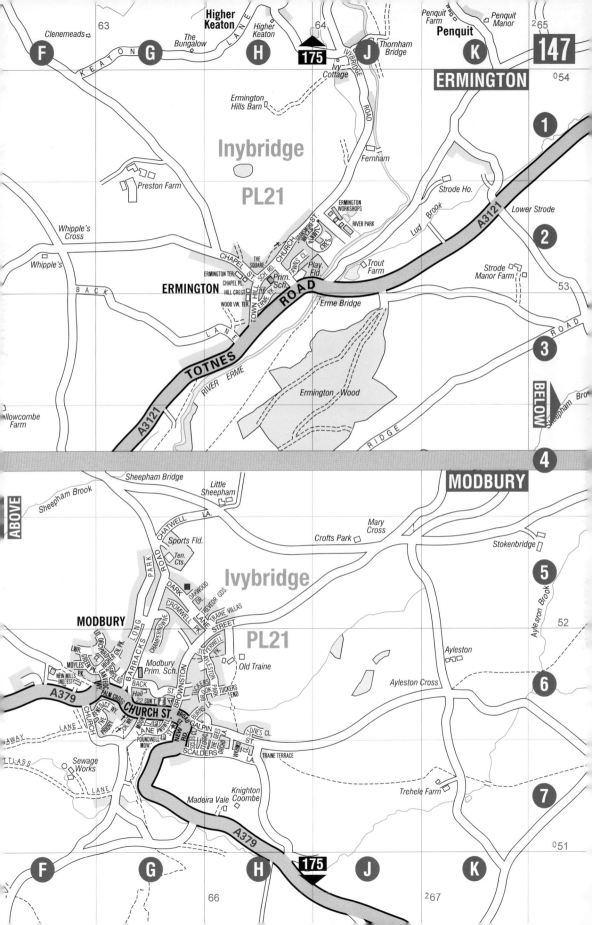

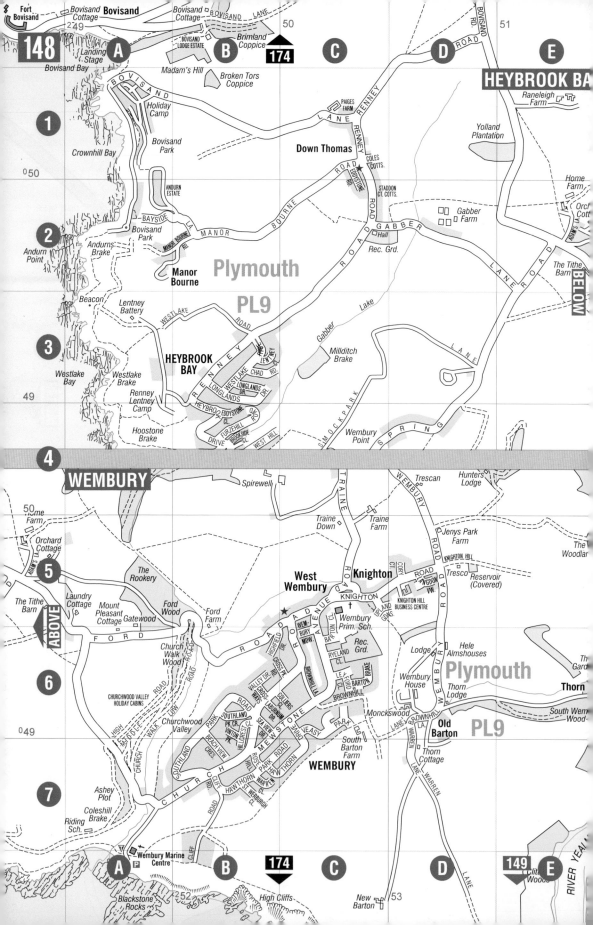

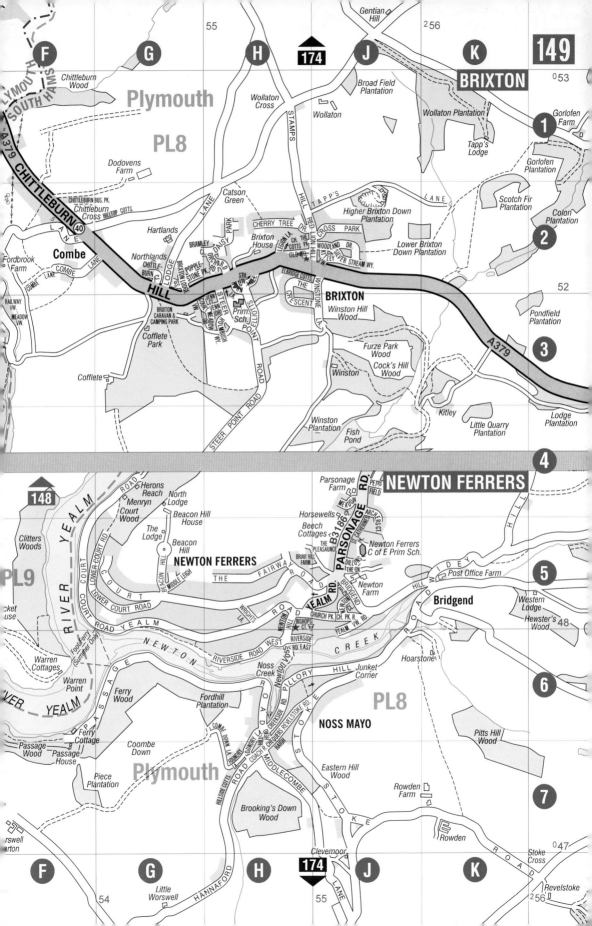

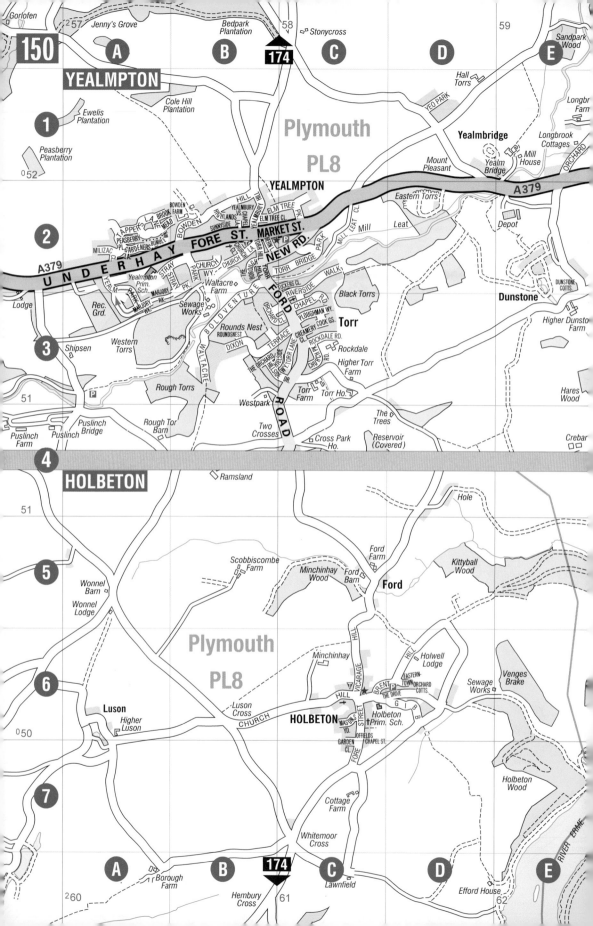

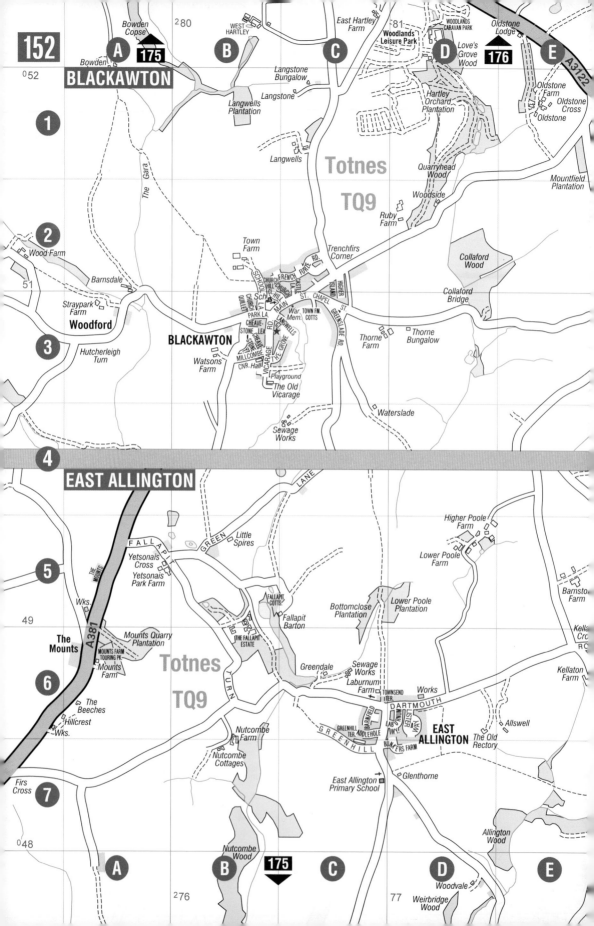

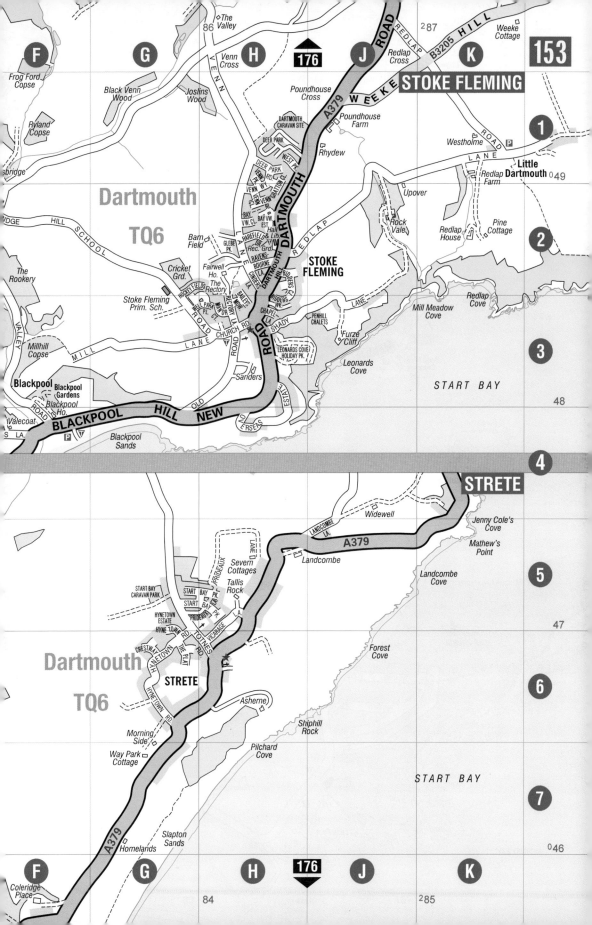

STOKE FLEMING

STRETE

Map Labels (Top Section)

F — Frog Ford Copse, Ryland Copse, S'bridge
G — Black Venn Wood, Joslins Wood, 86 The Valley, Venn Cross
H — Venn Cross
176
J — Redlap Cross
K — Weeke Cottage, 287, B3205 HILL

287 Poundhouse Cross
A379 WEEKE ROAD
REDLAP

Dartmouth Caravan Site
Deer Park
Poundhouse Farm
Rhydew
West Pk
Deer Park Rd.
Venn Est.
Venn Cl.
Venn Rd.
Bay Vw. Cl.
Bay Vw. Est.
Harefield & Lib.
Hall
Rec. Grd.
Ravens
Bourne
Bidders Wk.

Westholme
Little Dartmouth 049
Redlap Farm
Upover
Rock Vale
Redlap House
Pine Cottage

Dartmouth TQ6

School Hill
The Rookery
Cricket Grd.
Fairwell Ho.
The Rectory
Stoke Fleming Prim. Sch.
Hockey Fields
Glebe Pk.
Bailey's Well Pk.
Manor Dr.
Chapel La.
Shady La.
Church Rd.
Leonards Cove Holiday Pk.
Sanders

STOKE FLEMING

Penhill Chalets
Furze Cliff
Leonards Cove
Mill Meadow Cove
Redlap Cove

1
2
3

START BAY

48

Millhill Copse
Valley

Blackpool
Blackpool Gardens
Blackpool Ho.
Valecoat
S La.

BLACKPOOL HILL NEW ROAD
MILL LANE
OLD ROAD
OVERSEAS ESTATE

Blackpool Sands

4

Map Labels (Bottom Section)

STRETE

Widewell
LANDCOMBE LA.
A379
Landcombe
Jenny Cole's Cove
Mathew's Point
Landcombe Cove

Severn Cottages
Tallis Rock
Start Bay Caravan Park
Start Bay Pk.
Prideaux
Hynetown Estate
Hyne Town Rd.
Crestway
Hynetown Rd.
Totnes Rd.
Vicarage
The Plat

Dartmouth TQ6

STRETE

Morning Side
Way Park Cottage
Asherne
Shiphill Rock
Pilchard Cove
Forest Cove

5
6
7

47

START BAY

A379
Homelands
Slapton Sands
Coleridge Place

046

F
G
84
H
176
285
J
K

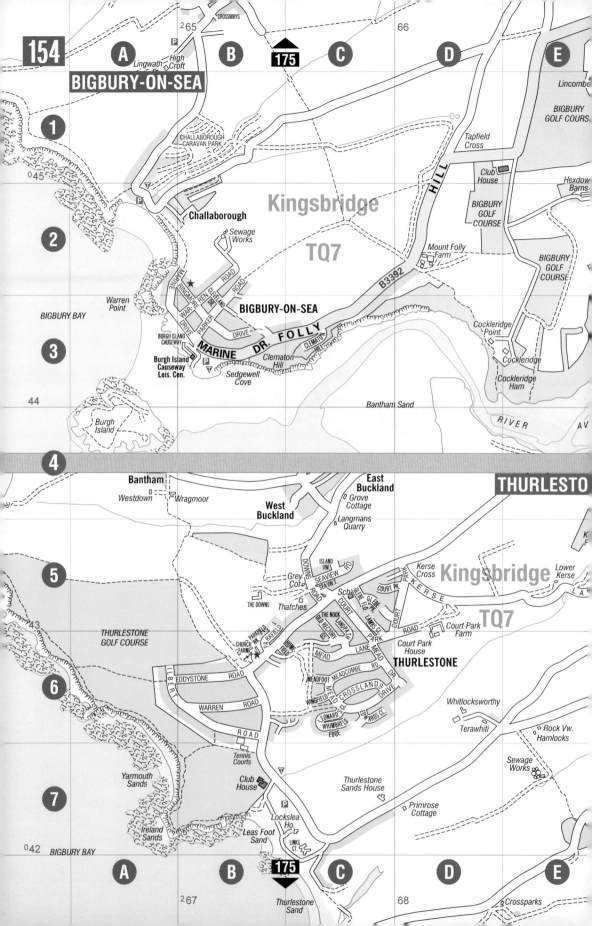

BIGBURY-ON-SEA

A Lingwath · High Croft
B ▲ **175**
C 66
D
E Lincombe

265 CROSSWAYS

BIGBURY GOLF COURS

1

CHALLABOROUGH CARAVAN PARK

Tapfield Cross

HILL

Club House

BIGBURY GOLF COURSE

Hexdow Barns

045

Kingsbridge

Challaborough

Mount Folly Farm

BIGBURY GOLF COURSE

2

TQ7

Sewage Works

B3392

Warren Point

MARINE ROAD · REN · PARKER · CASTLELAND · RINGMORE · WAR · DRIVE

BIGBURY-ON-SEA

Cockleridge Point

BIGBURY BAY

DRIVE

DR. FOLLY

CLEMATO HILL

Cockleridge

3

BURGH ISLAND CAUSEWAY

Burgh Island Causeway Leis. Cen.

Clematon Hill

Sedgewell Cove

Cockleridge Ham

44

Bantham Sand

RIVER AV

Burgh Island

4

Bantham

East Buckland

THURLESTO

Westdown · Wragmoor

West Buckland

Grove Cottage

Langmans Quarry

Kerse Cross

Lower Kerse

5

KF

ISLAND VW.

SEAVIEW · SEA VW. T.

Grey Cot.

COURT PARK

Kingsbridge

43

THE DOWNS

Thatches

DOWNS ROAD

Sch.

BERE TER. · GLEBE

COURT

Schl

COURT PK

COURT PK.

Court Park Farm

TQ7

THURLESTONE GOLF COURSE

THE NOOK

OLD RECTORY

LANGMA

LAMB'S CL

COURT PARK · MEAD

Court Park House

THURLESTONE

CHURCH FARM

PARKFIELD WK. · PARKFIELD

NUM.

LANE

MEAD

RD.

6

ILBERT · EDDYSTONE ROAD

WINGFIELD · MEAD · MEADFOOT · MEADCOMBE · CROSSLANDS DRIVE

Whitlocksworthy

WARREN ROAD

LEONARD'S CL. · WHIMBRE'L'S · EDGE

AROS CL.

Terawhiti

Rock Vw. Hamlocks

ROAD

Sewage Works

Tennis Courts

7

Yarmouth Sands

Club House

Thurlestone Sands House

Primrose Cottage

Lockslea Ho.

Ireland Sands

Leas Foot Sand

LINKS CT.

042 *BIGBURY BAY*

A
B ▲ **175**
C 68
D
E Crossparks

267

Thurlestone Sand

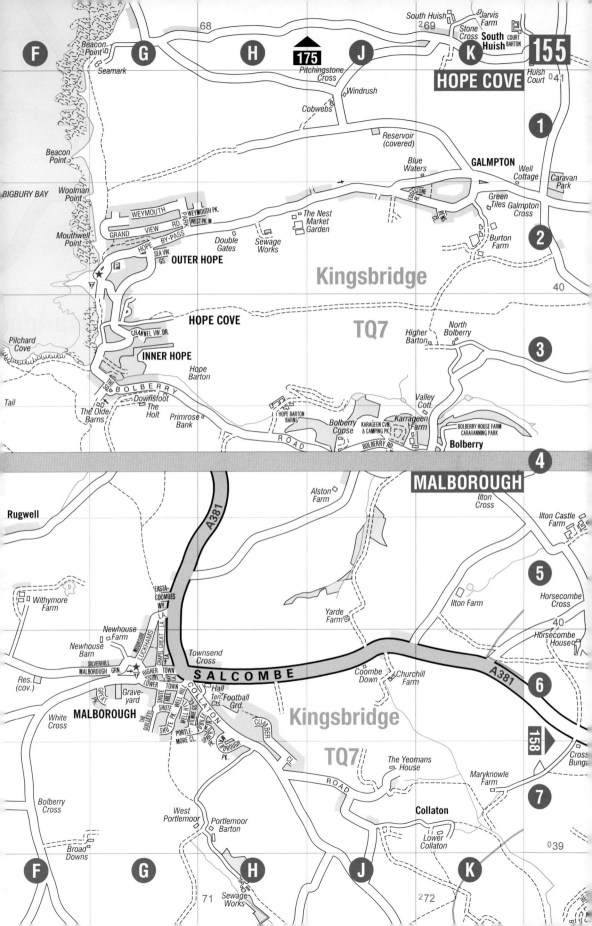

F G H J K

68

South Huish
269

Jarvis
Farm

Stone
Cross

South
Huish

COURT
BARTON

Huish
Court 041

175
Pitchingstone
Cross

Windrush

Cobwebs

Reservoir
(covered)

Blue
Waters

GALMPTON

Well
Cottage

Caravan
Park

1

BIGBURY BAY

Beacon
Point

Woolman
Point

Mouthwell
Point

WEYMOUTH
PARK

WEYMOUTH PK.
WEST PK. M

GRAND VIEW RD.

HOPE BY-PASS

SEA VW.
GS.

OUTER HOPE

Double
Gates

The Nest
Market
Garden

Sewage
Works

FODDSTONE RD

BENS
CL.

Green
Tiles

Galmpton
Cross

Burton
Farm

2

Beacon
Point

Seamark

Kingsbridge

40

Pilchard
Cove

Tail

CHANNEL VW. DR.

HOPE COVE

INNER HOPE

Hope
Barton

THE
SID

BOLBERRY

Downsfoot

The
Holt

Primrose
Bank

TQ7

Higher
Barton

North
Bolberry

3

The Olde
Barns

ROAD

HOPE BARTON
BARNS

Bolberry
Copse

KARAGEEN CVN
& CAMPING PK.

Karageen
Farm

BOLBERRY RD.

Valley
Cott.

BOLBERRY HOUSE FARM
CARAVANNING PARK

Bolberry

4

MALBOROUGH

Alston
Farm

Ilton
Cross

Ilton Castle
Farm

Rugwell

A381

EASTA-
COOMBES
WY.
L.A.

Withymore
Farm

Newhouse
Farm

Newhouse
Barn

SILVERHILL
MALBOROUGH
GRN.

MOORSIDE

BUCKHAMS

Res.
(cov.)

CHAPEL GREAT LA.

Higher
Town

Lower
Town

Townsend
Cross

S A L C O M B E

Yarde
Farm

Ilton
Farm

Horsecombe
Cross

5

40

Horsecombe
House

6

A381

White
Cross

MALBOROUGH

GREAT
PK.

Graveyard

THE QUILLETS

SHUTE PK.

SHUTE HILL

WELL HILL

PLIMHILL

PORTLE-
MORE CL.

SMALL
PK.

COLLATON

CUMBER CL.

PINE CL.

Hall
Ten.
Cts.

Football
Grd.

Coombe
Down

Churchill
Farm

Kingsbridge

TQ7

The Yeomans
House

Maryknowle
Farm

158

Cross
Bunga

7

Bolberry
Cross

Broad
Downs

West
Portlemoor

Portlemoor
Barton

ROAD

Collaton

Lower
Collaton

039

F G H J K

71

Sewage
Works

272

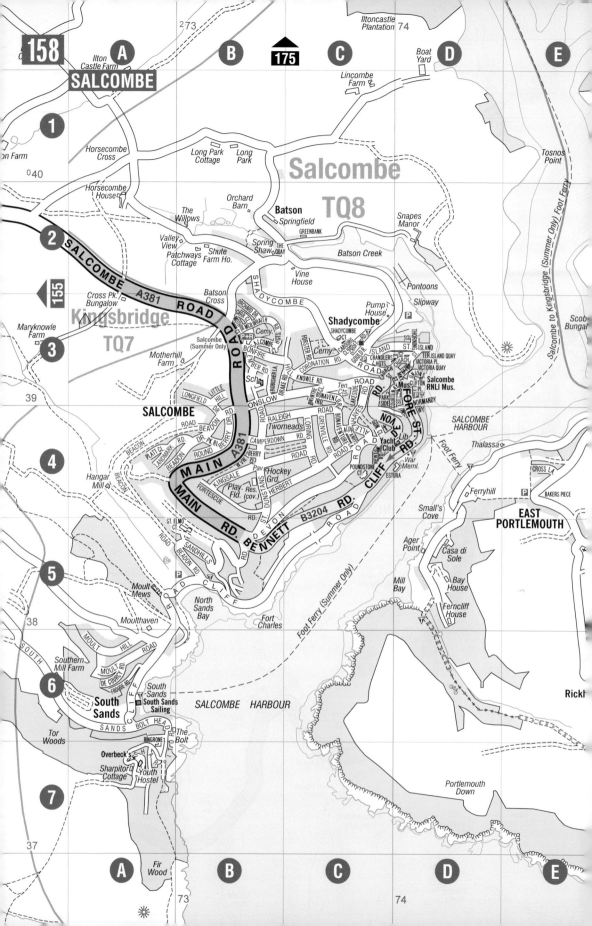

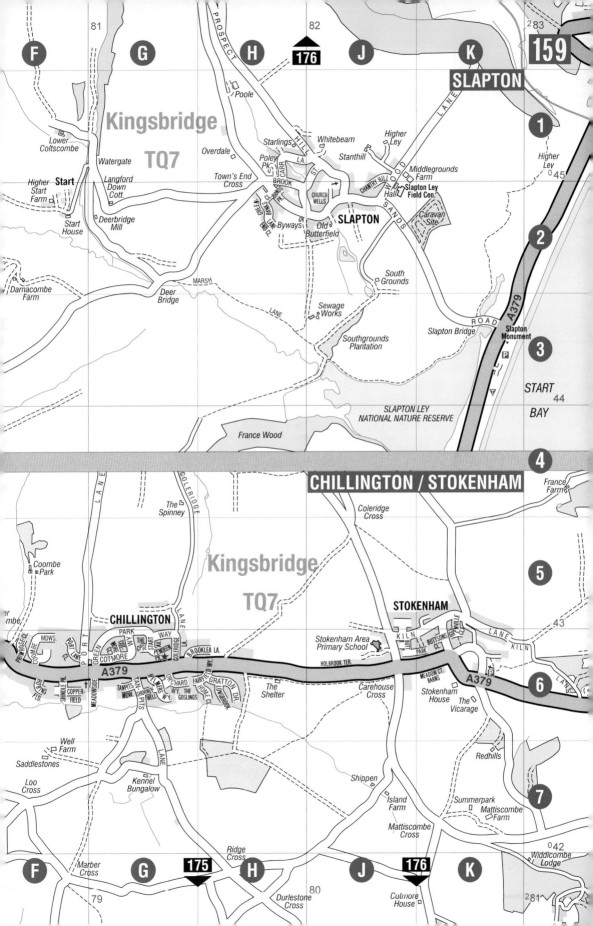

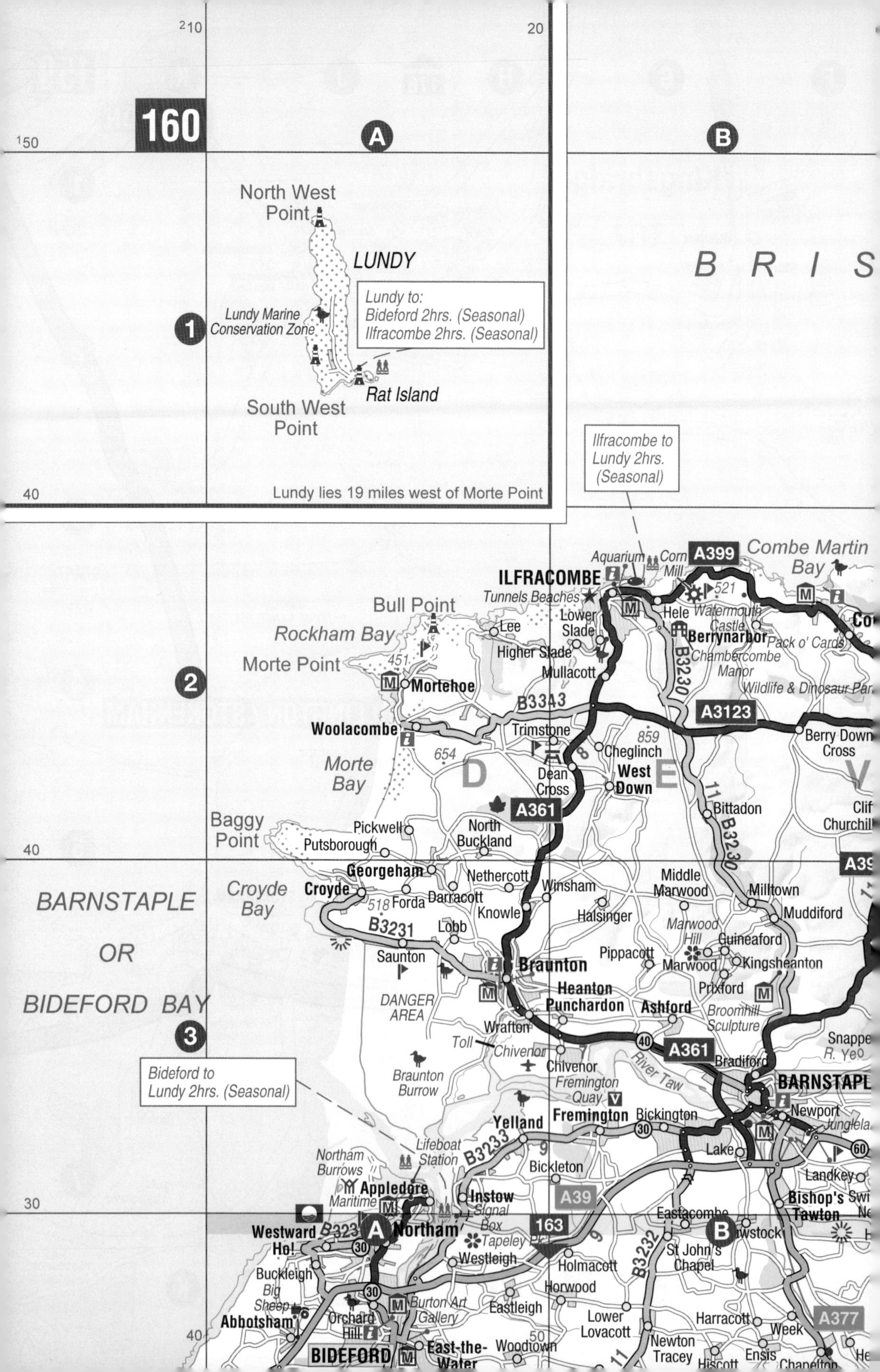

A

B

LUNDY

North West Point

Lundy Marine Conservation Zone

South West Point

Rat Island

Lundy to:
Bideford 2hrs. (Seasonal)
Ilfracombe 2hrs. (Seasonal)

Lundy lies 19 miles west of Morte Point

1

B R I S

Ilfracombe to Lundy 2hrs. (Seasonal)

2

Aquarium Corn Mill **A399** Combe Martin Bay

ILFRACOMBE

Tunnels Beaches Hele Watermouth Castle Co

Lower Slade **Berrynarbor** Pack o' Cards

Higher Slade *Chambercombe Manor*

Mullacott **B3230** *Wildlife & Dinosaur Par*

Bull Point

Rockham Bay

Morte Point 451 **B3343**

Lee

Trimstone **A3123** Berry Down Cross

Mortehoe

859 Cheglinch

Woolacombe 654 **West Down**

Bittadon Clif Churchill

Morte Bay **D** **E**

Dean Cross **A361** **B3230** **A39**

Baggy Point Pickwell North Buckland

Putsborough Middle Marwood **Milltown**

Georgeham Nethercott Winsham Muddiford

Croyde Bay **Croyde** Forda Darracott Halsinger *Marwood Hill* Guineaford

518 Knowle Pippacott Marwood Kingsheanton

B3231 Lobb Prixford

Saunton **Braunton** **Heanton Puncardon** Ashford *Broomhill Sculpture*

2

DANGER AREA Wrafton River Taw Bradiford Snappe R. Yeo

Toll Chivenor **BARNSTAPL**

Chivenor Fremington Quay Newport Junglela

Braunton Burrow **Fremington** Bickington Lake Landkey

Bideford to Lundy 2hrs. (Seasonal)

3

Yelland **B3333** Bickleton **Bishop's Tawton**

Lifeboat Station **B3233** wstock

Northam Burrows Signal Box **A39** Eastacombe

Appledore **Instow** Tapeley P **163** St John's Chapel

Maritime **A39** **B3232**

Westward Ho! **B323** **A** **Northam** Westleigh Holmacott **B**

Buckleigh Horwood

Big Sheep **30** Burton Art Gallery Eastleigh Lower Lovacott Harracott Week

Abbotsham Orchard Hill Woodtown Newton Tracey **A377**

BIDEFORD **East-the-Water** Hiscott Ensis Chapelt

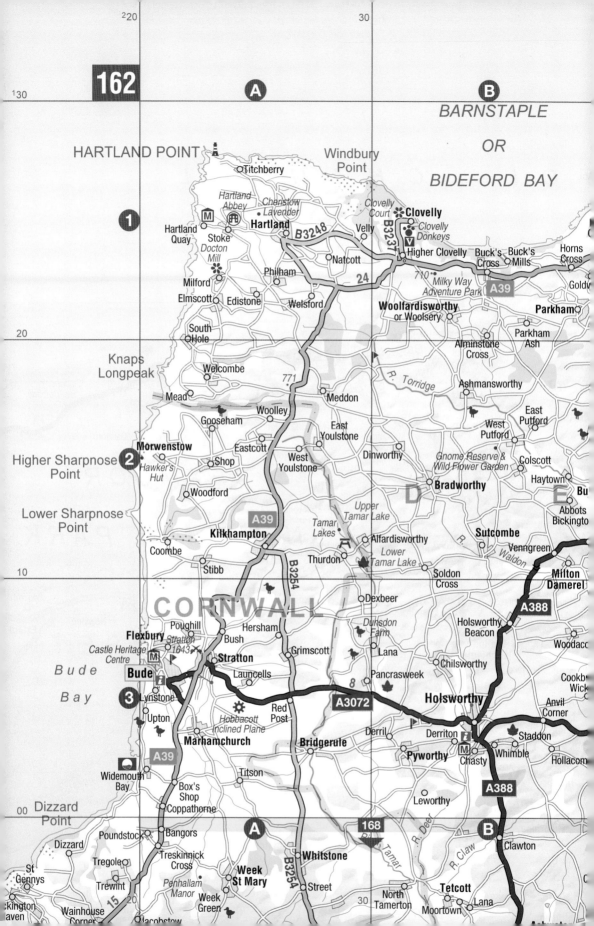

BARNSTAPLE

OR

BIDEFORD BAY

HARTLAND POINT

Titchberry

Windbury
Point

⓵

Hartland
Abbey

Cheristow
Lavender

Clovelly
Court

Clovelly

Hartland
Quay

Ⓜ

Hartland

B3248

Velly

B3237

Clovelly
Donkeys

Stoke
Docton
Mill

Natcott

Higher Clovelly

Buck's
Cross

Buck's
Mills

Horns
Cross

Milford

Philham

710

Milky Way
Adventure Park

A39

Goldv

Elmscott

Edistone

Welsford

Woolfardisworthy
or Woolsery

Parkham

South
Hole

Alminstone
Cross

Parkham
Ash

130 20

Knaps
Longpeak

Welcombe

771

R. Torridge

Ashmansworthy

Mead

Woolley

Meddon

East
Putford

Gooseham

Woolley

East
Youlstone

West
Putford

Colscott

Morwenstow

⓶

Eastcott

Dinworthy

Gnome Reserve &
Wild Flower Garden

Haytown

Higher Sharpnose
Point

Hawker's
Hut

Shop

West
Youlstone

Bradworthy

Ⓓ

Ⓔ

Bu

Woodford

Lower Sharpnose
Point

A39

Upper
Tamar Lake

Sutcombe

Abbots
Bickingto

Tamar
Lakes

Venngreen

**Milton
Damerel**

Coombe

Kilkhampton

B3254

Alfardisworthy

R. Waldon

Stibb

Thurdon

Lower
Tamar Lake

Soldon
Cross

A388

130 10

CORNWALL

Dexbeer

Dunsdon
Farm

Holsworthy
Beacon

Woodacc

Poughill

Hersham

Lana

Chilsworthy

Cookb'
Wick

Flexbury

Bush

Grimscott

Stratton
1643

Stratton

Pancrasweek

Holsworthy

Anvil
Corner

Castle Heritage
Centre

Ⓜ

8

A3072

Bude

Ⓘ

Launcells

Derril

Derriton

Staddon

Ⓜ

Bude

Lynstone

⓷

Red
Post

Bridgerule

Pyworthy

Chasty

Whimble

Hollacom

Bude

Bay

Upton

Hobbacott
Inclined Plane

Marhamchurch

Leworthy

A388

Widemouth
Bay

A39

Titson

Dizzard
Point

130 00

Box's
Shop
Coppathorne

Ⓐ

168

Ⓑ

Poundstock

Bangors

Clawton

Dizzard

Treskinnick
Cross

Whitstone

R. Deer

R. Claw

St
Gennys

Tregole

Trewint

Penhallam
Manor

**Week
St Mary**

B3254

Street

North
Tamerton

Tetcott

Lana

Moortown

kington
aven

15

20

Wainhouse
Corner

Macobstow

Week
Green

30

R. Tamar

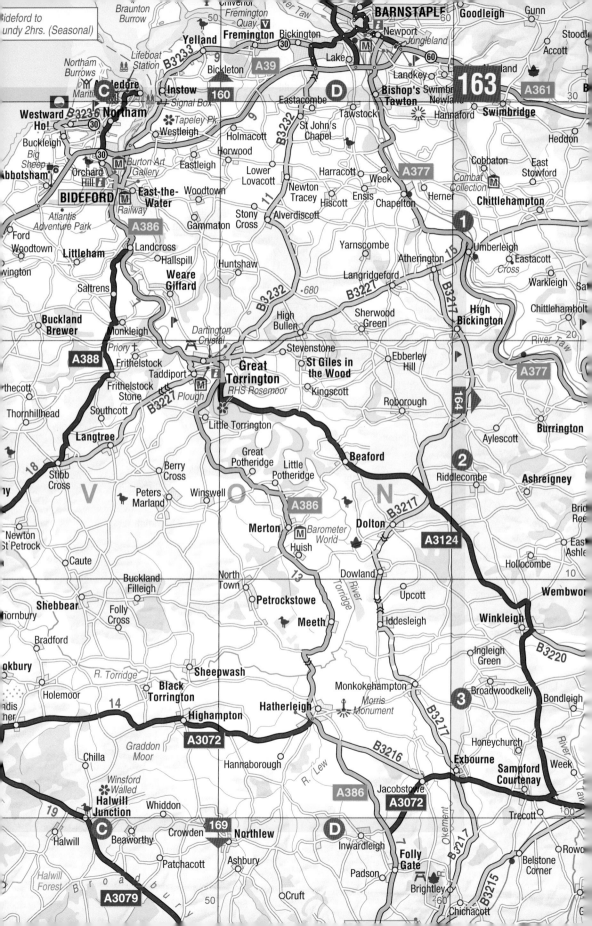

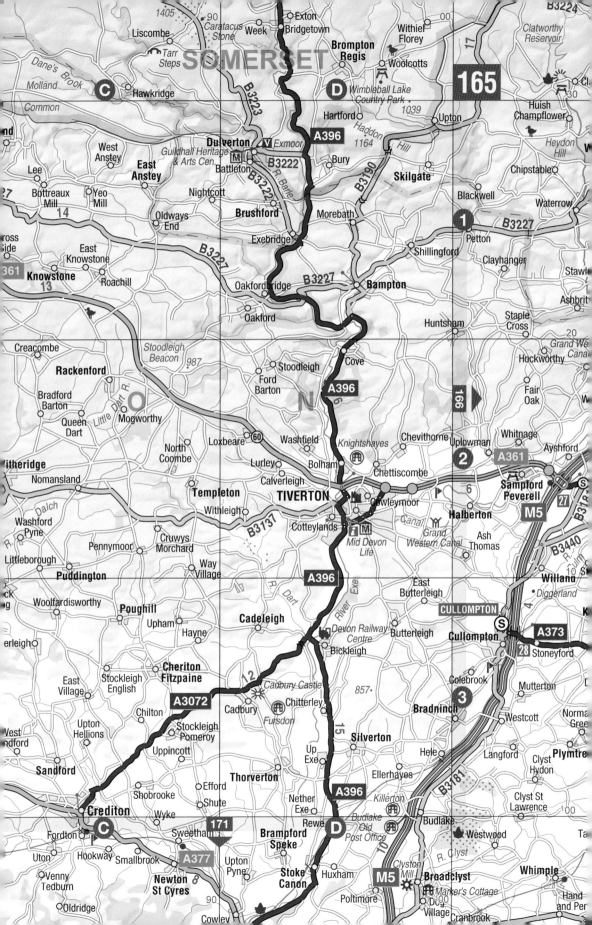

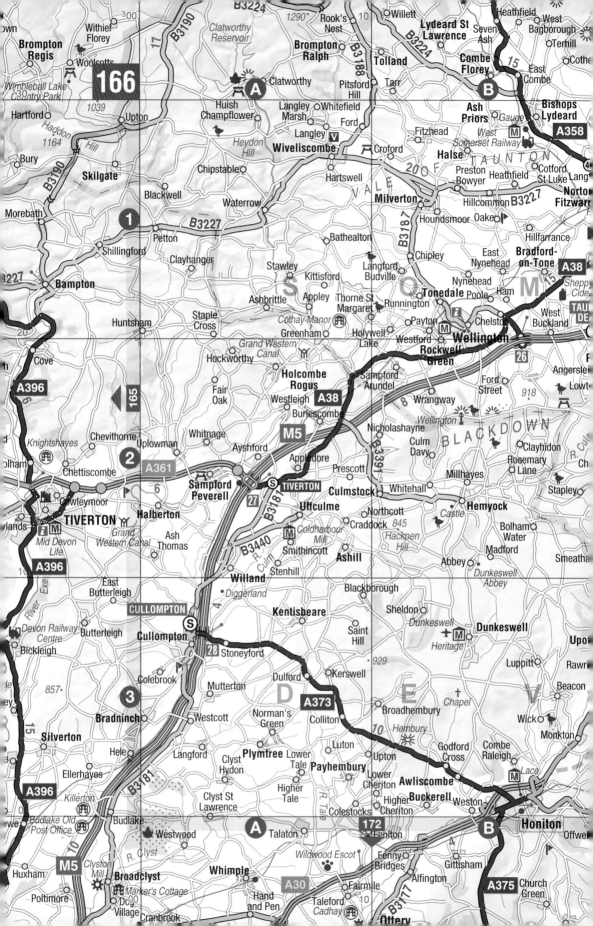

167

Huntstile · North Petherton · M5 · A38 · 24 · Pumping Station · Middlezoy · 40 Greylake · Henley · Beer · High Ham · King's Sedge Moor

Fyne Court · Broomfield · Shearston · North Newton · Thorngrove · Northmoor Green or Moorland · A361 22 · Othery · 30 · Bowdens · Low Ham · Pitney · 30

Kingston St Mary · C · Thurloxton · Adsborough · Maunsel Lock Canal Centre · Bankland · King Alfred's · Pathe · Burrow Mump · DANGER AREA · Stembridge

Hestercombe · West Monkton · Hedging · West Newton · West Lyng · Burrowbridge · Athelney · Statthe · Aller · A372 · Pict's Hill · Langport · 1645

Upper Cheddon · Cheddon Fitzpaine · A3259 · Durston · Creech Heathfield · Charlton · East Lyng · Willows & Wetlands · Woodhill · Oath · Wick · Portfield · Huish Episcopi · Pibsbury · Langport

Staplegrove · Monkton Heathfield · Creech St Michael · Meare Green · Stoke St Gregory · R. Parrett · R. Tone · A378 · Drayton · 1 · Muchelney · Priest's House · Muchelney Ham

Bathpool · Ruishton · North Curry · Huntham · West Sedge Moor · Burton Pynsent · Curry Rivel · B3168 · Abbey · Midelney

Bishop's Hull · 40 · 25 · Henlade · Thornfalcon · Ham · Knapp · Helland · Swell · Isle · R. Isle · Thorney

TAUNTON · P+R · Haydon · Stoke St Mary · Lillesdon · Newport · 15 · Fivehead · Swell · A378 · Hambridge · Somerset Distillery · Kingsbury Episcopi

A358 · 30 · Shoreditch · Wrantage · Meare Green · Curry Mallet · Isle Brewers · Lock-up · Coat · Stembridge 20

Galmington · M · Orchard Portman · Thurlbear · Hatch · Isle Abbotts · New Cross · East Lambrook · West Lambrook · Mid Manor

Trull · Corfe · Staple Fitzpaine · Slough Green · West Hatch · Hatch Beauchamp · Beercrocombe · Westport · Barrington Court · Lambrook · South Petherton

Sellick's Green · Howleigh · Blagdon Hill · Bickenhall · Curland · Stewley · RNAS Merryfield · Puckington · Ilford · B3168 · Barrington · Shepton Beauchamp · A303

Staple Hill · 1034 · Curland Common · Ashill · Rapps · Ilton · Stocklinch · Hurcott · Moor · Wigborough

Blindmoor · Hare · Windmill Hill · Horton Cross · Winterhay Green · Whitelackington · 2 · Seavington St Michael · Over Stratton · Lopen

Blackwater · Broadway · Horton · Ilminster · Kingstone · Seavington St Mary · Allowenshay · Merriott

Otterford · Birchwood · Buckland St Mary · Ham · A303 · Donyatt · Sea · Dowlish Wake · Dinnington · Hinton St George

Royston Water · Bishopswood · Newtown · 50 · Beetham · Street Ash · Combe St Nicholas · Peasmarsh · Knowle St Giles · Cricket Malherbie · Chillington · Broadshard · A356

B3170 · Marsh · Northay · Whitestaunton · Wadeford · Nimmer · Hornsbury · Cudworth · Crewkerne · A30

Howley · Cuttiford's Door · Crimchard · 40 · Chaffcombe · Lydmarsh · Purtington · Roundham · Heritage Centre · Misterton

Newcott · Yarcombe · A30 · Wambrook · M · Lakes & Gdns · Cricket St Thomas · Hewish · B3165

Crawley · Chard · B3162 · Street · Whatley · Woolminstone · Clapton · Seaborough

14 · Burridge · Forton · Winsham · Wayford · B3162 · Drimpton · A3066 · Littlewindsor

A30 · Stockland · Holy City · Tatworth · Perry Street · Bridge · Horn Ash · 3 · Greenham · B3164

Millhayes · Furley · Chardstock · South Chard · Chard Junction · Forde Abbey · Laymore · Thorncombe · Burstock · Hursey

Heathstock · Membury · Birchill · A358 · Tytherleigh · Holditch · Hewood · Blackdown · Broadwindsor · B3164

Ham · Castle · Alston · South Common · Wadbrook · Lower Holditch · Birdsmoorgate · Marshalsea · Stoke Abbott

Wilmington · Turfmoor · Churchill · DORSET · Bettiscombe · Pilsdon Pen · Blackney · North Bowood

10 · Burrow Farm · Loughwood Meeting House · C · Smallridge · Weycroft · 173 · Hawkchurch · Marshalsea · Pilsdon · Marshwood · South Bowood

Dalwood · B3165 · D · Lambert's Castle · Fishpond Bottom · Coney's Castle · Filford

A35 · Kilmington · Shute · Axminster · Blackpool Corner · Raymond's Hill · Monkton Wyld · Wootton Fitzpaine · Whitchurch · Broadoak

Seaton Junction · Hampton · Shute Barton · Abbey Gate · 30 · Penn · Marshwood Vale · R. Char · A358

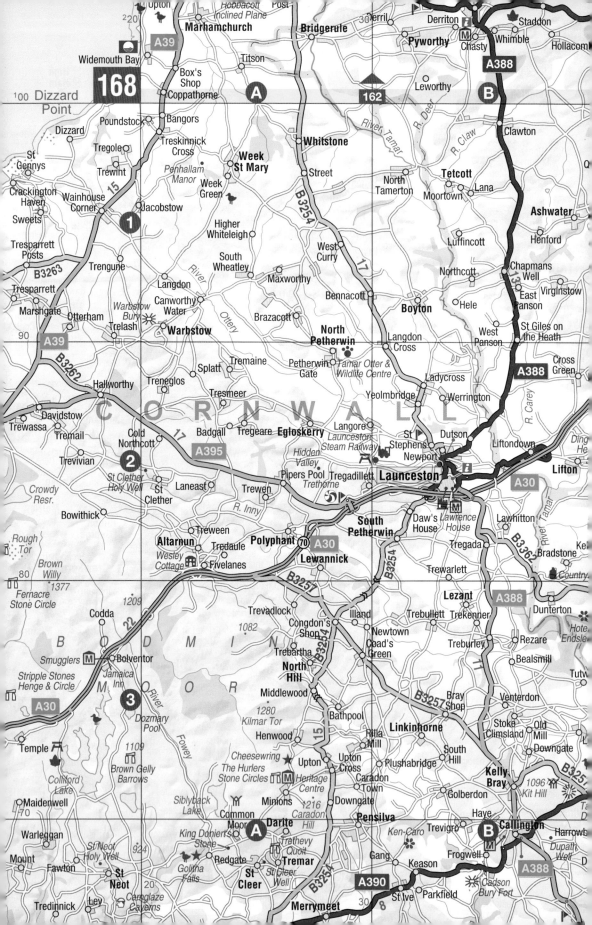

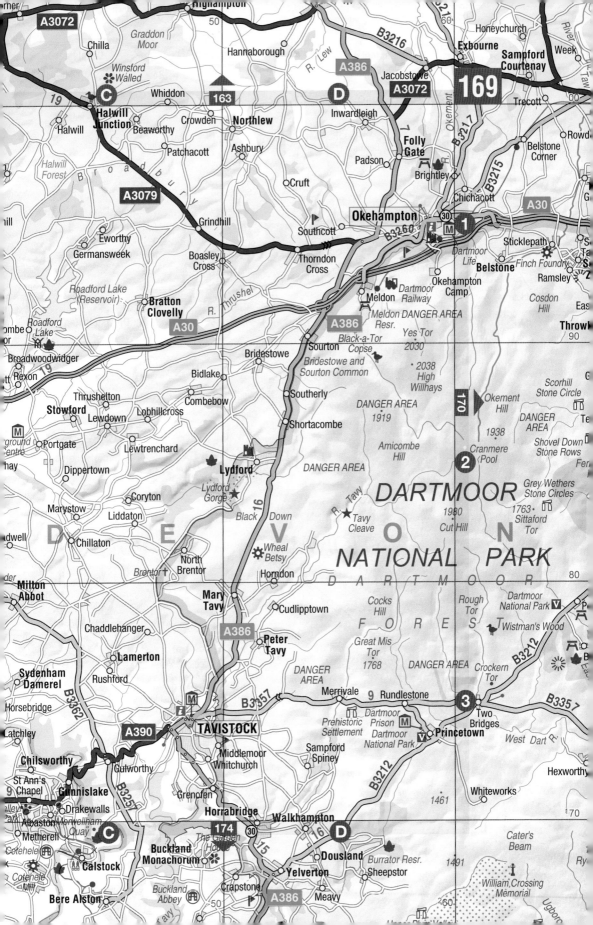

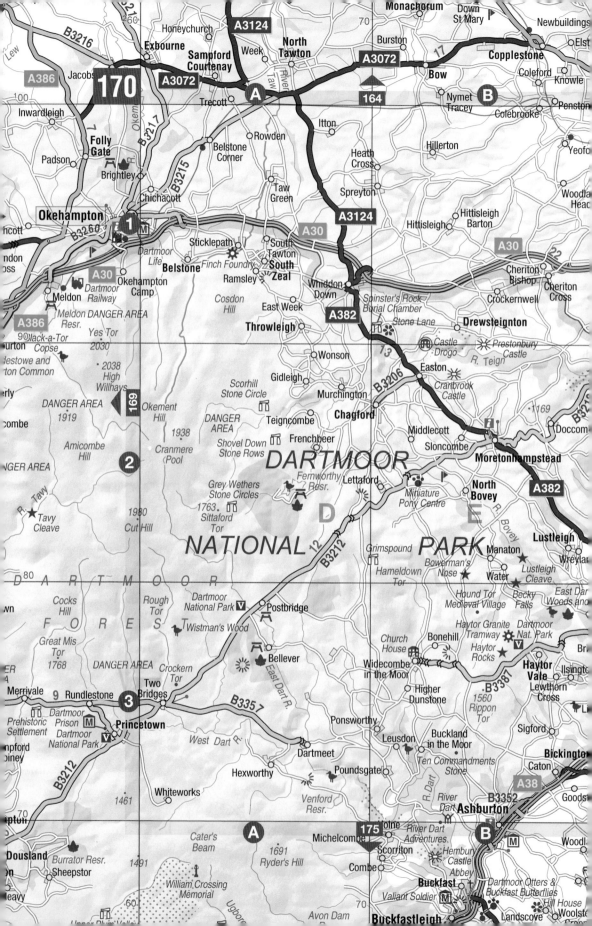

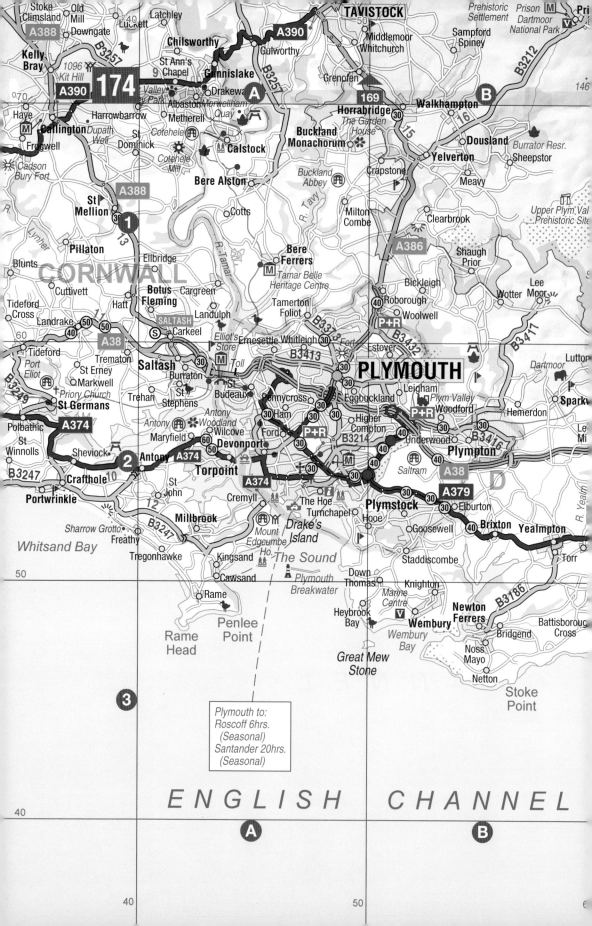

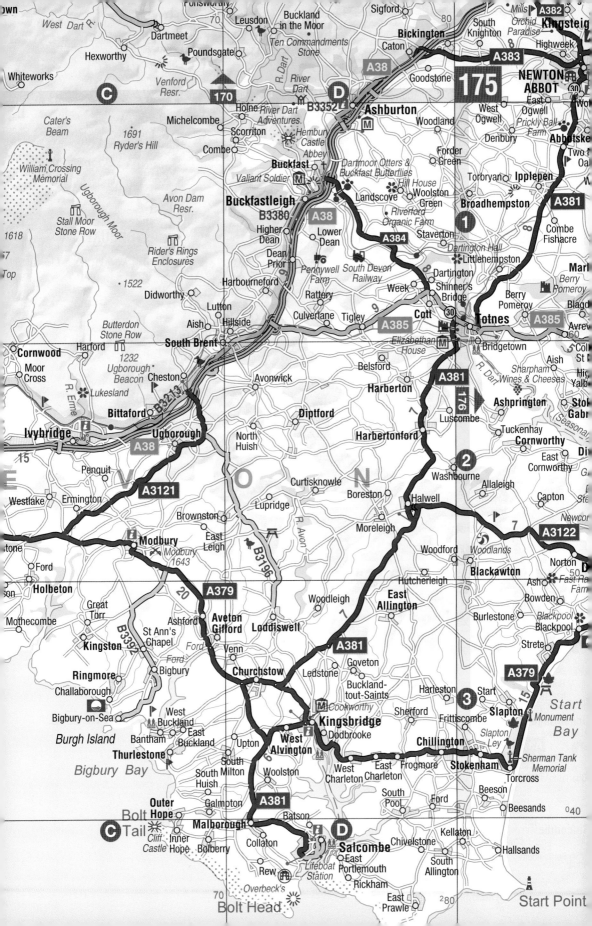

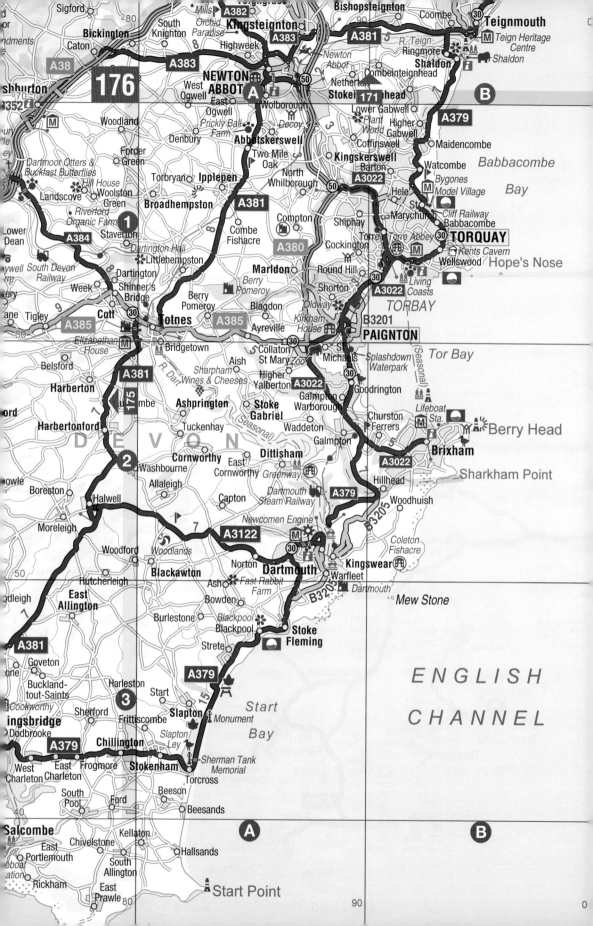

INDEX

Including Streets, Places & Areas, Industrial Estates,
Selected Flats & Walkways, Service Areas, Stations and Selected Places of Interest.

HOW TO USE THIS INDEX

1. Each street name is followed by its Postcode District, then by its Locality abbreviation(s) and then by its map reference;
   e.g. **Abbotsbury Rd.** TQ12: New A . . . . 7E **104** is in the TQ12 Postcode District and the Newton Abbot Locality and is to be found in square 7E on page **104**.
   The page number is shown in bold type.

2. A strict alphabetical order is followed in which Av., Rd., St., etc. (though abbreviated) are read in full and as part of the street name;
   e.g. **Bow La.** appears after **Bowland Cl.** but before **Bowley Mdw.**

3. Streets and a selection of flats and walkways that cannot be shown on street map pages **10-159**, appear in the index with the thoroughfare to which they are connected shown in brackets; e.g. **Abbeyfield Ho.** *TQ14: Teignm . . . . 4J **107** (off Heywoods Rd.)*

4. Addresses that are in more than one part are referred to as not continuous.

5. Places and areas are shown in the index in **BLUE TYPE** and the map reference is to the actual map square in which the town centre or area is located and not to the place name shown on the map. Map references for entries that appear on street map pages **10-159** are shown first, with references to road map pages **160-176** shown in brackets;
   e.g. **ABBOTSKERSWELL . . . .6E 108 (1A 176)**

6. An example of a selected place of interest is **Bishopsteignton Mus. of Rural Life 3C 106**

7. Transport hub examples:
   Axminster Station (Rail) . . . .4G 89 (1C 173); Seaton Stop (Seaton Tramway) . . . .5F 87 (1C 173); Barnstaple Bus Station . . . .4F 19; Dartmouth Park & Ride 7C 124

8. Service Areas are shown in the index in **BOLD CAPITAL TYPE**; e.g. **CULLOMPTON SERVICE AREA . . . .3H 45 (3A 166)**

9. Map references for entries that appear on large scale pages **6-9** & **124** are shown first, with small scale map references shown in brackets;
   e.g. **Alphington St.** EX2: Exe 6C **6** (7E **64**)

GENERAL ABBREVIATIONS

All. : Alley
Apts. : Apartments
App. : Approach
Arc. : Arcade
Av. : Avenue
Bk. : Back
Bri. : Bridge
B'way. : Broadway
Bldg. : Building
Bldgs. : Buildings
Bungs. : Bungalows
Bus. : Business
Cvn. : Caravan
C'way. : Causeway
Cen. : Centre
Chu. : Church
Cir. : Circus
Cl. : Close
Comn. : Common
Cnr. : Corner
Cott. : Cottage
Cotts. : Cottages
Ct. : Court
Cres. : Crescent
Cft. : Croft
Dr. : Drive
E. : East
Emb. : Embankment
Ent. : Enterprise
Est. : Estate
Fld. : Field
Flds. : Fields
Gdn. : Garden
Gdns. : Gardens
Gth. : Garth
Ga. : Gate
Gt. : Great
Grn. : Green
Gro. : Grove
Hgts. : Heights
Ho. : House
Ho's. : Houses
Ind. : Industrial
Info. : Information
Intl. : International
Junc. : Junction
La. : Lane
Lit. : Little
Lwr. : Lower
Mnr. : Manor
Mans. : Mansions
Mkt. : Market
Mdw. : Meadow
Mdws. : Meadows
M. : Mews
Mt. : Mount
Mus. : Museum
Nth. : North
Pde. : Parade
Pk. : Park
Pas. : Passage
Pl. : Place
Pct. : Precinct
Prom. : Promenade
Res. : Residential
Ri. : Rise
Rd. : Road
Rdbt. : Roundabout
Shop. : Shopping
Sth. : South
Sq. : Square
Sta. : Station
St. : Street
Ter. : Terrace
Twr. : Tower
Trad. : Trading
Up. : Upper
Va. : Vale
Vw. : View
Vs. : Villas
Vis. : Visitors
Wlk. : Walk
W. : West
Yd. : Yard

LOCALITY ABBREVIATIONS

Abbey Gate: EX13 . . . . Abb G
Abbotsham: EX39 . . . . A'sham
Abbotskerswell: TQ12 . . . . A'well
Aish: TQ9-10 . . . . Aish
Alphington: EX2 . . . . Alph
Appledore: EX39 . . . . App
Ashburton: TQ13 . . . . Ashb
Ashford: EX31 . . . . Ashf
Ashill: EX15 . . . . A'hill
Ashley: EX16 . . . . Ashy
Ash Thomas: EX16 . . . . Ash T
Aveton Gifford: TQ7 . . . . Ave G
Awliscombe: EX14 . . . . Awli
Axminster: EX13 . . . . Axmin
Axmouth: EX12 . . . . Axmth
Aylesbeare: EX5 . . . . Ayle
Bampton: EX16 . . . . Bam
Barbrook: EX35 . . . . Bar
Barnstaple: EX31-32 . . . . B'aple
Batson: TQ8 . . . . Bat
Beaford: EX19 . . . . Bea
Beer: EX12 . . . . Beer
Bere Alston: PL20 . . . . Bere A
Bere Ferrers: PL20 . . . . Bere F
Berrynarbor: EX34 . . . . Ber
Berry Pomeroy: TQ9 . . . . Berr P
Bickington: EX31 . . . . Bick
Bickleigh: PL6 . . . . Bickl
Bicton: EX9 . . . . Bic
Bideford: EX39 . . . . Bide
Bigbury-on-Sea: TQ7 . . . . Bigb S
Bishop's Tawton: EX32 . . . . B Taw
Bishopsteignton: TQ14 . . . . Bi'ton
Bittaford: PL21 . . . . Bitta
Blackawton: TQ9 . . . . Blacka
Blackpool: TQ6 . . . . Blackp
Blagdon: TQ3 . . . . Blag
Bolberry: TQ7 . . . . Bolb
Bolham: EX16 . . . . Bolh
Boode: EX33 . . . . Boo
Bovey Tracey: TQ13 . . . . Bov T
Bovisand: PL9 . . . . Bovis
Bow: EX17 . . . . Bow
Bradninch: EX5 . . . . Bradn
Bradworthy: EX22 . . . . Bradw
Brampford Speke: EX5 . . . . Bram S
Branscombe: EX10,EX12 . . . . Brans
Bratton Fleming: EX31-32 . . . . Brat F
Braunton: EX33 . . . . Brau
Bridestowe: EX20 . . . . Brid
Bridford: EX6 . . . . Bridf
Brixham: TQ5 . . . . Brixh
Brixton: PL8 . . . . Brixt
Broadclyst: EX5 . . . . Broadc
Broadsands: TQ4 . . . . Broads
Buckfast: TQ11 . . . . Buck
Buckfastleigh: TQ11 . . . . B'leigh
Buckland Brewer: EX39 . . . . Buck B
Buckland Monachorum: PL20 . . . . Buck M
Budleigh Salterton: EX9 . . . . Bud S
Burlescombe: EX16 . . . . Burl
Calverleigh: EX16 . . . . Calv
Cargreen: PL12 . . . . Car
Chagford: TQ13 . . . . Chag
Chawleigh: EX18 . . . . Chaw
Cheriton Bishop: EX6,EX31 . . . . Cher
Cheriton Fitzpaine: EX17 . . . . Cher F
Chettiscombe: EX16 . . . . Chet
Chevithorne: EX16 . . . . Chev
Chichacott: EX20 . . . . Chich
Chillington: TQ7 . . . . Chil
Chittlehampton: EX37 . . . . C'ton
Chivenor: EX31 . . . . C'nor
Chrisrow: EX6 . . . . Chri
Chudleigh: TQ13 . . . . Chud
Chudleigh Knighton: TQ13 . . . . Chud K
Chulmleigh: EX18 . . . . Chul
Churchstow: TQ7 . . . . Chur
Churston Ferrers: TQ5 . . . . Chur F
Clayhidon: EX15 . . . . Clay
Clovelly: EX39 . . . . Clov
Clyst Honiton: EX5 . . . . Clyst H
Clyst St George: EX3 . . . . Clyst G
Clyst St Mary: EX5 . . . . Clyst M
Cockwood: EX6 . . . . Cockw
Coffinswell: TQ12 . . . . Coff
Colaton Raleigh: EX10 . . . . Col R
Coldridge: EX17 . . . . Cold
Collaton St Mary: TQ4 . . . . Coll M
Collipriest: EX16 . . . . Colli
Colyford: EX24 . . . . Colyf
Colyton: EX24 . . . . Colyt
Combeinteignhead: TQ12 . . . . C'head
Combe Martin: EX34 . . . . C Mar
Combe Raleigh: EX14 . . . . Com R
Compton: TQ3 . . . . Comp
Coombelake: EX11 . . . . Coom
Copplestone: EX17 . . . . Cop
Cornwood: PL21 . . . . Corn
Countess Wear: EX2 . . . . Cou W
Cowley: EX5 . . . . Cowl
Craddock: EX15 . . . . Crad
Cranbrook: EX5 . . . . Cran
Cranford: EX39 . . . . Cran
Crapstone: PL20 . . . . C'stone
Crediton: EX17 . . . . Cred
Cremyll: PL10 . . . . Crem
Croyde: EX33 . . . . Croy
Cullompton: EX15 . . . . Cull
Culmstock: EX15 . . . . Culm
Daccombe: TQ12 . . . . Dacc
Dainton: TQ12 . . . . Dain
Dartington: TQ9 . . . . Darti
Dartmouth: TQ6 . . . . Dartm
Dawlish: EX7 . . . . Daw
Dawlish Warren: EX7 . . . . Daw W
Denbury: TQ12 . . . . Den
Devonport: PL1-2 . . . . Dev
Dittisham: TQ6 . . . . Ditt
Doddiscombsleigh: EX6 . . . . Dodd
Dolton: EX19 . . . . Dol
Dousland: PL20 . . . . Dous
Down Thomas: PL9 . . . . Down T
Drakelands: PL7 . . . . Drak
Dunkeswell: EX14 . . . . Dunk
Dunsford: EX6 . . . . Dunsf
Dunstone: PL8 . . . . Dunst
East Allington: TQ9 . . . . E All
East Budleigh: EX9 . . . . E Bud
Eastdon: EX6 . . . . E'don
East Ogwell: TQ12 . . . . E Ogw
East Portlemouth: TQ8 . . . . E Port
Ebford: EX3 . . . . Ebf
Elburton: PL9 . . . . Elb
Ermington: PL21 . . . . Erm
Exbourne: EX20 . . . . Exbo
Exeter: EX1-2,EX4 . . . . Exe
Exminster: EX2,EX6 . . . . Exmin
Exmouth: EX8 . . . . Exmth
Exton: EX3 . . . . Ext
Feniton: EX14 . . . . Fen
Filham: PL21 . . . . Fil
Forda: EX33 . . . . Forda
Fremington: EX31 . . . . Frem
Galmpton: TQ5,TQ7 . . . . Galm
Georgeham: EX33 . . . . Geo
George Nympton: EX36 . . . . G Nym
Gittisham: EX14 . . . . Gitt
Goodrington: TQ4 . . . . Good
Gosford: EX11 . . . . Gos
Goveton: TQ7 . . . . Gov
Great Torrington: EX38 . . . . G Tor
Haccombe: TQ12 . . . . Hacc
Halberton: EX16 . . . . Hal
Half Moon Village: EX5 . . . . Half M
Harberton: TQ9 . . . . Harb
Harbertonford: TQ9 . . . . H'ford
Harcombe: EX10 . . . . Harc
Harcombe Bottom: DT7 . . . . Harc B
Harford: PL21 . . . . Harf
Harpford: EX10 . . . . Harp
Hartland: EX39 . . . . Hart
Hatherleigh: EX20 . . . . Hath
Heathfield: TQ12 . . . . H'fld
Heavitree: EX1-2 . . . . Heav
Hele: EX5 . . . . Hele
Hemerdon: PL7 . . . . Hem
Hemyock: EX15 . . . . Hemy
Heybrook Bay: PL9 . . . . Hey B
High Bickington: EX37 . . . . High B
Higher Clovelly: EX39 . . . . High C
Higher Metcombe: EX11 . . . . High M

Hillhead: TQ5 . . . . .Hill
Holbeton: PL8 . . . . .Holb
Holcombe: EX7 . . . . .Holc
Holcombe Rogus: TA21 . . . . .Holc R
Holsworthy: EX22 . . . . .Hols
Honiton: EX14 . . . . .Hon
Hooe: PL9 . . . . .Hooe
Hope: TQ7 . . . . .Hope
Horndon: PL19 . . . . .Horn
Horrabridge: PL20 . . . . .Horr
Huish: EX20 . . . . .Huish
Huxham: EX5 . . . . .Hux
Ide: EX2 . . . . .Ide
Ilfracombe: EX34 . . . . .Ilfra
Instow: EX39 . . . . .Ins
Ipplepen: TQ12 . . . . .Ipp
Ivybridge: PL21 . . . . .Ivy
Kenn: EX6 . . . . .Kenn
Kennford: EX6 . . . . .Kennf
Kentisbeare: EX15 . . . . .Kent
Kenton: EX6 .Kenton
Kilmington: EX13 . . . . .Kilm
Kingsbridge: TQ7 . . . . .Kingsb
Kingskerswell: TQ12 . . . . .Kingsk
Kingsteignton: TQ12 . . . . .Kingst
Kingswear: TQ6 . . . . .Kingsw
Knowle: EX9,EX33 . . . . .Know
Lamerton: PL19 . . . . .Lam
Landkey: EX32 . . . . .Land
Lapford: EX17 . . . . .Lap
Lee Mill: PL21 . . . . .L Mill
Lee Moor: PL7 . . . . .L Moor
Lewdown: EX20 . . . . .Lew
Lifton: PL16 .Lift
Littleham: EX8,EX39 . . . . .Lit
Littlehempston: TQ9 . . . . .L'ton
Little Torrington:
    EX38 . . . . .Lit T
Liverton: TQ12 . . . . .Live
Lobb: EX33 .Lob
Loddiswell: TQ7 . . . . .Lodd
Longdown: EX6 . . . . .Long
Lower Dean: TQ11 . . . . .Lwr D
Lustleigh: TQ13 . . . . .Lust
Lutton: PL21 . . . . .Lutt
Lydford: EX20 . . . . .Lyd
Lyme Regis: DT7 . . . . .Lym R
Lympstone: EX8 . . . . .Lymp
Lynmouth: EX35 . . . . .Lynm
Lynton: EX35 . . . . .Lynt
Maidencombe: TQ1 . . . . .Maid
Malborough: TQ7 . . . . .Malb
Marldon: TQ3 . . . . .Marl

Marsh Barton: EX2 . . . . .Mar B
Marsh Green: EX5 . . . . .Mar G
Mary Tavy: PL19 . . . . .Mary T
Matford: EX2 . . . . .Matf
Meavy: PL20 . . . . .Meavy
Merton: EX20 . . . . .Mert
Metcombe: EX11 . . . . .Metc
Millbrook: PL10 . . . . .Millb
Milton Abbot: PL19 . . . . .Mil A
Modbury: PL21 . . . . .Modb
Monkton: EX14 . . . . .Monk'n
Monkton Wyld: DT6 . . . . .Monk W
Moorhaven: PL21 . . . . .Moor
Morchard Bishop: EX17 . . . . .Morc
Moretonhampstead: TQ13 . . . . .More
Mortehoe: EX34 . . . . .Mort
Musbury: EX13 . . . . .Mus
Nadderwater: EX4 . . . . .Nad
Netherton: TQ12 . . . . .N'ton
Newton Abbot: TQ12 . . . . .New A
Newton Ferrers: PL8 . . . . .New F
Newton Poppleford: EX10 . . . . .New P
Newton St Cyres: EX5 . . . . .New C
Northam: EX39 . . . . .Nort
North Buckland: EX33 . . . . .N Buck
North Molton: EX36 . . . . .N Mol
Northmostown: EX10 . . . . .N'town
North Tawton: EX20 . . . . .N Taw
North Whilborough: TQ12 . . . . .N Whil
Norton: TQ6 .Nort
Noss Mayo: PL8 . . . . .Noss M
Nymet Rowland: EX17 . . . . .Nym R
Offwell: EX14 . . . . .Offw
Okehampton: EX20 . . . . .Oke
Otterton: EX9 . . . . .Ott'n
Ottery St Mary: EX11 . . . . .Ott M
Paignton: TQ3-4 . . . . .Paig
Pinhoe: EX1,EX4-5 . . . . .Pin
Plymouth: PL1-6 . . . . .Plym
Plympton: PL7 . . . . .Plymp
Plymstock: PL9 . . . . .Plyms
Poltimore: EX4 . . . . .Polt
Preston: TQ3 . . . . .Pres
Princetown: PL20 . . . . .Prin
Putsborough: EX33 . . . . .Puts
Raymond's Hill: EX13 . . . . .Ray H
Rewe: EX5 . . . . .Rewe
Roborough: EX19,PL6 . . . . .Robo
Rockbeare: EX5 . . . . .Rock
Roundswell: EX31 . . . . .Rou
St Giles on the Heath: PL15 . . . . .St G
Salcombe: TQ8 . . . . .Salc
Saltash: PL12 . . . . .Salt

Sampford Peverell: EX16 . . . . .Sam P
Sandy Bay: EX8 . . . . .San B
Saunton: EX33 . . . . .Saunt
Seaton: EX12 . . . . .Seat
Shaldon: TQ14 . . . . .Shal
Shebbear: EX21 . . . . .Sheb
Shillingford Abbot: EX2 . . . . .Shil A
Shirwell: EX31 . . . . .Shir
Shute: EX13 .Shute
Sidbury: EX10 . . . . .Sidb
Sidford: EX10 . . . . .Sidf
Sidmouth: EX10 . . . . .Sidm
Silverton: EX5 . . . . .Silv
Slapton: TQ7 . . . . .Slap
Smallridge: EX13 . . . . .Smal
South Brent: TQ10 . . . . .S Bre
Southerton: EX11 . . . . .S'ton
South Huish: TQ7 . . . . .S Hui
South Milton: TQ7 . . . . .S Mil
South Molton: EX36 . . . . .S Mol
South Tawton: EX20 . . . . .S Taw
South Zeal: EX20 . . . . .S Zeal
Sowton: EX1-2,EX5 . . . . .Sow
Sparkwell: PL7 . . . . .Spa
Spriddlestone: PL9 . . . . .Spri
Staddiscombe: PL9 . . . . .Stad
Starcross: EX6-7 . . . . .Star
Sticklepath: EX20 . . . . .Stic
Stoke Canon: EX5 . . . . .Sto C
Stoke Fleming: TQ6 . . . . .Sto F
Stoke Gabriel: TQ9 . . . . .Sto G
Stokeinteignhead:
    TQ12,TQ14 . . . . .S'head
Stokenham: TQ7 . . . . .Stoke
Stoneycombe: TQ12 . . . . .Ston
Stowford: EX10 . . . . .Stow
Strete: TQ6 .Strete
Swimbridge: EX32 . . . . .Swim
Taleford: EX11 . . . . .Tale
Tamerton Foliot: PL5 . . . . .Tam F
Tavistock: PL19 . . . . .Tavi
Tawstock: EX31 . . . . .Taw
Tedburn St Mary: EX6 . . . . .Ted M
Teigngrace: TQ12 . . . . .Teigng
Teignmouth: TQ14 . . . . .Teignm
Thorverton: EX5 . . . . .Thor
Thurlestone: TQ7 . . . . .Thur
Tinhay: PL16 . . . . .Tin
Tipton St John: EX10 . . . . .Tip J
Tiverton: EX16 . . . . .Tive
Topsham: EX3 . . . . .Top
Torpoint: PL11 . . . . .Torp

Torquay: TQ1-2 . . . . .Torq
Torr: PL8 . . . . .Torr
Totnes: TQ9 .Tot
Trewetha: PL19 . . . . .T'tha
Two Mile Oak: TQ12 . . . . .Two O
Two Potts: EX34 . . . . .T Pot
Uffculme: EX15 . . . . .Uff
Ugborough: PL21 . . . . .Ugb
Up Exe: EX5 .Up E
Uplowman: EX16 . . . . .U'man
Uplyme: DT7 . . . . .Uply
Upper Dean: TQ11 . . . . .Upp D
Velator: EX33 . . . . .Vel
Venn Ottery: EX11 . . . . .Ven O
Waddeton: TQ5 . . . . .Wadd
Walkhampton: PL20 . . . . .Walk
Ware: DT7 . . . . .Ware
Washfield: EX16 . . . . .Wash
Wembury: PL9 . . . . .Wem
West Alvington: TQ7 . . . . .W Alv
West Charleton: TQ7 . . . . .W Cha
West Clyst: EX1 . . . . .W Cly
West Hill: EX11 . . . . .W Hill
Westleigh: EX39 . . . . .West
Weston: EX14 . . . . .W'ton
Westward Ho!: EX39 . . . . .W Ho
Weycroft: EX13 . . . . .Wey
Whimple: EX5 . . . . .Whim
Whipton: EX1,EX4 . . . . .Whip
Whitchurch: PL19 . . . . .Whit
Whitestone: EX4 . . . . .White
Whitford: EX13 . . . . .Whit
Wiggaton: EX11 . . . . .Wigg
Wilcove: PL11 . . . . .Wilc
Willand: EX15 . . . . .Will
Winkleigh: EX19 . . . . .Wink
Winsham: EX33 . . . . .Win
Witheridge: EX16 . . . . .W'ridge
Wonford: EX2 . . . . .Won
Woodbury: EX5 . . . . .W'bury
Woodbury Salterton: EX5 . . . . .Wood S
Woolacombe: EX34 . . . . .Wool
Woolsery: EX39 . . . . .Wools
Worston: PL8 . . . . .Wors
Wotter: PL7 . . . . .Wot
Wrafton: EX33 . . . . .Wraf
Wrangaton: TQ10 . . . . .Wran
Wyke Green: EX13 . . . . .Wy G
Yealmpton: PL8 . . . . .Y'ton
Yelland: EX31 . . . . .Yell
Yelverton: PL20 . . . . .Yelv

A

Abbeville Cl. EX2: Exe 2H **71**
ABBEY 2B **166**
Abbey Cl. EX13: Axmin 5G **89**
    PL20: C'stone 6C **126**
    TQ13: Bov T 4B **92**
    TQ14: Teignm 2J **107**
Abbey Ct. EX2: Sow 7E **66**
    PL1: Plym 5F **9**
    PL19: Tavi 3J **59**
Abbey Cres. TQ2: Torq 2C **116**
Abbeyfield TQ1: Torq 5D **112**
Abbeyfield Ho. TQ14: Teignm 4J **107**
    (off Heywoods Rd.)
Abbeyford Ct. EX20: Oke 3C **48**
Abbeyford Woods Forest Walks . . .1D **169**
Abbeyford Woods Picnic Site 1D **169**
ABBEY GATE 6G **89** (1C **173**)
Abbey Ga. La.
    EX13: Abb G, Wy G 7G **89**
Abbey Grange Cl. TQ11: Buck 2C **98**
Abbey La. EX13: Abb G 6F **89**
    PL20: C'stone 6C **126**
Abbeymead M. PL19: Tavi 4J **59**
Abbey Mdw. PL20: C'stone 6C **126**
    TQ11: Buck 2C **98**
Abbey Park 2B **116**
Abbey Pl. PL1: Plym 5E **8** (3J **141**)
    PL19: Tavi 3H **59**
    (Bannawell St.)
    PL19: Tavi 4J **59**
    (Dolvin Rd.)
Abbey Ri. EX20: Oke 2D **48**
    PL19: Tavi 4J **59**
Abbey Rd. EX4: Exe 1K **7** (4J **65**)
    EX14: Dunk 5H **47**
    EX31: B'aple 2D **18**
    TQ2: Torq 1C **116**
    TQ13: Bov T 3B **92**
Abbey Vw. EX10: Sidm 5D **84**
Abbot Rd. PL21: Ivy 3E **144**
ABBOTS BICKINGTON 2B **162**
ABBOTSBURY 1E **108**
Abbotsbury Rd. TQ12: New A 7E **104**
Abbotsbury Way PL2: Plym 3E **134**
Abbots Cl. EX39: Wools 2B **28**
    PL21: L Mill 5C **144**

Abbots Ct. PL21: Ivy 4E **144**
Abbots Dr. EX39: Bide 5J **23**
Abbotsfield PL19: Tavi 5F **59**
Abbotsfield Cl. PL19: Tavi 5F **59**
Abbotsfield Cres. PL19: Tavi 5F **59**
ABBOTSHAM 4A **22** (1C **163**)
Abbotsham Rd.
    EX39: A'sham, Bide 3A **22**
Abbotshill Cvn. Pk. 6D **108**
ABBOTSKERSWELL 6E **108** (1A **176**)
Abbots Mdw. EX37: C'ton 5H **25**
Abbotsridge Dr. TQ12: E Ogw 3C **108**
Abbots Rd. EX4: Exe 1K **7** (4H **65**)
Abbotswood TQ12: Kingst 3J **105**
    TQ12: Kingst 3J **105**
Abbott Cl. EX11: Ott M 3D **80**
Abbotts Hill EX33: Brau 4J **15**
Abbotts Pk. PL21: Corn 7J **129**
Abbotts Rd. PL3: Plym 6K **135**
Abbrook Av. TQ12: Kingst 2G **105**
Abelia Cl. TQ3: Paig 6E **114**
Abercromby Ho. EX2: Exe 3J **71**
    (off Turnstone Rd.)
Aberdeen Av. PL5: Plym 1J **135**
Abingdon Rd. PL4: Plym 1F **9** (1K **141**)
Abney Cres. PL6: Plym 4C **132**
Above Town
    TQ6: Dartm 2A **124** (6F **125**)
Aboveway EX6: Exmin 3D **74**
Abyssinia Ct. EX32: B'aple 6G **19**
    (off Abyssinia Ter.)
Abyssinia Ter. EX32: B'aple 6G **19**
Acacia Cl. EX39: Bide 4D **22**
    TQ12: Kingst 6H **105**
Academic La. EX18: Chul 6C **32**
Acadia Rd. TQ1: Torq 2G **117**
ACCOTT 3C **161**
Acer Ter. EX6: Cher 3D **62**
Ackland Cl. EX21: Sheb 6J **29**
Acklington Pl. PL5: Plym 6D **130**
Ackrells Hill TQ9: L'ton 1H **103**
Acland Ct. EX33: Brau 3J **15**
Acland Pk. EX14: Fen 1G **53**
Acland Rd. EX4: Exe 2G **7** (5G **65**)
    EX5: Broadc 6C **52**
    EX32: Land 1C **24**
    PL21: Ivy .3E **144**
    TQ8: Salc .4C **158**

Aclands EX36: S Mol 6D **26**
Acland Ter. EX4: Exe 2G **7** (5F **65**)
Acorn Gdns. PL7: Plymp 3A **138**
Acorn Gro. EX32: B'aple 5H **19**
The Acre TQ13: Chag 3H **61**
Acre Cotts. PL1: Dev 1E **140**
Acre La. TQ1: Torq 7G **113**
Acre Pl. PL1: Dev 1E **140**
Activate Sports & Leisure 3B **136**
Adams Cl. PL5: Plym 2D **134**
Adam's La. PL9: Down T 2E **148**
Adcroft Ri. EX13: Mus 7D **90**
Addington Cl. EX4: Exe 1E **6** (5F **65**)
Addison Cl. EX4: Exe 6B **64**
Addison Rd. PL4: Plym 2F **9** (1H **141**)
    TQ4: Paig .2G **119**
    TQ12: New A 2H **109**
Addlehole TQ9: E All 6C **152**
Addlepool Bus. Cen.
    EX3: Clyst G 6H **73**
Adelaide Ct. EX2: Exe 7B **6**
Adelaide La. PL1: Plym 5A **8** (3G **141**)
Adelaide Pl. PL1: Plym 4A **8** (2G **141**)
Adelaide St. PL1: Plym 4A **8** (2G **141**)
    PL2: Plym .6E **134**
Adelaide St. Ope
    PL1: Plym 4A **8** (2G **141**)
    PL1: Plym .2C **8**
Adela Rd. PL11: Torp 1A **140**
Adelphi La. TQ4: Paig 2J **119**
Adelphi Mans. TQ4: Paig 2J **119**
    (off Adelphi Rd.)
Adelphi Rd. TQ4: Paig 1J **119**
Adley La. TQ13: Chag 1J **61**
Admiral Ct. 7B **124**
Admirals Ct. EX8: Exmth 6C **76**
    EX39: Nort 5E **20**
Admiral's Hard PL1: Plym 4F **141**
Admirals Wlk. EX8: Exmth 2F **77**
    TQ14: Teignm 1G **107**
Admiral Swimming Cen. 4F **123**
Admiralty Cotts. PL1: Plym 5F **141**
Admiralty Rd. PL1: Plym 4F **141**
    PL5: Plym .1B **134**
Admiralty St. PL1: Plym 4F **141**

Admiralty St. La. W. PL1: Plym 4F **141**
Admiral Vernon Ct. EX2: Alph 5E **70**
    (off Chudleigh Rd.)
Admiral Way EX2: Cou W 5B **72**
Adrian Cl. EX39: Bide 1F **23**
ADSBOROUGH 1C **167**
Adwell La. EX33: N Buck 4E **14**
Afflington Rd. PL9: Plyms 3E **142**
Agatha Cl. PL6: Plym 4K **131**
Agaton Fort Rd. PL5: Plym 7E **130**
Agaton Rd. PL5: Plym 1D **134**
Aggett Gro. TQ13: Bov T 4E **92**
Aidan Av. EX32: B'aple 7H **19**
Ailescombe Dr. TQ3: Paig 1F **119**
Ailescombe Rd. TQ3: Paig 1F **119**
Ainslie Ter. PL2: Plym 4D **134**
Airborne Dr. PL6: Plym 6C **132**
    (not continuous)
Aire Gdns. PL3: Plym 6D **136**
Airfield Ind. Est. EX14: Dunk 5G **47**
AISH
    TQ9 . . . . .2A **176**
    TQ10 . . . . .1A **100** (1C **175**)
Aish La. TQ10: Aish, S Bre 1A **100**
Aish Pk. EX21: Sheb 6J **29**
Aish Rd. TQ4: Paig 5A **118**
    TQ9: Sto G 3B **152**
Alandale Cl. TQ14: Teignm 3J **107**
Alandale Rd. TQ14: Teignm 3J **107**
Alansway EX11: Ott M 4B **80**
A la Ronde 1C **76** (2A **172**)
Albacore Dr. PL6: Plym 5C **132**
Albany Cl. TQ3: Paig 7H **115**
Albany Ct. EX8: Exmth 2G **77**
Albany Rd. TQ3: Pres 5G **115**
Albany St. PL1: Dev 2D **140**
    TQ12: New A 1F **109**
ALBASTON .3C **169**
Albatross Rd. EX2: Cou W 4C **72**
Albemarle Vs. PL1: Plym 1E **140**
Alberta Vs. TQ14: Teignm 5E **107**
Alberta Cres. EX4: Exe 3J **65**
Albert Cl. EX17: Cred 6H **39**
Albert Cl. EX34: Ilfra 2J **11**
    (off Mill Head)
    TQ1: Torq .1D **116**
Albertha Cl. PL4: Plym 2G **9** (1A **142**)
Albert La. EX32: B'aple 4F **19**

Albert Pl. EX8: Exmth 6C 76
EX39: Bide 4E 22
TQ6: Dartm 1A 124 (6F 125)
Albert Rd. EX17: Cred 5H 39
PL2: Dev 1D 140
TQ1: Torq 1D 116
Albert St. EX1: Exe 2H 7 (5G 65)
EX7: Daw 4G 97
Albert Ter. EX13: Axmin 3H 89
PL20: Prin 6D 60
TQ2: New A 1F 109
TQ13: Bov T 4B 92
Albion Bungs. PL11: Torp 1A 140
Albion Cl. EX12: Seat 4D 86
Albion Ct. EX8: Exmth 6C 76
                            (off Albion Pl.)
PL11: Torp 1A 140
                    (off Gravesend Gdns.)
TQ5: Brixh 5E 122
Albion Dr. PL2: Plym 4G 135
Albion Gdns. TQ7: Kingsb 3F 157
TQ12: New A 1A 72
Albion Hill EX8: Exmth 5D 76
TQ12: New A 2F 109
Albion Pl. EX4: Exe 1H 7 (5G 65)
EX8: Exmth 5C 76
EX36: S Mol 6C 26
Albion Rd. PL11: Torp 1A 140
Albion St. EX4: Exe 6A 6 (7D 64)
EX8: Exmth 5C 76
TQ14: Shal 6G 107
Albion Ter. EX8: Exmth 5C 76
                    (off Henrietta Rd.)
Alcester Cl. PL2: Dev 7D 134
Alcester St. PL2: Dev 7E 134
Aldborough Ct. EX8: Exmth 6E 76
Aldens Grn. EX2: Alph 5E 70
Aldens Rd. EX2: Alph 5E 70
Alden Wlk. PL6: Plym 4C 136
Alder Cl. TQ12: New A 4J 109
TQ14: Teignm 3H 107
Alder Glade EX31: Rou 6B 18
Alderney Rd. PL6: Plym 3A 132
Alder Rd. PL19: Tavi 6J 59
Aldersley Wlk. PL6: Plym 3B 136
Alderson Dr. EX2: Sow 7C 66
Alders Way TQ4: Paig 4D 118
Aldrin Rd. EX4: Exe 2G 65
Alexander Ho. EX2: Exe 3J 71
                    (off Turnstone Rd.)
Alexander Pl. EX11: Ott M 3C 80
Alexander Wlk. EX2: Won 7C 66
The Alexandra Cinema 1E 108
Alexandra Cl. EX17: Cred 5F 39
PL9: Elb 4J 143
Alexandra Ct. EX32: B'aple 4F 19
Alexandra Dr. EX20: Bere A 2D 128
Alexandra Ho. TQ12: New A 2H 109
Alexandra La. TQ1: Torq 1D 116
Alexandra M. EX6: Star 1E 96
Alexandra Pl. PL4: Plym 1G 9 (7K 135)
Alexandra Rd. EX7: Daw 4G 97
EX13: Axmin 4G 89
EX17: Cred 5F 39
EX32: B'aple 3E 18
PL2: Plym 6E 134
PL4: Plym 1G 9 (7A 136)
PL6: Plym 1A
                    (off Morshead Rd.)
TQ1: Torq 7D 112
TQ2: New A 2G 109
Alexandra Ter. EX4: Exe 1J 7 (5H 65)
EX5: Broadc 2K 67
EX6: Star 1E 96
                    (off Royal Way)
EX8: Exmth 6B 76
EX16: Tive 4B 40
                    (off John St.)
EX36: S Mol 5C 26
                    (off North St.)
EX39: Bide 2E 22
PL2: Plym 6E 134
TQ9: Tot 5E 102
TQ12: New A 2F 109
TQ14: Teignm 5H 107
Alexandra Way EX17: Cred 5F 39
Alexandria Ind. Est. EX10: Sidm 4B 84
EX15: Cull 3J 45
Alexandria Rd. EX10: Sidm 4B 84
ALFARDISWORTHY 2A 162
ALFINGTON 1B 172
Alfington Rd. EX11: Ott M . . .4K 53, 2D 80
Alford Cl. EX1: Whip 5B 66
Alford Cres. EX1: Whip 5A 66
Alford Pasture EX5: Rock 3C 68
Alford Ter. EX35: Lynt 2G 13
Alfranza Cl. EX1: Heav 6A 66
Alfred Pl. PL2: Plym 6E 134
Alfred Rd. PL2: Plym 6E 134
Alfred St. PL1: Plym 6D 8 (3J 141)
Alfriston Rd. TQ3: Paig 7D 114
Alger Wlk. PL6: Plym 4K 131
Alice La. PL1: Plym 4B 8
Alice St. PL1: Plym 4A 8 (2G 141)
Alice Templer Cl. EX2: Won 2J 71
Alison Rd. TQ3: Pres 5G 115
Alive Fitness & Sport 3H 107
ALLALEIGH 2A 176
Allen Bank EX32: B'aple 6F 19

Allenby Rd. PL2: Plym 5F 135
Allen Cl. EX16: Tive 3F 41
Allendale Rd. PL4: Plym 1F 9 (1K 141)
Allenhayes La. TQ8: Salc 4C 158
Allenhayes Rd. TQ8: Salc 4C 158
Allens Rd. PL21: Ivy 3H 145
Allenstyle Cl. EX31: Yell 6C 16
Allenstyle Dr. EX31: Yell 6B 16
Allenstyle Gdns. EX31: Yell 6C 16
Allenstyle Vw. EX31: Yell 6B 16
Allenstyle Way EX31: Yell 6C 16
ALLER
TA10 . . . . .1D 167
TQ12 . . . . .6J 109
Aller Brake Rd. TQ12: New A 4H 109
Aller Cl. TQ12: Kingsk 6J 109
ALLERCOMBE 5K 69 (1A 172)
Allercombe La. EX5: Rock 5K 69
Aller Hill EX7: Daw 4F 97, 5F 97
Aller Mills TQ12: Kingsk 6J 109
Allern La. PL5: Tam F 1J 131
ALLER PARK 3J 109
Aller Pk. Rd. TQ12: New A 4J 109
Aller Rd. EX19: Dol 6H 31
TQ12: Kingsk 6J 109
Allerton Wlk. PL6: Plym 4C 136
Aller Va. Cl. EX2: Won 1A 72
Alleyn Ct. EX12: Seat 5D 86
Alleyn Gdns. PL3: Plym 3K 135
Allhalland St. EX39: Bide 3F 23
Allhallows Ct. EX4: Exe 5C 6 (7E 64)
EX14: Hon 3F 55
                    (off Northcote La.)
Allhallows Museum of Lace &
    Local Antiquities 3F 55 (3B 166)
All Hallows Rd. TQ3: Pres 4J 115
Alliance Ct. EX14: Hon 5C 54
Allington Mead EX4: Exe 2D 64
Allotment Gdns. EX4: Exe 2D 64
Allotment La. PL7: Plymp 6B 138
ALLOWENSHAY 2D 167
All Saints Cl. EX9: E Bud 1D 82
All Saints Ct. EX14: Hon 4D 54
All Saint's Rd. EX10: Sidm 6B 84
TQ1: Torq 7E 112
Alma Cotts. PL4: Plym 5J 9 (3A 142)
EX14: Hon 3F 55
Alma La. EX10: Sidm 6D 84
Alma Pl. EX2: Heav 7J 65
                    (off Sivell Pl.)
Alma Rd. PL3: Plym 1B 8 (6G 135)
TQ5: Brixh 3E 122
Alma Steps TQ6: Kingsw 7G 125
                    (off Beacon Rd.)
Alma St. PL4: Plym 5J 9 (3A 142)
Alma Villa Ri. EX5: Cran 4B 68
Almeria Ct. PL7: Plymp 5A 138
ALMINSTONE CROSS 1B 162
Almond Cl. EX31: Rou 7B 18
Almond Dr. PL7: Plymp 3E 138
The Alpha Cen. EX2: Sow 7E 66
Alpha Pl. EX39: App 2H 21
Alpha St. PL1: Heav 6J 65
Alpha Ter. TQ9: Tot 5D 102
Alphin Brook Ct. EX2: Mar B 4F 71
Alphin Brook Rd. EX2: Mar B 4F 71
ALPHINGTON 4E 70 (1D 171)
Alphington Rd. EX2: Exe 7C 6 (3E 70)
Alphington Spur EX2: Exe 4D 70
Alphington St. EX2: Exe 6C 6 (7E 64)
Alpine Park 4F 137
Alpine Rd. TQ1: Torq 1D 116
Alsa Brook Mdw. EX16: Tive 2C 40
ALSTON 3D 167
Alstone Rd. EX16: Tive 5F 41
Alston La. TQ5: Chur F 6J 121
Alston Ter. PL7: Plymp 3A 138
Alston Ter. EX8: Exmth 6B 76
ALSWEAR .1B 164
Alswear New Rd.
    EX36: G Nym, S Mol 7D 26
Alswear Old Rd. EX36: S Mol 7C 26
Altamira EX3: Top 5B 74
ALTARNUN 2A 168
Alton Pl. PL4: Plym 1G 9 (1K 141)
Alton Rd. PL4: Plym 1F 9 (1K 141)
Aluric Ri. TQ12: New A 7J 105
ALVERDISCOTT 1D 163
Alverdiscott Rd. EX39: Bide 4H 23
Alverdiscott Rd. Ind. Est.
    EX39: Bide 5J 23
Alver Grn. EX39: Bide 4J 23
Alvington St. PL4: Plym 6K 9 (3B 142)
Alvington Ter. TQ7: Kingsb 5F 157
                    (off W. Alvington Hill)
ALWINGTON 1C 163
Alwin Pk. PL6: Plym 5B 132
Alwyns Cl. TQ14: Teignm 4J 107
                    (off Lwr. Brimley Rd.)
Amacre Dr. PL9: Hooe 6C 142
Amados Cl. PL7: Plymp 7J 137
Amados Dr. PL7: Plymp 7K 137
Amados Ri. PL7: Plymp 7K 137
Ambassador Dr. EX1: Sow 5D 66
Ambassador Ho. TQ4: Paig 2J 119

Amber Ri. EX1: Pin 3G 67
Ambleside Pl. PL6: Plym 1E 136
Amersham Ct. EX2: Won 1K 71
                    (off Wonford St.)
Amethyst Dr. TQ14: Teignm 2J 107
AMF Bowling
    Torquay 2E 116
Amherst Rd. PL3: Plym 1B 8 (1H 141)
Amherst Rd. La. East
    PL3: Plym 1B 8 (7H 135)
Amity Pl. EX3: Top 6B 74
PL4: Plym 2G 9 (1K 141)
Amory Pl. EX36: S Mol 6C 26
                    (off Cooks Cross)
Amory Rd. EX16: Tive 6C 40
Amyas Way EX39: Nort 6F 21
Amyatts Ter. EX10: Sidm 7C 84
                    (off Church St.)
The Anchorage TQ4: Paig 2J 119
                    (off Belle Vue Rd.)
Anchorage Ct. TQ5: Brixh 3G 123
The Anchor Cen. TQ7: Kingsb 4G 157
                    (off Bridge St.)
Anchor Row EX2: Cou W 6C 72
Anchorwood Bank EX31: B'aple 5C 18
Anchorwood Bank Development
    EX31: B'aple 4D 18
Anderton Cl. PL19: Whit 7K 59
Anderton Ct. PL19: Whit 7K 59
Anderton La. PL19: Whit 7K 59
Andor Av. TQ12: Kingst 4G 105
Andrea Ct. TQ14: Teignm 4H 107
                    (off Yannon Dr.)
Andrew Cl. EX10: Sidm 2A 84
Andrew Rd. EX31: B'aple 7D 18
Andrews Pk. TQ9: Sto G 3B 120
Andrew's Wood Nature Reserve . . .2D 175
Andurn Cl. PL9: Elb 6J 143
Andurn Est. PL9: Down T 2A 148
Angel Hill EX16: Tive 4C 40
Angel M. EX14: Hon 3F 55
                    (off Silver St.)
Angel Ter. EX16: Tive 4C 40
                    (off Angel Hill)
ANGERSLEIGH 2B 166
Anna Mill Bus. & Distribution Pk.
    TQ10: Wran 3E 146
Anne Cl. EX4: Exe 3H 65
Anne Cres. EX31: B'aple 7C 18
Anning Rd. DT7: Lym R 4J 91
EX5: Pin .4F 67
Ann's Pl. PL3: Plym 7F 135
Anson Ho. PL1: Plym 3B 8
Anson Pl. PL2: Dev 7E 134
PL4: Plym 4K 9 (2B 142)
Anson Rd. EX8: Exmth 2E 76
Ansteys Cres. EX16: Tive 5F 41
Ansteys Ct. TQ1: Torq 1G 117
Anstey's Cove Rd. TQ1: Torq 7G 113
Anstey Way EX39: Ins 3K 21
Anstis Ct. EX10: Sidm 3B 84
Anstis St. PL1: Plym 3A 8 (2G 141)
Anthea Rd. TQ3: Pres 5F 115
Anthony Pk. PL19: Tavi 3K 59
                    (off Parkwood Rd.)
Anthony Rd. EX1: Heav 6J 65
Antonine Cres. EX4: Exe 6B 64
ANTONY 2A 174
Antony Gdns. PL2: Plym 3H 135
Antrim Ter. TQ9: Tot 5E 102
ANVIL CORNER 3B 162
Anzac Av. PL5: Plym 6C 132
Anzac St. TQ6: Dartm 1A 124 (6F 125)
Apollo Ct. PL4: Plym 4C 142
Appleby Wlk. PL5: Plym 6J 131
Apple Cl. EX8: Exmth 1D 76
APPLEDORE
    EX16 . . . . .2A 166
    EX39 . . . . .3H 21 (3A 160)
Appledore Cl. EX15: Cull 4G 45
Appledore Lifeboat Station
    . . . . .2G 21 (3A 160)
Apple Dr. EX15: Will 4D 44
Apple Farm Grange EX2: Sow 2D 72
Applegarth Av. TQ12: New A 6B 104
Applegarth Cl. TQ12: New A 7B 104
Applehayes EX8: Exmth 7E 76
Apple La. EX2: Sow 2D 72
Applemede EX5: Silv 1G 51
Apple Orchard EX38: G Tor 3A 30
Appleton Tor Cl. PL3: Plym 5F 137
Apple Tree Cl. EX16: W'ridge 6J 33
TQ13: Chud K 6A 94
Appletree Cl. EX15: Uff 7G 43
EX32: B'aple 5J 19
                    (not continuous)
Appletree Gdns. EX39: Nort 1F 23
Appletree M. EX39: App 2H 21
Apple Wharf TQ9: Tot 6F 103
APPLEY 1A 166
April Cl. EX8: Exmth 1D 76
Apsley Ct. PL4: Plym 1D 8 (1J 141)
Apsley Ho. TQ1: Torq 3E 116

Apsley Rd. PL4: Plym 1E 8 (1J 141)
Apsley Ter. EX33: Brau 3K 15
EX34: Ilfra .3J 11
                    (off Highfield Rd.)
Apsley Vs. EX34: Ilfra 3J 11
Apters Hill TQ5: Brixh 3E 122
                    (off Middle St.)
Aptor La. TQ3: Marl 2A 114
The Arboretum TQ3: Blag 7A 114
The Arbour PL6: Plym 5K 131
Arbour Cl. EX34: Ilfra 4H 11
The Arcade EX20: Oke 3B 48
                    (off Fore St.)
Arcade Rd. EX34: Ilfra 2H 11
Arcadia PL9: Elb 6K 143
Arcadia Rd. PL9: Elb 6K 143
The Arch EX5: W'bury 5B 78
Arch Cotts. TQ12: Kingst 4G 105
Archers Cl. PL8: New F 4J 149
Archer Ter. PL1: Plym 3C 8 (2H 141)
Archery Cl. TQ7: Kingsb 2F 157
The Arches EX2: Exe 7B 6
Archibald Rd. EX1: Exe 4G 7 (6G 65)
Archipark EX32: Swim 2H 25
Architects Way PL5: Plym 3A 134
Arcot Gdns. EX10: Sidm 4C 84
Arcot Pk. EX10: Sidm 4C 84
Arcot Rd. EX10: Sidm 4C 84
Arden Cl. EX9: Bud S 7C 82
Arden Dr. TQ2: Torq 7K 111
Arden Gro. PL2: Plym 3H 135
Ardenney Ct. EX8: Exmth 7E 76
Arena Pk. EX4: Whip 3A 66
Argent Ct. EX16: Tive 4D 40
                    (off Bartows C'way.)
Argus Cl. EX14: Hon 3G 55
Argyle Ter. TQ9: Tot 5D 102
Argyll M. EX4: Exe 3D 64
Argyll Rd. EX4: Exe 2E 64
Arimoor Gdns. PL19: Tavi 4K 59
Ark Pottery 7D 80 (1B 172)
Ark Royal Av. EX2: Cou W 5B 72
Ark Royal Cl. PL5: Plym 3C 134
Arkwright Gdns. PL5: Plym 1E 134
Arley Cl. PL6: Plym 4C 132
ARLINGTON 2C 161
Arlington Court 3C 161
Arlington Court Nature Walk 2C 161
Arlington Pl. EX34: Wool 6B 10
Arlington Rd. EX34: Wool 6A 10
PL4: Plym 7A 136
Arlington Ter. EX33: Brau 5J 15
Armada Cen. 3D 8 (2J 141)
Armada Cl. EX12: Seat 3E 86
Armada Ct. EX3: Top 5B 74
PL19: Tavi 5H 59
Armada Cres. TQ2: Torq 7J 111
Armada Dr. TQ14: Teignm 1G 107
Armada Memorial 7E 8 (4J 141)
Armada St. PL4: Plym 2F 9 (1K 141)
Armada Way EX39: W Ho 6A 20
PL1: Plym 7D 8 (3J 141)
                    (not continuous)
Armlet Row EX1: Pin 3F 67
Armstrong Av. EX4: Exe 2G 65
Armytage Rd. EX9: Bud S 5C 82
Arnison Cl. PL9: Plyms 7F 143
Arnold Cres. EX16: Tive 6B 40
Arnold's Point PL4: Plym 1D 142
Arnside Cl. PL6: Plym 7E 132
Arran Cl. TQ2: Torq 3A 112
Arrow Field Rd. EX1: Pin 3G 67
Arscott Gdns. PL9: Hooe 7D 142
Arscott La. PL9: Hooe 7D 142
Arthington TQ1: Torq 6B 112
Art Ho. EX1: Exe 5D 6
Arthurs Ct. EX8: Exmth 6F 77
Arthurs Lea EX39: A'sham 3A 22
Arthur's Rd. EX4: Whip 3K 65
Arthur Ter. PL11: Torp 2A 140
                    (off Bellevue Sq.)
Artillery Ct. EX2: Exe 2H 71
Artillery Pl. PL4: Plym 7H 9 (4A 142)
Artizan's Dwellings EX36: S Mol 6D 26
The Arts at Dartington 1D 102
Arun Cl. PL3: Plym 6D 136
Arundel Cl. EX2: Alph 5E 70
Arundel Cres. PL1: Plym 2B 8 (1H 141)
Arundell Cl. PL16: Lift 6B 56
Arundell Gdns. PL16: Lift 6B 56
Arundell Pl. TQ7: Lodd 3G 151
Arundell Rd. EX20: N Taw 6C 36
Arundel Ter. PL2: Dev 7E 134
                    (off Victoria Pl.)
Ascension Way TQ2: Torq 3B 112
Ascerton Cl. EX10: Sidm 5C 84
Ascerton Rd. EX10: Sidm 5C 84
ASH 3A 176
ASHBRITTLE 1A 166
Ashbrook St. PL9: Plyms 3E 142
Ashburn Cl. TQ13: Ashb 4G 99
Ashburn Gdns. TQ13: Ashb 3H 99

Ashburnham Rd. PL5: Plym 7F **131**
Ashburn Wlk. TQ4: Good 7H **119**
ASHBURTON 4H 99 (1D 175)
Ashburton By-Pass TQ13: Ashb 5G **99**
Ashburton Cl. TQ13: Bov T 6B **92**
Ashburton Information Centre
. . . . .4G 99 (1D 175)
Ashburton Mus. 4H 99 (1D 175)
Ashburton Rd. TQ9: Darti, Tot . . .2B **102**
TQ11: B'leigh 3D **98**
TQ12: New A 6A **104**
TQ13: Bov T 6B **92**
Ashburton Swimming Pool 4H **99**
ASHBURY 1D **169**
Ashbury Hotel Golf Courses 1D **169**
Ash Cl. PL20: Yelv 5F **127**
Ashclyst Forest Walks 1A **172**
Ashclyst Vw. EX5: Broadc 6D **52**
ASHCOMBE 3D **171**
Ashcombe Cl. PL7: Plymp 4K **137**
Ashcombe Rd. EX7: Daw 4F **97**
Ash Ct. EX17: Cred 5H **39**
PL21: Ivy, L Mill 4D **144**
Ashcroft Rd. EX1: Sow 6B **66**
Ashculm Turbary Nature Reserve
. . . . .2B **166**
Ashdown Cl. PL6: Plym 7F **133**
Ashdown Wlk. PL6: Plym 7F **133**
Ash Dr. EX15: Cull 2H **45**
EX36: S Mol 5D **26**
Asheldon Rd. TQ1: Torq 1G **117**
Ashery Dr. PL9: Hooe 6D **142**
Ashes Rd. EX13: Shute 2A **88**
Ash Farm Cl. EX1: Pin 3E **66**
Ashfield Cl. EX8: Exmth 3G **77**
EX31: Ashf 1K **17**
Ashfield Gdns. TQ2: Torq 2A **116**
Ashfield Rd. TQ2: Torq 1A **116**
Ashfield Ter. EX39: Nort 5F **21**
(off Diddywell Rd.)
ASHFORD
EX31 . . . . .3B **160**
TQ7 . . . . .4H 151 (3C 175)
Ashford Cl. PL3: Plym 7B **136**
Ashford Cres. PL3: Plym 7B **136**
Ashford Hill PL4: Plym 7B **136**
Ashford Rd. EX3: Top 5A **74**
PL4: Plym 7A **136**
Ash Gro. EX8: Exmth 2D **76**
EX12: Seat 2E **86**
PL2: Plym 4E **134**
PL21: Ivy 4J **145**
Ashgrove Rd. TQ13: Bov T 7B **92**
ASH HILL 3C **106**
Ash Hill TQ14: Bi'ton 3C **106**
Ash Hill Cl. EX12: Beer 7A **86**
Ash Hill Rd. TQ1: Torq 7C **112**
ASHILL
EX15 . . . . .2A **166**
TA19 . . . . .2D **167**
Ashlar Row EX1: Pin 3F **67**
Ashleigh EX2: Alph 5D **70**
Ashleigh Cl. EX4: Exe 6C **64**
PL5: Tam F 3H **131**
TQ2: Torq 2B **112**
TQ14: Teignm 2H **107**
Ashleigh Ct. TQ1: Torq 3F **117**
Ashleigh Cres. EX32: B'aple 5G **19**
Ashleigh Dr. TQ14: Teignm 2H **107**
Ashleigh La. PL5: Tam F 1J **131**
Ashleigh Mt. TQ14: Teignm 2H **107**
Ashleigh Mt. Rd. EX4: Exe 6B **64**
Ashleigh Pk. EX16: Bam 3J **33**
TQ14: Teignm 2H **107**
Ashleigh Ri. TQ14: Teignm 2H **107**
Ashleigh Rd. EX8: Exmth 5D **76**
EX14: Hon 3E **54**
EX32: B'aple 4F **19**
TQ7: Kingsb 5E **156**
Ashleigh Vs. TQ9: Tot 6D **102**
(off Plymouth Rd.)
Ashleigh Way PL7: Plymp 5F **139**
TQ14: Teignm 2H **107**
ASHLEY 7B **40**
Ashley Bk. La. EX16: Ashy 7B **40**
Ashley Brake EX11: W Hill 4H **79**
Ashley Cl. EX15: Uff 5J **43**
Ashley Cres. EX10: Sidm 3B **84**
Ashley Ho. EX8: Exmth 6D **76**
Ashley Pl. PL1: Plym 2B **8**
Ashley Priors La. TQ1: Torq 1E **112**
Ashley Ri. EX16: Ashy 7B **40**
Ashley Rd. EX15: Uff 6H **43**
EX20: Oke 3C **48**
Ashley Ter. EX34: Ilfra 3H **11**
(off St Brannock's Pk. Rd.)
EX39: Bide 4E **22**
(off Royston Rd.)
Ashley Way EX7: Daw 3J **97**
ASHMANSWORTHY 2B **162**
Ashmead Gro. EX33: Brau 4H **15**
ASH MILL 1B **164**
ASHMILL 1B **168**
Ashmill Ct. TQ12: New A 7C **104**
Ash Moor Nature Reserve 3D **163**
Ashmoor Sports Cen. 2J **99**
Ashmore Ct. EX2: Exe 7C **6**
Ash Pk. EX7: Holc 7F **97**

Ash Pk. Gdns. EX7: Holc 7F **97**
Ashplants Cl. EX19: Wink 2C **36**
EX39: Bide 3C **22**
ASHPRINGTON 2A **176**
ASH PRIORS 1B **166**
ASHREIGNEY 2A **164**
Ashridge Gdns. PL5: Plym 1G **135**
Ash Rd. EX33: Brau 4K **15**
TQ12: Kingst 5H **105**
ASH THOMAS 2A **166**
Ashton Cl. PL6: Plym 4D **132**
Ashton Ct. TQ12: Kingst 2H **105**
Ashton Cres. EX33: Brau 5H **15**
Ashton Rd. EX2: Mar B 3E **70**
Ashton Ter. TQ1: Torq 1G **117**
Ashtree Cl. PL6: Plym 3E **132**
Ashtree Gro. PL9: Elb 4K **143**
Ash Va. PL16: Lift 6A **56**
Ash Way TQ12: New A 3J **109**
ASHWATER 1B **168**
ASHWELL 2A **106**
Ashwood TQ10: S Bre 1B **100**
Ashwood Cl. PL7: Plymp 4E **138**
TQ7: Lodd 3G **151**
Ashwood Ct. TQ12: New A 2H **109**
(off Marychurch Rd.)
Ashwood Pk. TQ7: Lodd 3G **151**
Ashwood Pk. Rd. PL7: Plymp 3F **139**
Ashwood Rd. EX2: Exe 2E **70**
Aspen Cl. EX2: Won 1B **72**
EX14: Hon 5C **54**
EX15: Will 3E **44**
PL19: Tavi 6J **59**
Aspen Dr. TQ12: New A 4J **109**
Aspen Gdns. PL7: Plymp 4E **138**
Aspen Gro. EX31: Frem 7E **16**
Aspen Way EX16: Tive 1E **40**
TQ4: Paig 4D **118**
Astley Corte EX20: Oke 3A **48**
Astley Park 4F **123**
Astor Dr. PL4: Plym 1D **142**
Aswell Orchard TQ7: Lodd 3H **151**
(off Little Gate)
ATHELNEY 1D **167**
Athelstan Cl. EX13: Axmin 5G **89**
Athelstan Rd. EX1: Exe 4G 7 (6G **65**)
Athenaeum La.
PL1: Plym 5C 8 (3H **141**)
Athenaeum Pl.
PL2: Plym 5D 8 (3J **141**)
Athenaeum St.
PL1: Plym 6C 8 (3H **141**)
ATHERINGTON 1D **163**
Atherton La. TQ9: Tot 6E **102**
Atherton Pl. PL2: Dev 7D **134**
(off Charlotte St.)
Atherton Way EX16: Tive 5G **41**
Athlone Ho. PL1: Plym 5A **8**
Atkinson Cl. EX4: Whip 3K **65**
Atlantic Bldg. PL4: Plym . . .7H 9 (4A **142**)
Atlantic Cl. EX34: Ilfra 2H **11**
(off Northfield Rd.)
Atlantic Village EX39: Bide 5B **22**
Atlantic Way EX39: W Ho 5B **20**
Atlantis Adventure Pk. 5A 22 (1C **163**)
Atlas Ho. EX1: Exe 4J **7**
The Atrium TQ1: Torq 1F **117**
Attwater Ct. PL19: Lam 6C **58**
Attwill's Almshouses
EX4: Exe 1B 6 (5D **64**)
Attwood M. PL3: Plym 7G **135**
Attwyll Av. EX2: Won 7K **65**
Atway Cl. TQ13: Bov T 3B **92**
Atwill-Kingdon Almshouses
EX1: Exe 4K **7**
Auckland Rd. PL2: Plym 6F **135**
Auctioneers Cl. PL7: Plymp 4A **138**
Auction Pl. EX13: Axmin 4H **89**
Auction Way EX39: Wools 2B **28**
Audley Av. TQ2: Torq 5B **112**
Audley Ri. TQ12: New A 3K **109**
Augustine Cl. EX12: Seat 4D **86**
Augustus Ho. EX4: Exe 2E 6 (5F **65**)
Aunay Cl. EX22: Hols 1D **34**
Austen Cl. EX4: Whip 4B **66**
Austin Av. PL2: Plym 5F **135**
Austin Cres. PL6: Plym 2D **136**
Authers Hgts. EX16: Tive 6B **40**
Avalon Cl. EX4: Whip 2K **65**
Aveland Rd. TQ1: Torq 6E **112**
Avent Wlk. PL7: Plymp 2C **138**
The Avenue EX3: Ext 2G **75**
EX12: Seat 5E **86**
EX16: Tive 5E **40**
PL21: L Mill 5A **144**
TQ12: New A 1F **109**
TQ13: Bov T 5C **94**
Avenue Cl. DT7: Lym R 5J **91**
Av. Mezidon-Canon EX14: Hon . . .4G **55**
Avenue Rd. DT7: Lym R 5J **91**
EX34: Ilfra 2H **11**
TQ2: Torq 7A **112**
TQ12: Kingsk 7K **109**
TQ13: Bov T 4B **92**
Avenue Ter. TQ5: Chur F 3A **122**
Avery Hill TQ12: Kingst 3H **105**
AVETON GIFFORD 6H 151 (3C **175**)

Aviemore Ind. Est. EX31: B'aple . . .6C **18**
Avoca Av. TQ1: Torq 7B **112**
Avocet Dr. EX3: Ext 1G **75**
Avocet Rd. EX2: Sow 6E **66**
Avon Cl. PL3: Plym 5E **136**
TQ10: S Bre 2C **100**
Avondale Gdns. PL5: Plym 2B **100**
Avondale Rd. EX2: Won 7K **65**
EX8: Exmth 4F **77**
Avondale Ter. PL7: Plymp 6D **134**
Avon La. EX39: W Ho 5C **20**
Avon Rd. EX39: Bide 4H **23**
TQ2: Torq 6H **111**
Avranches Av. EX17: Cred 5F **39**
AWLISCOMBE 1A 54 (3B **166**)
EX2: Mar B, Matf 5G **71**
Axe Cliffe Vw. EX12: Seat 5E **86**
Axe Cliff Golf Course 5H 87 (2C **173**)
Axe Valley Cvn. Pk. 4F **87**
Axe Valley Cl. EX13: Ray H 1D **90**
Axeview Rd. EX12: Seat 3D **86**
Axe Yacht Club 4A **87**
AXMINSTER 3H 89 (1D **173**)
Axminster Heritage Cen. 4H **89**
(off Silver St.)
Axminster Leisure Cen. 3J **89**
Axminster Rd. EX13: Mus 7C **90**
EX14: Hon 4H **55**
Axminster Station (Rail) . . .4G 89 (1C **173**)
Axminster Tourist Information Point
. . . . .4H 89 (1D **173**)
AXMOUTH 3H 87 (1C **173**)
Axmouth Rd. EX12: Axmth 5G **87**
Axmouth to Lyme Regis Undercliffs
. . . . .7F 91 (2D **173**)
AXTOWN 6E **126**
Axtown La. PL20: Yelv 7E **126**
Aycliffe Gdns. PL7: Plymp 6D **138**
AYLESBEARE 1A **172**
Aylesbeare Common Nature Reserve
. . . . .1A **172**
Aylesbeare Common Nature Trail
. . . . .2A **172**
Aylesbury Cres. PL5: Plym 5G **131**
AYLESCOTT 2A **164**
Ayleston Pk. PL21: Modb 6H **147**
Aylwin Cl. PL7: Plymp 3B **138**
Ayres Cl. EX39: Bide 4H **23**
AYREVILLE 2A 118 (1A **176**)
Ayreville Rd. PL2: Plym 4G **135**
Aysha Gdns. EX39: W Ho 5C **20**
AYSHFORD 1E 42 (2A **166**)
Ayshford EX15: Uff 6H **43**
Azalea Cl. EX14: Dunk 7H **47**
Azes La. EX32: B'aple 4F **19**
Azure Sth. PL1: Plym 7C **8**

B

BABBACOMBE 6F 113 (1B **176**)
Babbacombe Bus. Pk.
TQ1: Torq 6F **113**
(not continuous)
Babbacombe Cliff Railway
. . . . .5E 112 (1B **176**)
Babbacombe Cl. PL6: Plym 3F **137**
Babbacombe Corinthian Sailing Club
. . . . .5D **112**
(off Fore St.)
Babbacombe Downs Rd.
TQ1: Torq 5E **112**
Babbacombe Model Village
. . . . .5E 112 (1B **176**)
Babbacombe Rd. TQ1: Torq 5E **112**
Babbacombe Theatre 6F **113**
Babbage Rd. TQ9: Tot 5E **102**
Babbages EX31: Bick 5K **17**
Babbage Way EX5: Clyst H 5F **67**
Babblebrook M. EX1: Pin 4E **66**
Bableigh Cl. EX39: Buck B 2H **29**
Bableigh Rd. EX32: Land 2B **24**
Babylon La. EX5: Silv 4G **51**
Backaborough La. EX39: Bide 4E **22**
(off Capern Rd.)
Backfield EX39: App 3H **21**
Back La. EX5: Bradn 3A **52**
EX10: N'town 5J **81**
EX10: New P 5G **81**
EX18: Chul 6B **32**
EX20: Mert 5B **30**
EX20: Stic 1G **49**
EX36: N Mol 2C **26**
EX37: C'ton 5J **25**
PL7: Plymp 5B **138**
PL21: Erm 2F **147**
PL21: Lutt 7G **129**
Back La. Ind. Est. EX18: Chul 5B **32**
Back Rd. TQ12: New A 1E **108**
(not continuous)
The Backs TQ6: Dartm 4E **124**
Back St. EX5: Bradn 1C **52**
EX16: Bam 2H **33**
EX39: Wools 2B **28**
PL21: Modb 6G **147**
BADGALL 2A **168**
Badgaver La. EX34: C Mar 7E **12**

Badger Cl. EX2: Won 7C **66**
EX10: New P 6F **81**
EX14: Hon 2H **55**
TQ3: Pres 5F **115**
TQ6: Dartm 5D **124**
Badgers Cl. PL21: Ivy 4E **144**
TQ7: Kingsb 5F **157**
TQ12: Kingst 3G **105**
Badgers Grn. TQ7: Kingsb 5F **157**
Badgers Holt EX20: Oke 3A **48**
(off Oaklands Dr.)
Badgers Way TQ13: Bov T 4C **92**
Badger Vw. PL9: Plyms 7F **143**
Badger Way EX5: Cran 2D **68**
Bad Homburg Way
EX2: Mar B, Matf 5G **71**
Badlake Cl. EX7: Daw 3F **97**
Badlake Hill EX7: Daw 3F **97**
Badon Cl. EX4: Whip 2K **65**
Bagshot Av. EX2: Exe 2G **71**
Baileys Mdw. TQ6: Sto F 3H **153**
Bailey St. EX4: Exe 3E 6 (6F **65**)
Bainbridge Av. PL3: Plym 4A **136**
Bainbridge Ct. PL7: Plymp 2A **138**
Baker Cl. EX10: Sidm 2B **84**
Bakers Cl. PL7: Plymp 4F **139**
Bakers Ct. La. EX35: Lynt 2G **13**
Baker's Hill EX16: Tive 4A **40**
TQ7: Ave G 6H **151**
TQ12: New A 1E **108**
Bakers M. EX15: Cull 4A **45**
(off Fore St.)
Bakers Piece TQ8: E Port 4E **158**
Bakers Pl. PL1: Dev 3E **140**
Baker St. EX2: Won 5K 7 (7H **65**)
Bakers Vw. TQ12: New A 1D **108**
Bakers Way EX4: Pin 4C **66**
Bakery La. EX8: Exmth 5C **76**
Bakery Way EX32: Land 2B **24**
Bala Brook Cl. TQ5: Brixh 6B **122**
Baldwin Cl. EX20: Oke 2D **48**
Baldwin Dr. EX20: Oke 3D **48**
Balfour Cl. EX14: Hon 4H **55**
Balfour Gdns. EX10: Sidm 4B **84**
Balfour Mnr. EX10: Sidm 5A **84**
Balfour M. EX10: Sidm 5B **84**
Balfour Rd. EX10: Sidm 3B **84**
Balfours EX10: Sidm 3B **84**
Balfour Ter. EX13: Kilm 2B **88**
PL2: Dev 7D **134**
Balkwill Rd. TQ7: Kingsb 5E **156**
Balland La. TQ13: Ashb 3J **99**
Balland Gdns. PL5: Plym 2H **135**
Balland Gro. EX10: Sidf 1E **84**
Ballards Cres. EX31: Yell 7B **16**
Ballards Gro. EX31: Yell 7B **16**
Balleroy Cl. EX21: Sheb 6J **29**
Ball Hill EX17: Cher F 1K **39**
Ball Hill La. EX20: Oke 3D **48**
Ballhill La. EX16: Bam 3F **33**
Ball Mdw. EX20: Oke 3D **48**
Ball's Farm Rd. EX2: Exe, Ide 3B **70**
Balmoral Av. PL2: Plym 6E **134**
Balmoral Cl. TQ12: New A 2H **109**
Balmoral Cres. EX20: Oke 3D **48**
Balmoral Gdns. EX3: Top 5B **74**
Balmoral Ho. EX31: B'aple 2D **18**
Balmoral Ter. EX34: Ilfra 3H **11**
(off St Brannock's Pk. Rd.)
Baltic Way TQ9: Tot 7F **103**
Baltic Wharf TQ9: Tot 7F **103**
Baltic Wharf Bus. Pk. TQ9: Tot 7F **103**
Bampfylde Cl. EX4: Polt 6A **52**
EX16: Tive 5F **41**
Bampfylde La. EX1: Exe 3E **6**
Bampfylde Rd. TQ2: Torq 1B **116**
Bampfylde St. EX1: Exe 3F 7 (6F **65**)
Bampfylde Way PL6: Plym 4J **131**
BAMPTON 2H 33 (1D **165**)
Bampton Castle 1H **33**
Bampton Cl. TQ3: Marl 4D **114**
Bampton Communication Mus. 2H **33**
Bampton Heritage Centre 2H **33**
Bampton Rd. PL6: Plym 2F **137**
Bampton St. EX16: Tive 4D **40**
Banbury Pk. TQ2: Torq 5J **111**
Banfield Way EX14: Hon 5E **54**
BANGORS 1A **168**
Bank End EX39: Bide 1G **23**
(off Chanters Rd.)
BANKLAND 1D **167**
Bank La. TQ5: Brixh 3E **122**
TQ9: Tot 6E **102**
Banksia Cl. EX16: Tive 1E **40**
Bankside EX8: Exmth 1E **76**
Bank St. TQ12: New A 1E **108**
TQ14: Teignm 5J **107**
Bank Ter. EX34: Wool 6B **10**
Bannawell St. PL19: Tavi 3H **59**
Banner Ct. TQ3: Paig 1G **119**
(off Winner St.)
BANTHAM 4A 154 (3C **175**)
Bantham M. PL4: Plym 1F 9 (7K **135**)
Baptist Chapel Ct. EX17: Cred 6H **39**
(off High St.)

Baptist La. TQ7: Kingsb 4F **157**
　　(off Fore St.)
TQ8: Salc 4C **158**
　　(off Devon Rd.)
Bapton Cl. EX8: Exmth 2D **76**
Bapton La. EX8: Exmth 3D **76**
Barberry Cl. EX4: Whip 4K **65**
Barber's La. DT7: Uply 4G **91**
BARBICAN 7F **9** (3J **141**)
The Barbican PL1: Plym 6F **9**
　　(New St.)
PL1: Plym 6G **9** (3K **141**)
　　(White La.)
Barbican App. PL4: Plym . . .6J **9** (3A **142**)
Barbican Cl. EX32: B'aple 5F **19**
Barbican Ct. EX4: Exe 5B **6**
PL4: Plym .6F **9**
Barbican La. EX32: B'aple 5G **19**
Barbican Leisure Pk. 6J **9** (3A **142**)
Barbican Pl. EX32: B'aple 5F **19**
　　(off Trinity St.)
Barbican Rd. EX32: B'aple 5F **19**
PL7: Plymp 5B **138**
Barbican Steps EX4: Exe 5C **6** (6E **64**)
Barbican Ter. EX32: B'aple 5F **19**
Barbican Theatre 7G **9** (4K **141**)
BARBROOK .2D **161**
Barbrook Rd. EX35: Bar, Lynt 4G **13**
Barbury Cres. PL6: Plym 2C **132**
Barchington Av. TQ2: Torq 2B **112**
Barcombe Hgts. TQ3: Pres 6G **115**
Barcombe La. TQ3: Pres 6H **115**
Barcombe M. TQ3: Pres 6H **115**
Barcombe Rd. TQ3: Pres 6G **115**
Barcote Wlk. PL6: Plym 2D **136**
Bardsey Cl. PL6: Plym 3B **132**
Barewell Cl. TQ1: Torq 5D **112**
Barewell Rd. TQ1: Torq 5D **112**
Barfield Cl. EX19: Dol 6J **31**
Barfield Rd. EX19: Dol 6H **31**
Barham Av. TQ14: Teignm 2K **107**
Baring Cotts. TQ9: Tot 6F **103**
Baring Ct. EX2: Exe 7F **7**
EX20: Lew 1A **56**
Baring Cres. EX1: Exe 5J **7** (6H **65**)
Baring St. PL4: Plym 2H **9** (1A **142**)
Baring Ter. EX2: Exe 7F **7** (1F **71**)
Barkers Way EX20: N Taw 6B **36**
Barlands Way EX19: Dol 6H **31**
Barle Cl. EX2: Sow 1C **72**
Barle Ct. EX16: Tive 1E **40**
Barley Cl. EX15: Cull 5G **45**
Barleycorn EX5: Cran 3C **68**
　　(off Brooks Warren)
Barleycorn Flds. EX32: Land 2B **24**
Barley Farm Rd. EX4: Exe 1B **70**
Barley La. EX4: Exe 6A **64**
Barley Mkt. St. PL19: Tavi 3J **59**
Barley Mt. EX4: Exe 7B **64**
Barley Wlk. EX6: Star 1D **96**
Barline EX12: Beer 7B **86**
Barlow Gdns. PL2: Plym 4G **135**
Barlow Rd. EX3: B'aple 2F **19**
Barnade Vw. EX1: Pin 3F **67**
Barnardo Rd. EX2: Exe 7F **7** (1G **71**)
Barnards Farm EX12: Beer 7B **86**
Barnards Hill La. EX12: Seat 2D **86**
Barn Cinema 1D **102**
Barn Cl. EX21: Sheb 6J **29**
EX32: B'aple 6H **19**
PL7: Plymp 5G **139**
PL21: Ivy 3E **144**
TQ9: Tot 5D **102**
Barn Cl. La. EX12: Axmth 5J **87**
Barn Ct. TQ5: Chur F 4A **122**
Barn Ct. Rd. TQ9: Tot 6H **103**
Barndale Cres. PL6: Plym 4C **132**
BARNE BARTON 3B **134**
Barne Cl. PL5: Plym 3B **134**
Barne La. PL5: Plym 2C **134**
Barne Rd. PL5: Plym 3B **134**
Barnes Cl. EX14: Hon 5E **54**
EX15: Will 3C **44**
Barnes Mdw. DT7: Uply 3A **91**
BARNFIELD 4G **7** (6G **65**)
Barnfield EX17: Cred 6H **39**
TQ9: E All 6C **152**
Barnfield Av. EX8: Exmth 5F **77**
Barnfield Cl. EX17: Cred 7H **39**
EX33: Brau 5K **15**
TQ5: Galm 3J **121**
Barnfield Cres.
EX1: Exe 4F **7** (6F **65**)
Barnfield Dr. PL7: Plymp 4F **139**
Barnfield Hill EX1: Exe 4G **7** (6G **65**)
Barnfield Rd. EX1: Exe 4F **7** (6F **65**)
　　(not continuous)
TQ2: Torq 4K **115**
TQ3: Paig 7F **115**
TQ5: Brixh 4G **123**
Barnfield Ter. TQ5: Chur F 3A **122**
TQ12: A'well 6E **108**
Barnfield Theatre 4F **7** (6F **65**)
Barnfield Wlk. TQ7: Kingsb 3F **157**
The Barnhay TQ9: Sto G 4B **120**
Barn Hayes EX10: Sidm 3A **84**

Barn Hill EX17: Cop 4A **38**
Barnhill Rd. TQ12: Kingsk 1G **111**
Barnicott Cl. PL8: New F 5J **149**
Barningham Gdns.
PL6: Plym 4B **132**
Barn La. EX9: Bud S 5B **82**
Barn Orchard EX5: Cran 3B **68**
Barn Owl Cl. TQ2: Torq 2K **111**
Barn Pk. EX17: Cred 6H **39**
EX33: Wraf 7K **15**
TQ9: Sto G 3B **120**
TQ11: B'leigh 5B **98**
TQ12: Live 4G **93**
Barn Pk. Cl. TQ12: Ipp 6J **101**
Barn Pk. Cotts. PL9: Plyms 4E **142**
　　(off Millway Pl.)
Barn Pk. Rd. EX31: Frem 6E **16**
PL3: Plym 6J **135**
Barnpark Rd. TQ14: Teignm 4J **107**
Barn Pk. Ter. TQ14: Teignm 3J **107**
Barn Pk. Vw. EX20: Lew 1A **56**
Barnridge EX8: Lymp 6H **75**
Barn Rd. TQ4: Good 5J **119**
Barns Cl. EX5: Bradn 3B **52**
TQ12: Kingst 5H **105**
Barnsey Gdns. TQ13: Ashb 2G **99**
Barnsfield La. TQ11: B'leigh 4B **98**
Barnshill Cl. EX17: Cher F 2J **39**
Barnshill Ct. EX17: Cher F 2J **39**
　　(off Barnshill Cl.)
Barnsley Cl. TQ14: Teignm 4J **107**
Barnsley Dr. TQ14: Teignm 4J **107**
Barns Pas. EX34: Ilfra 3H **11**
　　(off High St.)
Barns Rd. EX9: Bud S 6D **82**
BARNSTAPLE 4E **18** (3B **160**)
Barnstaple Bus Station 4F **19**
Barnstaple Castle Mound 4E **18**
Barnstaple Hill EX32: Swim 2G **25**
Barnstaple Pannier Mkt. 4E **18**
Barnstaple Park & Ride 7F **19**
Barnstaple Retail Pk. 5E **18**
Barnstaple Station
(Rail) 5E **18** (3B **160**)
Barnstaple St. EX19: Wink 2C **36**
EX36: S Mol 6C **26**
EX39: Bide 4G **23**
Barnstaple Tourist Information Centre
. . . . .5E **18** (3B **160**)
Barnstaple Western By-Pass
EX31: B'aple 3C **18**
Barnstone Ct. EX2: Alph 5D **70**
Barnwood Cl. PL9: Hooe 7F **143**
Barometer World 5B **30** (2D **163**)
Baron Ct. EX31: Rou 7A **18**
Baron's Pyke PL21: Ivy 5J **145**
Baron Rd. PL20: Dous 4K **127**
Baron Way EX31: Rou 7A **18**
TQ12: New A 1A **109**
Barossa Pl. PL11: Torp 2A **140**
Barossa Rd. PL11: Torp 1A **140**
Barrack La. EX2: Shil A 7D **70**
Barrack Pl. PL1: Plym 3F **141**
Barrack Rd.
EX2: Exe, Won 5K **7** (7H **65**)
EX11: Ott M 4A **80**
PL20: Prin 6C **60**
Barracks Hill TQ9: Darti, Tot 4B **102**
Barracks Rd. EX31: Frem 5F **17**
TQ12: Modb 6G **147**
Barrack St. PL1: Dev 2D **140**
Barradon Ct. TQ2: Torq 1C **112**
Barrel Cl. EX11: Ott M 4B **80**
Barrie Gdns. PL5: Plym 2K **135**
BARRINGTON 2D **167**
Barrington Ho. TQ1: Torq 1G **117**
　　(off Barrington Rd.)
Barrington Mead EX10: Sidm 6C **84**
　　(off Salcombe Rd.)
Barrington Rd. TQ1: Torq 1G **117**
Barrington St. EX16: Tive 4D **40**
Barris EX17: Lap 2J **37**
Barrowdale Cl. EX8: Exmth 1E **76**
Bar's La. EX9: Ott'n 5K **83**
Bartholomew Rd. PL2: Plym 6F **135**
Bartholomew St. E.
EX4: Exe 4C **6** (6E **64**)
Bartholomew St. W.
EX4: Exe 5C **6** (7E **64**)
Bartholomew Ter. EX4: Exe 5C **6**
BARTON 3B **112** (1B **176**)
Barton Acorn Youth Community &
　　Sports Cen. 3C **112**
Barton Av. EX33: Brau 5J **15**
PL2: Plym 6D **134**
TQ3: Paig 1F **119**
Barton Brake PL9: Wem 6C **148**
Barton Cleave EX31: Bick 7K **17**
Barton Cl. EX3: Ext 1G **75**
TQ9: Sto C 6J **51**
EX10: Sidm 7B **84**
　　(off The Triangle)
EX17: Cher F 2H **39**
EX20: N Taw 7B **36**
EX20: Oke 3C **48**

Barton Cl. EX33: Brau 6K **15**
PL7: Plymp 4F **139**
PL9: Wem 6C **148**
TQ3: Paig 7F **115**
TQ7: Kingsb 5G **157**
Barton Cl. EX1: Whip 5B **66**
EX10: Sidm 7B **84**
　　(off The Triangle)
EX34: Wool 6A **10**
Barton Cres. EX7: Daw 4F **97**
TQ3: Paig 7F **115**
Barton Dr. EX32: B'aple 5H **19**
TQ3: Paig 7F **115**
TQ12: New A 1C **108**
Barton Gdns. TQ3: Paig 7F **115**
Barton Ga. La. EX34: C Mar 6A **12**
Barton Hill EX7: Daw 4G **97**
EX20: N Taw 7B **36**
EX34: Ber 2D **12**
Barton Hill Rd. TQ2: Torq 4B **112**
Barton Hill Way TQ2: Torq 3A **112**
Barton La. EX2: Shil A 7B **70**
EX7: Daw 4F **97**
EX16: W'ridge 6H **33**
EX33: Brau 5J **15**
EX34: Ber 3C **12**
Barton La. Cl. EX33: Brau 6J **15**
Barton Leys TQ9: Berr P 4K **103**
Barton Lodge EX8: Exmth 6D **76**
Barton Mdw. Rd. EX37: High B 2B **32**
Barton M. EX3: Ext 2G **75**
EX11: Ven O 2F **81**
Barton Orchard EX10: Tip J 1J **81**
Barton Paddocks EX10: Tip J 1J **81**
Barton Ri. EX10: Tip J 1J **81**
EX14: Fen 2J **53**
Barton Rd. EX2: Exe 7A **6** (1C **70**)
EX16: Tive 2D **40**
EX20: Oke 3C **48**
EX32: B'aple 5J **19**
EX34: Wool 6A **10**
EX39: Buck B 2H **29**
PL9: Hooe 5C **142**
TQ1: Torq 6A **112**
TQ2: Torq 5A **112**
TQ3: Paig 7F **115**
Barton Rd. Ind. Units
TQ2: Torq 5A **112**
The Bartons EX1: Heav 7A **66**
　　(off Honiton Rd.)
Barton St. EX20: N Taw 7B **36**
Barton Ter. EX7: Daw 4G **97**
Barton Tors EX39: Bide 4H **23**
BARTON TOWN 2C **161**
Barton Vs. EX7: Daw 4F **97**
Bartows C'way. EX16: Tive 3D **40**
Barum Cl. TQ3: Paig 7J **115**
Barum Ct. EX32: B'aple 5F **19**
Barum Gate Bus. Pk.
EX32: B'aple 6J **19**
Bary Cl. EX17: Cher F 2J **39**
Bary La. EX17: Cher F 2J **39**
Bascombe Cl. TQ5: Chur F 2K **121**
Bascombe Rd. TQ5: Chur F 2J **121**
Basepoint Bus. Cen.
EX2: Mar B 5H **71**
Basinghall Cl. PL9: Plyms 7F **143**
Basket Ope PL4: Plym 6F **9**
Bassett Cl. EX33: Brau 5J **15**
Bassetts Cl. EX17: Cop 6C **38**
EX39: Nort 4E **20**
Bassetts Gdns. EX8: Exmth 2F **77**
Bastard's La. EX38: G Tor 1B **30**
Batavia Dr. EX2: Cou W 4C **72**
Bate Cl. EX2: Alph 4D **70**
Bath Cl. EX14: Fen 2G **53**
Bath Ct. EX39: W Ho 4E **20**
BATHEALTON 1A **166**
Batherm Cl. EX16: Bam 3H **33**
Bathern Rd. EX2: Sow 1C **72**
Bath Hotel Rd. EX39: W Ho 5B **20**
Bathill Camp Site 4G **121**
Bath La. PL1: Plym 5B **8** (3H **141**)
TQ2: Torq 1B **116**
Bath Pl. EX34: Ilfra 2H **11**
PL1: Plym 5B **8**
Bath Pl. W. PL1: Plym 5B **8**
BATHPOOL
PL15 . . . . .3A **168**
TA2 . . . . .1C **167**
Bath Rd. EX8: Exmth 6C **76**
Bath St. PL1: Plym 6B **8** (3H **141**)
Bath Ter. EX39: Ins 5J **21**
TQ14: Teignm 5J **107**
Batson Gdns. TQ4: Paig 3G **119**
Bats Roost EX5: Rock 2C **68**
Battershall Cl. PL9: Plyms 7G **143**
Batter St. PL4: Plym 5F **9** (3K **141**)
Battersway Rd. TQ4: Paig 3E **118**
Battery Gdns. 2E **122**
Battery La. PL19: Tavi 3J **59**
Battery St. PL1: Plym 4A **8** (2G **141**)
　　(not continuous)
BATTISBOROUGH CROSS 3C **175**
Battishorne Way EX14: Hon 5D **54**
BATTLEDOWN CROSS 6K **29**

Battle Rd. TQ12: H'fld 2J **93**
BATTLETON 1D **165**
Batts Combe M. PL9: Plyms 3E **142**
Batt's La. EX11: Ott M 4C **80**
Bavent Cl. EX5: Sto C 7J **51**
Baxter Cl. EX2: Sow 2C **72**
Bayard's Cove
TQ6: Dartm 2B **124** (6F **125**)
Bayard's Cove Fort 2B **124** (7F **125**)
Bayards Cove Steps TQ6: Dartm 2B **124**
　　(off Lower St.)
Bayard's Hill
TQ6: Dartm 2B **124** (6F **125**)
Bay Cl. EX12: Seat 6F **87**
Baydon Cl. PL6: Plym 2D **136**
Bayly's Rd. PL9: Plyms 5C **142**
Baymount Rd. TQ3: Paig 7G **115**
Bay Rd. EX9: Ott'n 6K **83**
Bayside La. PL9: Down T 2A **148**
Bayswater Rd.
PL1: Plym 2C **8** (1H **141**)
Baythorpe Lodge TQ2: Torq 4A **116**
　　(off Livermead Hill)
Baytor Ind. Est. TQ4: Paig 4E **118**
Baytree Cl. PL6: Plym 4E **132**
　　(off Elm Rd.)
Baytree Gdns. PL2: Plym 4F **135**
Bay Trees EX6: Kennf 2G **95**
Bay Vw. TQ3: Pres 5K **115**
Bay Vw. Clo. EX33: Croy 3C **14**
Bay Vw. Cl. TQ6: Sto F 2H **153**
Bay Vw. Ct. EX39: Nort 6E **20**
Bay Vw. Dr. TQ14: Teignm 3J **107**
Bay Vw. Est. TQ6: Sto F 2H **153**
Bay Vw. Farm Cvn. & Camping Pk.
. . . . .3C **14**
Bay Vw. Rd. DT7: Lym R 4J **91**
EX34: Wool 5A **10**
EX39: Nort 6B **20**
TQ1: Torq 6F **113**
TQ4: Paig 1J **119**
Bay Vw. Steps TQ5: Brixh 3F **123**
　　(off King St.)
Bazley Sq. EX1: Pin 4D **66**
Beach App. TQ5: Brixh 3F **123**
　　(off Pump St.)
Beach Rd. EX7: Daw W 7E **96**
EX12: Seat 6F **87**
EX33: Croy 1B **14**
EX34: Wool 6A **10**
EX39: W Ho 5C **20**
TQ1: Torq 6F **113**
TQ4: Paig 1J **119**
Beachside Holiday Pk. 5A **20**
Beach St. EX7: Daw 4H **97**
Beach Vw. Cres. PL9: Wem 7B **148**
Beach Wlk. TQ4: Good 5J **119**
BEACON 3B **166**
The Beacon EX8: Exmth 6C **76**
Beacon Av. EX4: Whip 4J **65**
Beacon Castle EX34: Ilfra 2G **11**
Beacon Cl. PL21: Ivy 3G **145**
Beacon Down Av. PL2: Plym 3G **135**
Beacon Heath EX4: Whip 3A **66**
Beacon Hgts. EX33: Brau 4K **15**
BEACON HILL 1B **66**
Beacon Hill EX5: Bradn 1B **52**
EX8: Exmth 6C **76**
PL8: New F 5G **149**
TQ1: Torq 3D **116**
EX4: Exe 3K **65**
EX15: Cull 1F **45**
TQ6: Kingsw 7G **125**
BEACON PARK 4G **135**
Beacon Pk. Rd. PL2: Plym 5F **135**
Beacon Pl. EX8: Exmth 6C **76**
Beacon Quay TQ1: Torq 3D **116**
Beacon Ri. EX18: Chul 6C **32**
Beacon Rd. EX5: Bradn 1C **52**
PL21: Ivy 3G **145**
TQ6: Kingsw 7G **125**
TQ8: Salc 4A **158**
Beacon Roman Fortlet 2C **161**
Beacon Ter. TQ1: Torq 3D **116**
　　(off Beacon Hill)
Beacon Vw. PL21: Bitta 4C **146**
TQ9: Darti 3B **102**
Beadle Ct. PL19: Tavi 5H **59**
Beadon Dr. TQ8: Salc 4A **158**
Beadon Rd. TQ8: Salc 4B **158**
BEAFORD 3H **31** (2D **163**)
Beagle Rd. PL1: Dev 3E **140**
Beal Farm M. TQ13: Chud K 6B **94**
BEALSMILL 3B **168**
Beanhay Cl. TQ12: Live 4G **93**
Beans Mdw. EX20: Oke 3B **48**
Beara La. EX31: Brat F 5J **13**
EX34: C Mar 7E **12**
Beardown Rd. EX20: Oke 3E **48**
Beards Rd. EX31: Frem 6F **17**
Beare Bri. Rd. EX20: Oke 2C **48**
Beare Cl. PL9: Hooe 7C **142**
Beare Copse La. EX19: Wink 3D **36**
Beare Farm Cotts. EX20: Dowe 1B **48**
Bear La. EX9: Know 4A **82**
Bearne's La. TQ12: New A 1E **108**
　　(off Bank St.)
Bearsdown Cl. PL6: Plym 3D **136**

Bearsdown Rd. PL6: Plym 3D 136
Bear St. EX1: Exe 5E 6 (7F 65)
 EX32: B'aple 4E 18
Beatlands Rd. EX10: Sidm 6C 84
Beatrice Av. PL2: Plym 4H 135
 PL4: Plym 2J 9 (1A 142)
Beattie Rd. PL5: Plym 3A 134
Beatty Av. EX2: Cou W 5B 72
Beatty Cl. PL6: Plym 6B 132
Beatty Way TQ6: Dartm 4F 125
Beauchamp Cres. PL2: Plym 4H 135
Beauchamp Rd. PL2: Plym 4H 135
Beaudyn Wlk. PL6: Plym 4D 136
Beaufort Cl. EX16: Sam P 2B 42
 PL5: Plym 3B 134
Beaufort Ho. PL4: Plym 5G 9
Beaufort Rd. EX2: Exe 7B 6 (1E 70)
Beaufort Wlk. EX32: B'aple 3G 19
Beauly Cl. PL7: Plymp 4D 138
Beaumaris Gdns. PL3: Plym 3A 136
Beaumaris Rd. PL3: Plym 4A 136
Beaumont Av.
 PL4: Plym 3G 9 (2K 141)
Beaumont Cl. TQ2: Torq 7K 111
 TQ12: Live 4F 93
Beaumont Lodge TQ3: Paig 7H 115
Beaumont Pk.
 PL4: Plym 3H 9 (2A 142)
Beaumont Pl. PL4: Plym 4G 9 (2K 141)
Beaumont Rd.
 PL4: Plym 4G 9 (2A 142)
 TQ12: New A 2F 109
Beaumont St. PL2: Plym 6F 135
Beauvale Cl. EX11: Ott M 3D 80
Beaver Rd. EX22: Bradw 5B 28
Beavers Brook Cl. TQ3: Pres 4H 115
Beavor La. EX13: Axmin 3J 89
BEAWORTHY 1C 169
Beaworthy Cl. EX2: Exe 3D 70
Becket Rd. TQ13: Bov T 4C 92
Beckets Rd. TQ7: Kingsb 4G 157
Beckford Cl. PL7: Plymp 4D 138
Beckham Pl. PL3: Plym 5B 136
Becklake Cl. EX31: Rou 7K 17
Beckley Ct. PL1: Plym 3E 8 (2J 141)
Beck's Sq. EX16: Tive 5C 40
 (off St George's Way)
Becky Falls 2B 170
Bede Gdns. PL5: Plym 2H 135
BEDFORD BRIDGE 1D 126
Bedford Gro. PL21: Ivy 4H 145
Bedford Ho. EX1: Exe 4E 6
 (off Bedford St.)
Bedford Pk. PL4: Plym 2G 9 (1K 141)
 PL20: Bere A 2C 128
 (off Bedford St.)
Bedford Pk. Vs.
 PL4: Plym 1G 9 (1K 141)
Bedford Pl. PL19: Tavi 4J 59
 (off Plymouth Rd.)
 PL20: Bere A 1C 128
 PL20: Horr 2E 126
Bedford Rd. PL9: Plyms 4F 143
 PL20: Horr 2E 126
 TQ1: Torq 5F 113
Bedford Row EX32: B'aple 4E 18
Bedford Sq. EX10: Sidm 7C 84
 PL19: Tavi 4J 59
Bedford St. EX1: Exe 4E 6 (6F 65)
 EX32: B'aple 4F 19
 (off Buller Rd.)
 PL2: Plym 6E 134
 PL20: Bere A 2C 128
Bedford Ter. PL4: Plym 2F 9 (1K 141)
Bedford Way PL1: Plym 5E 8 (2J 141)
Bedland's La. EX9: Bud S 5A 82
Beech Av. EX4: Exe 3K 65
 PL4: Plym 6K 9 (4B 142)
Beech Bank EX39: Bide 5C 22
Beech Cl. EX5: Broadc 6D 52
 EX10: New P 6F 81
 EX14: Hon 5D 54
 EX15: Will 4D 44
 EX31: Rou 7A 18
 PL19: Tavi 7J 59
 TQ9: Tot 5B 102
Beech Cl. PL6: Plym 5E 132
Beech Cres. PL20: Prin 6C 60
Beech Cft. EX15: Cull 2H 45
Beechcroft Rd. PL2: Plym 4G 135
 PL3: Plym 5B 136
Beechdown Ct. TQ4: Coll M 3A 118
Beechdown Pk. TQ4: Coll M 3B 118
Beech Dr. TQ12: Ipp 6J 101
The Beeches EX39: Wools 2B 28
 PL20: Yelv 5G 127
Beeches Av. PL20: Yelv 5F 127
 TQ2: Torq 3A 112
Beechfield Av. PL20: W'bury 6B 78
Beechfield Cl. EX31: Frem 2E 16
 (off Thornlea Av.)
Beechfield Gro. PL3: Plym 5K 135
Beechfield Pl. TQ2: Torq 3B 112
Beechfield Rd. EX31: Frem 6E 16
Beech Gro. EX31: B'aple 2E 18
 EX33: Brau 3H 15
 EX36: S Mol 5D 26

Beech Gro. Ter. EX31: B'aple 2E 18
Beech Pk. EX11: W Hill 4H 79
 EX17: Cred 5J 39
 EX31: Frem 6F 17
Beech Rd. EX5: Rock 3E 68
 EX16: Tive 3E 40
 PL21: L Mill 5A 144
Beech Rd. Bus. Pk.
 PL21: L Mill 4C 144
Beech Tree Dr. EX16: Tive 3B 40
Beech Tree Mdw. EX20: Brid 3J 57
Beech Trees La. TQ12: Ipp 5F 101
Beech Wlk. EX14: Gitt, Hon 7C 54
Beechway EX8: Exmth 4D 76
Beechwood Av. EX31: B'aple 6C 18
 PL4: Plym 1E 8 (7J 135)
 TQ12: New A 3H 109
 TQ13: Bov T 7B 92
Beechwood Cl. EX31: B'aple 5C 18
Beechwood Cl. TQ14: Teignm 2F 107
Beechwood Cres. PL2: Plym 4H 135
Beechwood Dr. TQ7: Kingsb 4G 157
Beechwood Pk. TQ7: Lodd 2G 151
Beechwood Ri. PL6: Plym 2F 137
Beechwood Rd. TQ13: Chud 2B 94
Beechwood Ter. PL4: Plym 7J 135
Beechwood Way PL7: Plymp 4G 139
BEENLEIGH 5E 100
BELSTONE .1A 170
BEERCROCOMBE 1D 167
Beer Head Cvn. Pk. 7B 86
Beer Heights Light Railway 7A 86
Beer Hill EX12: Seat 6C 86
Beer Quarry Caves 2C 173
Beer Rd. EX12: Seat 6C 86
Beer Sailing Club 7B 86
Beers Hill EX17: Cop 6A 38
Beers Ter. EX6: Kennf 1G 95
BEESANDS .3A 176
BEESON 3A 176
Beeston Wlk. PL3: Plym 4D 136
Beethulm Vista Rd. TQ5: Brixh 2E 122
Belair Ct. PL1: Plym 4H 135
Belair Vs. PL2: Plym 4H 135
 (off Montpelier Rd.)
Belfield Av. TQ3: Marl 4D 114
Belfield Cl. TQ3: Marl 3D 114
Belfield Ri. TQ3: Marl 3D 114
Belfield Rd. TQ3: Paig 7E 114
Belfield Way TQ3: Marl 3D 114
Belgrave Cl. EX9: Bud S 7B 82
Belgrave La. PL4: Plym 7K 135
Belgrave M. TQ2: Torq 1B 116
Belgrave Rd.
 EX1: Exe 3G 7 (6G 65)
 PL4: Plym 7K 135
 TQ2: Torq 1B 116
 TQ12: New A 3J 109
Belgrave Ter. TQ14: Teignm 4J 107
Belgravia Ter. TQ6: Kingsw 6G 125
Bellaire EX31: B'aple 2D 18
Bellaire Dr. EX31: B'aple 2D 18
Bellamarsh La. TQ13: Chud K 5B 94
Bellamy Cl. PL6: Plym 2B 136
Bella Vista Rd. TQ5: Brixh 2E 122
Belle Acre Cl. PL3: Plym 5A 136
Belle Av. EX17: Cred 6G 39
Belle Ct. EX17: Cred 6G 39
Belle Cross Rd. TQ7: Kingsb 3H 157
Belle Hill TQ7: Kingsb 3G 157
Belle Isle Dr. EX2: Exe 1G 71
Belle Mdw. Ct. EX32: B'aple 4E 18
 (off Albert La.)
Belle Mdw. Rd. EX32: B'aple 5E 18
Belle Pde. EX17: Cred 6H 39
Belle Vue Av. EX35: Lynt 2G 13
Belle Vue Cl. EX6: Kenn 3J 95
Belle Vue Cross EX38: G Tor 1E 30
Belle Vue Dr. PL9: Hooe 7C 142
Belle Vue Ri. PL9: Hooe 7C 142
Belle Vue Rd. EX4: Exe 2D 64
 EX8: Exmth 4C 76
 PL9: Hooe 7D 142
 TQ4: Paig 2J 119
 TQ7: Kingsb 4G 157
Bellevue Sq. PL11: Torp 2A 140
Belle Vue Ter. EX6: Kennf 2H 95
 EX15: Cull 3H 45
 EX39: Bide 3E 22
Bellflower Cl. PL6: Robo 1D 132
Bellingham Cres. PL7: Plymp 5E 138
Belliver Ind. Est. PL6: Robo 1C 132
Belliver Way PL6: Robo 1C 132
Bell La. TQ3: Blag 7B 114

Bell Pk. PL7: Plymp 2D 138
Bellrock Cl. TQ2: Torq 2D 112
Bell St. EX9: Ott'n 6H 83
Belmont EX32: B'aple 4F 19
Belmont Av. EX34: C Mar 6A 12
 EX34: Ilfra 3G 11
Belmont Cl. EX16: Tive 3D 40
 TQ12: Kingst 2H 105
Belmont Ct. EX16: Tive 3D 40
Belmont Ho. EX4: Exe 1H 7 (5G 65)
Belmont Pl. PL3: Plym 7F 135
Belmont Rd. EX1: Exe 2H 7 (5G 65)
 EX16: Tive 3D 40
 EX32: B'aple 3F 19
 EX34: Ilfra 3G 11
 PL21: Ivy 5G 145
 TQ1: Torq 7D 112
 TQ5: Brixh 4E 122
Belmont St.
 PL1: Plym 4B 8 (2H 141)
Belmont Ter. EX8: Exmth 3E 76
 (off Causeway)
 EX12: Beer 7B 86
 TQ9: Tot .5E 102
 TQ10: S Bre 1C 100
Belmont Vs. PL3: Plym 1F 141
Belstone Av. EX4: Exe 3D 64
 TQ12: New A 6B 104
Belvidere Rd. EX4: Exe 3D 64
Belvoir Rd. EX39: Bide 3E 22
Benbow St. PL2: Dev 7E 134
Bench Tor Cl. TQ2: Torq 5H 111
Bendarroch Rd. EX11: W Hill 3G 79
Bendle La. EX36: N Mol 2E 26
Bendley Hill EX16: W'ridge 5J 33
Benedict Cl. TQ14: Teignm 2J 107
Benedicts Cl. TQ12: Live 4G 93
Benedicts Rd. TQ12: Live 4G 93
Benedict Way PL21: Modb 6G 147
Ben Jonson Cl. TQ2: Torq 7K 111
Benlears Acre TQ12: Live 4G 93
BENNACOTT 1A 168
BENNAH 2C 171
Bennett Cl. EX2: Alph 5D 70
Bennett Rd. TQ8: Salc 5B 158
Bennetts Cl. EX12: Brans 6J 85
Bennetts Hill EX10: Sidm 3A 84
Bennett Sq. EX4: Whip 4K 65
Bennett St. PL1: Dev 3D 140
Benning Cl. EX31: B'aple 3B 18
Bens Cl. TQ7: Galm 2K 155
Benson Cl. EX16: W'ridge 6H 33
Benson Dr. EX39: Nort 6F 21
Benton Rd. EX32: Brat F 6J 13
Ben Venue Cl. TQ1: Torq 1E 116
Berachah Rd. TQ1: Torq 7D 112
Bere Alston Station
 (Rail) 1A 128 (1A 174)
Berea Rd. TQ1: Torq 7E 112
BERE FERRERS 6C 128 (1A 174)
Bere Ferrers Station
 (Rail) 6B 128 (1A 174)
Beresford St. PL2: Plym 7F 135
Berkeley Av. TQ2: Torq 4J 111
Berkeley Cotts. PL1: Plym 1F 141
Berkeley Pl. FX34: Ilfra 3H 11
 (off Highfield Rd.)
Berkeley Ri. TQ2: Torq 4J 111
Berkeley Sq. PL6: Plym 7A 132
Berkeley Way PL21: Ivy 5H 145
Berkshire Cl. TQ12: E Ogw 4C 108
Berkshire Dr. EX4: Exe 1B 70
 PL2: Plym 6E 134
Berman Ct. TQ12: New A 1E 108
 (off Clarendon Rd.)
Bernadette Cl. EX4: Whip 3B 66
Bernice Cl. PL4: Plym 7C 136
Bernice Ter. PL4: Plym 7B 136
Berretts Way TQ12: Live 4H 93
Berrow Pk. Rd. PL3: Plym 4J 135
Berry Av. TQ3: Paig 1F 119
Berryball Cl. EX20: Oke 2C 48
Berrybrook Mdw.
 EX6: Exmin 3D 74
Berry Cl. EX8: Exmth 4G 77
 TQ8: Salc 4B 158
 TQ12: A'well 6E 108
BERRY CROSS 2C 163
BERRY DOWN CROSS 2B 160
Berry Dr. TQ3: Paig 1F 119
Berry Head Country Pk.
 . . . . .3H 123 (2B 176)
Berry Head Fortifications 2J 123
Berry Head Gdns.
 PL6: Plym 2K 135

Berry Head National Nature Reserve
 . . . . .4H 123 (2B 176)
Berry Head Rd. TQ5: Brixh 3F 123
Berry Hill EX12: Beer 6B 86
 EX12: Brans 6F 85
 TQ14: Bi'ton 3B 106
Berry La. EX6: Dunsf 5B 62
 EX12: Beer 6B 86
 EX34: Ber 2E 12
 TQ12: Kingst 4H 105
Berry Mdw. TQ12: Kingst 5H 105
BERRYNARBOR 3C 12 (2B 160)
Berry Pk. Cl. PL9: Plyms 6F 143
Berry Pk. Rd. PL9: Plyms 5F 143
BERRY POMEROY 4K 103 (1A 176)
Berry Pomeroy Castle 1A 176
Berry Rd. EX32: B'aple 5H 19
 EX33: Brau 3K 15
 TQ3: Paig 1F 119
Berry Sq. TQ4: Paig 1J 119
 (off Beach Rd.)
Berrys Wood TQ12: New A 1C 108
Berthon Rd. PL5: Plym 4A 134
Berwick Av. PL5: Plym 7K 131
Besigheim Way TQ12: New A 1H 109
Besley Cl. EX16: Tive 5F 41
Besley Ct. EX2: Mar B 2E 70
Best Pk. EX5: Cran 3B 68
Bestridge Mdw. EX32: Swim 2H 25
Best's La. EX38: G Tor 1C 30
Bethany Gdns. PL2: Plym 3H 135
Bethel Ter. TQ1: Torq 1D 116
 (off Princes Rd.)
Betjeman Cl. EX10: Sidm 2A 84
Betjeman Dr. EX8: Exmth 1E 76
Betjeman Wlk. PL6: Plym 7H 131
Betony Ri. EX2: Won 2B 72
BETTISCOMBE 1D 173
Betton Way TQ13: More 6H 61
Bettsmead EX4: Whip 3K 65
Bettsmead Cl. EX4: Whip 4K 65
Beuvron Cl. EX39: Wools 2B 28
Bevan Rd. EX1: Whip 5A 66
Bevan Rd. EX1: Whip 5B 66
 EX32: B'aple 5F 19
Beverley Bay Cvn. Pk. 6H 119
Beverley Cl. EX2: Won 1A 72
Beverley Gdns. TQ13: Ashb 2J 99
Beverley Pk. TQ4: Good 6H 119
Beverley Ri. TQ5: Brixh 4D 122
Beverley Rd. PL3: Plym 7D 136
Beverley Vw. Holiday Pk. 6H 119
Beverston Way PL6: Plym 2C 132
Bevil Cl. EX39: Bide 4E 22
Bevin Ct. EX17: Cred 6J 39
Bewhay Gdns. TQ9: Darti 3B 102
Bewley Hill EX17: Cop 6D 38
Bewsley La. EX17: Cop 5D 38
Bexley La. TQ2: Torq 1B 116
Beyrout Cotts. PL1: Dev 1E 140
 (off Beyrout Pl.)
Beyrout Pl. PL1: Dev 1E 140
Bhutan Cl. EX14: Hon 4G 55
Bias La. EX33: Brau 4J 15
 (off Chaloner's Rd.)
Bicclescombe EX34: Ilfra 4H 11
 (off Bicclescombe Gdns.)
Bicclescombe Gdns. EX34: Ilfra 4H 11
Bicclescombe Pk. Rd. EX34: Ilfra 4H 11
BICKENHALL 2C 167
Bickern Rd. PL11: Torp 1A 140
Bickford La. TQ14: Teignm 5J 107
Bickfords Grn. TQ12: Live 4G 93
Bickham Pk. Rd. PL3: Plym 5J 135
Bickham Rd. PL5: Plym 1C 134
BICKINGTON
 EX31 . . . . .6K 17 (3B 160)
 TQ12 . . . . .3B 170
Bickington Hill EX31: Bick 6K 17
Bickington Lodge EX31: Bick 5J 17
Bickington Pk. EX31: Bick 6K 17
Bickington Rd. EX31: B'aple, Bick 5H 17
Bickington Steam Railway 5H 93
BICKLEIGH
 EX16 . . . . .3D 165
 PL6 . . . . .1H 133 (1B 174)
Bickleigh Cl. EX4: Pin 2C 66
 PL6: Plym 2B 136
Bickleigh Down Rd. PL6: Robo 2D 132
BICKLETON .3B 160
Bickley Rd. TQ12: Ipp, Ston 5B 110
Bickwell Ho. La. EX10: Sidm 5A 84
Bickwell La. EX10: Sidm 4A 84
Bickwell Valley EX10: Sidm 6A 84
BICTON 5F 83
Bicton Cl. PL6: Plym 2E 136
Bicton Gardens 5F 83 (2A 172)
Bicton Pl. EX1: Heav 4K 7 (6J 65)
 EX8: Exmth 6C 76
Bicton St. EX8: Exmth 6C 76
 EX32: B'aple 3F 19
Bicton Vs. EX8: Exmth 6D 76
Bicton Woodland Railway 4F 83
Biddamoor La. EX19: Bea 2G 31
Bidder Dr. TQ13: More 7J 61
Bidders Cl. TQ6: Sto F 2H 153
Bidders Wlk. TQ6: Sto F 3H 153

Biddiblack Way EX39: Bide 3H 23
Biddick Dr. PL2: Plym 5E 134
Biddington Way EX14: Hon 5D 54
BIDEFORD 3F 23 (1C 163)
Bideford Arts Cen. 3F 23
(off The Quay)
Bideford Bus. Pk. EX39: Bide 5K 23
Bideford Quay Fountain 3G 23
Bideford Railway Museum 1C 163
Bideford Railway Museum &
Tarka Trail Vis. Cen. 4G 23
Bideford Tourist Information Centre
. . . . .2F 23 (1C 163)
Bideford Wlk. PL6: Plym 3F 137
BIDLAKE .2D 169
Bidmead Cl. EX8: Lit 5G 77
Bidna La. EX3: Nort 4G 21
Bidwell Brook Dr. TQ4: Good 6H 119
Bidwell La. EX5: Thor 1B 50
Bidwell Wlk. TQ4: Good 6H 119
Biera Vw. TQ13: Chag 2H 61
Bigadon La. TQ11: B'leigh 6D 98
BIGBURY .3C 175
Bigbury Golf Course 1D 154 (3C 175)
BIGBURY-ON-SEA 3B 154 (3C 175)
Bigbury Wlk. PL6: Plym 3F 137
Bigbury Way TQ2: Torq 3D 112
Biggin Hill PL5: Plym 5E 130
The Big Sheep 4A 22 (1C 163)
Bilbie Cl. EX15: Cull 4F 45
Bilbury St. PL4: Plym 4F 9 (2K 141)
BILLACOMBE 4G 143
Billacombe Rd. PL9: Plyms 3D 142
Billacombe Vs. PL9: Plyms 4G 143
The Bill Douglas Cinema Mus.
. . . . .4E 64 (1D 171)
Billing Cl. PL6: Plym 4J 131
Billington Cl. PL6: Plym 3C 136
Bilton Ter. EX39: Bide 4F 23
(off Buttgarden St.)
Biltor Rd. TQ12: Ipp 7G 101
Bimbom La.
EX13: Kilm, Shute 4A 88
Bindon Rd. EX4: Pin 2D 66
Binford Cl. EX1: Whip 6A 66
Bingfield Cl. TQ1: Torq 1E 116
Bingham Cres. EX32: B'aple 4G 19
Binkham Hill PL20: Yelv 5H 127
Bircham Valley
Local Nature Reserve 7C 132
Bircham Vw. PL6: Plym 2D 136
(not continuous)
Birch Cl. PL6: Plym 3F 133
Birch End EX5: Rock 4F 69
Birchen La. EX16: Tive 5C 40
The Birches PL6: Plym 4E 132
Birchfield Av. PL2: Plym 5G 135
Birch Gro. EX11: W Hill 5H 79
BIRCHILL .3D 167
Birchland Rd. PL7: Spa 1K 139
Birchland Way PL7: Spa 1J 139
Birch La. EX17: Morc 2A 38
EX31: Rou 7B 18
Birchlea Cl. TQ13: Bov T 7B 92
Birch Pond Rd. PL9: Plyms 5E 142
Birch Rd. EX8: Lymp 6H 75
EX32: Land 1B 24
(not continuous)
TQ12: New A 3J 109
Birch Wlk. TQ2: Torq 5J 111
Birch Way EX5: Rock 3E 68
BIRCHWOOD 2C 167
Birchwood Cl. PL19: Tavi 6J 59
TQ9: Tot 6D 102
Birchwood Gdns. PL7: Plymp 2D 138
Birchwood Rd. EX8: Exmth 2F 77
Birchy Barton Hill EX1: Heav 7A 66
Birdcage La. EX11: Ott M 1J 79
Bird Cl. EX1: Pin 3D 66
Birdie Wlk. EX2: Cou W 4C 72
Bird of Prey Viewpoint 2C 171
BIRDSMOORGATE 3D 167
Birdswell La. EX34: Ber 3B 12
Birdwood Ct. TQ9: Tot 6E 102
Birdwood Cres. EX39: Bide 3C 22
Birkbeck Cl. PL7: Plymp 2B 138
Birkett Cl. EX2: Won 1B 72
Birks Grange EX4: Exe 3D 64
BISH MILL .1B 164
Bishop Ct. EX24: Colyt 6C 88
Bishops Av. TQ14: Bi'ton 4B 106
Bishops Cl. EX6: Star 1E 96
PL21: Ivy 3J 145
TQ1: Torq 2H 117
BISHOPS CLYST 2F 73
Bishops Ct. PL8: New F 5H 149
TQ13: Chud 2C 94
TQ14: Bi'ton 3B 106
Bishops Ct. Ind. Est. EX2: Sow 1D 72
Bishop's Ct. La. EX5: Clyst M 1H 73
Bishop's Ct. Rd.
EX5: Clyst H, Clyst M 2F 73
Bishops Dr. EX17: Cop 6C 38
BISHOP'S HULL 1C 167
BISHOPS LYDEARD 1B 166
Bishops Mead TQ10: S Bre 1B 100
Bishops Mdw. EX17: Morc 1B 38
BISHOP'S NYMPTON 1B 164

Bishops Pl. PL1: Plym 7B 8 (4H 141)
TQ3: Paig 1H 119
Bishops Ri. EX15: Kent 6A 46
TQ1: Torq 2J 117
BISHOP'S TAWTON 6B 24 (3B 160)
Bishop's Tawton Rd.
EX32: B'aple, B Taw 7G 19
BISHOPSTEIGNTON 3B 106 (3D 171)
Bishopsteignton Ho.
TQ14: Bi'ton 3A 106
Bishopsteignton Mus. of Rural Life
. . . . .3C 106
Bishopsteignton Rd.
TQ14: Teignm 5E 106
Bishopstone Gdns. TQ3: Pres 6J 115
Bishop's Wlk. TQ1: Torq 7H 113
Bishop's Way EX2: Sow 2D 72
BISHOPSWOOD 2C 167
Bishop Westall Ho. EX2: Exe 6E 6
(off Good Shepherd Dr.)
Bishop Westall Rd. EX2: Cou W 3K 71
Bishop Wilfrid Rd. TQ14: Teignm 3F 107
Bitney La. TQ12: A'well 7F 109
BITTADON .3A 160
BITTAFORD 3C 146 (2C 175)
Bittaford Ter. PL21: Bitta 4C 146
Bittaford Wood PL21: Bitta 4C 146
Bittaford Wood Pk. Homes 4C 146
Bittern Ind. Units EX2: Sow 7D 66
Bittern Rd. EX2: Sow 6D 66
Bitton Av. TQ14: Teignm 4H 107
Bitton Ct. TQ14: Teignm 4H 107
Bitton Pk. Rd. TQ14: Teignm 4H 107
(not continuous)
Blachford Cl. PL21: Corn 6J 129
Blachford Rd. PL21: Ivy 3F 145
Blackabrook Av. PL20: Prin 6C 60
Blackadon Nature Reserve 3B 170
Blackalder Ter. PL7: L Moor 1J 129
Blackall Gdns. PL6: Plym 4J 131
Blackall Rd. EX4: Exe 2E 6 (5F 65)
Black-a-Tor Copse
National Nature Reserve 2D 169
BLACKAWTON 3B 152 (2A 176)
Blackball La. TQ5: Brixh 2E 122
Blackberry Cl. PL9: Plyms 4E 142
TQ9: Tot 7G 103
Blackberry La. PL9: Plyms 4F 143
Blackberry Way TQ12: Kingst 2H 105
BLACKBOROUGH 3A 166
Blackboy Rd. EX4: Exe 1H 7 (5G 65)
Blackbrook Av. TQ4: Good 6H 119
Blackbrook Cl. PL20: Walk 2J 127
Blackbrook Wlk. TQ4: Good 6H 119
Blackbury Camp 1B 172
BLACK DOG 3C 165
BLACKDOWN
DT8 . . . . .3D 167
PL19 . . . . .1B 60
Blackdown Pk. EX15: Will 3C 44
Blackdown Rings Picnic Site 2D 175
Blackdown Vw. EX15: Hemy 1G 47
EX16: Sam P 2A 42
Blackenway La. TQ12: Coff 5K 109
Blackett Cl. PL21: Ivy 4J 145
Blackeven Cl. PL6: Robo 1E 132
Blackeven Hill PL6: Robo 1E 132
Blackfriars Cl. PL1: Plym 6F 9
Blackfriars Ope PL1: Plym 6F 9
BLACKHAVEN 4H 67
Blackhaven Cl. TQ4: Good 7H 119
BLACKHORSE 4H 67
Blackhorse La. EX5: Clyst H 4G 67
Black Lion Ct. EX14: Hon 3F 55
BLACKMOOR GATE 2C 161
Blackmore Cl. EX8: Exmth 3G 77
Blackmore Cres. PL6: Plym 4J 131
Blackmore Dr. EX10: Sidm 6C 84
Blackmore La. EX39: Bide 3C 22
Blackmore M. EX2: Won 1B 72
Blackmore Rd. EX16: Tive 5F 41
Blackmore's Path EX35: Lynt 2G 13
Blackmore Theatre 6C 76
Blackmore Vw. EX10: Sidm 6C 84
(off May Ter.)
BLACKNEY .1D 173
BLACKPOOL
PL8 . . . . .7G 139
TQ6 . . . . .4F 153 (3A 176)
TQ12 . . . . .5F 93
BLACKPOOL CORNER 1D 173
Blackpool Gdns. 3F 153 (3A 176)
Blackpool Hill TQ6: Blackp 4F 153
Blackpool Rd. EX17: Bow 6K 37
Blackpool Sands 3A 176
Blackpool Valley Rd.
TQ6: Blackp 2F 153
Blackpost La. TQ9: Tot 6H 103
Blacksmith La. TQ10: Wran 2E 146
Blackstone Cl. PL9: Elb 6J 143
Blackstone Rd. TQ12: Ipp 7H 101
Black Swan Bus. Pk. EX7: Daw 7C 96
Black Swan Ter. EX7: Daw 7C 96
Blackthorn Av. EX16: Tive 2F 41
Blackthorn Cl. EX10: Sidm 2A 84
EX14: Hon 5F 55
PL5: Plym 7G 131
PL6: Plym 2E 132
Blackthorn Cres. EX1: Whip 6B 66

Blackthorn Dr. PL21: Ivy 5J 145
Blackthorn La. EX5: Cran 2E 68
Blackthorn Way TQ4: Paig 3D 118
BLACK TORRINGTON 3C 163
BLACKWATER 2C 167
Blackwater Rd. EX15: Culm 3D 26
BLACKWELL 1A 166
Blackwood Path TQ10: Wran 1B 146
Bladon Cl. TQ12: New A 3G 109
BLAGDON 1B 118 (1A 176)
Blagdon EX17: Cred 6J 39
Blagdon Ct. EX17: Cred 6J 39
BLAGDON HILL 2C 167
Blagdon Pl. EX17: Cred 6J 39
(off Exhibition Rd.)
Blagdon Ri. EX17: Cred 5J 39
Blagdon Rd. TQ3: Blag 7A 114
Blagdon Vs. PL5: Plym 1B 134
Blake Cl. TQ1: Torq 5D 112
Blake Gdns. PL5: Plym 7H 131
Blakeland Rd. EX31: Frem 6E 16
Blakeney Rd. TQ9: Plyms 3E 142
Blakes Hill Rd.
EX32: Land, Swim 1B 24
Blakeslee Dr. EX2: Cou W 4C 72
Blanchard Pl. PL7: Plymp 2B 138
Blandford Rd. PL3: Plym 6B 136
Blangy Cl. EX20: N Taw 7C 36
Blatchcombe Dr. TQ3: Paig 7F 115
Blatchcombe Rd. TQ3: Paig 7F 115
Blatchford La. EX20: Brid 1J 57
Blatchford Ct. EX20: Oke 3B 48
Blatchmore La. TQ6: Dartm 7D 124
Blaxton La. PL5: Tam F 7E 128, 1H 131
Bleachfield Ri. EX13: Axmin 3J 89
Blenheim Cl. TQ1: Torq 2G 117
TQ12: New A 7D 104
Blenheim Ct. EX2: Matf 4F 71
EX15: Will 3D 44
Blenheim Dr. EX15: Will 3D 44
Blenheim La. EX20: Exbo 6J 35
Blenheim Rd. EX2: Alph 3E 70
PL4: Plym 2F 9 (1K 141)
Blenheim Ter. PL19: Lam 5B 58
TQ13: Bov T 4B 92
Bligh Cl. TQ14: Teignm 1G 107
Blind La. EX5: Hux 7K 51
EX34: Ber 3B 12
BLINDMOOR 2C 167
Blindwell Av. TQ12: Kingst 4H 105
Blindwell Cres. EX5: Cran 2F 69
Blindwylle Rd. TQ2: Torq 1A 116
Blogishay La. TQ13: Ashb 4H 99
Bloomball Cl. PL3: Plym 5C 136
Blossom Cl. EX14: Dunk 7H 47
Blossom Hill EX14: Dunk 7H 47
Blue Ball Hill TQ9: Tot 6E 102
Bluebell Av. EX16: Tive 2F 41
Bluebell Cl. EX22: Seat 3F 87
Bluebell Rd. EX14: Dunk 7H 47
Bluebell St. PL6: Plym 1B 136
Bluebell Way PL19: Lam 5K 59
Blueberry Downs EX9: Bud S 6E 82
Blueboy La. EX1: Exe 3F 7
(off Dix's Field)
Blue Boy Sq. EX1: Exe 3F 7
Blue Cedar Ct. EX8: Exmth 6D 76
Bluehayes La. EX5: Broadc 3A 68
Blue Haze Cl. PL6: Plym 5E 132
Blue Ridge Rd. TQ13: Bov T 7B 92
Bluewater Est. PL7: Plymp 2D 138
Bluewater Holiday Homes 7E 96
Blue Waters TQ13: Bov T 7B 92
Blue Waters Dr. DT7: Lym R 5G 91
TQ4: Broads 7J 119
Blue Waters Ind. Est.
TQ13: Bov T 6B 92
Blundell's Av. EX16: Tive 4F 41
Blundell's Rd. EX16: Tive 4D 40
(not continuous)
BLUNTS 1A 174
Blunts La. PL6: Plym 6D 132
Blyth Ct. EX39: W Ho 6A 20
Blythe Way TQ4: Paig 3D 118
Blythswood Cres. TQ1: Torq 6D 112
Boarden Barn EX8: Exmth 6D 76
Boards Ct. EX39: Bide 4G 23
Bockland Cl. EX15: Cull 4F 45
Boconnic La. PL20: Yelv 5G 127
Bodley Cl. EX1: Whip 6A 66
Bodley Ho. EX1: Whip 5A 66
Bodmin Rd. PL5: Plym 6G 131
Bodmin St. EX22: Hols 3B 34
Body Hayes Cl. TQ9: Sto G 4A 120
Bogmoor La. EX5: Whim 4F 53
Bogons Ct. TQ9: Tot 7F 103
Bohemia Vs. EX10: Sidm 5B 84
Bohelland Rd. EX9: Bud S 6D 82

Bolham Rd. EX16: Bolh, Tive 1C 40
BOLHAM WATER 2B 166
Bolt Head TQ8: Salc 6A 158
Bolt Ho. Cl. PL19: Tavi 4G 59
Bolton Ct. TQ5: Brixh 4E 122
(off Windmill Hill)
Bolton St. TQ5: Brixh 4E 122
Bolt Tail Cliff Castle 3C 175
BOLVENTOR 3A 168
Bonair Cl. TQ5: Brixh 5E 122
Bonaventure Cl. TQ8: Salc 3C 158
Bonaventure Rd. TQ8: Salc 3C 158
BONDLEIGH 3A 164
Bond's La. EX5: W'bury, Wood S 4A 78
Bonds Mdw. TQ13: Bov T 3B 92
Bond Spear Ct. PL1: Plym 7B 8
Bond St. EX19: Bea 2H 31
PL6: Plym 4K 131
PL21: Corn 6J 129
Bonehayne & Purlbridge Rd.
EX24: Colyt 5A 88
BONEHILL .3B 170
Bonfire Hill TQ8: Salc 3B 158
Bonfire La. EX5: W'bury 5B 78
Bonhay Cl. EX6: Star 1E 96
Bonhay Ho. EX4: Exe 1B 6
(off Bonhay Rd.)
Bonhay Rd. EX4: Exe 2A 6 (5D 64)
EX6: Star 1E 96
Boniface Ct. EX17: Cred 6J 39
Boniface La. PL5: Plym 1K 135
Bonners C'way. EX13: Axmin 2K 89
Bonners Dr. EX13: Axmin 3K 89
Bonners Glen EX13: Axmin 3K 89
Bonnicott La. EX33: Croy 3B 14
Bonnington Gro. EX1: Heav 6J 65
Bonville Cl. EX1: Whip 5A 66
Bonville Cres. EX16: Tive 5G 41
Bonville Dr. PL21: Ivy 5J 145
Bonville Rd. PL6: Plym 4J 131
BOOBERY 1B 42
Booery EX16: Sam P 2A 42
Boode Rd. EX33: Boo, Brau 3K 15
BOOHAY 4K 125
Boon's La. TQ7: Kingsb 4F 157
(off Ropewalk)
Boon's Pl. PL1: Plym 2D 8 (1J 141)
Booth Way EX8: Exmth 2D 76
Border Rd. EX14: Hon 4D 54
BORESTON .2D 175
Boringdon Av. PL5: Plym 3C 134
Boringdon Cl. PL7: Plymp 2A 138
Boringdon Hill PL7: Plymp 2B 138
Boringdon Pk. PL21: Ivy 4E 144
Boringdon Pk. Golf Course 3J 137
Boringdon Rd. PL7: Plymp 3A 138
PL9: Hooe 5B 142
Boringdon Ter. PL7: Plymp 3A 138
PL9: Hooe 5B 142
PL9: Plyms 4G 143
Boringdon Vs. PL7: Plymp 3A 138
The Borough PL8: Y'ton 2B 150
Borough Cl. TQ4: Paig 4E 118
Borough Pk. Rd. TQ3: Paig 2D 118
TQ9: Tot 5E 102
Borough Rd. EX34: C Mar 5A 12
EX38: G Tor 2D 30
TQ1: Torq 4D 112
TQ4: Paig 3D 118
Borough Vw. EX38: G Tor 2D 30
Borrowdale Cl. PL6: Plym 5J 131
Borthay Orchard TQ12: A'well 6E 108
Boscastle Gdns. PL2: Plym 3H 135
Boscawen Pl. PL2: Dev 7D 134
TQ14: Teignm 4H 107
Boshill Hill EX24: Colyt 1H 87
Bossell Ho. TQ11: B'leigh 5C 98
(off Bossell Pk.)
Bossell Pk. TQ11: B'leigh 5C 98
Bossell Rd. TQ11: B'leigh 5C 98
Bossell Ter. TQ11: B'leigh 5C 98
Boston Cl. PL9: Plyms 5C 142
Bosun Cl. TQ2: Cou W 6C 72
Bosuns Point TQ4: Good 3J 119
Boswell Cl. PL5: Plym 1G 135
Boswell's La. EX20: N Taw 5D 36
Boswell Way EX17: Seat 4D 86
Bottle Bri. Hill TQ13: Chud 1D 94
Bottle Pk. PL21: L Mill 5A 144
Bottom La. EX13: Mus 5D 90
Bottompark La. TQ2: Torq 2B 112
Bottoms La. EX33: Geo 6D 14
TQ12: Dacc 1A 112
BOTTREAUX MILL 1C 165
BOTUS FLEMING 1A 174
Boucher Rd. EX9: Bud S 6D 82
BOUCHERS HILL 5B 36
Boucher Way EX9: Bud S 6D 82
Bouchiers Cl. EX20: N Taw 5B 36
Boughmore La. EX10: Sidm 6A 84
Boughmore Rd. EX10: Sidm 6A 84
Boughthayes PL19: Tavi 4G 59
Boughthayes Est. PL19: Tavi 5G 59
Boulden Cl. PL7: Plymp 4F 139
Boulder Clay Way EX31: Bick 7K 17
Boulder Cl. PL6: Plym 1D 132
Boundary Cl. TQ12: Kingsk 6J 109
Boundary Pk. EX12: Seat 3E 86

Boundary Pl.—Britten Dr.

Boundary Pl. PL6: Plym 3D 132
Boundary Rd. PL20: Dous 4K 127
TQ2: Torq 1K 115
Bounds Pl.
PL1: Plym 6B 8 (3H 141)
Bounsells La. EX20: Mert 5B 30
Bounty Gro. EX2: Cou W 5B 72
Bourchier Cl. EX16: Bam 1H 33
Bourchier Dr. EX16: Bam 1H 33
Bourne Cl. PL3: Plym 5E 136
Bourne Ct. TQ5: Brixh 6B 122
Bourne Rd. TQ12: Kingsk 7K 109
Bourn Ri. EX4: Pin 2C 66
Bournville Pl. EX16: Tive 3E 40
Bourton La. TQ9: Tot 5F 103
Bourton Rd. TQ9: Tot 5G 103
The Bourtons TQ9: Tot 4F 103
Boutport St. EX31: B'aple 3E 18
Bovemoor's La. EX2: Won 7J 65
Bove Pk. Rd. TQ2: Torq 1C 112
Bovey Heath Battle Site 3C 171
Bovey La. EX12: Beer 5A 86
BOVEY TRACEY 4B 92 (3C 171)
Bovey Tracey Golf Course 2A 92
Bovey Tracey Heritage Cen.
. . . . .4B 92 (3C 171)
Bovey Tracey Information Centre
. . . . .4B 92 (3C 171)
Bovey Tracey Rd. TQ12: New A 4B 104
Bovey Tracey Swimming Pool 5B 92
Boville La. PL9: Elb 5K 143
BOVISAND 1B 148
Bovisand La.
PL9: Bovis, Down T 1A 148
PL9: Bovis, Stad 1B 148
Bovisand Lodge Est.
PL9: Bovis 1B 148
Bovisand Rd. PL9: Stad 1D 148
BOW 5H 37 (3B 164)
Bowcombe Rd. TQ7: Kingsb 6J 157
BOWD 2B 172
BOWDEN 3A 176
Bowden Farm PL8: Y'ton 2B 150
BOWDEN GREEN 5D 22
Bowden Grn. EX39: Bide 5D 22
Bowden Hill EX17: Cred 6J 39
PL8: Y'ton 2B 150
TQ12: New A 2F 109
TQ13: Ashb 4F 99
Bowden Pk. Rd. PL6: Plym 2B 136
Bowden Rd. TQ12: Ipp 6J 101
BOWDENS 1D 167
Bowdens Cl. TQ13: Bov T 4B 92
Bowdens Pk. PL21: Ivy 5F 145
Bowe Ct. EX1: Exe 1J 7
Bowen Ct. EX33: Brau 5J 15
Bowering Ct. *EX32: B'aple* *6G 19*
(off Cyprus Ter.)
Bowerland Av. TQ2: Torq 1B 112
Bowerman's Nose 2B 170
Bowers Pk. Dr. PL6: Plym 3F 133
Bowers Rd. PL2: Plym 6G 135
Bowhay La. EX4: Exe 7A 64
EX34: C Mar 7C 12
Bowhays Wlk. PL6: Plym 4D 136
Bowhill 1C 70
Bowhill EX5: Bradn 1D 52
BOWITHICK 2A 168
Bowker Ho. PL21: L Mill 5A 144
Bowland Cl. TQ4: Paig 5G 119
Bow La. TQ13: More 7H 61
Bowley Mdw. EX5: Bradn 2B 52
Bowling Grn. *TQ13: Ashb* *4H 99*
(off Whistley Hill)
Bowling Grn. Chalets 6J 91
Bowling Grn. La. EX14: Hon 4F 55
EX20: Hath 2G 35
EX34: C Mar 7C 12
Bowling Green Marsh
Bird Sanctuary 7C 74
Bowling Green Marsh
Nature Reserve 6C 74
Bowling Grn. Rd. EX3: Top 6C 74
Bowling Grn. Vw. EX15: Cull 6G 45
Bowmans Mdw. EX20: Hath 1H 35
Bow Mill La. EX17: Bow 5G 37
Bowring Cl. EX1: Whip 5A 66
Bowring Mead TQ13: More 7J 61
Bowring Pk. TQ13: More 7J 61
Bowringsleigh Pl. TQ7: Kingsb 4E 156
Bow Rd. TQ9: H'ford 6C 100
The Box 3F 9 (2K 141)
Boxfield Rd. EX13: Axmin 4H 89
Boxhill Cl. PL5: Plym 7G 131
Boxhill Gdns. PL2: Plym 3H 135
BOX'S SHOP 3A 162
Boyce Ct. TQ2: Torq 5A 112
Boyce Pl. EX16: Tive 4B 40
Boyds Dr. TQ14: Teignm 4J 107
Boyes Cl. EX16: Hal 6C 42
Boyne Rd. EX9: Bud S 5C 82
BOYTON .1B 168
Bracken Cl. EX14: Hon 6C 54
PL6: Plym 2E 132
TQ12: New A 3J 109
Brackendale EX8: Exmth 1E 76
Brackendown EX11: W Hill 6H 79
Bracken Ri. TQ4: Broads 2J 121
Bracken Way *EX7: Daw W* *7D 96*
(off Beechwood Cres.)
Brackenwood EX8: Exmth 3E 76
Bradden Cres. TQ5: Brixh 4C 122
Braddicks Holiday Cen. 5A 20
Braddons Cliffe TQ1: Torq 2D 116
Braddons Hill PL7: Plymp 4J 137
Braddons Hill Rd. E. TQ1: Torq 2D 116
Braddons Hill Rd. W. TQ1: Torq 2D 116
Braddons St. TQ1: Torq 2D 116
Bradfield Cl. PL6: Plym 2F 137
Bradfield Rd. EX4: Pin 3C 66
BRADFORD 3C 163
BRADFORD BARTON 2C 165
Bradford Cl. EX8: Exmth 1E 76
PL6: Plym 4C 136
Bradford Ct. EX39: Nort 6F 21
BRADFORD-ON-TONE 1B 166
Bradham Ct. EX8: Exmth 4F 77
Bradham La. EX8: Exmth 3E 76
BRADIFORD 2D 18 (3B 160)
Bradiford EX31: B'aple 2D 18
BRADLEY 6E 92
Bradley 2C 108 (3C 171)
Bradley Ct. TQ12: New A 1E 108
Bradley La. TQ12: New A 1D 108
Bradley Pk. Rd. TQ1: Torq 5C 112
Bradley Rd. PL4: Plym 7A 136
TQ12: New A 3D 108
TQ13: Bov T 3D 92
Bradman Way EX2: Mar B 3E 70
BRADNINCH 1C 52 (3A 166)
Bradninch Pl. EX4: Exe 3E 6
BRADSTONE 2B 168
Bradwell Rd. EX34: Ilfra 3G 11
BRADWORTHY 5B 28 (2B 162)
Braeburn Pl. TQ5: Brixh 5E 122
Braemar Cl. PL7: Plymp 5F 139
Braeside M. TQ4: Good 3J 119
Braeside Rd. TQ2: Torq 1C 112
TQ4: Good 3J 119
Braggs' Hill EX37: High B 3A 32
Brahms Way EX32: B'aple 4H 19
Braidwood Ter. La. PL4: Plym 1G 9
Brakefield TQ10: S Bre 2C 100
Brakeridge Cl. TQ5: Chur F 2J 121
Brake Rd. PL5: Plym 1K 135
Brake Wood Cl. EX31: Frem 6E 16
Bramble Cl. EX9: Bud S 6D 82
EX10: Sidm 2C 84
PL3: Plym 4C 136
TQ2: Torq 1K 115
TQ9: Darti 3B 102
Bramble Hill Ind. Est.
EX14: Hon 3E 54
Bramble La. EX14: Hon 4D 54
EX17: Cred 5K 39
Bramble Path EX32: Land 2C 24
Bramble Wlk. EX31: Rou 6A 18
PL6: Plym 4D 136
Bramfield Pl. PL6: Plym 4E 136
Bramley Av. EX1: Heav 6B 66
Bramley Cl. EX6: Kenton 6J 95
EX15: Will 4D 44
EX16: Tive 1D 40
PL8: Brixt 2G 149
Bramley Gdns. EX5: Whim 7G 53
Bramley Mdw. EX32: Land 2D 24
Bramley Rd. PL3: Plym 7D 136
The Bramleys EX14: Hon 2H 55
BRAMPFORD SPEKE 5G 51 (1D 171)
Brancker Rd. PL2: Plym 5H 135
Brand Cl. EX14: Hon 5F 55
BRANDIS CORNER 3C 163
Brandis Pk. TQ7: Slap 2H 159
Brandize Pk. EX20: Oke 5B 48
Brandon Rd. PL3: Plym 7D 136
Brandreth Rd. PL3: Plym 5A 136
Brand Rd. EX14: Hon 5F 55
Branksome Cl. TQ3: Pres 4J 115
Brannam Ct. EX31: Rou 7A 18
Brannam Cres. EX31: Rou 7K 17
Brannams Sq. *EX32: B'aple* *5F 19*
(off Kiln La.)
Brannams Wlk. *EX32: B'aple* *5F 19*
(off Litchdon St.)
BRANSCOMBE 6H 85 (2B 172)
Branscombe Cl. EX4: Exe 7B 64
EX24: Colyf 1F 87
TQ1: Torq 7F 113
Branscombe Forge 6H 85 (2B 172)
Branscombe Gdns. PL5: Plym 7F 131
Branscombe La. EX7: Daw 7A 96
Branscombe Old Bakery . . .6H 85 (2B 172)
Branscombe Rd. EX16: Tive 4F 41
Branson Ct. PL7: Plymp 4F 139
Brantwood Cl. TQ4: Good 3G 119
Brantwood Cres. TQ4: Good 4G 119
Brantwood Dr. TQ4: Good 3G 119
BRATTON CLOVELLY 1C 169
BRATTON FLEMING 6H 13 (3C 161)
BRAUNTON 4J 15 (3A 160)
Braunton & District Mus.
. . . . .4J 15 (3A 160)
Braunton Burrows
National Nature Reserve 3A 160
Braunton Countryside Cen. *4J 15*
(off Caen St.)
Braunton Gt. Fld. EX33: Brau 5G 15
Braunton Rd. EX31: B'aple 2B 18
Braunton Tourist Information Centre
. . . . .4J 15 (3A 160)
Braunton Wlk. PL6: Plym 3F 137
Bray Cl. PL19: Tavi 4G 59
BRAYFORD 3C 161
Brayford Cl. PL5: Plym 7G 131
Brayhams Ter. EX20: Oke 2C 48
Bray Rd. EX22: Hols 1C 34
Brays Cl. EX17: Cred 6H 39
BRAY SHOP 3B 168
BRAZACOTT 1A 168
Breakneck Hill TQ14: Teignm 1H 107
Breakwater Ct. TQ5: Brixh 2G 123
Breakwater Hill
PL4: Plym 7J 9 (4B 142)
Breakwater Ind. Est. PL9: Plyms . . .4D 142
Breakwater Rd. PL9: Plyms 4D 142
Brean Down Cl. PL3: Plym 5K 135
Brean Down Rd. PL3: Plym 4K 135
Brecon Cl. EX39: Bide 4J 23
PL3: Plym 4B 136
TQ4: Coll M 3D 118
Bredon Ct. EX2: Exe 5K 7
Bredon La. EX9: Ott'n 5J 83
BRENDON 2D 161
Brendon Hill EX17: Cop 4E 38
The Brendons EX16: Sam P 1B 42
Brendons Av. TQ2: Torq 3J 115
Brennacott Pl. *EX39: Bide* *5C 22*
(off Brennacott Rd.)
Brennacott Rd. EX39: Bide 5C 22
Brent Cl. EX5: W'bury 5C 78
Brentford Av. PL5: Plym 5G 131
Brent Hill PL8: Holb 6C 150
Brent Knoll Rd. PL3: Plym 5K 135
Brent Mill Bus. Pk.
TQ10: S Bre 2B 100
Brenton Rd. EX6: Kennf 1G 95
Brentor Cl. EX4: Exe 4C 64
Brentor Rd. PL4: Plym 2C 142
PL19: Mary T 1A 60
Brentor St Michael's Church 2C 169
Brent Rd. TQ3: Paig 1G 119
Brentwood Gdns. *EX34: Ilfra* *3K 11*
(off Channel Vw.)
Brest Rd. PL6: Plym 6B 132
Brest Way PL6: Plym 7B 132
Bretonside PL4: Plym 5F 9 (3K 141)
Breton Way EX8: Exmth 3G 77
Bretteville Cl. EX5: W'bury 5C 78
TQ13: Chag 2H 61
Brett Wlk. PL7: Plymp 2C 138
Brewer Av. EX13: Axmin 2J 89
Brewer Rd. EX32: B'aple 5H 19
Brewers Ct. EX2: Exe 7C 6 (1E 70)
Brewery Ct. *EX7: Daw* *4H 97*
(off High St.)
Brewery La. *EX1: Heav* *7J 65*
(off North St.)
EX10: Sidm 5B 84
TQ5: Brixh *3E 122*
(off Market St.)
Brewhouse 4E 140
Brewin Rd. EX16: Tive 5C 40
Briar Cl. EX8: Exmth 4F 77
EX14: Hon 6F 55
Briar Cres. EX2: Won 3J 71
Briardale Rd. PL2: Plym 5E 134
Briar Hill Farm PL8: New F 5H 149
Briarleigh Cl. PL6: Plym 1G 137
Briar Rd. PL3: Plym 4A 136
Briar Tor PL20: Yelv 5G 127
Briary La. TQ1: Torq 1D 116
Briary M. TQ1: Torq 2F 117
Brickfields Cl. PL1: Dev 2E 140
Brickfields Sports Cen. 2E 140
Brickfields Stadium 2E 140
Brickfield Ter. *EX16: Tive* *4D 40*
(off Martins La.)
Brickhouse Dr. EX16: Tive 2D 40
Brickhouse Hill EX16: Tive 2D 40
(not continuous)
Brick Kiln Cl. EX4: Pin 3B 66
Brickyard La. EX6: Star 1D 96
Brid Cl. EX20: Brid 3H 57
Bridespring Rd. EX4: Exe 3J 65
Bridespring Wlk. EX4: Exe 3J 65
BRIDESTOWE 3H 57 (2D 169)
Bridewell Ct. EX16: Tive 5C 40
BRIDFORD 1F 63 (2C 171)
Bridford Rd. EX2: Mar B 3F 71
EX6: Bridf, Chri 1H 63
BRIDGE 3D 167
The Bridge PL1: Plym 7B 8
Bridge Bldgs. EX16: Tive 4C 40
Bridge Chambers Bus. Cen.
EX31: B'aple 4E 18
Bridge Cotts. EX4: Exe 1G 7 (4G 65)
EX9: E Bud 2D 82
EX9: Know 5A 82
Bridge Ct. EX4: Exe 3C 6
EX32: Land 2B 24
TQ9: Tot 5D 102
TQ13: Chud 6C 92
Bridge Cft. TQ13: Ashb 3G 99
BRIDGE END 5J 81
Bridgefield *EX11: Ott M* *3D 80*
(off Chineway Rd.)
Bridge Hill EX3: Top 5B 74
Bridgehill Gth. EX3: Top 5B 74
Bridgelands Cl. PL5: Plym 1A 134
Bridgeland St. EX39: Bide 3F 23
Bridge La. EX39: Ins 3K 21
Bridge Mill La. PL21: Corn 7H 129
BRIDGEND 5K 149 (3B 174)
Bridgend Hill PL8: New F 5J 149
Bridge Pk. PL21: Ivy 4H 145
Bridge Plats Way EX39: Bide 3C 22
BRIDGE REEVE 2A 164
Bridge Retail Pk.
Torquay 5A 112
Bridge Rd. EX2: Cou W, Exmin 6J 71
EX6: Exmin 6J 71
EX8: Exmth 4C 76
EX9: Bud S 5D 82
TQ2: Torq 1B 116
TQ5: Chur F 3K 121
TQ5: Hill 7J 123
TQ6: Kingsw 3G 125
TQ9: Tot 5B 102
TQ14: Shal 6G 107
BRIDGERULE 3A 162
Bridgeside *TQ9: H'ford* *6B 100*
(off Woodland Rd.)
Bridge Site EX36: N Mol 2D 26
Bridge St. DT7: Lym R 5K 91
EX10: Sidb 2H 85
EX15: Uff 6H 43
EX16: Tive 4C 40
EX20: Hath 2H 35
EX39: Bide 4F 23
TQ7: Kingsb 4G 157
TQ11: B'leigh 4C 98
TQ12: Ipp 6H 101
Bridge St. Ho. *TQ12: New A* *1E 108*
(off Bank St.)
Bridge Ter. EX16: Bam 2H 33
EX16: Tive 4C 40
BRIDGETOWN
TA22 .1D 165
TQ9 . . . . .6G 103 (1A 176)
Bridgetown TQ9: Tot 6F 103
Bridgetown Ct. TQ9: Tot 6F 103
Bridgetown Hill TQ9: Tot 6F 103
Bridge Vw. EX5: Rock 3F 69
EX12: Brans 6H 85
PL5: Plym 3C 134
Bridgewater Gdns. TQ9: Tot 6G 103
Bridge Way EX4: Exe 4D 6
Bridgwater Cl. PL6: Plym 2C 136
Bridle Cl. PL7: Plymp 2E 138
TQ4: Good 7H 119
The Bridle Path TQ9: Tot 7E 102
BRIDPORT 1D 173
Bridwell Av. EX15: Uff 7F 43
Bridwell Cl. PL5: Plym 3D 134
Bridwell La. Nth. PL5: Plym 3D 134
Bridwell Rd. PL5: Plym 3D 134
BRIGHTLEY 1A 170
Brightley Rd. EX20: Oke 1C 48
Bright Vw. EX20: Oke 4A 48
Brimacombe Rd. EX39: Hart 2H 27
Brimblecombe Rd. EX31: Yell 7C 16
Brim Brook Ct. *TQ2: Torq* *5H 111*
(off Chinkwell Ri.)
Brimhay TQ9: Darti 3B 102
Brim Hill TQ1: Maid 1J 113
Brimhill Cl. PL7: Plymp 6E 138
Brimhill La. PL19: Horn 1E 60
Brimlands TQ5: Brixh 4D 122
Brimlands Ct. *TQ5: Brixh* *4D 122*
(off New Rd.)
BRIMLEY .3C 171
Brimley Bus. Pk. TQ13: Bov T 6B 92
Brimley Ct. TQ13: Bov T 6A 92
Brimley Cross TQ13: Bov T 6A 92
Brimley Dr. TQ14: Teignm 4J 107
Brimley Gdns. TQ13: Bov T 6B 92
Brimley Grange TQ13: Bov T 6A 92
Brimley Halt TQ13: Bov T 6B 92
Brimley La. TQ13: Bov T 6A 92
Brimley Pk. TQ13: Bov T 6B 92
Brimley Rd. TQ13: Bov T 6A 92
Brimley Va. TQ13: Bov T 5B 92
Brimpenny Rd. EX8: Exmth 3E 76
Brinchcombe M. PL9: Plyms 3E 142
Brinkburn Ct. EX10: Sidm 7B 84
Briseham Cl. TQ5: Brixh 5F 123
Briseham Rd. TQ5: Brixh 5F 123
Brismar Wlk. PL6: Plym 4D 136
Bristol Row PL20: Bere F 6C 128
Britannia Av. TQ6: Dartm 6C 124
Britannia Mus. 5E 124
Britannia Pl. PL4: Plym 2C 142
Britannia Row *EX34: Ilfra* *2J 11*
(off Broad St.)
Britannia Way EX39: W Ho 5D 20
Britcheston Cl. PL9: Spri 7H 143
Briton St. EX16: Bam 2H 33
Briton St. La. EX6: Dunsf 6C 62
Brittany Rd. EX8: Exmth 1E 76
Brittany St. PL1: Plym 5A 8 (3G 141)
Britten Dr. EX2: Won 7A 66
EX32: B'aple 4G 19

Britton Cl.—Budleigh Salterton

Britton Cl. EX16: Hal 6C 42
The Brittons EX33: Brau 5K 15
Brittons Cl. EX33: Brau 5K 15
Briwere Rd. TQ1: Torq 6A 112
BRIXHAM 3F 123 (2B 176)
Brixham Battery Heritage Cen.
. . . . .2D 122 (2B 176)
Brixham Ent. Est. TQ5: Brixh 4F 123
Brixham Heritage Mus. . . .3E 122 (2B 176)
Brixham Holiday Pk. 2D 122
Brixham Leisure Cen. 4F 123
Brixham Park & Ride 3K 121
Brixham Rd. TQ4: Good, Paig 3E 118
TQ5: Brixh, Chur F 3K 121
TQ6: Kingsw 6H 125
Brixham Theatre 3E 122
Brixham Wlk. PL6: Plym 3F 137
Brixham Yacht Club 2F 123
BRIXINGTON 2F 77
Brixington Dr. EX8: Exmth 2F 77
Brixington La. EX8: Exmth 3E 76
(not continuous)
Brixington Pde. EX8: Exmth 2F 77
BRIXTON 2H 149 (2B 174)
Brixton Cvn. & Camping Pk. 3G 149
Brixton Lodge Gdns. PL8: Brixt 2G 149
Broadacre Dr. TQ5: Brixh 3F 123
Broad Cl. EX17: Cred 6F 39
EX36: N Mol 2D 26
Broadclose Rd. EX31: B'aple 6C 18
BROADCLYST 5C 52 (1D 171)
Broadclyst Leisure Cen.
EX5: Broadc 7D 52
Broadclyst Rd. EX5: Whim 5F 53
BROADCLYST STATION 1K 67
Broadfield Rd. EX32: B'aple 5F 19
Broadfields Rd. EX2: Won 7B 66
Broadgate EX1: Exe 4D 6 (6E 64)
Broadgate Cl. EX31: B'aple 2D 18
EX33: Brau 4J 15
Broadgate Cres. TQ12: Kingsk 1F 111
Broadgate La. EX17: Morc 2C 38
Broadgate Rd. TQ12: Kingsk 7J 109
Broadhays Dr. EX5: Cran 2F 69
BROADHEMBURY 3B 166
BROADHEMPSTON 1A 176
Broadland Gdns. PL9: Plyms 4H 143
Broadland La. PL9: Plyms 4G 143
BROADLANDS 1C 108
Broadlands EX5: Thor 3A 50
EX39: Bide 4J 23
EX39: Nort 4E 20
TQ14: Shal 6G 107
Broadlands Av. TQ12: New A 1D 108
Broadlands Cl. PL7: Plymp 6D 138
Broadlands Ct. TQ12: New A 1D 108
Broadlands Rd. TQ4: Paig 3G 119
Broad La. EX16: Tive 5B 40
EX33: Brau, Lob 2F 15
EX39: App 3G 21
Broadleaf Cl. EX1: Pin 4D 66
Broad Leaf Pk. TQ14: Teignm 2K 107
Broadley Ct. PL6: Robo 1C 132
Broadley Dr. TQ2: Torq 3J 115
Broadley Pk. Rd. PL6: Robo 1B 132
Broadmead EX5: W'bury 5B 78
EX8: Exmth 2F 77
Broadmead Bungs. EX32: B'aple 7H 19
Broadmeade Ct. TQ12: New A 2G 109
Broadmead Gdns. EX35: Lynt 2G 13
Broadmeadow Av. EX4: Exe 1C 70
Broadmeadow Ind. Est.
TQ14: Teignm 4F 107
Broadmeadow La.
TQ14: Bi'ton, Teignm 3E 106
Broadmeadow Sports Cen. 4F 107
Broadmeadow Vw.
TQ14: Teignm 3F 107
Broadmoor La. EX20: Oke 3A 48
BROAD OAK 5H 79 (1A 172)
BROADOAK 1D 173
Broadoak Cl. EX11: W Hill 5H 79
Broad Oak Cres. TQ9: Tot 6F 103
Broadoaks PL7: L Moor 2H 129
Broad Pk. PL9: Plyms 5D 142
TQ6: Dartm 6D 124
Broadpark EX5: Bram S 6F 51
EX20: Oke 3D 48
TQ13: Ashb 2H 99
TQ13: Bov T 6A 92
Broad Pk. Av. EX34: Ilfra 4G 11
Broad Pk. Cl. EX33: Croy 2C 14
EX34: Ilfra 4G 11
Broad Pk. Cres. EX34: Ilfra 4G 11
Broad Pk. Rd. PL3: Plym 5J 135
PL20: Bere A 1B 128
Broadpark Rd. EX8: Exmth 3E 76
TQ2: Torq 3J 115
TQ3: Paig 6F 115
Broadparks Av. EX4: Pin 2D 66
Broadparks Cl. EX4: Pin 2D 66
Broad Pk. Ter. EX20: N Taw 6C 36
Broad Path EX15: Uff 5H 43
Broadpath TQ9: Sto G 4B 120
(not continuous)
Broad Reach TQ4: Broads 1J 121
Broadridge Cl. TQ12: New A 7A 104
Broad Rd. TQ6: Kingsw 3K 125
BROADSANDS 1H 121
Broadsands Av. TQ4: Broads 1J 121
Broadsands Bend TQ4: Broads 7J 119
Broadsands Ct. TQ4: Broads 1H 121
Broadsands Gdns. TQ5: Chur F 2J 121
Broadsands Pk. Rd.
TQ4: Broads 7J 119
Broadsands Pitch & Putt Course . . .1A 122
Broadsands Rd. TQ4: Broads 1H 121
BROADSHARD 2D 167
Broad Steps *TQ5: Brixh* . . . . *.3E 122*
(off Higher St.)
Broadstone TQ6: Dartm . . .1A 124 (5F 125)
Broadstone Pk. Rd.
TQ2: Torq 3K 115
Broad St. DT7: Lym R 5K 91
EX11: Ott M 4C 80
EX34: Ilfra 2J 11
EX36: S Mol 6C 26
PL16: Lift 6B 56
PL21: Modb 6G 147
Broad Vw. TQ9: Darti 3B 102
Broadview EX5: Broadc 6C 52
Broadwalk Ho. EX1: Exe 4F 7
BROADWAY 2D 167
Broadway EX2: Exe 2C 70
EX5: W'bury 6B 78
EX5: Whim 6G 53
EX10: Sidm 5A 84
EX31: Frem 6G 17
The Broadway EX8: Exmth 4G 77
PL9: Plyms 5F 143
Broadway Av. TQ12: Kingst 3G 105
B'way. Hill EX2: Exe 2B 70
Broadway La. EX33: Croy 1C 14
Broadway Rd. TQ12: Kingst 3F 105
BROADWINDSOR 3D 167
BROADWOODKELLY 3A 164
BROADWOODWIDGER 2C 169
Broady Strap EX31: Frem 6G 17
Brockey Wlk. EX2: Sow 1C 72
Brockhole La. PL7: Plymp 1B 138
Brock Ho. PL4: Plym 5F 9
Brockhurst Pk. TQ3: Marl 4D 114
Brockley Rd. PL3: Plym 7D 136
Brocks La. TQ12: Teigng 1C 104
Brockton Gdns. PL6: Plym 4C 132
Brodick Cl. EX4: Exe 3G 65
Bromhead Ct. PL6: Plym 3B 136
Bromhill La. EX33: N Buck 5E 14
Bromley Pl. PL2: Plym 7F 135
Brompton Gdns. TQ1: Torq 1G 117
BROMPTON RALPH 1A 166
BROMPTON REGIS 1D 165
Bronescombe Av. TQ14: Bi'ton 3C 106
Bronshill M. TQ1: Torq 7D 112
Bronshill Rd. TQ1: Torq 7D 112
Bronte Ct. EX8: Exmth 5E 76
Bronte Ho. EX2: Won 2J 71
Bronte Pl. PL5: Plym 2J 135
Bronzerock Vw. EX7: Holc 7F 97
BROOK 7H 59
Brook Cl. EX1: Whip 4A 66
EX7: Holc 7F 97
EX10: Sidf 1D 84
PL7: Plymp 6D 138
TQ13: Bov T 4B 92
Brook Ct. EX31: Rou 6A 18
TQ5: Brixh 4D 122
Brookdale EX11: Ott M 3D 80
Brookdale Av. EX34: Ilfra 3G 11
Brookdale Cl. TQ5: Brixh 4D 122
Brookdale Ct. TQ5: Brixh 4D 122
Brookdale Pk. TQ5: Brixh 4D 122
Brookdale Ter. EX7: Daw 4H 97
EX32: B'aple . . . . *.5G 19*
(off Victoria St.)
BROOKEADOR 7J 109
Brooke Av. EX2: Won 2J 71
Brooke Cl. PL12: Salt 1A 134
Brookedor TQ12: Kingsk 7J 109
Brookedor Gdns. TQ12: Kingsk 7J 109
Brooke Rd. EX16: W'ridge 6H 33
Brookfield EX39: Bide 5D 22
Brookfield Cl. EX33: Brau 5J 15
PL7: Plymp 4E 138
TQ3: Pres 6J 115
TQ12: Kingst 3H 105
Brookfield Ct. *TQ13: Chud* . . . . *.1D 94*
(off New Exeter St.)
Brookfield Dr. EX24: Colyt 6D 88
TQ14: Teignm 2J 107
Brookfield Gdns. EX2: Alph 4E 70
Brookfield M. EX4: Exe 1C 6 (5E 64)
Brookfield Orchard
TQ12: Kingst 4H 105
Brookfield Pl. EX34: Ilfra 3H 11
Brookfield Rd. EX9: E Bud 1D 82
Brookfield St. EX39: Bide 4G 23
Brook Gdns. PL21: Ugb 6E 146
Brook Grn. Ter. EX4: Exe 1G 7 (5G 65)
Brook Haven Cl. TQ12: Kingsk 7J 109
Brookhayes Cl. EX8: Exmth 4D 76
Brookhill TQ6: Kingsw 7H 125
Brook Ho. *EX7: Daw* . . . . *.4F 97*
(off Church St.)
Brooking Cl. PL6: Plym 2B 136
Brookingfield Cl. PL7: Plymp 6K 137
Brooklands EX2: Exe 3J 71
EX7: Daw . . . . *.4G 97*
(off Alexandra Rd.)
TQ9: Tot 6G 103
Brooklands Ct. PL6: Plym 7K 131
Brooklands Farm Cl. EX13: Kilm 3C 88
Brooklands La. TQ2: Torq 2A 116
Brooklands Orchard EX11: Ott M 3D 80
EX13: Kilm 3C 88
Brooklands Rd. EX8: Exmth 3F 77
Brookland Ter. *EX11: Ott M* . . . . *.4D 80*
(off Brook St.)
Brook La. EX10: Sidf 1D 84
PL19: Tavi 6H 59
TQ14: Shal 6F 107
Brookleigh Av. EX1: Heav 7A 66
Brooklyn Cl. EX1: Sow 6C 66
Brooklyn Pk. EX8: Exmth 3E 76
Brook Mead PL8: Y'ton 2A 150
(not continuous)
Brook Mdw. EX8: Exmth 3E 76
EX10: New P 5H 81
EX36: S Mol 6D 26
Brook Mdw. Ct. EX9: Bud S 6A 82
Brook Orchard TQ12: Kingsk 7J 109
Brook Rd. EX9: Bud S 7C 82
EX15: Cull 5G 45
EX19: Dol 6H 31
PL21: Ivy 4H 145
TQ12: Ipp 6H 101
Brookside EX8: Lymp 6G 75
EX10: Sidm 3B 84
EX31: Bick 6K 17
TQ7: Kingsb 5F 157
Brookside Cl. EX13: Kilm 2B 88
PL9: Hey B 4B 148
TQ14: Teignm 4G 107
Brookside Cres. EX4: Whip 2A 66
Brookside Pathway *TQ9: Darti* . . . . *.3D 102*
(off Nellies Wood Vw.)
Brookside Vs. EX34: C Mar 7C 12
Brook St. EX7: Daw 4G 97
EX11: Ott M 4C 80
EX16: Bam 2H 33
PL19: Tavi 3J 59
TQ7: Slap 1H 159
Brooks Warren EX5: Cran 3C 68
Brook Ter. EX12: Axmth 3H 87
Brookvale Cl. TQ14: Shal 7F 107
Brookvale Orchard TQ14: Shal 7F 107
Brook Vw. TQ9: Tot 5B 102
Brook Way TQ12: Kingst 1G 105
Brookway EX1: Whip 5A 66
Brookwood Cl. TQ10: S Bre 1B 100
Broomborough Ct. TQ9: Tot 6D 102
Broomborough Dr. TQ9: Tot 6C 102
Broom Cl. EX2: Won 7K 65
EX7: Daw 1J 97
Broome Cl. EX13: Axmin 3J 89
BROOMFIELD 1C 167
Broomfield Dr. PL9: Hooe 6C 142
Broomhill EX6: Chri 1K 63
EX16: Tive 4B 40
TQ13: Chag 2J 61
Broomhill Sculpture Gardens 3B 160
Broomhill Way TQ2: Torq 4A 112
Broomhouse Pk. EX16: W'ridge 6H 33
Broom Pk. EX5: Cran 3B 68
EX20: Oke 2E 48
PL9: Hooe 7E 142
TQ2: Torq 2B 112
TQ9: Darti 2A 102
Broom Pk. Hill TQ9: Darti 1A 102
Broughton Cl. PL3: Plym 4A 136
Brow Hill TQ12: H'fld 2K 93
Brownhill La. PL9: Wem 6C 148
Brownhills Rd. TQ12: New A 1D 108
Browning Cl. EX2: Won 1K 71
Browning Ct. EX2: Exe 7B 6
Browning Rd. PL2: Plym 6F 135
Brownings End TQ12: E Ogw 3C 108
Brownings Mead EX6: Dunsf 7C 62
Brownings Wlk. TQ12: E Ogw 3C 108
Brownlands Cl. EX10: Sidm 5D 84
Brownlands Rd. EX10: Sidm 5D 84
Brownlees EX6: Exmin 2C 74
Brownlow St. PL1: Plym 3G 141
Brown's Bri. La. EX15: Will 2A 44
Browns Bri. Rd. TQ2: Torq 3K 111
Brownscombe Cl. TQ3: Marl 4D 114
Brown's Hill TQ6: Dartm 1A 124
BROWNSTON 2C 175
BROWNSTONE 3B 164
Brownstone Rd. TQ6: Kingsw 7K 125
Brownston St. PL21: Modb 6G 147
Broxton Dr. PL9: Plyms 3E 142
Brunel Av. PL2: Plym 6E 134
TQ2: Torq 1D 112
Brunel Cl. EX4: Exe 2A 6 (5D 64)
TQ14: Teignm 3J 107
Brunel Ct. EX7: Daw 4H 97
Brunel M. *TQ2: Torq* . . . . *.2B 116*
(off Solsbro Rd.)
Brunel Rd. EX6: Star 1D 96
EX15: Cull 2K 45
TQ4: Broads 1J 121
TQ12: New A 1G 109
Brunel Ter. PL2: Plym 6E 134
Brunel Vw. EX6: Exmin 1D 74
Brunel Way PL1: Plym 6A 8 (3G 141)
PL21: Ivy 3J 145
Brunenburg Way EX13: Axmin 5H 89
Brunswick Pl. EX7: Daw 4G 97
PL2: Dev 7E 134
Brunswick Rd.
PL4: Plym 5J 9 (3A 142)
Brunswick Sq. *TQ1: Torq* . . . . *.7B 112*
(off Teignmouth Rd.)
Brunswick St. EX4: Exe 6A 6 (7D 64)
TQ14: Teignm 5J 107
Brunswick Ter. TQ1: Torq 7B 112
BRUSHFORD
EX18 .3A 164
TA22 .1D 165
Brutus Cen. *TQ9: Tot* . . . . *.6E 102*
(off Station Rd.)
Brymon Way PL6: Plym 6C 132
Brynhyfryd Gdns. EX31: B'aple 7B 18
Brynmoor Cl. PL3: Plym 4B 136
Brynmoor Pk. PL3: Plym 4B 136
Brynmoor Wlk. PL3: Plym 5B 136
Brynsworthy La. EX31: Bick, Rou 7K 17
Brynsworthy Pk. EX31: Rou 6A 18
Brynworthy Ct. EX31: Rou 7K 17
Buchanan Cl. EX14: Hon 5E 54
BUCKERELL 3B 166
Buckerell Av. EX2: Exe 2H 71
Buckeridge Av. TQ14: Teignm 3H 107
Buckeridge Rd. TQ14: Teignm 2H 107
BUCKFAST 2C 98 (1D 175)
Buckfast Abbey 2D 98 (1D 175)
Buckfast Cl. PL2: Plym 3E 134
PL21: Ivy 5H 145
TQ11: Buck 3D 98
BUCKFASTLEIGH 4C 98 (1D 175)
Buckfastleigh Holy Trinity Church
Viewpoint 1D 175
Buckfastleigh Station
South Devon Railway
. . . . .4E 98 (1D 175)
Buckfastleigh Swimming Pool 5C 98
Buckfast Rd. TQ11: Buck 2D 98
Buckingham Cl. EX8: Exmth 5G 77
EX36: S Mol 7C 26
Buckingham Orchard TQ13: Chud K . . .5B 94
Buckingham Pl. PL5: Plym 1C 134
Buckingham Rd. EX2: Sow 2C 72
BUCKLAND 2J 109
Buckland Abbey 7A 126 (1A 174)
Buckland Brake TQ12: New A 2H 109
BUCKLAND BREWER 2H 29 (1C 163)
Buckland Cl. EX39: Bide 5D 22
PL7: Plymp 2A 138
Buckland Ct. PL20: C'stone 6C 126
Buckland Cross EX33: Brau 3H 15
BUCKLAND FILLEIGH 3C 163
Buckland Hgts. TQ12: New A 1J 109
BUCKLAND IN THE MOOR 3B 170
BUCKLAND MONACHORUM
. . . . .5A 126 (1A 174)
Buckland Rd. EX33: Geo 5C 14
EX39: Bide, Lit 7B 22
TQ12: New A 2H 109
(Buckland Brake, not continuous)
TQ12: New A 1J 109
(Haytor Dr.)
BUCKLAND ST MARY 2C 167
Buckland St. PL1: Plym 5C 8 (3H 141)
Buckland Ter. PL20: Yelv 5F 127
BUCKLAND-TOUT-SAINTS 3D 175
Buckland Vw. EX39: Buck B 2H 29
TQ12: New A 7G 105
Buckland Wlk. EX6: Exmin 1B 74
BUCKLEIGH 6B 20 (1C 163)
Buckleigh Grange EX39: W Ho 6B 20
Buckleigh Rd. EX39: W Ho 6B 20
Buckle Ri. EX1: Pin 3G 67
Buckley Rd. EX10: Sidb 3J 85
Buckley St. TQ8: Salc 3D 158
Bucknall Cl. EX12: Brans 6H 85
Bucknill Cl. EX6: Exmin 2C 74
Bucks Cl. TQ13: Bov T 4C 92
BUCK'S CROSS 1B 162
Bucks La. TQ13: Bov T 4C 92
BUCK'S MILLS 1B 162
Buckthorn Ct. PL6: Plym 4H 131
Buckwell Cl. TQ7: Kingsb 3G 157
Buckwell Rd. TQ7: Kingsb 3G 157
Buckwell St. PL1: Plym 5F 9 (3K 141)
Buctor Pk. PL19: Tavi 5F 59
Buddle Cl. PL9: Plyms 7H 143
PL19: Tavi 3H 59
PL21: Ivy 4J 145
Buddle La. EX4: Exe 7C 64
EX20: Hath 2H 35
BUDE 3A 162
Bude Hill EX19: Wink 3E 36
Bude St. EX1: Exe 3F 7 (6F 65)
EX39: App 3H 21
BUDLAKE 3D 165
Budlake Old Post Office 1D 171
Budlake Rd. EX2: Matf 4F 71
Budleigh Cl. PL9: Plyms 7G 143
TQ1: Torq 7F 113
Budleigh Hill EX9: E Bud 2D 82
BUDLEIGH SALTERTON . . .7C 82 (2A 172)

Budleigh Salterton Information Centre
. . . . .7C 82 (2A 172)
Budshead Grn. PL5: Plym 6H 131
Budshead Rd. PL5: Plym 7E 130
PL6: Plym 7K 131
Budshead Way PL6: Plym 1K 135
Budshead Wood
Local Nature Reserve 6F 131
Buena Vista Cl. PL6: Plym 4E 132
Buena Vista Dr. PL6: Plym 4D 132
Buena Vista Gdns. PL6: Plym 4D 132
Buena Vista Way PL6: Plym 4D 132
Bugle Pl. TQ12: New A 6A 104
Bulgis Pk. EX36: S Mol 5B 26
BULKWORTHY 2B 162
Bullands Cl. TQ13: Bov T 3B 92
Bull Ct. EX31: B'aple 4E 18
Bulleid Cl. PL2: Plym 4E 134
Bullens Cl. EX5: Thor 3A 50
Bullen St. EX5: Thor 2A 50
Buller Cl. EX15: Cull 3H 45
PL7: Plymp 5C 138
PL11: Torp 1A 140
Buller Ct. EX2: Exe 7A 6 (1D 70)
Buller Ho. EX2: Exe 3J 71
(off Turnstone Rd.)
Buller Rd. EX4: Exe 6A 6 (7D 64)
EX17: Cred 5G 39
EX32: B'aple 4F 19
PL11: Torp 1A 140
TQ12: New A 2G 109
Bullfinch Cl. EX15: Cull 5F 45
Bull Hill EX31: B'aple 2E 18
EX39: Bide 4F 23
Bull Mdw. Rd. EX2: Exe 6F 7 (7F 65)
Bullow Vw. EX19: Wink 3C 36
Bull Point PL5: Plym 3A 134
Bull Point Barracks PL5: Plym . . .3A 134
Bull Point Lighthouse 2A 160
Bull Ring TQ13: Ashb 4H 99
Bulls Ct. EX24: Colyt 6D 88
Bulmer Rd. PL4: Plym 4K 9 (2B 142)
Bulteel Gdns. PL6: Plym 3K 131
BULVERTON 4A 84
Bulverton Pk. EX10: Sidm 4A 84
Bulwark Cl. PL5: Plym 2J 135
Bumble Wlk. PL8: Y'ton 2A 150
Bunclarks PL21: Lutt 7G 129
(off Old Rd.)
Bunkers Farm TQ9: E All 7D 152
Bunker Sq. EX2: Cou W 3C 72
Bunn Rd. EX8: Exmth 1F 77
Bunting Cl. TQ12: E Ogw 3D 108
TQ14: Teignm 3G 107
The Buntings EX6: Exmin 2B 74
Bunting Way EX7: Daw 6G 97
Bunts La. EX12: Seat 5C 86
Bunyan Cl. PL5: Plym 1H 135
Burch Cl. EX8: Exmth 2C 76
Burch Gdns. EX7: Daw 1H 97
Burdouns Way
TQ12: Kingst, New A 1H 105
Burgh Island C'way. TQ7: Bigb S . .3A 154
Burgh Island Causeway
Leisure Cen. 3A 154
Burgmanns Hill EX8: Lymp 6F 75
Burke Rd. TQ9: Tot 5F 103
The Burlands EX14: Fen 2G 53
Burleigh La. PL3: Plym 4J 135
Burleigh Mnr. PL3: Plym 4J 135
Burleigh Pk. Rd. PL3: Plym 5J 135
Burleigh Rd. TQ2: Torq 6J 111
BURLESCOMBE 2A 166
BURLESTONE 3A 176
Burlington Cl. EX38: B'aple 7G 19
Burlington Gro. EX32: B'aple 7G 19
Burnard Cl. PL6: Plym 3K 131
Burnards Cl. EX24: Colyt 6C 88
Burnards Fld. Rd. EX24: Colyt 6C 88
Burnet Cl. EX2: Won 2B 72
Burnet Rd. TQ12: New A 6A 104
Burnett Rd. PL6: Plym 3A 136
Burnham Ct. TQ12: Kingst 4H 105
(off Orchid Av.)
Burnham Pk. Rd. PL3: Plym 4J 135
Burniston Cl. PL7: Plymp 6D 138
Burnley Cl. TQ12: New A 7A 104
Burnley Rd. TQ12: New A 7A 104
Burn River Ri. TQ2: Torq 5H 111
Burns Av. EX2: Won 2J 71
PL5: Plym 1G 135
Burnside EX8: Exmth 3D 76
Burnside Rd. EX34: Ilfra 5G 11
Burns La. PL21: Modb 6G 147
Burnthouse Hill EX8: N Whil 5E 110
Burnthouse La. EX2: Won 2J 71
Burnt Oak EX10: Sidb 3H 85
BURRATON 2A 174
Burrator Av. TQ20: Prin 6C 60
Burrator Dr. EX4: Exe 5B 64
Burrator Gdns. PL2: Plym 4E 134
Burrator Reservoir
Woodland Walks 1B 174
Burrator Rd. PL20: Dous 4K 127
BURRIDGE 3D 167
Burridge Av. TQ2: Torq 1K 115
Burridge La. TQ2: Torq 1C 116

Burridge Rd. EX5: Bram S 7F 51
TQ2: Torq 1K 115
BURRINGTON 2A 164
Burrington Bus. Pk. PL5: Plym 2F 135
Burrington Ind. Est. PL5: Plym 2F 135
Burrington Rd. PL5: Plym 2F 135
Burrington Way PL5: Plym 2F 135
Burrough Flds. EX5: Broadc 3B 68
Burrough Lawn EX39: Nort 6F 21
(off Burrough Rd.)
Burrough Rd. EX39: Nort 6F 21
BURROW
EX5 . . . . .5E 52
EX10 . . . . .5F 81 (2A 172)
The Burrow EX12: Seat 6F 87
BURROWBRIDGE 1D 167
Burrow Cl. EX10: New P 5F 81
The Burrowe EX17: Cred 6H 39
Burrow Farm Gardens 1C 173
Burrow Hill PL9: Plyms 6F 143
Burrow Rd. EX5: Broadc 5D 52
EX12: Seat 6F 87
EX34: Ilfra 3H 11
Burrows Centre 2D 20
Burrows Cl. EX33: Brau 5H 15
Burrows La. EX39: App 3F 21
Burrows Pk. EX33: Brau 5H 15
(not continuous)
Burrows Way EX39: Nort 4E 20
Burscombe La. EX10: Sidb, Sidf . . .1B 84
BURSCOTT 6G 27
Bursledon Ct. EX7: Daw 4J 97
(off E. Cliff Rd.)
BURSTOCK 3D 167
BURSTON 3B 164
Burton Art Gallery & Mus.
. . . . .2F 23 (1C 163)
Burton Cl. PL6: Plym 4C 132
Burton Pl. TQ5: Brixh 4E 122
Burton St. TQ5: Brixh 5E 122
Burton Villa Cl. TQ5: Brixh 4E 122
Burvill St. EX35: Lynt 2G 13
Burwell Cl. PL6: Plym 6F 133
Burwood La. EX38: G Tor 2D 30
Burwood La. EX38: G Tor 3E 30
Burwood Pl. TQ14: Teignm 3K 107
Burwood St. EX38: G Tor 2D 30
BURY 1D 165
The Bury EX5: Thor 2A 50
Bury Rd. TQ12: New A 7E 104
BUSH 3A 162
Bushell Rd. TQ12: New A 7D 104
The Bushens EX32: B Taw 6A 24
Bushes La. EX12: skmth 3K 87
Bushmead Av. TQ12: Kingsk 7K 109
Bush Pk. PL6: Plym 7G 133
Butchers La. TQ10: S Bre 1B 100
(off Stockbridge La.)
Butcher's Moor La. EX19: Wink 1B 36
Butchers Row EX31: B'aple 4E 18
EX39: Bide 4F 23
(off Market Pl.)
Butcombe La. EX17: Morc 3E 38
Bute Rd. PL4: Plym 7B 136
Butland Av. EX17: Cred 3J 115
Butland Rd. TQ12: Kingst 3G 105
Butler Cl. EX16: Tive 5E 40
PL6: Plym 4C 132
Buttercombe Cl. TQ12: E Ogw 4C 108
Buttercup Cl. EX12: Seat 2F 87
Buttercup Cl. EX15: Will 3E 44
PL6: Plym 1B 136
Buttercup Wlk. EX7: Daw 3H 97
Buttercup Way TQ12: New A 6A 104
Butterdon Stone Row 2C 175
Butterdon Wlk. PL21: Ivy 4K 145
Butterlake TQ3: Marl 2D 114
BUTTERLEIGH 3D 165
Butterleigh Dr. EX16: Tive 5E 40
Butterpark PL21: Ivy 4H 145
Buttersby La. PL4: Plym 2K 9
Buttery Cl. EX14: Hon 5F 55
Buttery Rd. EX14: Hon 5F 55
Buttgarden St. EX39: Bide 4F 23
Buttlands Ind. Est. TQ12: Ipp 6J 101
Button La. EX31: Brat F 4H 13
PL21: Ivy 5J 145
Butt Pk. TQ20: Buck M 5A 126
Butt Pk. PL5: Plym 1G 135
Butt Parks EX17: Cred 7J 39
Butt Pk. Ter. TQ7: Chur 1B 156
BUTTS 6B 62
The Butts EX24: Colyt 6C 88
TQ7: Lodd 1G 151
Butts Cl. EX6: Bridf 1F 63
EX14: Hon 6E 54
EX16: W'ridge 6J 33
Butts Ct. EX2: Heav 7K 65
Buttsford Ter. PL21: L Mill 5A 144
(off New Pk. Rd.)
Butts Hill EX6: Kenton 6H 95
EX11: Ott M 3D 80
TQ3: Blag 6B 114
Butts La. EX6: Chri 4J 63
Buttsons Cl. TQ7: Stoke 6K 159

Butts Path EX33: Brau 4J 15
(not continuous)
Butts Rd. EX2: Heav 7K 65
EX11: Ott M 3D 80
Butts Way EX20: N Taw 6B 36
Buzzacott Cl. EX34: C Mar 7D 12
Buzzacott La. EX34: C Mar 7D 12
Buzzard Rd. PL19: Whit 7K 59
Buzz Bingo
Plymouth, Charles Cross 4F 9
Torquay 1C 116
Byard Cl. PL5: Plym 2D 134
Bydown EX32: Swim 4H 25
The Byes EX10: Sidm 6C 84
Byes Cl. EX10: Sidf 2D 84
Byeside Rd. EX10: Sidm 2D 84
Byes Cl. EX10: Sidm 2D 84
Byes La. EX10: Sidf 2E 84
Byeways Cl. EX31: Frem 6G 17
Bygones
Torquay 5E 112 (1B 176)
Byland Rd. PL3: Plym 5B 136
Byng Cl. TQ12: New A 7J 105
Byron Av. PL5: Plym 1G 135
Byron Cl. EX31: B'aple 2E 18
Byron Rd. EX2: Won 7B 66
TQ1: Torq 5C 112
Byron Way EX8: Exmth 7K 75
Byslades Intl. Touring Pk. 2A 114
BYSTOCK 1H 77 (2A 172)
Bystock Cl. EX4: Exe 2C 6 (5E 64)
Bystock M. EX8: Exmth 1G 77
Bystock Nature Reserve 2A 172
Bystock Rd. EX8: Exmth 1F 77
Bystock Ter. EX4: Exe 2C 6 (5E 64)
Byter Mill La. TQ9: Sto G 1A 120

C

Cabbage Hill TQ13: Ashb 5G 99
Cabourg Cl. TQ8: Salc 3C 158
CADBURY 3D 165
Cadbury Castle 3D 165
Cadbury Cl. EX1: Sow 5C 66
Cadbury Gdns. EX9: E Bud 1D 82
Caddsdown Ind. Pk. EX39: Bide . . .6C 22
Caddy Pl. EX2: Cou W 3C 72
Caddywell La. EX38: G Tor 2D 30
Caddywell Mdw. EX38: G Tor 2D 30
CADELEIGH 3D 165
Cadet La. EX31: Frem 5F 17
Cadewell Cres. TQ2: Torq 4K 111
Cadewell La. TQ2: Torq 5J 111
Cadewell Pk. Rd. TQ2: Torq 4J 111
. . . . .2A 80 (1A 172)
Cadhay Cl. EX11: Ott M 4A 80
Cadhay La. EX11: Coom, Ott M . . .2A 80
Cad La. TQ13: Ashb 4H 99
(off Stapleton La.)
Cadleigh Cl. PL21: L Mill 5C 144
Cadleigh La. PL21: Ivy 4D 144
CADLEIGHPARK 5C 144
Cadover Cl. PL6: Plym 2B 136
Cadwell Rd. TQ3: Paig 7H 115
Caen Fld. EX33: Brau 5J 15
Caen Fld. Shop. Cen. 4J 15
Caen Gdns. EX33: Brau 4J 15
Caen St. EX33: Brau 4J 15
Caen Vw. EX33: Brau 5H 15
Caernarvon Gdns. PL2: Plym 4G 135
Cairn Pleasure Ground & Old Railway
Nature Reserve 5G 11 (2B 160)
Cairn Rd. EX34: Ilfra 4H 11
Cairnside EX34: Ilfra 5H 11
Cake Down La. EX36: S Mol 6E 26
Calder Cl. PL3: Plym 5C 136
Caldicot Gdns. PL6: Plym 2C 132
Caledonia Cl. PL7: Plymp 4E 138
Calf St. EX38: G Tor 2C 30
California Cl. EX4: Exe 1G 65
California Gdns. PL3: Plym 5E 136
Callards Combe La. EX18: Chul 5A 32
CALLINGTON 3B 168
Callington Rd.
PL19: Tavi, T'tha 6F 59
Calm La. EX10: N'town 7J 81
CALSTOCK 1A 174
Calstock Cl. PL2: Plym 3H 135
Calstock Station (Rail) 1A 174
Calthorpe Rd. EX4: Exe 4J 65
Calvados Ho. EX32: B'aple 4F 19
(off Bevan Rd.)
Calvados Pk. TQ12: Kingst 4J 105
Calverleigh Cl. EX38: G Tor 1D 30
Calverford Rd. EX38: G Tor 2D 30
Camber Rd. PL1: Plym 7A 8 (4G 141)
Camborne Cl. PL5: Plym 5F 131
Camborne Cres. TQ4: Good 7H 119
Cambrian Cl. TQ4: Coll M 3D 118
Cambridge Gro. EX34: Ilfra 3J 11
Cambridge Rd. PL2: Plym 6E 134
TQ1: Torq 4D 112
TQ5: Brixh 4C 122
Cambridge St. EX4: Exe 6A 6 (7D 64)

Cambridge Ter. EX4: Exe 2G 7
(off Well St.)
EX10: Sidm 6C 84
(off Salcombe Rd.)
Cambridge Way EX15: Cull 4F 45
Camden Ct. PL4: Plym 3G 9
Camden Pl. PL4: Plym 3G 9
Camden Rd. TQ1: Torq 1D 116
Camden St. PL4: Plym 3G 9 (2K 141)
Camellia Cl. EX16: Tive 2F 41
TQ5: Chur F 2K 121
Camelot Cl. EX4: Whip 3K 65
CAMEL'S HEAD 4D 134
Cameron Cl. EX16: Tive 5B 40
Cameron Dr. PL21: Ivy 4E 144
Cameron Way PL6: Plym 2C 136
Camfield Dr. EX16: Tive 2F 41
Camilla Cl. EX4: Exe 2E 6
Camilla Ter. PL2: Plym 4J 135
Camomile Way TQ12: New A 6A 104
Campbell Rd. PL3: Plym 5G 143
Camperdown Rd. TQ8: Salc 4B 158
Camperdown St. PL2: Plym 7D 134
Camperdown St. La. Nth.
PL2: Plym 7D 134
(off Camperdown St.)
Camperdown Ter. EX8: Exmth 6A 76
Campion Cl. PL7: Plymp 4F 139
Campion Cl. EX15: Will 3D 44
Campion Dr. EX32: B'aple 4K 19
Campion Gdns. EX2: Won 2A 72
Campion Pl. TQ12: New A 6A 104
Campion Ri. PL19: Tavi 3K 59
Campion Vw. PL6: Plym 2F 133
Campion Way EX14: Hon 6C 54
Camplehaye Cotts. PL19: Lam 6C 58
Cample Haye Vs. PL5: Plym 2A 134
(off Little Ash Rd.)
Camp Rd. EX20: Oke 5C 48
Canaan Way EX11: Ott M 4C 80
Canada Hill TQ12: E Ogw 3C 108
Canal Banks EX2: Exe 2F 71
Canal Hill EX16: Tive 5E 40
Canal Rd. EX22: Hols 1D 34
PL19: Tavi 4H 59
Canal Way TQ12: Kingst 5G 105
Canberra Cl. EX4: Exe 2H 65
Canberra Rd. PL6: Plym 6C 132
The Candar EX34: Ilfra 2H 11
Candish Dr. PL9: Elb 7K 143
Candy's Path EX8: Lymp 6G 75
Canefields Av. PL7: Plymp 6E 138
Cane's Cotts. PL8: Brixt 2H 149
(off Elliotts Hill)
Canhaye Cl. PL7: Plymp 6D 138
Cann Bri. School PL6: Plym 1E 136
Cann Cotts. PL5: Tam F 4H 131
Cann Gdns. PL6: Plym 4J 131
Cannington Rd. EX16: W'ridge 6H 33
Cann Pk. EX14: Awli 2K 93
Cannon St. PL1: Dev 2C 140
Cannon St. Flats PL1: Dev 2C 140
(off Cannon St.)
Cann Wood
Local Nature Reserve 4G 131
Cann Woods Forest Walk 2B 174
Cann Woods Picnic Site 2B 174
Cann Wood Vw. PL6: Plym 3F 133
Canon Ho. EX1: Sow 4F 7
Canons Cl. TQ14: Bi'ton 3B 106
Canons Ga. TQ5: Brixh 6G 59
Canons Way PL19: Tavi 6G 59
Canonteign Falls 2C 171
Canonteign Falls Nature Trails 2C 171
Canon Way EX2: Alph 5E 70
Canterbury Cl. EX14: Fen 2G 53
PL21: Ivy 5J 145
Canterbury Dr. PL5: Plym 6G 131
Canterbury Rd. EX4: Exe 5B 64
Canterbury Way EX8: Exmth 1G 77
CANWORTHY WATER 1A 168
Capel Cl. EX8: Lit 5H 77
Capel Cotts. EX8: Exmth, Lit 4H 77
Capel La. EX8: Exmth, Lit 4H 77
Capern Cl. EX33: Wraf 6K 15
Capern Rd. EX39: Bide 4E 22
Capper Cl. EX10: New P 5G 81
Capra Cl. TQ12: New A 7J 105
Caprera Pl. PL4: Plym 2D 8
Caprera Ter. La. PL4: Plym . .2D 8 (1J 141)
Capstone Ct. EX34: Ilfra 3K 11
Capstone Cres. EX34: Ilfra 2J 11
Capstone Pde. EX34: Ilfra 1H 11
Capstone Pl. EX34: Ilfra 2J 11
(off Capstone Rd.)
Capstone Rd. EX34: Ilfra 2J 11
Captains Gdns. PL5: Plym 2K 135
Captains Rd. TQ12: Kingst 3G 105
CAPTON .2A 176
Caradon Cl. PL6: Plym 5B 132
Caradon Ct. TQ12: Kingst 2E 126
CARADON TOWN 3A 168
Carbeile Rd. PL11: Torp 2A 140
Carberry Av. EX8: Exmth 3C 76
CARADON TOWN 3A 168
Carbis Cl. PL5: Plym 6G 131
Carders Ct. EX2: Exe 6C 6 (7E 64)
Cardiff Cl. PL7: Plymp 5E 138
Cardigan Rd. PL6: Plym 2D 136
Cardinal Av. PL5: Plym 3C 134

Careswell Av.—Chapel Way

Careswell Av. PL2: Plym 3E 134
Carew Av. PL5: Plym 7G 131
Carew Gdns. PL5: Plym 7G 131
TQ12: New A 1J 109
Carew Gro. PL5: Plym 7G 131
Carew Rd. EX16: Tive 2D 40
Carew Ter. PL11: Torp 2A 140
Carew Wharf PL11: Torp 2B 140
Carey Rd. TQ6: Dartm 6C 124
CARGREEN 1A 130 (1A 174)
Carhaix Way EX7: Daw 2H 97
Carisbrooke Rd. PL6: Plym 2D 136
CARKEEL 1A 174
Carlile Rd. EX2: Won 7K 65
TQ5: Brixh 3C 122
Carling Ct. TQ7: Kingsb 5F 157
Carlisle Rd. PL5: Plym 7H 131
Carlisle St. TQ12: New A 1F 109
Carlton Cl. PL3: Plym 6C 136
TQ3: Pres 4J 115
Carlton Dr. TQ3: Pres 4J 115
Carlton Hill EX8: Exmth 7C 76
Carlton Pl. TQ14: Teignm 5J 107
Carlton Rd. EX2: Won 1A 72
TQ1: Torq 7E 112
Carlton Ter. EX7: Daw 4H 97
EX32: B'aple 5F 19
(off Barbican Rd.)
PL1: Plym 3A 8 (2G 141)
PL4: Plym 3J 9 (2A 142)
PL5: Plym 3D 134
Carlyle Av. EX32: B'aple 3F 19
Carlyon Cl. EX1: Heav 6K 65
Carlyon Gdns. EX1: Heav 6K 65
Carmarthen Rd. PL4: Plym 2C 142
Carmel Gdns. PL19: Tavi 4G 59
Carnac Dr. EX7: Daw 2H 97
Carnegie Nth. *EX39: Nort 6F 21*
(off Clevelands Pk.)
Carnegie Sth. *EX39: Nort 6F 21*
(off Clevelands Pk.)
Carnegie Wlk. EX2: Cou W 4D 72
Carnock Rd. PL2: Plym 3J 135
Carolina Gdns. PL2: Plym 4E 134
Caroline Av. EX2: Cou W 4C 72
Caroline Cl. EX8: Exmth 3F 77
TQ12: Kingsk 2G 111
Caroline Pl. PL1: Plym 3F 141
Carousel Ct. EX4: Exe 7A 6 (1D 70)
Carpenter Cl. EX4: Exe 4C 6 (6E 64)
EX16: Tive 5C 40
Carpenter Rd. PL9: Plyms 4G 143
Carpenters Ct. *TQ12: New A 2F 109*
(off Church Rd.)
Carradale Rd. PL6: Plym 4D 136
Carr Cl. TQ8: Salc 3B 158
Carrington Pl. EX14: Hon 4G 55
Carrington Ter. *EX32: B'aple 3F 19*
(off Yeo Vale Rd.)
Carrionpit La. EX19: Wink 2C 36
The Carrions TQ9: Tot 6E 102
Carr La. TQ7: Slap 1H 159
Carroll Rd. PL5: Plym 7H 131
Carrolls Way PL9: Spri 7H 143
Carron La. PL6: Robo 1E 132
Carslake Cl. EX10: Sidm 3D 84
Carswells TQ12: Kingsk 7J 109
Carter Av. EX8: Exmth 4C 76
Carter Rd. PL21: Ivy 3H 145
Cartwright Cres. TQ14: Teignm 3F 107
Cary Av. TQ1: Torq 6E 112
Cary Castle TQ1: Torq 5D 112
Cary Castle Dr. TQ1: Torq 5D 112
Cary Pde. TQ2: Torq 2D 116
Cary Pk. TQ1: Torq 6D 112
Cary Pk. Rd. TQ1: Torq 6E 112
Cary Rd. TQ2: Torq 2C 116
TQ3: Pres 5G 115
Caseberry La. EX5: Bradn 3A 52
Case Gdns. EX12: Seat 4F 87
Cassiobury Way TQ2: Torq 3A 112
Castle EX12: Brans 6J 85
Castle Acre Gdns. PL3: Plym 6C 136
Castle Bank Gdns. PL3: Plym 6C 136
Castle Barbican PL7: Plymp 5B 138
Castlebar Cl. EX16: Tive 5E 40
Castle Carey Gdns. PL3: Plym 6C 136
Castle Cir. TQ1: Torq 1C 116
Castle Cir. Ct. TQ1: Torq 1C 116
Castle Ct. EX32: Land 2C 24
TQ9: Tot 6D 102
Castle Drogo 1B 170
Castle Dyke La. PL1: Plym 6F 9
Castle Farm EX11: W Hill 4J 79
Castle Ga. EX6: Kenton 6J 95
Castle Ham Lodge EX20: Oke 4B 48
Castlehayes Gdns. PL7: Plymp 5B 138
Castle Hgts. EX35: Lynt 2H 13
Castle Hill EX12: Seat 6E 86
EX13: Axmin 3H 89
EX34: Ber 3C 12
EX34: Ilfra 2J 11
EX35: Lynt 2H 13
Castle Hill Av. EX34: Ilfra 3J 11
Castle Hill Gardens 1A 164
Castle Hill Gdns. EX38: G Tor 2C 30
Castle Hill Vw. EX10: Sidf 1D 84
Castle Hill Vis. Cen. 3C 30
Castle La. EX5: W'bury 5C 78
EX8: Lit .5H 77
EX20: Oke 5A 48
PL7: Plymp 5B 138
TQ1: Torq 1D 116
(not continuous)
TQ3: Comp 7C 110
TQ9: Blacka 2C 152
Castleman Way EX15: Cull 3K 45
Castle Mdw. EX39: Buck B 1H 29
Castle M. EX13: Axmin 3H 89
Castle Mill EX32: Land 2C 24
Castle Mt. EX4: Exe 1D 6 (5E 64)
Castle Pk. EX15: Hemy 2G 47
Castle Pk. Cl. TQ4: Paig 6F 119
Castle Pk. Dr. TQ4: Paig 6F 119
Castle Pk. Rd. EX32: B'aple 6K 19
Castle Pk. Way TQ4: Paig 7F 119
Castle Quay EX31: B'aple 4E 18
Castle Quay Ct. EX31: B'aple 4D 18
Castle Ri. PL3: Plym 7C 136
Castle Rd. EX20: Oke 4B 48
TQ1: Torq 1C 116
TQ6: Dartm 7G 125
TQ6: Kingsw 7G 125
Castle Rock EX34: Mort 4A 10
Castle St. EX4: Exe 3E 6 (6F 65)
EX13: Axmin 3H 89
EX16: Bam 2H 33
EX16: Tive 4D 40
EX19: Wink 2C 36
EX31: B'aple 4E 18
EX34: C Mar 7C 12
EX38: G Tor 2C 30
Castle St. EX39: Nort 6E 20
PL1: Plym 6F 9 (3K 141)
TQ9: Tot 5E 102
Castle Ter. EX34: Ilfra 3J 11
Castleton Cl. PL3: Plym 7B 136
Castle Vw. EX24: Colyt 6D 88
Castle Vw. Ter. *TQ9: Tot 5E 102*
(off Castle St.)
Castle Way TQ12: New A 7B 104
Castlewood Av. TQ12: New A 6B 104
Castor Cl. TQ5: Brixh 5F 123
Castor La. TQ4: Good 6H 119
Castor Rd. TQ5: Brixh 5E 122
The Catacombs 4C 6
Catalina Cl. EX14: Dunk 7H 47
Catalina Vs. PL9: Hooe 6B 142
Cat & Fiddle Pk. EX5: Clyst M 2K 73
Cater Rd. EX32: B'aple 5G 19
Catford Ct. EX15: Kent 6A 46
Cathcart Av. PL4: Plym 2C 142
Cathedral Cl. EX1: Exe 4E 6 (6F 65)
Cathedral St. PL1: Plym 3B 8 (2H 141)
Cathedral Yd. EX1: Exe 4D 6 (6E 64)
Catherine Cl. EX16: Tive 3E 40
Catherine Cres. TQ4: Paig 3F 119
Catherine Sq. EX1: Exe 4E 6
Catherine St. EX1: Exe 4E 6 (6F 65)
PL1: Plym 5E 8 (3J 141)
CATHERSTON LEWESTON 1D 173
Catnip Cl. EX13: Axmin 3J 89
CATON 3B 170
Cator TQ9: Sto G 3B 120
Catshole La. EX39: Bide 5E 22
CATTEDOWN 7K 9 (4B 142)
Cattedown Rd. PL4: Plym 5K 9 (3B 142)
(Embankment Rd.)
PL4: Plym 7K 9 (4B 142)
(Esso Wharf Rd.)
CATTEDOWN RDBT. 5J 9 (3A 142)
Catterick Cl. PL5: Plym 5D 130
Cattewater Rd. PL4: Plym 3C 142
Cauleston Cl. EX8: Exmth 2C 76
Caumont Cl. EX15: Uff 7F 43
Caunters Cl. TQ12: Ipp 6H 101
Causeway EX12: Beer 7B 86
Causeway Cl. EX39: Nort 5F 21
Causeway Cotts. EX12: Beer 6B 86
C'way. Cross TQ12: Ipp 6J 101
Causeway Vw. PL9: Hooe 5C 142
Causey Gdns. EX1: Pin 3D 66
Causey La. EX1: Pin 3D 66
CAUTE 2C 163
Cavalier Rd. TQ12: H'fld 1H 93
Cavalry Dr. TQ12: H'fld 3J 93
Cavell Way EX20: Oke 2C 48
Cavendish Cl. EX7: Daw 3F 97
Cavendish Pl. EX35: Lynt 2G 13
Cavendish Rd. EX1: Heav 3K 7 (6H 65)
PL4: Plym 3C 142
Cavern Rd. TQ1: Torq 1D 116
TQ5: Brixh 4E 122
Caversham Cl. EX6: Chri 3J 63
Cavie Cres. EX33: Brau 4G 15
Cavie Rd. EX33: Brau 4G 15
Cawley Av. EX13: Axmin 2K 89
CAWSAND .2A 174
Cawsand Vw. *EX20: Exbo 6J 35*
(off High St.)
Caxton Gdns. PL5: Plym 2H 135
Caxton Row EX16: Tive 2D 40
Cayley Way PL5: Plym 1E 134
Cayman Cl. TQ2: Torq 2A 112
Cecil Av. PL4: Plym 2K 9 (1B 142)
TQ3: Pres 6H 115
Cecil Cotts. PL1: Plym 4A 8 (2G 141)
Cecilia Rd. TQ3: Pres 5H 115
Cecil M. TQ3: Paig 7H 115
Cecil Rd. EX2: Exe 7B 6 (1D 70)
TQ3: Paig 1G 119
Cecil St. PL1: Plym 3B 8 (2H 141)
Cedar EX7: Daw W 7D 96
Cedar Av. PL9: Hooe 7D 142
Cedar Cl. EX5: Rock 3E 68
EX8: Exmth 1F 77
EX12: Seat 3E 86
EX13: Axmin 4H 89
EX14: Hon 4E 54
TQ14: Teignm 2K 107
Cedar Ct. EX5: Rock 3E 68
Cedar Ct. Rd. TQ1: Torq 6D 112
Cedarcroft Rd. PL2: Plym 4G 135
Cedar Dr. TQ7: Lodd 2G 151
Cedar Gdns. EX13: Axmin 4H 89
Cedar Gro. EX31: Rou 7A 18
Cedar Rd. EX16: Tive 3F 41
TQ3: Pres 5J 115
TQ12: New A 4J 109
The Cedars EX14: Hon 2H 55
TQ9: Tot 5G 103
Cedars Pk. EX31: B'aple 5A 18
Cedars Rd. EX2: Exe 7F 7 (7F 65)
TQ1: Torq 1E 116
Cedar Units TQ9: Darti 3B 102
Cedar Way EX39: Bide 5C 22
TQ5: Brixh 6C 122
Celandine Cl. EX12: Seat 3F 87
Celandine Gdns. PL7: Plymp 4F 139
Celandine Lawns EX15: Will 3D 44
Celia Cres. EX4: Whip 2K 65
Celtic Ct. *EX7: Daw 3H 97*
(off Celtic Flds.)
Celtic Flds. EX7: Daw 3H 97
Cembra Cl. EX14: Hon 4G 55
Cemetery La. EX5: Bradn 2C 52
Centenary Rd. PL1: Dev 2D 140
Centenary Way TQ2: Torq 3J 111
TQ13: Bov T 4E 92
Central Av. EX2: Cou W 6C 72
EX4: Whip 2A 66
EX22: Hols 2B 34
PL21: L Mill 4B 144
TQ3: Paig 7H 115
Central Cinema 4E 18
The Central Cinema 2D 116
Central Park 1D 8 (7H 135)
Central Pk. Av. PL4: Plym . . .1C 8 (1H 141)
Central Pk. Towers
PL4: Plym 1D 8 (1J 141)
Central Rd. PL1: Plym 7C 8 (4H 141)
Centre Ct. PL21: Moor 2C 146
Centry Ct. TQ5: Brixh 4G 123
Centry Rd. TQ5: Brixh 4G 123
Century Dr. EX39: Nort 6D 20
Century Quay PL4: Plym 5G 9
Ceramic Ter. *EX32: B'aple 5F 19*
(off Trinity St.)
Chaddiford La. EX31: B'aple 2C 18
CHADDLEHANGER 3C 169
CHADDLEWOOD 4F 139
Chaddlewood Av.
PL4: Plym 2J 9 (1A 142)
Chaddlewood Cl. PL7: Plymp 4C 138
Chaddlewood District Cen.
PL7: Plymp 4F 139
Chad Rd. PL9: Hey B 3B 148
CHAFFCOMBE 2D 167
Chaffcombe La. EX17: Cop 6A 38
Chaffinch Dr. EX15: Cull 5F 45
CHAGFORD 2H 61 (2B 170)
Chagford Cross TQ13: More 6G 61
Chagford Swimming Pool 1J 61
Chagford Wlk. PL6: Plym 3F 137
Chains Rd. EX16: Sam P 2A 42
Chalfield Cl. TQ2: Torq 2B 112
CHALLABOROUGH 2B 154 (3C 175)
Challaborough 3C 175
Challaborough Cvn. Pk. 1B 154
Challabrook La. TQ13: Bov T 5A 92
CHALLACOMBE 2C 161
Challacombe Cl. *EX32: Land 2C 24*
(off Blakes Hill Rd.)
Challacombe Hill EX34: Wool 7A 10
Challacombe Hill Rd.
EX34: Wool 6A 10
Challgood Cl. PL9: Plyms 7G 143
Challgood Ri. PL9: Plyms 7G 143
Challock Cl. PL6: Plym 6E 132
Challowell La. EX33: Brau 2H 15
Challycroft Rd. TQ5: Brixh 7C 122
Chaloner's Rd. EX33: Brau 3J 15
CHAMBERCOMBE 3K 11
Chambercombe La. EX34: Ilfra 4K 11
Chambercombe Manor 2B 160
Chambercombe Pk. Rd.
EX34: Ilfra 3K 11
Chambercombe Pk. Ter.
EX34: Ilfra 3K 11
Chambercombe Rd. EX34: Ilfra 3K 11
Chambercombe Ter. EX34: Ilfra 3K 11
Chamberlain Rd.
EX2: Exe 7D 6 (1E 70)
Chamberlayne Dr. PL7: Plymp 3B 138
Chambers Cl. EX10: Sidm 2B 84
Champernowne PL21: Modb 6G 147
Champernowne Cres. EX34: Ilfra 3K 11
Chancel Ct. EX4: Pin 3C 66
Chancel La. EX4: Pin 3C 66
Chancellor's Way EX4: Whip 2K 65
Chandlers Ct. EX39: Ins 3K 21
Chandlers Hgts. TQ8: Salc 3C 158
Chandlers La. EX10: Sidm 5C 84
Chandlers Wlk. EX2: Exe 7D 6 (1E 70)
Chandlers Way EX34: Ilfra 5H 11
Channel Pk. Av. PL3: Plym 6C 136
Channel Vw. EX34: Ilfra 4K 11
EX34: Mort 3B 10
Channel Vw. Dr. TQ7: Hope 3G 155
Channel Vw. La. EX7: Holc 7F 97
Channel Vw. Ter.
PL4: Plym 2K 9 (1B 142)
Chanter Ct. EX2: Cou W 3K 71
Chanter's Hill EX32: B'aple 4G 19
Chanters Rd. EX39: Bide 2F 23
(not continuous)
Chantry Av. EX39: Bide 2F 23
Chantry Cl. TQ14: Teignm 2K 107
Chantry Hill TQ7: Slap 2J 159
Chantry Mdw. EX2: Alph 5E 70
Chantry Orchard EX24: Colyt 5C 88
Chantry Pl. EX24: Colyt 5C 88
Chantry Rd. PL7: Plymp 6J 137
The Chapel *TQ9: Tot 6F 103*
(off The Plains)
Chapel Cl. EX16: Hal 6D 42
EX33: Brau 4J 15
PL20: Horr 2E 126
Chapel Cotts. PL7: L Moor 1J 129
Chapel Ct. *EX2: Alph 4E 70*
(off Church Rd.)
EX32: Swim 3H 25
TQ1: Torq 6B 112
TQ9: Sto G 3B 120
TQ13: Chud 1D 94
Chapeldown Rd. PL11: Torp 2A 140
Chapel Downs Dr. EX17: Cred 5F 39
Chapel Downs Rd. EX17: Cred 5F 39
Chapel Flds. TQ10: S Bre 1B 100
Chapel Hgts. PL19: Tavi 3J 59
Chapel Hill EX3: Clyst G 7H 73
EX8: Exmth 6C 76
EX9: Bud S 6C 82
EX15: Uff 6H 43
EX17: Cher F 1K 39
TQ12: New A 1E 108
Chapel La. EX10: Col R 2G 83
EX11: Ott M 3D 80
EX34: C Mar 6B 12
PL8: Y'ton 2B 150
PL19: Mary T 1B 60
PL20: Horr 2E 126
PL21: Lutt 7G 129
TQ6: Dartm 2A 124
TQ6: Sto F 3H 153
TQ7: Malb 6G 155
TQ9: Tot 6F 103
TQ12: Live 4G 93
Chapel Mdw. PL20: Buck M 5A 126
Chapel of St Lawrence *4H 99*
(off East St.)
Chapel Pk. Cl. EX39: Bide 3H 23
Chapel Pl. EX3: Top 5B 74
PL21: Erm 2H 147
PL21: Ivy 4H 145
Chapel Rd. EX2: Alph 4E 70
EX5: Bram S 5G 51
EX8: Lymp 6F 75
EX10: Sidm 7C 84
PL8: Torr 3C 150
TQ12: New A 1G 109
Chapel Row EX12: Brans 6F 85
PL11: Torp 1A 140
Chapel St. EX1: Exe 4E 6 (6F 65)
EX8: Exmth 6C 76
EX9: Bud S 7C 82
EX10: Sidb 3H 85
EX10: Sidm 7C 84
EX12: Axmth 3H 87
EX14: Hon 3F 55
EX16: Tive 4D 40
EX17: Morc 1B 38
EX19: Dol 6H 31
EX22: Hols 2C 34
EX33: Brau 5J 15
EX33: Geo 5B 14
EX39: Bide 3F 23
EX39: Wools 2B 28
PL1: Dev 2D 140
PL4: Plym 3F 9 (2K 141)
PL8: Holb 6C 150
PL16: Lift 6B 56
PL19: Tavi 4H 59
PL20: Bere A 2C 128
PL21: Erm 2H 147
TQ9: Blacka 3C 152
TQ11: B'leigh 4C 98
Chapel St. Ope PL1: Dev 2D 140
CHAPELTON 1D 163
Chapelton Station (Rail) 1D 163
Chapel Vs. PL7: L Moor 1J 129
Chapel Way PL3: Plym 5B 136

Chapel Wood Nature Trails 2A 160
CHAPMANS WELL 1B 168
Chapple Cl. EX6: Star 2E 96
Chapple Cross TQ13: Bov T 6A 92
Chapple Rd. EX16: W'ridge 6H 33
  TQ13: Bov T 5A 92
CHARD 3D 167
Chard Av. EX5: Whim 6G 53
Chard Barton PL5: Plym 7G 131
CHARD JUNCTION 3D 167
Chard Rd. EX1: Heav 6K 65
  EX13: Axmin, Wey 3J 89
  PL5: Plym 1C 134
Chards Orchard EX6: Kennf 1G 95
CHARDSTOCK 3D 167
Chardstock Cl. EX1: Sow 6C 66
Chard St. EX13: Axmin 3H 89
Charfield Dr. PL6: Plym 2B 136
Charingthay Ea. EX4: Exe 4H 65
Chariot Dr. TQ12: Kingst 5J 105
Charlbury Dr. PL9: Plyms 3E 142
Charlemont Rd. TQ14: Teignm . . .1H 107
CHARLES 3C 161
Charles Av. EX39: Bide 2F 23
Charles Church 4F 9
Charles Cross PL4: Plym 4F 9 (2K 141)
Charles Cross Centre 4F 9 (2K 141)
Charles Dart Cres. EX32: B'aple . .3F 19
Charles Darwin Rd. PL1: Dev 3E 140
Charles Hankin Cl. PL21: Ivy 5J 145
Charles Hudson La.
  EX31: B'aple 2F 19
Charles Rd. EX14: Hon 3F 55
  TQ12: Kingst 3G 111
Charles St. EX8: Exmth 5C 76
  EX32: B'aple 3E 18
  PL1: Plym 3F 9 (2K 141)
  TQ6: Dartm 1A 124 (6F 125)
Charles Ter. PL3: Plym 5B 136
Charlestown Rd. TQ3: Paig 7D 114
Charleton Way TQ7: W Cha 7K 157
Charlotte Cl. TQ2: Torq 5B 112
Charlotte M. EX2: Exe 5F 7
  (off Pavilion Pl.)
Charlotte St. EX17: Cred 6J 39
  PL2: Dev 7D 134
CHARLTON 1C 167
Charlton Ct. TQ14: Teignm 5J 107
  (off Bank St.)
Charlton Cres. PL6: Plym 1B 136
Charlton Ho. EX7: Daw 4H 97
  (off E. Cliff Rd.)
Charlton Rd. PL6: Plym 7A 132
Charlton Ter. PL21: Ivy 4H 145
Charlwood Ct. TQ1: Torq 5E 112
CHARMOUTH 1D 173
Charmouth Cl. DT7: Lym R 4K 91
  TQ1: Torq 7F 113
Charmouth Ho. DT7: Lym R 5H 91
  (off Portland Ct.)
Charmouth Rd. DT7: Lym R 3K 91
  EX13: Ray H 2C 90
Charnhill Cl. PL9: Elb 6H 143
Charnhill Way PL9: Elb 6H 143
Charnley Av. EX4: Exe 7B 64
Charter Cl. EX16: Tive 4A 40
Charter Ho. EX31: Rou 7K 17
Charter Rd. EX13: Axmin 2J 89
Chartwell Cl. TQ3: Paig 7E 114
Chartwell Dr. TQ12: New A 7D 104
Charwell Mdw. EX5: Bradn 2C 52
The Chase EX3: Top 7C 72
  EX14: Hon 2G 55
  EX20: Oke 2D 48
  PL21: Ivy 5H 145
CHASTY 4C 34 (3B 162)
Chasty La. EX22: Hols 4C 34
Chatham Cl. EX8: Exmth 3F 77
Chatsworth Gdns. PL5: Plym 7E 130
Chatsworth Rd. TQ1: Torq 7D 112
Chatto Rd. TQ1: Torq 6C 112
Chatto Way TQ1: Torq 6C 112
Chatwell La. PL21: Modb 5G 147
Chaucer Av. EX2: Won 2J 71
Chaucer Gro. EX4: Whip 4J 65
Chaucer Ri. EX8: Exmth 7K 75
Chaucer Rd. PL19: Tavi 4K 59
Chaucer Way PL5: Plym 2G 135
Chaves Cl. EX16: Tive 5F 41
CHAWLEIGH 2B 164
Chawleigh Hill EX18: Chaw, Chul . .7D 32
Chawleigh Week Hill
  EX18: Chaw 7B 32
Chawleigh Week La.
  EX18: Chaw 7A 32
Cheavestone Lea TQ9: Blacka 3B 152
Cheavestone Ter. TQ9: Blacka 3B 152
CHEDDON FITZPAINE 1C 167
Chedworth St. PL4: Plym . . .3G 9 (2K 141)
Cheeke St. EX1: Exe 3G 7 (6G 65)
Cheese La. EX10: Sidm 6A 84
Cheffers M. EX2: Cou W 6C 72
CHEGLINCH 2B 160
CHELDON 2B 164
Chelmer Cl. PL7: Plymp 4D 138
Chelmsford Pl. PL5: Plym 6H 131
Chelmsford Rd. EX4: Exe 6A 64
Chelsea Pl. TQ14: Teignm 4H 107

Chelson Gdns. PL6: Plym 7F 133
CHELSTON
  TA21 .1B 166
  TQ2 . . . . .2A 116
Chelston Rd. TQ2: Torq 3A 116
  TQ12: New A 7E 104
Cheltenham Cl. EX4: Exe 5B 64
Cheltenham Pl.
  PL4: Plym 1G 9 (1K 141)
Cheltenham Vs. PL4: Plym 1H 9
Chelwood Gro. PL7: Plymp 4C 138
Cheney's La. EX14: Hon 1H 55
Chepstow Av. PL6: Plym 2D 132
Chepstow Cl. EX2: Cou W 5A 72
Cheques Haigh PL8: Noss M 6H 149
Chercombe Bri. Rd.
  TQ12: New A 1A 108
Chercombe Cl. TQ12: New A 7B 104
Chercombe Valley Rd.
  TQ12: New A 7B 104
Cheristow Lavender 1G 27 (1A 162)
Cheriswood Av. EX8: Exmth 3F 77
Cheriswood Cl. EX8: Exmth 3F 77
CHERITON 2D 161
CHERITON BISHOP 2C 62 (1B 170)
Cheriton Cl. PL5: Plym 7F 131
CHERITON CROSS 2C 62 (1B 170)
CHERITON FITZPAINE . .2H 39 (3C 165)
Cherry Arbour EX32: B'aple 6H 19
Cherry Brook Dr. TQ4: Good 7H 119
Cherry Brook Sq. TQ4: Good 7H 119
Cherry Brook Wlk. TQ4: Good 6H 119
Cherry Cl. EX8: Exmth 1E 76
  EX14: Hon 5C 54
  EX15: Will 4D 44
  EX16: Tive 3D 40
  EX17: Cher F 2J 39
Cherry Cross TQ9: Tot 7E 102
Cherry Dr. EX12: Seat 5E 86
  EX17: Cred 6H 39
  TQ3: Paig 7G 115
Cherry Gro. EX2: Won 1K 71
Cherry Gro. EX38: B'aple 7H 19
Cherry Mdw. EX17: Cher F 2J 39
Cherry Pk. EX39: App 3G 21
Cherry Pk. Cl. TQ2: Torq 4K 115
  EX5: Rock 3E 68
Cherry Tree Cl. EX4: Exe 1D 64
Cherry Tree Dr. EX32: Land 2B 24
  PL8: Brixt 2I 149
Cherry Tree Farm Campsite 1B 14
Cherry Tree Gdns. EX16: Tive 3E 40
Cherry Tree La. PL7: Plymp 5D 138
Cherry Tree Rd. EX13: Axmin 3J 89
Cherry Tree Way EX5: Rock 3E 68
Cherrywood Cl. TQ12: New A 7B 104
Cheshire Dr. PL6: Plym 4H 131
Cheshire Rd. EX8: Exmth 2G 77
Chester Cl. EX4: Exe 5B 64
Chester Ct. EX8: Exmth 4H 77
  (off Manchester Rd.)
Chesterfield Rd. PL3: Plym 7C 136
Chester Pl. PL4: Plym 1G 9 (7K 135)
Chester Ter. EX32: B'aple 5F 19
  (off Barbican Rd.)
Chesterton Cl. PL5: Plym 7H 131
Chestnut Av. EX2: Won 2K 71
  EX15: Cull 5H 45
  PL9: Hooe 7D 142
  TQ2: Torq 2B 116
  TQ6: Dartm 5E 124
Chestnut Cl. EX6: Cher 2C 62
  EX8: Exmth 1E 76
  EX12: Seat 3E 86
  EX17: Cred 5J 39
  EX33: Brau 4K 15
  PL19: Lam 5C 58
  PL19: Tavi 7K 59
  PL20: Bere A 2B 128
Chestnut Ct. EX2: Alph 5E 70
  TQ13: Chud 1D 94
Chestnut Cres. EX5: Sto C 7J 51
  TQ13: Chud 1D 94
Chestnut Dr. EX15: Will 4C 44
  EX39: Bide 5C 22
  TQ5: Brixh 6C 122
  TQ12: Kingst 5J 105
  TQ12: New A 3K 109
Chestnut Gro. TQ6: Dartm 5C 124
Chestnut M. EX14: Fen 2J 53
Chestnut Rd. EX16: Tive 3F 41
  PL3: Plym 4J 135
Chestnut Ter. PL19: Lam 6C 58
Chestnut Wlk. EX7: Daw 5F 97
Chestnut Way EX10: New P 5H 81
  EX14: Hon 5D 54
  TQ7: Lodd 6J 157
CHESTON 1E 146 (2C 175)
CHESTWOOD 5A 24
Chestwood Av. EX31: B'aple 6B 18
Chestwood Cl. EX31: B'aple 6C 18
CHETTISCOMBE 1F 41 (2D 165)
CHEVITHORNE 2D 165
Cheyne Beach EX34: Ilfra 2J 11
Cheynegate La. EX4: Pin 1B 66
Cheyne Ri. EX4: Pin 2C 66
CHICHACOTT 1E 48 (1A 170)
Chichacott Rd. EX20: Chich, Oke . .2D 48

Chichester Cl. EX8: Exmth 5E 76
  EX32: B'aple 7G 19
  EX34: Ilfra 4G 11
  EX39: Ins 2K 21
  TQ14: Teignm 1G 107
Chichester Ct. EX32: B'aple 4H 19
  (off Valley Cl.)
  PL20: Horr 2E 126
Chichester Cres. EX32: B'aple 7G 19
Chichester Ho. EX2: Won 7A 66
  PL1: Plym 6C 8 (3H 141)
Chichester M. EX1: Exe 4F 7 (6F 65)
Chichester Pk. EX34: Wool 6B 10
Chichester Pl. EX16: Tive 5G 41
Chichester Rd. EX32: B'aple 7G 19
Chichester's Yd. EX33: Brau 5J 15
  (off Exeter Rd.)
Chichester Way EX9: E Bud 1D 82
  EX39: W Ho 6B 20
  TQ12: New A 1H 109
CHIDEOCK 1D 173
Chideock Ct. DT7: Lym R 5H 91
  (off Clappentail La.)
Chieftain Way EX2: Exe 7A 6 (1D 70)
Chilcote Cl. TQ1: Torq 5E 112
Chilcott Cl. EX16: Tive 5G 41
Children's Adventure Land 6C 44
Childrey Gdns. PL6: Plym 2D 136
Childrey Wlk. PL6: Plym 2D 136
CHILLA 3C 163
CHILLATON 2C 169
CHILLINGTON
  TA17 .2D 167
  TQ7 . . . . .6G 159 (3D 175)
Chillpark Brake EX5: Broadc 2J 67
Chilmark Cl. PL9: Plyms 3E 142
Chilpark EX31: Frem 6E 16
CHILSWORTHY
  EX22 . . . . .3B 162
  PL18 . . . . .3C 169
Chiltern Cl. TQ2: Torq 3K 115
CHILTON .3C 165
Chilton Av. TQ14: Teignm 3J 107
Chilton Cl. PL6: Plym 4C 136
China Blue 5E 102
Chineway Gdns. EX11: Ott M 3E 80
Chineway Rd. EX11: Ott M 3D 80
Chingswell St. EX39: Bide 3F 23
Chinkwell Ri. TQ2: Torq 5H 111
Chinon Cl. EX16: Tive 2G 41
Chinon Pl. EX18: Tive 2A 40
Chinston Cl. EX14: Awli 1A 54
Chipley Ho. EX4: Exe 3D 64
  (off Copplestone Dr.)
Chiseldon La. TQ5: Brixh 7E 122
CHITTERLEY 3D 165
Chittleburn Bus. Pk. PL8: Brixt 2F 149
Chittleburn Cl. PL8: Brixt 2G 149
Chittleburn Hill PL8: Brixt 1F 149
CHITTLEHAMHOLT 1A 164
CHITTLEHAMPTON 5J 25 (1A 164)
CHIVELSTONE 3D 175
CHIVENOR 1E 16 (3A 160)
Chivenor Airfield 1B 16 (3A 160)
Chivenor Av. PL5: Plym 6C 130
Chivenor Cvn. Pk. 1E 16
Chivenor Ind. Est. EX31: C'nor 1E 16
Chiverstone La. EX6: Kenton 5G 95
Chiverstone Rd. EX6: Kenton 5G 95
Choak Wlk. TQ13: Bov T 4E 92
Chockenhole La. EX9: Ott'n 5J 83
Chockland Rd. TQ12: Kingst 2G 105
Chollacott Cl. PL19: Tavi 6J 59
Chollacott La. PL19: Whit 6K 59
Chope Rd. EX39: Nort 6E 20
Chopes Cl. EX39: Bide 5J 23
Christian Mill Bus. Pk.
  PL6: Plym 6K 131
Christina Pde. TQ9: Tot 6G 103
Christina Pk. TQ9: Tot 6G 103
CHRISTOW 4J 63 (2C 171)
Christow Rd. EX2: Mar B 3E 70
Chrystel Cl. EX10: Tip J 1J 81
Chubb Dr. PL3: Plym 7G 135
Chubb Rd. EX39: Bide 5H 23
Chubby Cft. Cl. EX39: Hart 3J 27
CHUDLEIGH 1C 94 (3C 171)
Chudleigh Av. EX39: Bide 3G 23
Chudleigh Community Swimming Pool
 . . . . .2C 94
Chudleigh Fort 4G 23
CHUDLEIGH KNIGHTON . .6A 94 (3C 171)
Chudleigh Knighton Heath
  Nature Reserve 6A 94 (3C 171)
Chudleigh Rd. EX2: Alph, Matt 5E 70
  EX39: Bide 4G 23
  PL4: Plym 7B 136
  TQ12: Kingst 2F 105
Chudleigh Rocks 3B 94
Chudleigh Ter. EX39: Bide 6J 39

Chudley Cl. EX8: Exmth 3F 77
Chugg's Orchard EX33: Croy 2D 14
Chuley Hill TQ13: Ashb 5H 99
Chuley Rd. TQ13: Ashb 5H 99
CHULMLEIGH 6C 32 (2A 164)
Chulmleigh Golf Course
 . . . . .6C 32 (2A 164)
Chulmleigh Hill EX18: Chul 6C 32
Chulmleigh Rd. EX17: Morc 1A 38
  EX19: Wink 2C 36
Chulmleigh Sports Cen. 5C 32
Church Av. EX20: Oke 3A 48
  PL19: Lam 6D 58
Church Cl. EX5: Broadc 5C 52
  EX17: Lap 2K 37
  EX18: Chul 6C 32
  EX19: Dol 7H 31
  EX31: Brat F 6H 13
  PL7: Plymp 4J 137
  PL8: Y'ton 2B 150
  TQ6: Dartm 1B 124 (6F 125)
  TQ7: Kingsb 4G 157
  TQ9: Tot 6E 102
Church Cotts. PL8: Brixt 2H 149
  TQ3: Marl 2D 114
Church Ct. TQ12: Kingst 5H 105
  TQ12: New A 1E 108
Church Cross TQ11: B'leigh 3C 98
Church Elm La. EX32: Colyf 1F 87
Church End Rd. TQ12: Kingsk 7J 109
Chu. Farm TQ7: Thur 6B 154
Churchfield EX39: App 2H 21
Churchfields TQ6: Dartm 6D 124
Churchfields Dr. TQ13: Bov T 4C 92
Churchfields W. TQ6: Dartm 6D 124
Churchford Rd. EX33: Know 1K 15
CHURCH GREEN 1B 172
Church Gro. EX32: B'aple 6G 19
Church Hill EX4: Pin 1B 66
  EX6: Ted M 5H 49
  EX9: Ott'n 6G 83
  EX12: Beer 7B 86
  EX13: Mus 7C 90
  EX14: Awli 1A 54
  EX14: Hon 4G 55
  EX19: Wink 2C 36
  EX31: Frem 6F 17
  EX34: Ilfra 3G 11
  EX35: Lynt 2H 13
  PL6: Plym 2C 136
  PL7: Spa 1J 139
  PL8: Holb 6B 150
  PL19: Whit 7K 59
  TQ3: Marl 2D 114
  TQ6: Kingsw 7G 125
  TQ9: Blacka 2B 152
  TQ11: B'leigh 3C 98
Church Hill Cl. TQ9: Blacka 2B 152
Church Hill Cotts. TQ3: Marl 3D 114
Church Hill E. TQ5: Brixh 3E 122
Church Hill La. EX33: Know 1K 15
Church Hill Rd. PL9: Hooe 6B 142
Church Hill W. TQ5: Brixh 3E 122
Church House 3B 170
Church Ho. Cl. TQ13: Chud K 6B 94
CHURCHILL
  EX13 . . . . .3D 167
  EX31 . . . . .2B 160
Churchill Av. EX7: Daw 5G 97
Churchill Cl. EX6: Kenton 6H 95
  EX32: B'aple 3G 19
Churchill Cotts. PL21: Ugb 6D 146
Churchill Dr. EX7: Lymp 5G 75
  TQ5: Brixh 4E 122
  (off Bolton St.)
Churchill Cres. EX36: S Mol 7C 26
Churchill Dr. EX17: Cred 5G 39
  TQ14: Teignm 3J 107
Churchill Ri. EX13: Axmin 2J 89
Churchill Rd. EX2: Exe 7A 6 (1C 70)
  EX8: Exmth 2F 77
  EX16: Tive 4A 40
  EX39: Bide 5H 23
  PL19: Whit 7K 59
Churchills EX15: Hemy 2G 47
The Churchills TQ12: New A 7D 104
Churchills Ri. EX15: Hemy 2G 47
Churchill Way EX39: App, Nort 6E 20
  PL3: Plym 5K 135
CHURCHINFORD 2C 167
Church Lake EX32: Land 2B 24
Churchlands EX17: Bow 5J 37
Churchlands Cl. PL6: Plym 3F 133
Churchlands Rd. PL6: Plym 2F 133
Church La. EX2: Exe 7B 6 (1D 70)
  EX2: Won 6K 7 (7J 65)
  EX4: Exe 2F 7 (5F 65)
  EX4: Pin 2C 66
  EX5: Broadc 5C 52
  EX5: Clyst M 3G 73
  EX6: Bridf 1F 63
  EX6: Cher 1C 62
  EX6: Chri 4K 63
  EX9: E Bud 1D 82
  EX10: Sidm 7C 84
  EX14: Fen 2J 53
  EX17: Cred 6J 39

Church La. EX19: Wink 2C **36**
　(off High St.)
EX20: Hath 1H **35**
EX22: Hols 2C **34**
EX31: B'aple 4E **18**
　(off High St.)
EX32: Swim 3H **25**
EX38: G Tor 2B **30**
PL8: Y'ton 3B **150**
PL12: Car 1A **130**
PL19: Tavi 4J **59**
PL21: Modb 6F **147**
PL21: Moor 3C **146**
TQ2: Torq 1B **116**
TQ7: W Cha 7J **157**
TQ8: Salc 3D **158**
Church Lea PL19: Whit 7K **59**
Church Mdw. EX20: Oke 3A **48**
EX32: Land 2B **24**
EX37: High B 2B **32**
PL21: Ivy 5E **144**
Church M. TQ12: Kingst 5H **105**
Church Pk. PL8: New F 5J **149**
PL20: Horr 2E **126**
PL21: Corn 7H **129**
Church Pk. Ct. PL6: Plym 2F **133**
Church Pk. Rd. PL6: Plym 2F **133**
PL8: New F 5J **149**
PL8: Torr 3C **150**
Church Path EX2: Exe 7B **6** (1D **70**)
EX3: Top 5B **74**
EX4: Exe 2B **6** (5D **64**)
EX8: Lymp 6G **75**
EX16: Hal 6C **42**
EX20: Oke 3A **48**
EX31: B'aple 2D **18**
PL1: Dev 2F **141**
TQ3: Paig 1H **119**
TQ12: Ipp 6G **101**
TQ12: New A 6D **104**
T13: Ashb 4H **99**
Church Path La. EX2: Heav 7K **65**
Church Path Rd. EX2: Exe 2C **70**
Church Path Ter. EX8: Lymp 7G **75**
Chu. Quillet TQ9: Blacka 3B **152**
Church Rd. EX2: Alph 3E **70**
EX2: Exe 7A **6** (1D **70**)
EX5: Silv 2H **51**
EX5: Whim 6G **53**
EX6: Cockw, Star 4C **96**
EX8: Exmth 5C **76**
EX8: Lymp 6G **75**
EX10: Col R 3H **83**
EX33: Geo 5B **14**
EX34: Ilfra 3G **11**
PL7: Plymp 5C **138**
PL9: Plyms 5F **143**
PL9: Wem 7B **148**
TQ1: Torq 4D **112**
TQ2: Torq 2C **112**
TQ5: Chur F 3A **122**
TQ6: Dartm 5D **124**
TQ6: Sto F 3H **153**
TQ12: E Ogw 3A **108**
TQ12: New A 2F **109**
TQ14: Bi'ton 3C **106**
Church Row EX12: Brans 6G **85**
PL21: Ugb 6E **146**
Church Row La. PL5: Tam F 4H **131**
Church Side EX5: Clyst H 5J **67**
CHURCHSTANTON 2B **166**
Chu. Steps EX5: W'bury 5B **78**
　(off Church Stile La.)
Church Stile La. EX5: W'bury 5B **78**
CHURCHSTOW 1B **156** (3D **175**)
Churchstow Wlk. PL6: Plym 3F **137**
Church St. DT7: Lym R 5K **91**
DT7: Uply 3G **91**
EX2: Heav 7J **65**
EX5: Bradn 1C **52**
EX6: Kenton 6H **95**
EX6: Star 1E **96**
EX7: Daw 4F **97**
EX8: Exmth 6C **76**
EX10: Sidb 2J **85**
EX10: Sidf 1D **84**
EX10: Sidm 7C **84**
EX12: Axmth 3H **87**
EX13: Axmin 4H **89**
EX14: Hon 3H **54**
EX15: Cull 4H **45**
EX16: Tive 4C **40**
EX16: W'ridge 5H **33**
EX17: Cred 6J **39**
EX17: Morc 1C **38**
EX18: Chul 6C **32**
EX19: Dol 6H **31**
EX20: Oke 3B **48**
EX24: Colyt 5D **88**
EX33: Brau 3J **15**
EX34: C Mar 7C **12**
EX34: Ilfra 3H **11**
EX36: S Mol 6C **26**
PL3: Plym 7F **135**
PL21: Erm 2H **147**
PL21: Modb 6G **147**
TQ2: Torq 1B **116**

Church St. TQ3: Paig 1H **119**
TQ5: Brixh 3E **122**
TQ7: Kingsb 4G **157**
TQ8: Salc 3C **158**
TQ10: S Bre 1B **100**
TQ11: B'leigh 4C **98**
TQ12: Kingst 5H **105**
Church Ter. EX2: Heav 5K **7** (7J **65**)
EX16: Bam 2H **33**
EX24: Colyt 5D **88**
　(off Lwr. Church St.)
CHURCHTOWN 2C **161**
Churchtown PL21: Corn 7H **129**
Churchtown Cl. PL21: Corn 7J **129**
Church Vw. EX6: Kenton 6J **95**
　(off Kenton Hill)
EX7: Daw 4F **97**
EX11: Ott M 4C **80**
PL16: Lift 6B **56**
PL20: Walk 2J **127**
TQ12: Kingst 5H **105**
　(off Greenhill Rd.)
TQ13: Chud 1C **94**
Church Wlk. EX38: G Tor 2B **30**
EX39: Bide 4F **23**
　(off Buttgarden St.)
PL9: Wem 7A **148**
PL21: Modb 6G **147**
TQ9: Sto G 4B **120**
Churchward Rd. TQ3: Paig 1H **119**
Church Way PL8: Y'ton 2B **150**
TQ12: Coff 7K **109**
TQ12: New A 3H **109**
Churchway PL5: Plym 3D **134**
Chu. Wells TQ7: Slap 2J **159**
TQ1: Torq 6E **112**
Churchwood Valley Holiday Cabins
　. . . . . .6A **148**
Church Yd. EX36: S Mol 6C **26**
Churscombe Grn. TQ3: Marl 4E **114**
Churscombe Pk. TQ3: Marl 4D **114**
Churscombe Rd. TQ3: Marl 4D **114**
Churston B'way. TQ4: Broads 1H **121**
Churston Cl. TQ5: Galm 3J **121**
Churston Golf Course 2J **121** (2A **176**)
Churston Go-Karts 3K **121**
Churston Ri. EX12: Seat 4C **86**
Churston Rd. TQ5: Chur F 4A **122**
Churston Station
Dartmouth Steam Railway
　. . . . . .3J **121** (2A **176**)
Churston Way TQ5: Brixh 4C **122**
Chute St. EX1: Exe 2H **7** (5G **65**)
Cinders La. TQ6: Sto F 2H **153**
Cintra Ter. EX39: Bide 1F **23**
Cineworld IMAX 5F **9** (3K **141**)
Cistern St. TQ9: Tot 6D **102**
Citadel Hill PL1: Plym 7E **8** (4J **141**)
Citadel Ope PL1: Plym 6F **9**
Citadel Rd. PL1: Plym 6B **8** (3H **141**)
Citadel Rd. E.
PL1: Plym 6E **8** (3K **141**)
City Arc. EX4: Exe 5D **6**
City Bank EX1: Exe 4D **6**
City Bus. Pk. PL3: Plym 7F **135**
City Ind. Est. EX2: Exe 7E **6** (1F **71**)
Claddon La. TQ1: Maid 1C **112**
Clampet La. TQ14: Teignm 5J **107**
　(off Fore St.)
Clampitt Cl. TQ12: Ipp 7H **101**
Clampitt Rd. TQ12: Ipp 6H **101**
Clampitts EX15: Cull 5G **45**
Clanage Cross TQ14: Bi'ton 2A **106**
Clanage St. TQ14: Bi'ton 3B **106**
CLAPHAM 2C **171**
Clappentail Cl. DT7: Lym R 4H **91**
Clappentail La. DT7: Lym R 5H **91**
Clappentail Pk. DT7: Lym R 5H **91**
Clapperbrook La. EX2: Alph 4E **70**
Clapper La. EX14: Com R, Hon . . .2F **55**
Clapp's La. EX12: Beer 7B **86**
Clapps La. EX11: Ott M 4C **80**
EX12: Seat 5F **87**
CLAPTON 3D **167**
CLAPWORTHY 1A **164**
Clara Pl. EX3: Top 5A **74**
Claredale Rd. EX8: Exmth 6D **76**
Clare Dr. EX16: Tive 2F **41**
Claremont Av. TQ12: Kingsk 1G **111**
Claremont Fld. EX11: Ott M 5C **80**
Claremont Gro. EX2: Exe 7G **7** (1G **71**)
EX8: Exmth 5D **76**
Claremont La. EX8: Exmth 5E **76**
Claremont Pl. EX20: Hath 1H **35**
Claremont St.
PL1: Plym 2C **8** (1H **141**)
Clarence Pl. PL1: Plym 4E **140**
Clarence Cotts. EX34: Ilfra 2H **11**
　(off Belvedere Rd.)
Clarence Ct. EX8: Exmth 5C **76**
　(off Meadow St.)
PL1: Plym 2G **141**
Clarence Hill
TQ6: Dartm 1A **124** (6F **125**)
Clarence Pl. EX4: Exe 1G **7** (5G **65**)
PL1: Plym 4A **8** (2G **141**)
PL2: Dev 7D **134**

Clarence Rd. EX4: Exe 6A **6** (7D **64**)
EX8: Exmth 5C **76**
EX9: Bud S 5C **82**
PL11: Torp 1A **140**
Clarence St.
TQ6: Dartm 1B **124** (5F **125**)
Clarendon Cl. TQ1: Torq 6B **112**
Clarendon Ct. TQ1: Torq 2E **116**
Clarendon Gdns. EX31: Rou 7B **18**
Clarendon La. PL2: Dev 1E **140**
Clarendon Rd. TQ12: Ipp 6H **101**
TQ12: New A 1E **108**
Clare Pl. PL4: Plym 6J **9** (3A **142**)
Clare St. PL21: Ivy 5G **145**
Clarke Cl. EX15: Uff 7F **43**
Clarke Mead EX2: Won 1B **72**
Clarke's La. EX33: Brau 1H **15**
Clarkes La. EX20: Mert 4H **27**
Clarks Barn Rd. TQ7: Lodd 3G **151**
Clark's Ct. EX15: Cull 4H **45**
CLATWORTHY 1A **166**
Claude Dix Cl. EX31: B'aple 3F **19**
CLAWTON 1B **168**
CLAYHANGER 1A **166**
CLAYHIDON 2B **166**
Clay Ho. TQ14: Teignm 4H **107**
　(off Clay La.)
CLAYLAND CROSS 3E **118**
Claylands Dr. TQ4: Paig 3F **119**
Claylands Vw. EX14: Hon 5E **54**
Clay La. EX8: Lymp 7G **75**
EX15: Uff 4G **43**
EX17: Cop 5B **38**
EX24: Colyt 6C **88**
TQ9: Darti 3C **102**
TQ13: Chud, Chud K 7A **94**
TQ14: Teignm 4H **107**
Claymans Pathway PL21: Ivy 3E **144**
Claypark Ter. TQ9: Sto G 1A **120**
Clay Pit Cl. EX5: Clyst M 2G **73**
Claypits Rd. EX31: Bick 7K **17**
Clay Pits Way TQ12: Kingst 1G **105**
Claytonia Cl. PL6: Robo 1D **132**
Clayton Pl. PL4: Plym 2C **142**
Clayton Rd. EX4: Exe 2B **6** (5D **64**)
PL4: Plym 2C **142**
CLEARBROOK 1B **174**
Clearbrook Av. PL5: Plym 2D **134**
Clearbrook (Leat) Viewpoint 1B **174**
Cleatlands Cl. TQ4: Paig 3E **118**
Cleave EX39: Nort 7G **21**
Cleaveanger La. EX17: Cold 4F **37**
Cleave Cl. EX6: Ted M 7J **49**
EX31: B'aple 5C **18**
Cleave Hill EX19: Dol 7G **31**
Cleaveland Ri. TQ12: E Ogw 3C **108**
Cleave Pk. EX31: Frem 6G **17**
Cleave Rd. EX31: B'aple 5C **18**
Cleaves Cl. EX5: Thor 2A **50**
Cleavewood Dr. EX39: Bide 4J **23**
Cleavewood Holiday Pk. 7C **10**
The Cleeve EX15: Culm 2B **46**
Cleeve Dr. PL21: Ivy 3F **145**
Cleeve Gdns. PL2: Plym 3F **135**
Cleland Ct. TQ14: Bi'ton 3B **106**
Clematon Hill TQ7: Bigb S 3C **154**
Clement Rd. PL7: Plymp 4E **138**
Clennon Av. TQ4: Good 3H **119**
Clennon Ct. TQ2: Torq 3C **112**
Clennon Dr. TQ4: Good 3H **119**
Clennon Gdns. TQ4: Good 3H **119**
Clennon Hgts. TQ4: Good 3H **119**
Clennon La. TQ2: Torq 3B **112**
TQ4: Paig 3G **119**
Clennon Pk. TQ4: Good 3H **119**
Clennon Ri. TQ4: Good 3H **119**
Clennon Summit TQ4: Good 3H **119**
Clerk Cl. EX8: Exmth 2E **76**
Cleve Cl. EX4: Exe 5B **64**
Clevedon Cl. EX4: Exe 3G **65**
Clevedon Pk. EX10: Sidm 5D **84**
Clevedon Pk. Av. PL2: Plym 5G **135**
Cleveland Ct.
EX1: Exe 2H **7** (5G **65**)
TQ4: Paig 2B **119**
Cleveland Dr. TQ7: Bigb S 2B **154**
Cleveland Gdns. EX1: Exe 2H **7**
Cleveland Rd. EX7: Daw 4H **97**
　(off High St.)
EX8: Exmth 6B **76**
Cleveland Rd.
PL4: Plym 3K **9** (2B **142**)
TQ2: Torq 7B **112**
TQ4: Paig 2J **119**
Clevelands Pk. EX39: Nort 6E **20**
Cleveland St. EX4: Exe 6A **6** (7D **64**)
Cleveland Ter. EX39: W Ho 5B **20**
　(off Atlantic Way)
Cleve La. EX4: Exe 5B **64**
Cleve Rd. EX4: Exe 6C **64**
Cleve Ter. TQ1: Torq 1G **117**
Cliff Bastin Cl. EX2: Won 1B **72**
Cliff Ct. EX7: Daw 4H **97**
Cliff Ho. TQ4: Paig 2K **119**
Cliff M. TQ4: Paig 2K **119**
Clifford Av. TQ12: Kingst 2G **105**

Clifford Cl. EX1: Whip 5A **66**
PL5: Plym 1D **134**
TQ12: Kingst 4H **105**
TQ13: Chud 1C **94**
TQ14: Shal 6G **107**
Clifford Dr. TQ12: H'fld 2J **93**
Clifford Gdns. EX17: Cred 5H **39**
Clifford Rd. EX4: Exe 4J **65**
Clifford St. TQ12: Kingst 4H **105**
TQ13: Chud 1C **94**
Cliff Pk. Av. TQ4: Good 4J **119**
Cliff Pk. Ct. TQ4: Good 4J **119**
Cliff Pk. Rd. TQ4: Good 5J **119**
Cliff Path EX9: Bud S 7A **82**
Cliff Rd. EX9: Bud S 7C **82**
EX10: Sidm 7C **84**
PL1: Plym 7B **8** (4H **141**)
PL9: Wem 7B **148**
TQ2: Torq 4A **116**
TQ4: Paig 2K **119**
TQ8: Salc 6A **158**
TQ14: Teignm 2K **107**
The Cliffs EX7: Daw 6H **97**
Cliffside Rd. TQ1: Torq 5E **112**
Cliff Ter. EX9: Bud S 7C **82**
CLIFTON 2C **161**
Clifton Av. PL7: Plymp 2B **138**
Clifton Bank TQ3: Paig 1G **119**
Clifton Cl. PL7: Plymp 2B **138**
TQ3: Paig 1F **119**
Clifton Ct. EX1: Exe 2J **7**
EX34: Ilfra 3H **11**
　(off High St.)
EX39: W Ho 6A **20**
Clifton Cres. TQ3: Paig 1G **119**
Clifton Gdns. TQ3: Paig 1G **119**
Clifton Gro. TQ1: Torq 2F **117**
TQ3: Paig 1G **119**
Clifton Hill EX1: Exe 2J **7** (5H **65**)
Clifton Hill Driving Range 3J **7**
Clifton Hill Sports Centre & Ski Slope
　. . . . . .3J **7** (5H **65**)
Clifton Pl. EX7: Daw 4F **97**
EX34: Ilfra 3H **11**
　(off Belvedere Rd.)
PL4: Plym 1G **9** (1K **141**)
TQ8: Salc 3D **158**
Clifton Rd. EX1: Exe 3H **7** (6G **65**)
TQ3: Paig 1F **119**
Clifton St. EX1: Exe 3H **7** (6G **65**)
EX31: B'aple 5E **18**
EX39: Bide 4G **23**
PL4: Plym 2G **9** (1K **141**)
Clifton Ter. EX31: B'aple 5D **18**
EX39: Nort 5F **21**
　(off Northcott Gdns.)
TQ1: Torq 2D **116**
Climsland Rd. TQ4: Paig 2G **119**
Clinton Av. EX4: Exe 1K **7** (4H **65**)
PL4: Plym 1K **9** (1B **142**)
Clinton Cl. EX9: Bud S 5B **82**
Clinton Gdns. EX20: Mert 5B **30**
Clinton Ri. EX12: Beer 6C **86**
Clinton Rd. EX32: B'aple 7G **19**
Clinton Sq. EX8: Exmth 6B **76**
Clinton St. EX4: Exe 6A **6** (7D **64**)
EX20: Mert 5B **30**
　(off Clinton Gdns.)
EX32: B'aple 6G **19**
EX38: G Tor 2A **30**
　(off New St.)
Clipper Quay EX2: Exe 7E **6** (1F **71**)
Clipper Wharf EX8: Exmth 6A **76**
　(off Shelly Rd.)
Cliston Av. EX8: Exmth 2F **77**
Clittaford Rd. PL6: Plym 4K **131**
Clittaford Vw. PL6: Plym 3K **131**
Cliveden Rd. EX39: Bide 5J **23**
Cloake Pl. PL12: Car 1A **130**
Cloakham Dr. EX13: Axmin 2J **89**
Cloakham Lawn Sports Cen. 2J **89**
Clobells TQ10: S Bre 2B **100**
Cloford Cl. PL9: Plyms 3E **142**
Cloister Rd. EX4: Exe 5A **65**
The Cloisters EX1: Exe 5E **6** (6F **65**)
Cloisters Gth. EX1: Exe 4E **6**
　(off Cathedral Cl.)
Clonway PL20: Yelv 5F **127**
Clooneavin Path EX35: Lynm 2H **13**
The Close EX7: Holc 7G **97**
EX12: Seat 5E **86**
EX16: Tive 2F **41**
EX32: B'aple 4H **19**
PL20: Bere A 2C **128**
TQ4: Broads 7J **119**
TQ5: Brixh 3D **122**
Cloutman's La. EX33: Croy 2C **14**
CLOVELLY 5H **27** (1B **162**)
Clovelly Apts. EX34: Ilfra 3H **11**
　(off Oxford Pk.)
Clovelly Cl. EX39: Bide 4D **22**
Clovelly Court Gdns. 4G **27** (1B **162**)
Clovelly Donkeys 5H **27** (1B **162**)
Clovelly Dykes 7G **27**
Clovelly Fisherman's Cottage 5H **27**
Clovelly Gdns. Nth. EX39: Bide . . .4E **22**

Clovelly Gdns. Sth. EX39: Bide 4E 22
Clovelly Lifeboat Station 5H 27
Clovelly Ri. EX7: Daw 5G 97
   TQ3: Paig 1E 118
Clovelly Rd. EX39: Bide 5A 22
   PL4: Plym 7K 9 (4B 142)
Clovelly Rd. Ind. Est.
   EX39: Bide 5B 22
Clovelly Vw. PL9: Hooe 5B 142
Clovelly Visitor Cen. 5G 27 (1B 162)
Clover Av. EX4: Exe 4B 64
Clover Cl. TQ4: Paig 5E 118
Cloverdale Cl. DT7: Lym R 4K 91
Clover Dr. EX7: Daw 3G 97
   EX15: Cull 5G 45
Clover Ri. PL6: Plym 2F 133
Clover Way EX32: B'aple 5K 19
   TQ12: New A 6A 104
Clowance Cl. PL1: Dev 3E 140
Clowance La. PL1: Dev 3D 140
Clowance La. Flats PL1: Dev 3D 140
   (off Clowance La.)
Clowance St. PL1: Dev 3D 140
   (not continuous)
Cluden Rd. EX39: Nort 6E 20
Cludens Cl. EX2: Alph 5E 70
Clumpit La. EX4: Kenton 4F 95
Clydesdale Ct. EX4: Exe 3D 64
Clydesdale Ho. EX4: Exe 3D 64
   (off Clydesdale Rd.)
Clydesdale Ri. EX4: Exe 3D 64
Clydesdale Rd. EX4: Exe 3D 64
Clyde St. PL2: Plym 6E 134
Clyst Av. EX5: Broadc 2K 67
   TQ5: Brixh 6C 122
Clyst Halt Av. EX2: Sow 2D 72
Clyst Hayes Ct. EX9: Bud S 6A 82
Clyst Hayes Gdns. EX9: Bud S 6A 82
Clyst Heath EX2: Sow 2C 72
CLYST HONITON 4J 67 (1D 171)
CLYST HYDON 3A 166
Clyston Mill 5C 52 (1D 171)
Clyst Rd. EX3: Top 7G 72
CLYST ST GEORGE 7H 73 (2D 171)
CLYST ST LAWRENCE 3A 166
CLYST ST MARY 2F 73 (1D 171)
Clystside EX5: Clyst H 4J 67
Clyst Valley Rd. EX5: Clyst M 3G 73
Coach Dr. EX39: Bide 6F 23
The Coach Ho. TQ3: Paig 7J 115
   (off Steartfield Rd.)
Coach Ho. La. TQ2: Torq 2A 116
Coach Ho. M. PL9: Elb 6J 143
   TQ13: Chud 2C 94
Coach Pl. TQ12: New A 2F 109
Coach Rd. EX5: Silv 2H 51
   PL8: Noss M 7H 149
   TQ12: New A 3E 108
The Coach Ho. DT7: Harc B 1G 91
COAD'S GREEN 3A 168
Coaker Rd. EX1: Pin 2E 66
Coastguard Cotts. EX7: Daw 4J 97
   TQ1: Torq 4E 116
Coastguard Hill EX9: Bud S 7D 82
Coastguard Rd. EX9: Bud S 6D 82
Coast Vw. Holiday Pk. 7G 107
COAT 1D 167
Coates Rd. EX2: Won 7A 66
Coaver Club 7H 7 (1G 71)
COBB 6J 91
COBBATON 1A 164
Cobbaton Combat Collection 1A 164
Cobbett Rd. PL5: Plym 2G 135
Cobb La. PL9: Plyms 6G 143
Cobblestone La. PL1: Plym 3F 141
   (off Brownlow St.)
Cobb Rd. DT7: Lym R 6J 91
Cobb Ter. DT7: Lym R 6J 91
Cobden La. EX5: Whim 2J 69
Cobham Cl. PL6: Plym 4D 132
Cobley Ct. EX4: Pin 4C 66
Cob Mdw. EX20: Hath 2H 35
Cobourg St. PL1: Plym 3E 8 (2J 141)
COBURG 2B 94 (3C 171)
Coburg Cres. TQ13: Chud 2B 94
Coburg Field 7C 84
Coburg Grn. EX2: Sow 1C 72
Coburg Pl. EX15: Cull 1H 45
   TQ2: Torq 2D 116
   (off Warren Rd.)
Coburg Rd. EX10: Sidm 7B 84
Coburg Ter. EX10: Sidm 7B 84
   EX34: Ilfra 2J 11
Cockhaven Cl. TQ14: Bi'ton 4B 106
Cockhaven Mead TQ14: Bi'ton 4B 106
Cockhaven Rd. TQ14: Bi'ton 4B 106
COCKINGTON 2J 115 (1A 176)
Cockington Cl. PL6: Plym 2F 137
Cockington Country Pk. . .2J 115 (1A 176)
Cockington Court Craft Cen. 2H 115
Cockington La. TQ2: Torq 1J 115
   TQ3: Pres 5J 115
Cockington Rd. TQ3: Marl 3F 115
Cockington Wlk. PL6: Plym 2D 136
Cockles La. EX17: Cred 6J 39
Cockles Ri. EX17: Cred 6J 39
Cockpit Hill EX15: Cull 4H 45
COCKWOOD 3E 96 (2D 171)

CODDA 3A 168
CODDEN 6D 24
Codden Beacon 1D 163
Coddiford Hill EX17: Cher F 1H 39
Codrington Ct. EX1: Exe 3H 7
Codrington St.
   EX1: Exe 3H 7 (6G 65)
Coffins La. EX6: Exmin 3B 74
COFFINSWELL 1A 176
Coffinswell La. TQ12: Kingsk 1G 111
COFTON 4C 96
Cofton Cl. EX6: Cockw 4E 96
Cofton Country Holidays 4C 96
Cofton Hill EX6: Cockw 3E 96
Cofton Rd. EX2: Mar B 4G 71
Coker Av. TQ2: Torq 1B 112
Colands Ct. EX2: Alph 5D 70
Colaton La. EX5: Thor 1B 52
COLATON RALEIGH 3J 83 (2A 172)
Colaton Ter. EX10: Sidm 6A 84
   (off Cotmaton Rd.)
Colborne Rd. PL6: Plym 1B 136
Colcombe Rd. EX24: Colyt 4D 88
COLDEAST 3F 93 (3C 171)
Coldharbour EX15: Uff 7G 43
   EX39: Bide 3F 23
   TQ9: Tot .6G 103
Coldharbour Mill Mus. 7G 43 (2A 166)
Coldharbour Rd. EX16: Tive 5A 40
COLD NORTHCOTT 2A 168
Coldrenick St. PL5: Plym 2B 134
COLDRIDGE 3A 164
Coldstream Gdns. EX20: Mert 5B 30
Coldstream Pl. EX39: Bide 4E 22
   (off Clovelly Rd.)
Coldwell La. EX2: Axmth 4H 87
Coldwell La. Ter. EX12: Axmth 3H 87
Coleberd Cl. EX11: Ott M 3D 80
COLEBROOK
   EX15 . . . . .6F 45 (3A 166)
   PL7 . . . . .3B 138
COLEBROOKE 1B 170
Colebrook La. PL7: Plymp 2B 138
Colebrook Rd. PL5: Plym 2C 134
   PL7: Plymp 3B 138
COLEFORD .3B 164
Cole La. PL21: Ivy 3H 145
   (Carter Rd.)
   PL21: Ivy .7F 145
   (Keaton La.)
Coleman Av. TQ14: Teignm 3G 107
Coleman Cl. EX16: Tive 3G 41
Coleman Dr. PL9: Plyms 7G 143
Cole Mdw. EX37: High B 3C 32
Cole Moore Mdw. PL19: Tavi 3H 59
Coleridge Av. PL6: Plym 1A 136
Coleridge Cl. EX8: Exmth 1E 76
Coleridge Ct. TQ2: Torq 3C 112
Coleridge Gdns.
   PL4: Plym 1K 9 (1B 142)
Coleridge La. TQ7: Chil 4G 159
Coleridge Rd. EX2: Exe 1C 70
   EX11: Ott M 3E 80
   EX16: Tive 4G 41
   PL4: Plym 1J 9 (7A 136)
Coles Cotts. PL7: Plymp 3B 138
   PL9: Down T 1C 148
Cole's Ct.
   TQ6: Dartm 2B 124 (6F 125)
Colesdown Hill PL9: Plyms 4H 143
Cole's La. TQ12: Kingsk 7J 109
Coles Mead EX16: Tive 4F 41
Coles M. EX2: Exe 7A 6 (1D 70)
Coles Mill Cl. EX22: Hols 2C 34
COLESTOCKS 3A 166
Coleton Fishacre 2B 176
Colin Campbell Ct.
   PL1: Plym 4C 8 (2H 141)
Colin Rd. TQ3: Pres 7J 115
Collabridge Hill EX6: Dunsf 5A 62
Collabridge La. EX6: Dunsf 6A 62
Collabridge Rd. EX6: Dunsf 5B 62
Collaford Cl. PL7: Plymp 6D 138
Collaford La. TQ6: Dartm 1A 124
Collapark TQ9: Tot 6C 102
COLLATON 7K 155 (3D 175)
Collaton Ct. TQ2: Torq 5J 111
Collaton Ho. TQ1: Torq 2F 117
   (off Old Torwood Rd.)
Collaton M. TQ4: Coll M 3D 118
Collaton Rd. TQ2: Torq 4H 111
   TQ7: Malb 6G 155
COLLATON ST MARY 3D 118 (1A 176)
Collatons Wlk. EX17: Bow 6H 37
College TQ13: Bov T 3D 92
The College EX2: Ide 3A 70
   EX11: Ott M 3C 80
College Av. EX2: Exe 5H 7 (7G 65)
   PL4: Plym 6K 135
   PL19: Tavi 3K 59
College Cl. EX39: W Ho 6B 20
College Ct. EX15: Uff 7G 43
   EX31: B'aple 6C 18
College Dean Cl. PL6: Plym 5D 132
   EX39: Bide 3E 22
College La. EX15: Uff 6G 43
   EX2: Ide .3A 70
   PL4: Plym 7K 135

College Pk. Pl. PL3: Plym 6K 135
College Rd.
   EX1: Exe 5H 7 (7G 65)
   EX15: Cull 3H 45
   EX21: Sheb 6K 29
   PL2: Plym 6D 134
   TQ12: New A 3E 108
College Vw. EX16: Tive 2C 40
   PL3: Plym 7K 135
College Way EX1: Pin 5D 66
   TQ6: Dartm 1A 124 (5E 125)
Colleton Cl. EX8: Exmth 4E 76
Colleton Cres.
   EX2: Exe 6E 6 (7F 65)
Colleton Gro. EX2: Exe 7F 7 (1F 71)
Colleton Hill EX2: Exe 7E 6 (1F 71)
Colleton M. EX2: Exe 7F 7 (1F 71)
Colleton Row EX2: Exe 7F 7 (1F 71)
Colleton Way EX8: Exmth 4E 76
Collett Way TQ12: New A 1H 109
Colleybrook Cl.
   TQ12: Kingst 1G 105
Colley Cres. TQ3: Paig 1G 119
Colley End Pk. TQ3: Paig 1G 119
Colley End Rd. TQ3: Paig 1E 118
Colley Pk. Rd. TQ33: Brau 5J 15
Colliepriest Vw. EX16: Ashy 7B 40
Colliers Cl. PL9: Wem 6C 148
Colliers M. EX20: Oke 2B 48
Collin Cl. PL5: Plym 2C 134
Collingwood Av. PL4: Plym 3B 142
Collingwood Cl. TQ1: Torq 4E 116
   TQ6: Dartm 6C 124
Collingwood Rd. PL1: Plym 1F 141
   TQ4: Paig 2G 119
   TQ6: Dartm 6C 124
Collingwood Vs. PL1: Plym 1F 141
   (off Collingwood Rd.)
Collins Pk. EX9: E Bud 1D 82
Collins Rd. EX4: Exe 2G 65
   TQ9: Tot .5D 102
COLLIPRIEST 7C 40
Collipriest Rd.
   EX16: Colli, Tive 6C 40
COLLITON .3A 166
Colne Gdns. PL3: Plym 6C 136
Colombelles Cl. EX31: Frem 6F 17
Col. R.H. Maclaren Memorial 2D 161
COLSCOTT .2B 162
Colston Cl. PL6: Plym 4C 132
Colston Rd. IQ11: B'leigh 5E 98
Coltishall Cl. PL5: Plym 6E 130
Coltness Rd. PL9: Elb 7J 143
Coltsfield Cl. PL6: Plym 3C 136
Columbus Cl. PL5: Plym 1B 134
Colvin Cl. EX8: Exmth 5F 77
Colway Cl. DT7: Lym R 3J 91
Colway Cross TQ14: Teignm 2A 106
Colway La. DT7: Lym R 4J 91
   TQ13: Chud 1D 94
COLWAY MEAD 4J 91
Colwill M. TQ13: More 6H 61
Colwill Rd. PL6: Plym 7F 133
   TQ13: Bov T 7G 133
Colwill Wlk. PL6: Plym 7F 133
Colwyn Ct. TQ1: Torq 1G 117
Colwyn Rd. PL11: Torp 1A 140
COLYFORD 1F 87 (1C 173)
Colyford Common Local
   Nature Reserve 1G 87
Colyford Rd. EX12: Seat 4F 87
Colyford Stop
   Seaton Tramway 1G 87 (1C 173)
Coly Rd. EX14: Hon 5F 55
   EX24: Colyf, Colyt 6D 88
COLYTON 5D 88 (1C 173)
Colyton Hill EX13: Whit 6A 90
Colyton Local History Cen. 6D 88
Colyton Sports Cen. 1E 86
Colyton Stop
   Seaton Tramway 5E 88 (1C 173)
Colyvale EX24: Colyt 7D 88
Combas La. EX33: Croy 2D 14
COMBE
   PL8 . . . . .2F 149
   TQ11 . . . . .1D 175
Combe Bank TQ5: Brixh 4D 122
COMBEBOW 2C 169
Combe Down La. PL8: Noss M 6H 149
COMBE FISHACRE 1A 176
COMBE FLOREY 1B 166
COMBEINTEIGNHEAD 7A 106 (3D 171)
Combe La. PL8: Brixt 2F 149
   TQ5: Galm 6H 121
COMBE MARTIN 6B 12 (2B 160)
Combe Martin Beach Holiday Pk.
   . . . . .5A 12
Combe Martin Information Point
   . . . . .5A 12 (2B 160)
Combe Martin Mus. 5A 12 (2B 160)
Combe Martin Wildlife & Dinosaur Park
   . . . . .2B 160
COMBE PAFFORD 4C 112
Combe Pk. EX34: Ilfra 3K 11
COMBE RALEIGH 1E 54 (3B 166)
Combe Rd. TQ2: Torq 3D 112
COMBE ST NICHOLAS 2D 167
Combestone Tor Viewpoint 3A 170

Combined Court
   Exeter 5F 7 (7F 65)
   Plymouth 5E 8 (3J 141)
Combley Dr. PL6: Plym 6E 132
Combourg Cl. EX8: Exmth 1H 77
COMBPYNE .1C 173
Combpyne Rd. EX13: Mus 7C 90
COMBREW 6H 17
Combrew La. EX31: Bick 6H 17
Comer Cl. EX20: Exbo 6J 35
   (off High St.)
Comers La. EX34: C Mar 7C 12
Comilla Cl. EX8: Exmth 1E 76
Commanders Cut TQ6: Dartm 5E 124
   (off Chestnut Av.)
Commercial Ope PL4: Plym 6J 9
Commercial Pl. PL4: Plym 7J 9
Commercial Rd. EX2: Exe 6C 6 (7E 64)
   EX7: Daw 4H 97
   EX15: Uff .7G 43
   EX17: Cred 6K 39
   EX31: B'aple 4E 18
   PL4: Plym 6J 9 (3A 142)
   PL20: Horr 2E 126
   TQ4: Paig 1H 119
Commercial St. PL4: Plym 6J 9 (3A 142)
Commin's Rd. EX1: Heav 1K 7 (5J 65)
Commodore Cl. EX39: W Ho 5D 20
Common Hill EX12: Beer 7B 86
Common La. EX12: Beer 7B 86
   EX24: Colyf 2F 87
   TQ12: N Whil 3D 110
Commonmarsh La. EX17: Cred 6K 39
COMMON MOOR 3A 168
Commons Hill EX6: Chri 4G 63
Commons La. EX7: Daw 3G 97
   TQ14: S'head 7G 107
   TQ14: Shal 6F 107
Commons Old Rd. TQ14: Shal 6G 107
   (not continuous)
Company Rd. EX31: Frem 5F 17
Compass Dr. PL7: Plymp 2D 138
Compass Quay EX2: Exe 7E 6 (1F 71)
Compass Sth. TQ1: Torq 3H 117
COMPTON 7D 110 (1A 176)
Compton Av. PL3: Plym 6A 136
Compton Castle 7D 110 (1A 176)
Compton Ho. TQ1: Torq 6E 112
   (off Palermo Rd.)
Compton Knoll Cl. PL3: Plym 5B 136
Compton Leigh PL3: Plym 5B 136
Compton Pk. Rd. PL3: Plym 6A 136
Compton Pl. TQ1: Torq 4D 112
Compton Rd. TQ7: W Cha 7K 157
Compton Va. PL3: Plym 6B 136
Comyn Hill EX34: Ilfra 4K 11
Concorde Dr. EX32: B'aple 3H 19
Concorde Rd. EX8: Exmth 3G 77
Condor Dr. TQ2: Torq 3K 111
Condor Way TQ2: Torq 3K 111
Conduit La. EX39: Bide 3F 23
   (off The Quay)
Conduit Sq. TQ13: Chud 1C 94
Coney Av. EX32: B'aple 6G 19
Coney Ct. EX2: Exe 7D 6
Coney Pk. La. EX34: C Mar 7C 12
CONGDON'S SHOP 3A 168
Congella Rd. TQ1: Torq 7E 112
Congram's Cl. EX32: B'aple 6G 19
Congreve Gdns. PL5: Plym 2H 135
Conifer Cl. EX15: Cull 2H 45
Conifer M. EX2: Sow 2C 72
The Conifers TQ2: Torq 2D 112
   TQ13: Bov T 7B 92
Conigar Cl. PL5: Plym 2F 47
Conigar La. EX15: Hemy 3F 47
Coniston Cl. TQ5: Brixh 6C 122
Coniston Ct. TQ4: Paig 3G 119
Coniston Gdns. PL6: Plym 6A 132
Coniston Rd. TQ12: E Ogw 4C 108
Conker Gdns. PL7: Plymp 4E 138
Connaught Av. PL4: Plym 7K 135
Connaught Cl. EX10: Sidm 6B 84
Connaught La. PL4: Plym 7K 135
Connaught Pl. EX32: B'aple 4E 18
   (off Silver St.)
Connaught Rd. EX10: Sidm 6B 84
Conniford La. TQ12: Ipp 7H 101
Conqueror Dr. PL5: Plym 2K 135
Conrad Av. EX4: Whip 4A 66
Conrad Rd. PL5: Plym 2H 135
Consort Cl. PL3: Plym 4K 135
Constable Cl. PL5: Plym 1J 135
   (off Cowley Rd.)
Constance Pl. PL1: Plym 3A 8 (2G 141)
Constantine Cl. EX12: Seat 4D 86
Constantine Ho. EX4: Exe 2D 6
Constantine St.
   PL4: Plym 4G 9 (2K 141)
Constitution Hill EX32: B'aple 4G 19
Contour Hgts. TQ6: Kingsw 6G 125
Convent Cl. EX32: B'aple 7H 19
Convent Flds. EX10: Sidm 6A 84
Convent Rd. EX10: Sidm 5A 84
Conway Ct. EX1: Exe 5G 7 (7G 65)
Conway Cres. TQ4: Paig 2G 119
Conway Gdns. PL2: Plym 4G 135
Conway Rd. TQ4: Paig 2H 119

Conybeare Cl. EX4: Exe 5A 66
Conybeare St. EX39: Nort 6D 20
Conyngham Ct. PL6: Plym 3B 136
Cooban Ct. PL6: Plym 3B 136
COOKBURY 3C 163
COOKBURY WICK 3B 162
Cooke Dr. TQ12: Ipp 6J 101
Cooks Cl. TQ12: Kingst 4J 105
  TQ13: Ashb 3J 99
Cooks Ct. EX16: Tive 4D 40
Cooks Cross EX36: S Mol 7C 26
Cooks La. EX13: Ray H 1A 90
Cooks Mead DT7: Uply 2F 91
Cooksons Rd. EX6: Star 1D 96
Cookworthy Ct. TQ7: Kingsb . . .3F 157
Cookworthy Museum 3F 157 (3D 175)
Cookworthy Rd. PL2: Plym 5E 134
  TQ7: Kingsb 4F 157
The Coolings EX2: Exe 7E 6
COOMBE
  EX10 . . . . .1B 172
  EX23 . . . . .2A 162
  EX14 . . . . .2G 107 (3D 175)
The Coombe TQ5: Galm 3H 121
  TQ6: Dartm 5F 125
Coombe Av. TQ14: Teignm 4G 107
Coombe Ball Hill EX16: W'ridge . .6F 33
Coombe Cl. EX14: Hon 5F 55
  TQ6: Dartm 1A 124 (5F 125)
  TQ13: Bov T 4D 92
Coombe Cross TQ13: Bov T 4D 92
Coombe Dean Sports Cen. 6H 143
Coombe Dr. PL12: Car 1A 130
Coombefield La. EX13: Axmin . . .4H 89
Coombe Hayes EX10: Sidm 2C 84
Coombe Ho. La. TQ9: Aish 5A 118
COOMBELAKE 1A 80
Coombe La. EX13: Axmin 4H 89
  PL5: Tam F 4H 131
  PL12: Car 1A 130
  TQ2: Torq 4C 112
  TQ13: Bov T 4D 92
  TQ14: Teignm 2G 107
Coombe Mdw. TQ13: Bov T 5H 115
  TQ6: Dartm 5F 125
  TQ14: Shal 6D 106
The Coombes EX31: Rou 7K 17
Coombesend Rd. TQ12: Kingst . .4J 105
  (not continuous)
Coombesend Rd. E.
  TQ12: Kingst 4K 105
Coombeshead Rd. TQ12: New A . .7C 104
Coombe Shute TQ9: Sto G 4B 120
Coombe St. DT7: Lym R 5E 91
  EX1: Exe 5E 6 (7F 65)
Coombe Ter. EX12: Axmth 4J 87
Coombe Va. EX10: Tip J 1K 81
Coombe Va. Rd. TQ14: Teignm . .3G 107
Coombe Vw. PL2: Plym 4D 134
  (off Ainslie Ter.)
  TQ14: Teignm 2F 107
Coombe Way PL5: Plym 6E 134
  TQ14: Bi'ton 2C 106
Coopers Ct. EX16: Tive 5D 40
Coopers Dray EX5: Whim 5G 53
Coopers Dr. EX31: Nort 7A 18
Coopers Hill EX19: Wink 2C 36
Cooper St. EX39: Bide 3F 23
Coot Hide EX16: Sam P 2B 42
Copland La. TQ9: Tot 4B 102
Copland Mdws. TQ9: Tot 5C 102
Copleston Rd. PL6: Plym 5J 131
Copley Cl. TQ3: Paig 1F 119
Copley Dr. EX31: B'aple 6C 18
Coppard Mdws. PL7: Plym 5J 137
COPPATHORNE 3A 162
Copper Beech Way PL6: Plym . . .3D 132
Copper Cl. EX39: Wools 2B 28
Copperfield TQ7: Chil 6F 159
Copperfield Est. EX8: Exmth 3G 77
Copperfields PL20: Horr 2D 126
Coppers Pk. PL6: Plym 3F 133
Copperwood Cl. TQ13: Ashb 4G 99
Copp Hill La. EX9: Bud S 5C 82
The Coppice EX7: Daw 6G 97
  PL21: Ivy 5E 144
Coppice Cl. EX13: Ray H 2B 90
  EX31: Frem 5F 17
  EX32: B'aple 6K 19
Coppice Gdns. PL5: Plym 1K 135
Coppice Ga. EX32: B'aple 6H 19
Coppice Wood Dr. PL6: Plym . . .2D 132
Coppledown Gdns. EX9: Bud S . . .5A 82
COPPLESTONE 6D 38 (3B 164)
Copplestone Dr. EX4: Exe 3D 64
Copplestone Rd. EX10: Col R 2G 83
Copplestone Rd. EX9: Bud S 6C 82
Copplestone Station
  (Rail) 5C 38 (3B 164)
Copp Path EX7: Daw 5F 97
  (off Taylor Cl.)

Copp's Cl. EX39: Bide 2E 22
The Copse EX2: Cou W 6B 72
  EX8: Exmth 2G 77
  EX10: New P 5H 81
  EX20: Oke 2D 48
  EX31: Rou 6A 18
  TQ7: Chil 6G 159
  TQ9: Tot 5A 102
  EX4: Exe 4K 109
Copse Cl. PL7: Plymp 5A 138
Copseclose La. EX5: Cran 3B 68
Copse Rd. PL7: Plymp 5A 138
Copsey La. TQ12: Den 2J 101
Copthorne Gdns. PL9: Plyms 7G 143
Copydown La. EX5: Hele 1A 52
Copythorne Cl. TQ5: Brixh 4C 122
Copythorne Ct. EX10: Sidb 4C 122
Copythorne Rd.
  TQ5: Brixh, Chur F 3A 122
Coral Av. EX39: W Ho 5C 20
Coram Av. DT7: Lym R 6J 91
Coram Ct. DT7: Lym R 5J 91
Cordery Rd. EX2: Exe 2C 70
Corea Ter. PL1: Dev 2F 141
Corefields EX10: Sidf 2C 84
  EX10: Sidm 3B 84
Core Hill Rd. EX10: Sidb, Stow . . .1A 84
Core Hill Wood Nature Reserve . .1B 84
Coreway EX10: Sidf 2C 84
Coreway Cl. EX10: Sidf 2B 84
CORFE 2C 167
Corfe Av. PL3: Plym 4A 136
Corfe Cl. PL21: Ivy 5H 145
Corfe Cres. TQ2: Torq 5B 112
Corilhead Rd. EX33: Brau 2J 15
Coringdean Cl. PL6: Plym 4C 132
Coriolis Way Nth. EX1: Sow 5C 66
Coriolis Way Sth. EX1: Sow 6C 66
Cormelles Ct. EX34: C Mar 7C 12
Cormorant Cl. TQ2: Torq 2K 111
Cornacre Cl. TQ2: Torq 6J 111
Cornacre Rd. TQ2: Torq 7J 111
Cornborough Rd. EX39: W Ho . . .6A 20
Corner Brake PL6: Plym 3E 132
Corner La. EX17: Morc 1B 38
Corner La. EX16: Hal 6D 42
  EX34: C Mar 7C 12
Cornerstones TQ9: Tot 6E 102
  (off Warland)
Corn Exchange
  Exeter 5D 6 (7E 64)
Cornfield Gdns. PL7: Plymp 2E 138
Cornfield Grn. TQ2: Torq 3D 112
  (off Bellrock Cl.)
Cornflower Cl. EX15: Will 3E 44
  EX31: Rou 6A 18
Cornflower Hill EX4: Exe 4A 64
Cornflower Wlk. PL6: Plym 1C 136
Cornflower Cl. EX15: New A 6A 104
Cornhill EX11: Ott M 3C 80
  EX15: Hemy 3F 47
Cornlands EX16: Sam P 1B 42
Cornmarket St. EX38: G Tor 2C 30
  Corn Mill EX11: Ott M 4C 80
  (off Mill St.)
Cornmill Cres. EX2: Alph 4D 70
Corn Pk. TQ10: S Bre 2B 100
Corn Pk. Rd. TQ12: A'well 6D 108
CORNTOWN 7H 129
Cornwall Beach PL1: Dev 2C 140
Cornwall St. EX4: Exe 6A 6 (7D 64)
  PL1: Dev 2C 140
  PL1: Plym 4C 8 (2H 141)
  (not continuous)
  PL20: Bere A 2C 126
Cornwall St. Flats PL1: Dev 2C 140
  (off Cornwall St.)
CORNWOOD 6J 129 (2C 175)
Cornwood Rd. PL7: Plymp 5E 138
  PL21: Ivy 4E 144
CORNWORTHY 2A 176
Cornworthy Cl. PL7: Plymp 4F 135
Coronation Av. EX7: Daw 5G 97
Coronation Cotts. PL11: Torp 1A 140
Coronation Cres. EX15: Uff 6G 43
Coronation Pl. EX21: Sheb 6J 29
  PL5: Plym 3D 134
Coronation Rd. EX2: Won 1K 71
  EX39: Bide 4E 22
  TQ7: Kingsb 4G 157
  TQ8: Salc 3C 158
  TQ9: Tot 5E 102
  TQ12: Kingst 4H 105
  TQ12: New A 1D 108
Coronation St. EX32: B'aple 3E 18
  TQ14: Shal 6G 107
Coronation Ter. EX6: Star 1E 96
  EX34: Ilfra 2J 11
Corndale Rd. PL2: Plym 4G 135
Coronet Cl. EX2: Sow 2C 72
Corporation Cres. EX32: B'aple 7G 19
  (off Corporation Ter.)
Corporation Rd. PL2: Plym 4J 135
Corporation St. EX32: B'aple 6G 19
Corporation Ter. EX32: B'aple 6G 19
Corsham Cl. PL6: Plym 4C 132
Corsham Rd. TQ4: Paig 2G 119
Cory Cl. PL9: Wem 5D 148

CORYTON 2C 169
Coryton Cl. EX7: Daw 4G 97
Coryton La. EX13: Kilm 1B 88
Coscombe Cir. PL9: Plyms 3E 142
Cosdon Pl. PL6: Plym 2A 136
Costly St. PL21: Ivy 4H 145
Cosway Rd. EX16: Tive 3D 40
Cotehele Av. PL2: Plym 6E 134
  PL4: Plym 5K 9 (3B 142)
Cotehele Dr. TQ3: Paig 7D 114
Cotehele Woodland Walks 1A 174
Cotfield Cl. EX14: Hon 2G 55
Cotfield St. EX2: Exe 2F 71
Cotford Cl. EX10: Sidb 1J 85
Cotford Rd. EX10: Sidb 1J 85
Cotford Rd. EX10: Sidb 2J 85
COTFORD ST LUKE 1B 166
COTHELSTONE 1B 166
Cot Hill PL7: Plymp 6J 137
Cot Hill Cl. PL7: Plymp 5H 137
Cot Hill Dr. PL7: Plymp 6J 137
Cot Hill Trad. Est. PL7: Plymp 5H 137
Cotlands EX10: Sidm 7A 84
COTLEIGH 3C 167
Cot Mnr. EX32: B'aple 6A 84
  (off Landkey Rd.)
COTMATON 6A 84
Cotmaton Rd. EX10: Sidm 7A 84
Cotmore Cl. TQ5: Brixh 6C 122
  TQ7: Chil 6G 159
Cotmore Way TQ7: Chil 6G 159
Cotsford Cl. EX5: Clyst M 2G 73
Cotswold Cl. TQ2: Torq 3K 115
COTT 3B 102 (1D 175)
Cottage Cl. EX33: Know 1K 15
Cott. Homes EX36: S Mol 7D 26
  (off Alswear New Rd.)
Cottage M. PL7: Plymp 5B 138
Cottage Rd. EX16: Tive 3B 40
Cotterell Rd. EX5: Broadc 2K 67
Cotters La. EX15: Kent 6B 46
Cottey Brook EX16: Tive 5B 40
Cottey Cres. EX4: Whip 2K 65
COTTEYLANDS 5B 40 (2D 165)
Cottey Mdw. TQ12: Kingst 5H 105
Cottingham Cres. EX39: Bide 2E 22
Cottington Ct. EX10: Sidm 6B 84
Cottington Mead EX10: Sidm 6B 84
Cottisbourne TQ13: Chag 2H 61
Cott La. EX33: Croy 3C 14
  TQ9: Darti 3B 102
Cotton Cl. PL7: Plymp 5C 138
Cotton Rd. TQ9: Darti 2B 102
COTTS 1A 174
Couches La. EX5: W'bury 6C 78
COUCHILL 5C 86
Couchill Dr. EX12: Seat 4D 86
Couchill La. EX12: Seat 4D 86
Coulsdon Rd. EX10: Sidm 4C 84
Council La. EX5: Broadc 7E 52
Countess Pl. EX16: Tive 3E 40
COUNTESS WEAR 5A 72
Countess Wear Rd. EX2: Cou W . .4K 71
Counties Cres. EX6: Star 2E 96
COUNTISBURY 2D 161
Countisbury Cliffs 1D 161
Countisbury Hill EX35: Lynm 2B 161
Countryman Cider 2B 168
Countryside Mus. 5F 83
County Cl. PL7: Plymp 4D 138
County Court
  Barnstaple 4D 18
  Torquay & Newton Abbot 4A 112
County Gate Viewpoint 2D 161
Couper Mdws. EX2: Sow 2C 72
The Court EX6: Dunsf 6C 62
  PL6: Plym 3D 132
Ct. Barton TQ7: S Hui 1K 155
Ct. Barton Hill EX12: Beer 6B 86
Court Barton La. EX5: New C 7D 50
Ct. Barton M. PL19: Lam 5D 58
Court Dr. EX15: Cull 2H 45
Courtenay EX14: Hon 4D 54
Courtenay Cl. EX6: Star 1D 96
  EX24: Colyt 7D 88
Courtenay Dr. EX24: Colyt 7D 88
Courtenay Gdns. EX2: Alph 5D 70
  TQ12: New A 2F 109
Courtenay Mnr. TQ1: Torq 2E 116
  (off Grafton Rd.)
Courtenay Pk. TQ10: S Bre 2B 100
  TQ12: New A 1G 109
Courtenay Pl. TQ14: Teignm 5J 107
  (off Den Promenade)
Courtenay Rd. EX2: Exe 2E 70
  EX20: Oke 4C 48
  PL19: Tavi 5H 59
  TQ4: Good 5J 119
  TQ12: New A 1G 109
Courtenay St. PL1: Plym . . .5D 8 (2J 141)
  TQ8: Salc 3C 158
  TQ12: New A 1E 108
Courtenay Ter. EX6: Star 1E 96
  TQ8: Salc 3C 158
  (off Devon Rd.)
  TQ13: More 7J 61
Ct. Farm Barn TQ12: A'well 6E 108

Courtfield TQ9: Tot 6H 103
Courtfield Cl. EX11: W Hill 3H 79
Courtfield Rd. PL3: Plym 6A 136
Court Ga. Cl. TQ12: Ipp 7G 101
Ct. Grange TQ12: A'well 6D 108
Courthayes La. EX5: Thor 2B 50
Courtis Gdns. EX17: Cred 7J 39
Courtlage Wlk. TQ7: Kingsb 3F 157
Courtland Cres. PL7: Plymp 2A 138
Courtland Rd. TQ2: Torq 6H 111
  TQ3: Paig 7H 115
Courtlands Cl. PL19: Tavi 3H 59
Courtlands La. EX8: Exmth 7H 75
Courtlands Rd. PL19: Tavi 3H 59
  TQ12: New A 2G 109
Court La. EX12: Seat 4E 86
Court M. TQ12: New A 1E 108
  (off Wolborough St.)
Courtney Rd. EX16: Tive 3E 40
Ct. Orchard EX5: New C 6D 50
Court Pk. TQ7: Thur 5C 154
Court Pk. Rd. TQ7: Thur 5C 154
Court Rd. PL8: New F 5F 149
  (not continuous)
  TQ2: Torq 1J 115
  TQ12: A'well 6E 108
Court St. TQ13: More 7G 61
Court Vw. EX14: Dunk 7H 47
  PL8: Brixt 3G 149
Court Wlk. EX19: Wink 2C 36
Court Way EX16: Sam P 2B 42
Court Wood PL8: New F 4G 149
The Courtyard TQ12: New A 1E 108
  (off Wolborough St.)
Cousens Cl. EX7: Daw 2J 97
COVE 2D 165
Coventry Cl. EX14: Fen 2G 53
Coventry Farm Trad. Est.
  TQ12: Kingsk 3G 111
Coventry Rd. EX4: Exe 6C 64
Coverdale Cl. TQ3: Paig 1H 119
  (off Bishops Pl.)
Coverdale Pl. PL5: Plym 2G 135
Coverdale Rd. EX2: Exe 2E 70
  PL5: Plym 1H 119
Coverts Cl. EX31: Bick 7K 17
Covetts EX5: W'bury 5C 78
Cove Vw. Apts. EX34: Ilfra 2J 11
  (off Sommers Cres.)
Cowick Ct. EX2: Exe 3D 70
Cowick Hill EX2: Exe 2B 70
Cowick La. EX2: Exe 2B 70
Cowick Rd. EX2: Exe 7B 6 (1D 70)
Cowick St. EX4: Exe 7A 6 (1C 70)
Cow La. EX34: Ilfra 2H 11
COWLEY 1C 64 (1D 171)
Cowley Bri. Rd. EX4: Exe . . .1A 6 (1C 64)
COWLEYMOOR 3E 40 (2D 165)
Cowleymoor Rd. EX16: Tive 3E 40
Cowley Rd. PL5: Plym 7J 131
Cownhayne La. EX24: Colyt 5E 88, 7E 88
Cowpark Ter. EX39: Nort 2H 71
Cowper Av. EX2: Won 2H 71
Cowslip Cres. TQ12: New A 6A 104
Cowslip Mdw. EX7: Daw 2H 97
Cox's Cl. PL6: Plym 2C 136
COXSIDE 6J 9 (4A 142)
Coxs Steps TQ6: Dartm 1A 124
  (off Clarence Hill)
Cox Tor Cl. PL20: Yelv 5F 127
Cox Tor Rd. PL19: Tavi 4K 59
Coypool Park & Ride 5H 137
Coypool Rd. PL7: Plymp 5H 137
Coysh Sq. EX3: Top 5A 74
Crab Apple EX5: Rock 3D 68
Crabb La. EX2: Exe 3C 70
Crabbs Cl. PL15: St G 6C 34
Crabshell Hgts. TQ7: Kingsb 6G 157
  TQ7: Kingsb 6E 136
Crabtree Cl. EX5: Cran 2E 68
  PL3: Plym 6G 137
Crabtree Vs. PL3: Plym 6F 137
Crackington Av. EX4: Pin 3C 66
CRACKINGTON HAVEN 1A 168
Crackston Cl. PL6: Plym 4C 136
CRADDOCK 2A 166
Craddock Cl. EX22: Hols 1C 34
CRAFTHOLE 2A 174
Craig Cotts. EX5: Clyst M 2G 73
Craig Ct. EX10: Sidm 6D 84
Craigie Dr. PL1: Plym 3A 8 (2G 141)
Craigmore Av. PL2: Plym 6E 134
Cramber Cl. PL6: Robo 1D 132
  PL19: Tavi 5H 59
Crampit La. EX39: West 7J 21
Cranbourne Av. PL4: Plym . .2K 9 (1B 142)
CRANBROOK 3B 68 (1A 172)
Cranbrook Castle 2B 170
Cranbrook Rd. EX2: Won 7K 65
Cranbrook Station
  (Rail) 3A 68 (1D 171)
Cranbrook Wlk. EX1: Pin 5C 66
Crandford Cl. EX20: Brid 3H 57
Cranesbill Way TQ12: New A 6A 104
Cranes La. EX9: E Bud 1D 82
Cranfield PL7: Plymp 4K 137

CRANFORD 1E 28
Cranford EX10: Sidm 5C 84
Cranford Av. EX8: Exmth 6E 76
Cranford Cl. EX8: Exmth 6E 76
Cranford Cross EX39: Cran 1E 28
Cranford Hill Ho. EX8: Exmth 5F 77
Cranford Ho. EX8: Exmth 6F 77
Cranford Rd. TQ3: Pres 5G 115
Cranford Sports & Fitness Club 6E 76
Cranford Vw. EX8: Exmth 6E 76
Cranishaies La. EX5: Bradn 7F 45
Cranleigh Ter. EX34: C Mar 6B 12
                               (off King St.)
Cranley Gdns. TQ13: Chag 2H 61
Cranmere Ct. EX2: Matf 5G 71
Cranmere Pool 2A 170
Cranmere Rd. EX20: Oke 2E 48
   PL3: Plym 5B 136
Cranmore Vw. EX16: Ashy 7B 40
Crannaford La. EX5: Cran 2D 68
Crannafords Ind. Pk.
   TQ13: Chag 1K 61
Crantock Ter. PL2: Plym 6F 135
Craon Gdns. EX20: Oke 2D 48
CRAPSTONE 6C 126 (1B 174)
Crapstone Rd. PL20: Yelv 6E 126
Crapstone Ter. PL20: C'stone 6C 126
Crashaw Cl. PL5: Plym 7J 131
Craven Av. PL4: Plym 2K 9 (1B 142)
Crawford Gdns. EX2: Exe 2D 70
Crawford Rd. PL1: Plym . . .1A 8 (1G 141)
CRAWLEY 3C 167
CRAZE LOWMAN 1J 41
CREACOMBE 2C 165
Creadly La. EX3: Top 7E 72
Crealy Adventure Pk. & Resort . . .1A 172
Creamery Cl. PL8: Torr 3C 150
Crease La. PL19: Tavi 5F 59
CREDITON 6H 39 (3C 165)
Crediton La. EX6: Cher 1E 62
Crediton Rd. EX5: Cowl 1C 64
   EX20: Oke 3C 48
Crediton Station (Rail) . . .7K 39 (1C 171)
Crediton Wlk. PL6: Plym 3F 137
CREECH HEATHFIELD 1C 167
CREECH ST MICHAEL 1C 167
Creedy Rd. EX17: Cred 6J 39
   PL3: Plym 6D 136
Creedy Vw. EX5: New C 4C 50
Creek Rd. PL5: Plym 4C 134
   TQ6: Dartm 5D 124
Creekside Rd. PL8: Noss M 6H 149
Creely Cl. EX2: Alph 5F 71
Crelake Cl. PL19: Tavi 5J 59
Crelake Ind. Est. PL19: Tavi 5J 59
Crelake Pk. PL19: Tavi 5J 59
Crelake Vs. PL19: Tavi 5J 59
CREMYLL 5D 140 (2A 174)
Cremyll Rd. PL11: Torp 2A 140
Cremyll St. PL1: Plym 3F 141
The Crescent EX8: Exmth 4G 77
   EX13: Kilm 2B 88
   PL1: Plym 5C 8 (3H 141)
   PL8: Brixt 2H 149
   PL16: Lift 6B 56
   PL20: C'stone 6C 126
   TQ5: Brixh 5F 123
Crescent Av. EX31: B'aple 6C 18
   PL1: Plym 6C 8 (3H 141)
Crescent Av. M. PL1: Plym 6C 8
Crescent Ct. TQ6: Dartm 6D 124
                         (off Townstal Cres.)
Crescent Gdns. PL21: Ivy 3G 145
Crescent Mans. EX2: Exe 6G 7
Crescent Rd. PL21: Ivy 3G 145
Cressbrook Cl. PL6: Plym 1G 137
Cressbrook Dr. PL6: Plym 1G 137
Cressbrook Wlk. PL6: Plym 1F 137
Cresswell Cl. TQ12: Kingsk 7K 109
The Crestas TQ1: Torq 7E 112
Crestfield Ri. PL21: Ivy 4F 145
Crestfields TQ6: Strete 6G 153
                               (off Crestway)
Crest Hill TQ11: B'leigh 4C 98
Cresthill Rd. PL2: Plym 4G 135
Crest Vw. TQ4: Paig 2J 119
Crestway TQ6: Strete 6G 153
CREWKERNE 3D 167
Crewkerne Rd. EX13: Ray H 3B 90
Crewkerne Station (Rail) 3D 167
Cricket Cl. EX18: Chul 6D 32
The Cricketers EX13: Axmin 2H 89
Cricketers Grn. TQ2: Torq 5A 112
Cricketfield Cl. TQ13: Chud 1D 94
Cricket Fld. Ct. EX9: Bud S 6C 82
Cricket Fld. La. EX9: Bud S 6C 82
Cricket Fld. Rd. TQ12: New A 7F 105
Cricketfield Rd. TQ2: Torq 6A 112
Cricketfield Vw. TQ13: Chud 1D 94
Cricket La. TQ11: B'leigh 3B 98
CRICKET MALHERBIE 2D 167
CRICKET ST THOMAS 3D 167
Cricklepit La. EX1: Exe 6D 6
                         (off Commercial Rd.)
Cricklepit St. EX1: Exe 6D 6 (7E 64)
Cridlake EX13: Axmin 4J 89
CRIMCHARD 3D 167
Crimson King EX5: Cran 3C 68

Crispin Rd. TQ7: Kingsb 4F 157
Critchards EX5: W'bury 6C 78
Criterion Pl. EX8: Exmth 6C 76
                             (off Tower St.)
Crocken Tor Rd. EX20: Oke 3D 48
Crocker Ct. EX2: Exe 2E 70
Crockern Tor 3A 170
CROCKERNWELL 1B 170
Crockers Cl. EX31: Bick 7K 17
Crockers Way PL15: St G 6C 34
Crockwells Cl. EX6: Exmin 3D 74
Crockwells Rd. EX6: Exmin 3D 74
CROFORD 1B 166
The Croft EX20: S Zeal 3H 49
   TQ12: E Ogw 3A 108
Cft. Chase EX4: Exe 1B 70
Croft Cl. TQ12: E Ogw 3A 108
Croft Cl. TQ2: Torq 1C 116
                             (off Abbey Rd.)
Crofters Cl. PL21: Fil 5K 145
Cft. Hill TQ2: Torq 1C 116
Croft Ho. EX22: Hols 2C 34
Cft. Lee EX34: Ber 4C 12
Croft Mdw. TQ12: Ipp 6H 101
Cft. Orchard TQ12: Ipp 6H 101
Croft Pk. PL6: Plym 3D 132
                       (off Copper Beech Way)
Croft Rd. EX22: Hols 2C 34
   TQ2: Torq 1C 116
   TQ8: Salc 3C 158
   TQ12: E Ogw 3A 108
   TQ12: Ipp 6H 101
Croftside EX34: Ilfra 3H 11
Crofts Lea Pk. EX34: Ilfra 3K 11
Croftswood Gdns. EX34: Ilfra 4K 11
Croftswood Vs. EX34: Ilfra 3K 11
Croftview Ter. TQ8: Salc 3C 158
                             (off Island St.)
Crogg La. DT7: Uply 3G 91
Croker's Mdw. TQ13: Bov T 3B 92
Crokers Way TQ12: Ipp 6H 101
Cromartie Point TQ2: Torq 4A 116
                          (off Livermead Hill)
Cromartie Rd. PL4: Plym 3C 142
                            (off Cavendish Rd.)
Cromer Cl. PL6: Plym 3B 132
Cromer Wlk. PL6: Plym 3B 132
Cromwell Cl. EX38: G Tor 1E 30
Cromwell Ct. EX1: Heav 7K 65
Cromwell Ga. PL6: Plym 3D 132
Cromwell Pk. EX16: Tive 6G 41
   PL1: Modb 7A 136
Cromwell Rd. PL4: Plym 5K 9 (3B 142)
Cromwells Mdw. EX17: Cred 5K 39
Cromwells Way TQ13: Bov T 3B 92
Cromwell Ter. EX2: Won 7C 66
                           (off Sidmouth Rd.)
Crookeder Cl. PL9: Plyms 7H 143
Crooklake Hill EX5: Half M 7A 50
Crookmans Ct. EX32: B'aple 4H 19
Croppins Cl. TQ11: B'leigh 4D 98
Cropp La. PL2: Dev 7D 134
CROSS .2E 14
Cross Cl. EX31: Frem 6E 16
Crosscut Way EX14: Hon 4F 55
Cross Farm Ct. EX32: B Taw 6B 24
Cross Grange Trad. Est.
   TQ12: H'fld 1J 93
CROSS GREEN 2B 168
Cross Hill PL2: Dev 7D 134
   TQ12: C'head, N'ton 7A 106
Crossingfields Dr. EX8: Exmth 3C 76
Crossings Cl. PL19: Mary T 1B 60
Crosslands EX31: B'aple 5B 18
   TQ7: Thur 6C 154
Cross La. EX10: Sidm 7C 84
                              (off Fore St.)
   EX34: Ber 3C 12
   TQ8: E Port 4E 158
Crossley Cl. TQ12: Kingst 3H 105
Crossley Moor Rd. TQ12: Kingst . . .4H 105
Crossmead EX35: Lynt 2G 13
Cross Mdws. EX31: Rou 7K 17
Crossmead Vs. EX2: Exe 2A 70
Cross Pk. EX20: S Zeal 2H 49
   EX34: Ilfra 2H 11
   EX37: High B 3C 32
   PL8: Brixt 2J 149
   PL20: Buck M 5A 126
   TQ5: Brixh 5D 122
Crosspark TQ9: Tot 5G 103
Cross Pk. Av. TQ2: Torq 2A 136
Crosspark Av. TQ2: Torq 5J 111
Crosspark Cl. EX31: B'aple 2D 18
Cross Pk. Rd. PL6: Plym 2A 136
   PL9: Wem 6B 148
Cross Parks EX15: Cull 5F 45
Crossparks EX15: Ash T 7B 42
   TQ6: Dartm 7C 124
Cross Pk. Way PL6: Plym 2A 136
CROSS ROADS 1C 56
CROSS SIDE 1C 165
Cross St. EX12: Seat 5E 86
   EX31: B'aple 4E 18
   EX34: C Mar 5A 12
   EX35: Lynt 2G 13
   EX39: Nort 5E 20
   TQ13: More 6H 61

Cross Tree Cen. EX33: Brau 4J 15
Cross Vw. EX2: Alph 4E 70
   TQ11: Upp D 7B 98
Cross Vw. Ter. EX2: Ide 3B 70
Crossway PL7: Plymp 4K 137
   TQ4: Good 5J 119
Crossway Av. PL4: Plym 1C 142
Crossway Country Cvn. Pk. 1F 25
Crossways PL7: Spa 1J 139
   PL9: Wem 6B 148
   PL21: Corn 6J 129
The Crossways Shop. Cen. 1H 119
Crowbeare Mdw. EX38: G Tor 1D 30
CROWBOROUGH 5C 14
Crowborough La. EX33: Geo 5B 14
Crowborough Rd. EX33: Geo 5C 14
Crow Bri. EX15: Cull 4F 45
                             (not continuous)
Crowbridge Pk. EX15: Cull 5G 45
CROWDEN 1C 169
Crowden Cres. EX16: Tive 5F 41
Crowder Mdw. TQ10: S Bre 2C 100
Crowder Pk. TQ10: S Bre 2C 100
Crowder's Hill EX8: Exmth 1D 76
Crow Grn. EX15: Cull 4G 45
Crown & Anchor Way TQ3: Paig 1H 119
Crowndale Av. PL3: Plym 5B 136
Crowndale Rd. PL19: Tavi 7G 59
Crown Gdns. PL6: Plym 2B 136
CROWNHILL 2B 136
Crownhill Fort 7A 132 (2A 174)
Crown Hill EX16: Nad 5B 42
Crownhill Ct. TQ2: Torq 7A 112
Crownhill Cres. TQ5: Galm 3H 121
Crownhill Fort Rd. PL6: Plym 7A 132
Crownhill Pk. TQ2: Torq 7A 112
Crownhill Ri. TQ2: Torq 7A 112
Crownhill Rd. PL5: Plym 7E 130
   PL6: Plym 7H 131
Crownley La. TQ9: Sto G 3B 120
Crown Sq. TQ14: Shal 6G 107
Crown Way EX2: Sow 2C 72
Crow Pk. PL3: Plym 4A 136
Crowther's Hill
   TQ6: Dartm 2A 124 (6F 125)
Crow Vw. EX32: B'aple 4H 19
CROYDE 2D 14 (3A 160)
CROYDE BAY 1B 14
Croyde Bay Holiday Village 3B 14
Croyde Rd. EX33: Croy, Saunt 4A 14
Croydon Gdns. PL5: Plym 6D 130
Crozier Rd. PL4: Plym 7A 136
Crudges La. EX8: Exmth 5C 76
Cruffen La. EX33: Lob 1G 15
CRUFT .1D 169
CRUWYS MORCHARD 2C 165
Crystal Cl. TQ4: Good 5J 119
Cuckoo Down La. EX14: Hon 5H 55
Cuckoo La. DT7: Uply 4F 91
Cudhill Rd. TQ5: Brixh 4D 122
CUDLIPPTOWN 2E 60 (3D 169)
Cudmore Pk. EX16: Tive 6G 41
CUDWORTH 2D 167
Cuffe Rd. PL3: Plym 7G 135
Culbin Grn. PL6: Plym 3E 136
Culdrose Cl. PL5: Plym 7D 130
CULLOMPTON 4H 45 (3A 166)
Cullompton Hill EX5: Bradn 1D 52
CULLOMPTON SERVICE AREA
                              . . .3H 45 (3A 166)
Culm Cl. EX2: Sow 1C 72
   EX39: Bide 3H 23
   TQ2: Torq 5H 111
Culm Davy EX14: Dunk 7H 47
Culme Rd. PL3: Plym 6B 136
Culme Way EX14: Dunk 7G 47
Culm Gro. EX2: Sow 1C 72
Culm Haven EX15: Uff 6G 43
Culm Lea EX15: Cull 4K 45
CULMSTOCK 1B 46 (2B 166)
Culmstock Rd. EX15: Hemy 2F 47
Culm Valley Sports Cen. 5H 45
Culm Valley Way EX15: Uff 7F 43
CULVER .1C 171
Culver Cl. EX5: Bradn 2D 52
   EX16: Tive 6F 41
   PL6: Plym 3B 136
Culverdale TQ9: Tot 7G 103
Culver Gdns. EX10: Sidm 6C 84
Culver Ho. TQ13: Chud 1C 94
Culverland Cl. EX4: Exe 4G 65
Culverland Rd. EX4: Exe 4G 65
CULVERLANE 1D 175
Culver La. TQ13: Chud 1D 94
Culver Pk. Cl. TQ7: Kingsb 6H 157
Culvert Rd. EX5: Sto C 6J 51
Culver Way PL7: Plymp 3F 139
Culverwood Cl. PL7: Plymp 3F 139
Culvery Cl. EX5: W'bury 5C 78
Culvery Grn. TQ2: Torq 5H 111
Cumber Cl. TQ5: Brixh 3D 122
   TQ7: Malb 3D 155
Cumber Dr. TQ5: Brixh 3D 122
Cumberland Cl. EX8: Exmth 3F 77
Cumberland Dr. EX2: Sow 1C 72
Cumberland Grn. TQ5: Brixh 3D 122

Cumberland Rd. PL1: Dev 3E 140
Cumberland St. PL1: Dev 2D 140
Cumberland Way EX1: Pin, Sow 4D 66
Cummings Cross TQ12: Live 3F 93
Cundy Cl. PL7: Plymp 4H 137
Cunliffe Av. PL9: Hooe 6B 142
Cunningham Av. EX13: Axmin 2K 89
Cunningham Rd. EX8: Exmth 2F 77
   PL5: Tam F 2H 131
Curie M. EX2: Exe 1H 71
CURLAND 2C 167
CURLAND COMMON 2C 167
Curledge St. TQ4: Paig 2H 119
Curlew Cl. EX20: Oke 2A 48
   TQ2: Torq 2J 111
Curlew Dr. TQ7: W Cha 7J 157
Curlew M. PL3: Plym 7D 136
Curlew Way EX4: Exe 2F 65
   EX7: Daw 7C 96
Currington Mdw. EX31: Bick 6K 17
                             (not continuous)
CURRY MALLET 1D 167
CURRY RIVEL 1D 167
Cursons Way PL21: Ivy 4E 144
CURTISKNOWLE 2D 175
Curtis St. PL1: Dev 3D 140
Curve Acre EX33: Brau 5K 15
Curwood Cres. EX16: Tive 5C 40
Custance Ho. EX14: Hon 3F 55
                             (off Queen St.)
Custom Ho. Hill TQ14: Teignm 5H 107
Custom Ho. La.
   PL1: Plym 7B 8 (4H 141)
Custom House Vis. Cen. 6D 6
Cuthbert Cl. PL21: Ivy 4C 112
Cutlife La. EX39: Hart 3G 27
Cutterburrow La. EX33: Brau 5H 15
Cutters Wharf EX8: Exmth 6A 76
                            (off Shelly Rd.)
CUTTIFORD'S DOOR 2D 167
CUTTIVETT 1A 174
Cuxton Mdws. PL20: Buck M 5A 126
Cygnet Ind. Units EX2: Sow 7D 66
Cygnet Theatre 6E 6
Cypress Cl. EX14: Hon 6C 54
   PL7: Plymp 4F 139
   TQ2: Torq 1C 116
Cypress Ct. TQ4: Paig 2H 119
                            (off Fisher St.)
Cypress Dr. EX4: Exe 5C 64
Cyprus Gdns. EX8: Exmth 6E 76
                             (not continuous)
Cyprus Rd. EX8: Exmth 6D 76
Cyprus Ter. EX32: B'aple 6G 19

D

Dabby La. EX6: Cher 1D 62
Daccabridge Rd. TQ12: Kingsk 1F 111
DACCOMBE 1A 112
Daccombe Hill TQ12: Dacc 1A 112
Daccombe Mill La.
   TQ12: Coff, Kingsk 1G 111
Daddon Hill EX39: Nort 6D 20
Daddyhole Plain TQ1: Torq 4F 117
Daddyhole Rd. TQ1: Torq 3E 116
                             (not continuous)
Daggers Copse TQ12: New A 1C 108
Dagmar Rd. EX8: Exmth 6C 76
Dagmar St. TQ14: Shal 6G 107
Dagra La. TQ14: Shal 7D 106
Daimonds La. TQ14: Teignm 4H 107
DAINTON 4A 110
Dainton Bus. Pk. TQ12: H'fld 1K 93
Dainton Cl. TQ4: Good 5J 119
Dainton M. TQ4: Paig 2H 119
Dainton Pk. Golf Course
                               . . . . . .5K 101 (1A 176)
Dairy Cl. EX6: Exmin 3D 74
   TQ9: Tot 6H 103
The Dairy Estate EX4: Pin 4C 66
Dairy Hill TQ12: Torq 6J 111
Dairy La. PL1: Plym 2A 8 (1G 141)
   PL21: Ivy 4H 145
Daison Cotts. TQ1: Torq 6C 112
Daison Cres. TQ1: Torq 5D 112
Daisy La. TQ12: New A 6A 104
Daisy Links EX4: Exe 4A 64
Daisy Pk. PL8: Brixt 2H 149
Daisys Path TQ9: Sto G 3B 120
Dakota Way PL5: Clyst H 5A 68
Dale Av. PL6: Plym 4D 136
Dale Gdns. PL4: Plym 1E 8 (7J 135)
Dale Rd. PL4: Plym 1D 8 (7J 135)
Daleside Rd. EX4: Exe 3H 65
Daleswood Rd. PL19: Tavi 5G 59
Dalton Gdns. PL5: Plym 7D 130
Dalverton Ct. TQ5: Brixh 2E 122
DALWOOD 3C 167
Damage Barton Cvn. & Camping Site
                               . . . . .3D 10
Damerel Cl. PL1: Dev 2E 140
Damson Cl. EX15: Will 4D 44
Danby Hgts. Cl. TQ1: Torq 2G 117
Danby La. EX8: Exmth 5C 76
Danby Ter. EX8: Exmth 5C 76

Dandelion Pl.—Diggerland

Dandelion Pl. TQ12: New A 6A 104
Dane Ct. EX39: Nort 6F 21
Dane Heath Bus. Pk. TQ12: H'fld 1J 93
The Danes 1F 13
Daneshay EX39: Nort 5F 21
Danes Mead EX15: Cull 1H 45
Dane's Rd. EX4: Exe 1D 6 (5E 64)
Danesway EX4: Pin 2D 66
Danum Dr. PL7: Plymp 6E 138
Danvers Rd. TQ2: Torq 3B 112
Daphne Cl. TQ1: Torq 2F 117
D'arcy Ct. TQ12: New A 7F 105
Dares Orchard EX24: Colyf 1F 87
DARITE 3A 168
Darkey La. EX20: Oke 4A 48
PL16: Lift 6A 56
Darklake Cl. PL6: Plym 5F 133
Darklake La. PL6: Plym 2E 132
Darklake Pk. PL6: Plym 5F 133
Darklake Vw. PL6: Plym 5E 132
Dark La. EX5: Thor 2A 50
EX9: Bud S 6B 82
EX10: Sidm 4A 84
EX31: B'aple 2E 18
PL21: Modb 5G 147
Dark St. La. PL7: Plymp 4B 138
Darky La. EX18: Chaw 7C 32
TQ7: Kingsb 1E 156
Darnell Cl. EX10: Sidm 4C 84
Darracombe Cres. TQ12: New A 6B 104
DARRACOTT 6D 14 (3A 160)
Darracott EX38: G Tor 1D 30
Darracotts Ct. EX39: App 2H 21
Darran Cl. TQ12: Kingst 4J 105
Darran Rd. TQ12: Kingst 4J 105
Dart Av. EX2: Cou W 6C 72
TQ2: Torq 5J 111
Dartbridge Mnr. TQ11: B'leigh 3D 98
Dart Bri. Rd. TQ11: B'leigh 4D 98
Dart Bus. Cen. TQ9: Darti 2B 102
Dart Cl. EX31: C'nor 1D 16
PL3: Plym 5E 136
Dart Hill EX16: W'ridge 4G 33
DARTINGTON 2A 102 (1D 175)
Dartington Cl. EX38: G Tor 1D 30
Dartington Crystal 2C 163
Dartington Crystal Vis. Cen. 1B 30
Dartington Flds. EX38: G Tor 1D 30
Dartington Hall Gdns. 1D 102 (1A 176)
Dartington La. TQ9: Darti 4D 102
Dartington Vis. Cen. 1D 102
Dartington Wlk. EX6: Exmin 1B 74
PL6: Plym 3F 137
Dart Marina TQ6: Dartm 4F 125
Dart Marine Pk. TQ9: Tot 7F 103
DARTMEET 3A 170
Dartmeet Av. PL3: Plym 5C 136
Dartmoor Cvn. Pk. 7B 126
Dartmoor Cotts. PL7: Wot 1F 129
Dartmoor Country Holidays 1D 126
Dartmoor Ct. *TQ13: Bov T* *4B 92*
(off Station Rd.)
Dartmoor Nat. Pk. 2D 169
Dartmoor National Park Visitor Centre
Haytor 3B 170
Postbridge 3A 170
Princetown 7C 60 (3D 169)
Dartmoor Otters & Buckfast Butterflies 4E 98 (1D 175)
Dartmoor Prison Mus. 5B 60 (3D 169)
Dartmoor Railway
Dartmoor Railway 5C 48 (1D 169)
Dartmoor Vw. EX18: Chul 6C 32
PL4: Plym 1D 142
Dartmoor Way EX15: Cull 4F 45
Dartmoor Zoo 2B 174
DARTMOUTH 1B 124 (6F 125)
Dartmouth Cvn. Site 1H 153
Dartmouth Castle 7H 125 (2A 176)
Dartmouth Ct. *TQ6: Dartm* *2B 124*
(off Oxford St.)
Dartmouth Golf Course
Blackawton 2A 176
Dartmouth Hill TQ6: Sto F 2H 153
Dartmouth Leisure Cen. 7C 124
Dartmouth Mus. 1B 124 (6F 125)
Dartmouth Outdoor Heated
Swimming Pool 7D 124
Dartmouth Park & Ride 7C 124
Dartmouth Rd.
TQ4: Broads, Good, Paig 1H 119
TQ5: Chur F 2H 121
TQ6: Sto F 2H 153
TQ9: E All 6D 152
Dartmouth Steam Railway
Churston Station 3J 121 (2A 176)
Goodrington Station 3J 119 (2A 176)
Greenway Halt 5G 121 (2A 176)
Kingswear Station 6G 125 (2A 176)
Paignton Station 2H 119 (1A 176)
Dartmouth Steam Railway Vis. Cen. 6G 125
Dartmouth to Dartmouth Castle
Foot Ferry 1B 124 (7G 125)
Dartmouth to Dittisham
Foot Ferry 1B 124 (6F 125)
Dartmouth to Totnes
Foot Ferry 1B 124 (6G 125)
Dartmouth Visitor Centre 1B 124 (6F 125)
Dartmouth Wlk. PL6: Plym 3F 137
(not continuous)
Dartmouth Yacht Club 2B 124
Darton Gro. TQ9: Sto G 4B 120
Dart Pk. EX36: S Mol 6D 26
Dartridge La. EX18: Chul 6A 32
Dart Rock Climbing Cen. 4E 98
Darts Cl. PL15: St G 6C 34
Darts Farm EX3: Clyst G 5D 74
Dartside TQ9: Tot 4D 102
Dartside Ct. *TQ6: Dartm* *5F 125*
(off Clarence St.)
Dartside Quay TQ5: Galm 4G 121
Dart Valley Nature Reserve 3A 170
Dart Vw. Rd. TQ5: Galm 2H 121
Dart Vs. TQ9: Tot 7E 102
Dart Wlk. EX2: Sow 1C 72
Darwin Ct. EX2: Exe 6F 7 (7F 65)
TQ2: Torq 2B 112
Darwin Cres. PL3: Plym 6E 136
TQ2: Torq 2B 112
Dashpers TQ5: Brixh 5D 122
Dathan Cl. PL19: Tavi 4J 59
Daucus Cl. PL19: Tavi 5H 59
Davenham Cl. PL6: Plym 4C 132
Daveys Elm Vw. TQ4: Good 5H 119
David Cl. EX33: Brau 5J 15
PL7: Plymp 3C 138
David Lloyd Leisure
Exeter 2D 72
David Rd. TQ3: Paig 7G 115
Davids Cl. EX10: Sidb 1H 85
David's Hill EX33: Geo 5B 14
Davids La. PL21: Fil 6A 146
David Southgate Ct.
PL1: Plym 5A 8
DAVIDSTOW 2A 168
Davies Av. TQ4: Good 6H 119
Davies Cl. EX5: Silv 1H 51
Davis Av. TQ2: Torq 7K 111
Davis Ct. TQ12: New A 7D 104
Davis Rd. TQ6: Dartm 6C 124
Davy Rd. PL6: Plym 6D 132
Dawes Cl. TQ12: E Ogw 4C 108
Dawes La. PL9: Elb 7K 143
DAWLISH 4H 97 (3D 171)
Dawlish Bus. Pk. EX7: Daw 7C 96
Dawlish Leisure Cen. 2J 97
Dawlish Mus. 4G 97 (3D 171)
Dawlish Pk. Ter. EX8: Exmth 7H 75
Dawlish Rd. EX2: Alph, Matf 4E 70
EX2: Matf 6H 71
EX6: Exmin 6H 71
TQ14: Teignm 4J 107
Dawlish Sands Holiday Pk. 6E 96
Dawlish Station (Rail) 4H 97 (3D 171)
Dawlish St. TQ14: Teignm 4J 107
Dawlish Tourist Information Centre 4H 97 (3D 171)
Dawlish Wlk. PL6: Plym 4F 137
DAWLISH WARREN 7E 96 (3D 171)
Dawlish Warren 3D 171
Dawlish Warren Holiday Pk. 7E 96
Dawlish Warren
National Nature Reserve 3D 171
Dawlish Warren Rd.
EX6: Cockw, E'don 3E 96
EX7: Daw W, Star 3E 96
Dawlish Warren Station
(Rail) 7E 96 (3D 171)
Dawn Cl. EX1: Heav 6K 65
DAW'S HOUSE 2B 168
Daws Mdw. TQ12: Kingst 5H 105
Dawson Cl. PL5: Plym 2D 134
Daymond Dr. TQ13: Bov T 4E 92
Daymond Rd. PL5: Plym 1C 134
Days-Pottles La. EX6: Exmin 2A 74
Dayton Cl. PL6: Plym 1K 135
Deacon Cl. EX2: Alph 5E 70
Deacons Grn. PL19: Tavi 5G 59
Deadhorse La. EX13: Mus 7B 90
DEAN
EX31 2C 161
EX35 2D 161
Dean Clarke Gdns. EX1: Exe 5F 7
DEAN CROSS 2B 160
DEAN CROSS 5F 143
Dean Cross Rd. PL9: Plyms 5F 143
Deane Cl. EX33: Know 1K 15
Deanery Pl. EX1: Exe 5E 6
The Deanes EX16: Tive 5B 40
Dean Hill PL9: Plyms 5F 143
Dean Hill Rd. EX15: Will 5B 44
Dean Pk. Rd. PL9: Plyms 5E 142
DEAN PRIOR 1D 175
Dean Rd. PL7: Plymp 3A 138
Deans Cl. EX39: Nort 5E 20
TQ14: Bi'ton 3B 106
Deans La. EX36: S Mol 5D 26
Deans Mead EX10: Sidm 5B 84
Deans Pk. EX36: S Mol 5D 26
Dean St. EX2: Exe 6F 7 (7F 65)
EX17: Cred 6J 39
Debden Cl. PL5: Plym 6C 130
De Brionne Hgts. EX20: Oke 3C 48
De Courcy Rd. TQ8: Salc 6A 158
Decoy Country Pk. 3F 109 (1A 176)
Decoy Discovery Cen. 3G 109
Decoy Ind. Est. TQ12: New A 4G 109
Decoy Rd. TQ12: New A 2G 109
Deeble Cl. PL7: Plymp 2B 138
Deep Dene Cl. TQ5: Brixh 5C 122
Deepdene Pk. EX2: Exe 7J 7 (1H 71)
Deep La. EX17: Cred 5H 39
EX31: Brat F 7G 13
PL7: Plymp 7F 139
Deepway EX10: Sidb 2H 85
EX16: Tive 4F 41
Deepway Ct. EX6: Exmin 2C 74
Deepway Gdns. EX6: Exmin 2B 74
Deepway La. EX2: Matf 1A 74
EX6: Exmin 2B 74
EX12: Brans 6G 85
Deepways EX9: Bud S 5A 82
Deer Combe *TQ6: Sto F* *1H 153*
(off West Pk.)
Deerhill La. EX36: S Mol 4B 26
Deerhill Rd. EX36: S Mol 5B 26
Deer Leap PL19: Tavi 5K 59
Deer Pk. PL21: Ivy 4J 145
TQ6: Sto F 1H 153
Deer Pk. Av. TQ14: Teignm 3G 107
Deer Pk. Cl. PL19: Tavi 4J 59
TQ14: Teignm 3G 107
Deer Pk. Cres. PL19: Tavi 4J 59
Deer Pk. Dr. PL3: Plym 4D 136
TQ14: Teignm 3G 107
Deer Pk. La. PL19: Tavi 4J 59
Deer Pk. Rd. EX32: B'aple 7H 19
PL19: Tavi 4J 59
TQ6: Sto F 1H 153
TQ12: New A 3G 109
Deers Leap Cl. TQ3: Pres 4H 115
Deer Valley Rd. EX22: Hols 2B 34
Deer Wood Vw. EX32: B Taw 6B 24
Defoe Cl. PL5: Plym 1H 135
Delacombe Cl. PL7: Plymp 2C 138
De-la-Hay Av. PL3: Plym 1A 8 (1G 141)
Delamere Rd. PL6: Plym 4D 136
Delamore Cl. PL21: Ivy 4E 144
De La Pole Ct. *EX12: Seat* *5F 87*
(off Fore St.)
De La Rue Way EX4: Pin 3C 66
Delaware Gdns. PL2: Plym 4E 134
Delderfield Gdns. EX8: Exmth 6E 76
Delgany Dr. PL6: Plym 5B 132
Delgany Vw. PL6: Plym 5B 132
Delgany Vs. PL6: Plym 5B 132
Delia Gdns. EX5: Rock 4E 68
Delius Cres. EX2: Won 7B 66
The Dell PL7: Plymp 5J 137
PL19: Tavi 3H 59
Dell Ct. TQ12: New A 1F 109
The Den TQ14: Teignm 5J 107
Denbeigh Ter. EX10: Sidm 5C 84
Den Brook Cl. TQ1: Torq 7F 113
DENBURY 2H 101 (1A 176)
Denbury Ct. EX2: Mar B 5G 71
Denbury Down La. TQ12: Den 2G 101
Denbury Grn. TQ12: Den 2H 101
Denbury Rd. TQ12: Den, E Ogw 2J 101
Denby Ho. TQ4: Paig 2J 119
Den Cres. TQ14: Teignm 5J 107
Dendy Rd. TQ4: Paig 1H 119
Dene Cl. EX8: Exmth 3F 77
Denes Cl. EX32: Land 2B 24
Denes Rd. EX32: Land 2B 24
Dengie Cl. PL7: Plymp 4E 138
Denham Cl. PL5: Plym 1H 135
Dening Ct. EX8: Exmth 4D 76
Denise Cl. EX2: Alph 5E 70
Denmark Rd. EX1: Exe 5G 7 (7G 65)
EX8: Exmth 4F 77
Denners Way EX15: Uff 6H 43
Dennesdene Cl. EX8: Exmth 1D 76
Dennington Hill EX32: Swim 3G 25
Dennis Camp Rd. PL6: Plym 3B 132
Dennis Cl. PL5: Plym 4B 134
Dennysmead Ct. *EX4: Exe* *3D 64*
(off Glenthorne Rd.)
Den Prom. TQ14: Teignm 5J 107
Den Rd. TQ14: Teignm 5J 107
Denver Cl. EX3: Top 7D 72
Denver Rd. EX3: Top 7D 72
Denys Rd. TQ1: Torq 7E 112
TQ9: Tot 6E 102
Deptford Pl. PL4: Plym 2G 9 (1K 141)
Deptford Vs. EX31: B'aple 6B 18
Derby Rd. EX32: B'aple 3F 19
PL5: Plym 6H 131
TQ7: Kingsb 5G 157
Derick Rd. EX16: Tive 3B 40
Derncleugh Gdns. EX7: Holc 7G 97
Derrell Rd. TQ4: Paig 3G 119
DERRIFORD 6C 132
Derriford Bus. Pk. PL6: Plym 7B 132
Derriford Health & Leisure Cen. 7D 132
Derriford Pk. PL6: Plym 7B 132
Derriford Rd. PL6: Plym 6B 132
DERRIL 3B 162
DERRITON 3A 34 (3B 162)
Derry Av. PL4: Plym 1E 8 (1J 141)
Derry's Cross PL1: Plym 5C 8 (3H 141)
Derwent Av. PL3: Plym 6D 136
Derwent Rd. TQ1: Torq 6D 112
Desborough La.
PL4: Plym 4K 9 (2B 142)
Desborough Rd.
PL4: Plym 4J 9 (2A 142)
De Tracey Pk. TQ13: Bov T 4C 92
Dettingen Path *EX2: Won* *2H 71*
(off Barrack Rd.)
Deveron Cl. PL7: Plymp 4D 138
Devil's Cauldron 6G 57
Devington Pk. EX6: Exmin 1B 74
Devon & Cornwall Constabulary HQ 1C 72
The Devon Bird of Prey Cen. 4J 101
Devon Bus. Pk. EX15: Cull 3J 45
Devon Cliffs Holiday Pk. 7J 77
Devon County Showground 2J 73 (1D 171)
Devoncourt TQ5: Brixh 2G 123
Devondale Ct. EX7: Daw W 7E 96
Devon Ent. Facility PL6: Robo 1C 132
The Devon Guild of Craftsmen 4C 92
Devon Heath TQ13: Chud K 6A 94
Devon Heritage Centre 6D 66
Devon Ho. Dr. TQ13: Bov T 3D 92
Devon Ho. Flats TQ13: Bov T 3D 92
Devonia Cl. PL7: Plymp 2B 138
Devon M. *TQ13: Chud K* *6A 94*
(off Devon Heath)
Devon Pl. *TQ9: Tot* *6F 103*
(off Bridgetown)
DEVONPORT 1E 140 (2A 174)
Devonport Column 3D 140
Devonport Hill PL1: Dev 3E 140
Devonport Naval Heritage Centre 2D 140
Devonport Park 1D 140
Devonport Pk. PL1: Dev 2E 140
Devonport Playhouse *2D 140*
(off Fore St.)
Devonport Rd. PL1: Plym 2E 140
PL3: Plym 7F 135
Devonport Station
(Rail) 1E 140 (2A 174)
Devon Railway Centre 3D 165
Devon Rd. EX4: Exe 1K 7 (4J 65)
TQ8: Salc 5B 158
Devonshire Ct. EX14: Hon 5C 54
PL11: Torp 1A 140
Devonshire Gdns. EX20: N Taw 6C 36
Devonshire Health & Raquets Club 6C 132
Devonshire Ho. PL1: Plym 5B 8
TQ1: Torq 5E 112
Devonshire Pk. EX39: Bide 5F 23
Devonshire Pl. EX4: Exe 1G 7 (4G 65)
Devonshire Ri. EX16: Tive 5E 40
Devonshire Rd. EX14: Hon 5B 54
Devonshire Row PL20: Prin 6C 60
Devonshire St. PL4: Plym 3G 9
Devonshire Traditional Breeds Cen. 7K 39
Devonshire Way EX14: Hon 5D 54
Devon Sq. TQ7: Kingsb 4F 157
TQ12: New A 1F 109
Devons Rd. TQ1: Torq 6E 112
Devon Ter. PL3: Plym 7K 135
TQ9: Tot 6F 103
Devon Tors PL20: Yelv 6G 127
Devon Tors Rd. PL20: Yelv 5F 127
Devon Valley Holiday Village 6D 106
Devon Vw. EX7: Daw W 7E 96
Devon Windsurf & Canoe Cen. 3F 109
Dewar Wlk. PL5: Plym 1E 134
Dewberry Dr. EX31: Rou 6A 18
DEXBEER 3A 162
Deyman's Hill EX16: Tive 5D 40
Dial St. EX19: Wink 2C 36
Diamond Av. PL4: Plym 2H 9 (1A 142)
Diamond Rd. EX2: Exe 7D 6 (1E 70)
Diamond St. EX32: B'aple 5E 18
Diane Cl. EX8: Exmth 1F 77
TQ4: Good 6F 119
Diane Ct. *TQ4: Good* *6F 119*
(off Diane Cl.)
Dickens Dr. EX2: Won 2J 71
Dickens Rd. PL5: Plym 1G 135
Dickers Ter. TQ12: Kingst 4H 105
Dick Hills La. EX38: G Tor 2C 30
Dickiemoor La. PL5: Plym 1H 135
Dickna Cl. PL15: St G 6C 34
Dick Pym Cl. EX2: Won 1B 72
Diddywell Cl. EX39: Nort 4F 21
Diddywell Rd. EX39: Nort 5E 20
DIDWORTHY 1C 175
Dieppe Cl. *PL1: Dev* *2E 140*
(off St Nazaire App.)
Digby & Sowton Station
(Rail) 1D 72 (1D 171)
Digby Dr. EX2: Sow 2C 72
Digby Gro. PL5: Plym 5E 130
Digby Ho. EX2: Sow 2C 72
Digby Park & Ride 2C 72
Digby Rd. EX2: Sow 2B 72
Diggerland
Devon 6C 44 (3A 166)

Diggories La.—Earls Wood Dr.

Diggories La. EX14: Hon 3E 54
Dillons PL8: New F 5J 149
Dinan Way EX8: Exmth 7K 75
Dinan Way Trad. Est. EX8: Exmth 3H 77
Dince Hill Cl. EX5: Whim 6H 53
Dingle Rd. PL2: Plym 5F 135
PL7: Plymp 5K 137
Dingles Fairground Heritage Centre 2C 169
Dingwall Av. PL5: Plym 7K 131
Dinham Cres. EX4: Exe 4B 6 (6E 64)
Dinham M. EX4: Exe 4C 6
Dinham Rd. EX4: Exe 4C 6 (6E 64)
Dinnaton Golf Course 2E 144 (2C 175)
Dinneford St. EX5: Thor 2A 50
DINNINGTON 2D 167
Dinnis Cl. EX6: Ted M 7J 49
Dinosaurland Fossil Mus. 5K 91 (1D 173)
DINWORTHY 2B 162
Dipper Dr. PL19: Whit 7K 59
DIPPERTOWN 2C 169
DIPTFORD 2D 175
Diptford Cl. TQ4: Paig 4E 118
Discovery Hgts. PL1: Plym 3E 8
Discovery Rd. PL1: Dev 3E 140
Discovery Wharf *PL4: Plym* 5G 9 (off North Quay)
Distine Cl. PL3: Plym 4C 136
DITTISHAM 5C 120 (2A 176)
Dittisham Ct. TQ6: Ditt 5C 120
Dittisham Sailing Club 5D 120
Dittisham Wlk. PL6: Plym 3F 137
Ditton Ct. PL6: Plym 3B 136
Divett Dr. TQ12: Live 4F 93
Dixon Cl. TQ3: Paig 5E 114
Dixon Dr. EX5: Clyst M 2G 73
Dixon Pl. PL2: Dev 7E 134
Dixon Ter. PL8: Torr 3B 150
Dix's Fld. EX1: Exe 3F 7 (6F 65)
DIZZARD 1A 168
Doatshayne Cl. EX13: Mus 7D 90
Doatshayne La. EX13: Mus 7D 90 (not continuous)
Dobbin Arch TQ12: Kingsk 1F 111
Dobles Cl. EX22: Hols 1C 34
Dobles La. Ind. Est. EX22: Hols 1C 34
DOCCOMBE 2B 170
Dockray Cl. PL6: Plym 6E 132
Dock Rd. EX8: Exmth 6B 76
Dockyard Station (Rail) 7D 134 (2A 174)
Docton Mill Gardens 1A 162
Doctors Rd. TQ5: Brixh 5E 122
Doctors Steps *PL8: New F* 6G 149 (off Yealm Rd.)
Doctors Wlk. EX2: Ide 2A 70 (not continuous)
DODBROOKE 4H 157 (3D 175)
Dodbrooke Ct. TQ7: Kingsb 4G 157
DODDISCOMBSLEIGH 2C 171
Doddridge Cl. PL9: Plyms 7G 143
Doe Ct. EX38: G Tor 2C 30
Doggie La. EX34: Ilfra 5E 11
DOG VILLAGE 7D 52 (1D 171)
Doidges Farm Cl. PL6: Plym 3C 136
Dokkum Rd. EX17: Cred 7J 39
Dolbeare Bus. Pk. TQ13: Ashb 3J 99
Dolbeare Rd. TQ13: Ashb 3J 99 (not continuous)
Dolforgan Ct. EX8: Exmth 6C 76
Dolphin Bldg. PL4: Plym 7H 9 (4A 142)
Dolphin Cl. DT7: Lym R 5K 91
PL9: Plyms 6G 143
Dolphin Ct. EX39: Nort 5D 20
TQ5: Brixh 3E 122
TQ14: Shal 6G 107 (off Albion St.)
Dolphin Ct. Rd. PL9: Plyms 6G 143
TQ3: Pres 5F 115
Dolphin Cres. TQ3: Pres 5F 115
Dolphin Ho. PL4: Plym 5G 9
Dolphin Rd. EX12: Beer 7B 86
Dolphin Sq. PL9: Plyms 5G 143
Dolphin St. EX24: Colyt 5D 88
Dolphion Sq. TQ13: Bov T 4B 92
DOLTON 6H 31 (2D 163)
Dolton Cvn. Pk. 7G 31
Dolvin Rd. PL19: Tavi 4J 59
Domehayes Ter. *EX20: Oke* 3B 48 (off Church St.)
Dommett Cl. EX13: Axmin 2J 89
Donkey La. PL21: Ivy 4G 145
PL21: Ugb 6E 146
The Donkey Sanctuary 2B 172
Donn Gdns. EX39: Bide 3H 23
Donnington Dr. PL3: Plym 4C 136
DONYATT 2D 167
Doone Valley 2D 161
Doone Way EX34: Ilfra 4H 11
Dorchester Av. PL5: Plym 6J 131
Dorchester Gro. TQ2: Torq 4B 112
Dorchester Way EX8: Exmth 1F 77
Doreena Rd. PL9: Elb 5K 143
Doriam Cl. EX4: Exe 2F 65
Dormy Av. PL3: Plym 6A 136
Dornafield Cvn. Pk. 7A 108
Dornafield Cl. TQ12: Ipp 6H 101
Dornafield Dr. E. TQ12: Ipp 6H 101
Dornafield Dr. W. TQ12: Ipp 6H 101
Dornafield La. TQ12: Ipp, Two O 5H 101
Dornafield Rd. TQ12: Ipp 6H 101
Dorothy Ward La. PL1: Plym 6F 9 (3K 141)
Dorset Av. EX4: Exe 1B 70
Dorset Down Cres. EX15: Cull 4F 45
Dorset Pl. *EX14: Hon* 3F 55 (off New St.)
Dorsmouth Ter. PL7: Plymp 5B 138
Dosson Gro. TQ1: Torq 6A 112
DOTTERY 1D 173
Dotton Cl. EX1: Sow 6C 66
Dotton La. EX10: New P 1J 83
Doughy La. TQ12: Den 1H 101
Douglas Av. EX8: Exmth 7D 76
TQ5: Brixh 4G 123
Douglas Ct. EX8: Exmth 6E 76
Douglas Dr. PL9: Plyms 6H 143
Douglas Ho. *TQ14: Teignm* 4H 107 (off Bitton Pk. Rd.)
Douglass Rd. PL3: Plym 5D 136
Douro Ct. PL21: Ivy 4H 145
DOUSLAND 4K 127 (1B 174)
Dousland Rd. PL20: Dous, Yelv 6G 127
Dousland Ter. PL20: Dous 4K 127
Dove Cl. EX14: Hon 5E 54
EX15: Cull 5F 45
Dovedale Rd. PL2: Plym 4F 135
Dove Gdns. PL3: Plym 5E 136
Dove La. EX10: Sidm 7C 84
Dover Rd. PL6: Plym 7F 133
Dove Way EX2: Exe 2A 70
Dowell St. EX14: Hon 3E 54
Dower Ct. TQ3: Pres 6J 115
Dower Rd. TQ1: Torq 6C 112
DOWLAND 2D 163
DOWLANDS 1C 173
DOWLISH WAKE 2D 167
The Down PL20: Bere A 2C 128
Downaway La. TQ12: Dacc 1A 112
Down Cl. EX10: New P 6F 81
Down End EX33: Croy 3B 14
Downes Crediton Golf Course 7K 39 (1C 171)
Downeshead La. EX17: Cred 6J 39
Downfield Cl. TQ5: Brixh 5C 122
Downfield Dr. PL7: Plymp 4C 130
Downfield Wlk. PL7: Plymp 4C 138
Downfield Way PL7: Plymp 4C 138
DOWNGATE
PL14 3A 168
PL17 3B 168
Downgate Gdns. PL2: Plym 3J 135
Downham Gdns. PL5: Tam F 3H 131
Downhorne Pk. PL9: Plyms 6G 143
Down La. EX33: Brau 4K 15
EX33: Croy 3D 14
Downlea PL19: Tavi 5K 59
Down Pk. Dr. PL19: Tavi 5K 59
Down Rd. PL7: Plymp 4F 139
PL19: Tavi 5J 59
The Downs TQ7: Thur 5B 154
DOWN ST MARY 3B 164
Downshead La. EX17: Cred 6K 39
Downside Av. PL6: Plym 4D 136
Downs Rd. EX39: Ins 3K 21
TQ7: Thur 5C 154
DOWN THOMAS 1C 148 (2B 174)
Downton Cl. PL1: Plym 2A 8 (1G 141)
Down Vw. Rd. TQ12: Den 2H 101
The Doyle Cen. EX8: Exmth 4G 77
Dracaena Av. EX31: B'aple 5B 18
Dragons Hill DT7: Lym R 3K 91
Dragon's Mead EX13: Axmin 5G 89
Dragoon Cl. TQ12: H'fld 1H 93
Drake Av. EX2: Won 7C 66
EX31: Yell 1C 16
PL21: Ivy 4D 144
TQ2: Torq 7J 111
TQ14: Teignm 1G 107
Drake Cir. PL1: Plym 4F 9 (2J 141)
PL4: Plym 3F 9 (2K 141)
Drake Cl. EX15: Cull 3H 45
EX39: W Ho 6A 20
Drake Ct. PL4: Plym 3J 9 (2A 142)
PL5: Plym 6D 130
Drake Dr. TQ4: Good 5G 119
Drake Gdns. PL19: Tavi 5J 59
Drake La. TQ13: Bov T 4D 92
Drake Rd. PL19: Tavi 3H 59
TQ8: Salc 3B 158
TQ12: New A 1J 109
TQ13: Bov T 4D 92
Drake's Av. EX8: Exmth 4F 77
EX10: Sidf 2D 84
Drakes Cl. PL6: Plym 5A 132
Drakes Farm EX2: Ide 3B 70
Drakes Gdns. EX8: Exmth 4F 77
Drakes Mdw. EX17: Cher F 2H 39
Drake's Pk. PL20: Bere A 2C 128
Drakes Rd. EX4: Exe 7A 6 (1D 70)
TQ4: Paig 3E 118
Drake's Statue 7D 8 (4J 141)
Drakes Way *DT7: Lym R* 5K 91 (off Broad St.)
Drake Vs. PL19: Tavi 5H 59
DRAKEWALLS 3C 169
Drake Way PL9: Plyms 5F 143
Drapers Cl. EX34: C Mar 7D 12
Drax Gdns. PL6: Plym 3K 135
Draycott Cl. EX2: Won 1K 71
Dray Ct. *EX8: Exmth* 6C 76 (off Rolle Rd.)
DRAYFORD 2B 164
Drayford La. EX16: W'ridge 6G 33
DRAYTON 1D 167
Drayton Rd. PL5: Plym 2H 135
Drew's Cl. EX6: Star 1D 96
Drew's Fld. La. TQ3: Comp 6D 110
DREWSTEIGNTON 1B 170
Drew St. TQ5: Brixh 5E 122
Dreys Ct. EX1: Exe 4K 7 (6H 65)
DRIMPTON 3D 167
Drina La. PL5: Plym 1D 134
The Drive EX7: Daw 4H 97
EX9: Bic 5G 83
PL3: Plym 4K 135
PL8: Holb 6D 150
TQ5: Brixh 6E 122
TQ14: Bi'ton 3A 106
Droridge TQ9: Darti 3B 102
Droridge La. TQ9: Darti 3A 102
Drovers Way EX12: Seat 2E 86
PL21: Ivy 3E 144
Druid Rd. TQ13: Ashb 1F 99
Drummond Cl. PL2: Plym 4E 134
Drummond Pl. PL1: Dev 1E 140
Drummond Way PL20: Bere F 7B 128
Drum Way TQ12: H'fld 2J 93
Drunken Bri. Hill PL7: Plymp 1K 143
Drupe Farm Ct. EX10: Col R 3H 83
Dryburgh Cres. PL2: Plym 4F 135
Dry Cl. EX5: Rock 3D 68
Dryden Av. PL5: Plym 2H 135
Dryden Cl. EX8: Exmth 7K 75
Dryden Rd. EX2: Won 7K 7 (1J 71)
Dryfield EX6: Exmin 2D 74
Dry La. EX6: Chri 3J 63
Ducane Wlk. PL6: Plym 2C 136
Duchy Av. TQ3: Pres 4G 115
Duchy Dr. TQ3: Pres 4G 115
Duchy Gdns. TQ3: Pres 3G 115
Duchy Pk. TQ3: Pres 4G 115
Duchy Rd. EX14: Hon 5D 54
Duck La. EX20: Exbo 5J 35
Duckpool Rd. EX31: C'nor 1E 16
Ducks Orchard EX6: Exmin 3D 74
Duckspond Cl. TQ11: B'leigh 5B 98
Duckspond Rd. TQ11: B'leigh 5B 98
Duckworth Rd. EX2: Exe 1D 70
Duckworth St. PL2: Dev 7F 135
Dudley Gdns. PL6: Plym 3C 136
Dudley Rd. PL7: Plymp 6J 137
Dudley Vw. EX39: W Ho 6A 20
Dudley Way EX39: W Ho 6A 20
Duke of Cornwall Cl. EX8: Exmth 3G 77
Dukes Cl. EX9: Ott'n 6H 83
TQ3: Paig 1E 118
Dukes Cres. EX8: Exmth 3G 77
Dukes Mead EX15: Cull 5H 45
Dukes Orchard EX5: Bradn 2C 52
Duke's Rd. EX9: Bud S 5B 82
Dukes Rd. TQ9: Tot 6H 103
The Dukes Ryde PL9: Plyms 5G 143
Duke St. EX15: Cull 5H 45
EX36: S Mol 6C 26
PL1: Dev 2D 140
PL19: Tavi 4J 59
TQ6: Dartm 1A 124 (6F 125)
TQ7: Kingsb 4F 157
Dukes Wlk. EX2: Cou W 4C 72
Dukes Way EX13: Axmin 5G 89
DULFORD 3A 166
Dulings Mdw. EX17: Cop 6D 38
Duloe Gdns. PL2: Plym 3H 135
DULVERTON 1D 165
Dulverton M. TQ3: Paig 6E 114
Dumfries Av. PL5: Plym 7J 131
DUMPINGHILL 7K 29
Dunard *EX10: Sidm* 6B 84 (off All Saint's Rd.)
Dunboyne Ct. *TQ1: Torq* 5D 112 (off St Marychurch Rd.)
Duncannon La. TQ9: Sto G 4A 120
Duncannon Mead TQ9: Sto G 4B 120
Duncan St. PL1: Dev 3D 140
DUNCHIDEOCK 2C 171
Dunchideock Rd. EX2: Ide 5A 70
Dunclair Pk. PL3: Plym 6E 136
Duncombe Av. PL5: Plym 7E 130
Duncombe St. TQ7: Kingsb 3G 157
Dundas St. PL2: Dev 7F 135
Dundonald St. PL2: Dev 7E 134
The Dunes EX39: Ins 2K 21
Dune Vw. EX33: Brau 3G 15
EX39: W Ho 5C 20
Dune Vw. Rd. EX33: Brau 4G 15
DUNKESWELL 5H 47 (3B 166)
Dunkeswell Abbey 2B 166
Dunkeswell Airfield 5F 47 (3B 166)
Dunkeswell Bus. Pk. EX14: Dunk 5G 47
Dunkeswell Cl. PL2: Plym 3E 134
Dunkeswell Heritage Centre 3B 166
Dunley Wlk. PL6: Plym 2D 136
Dunlin Cl. EX7: Daw W 7C 96
Dunmere Rd. TQ1: Torq 7D 112
Dunmore Ct. TQ14: Shal 7H 107
Dunmore Dr. TQ14: Shal 7H 107
Dunnet Rd. PL6: Plym 4J 131
Dunning Ct. EX14: Hon 3E 54
Dunning Grn. EX31: B'aple 6B 18
Dunning Rd. TQ14: Teignm 2G 107
Dunning Wlk. *TQ14: Teignm* 2G 107 (off Lake Av.)
Dunns Cl. EX33: Wraf 6K 15
Dunn's Hill TA21: Holc R 1H 43
Dunraven Dr. PL6: Plym 5A 132
Dunrich Cl. EX2: Exe 5H 7 (7G 65)
Dunsdon Farm National Nature Reserve 3A 162
DUNSFORD 6C 62 (2C 171)
Dunsford Cl. EX8: Exmth 6F 77
Dunsford Gdns. EX4: Exe 2B 70
Dunsford Rd. EX2: Exe 2A 70
EX4: Exe 2A 70
Dunsford Way *EX16: Tive* 5C 40 (off Narrow La.)
Dunsford Woods Nature Reserve 2B 170
Dunsgreen La. EX15: Clay 1K 47
Dunster Cl. PL7: Plymp 5F 139
Dunsterville Rd. PL21: Ivy 3J 145
Dunster Wlk. EX6: Exmin 1B 74
DUNSTONE 2E 150 (2B 174)
Dunstone Av. PL9: Plyms 5H 143
Dunstone Cl. PL9: Plyms 5G 143
TQ3: Paig 5E 114
Dunstone Cotts. PL8: Dunst 2E 150
Dunstone Dr. PL9: Plyms 5G 143
Dunstone La. PL9: Elb 5J 143
Dunstone Pk. Rd. TQ3: Paig 5E 114
Dunstone Ri. TQ3: Paig 5E 114
Dunstone Rd. PL5: Plym 7E 130
PL9: Plyms 5G 143
Dunstone Vw. PL9: Elb, Plyms 5H 143
DUNTERTON 3B 168
Duntz Hill PL16: Lift 6B 56
Dunvegan Cl. EX4: Exe 4D 64
Durant Cl. EX20: N Taw 6B 36
Durban Rd. PL3: Plym 6J 135
Durbin Cl. EX14: Hon 4G 55
Dure La. EX36: N Mol 2D 26
Durham Av. PL4: Plym 2K 9 (1B 142)
Durham Cl. EX1: Whip 5B 66
EX8: Exmth 1F 77
TQ3: Pres 5H 115
Durham Cotts. PL1: Plym 2B 8
Durham Way EX14: Hon 5D 54
Durleigh Rd. TQ5: Brixh 4D 122
Durley Rd. EX12: Seat 5D 86
Durnford St. PL1: Plym 3F 141
Durnford St. Ope PL1: Plym 3F 141
Durrant Cl. EX39: Nort 7F 21
PL1: Dev 1D 140
Durrant La. EX39: Nort 7F 21
Durris Cl. PL6: Plym 6E 132
Durris Gdns. PL6: Plym 6E 132
Dursley Way EX39: Bide 3D 22
DURSTON 1C 167
Durwent Cl. PL9: Hooe 6B 142
DURYARD 2E 64
Duryard Halls EX4: Exe 2D 64
Dutchbarn La. EX2: Cou W 6C 72
Dutch Ct. EX3: Top 6B 74
DUTSON 2B 168
Duxford Cl. PL5: Plym 5D 130
Dyers Cl. EX33: Brau 4J 15
Dyers Ct. EX2: Exe 6C 6 (7E 64)
Dyers Mdw. EX10: Sidf 2E 84
Dyke Grn. Farm Camp Site 7G 27
Dymock Way PL21: Ivy 4E 144
Dymond Rd. EX39: Bide 4E 22
Dynevor Cl. PL3: Plym 4A 136

E

Eager Way EX6: Exmin 1B 74
Eagle Cl. PL7: Plymp 5F 139
TQ12: Kingst 1G 105
Eagle Cotts. EX4: Exe 5B 6 (7D 64)
Eagle Hurst Ct. *EX10: Sidm* 6B 84 (off Cotmaton Rd.)
Eagle Pl. TQ13: More 6H 61
Eagle Rd. PL7: Plymp 4F 139
Eagles Nest EX2: Exe 1A 70
Eagle Way EX2: Sow 7E 66
Eaglewood Cl. TQ2: Torq 3J 111
Eagle Yd. EX4: Exe 5C 6
Ealing Cl. TQ5: Brixh 5F 123
Earl Richards Rd. Nth. EX2: Exe 2H 71
Earl Richards Rd. Sth. EX2: Exe 3J 71
Earl's Acre PL3: Plym 1B 8 (7H 135)
Earls Ct. TQ1: Torq 7B 112
Earls Mill Rd. PL7: Plymp 3B 138
Earls Wood Cl. PL6: Plym 7G 133
Earls Wood Dr. PL6: Plym 7G 133

Earlswood Dr.—Elwick Gdns.

Earlswood Dr. TQ3: Paig 7D **114**
Easewell Farm Holiday Pk. 3B **10**
EASTACOMBE 1D **163**
Eastacoombes Way TQ7: Malb 5G **155**
EASTACOTT 1A **164**
Eastacott Cross 1A **164**
Eastacott La. EX34: Wool 6D **10**
EAST ALLINGTON 6C **152** (3D **175**)
EAST ANSTEY 1C **165**
EAST ASHLEY 2A **164**
East Av. EX1: Heav 3K **7** (5H **65**)
E. Ball Hill EX39: Hart 2J **27**
Eastbourne Ter. EX39: W Ho 4C **20**
EAST BUCKLAND
EX32 .... 3C **161**
TQ7 .... 4C **154** (3C **175**)
EAST BUDLEIGH 1D **82** (2A **172**)
E. Budleigh Rd.
EX9: Bud S, E Bud 2D **82**
(not continuous)
Eastbury Av. PL5: Plym 1F **135**
EAST BUTTERLEIGH 3D **165**
E. Challacombe La. EX34: C Mar 5D **12**
EAST CHARLETON 3D **175**
E. Cliff DT7: Lym R 5K **91**
E. Cliff Cl. EX7: Daw 3H **97**
Eastcliffe Ho. TQ14: Teignm 3K **107**
E. Cliff Gdns. EX7: Daw 3H **97**
E. Cliff Rd. EX7: Daw 3H **97**
Eastcliff Wlk. TQ14: Teignm 4K **107**
East Cl. EX16: W'ridge 6J **33**
EAST COMBE 1B **166**
EAST CORNWORTHY 5A **120** (2A **176**)
Eastcote Cl. PL6: Plym 4C **132**
EASTCOTT 2A **162**
East Dartmoor Woods & Heaths
National Nature Reserve 3B **170**
East Devon Golf Course 7A **82** (2A **172**)
EASTDON 5E **96**
EAST DOWN 2C **161**
East Dr. EX8: Exmth 3C **76**
Eastella Rd. PL20: Yelv 6G **127**
East End PL9: Plyms 4D **142**
East End Ter. TQ13: Ashb 2K **99**
Easter Ct. EX31: Rou 7A **18**
Easterdown Cl. PL9: Plyms 5G **143**
Easterfield La. TQ1: Torq 3D **112**
Easter Hill La. EX6: Star 2C **96**
Easter La. EX34: Ber 3C **12**
Easterley Ter. *EX31: B'aple 6B 18*
(off Bickington Rd.)
Eastern Av. EX2: Cou W 6B **72**
EX32: B'aple 5G **19**
Eastern Backway *TQ7: Kingsb 4G 157*
(off Church St.)
Eastern Esplanade TQ4: Paig 2J **119**
Eastern Rd. TQ13: Ashb 3J **99**
EASTERN TOWN 7C **84**
Easterntown PL8: Holb 6D **150**
Eastern Wood Rd.
PL7: Plymp 4G **139**
Easter St. EX32: B Taw 6B **24**
Eastfield EX11: W Hill 4H **79**
Eastfield Av. PL9: Hooe 6D **142**
Eastfield Cres. PL3: Plym 4B **136**
Eastfield Gdns. EX11: W Hill 4H **79**
Eastfield Orchard EX11: W Hill 4H **79**
EX15: Uff 5H **43**
Eastgate EX1: Exe 3F **7** (6F **65**)
East Gro. Rd. EX2: Exe 7G **7** (1G **71**)
East Hill EX33: Brau 4J **15**
EASTINGTON 3B **164**
Eastington La. EX17: Lap 2K **37**
Eastington Rd. EX17: Lap 1K **37**
East John Wlk. EX1: Exe 3J **7** (6H **65**)
E. Kingfisher La. *EX2: Exe 3J 71*
(off Turnstone Rd.)
EAST KNOWSTONE 1C **165**
Eastlake Ope PL1: Plym 4F **9** (2K **141**)
Eastlake St. PL1: Plym 3E **8** (2J **141**)
EAST LAMBROOK 2D **167**
Eastlands EX15: Hemy 2G **47**
EAST LEIGH
EX17 .... 3A **164**
PL21 .... 2C **175**
EASTLEIGH 1C **163**
Eastleigh Cl. EX13: Kilm 2C **88**
EAST LYNG 1D **167**
E. Mallard La. *EX2: Exe 3J 71*
(off Turnstone Rd.)
E. Mead EX15: Hemy 2G **47**
East Mdw. Rd. EX33: Brau 3G **15**
EAST NYNEHEAD 1B **166**
EAST OGWELL 3A **108** (3C **171**)
EASTON 2B **170**
Easton La. EX16: Sam P 2C **42**
E. Pafford Av. TQ2: Torq 3D **112**
EAST PANSON 1B **168**
East Pk. EX19: Wink 2D **36**
EX39: Wools 2B **28**
East Pk. Av. PL4: Plym 1E **8** (1J **141**)
East Pk. Cl. EX19: Wink 2D **36**
East Pk. Rd. EX32: B'aple 6J **19**
EAST PORTLEMOUTH 4E **158** (3D **175**)
EAST PRAWLE 3D **175**
EAST PUTFORD 2B **162**
E. Ridge Vw. EX39: Bide 4G **23**
EAST STOWFORD 1A **164**
East St. EX10: Sidm 7C **84**
EX15: Uff 6H **43**
EX17: Cred 6J **39**
EX18: Chul 6C **32**
EX20: Oke 3B **48**
EX32: B Taw 6B **24**
EX33: Brau 4J **15**
EX36: N Mol 2C **26**
EX36: S Mol 6D **26**
EX37: C'ton 5J **25**
EX38: G Tor 2C **30**
PL1: Plym 5A **8** (3G **141**)
(not continuous)
TQ2: Torq 7B **112**
TQ12: Den 2H **101**
TQ12: Ipp 6H **101**
TQ12: New A 1E **108**
TQ13: Ashb 4H **99**
TQ13: Bov T 3C **92**
East Ter. EX1: Heav 6K **65**
EX9: Bud S 6C **82**
EAST-THE-WATER 4G **23** (1C **163**)
EAST TOWN 7J **39**
East Town La. EX6: Kenton 6H **95**
East Vw. *PL3: Plym 7F 135*
(off Ann's Pl.)
East Vw. Pl. EX16: Tive 3E **40**
East Vw. Ter. EX39: Bide 4F **23**
EAST VILLAGE 3C **165**
East Wlk. EX12: Seat 6F **87**
E. Way PL21: L Mill 5B **144**
EAST WEEK 1A **170**
E. Wonford Hill EX1: Heav 7K **65**
Eastwood Cres. TQ12: New A 7B **104**
EAST WORLINGTON 2B **164**
EAST YOULSTONE 2A **162**
Eaton Ct. TQ14: Teignm 2H **107**
Eaton Dr. EX1: Exe 3G **7** (6G **65**)
Eaton Hall Dr. *TQ6: Dartm 5E 124*
(off Flagstaff Rd.)
Eaton Ho. EX1: Exe 3G **7**
Eaton Pl. TQ4: Paig 2H **119**
Eaton Villa *EX34: Ilfra 2J 11*
(off Montpelier Rd.)
EBBERLEY HILL 2D **163**
Ebberly Lawn EX32: B'aple 4F **19**
Ebberly Ter. *EX32: B'aple 4F 19*
(off Bear St.)
Ebdons Ct. *EX10: Sidm 7C 84*
(off Church St.)
Ebdon Way TQ1: Torq 7B **112**
Ebenezer Rd. TQ3: Paig 2G **119**
EBFORD 6E **74** (2D **171**)
Ebford La. EX3: Ebf 5E **74**
Ebrington Rd. EX2: Exe 2E **70**
Ebrington St. PL4: Plym 4G **9** (2K **141**)
TQ7: Kingsb 4G **157**
Echo Cres. PL5: Plym 1J **135**
Eco Way PL6: Plym 2D **132**
Eddy's La. EX32: B'aple 6G **19**
Eddystone Cl. PL3: Plym 5D **136**
PL9: Hey B 4B **148**
Eddystone Ri. TQ7: Galm 2J **155**
Eddystone Rd. PL9: Down T 1C **148**
TQ7: Thur 6B **154**
Eddystone Ter. PL1: Plym 7B **8** (4H **141**)
Eddy Thomas Wlk. PL5: Plym 6H **131**
Eden Cl. TQ5: Brixh 5E **122**
Eden Cotts. PL21: Ivy 4H **145**
Eden Gro. TQ3: Paig 7F **115**
Edenhurst Ct. *TQ1: Torq 3D 116*
(off Parkhill Rd.)
Eden Pk. TQ5: Brixh 5E **122**
Edens Ct. *TQ14: Teignm 4J 107*
(off Heywoods Rd.)
Eden Vale Rd. TQ3: Paig 6F **115**
Eden Valley Gdns. PL6: Plym 1E **136**
Eden Way EX10: Col R 3J **83**
Edgar Ter. PL4: Plym 7B **136**
Edgbaston Mead EX2: Won 1B **72**
EDGCOTT 3D **161**
Edgcumbe Av. PL1: Plym 2G **141**
Edgcumbe Dr. PL19: Tavi 3H **59**
Edgcumbe Pk. Rd. PL3: Plym 5J **135**
Edgcumbe St. PL1: Plym 3F **141**
Edgcumbe Ter. PL19: Mil A 2B **58**
PL20: Bere A 2C **128**
Edgecumbe Ho. PL1: Plym 5A **8**
Edgehill Theatre 2D **22**
Edgelands La. TQ12: Ipp 7G **101**
Edgeley Rd. TQ2: Torq 3C **112**
Edgerton Pk. Rd. EX4: Exe 1F **7** (4G **65**)
EDGINSWELL 5J **111**
Edginswell Cl. TQ2: Torq 4J **111**
Edginswell La. TQ2: Torq 4H **111**
TQ12: Kingsk 2F **111**
Edinburgh Cres. EX8: Lymp 5G **75**
Edinburgh Dr. EX4: Exe 6B **64**
Edinburgh Rd. TQ5: Brixh 5F **123**
Edinburgh St. PL1: Dev 3D **140**
Edinburgh Vs. TQ1: Torq 7B **112**
EDISTONE 1A **162**
Edith Av. PL4: Plym 1B **142**
Edith St. PL5: Plym 2C **134**
Edmonds Wlk. TQ1: Torq 7B **112**
Edmonton Cl. EX4: Exe 4K **65**
Edmund St. EX2: Exe 6C **6** (7E **64**)
Edna Ter. PL4: Plym 2C **142**
Edwards Cl. PL7: Plymp 5E **138**
TQ7: Thur 6C **154**
Edwards Ct. EX2: Sow 1C **72**
Edwards Dr. EX39: W Ho 5D **20**
PL7: Plymp 4E **138**
Edwards Rd. PL15: St G 6C **34**
Edwin Rd. EX2: Exe 2E **70**
Effingham Cres. PL3: Plym 4J **135**
EFFORD
EX17 .... 3C **165**
PL3 .... 6D **136**
Efford Crematorium 5D **136**
Efford Cres. PL3: Plym 5C **136**
Efford La. PL3: Plym 7C **136**
Efford Marsh
Local Nature Reserve 5F **137**
Efford Pathway PL3: Plym 5D **136**
Efford Rd. PL3: Plym 5C **136**
Efford Wlk. PL3: Plym 5C **136**
Egerton Cres.
PL4: Plym 3K **9** (2B **142**)
Egerton Pl. PL4: Plym 3K **9** (2B **142**)
Egerton Rd. PL4: Plym 4J **9** (2A **142**)
TQ1: Torq 7E **112**
EGGBUCKLAND 3C **136** (2A **174**)
Eggbuckland Rd. PL3: Plym 5A **136**
PL6: Plym 3C **136**
EGGESFORD 2A **164**
Eggesford Airfield 3A **164**
Eggesford Rd. EX19: Wink 3C **36**
Eggesford Station (Rail) 2A **164**
Egham Av. EX2: Exe 2G **71**
EGLOSKERRY 2A **168**
Egremont Rd. EX8: Exmth 4C **76**
Egret Cl. EX7: Daw 7C **96**
Egypt La. EX1: Exe 4E **6**
EX18: Chul 6C **32**
Eight Acre Dr. TQ4: Paig 6F **119**
Eight Acres Cl. PL7: Plymp 4F **139**
Elaine Cl. EX4: Whip 2K **65**
PL7: Plymp 6J **137**
Elba Cl. TQ4: Good 6J **119**
Elberry La. TQ4: Broads 1K **121**
TQ5: Chur F 4K **121**
Elbow La. PL19: Tavi 3J **59**
Elbridge Cotts. PL8: Brixt 2H **149**
ELBURTON 5K **143** (2B **174**)
Elburton Rd. PL9: Elb, Plyms 4H **143**
Elbury Cl. EX5: Broadc 6E **52**
Eldad Hill PL1: Plym 3A **8** (2G **141**)
Elderberry Way EX15: Will 3E **44**
Elder Cl. PL7: Plymp 4E **138**
Elder Gro. EX17: Cred 5K **39**
Eldertree Gdns. EX4: Exe 1B **6** (5D **64**)
Elford EX8: Exmth 7D **76**
Elford Cres. PL7: Plymp 2B **138**
Elford Dr. PL9: Plyms 5D **142**
Elfordleigh Golf Course 2B **174**
Elford Pk. PL20: Yelv 6G **127**
Elgar Cl. EX2: Won 7B **66**
EX32: B'aple 4H **19**
Elgin Cres. PL5: Plym 7K **131**
Elim Cl. EX10: Sidm 5C **84**
Elim Ct. PL3: Plym 6K **135**
Elim Ter. PL3: Plym 6K **135**
Eliot St. PL5: Plym 3D **134**
Elizabethan Ct. *EX2: Exe 6F 7*
(off Roberts Rd.)
Elizabethan House 6F **9**
Elizabethan Way
TQ14: Teignm 2K **107**
Elizabeth Av. EX4: Exe 4H **65**
TQ5: Brixh 7C **122**
Elizabeth Cl. DT7: Lym R 4K **91**
EX5: Whim 6G **53**
EX31: B'aple 7C **18**
PL21: Ivy 4K **145**
Elizabeth Ct. TQ2: Torq 1B **116**
TQ9: Tot 6H **103**
Elizabeth Dr. EX31: B'aple 6C **18**
Elizabeth Lea Cl. EX22: Bradw 5B **28**
Elizabeth Pl.
PL4: Plym 2F **9** (1K **141**)
Elizabeth Rd. EX8: Exmth 2E **76**
EX12: Seat 3E **86**
Elizabeth Sq. TQ12: New A 2J **109**
Elizabeth Way EX12: Seat 4E **86**
Elkins Hill TQ5: Brixh 3F **123**
ELLACOMBE 7D **112**
Ellacombe Chu. Rd. TQ1: Torq 7D **112**
Ellacombe Mdws. EX3: Clyst G 6H **73**
Ellacombe Rd. TQ1: Torq 7D **112**
Ellards Cl. EX2: Exe 2H **71**
ELLBRIDGE 1A **174**
ELLERHAYES 3D **165**
Ellerslie Ho. *TQ14: Shal 6H 107*
(off Marine Pde.)
Ellerslie Rd. EX31: B'aple 6A **18**
Ellesmere TQ1: Torq 2E **116**
Ellesmere Rd. TQ1: Torq 1G **117**
Ellimore Rd. TQ13: Lust 6G **63**
Ellington Ct. *TQ2: Torq 2C 116*
(off St Luke's Rd. Sth.)
Elliot Cl. EX11: Ott M 4B **80**
EX32: B'aple 5H **19**
Elliot Sq. PL11: Torp 1A **140**
Elliot St. PL1: Plym 7C **8** (4H **141**)
Elliott Cl. EX4: Exe 2H **65**
Elliott Ct. TQ12: Ipp 6H **101**
Elliot Ter. PL1: Plym 7D **8**
Elliot Ter. La.
PL1: Plym 7D **8** (4J **141**)
The Elliott Gallery 1K **15**
Elliott Gro. TQ5: Brixh 4C **122**
Elliott Plain TQ11: B'leigh 4D **98**
Elliott Rd. PL4: Plym 3B **142**
Elliott's Hill EX17: Morc 1E **38**
Elliotts Hill PL8: Brixt 3H **149**
Elliott Way EX2: Sow 7C **66**
Ellwood Rd. EX8: Exmth 2F **77**
Elm Bank TQ11: B'leigh 5B **98**
Elmbank Gdns. TQ4: Paig 2G **119**
Elmbank Rd. TQ4: Paig 2G **119**
Elmbridge Gdns. EX4: Exe 4D **64**
Elmbrook EX4: Exe 1B **6** (5E **64**)
Elm Cl. EX5: Broadc 6C **52**
PL19: Tavi 6J **59**
Elm Ct. EX6: Star 1E **96**
Elm Cres. PL3: Plym 7B **136**
Elm Cft. *PL6: Plym 4E 132*
(off Elm Rd.)
Elmcroft PL2: Plym 4G **135**
Elmcroft La. TQ12: Kingsk 7H **109**
Elmdale Rd. EX39: Bide 2F **23**
Elmdon Cl. EX4: Exe 3G **65**
Elm Dr. TQ12: Kingst 4H **105**
Elm Farm La. EX24: Colyf 1F **87**
Elmfield Cres. EX8: Exmth 2C **76**
Elmfield Rd. EX12: Seat 3E **86**
EX31: Bick 6J **17**
Elmfield Ter. *EX39: Nort 5F 21*
(off Oxmans La.)
Elmfield Way TQ12: Kingst 5H **105**
Elm Gro. EX8: Exmth 6B **76**
EX39: Bide 3E **22**
PL6: Plym 3C **136**
PL7: Plymp 4B **138**
TQ14: Teignm 1H **107**
Elm Gro. Av. EX3: Top 5B **74**
Elm Gro. Cl. EX7: Daw 3H **97**
Elm Gro. Dr. EX7: Daw 3H **97**
Elm Gro. Gdns. EX3: Top 5B **74**
Elm Gro. Rd. EX3: Top 7E **72**
EX4: Exe 1C **6** (5E **64**)
EX7: Daw 2H **97**
Elm Gro. Ter. EX24: Colyt 5D **88**
Elmhirst Dr. TQ9: Tot 6G **103**
Elmhurst Ct. TQ14: Teignm 4H **107**
Elm La. EX8: Lit 5H **77**
Elmlea Av. EX31: Frem 6E **16**
El Monte Cl. TQ14: Teignm 3H **107**
Elm Orchard *EX12: Axmth 3H 87*
(off Kemp's La.)
Elmore Way EX16: Tive 3E **40**
Elm Pk. PL10: Millb 5A **140**
TQ3: Paig 1F **119**
Elm Rd. EX8: Exmth 5E **76**
PL4: Plym 6A **136**
PL6: Plym 4E **132**
TQ5: Brixh 6C **122**
TQ12: New A 1F **109**
The Elms EX24: Colyf 1F **87**
PL3: Plym 1F **141**
TQ13: Chud 1C **94**
ELMSCOTT 1A **162**
Elmscott Ter. *EX39: Bide 3F 23*
(off Pitt La.)
Elmside EX4: Exe 1J **7** (5H **65**)
EX9: Bud S 6C **82**
EX15: Will 5D **44**
Elmside Cl. EX4: Exe 1J **7** (5H **65**)
Elmsleigh Ct. *TQ4: Paig 2H 119*
(off Elmsleigh Rd.)
Elmsleigh Pk. TQ4: Paig 2H **119**
Elmsleigh Rd. TQ4: Paig 2H **119**
Elms Mdw. EX19: Wink 3C **36**
Elm Ter. EX14: Hon 3G **55**
EX16: Tive 4B **40**
EX39: Ins 4K **21**
PL4: Plym 6A 136
(off Elm Rd.)
Elm Tree Cl. PL8: Y'ton 2B **150**
TQ2: Torq 3J **111**
Elm Tree Pk. PL8: Y'ton 2B **150**
Elm Wlk. TQ9: Tot 6G **103**
Elm Way EX10: Sidf 1C **84**
Elmwood Av. TQ12: New A 7B **104**
Elmwood Cl. PL6: Plym 5E **132**
Elmwood Cres. EX7: Daw 3H **97**
Elmwood Gdns. EX24: Colyf 1F **87**
Elmwood Pk. TQ7: Lodd 2G **151**
Elphinstone Rd. PL2: Plym 4H **135**
Elsdale Rd. TQ4: Paig 3G **119**
Elsdon EX11: W Hill 4J **79**
Elsdon La. EX11: W Hill 4J **79**
Elsie Pl. EX1: Sow 6C **66**
ELSTON 3B **164**
ELSTONE 2A **164**
Elston La. EX17: Cop 7E **38**
Elston Mdw. EX17: Cred 6F **39**
Elston Pk. TQ7: Chur 2A **156**
Elton Rd. EX4: Exe 1K **7** (4H **65**)
Elvestone *EX9: Bud S 7D 82*
(off Fore Street Hill)
Elvis Rd. EX8: Exmth 5F **77**
Elwick Gdns. PL3: Plym 6C **136**

Elwyn Rd.—Faraday Mill Bus. Pk.

Elwyn Rd. EX8: Exmth 5E 76
Ely Cl. EX4: Exe 6A 64
EX14: Fen 1G 53
Elysian Ct. EX36: S Mol 6D 26
Elysian Flds. EX10: Sidm 6B 84
The Embankment TQ14: Shal 6F 107
Embankment La. PL4: Plym 2C 142
Embankment Rd.
PL4: Plym 5K 9 (3B 142)
TQ7: Kingsb 5G 157
Embankment Rd. La. Nth.
PL4: Plym 2C 142
(off Grenville Rd.)
Emb. Rd. La. Sth.
PL4: Plym 5K 9 (3B 142)
The Embassy Cinema 2H 11
Ember Rd. TQ8: Salc 3B 158
Embleford Cres. TQ13: More 6H 61
Emblett Dr. TQ12: New A 7B 104
Emblett Hill Vw. TQ12: E Ogw 3C 108
Embridge Hill TQ6: Blackp 2F 153
Embury Cl. TQ12: Kingsk 1G 111
Emily Gdns. PL4: Plym 1J 9 (1A 142)
Emlyn Pl. TQ13: Bov T 4C 92
Emmanuel Cl. EX4: Exe 5A 6 (7D 64)
Emmanuel Rd. EX4: Exe 5A 6 (7D 64)
Emma Pl. PL1: Plym 3F 141
Emma Pl. Ope PL1: Plym 3F 141
Emmasfield EX8: Exmth 5F 77
Emmetts Pk. TQ13: Ashb 3J 99
Emmetts Pl. TQ12: A'well 6E 108
Emperor Way EX1: Sow 6D 66
Empire Ct. TQ1: Torq 6C 112
Empire Rd. TQ1: Torq 6C 112
Empsons Cl. EX7: Daw 4F 97
Empsons Hill EX7: Daw 4F 97
Endeavour Av. EX2: Cou W 5B 72
Endeavour Ct. PL1: Plym 1F 141
Endfield Cl. EX1: Heav 6A 66
Endsleigh EX5: Broadc 5C 52
Endsleigh Cres. EX5: Clyst H 5G 67
Endsleigh Gdns.
PL4: Plym 2F 9 (1K 141)
Endsleigh Pk. Rd. PL3: Plym 5J 135
Endsleigh Pl. PL4: Plym 2F 9 (1K 141)
Endsleigh Rd. PL9: Plyms 5D 142
Endsleigh Vw. PL21: Ivy 4E 144
Endurance Ct. PL1: Dev 2D 140
Energic Ter. EX15: Cull 3H 45
Enfield Cl. EX17: Cred 6F 39
Enfield Rd. TQ1: Torq 6E 112
England's Cl. EX10: Sidf 1E 84
English Riviera Visitor Information Cen.
. . . . . 3D 116 (1B 176)
Eningdale Rd. PL19: Tavi 5G 59
Ennerdale Gdns. PL6: Plym 6K 131
Ennerdale Way EX4: Exe 6C 64
Ennisfarne Rd. EX39: W Ho 5A 20
Ensign Ct. EX39: W Ho 5D 20
Ensign La. PL4: Plym 4K 9 (2B 142)
ENSIS 1D 163
Enterprise Cen. EX22: Bradw 5C 28
Enterprise Ct. PL11: Torp 2B 140
Ent. Dr. PL5: Plym 1J 135
Epping Cres. PL6: Plym 4E 136
Epworth Ter. PL2: Plym 6E 134
Erica Dr. TQ2: Torq 2B 112
Eric Rd. PL4: Plym 4K 9 (2B 142)
Erith Av. PL2: Plym 4E 134
Erle Gdns. PL7: Plymp 6C 138
Erlstoke Cl. PL6: Plym 2E 136
Erme Ct. PL21: Ivy 4H 145
Erme Dr. PL21: Ivy 4G 145
Erme Gdns. PL3: Plym 6D 136
Erme M. PL21: Ivy 5G 145
Erme Pk. PL21: Erm 3H 147
Erme Rd. PL21: Ivy 4H 145
Erme Ter. PL21: Ivy 4H 145
ERMINGTON 2H 147 (2C 175)
Ermington Rd. PL21: Ivy 5F 145
Ermington Ter. PL4: Plym 7K 135
PL21: Erm 2H 147
Ermington Workshops
PL21: Erm 2J 147
ERNESETTLE 6D 130 (2A 174)
Ernesettle Cres. PL5: Plym 7D 130
Ernesettle Grn. PL5: Plym 6D 130
Ernesettle La. PL5: Plym 5C 130
Ernesettle Rd. PL5: Plym 7D 130
Ernesettle Ter. *PL5: Plym 7D 130*
(off Ernesettle Rd.)
Ernsborough Ct. EX2: Exe 6G 7
Ernsborough Gdns. EX14: Hon 4E 54
Erril Retail Pk. 6J 137
Eskil Pl. EX38: G Tor 1B 30
Esmonde Gdns. PL5: Plym 3A 134
Esplanade EX8: Exmth 6B 76
EX12: Seat 6F 87
TQ14: Teignm 5J 107
The Esplanade EX10: Sidm 7B 84
EX34: Wool 5A 10
EX35: Lynm 1G 13
PL1: Plym 7D 8 (4J 141)
TQ4: Paig 2J 119
TQ6: Dartm 4E 124
Esplanade Rd. TQ3: Paig 7J 115
TQ4: Paig 2J 119
Essex Cl. EX4: Exe 2B 70
Essex St. PL1: Plym 2B 8 (1H 141)
ESSINGTON 6C 36
Essington Cl. EX8: Exmth 1D 76
Essington Ct. EX8: Exmth 1D 76
EX20: N Taw 6C 36
Essington La. EX20: N Taw 6C 36
Essington Rd. EX20: N Taw 6C 36
Esso Wharf Rd.
PL4: Plym 7K 9 (4B 142)
Esthwaite La. PL6: Plym 6B 132
ESTOVER 7F 133 (2B 174)
Estover Cl. PL6: Plym 6G 133
Estover Ind. Est. PL6: Plym 6G 133
Estover Rd. PL6: Plym 6F 133
Estuary Bus. Pk. EX31: Yell 6A 16
Estuary Ct. EX8: Exmth 6A 76
TQ14: Teignm 4F 107
Estuary Vw. EX8: Exmth 1C 76
EX9: Bud S 6D 82
EX31: Yell 7A 16
EX39: Nort 4F 21
TQ12: Kingst 5J 105
Estuary Way PL5: Plym 3B 134
Estura TQ8: Salc 4C 158
Ethelston's Cl. DT7: Uply 3F 91
Ethelwynne Brown Cl.
EX39: Bide 3G 23
Ethmar Ct. EX15: Will 3D 44
Eton Av. PL1: Plym 2D 8 (1J 141)
Eton Cl. EX39: Bide 2E 22
Etonhurst Cl. EX2: Sow 2C 72
Eton La. PL1: Plym 3D 8
Eton Pl. PL1: Plym 2D 8 (1J 141)
Eton St. PL1: Plym 3D 8 (1J 141)
Eton Ter. PL1: Plym 3C 8 (2H 141)
Eton Wlk. EX4: Exe 1A 70
Eugene Rd. TQ3: Pres 6J 115
Eureka Ter. *EX14: Hon 4F 55*
(off Jerrard Cl.)
TQ13: Bov T 3C 92
Europa Pk. 6D 10
Evans Fld. EX9: Bud S 5B 82
Evans Pl. PL2: Plym 6G 135
Eveleigh Cl. EX1: Pin 1D 66
TQ5: Brixh 5E 122
Eveleighs Ct. EX4: Exe 2F 7
Evelyn Pl. PL4: Plym 1F 9 (1K 141)
Evelyn St. PL5: Plym 2C 134
Evenden Ct. PL11: Torp 1A 140
Everest Dr. EX12: Seat 3E 86
Everett Pl. EX16: Tive 2E 40
Evergreen Cl. EX8: Exmth 1F 77
Evett Cl. EX8: Exmth 4G 77
Evil La. EX13: Axmin 3K 89
Evran Dr. EX8: Exmth 1G 77
EWORTHY 1C 169
EXBOURNE 5J 35 (3A 164)
Excalibur Cl. EX4: Whip 3K 65
Exchange St. PL4: Plym 6F 9
EXEBRIDGE 1D 165
EXE BRI. NTH. 6C 6 (7E 64)
Exebridge Retail Pk. 7C 6 (1E 70)
EXE BRI. STH. 6C 6 (7E 64)
Exe Cl. EX31: C'nor 1D 16
Exe Estuary Local Nature Reserve
. . . . . 7A 76
Exe Estuary Local Nature Reserve
East 2D 171
West 2D 171
Exe Gdns. PL3: Plym 4D 136
Exe Hill TQ2: Torq 5H 111
EXE ISLAND 5C 6 (7E 64)
Exe Reed Beds
Nature Reserve 7C 72 (2D 171)
Exe Sailing Club 6A 76
Exe St. EX3: Top 5B 74
EX4: Exe 4C 6 (6E 64)
EXETER 4E 6 (6F 65)
Exeter Airport 7B 68 (1A 172)
Exeter Airport Bus. Pk.
EX5: Clyst H 7B 68
Exeter Airport Ind. Est.
EX5: Clyst H 7B 68
Exeter & Devon Crematorium 3J 71
Exeter Arena Athletics Stadium 3A 66
Exeter Av. TQ2: Torq 4B 112
Exeter Bus. Pk. EX1: Sow 5D 66
Exeter Castle 3E 6 (6F 65)
Exeter Cathedral 4E 6 (6F 65)
Exeter Central Station
(Rail) 2D 6 (5E 64)
Exeter Chiefs RUFC 3D 72
Exeter City FC 1G 7 (5G 65)
Exeter Cl. EX14: Fen 2G 53
PL5: Plym 6C 130
Exeter Cross TQ12: Live 4H 93
Exeter Foyer EX1: Exe 6D 6
Exeter Ga. EX36: S Mol 7C 26
Exeter Golf & Country Club
. . . . . 5B 72 (1D 171)
Exeter Hill EX6: Kenton 5H 95
EX15: Cull 5G 45
EX16: Tive 5E 40
Exeter Inn Ct. *EX32: B'aple 5F 19*
(off Litchdon St.)
Exeter Phoenix 3E 6 (6F 65)
Exeter Picturehouse 5C 6
Exeter Racecourse 2D 171
Exeter Rd. EX2: Cou W 6C 72
EX3: Top 7D 72
EX5: Silv 3G 51
EX6: Kennf 1H 95
EX6: Star 5B 96
EX7: Daw 5B 96
EX8: Exmth 1C 76
EX10: New P 5F 81
EX11: Ott M 1G 79, 4A 80
EX14: Hon 4C 54
EX15: Cull 5G 45
EX16: Ashy, Tive 7B 40
EX17: Cred 7J 39
EX19: Wink 3C 36
EX20: Oke 3C 48
EX32: B Taw 5A 24
EX33: Brau, Wraf 5J 15
PL21: Fil, Ivy 4H 145
TQ10: S Bre 2B 100
TQ12: Kingst 1G 105
TQ12: Kingst, New A 5E 104
TQ12: New A 6C 104
TQ13: Chud 1D 94
TQ14: Teignm 2G 107
Exeter Rd. Ind. Est. EX20: Oke 2E 48
Exeter St David's Station
(Rail) 1A 6 (5D 64)
EXETER SERVICE AREA
. . . . . 1E 72 (1D 171)
Exeter Sports Academy 3F 71
Exeter St. EX20: N Taw 6B 36
PL4: Plym 5F 9 (2K 141)
TQ14: Teignm 4H 107
Exeter Tennis Cen. 3E 64
Exeter Tenpin 7E 6 (1F 71)
Exeter Trade Cen. EX2: Mar B 5H 71
Exeter Underground Passages 3F 7
Exeter Visitor Information 3F 7 (6F 65)
Exe Vale Rd. EX2: Cou W 4K 71
Exe Vale Ter. EX16: Tive 5C 40
Exe Valley Leisure Cen. 3C 40
Exe Vw. EX6: Exmin 2C 74
Exe Vw. Cotts. EX2: Exe 1F 71
EX4: Exe 1A 6 (4C 64)
Exe View Rd. EX8: Lymp 4K 75
EXFORD 3D 161
Exhibition Rd. EX17: Cred 6J 39
Exhibition Way EX4: Pin 3B 66
EXMINSTER 2D 74 (2D 171)
Exminster Hill EX6: Exmin 4D 74
Exmoor Cl. EX16: Tive 2E 40
Exmoor National Park
. . . . . 3H 13 (3D 161)
Exmoor National Park Centre
Lynton 1H 13 (2D 161)
Exmoor Vw. EX36: S Mol 5C 26
Exmoor Way EX15: Cull 4F 45
Exmoor Zoo 2C 161
EXMOUTH 6C 76 (2A 172)
Exmouth Ct. EX8: Exmth 6D 76
Exmouth Leisure Cen. 5B 76
Exmouth Lifeboat Station
. . . . . 7E 76 (3A 172)
Exmouth Mus. 5C 76 (2A 172)
Exmouth Pavilion 7C 76
Exmouth Quay 6A 76
Exmouth Rd.
EX3: Clyst G, Ebf, Ext 5E 74
EX5: Clyst M 3F 73
EX8: Exmth, Lymp 3H 75, 4H 75
EX9: Bud S, Know 6A 82
EX10: Col R, New P 3H 83
PL1: Dev 1E 140
(not continuous)
Exmouth Station (Rail) 5B 76 (2D 171)
Exmouth Tennis & Fitness Cen. 4D 76
Exmouth Tourist Info. Cen. 6C 76
Exmouth Tourist Information Service
. . . . . 6C 76 (2D 171)
Exon Bldgs. EX15: Cull 5G 45
Exonia Pk. EX2: Exe 2A 70
Explorer Ct. PL2: Plym 6G 135
Explorer Wlk. *TQ2: Torq 2B 112*
(off Kingsley Av.)
EXTON
EX3 . . . . . 1G 75 (2D 171)
TA22 . . . . . 1D 165
Exton La. EX3: Ext 1G 75
Exton Rd. EX2: Mar B 2F 71
Exton Station (Rail) 2G 75 (2D 171)
EXWICK 4B 64 (1D 171)
Exwick Ct. EX4: Exe 4C 64
Exwick Hill EX4: Exe 4C 64
Exwick La. EX4: Exe 5A 64
Exwick Rd. EX4: Exe 4C 64
Exwick Vs. EX4: Exe 5C 64
Eyewell Grn. EX12: Seat 4E 86
Eymore Dr. EX11: W Hill 5G 79
Eyrecourt Rd. EX12: Seat 6E 86

F

Factory Ope *EX39: App 3J 21*
(off The Quay)
Factory Row TQ2: Torq 1C 116
Fairacre Av. EX32: B'aple 6H 19
Fairby Cl. EX16: Tive 2E 40
Fairfax Dr. EX15: Cull 3H 45
Fairfax Gdns. EX2: Alph 3E 70
Fairfax Pl.
TQ6: Dartm 2B 124 (6F 125)
Fairfax Rd. TQ12: H'fld 1H 93
Fairfax Ter. PL2: Plym 7E 134
Fairfax Way EX11: Ott M 2E 80
EX38: G Tor 1E 30
Fair Fld. TQ10: S Bre 2C 100
Fairfield EX16: Sam P 2B 42
EX31: Brat F 7H 13
EX34: Ilfra 3J 11
PL7: Plymp 2B 138
Fairfield Av. EX4: Whip 4B 66
PL2: Plym 4H 135
Fairfield Cl. EX8: Exmth 6D 76
EX13: Axmin 4H 89
TQ7: Kingsb 5G 157
TQ13: Bov T 4B 92
Fairfield Gdns. EX14: Hon 4F 55
Fairfield Ho. *EX2: Exe 3J 71*
(off Turnstone Rd.)
Fairfield Pk. DT7: Lym R 4K 91
Fairfield Rd. EX2: Alph 5E 70
EX8: Exmth 6D 76
EX17: Cred 5H 39
TQ2: Torq 5B 112
TQ12: Kingsk 2G 111
Fairfield Ter. EX2: Exe 7B 6 (1D 70)
TQ12: New A 1F 109
Fairfield Way TQ7: Chil 6H 159
Fairhazel Dr. EX4: Exe 5C 64
Fairholme Rd. EX34: Wool 6A 10
Fairies Hill TQ11: B'leigh 3D 98
Fair Isle Cl. TQ2: Torq 3A 112
Fairlands Av. EX6: Chri 4J 63
Fairlawn Ct. EX10: Sidm 5C 84
Fairlawns Pk. TQ4: Good 5H 119
Fairlea Cl. EX7: Daw 1J 97
Fairlea Cres. EX39: Nort 6D 20
Fairlea Gdns. EX39: Nort 6D 20
Fairlea Rd. EX7: Daw 2H 97
Fairleigh EX10: New P 5G 81
Fairlynch Cl. EX33: Brau 3G 15
Fairlynch Gro. EX33: Brau 3H 15
Fairlynch La. EX33: Brau 3G 15
Fairlynch Mus. & Arts Cen.
. . . . . 7D 82 (2A 172)
Fairmead EX10: Sidm 2A 84
Fairmead Ct. EX1: Pin 3D 66
FAIRMILE 1A 80 (1A 172)
FAIR OAK 2A 166
Fair Oak Cl. EX5: Clyst H 7C 68
Fair Oak Ct. EX5: Clyst H 7B 68
Fair Oaks TQ14: Teignm 3G 107
Fairpark Cl. EX2: Exe 6G 7 (7G 65)
TQ13: Chud 2B 94
Fairpark Rd. EX2: Exe 6F 7 (7F 65)
Fairplace *EX20: Oke 3B 48*
(off Mill Rd.)
Fairplace Ter. *EX20: Oke 3B 48*
(off St James St.)
Fairseat Cl. TQ9: Tot 6F 103
Fair Vw. EX31: B'aple 3D 18
Fairview EX22: Bradw 6B 28
Fairview Av. EX5: Clyst M 3J 73
PL3: Plym 6E 136
Fair Vw. La. EX24: Colyf 7C 88
Fairview Pk. TQ13: Bov T 6B 92
Fair Vw. Rd. EX14: Hon 4F 55
Fairview Rd.
TQ6: Dartm 1A 124 (6E 124)
TQ12: Den 1H 101
Fairview Ter. EX1: Pin 3E 66
EX8: Exmth 5D 76
Fairview Way PL3: Plym 6F 137
Fairwater Cl. TQ12: Kingst 4J 105
Fairwaters TQ12: Kingst 3H 105
Fairway EX16: Tive 3K 41
EX39: App 3G 21
The Fairway EX4: Exe 3H 65
EX33: Brau 4F 15
PL8: New F 5H 149
Fairway Av. PL21: Ivy 4F 145
Fairway Cl. EX33: Brau 4G 15
TQ5: Chur F 3K 121
The Fairways EX39: W Ho 5C 20
FAIRY CROSS 1C 163
Fairy La. TQ11: B'leigh 5B 98
Falcon Rd. EX2: Sow 1D 72
PL1: Dev 3E 140
Falcon Way EX16: Tive 2E 40
Falkland Cl. EX4: Exe 2H 65
Falkland Dr. TQ12: Kingst 3J 105
Falkland Rd. TQ2: Torq 2B 116
Falkland Way TQ14: Teignm 2G 107
Fallapit Cotts. TQ9: E All 5B 152
The Fallapit Estate TQ9: E All 6B 152
Fallapit Turn TQ9: E All 5A 152
Falloway Cl. TQ2: Torq 3C 112
Fallowfield Cl. TQ12: New A 1J 109
Fallow Flds. EX32: B'aple 7H 19
Fallowfields TQ9: Tot 6C 102
Falmouth Cl. TQ2: Torq 5H 111
Fanshawe Way PL9: Hooe 6D 142
Faraday Ho. EX1: Exe 4K 7 (6H 65)
Faraday Mill Bus. Pk.
PL4: Plym 3C 142

Faraday Mill Trade Pk.
L4: Plym 3C **142**
Faraday Rd. PL4: Plym 3C **142**
Faringdon Rd. PL4: Plym 1C **142**
Farleigh Mdws. EX16: Tive 2A **40**
Farleys Ct. EX3: Top 5A **74**
The Farm EX5: Whim 6F **53**
Farm Cl. EX2: Won 1B **72**
EX31: Bick 7K **17**
PL7: Plymp 5K **137**
TQ12: Kingsk 6J **109**
Farm Ct. TQ5: Brixh 3G **123**
Farmer Frank's La. EX19: Wink . . .3C **36**
Farm Hill EX4: Exe 4A **64**
Farmhouse Av. EX1: Pin 4E **66**
Farm Ho. Ri. EX6: Exmin 2B **74**
Farm La. PL5: Plym 1G **135**
PL6: Plym 3C **136**
Farm Pk. EX5: Cran 3B **68**
Farm Rd. EX39: Bide 6B **22**
Farm Way EX14: Fen 2F **53**
Farmyard La. TQ3: Comp 7D **110**
Farnley Cl. PL6: Plym 4C **132**
The Farriers PL19: Lam 6C **58**
Farriers Cotts. PL7: Plymp 3B **138**
FARRINGDON 1A **172**
Farthing La. TQ3: Marl 4C **114**
Farthings La. EX10: New P 6F **81**
Far Vw. Rd. EX20: Oke 3C **48**
FARWAY 1B **172**
Farwell Rd. TQ9: Tot 6D **102**
Fast Rabbit Farm Gardens 2A **176**
Fatherford Rd. EX20: Oke 3D **48**
Faulkner Cl. TQ6: Dartm 6C **124**
Fawns Cl. PL21: Erm 2H **147**
FAWTON 3A **168**
Fay Rd. EX7: Daw 4H **97**
Featherbed La. EX8: Exmth 2C **76**
Featherstone Rd. EX8: Exmth 2C **76**
Federation Rd. PL3: Plym 7D **136**
Fegen Rd. PL5: Plym 2A **134**
Felixwell Ct. EX4: Exe 5A **6**
Fellowes La. PL1: Plym 1G **141**
Fellowes Pl. PL1: Plym 2F **141**
Fellowes Pl. La. Sth. PL1: Plym . . .2G **141**
(off Edgcumbe Av.)
Feltrim Av. EX2: Exe 2G **71**
FENITON 2G **53** (1A **172**)
Feniton Gdns. EX14: Fen 2G **53**
Feniton Station (Rail) 2F **53** (1A **172**)
Ferguson Cl. EX11: Ott M 4A **80**
Fern Bank TQ7: W Alv 5D **156**
Fernbank Av. PL21: Ivy 3E **144**
Fern Cl. EX20: Oke 2C **48**
PL7: Plymp 4E **138**
TQ5: Brixh 4F **123**
Ferncombe Cl. TQ12: Kingst 1H **105**
Ferncombe Dr. TQ12: Kingst 1H **105**
Ferndale TQ6: Dartm . . .2A **124** (6E **124**)
Ferndale Av. PL2: Plym 4D **134**
Ferndale Cl. EX14: Hon 6C **54**
PL6: Plym 2E **132**
Ferndale Gdns. EX2: Exe 1D **70**
Ferndale M. TQ2: Torq 6H **111**
Ferndale Rd. EX2: Exe 7B **6** (1D **70**)
PL2: Plym 4D **134**
TQ2: Torq 6H **111**
TQ14: Teignm 3H **107**
Ferndown Cl. EX39: Bide 3D **22**
Ferndown Rd. DT7: Lym R 5K **91**
Fernham Ter. TQ3: Paig 7H **115**
Fernhill Cl. PL21: Ivy 4F **145**
Fernicombe Cl. TQ3: Paig 7E **114**
Fernicombe Rd. TQ3: Paig 7E **114**
Fernleigh Ct. EX20: N Taw 6B **36**
Fernleigh Rd. PL3: Plym 6A **136**
Fern Mdw. EX20: Oke 2C **48**
PL19: Tavi 3K **59**
Fern Pk. EX34: Ilfra 3H **11**
Fernpark Cl. EX2: Exe 3H **71**
Fern Rd. TQ12: New A 4J **109**
Fern Ter. EX20: Prin 6C **60**
(off Heather Ter.)
Fern Way EX34: Ilfra 3H **11**
Fernworthy Cl. EX17: Cop 6D **38**
TQ2: Torq 6G **111**
Fernworthy Forest Walks 2A **170**
Fernworthy Gdns. EX17: Cop 6D **38**
Fernworthy Pk. EX17: Cop 6D **38**
Fernworthy Picnic Site 2A **170**
Fernworthy Reservoir Nature Reserve
. . . . .2A **170**
Ferrers Grn. TQ5: Chur F 4A **122**
Ferrers Rd. PL5: Plym 2D **134**
Ferrymans TQ5: Hill 6J **123**
Ferrymans Reach TQ14: Shal 6H **107**
(off Marine Pde.)
Ferryman Way EX2: Cou W 6C **72**
Ferry Rd. EX3: Top 5A **74**
PL1: Dev 1C **140**
Ferry St. PL11: Torp 1B **140**
Feversham Cl. PL7: Plymp 3E **138**
Field Cl. EX33: Brau 5H **15**
TQ3: Pres 4H **115**
EX39: Bide 3D **22**
Field End EX13: Axmin 4J **89**
The Fieldings EX37: C'ton 6H **25**

Field La. EX33: Brau 5H **15**
FILFORD 1D **173**
FILHAM 5K **145**
Filham Ind. Est. PL21: Ivy 4H **145**
(off Blair Rd.)
Filham Moor Cl. PL21: Ivy 5J **145**
Fillablack Rd. EX39: Bide 3H **23**
Fillace La. PL20: Horr 2E **126**
Fillace Pk. PL20: Horr 2E **126**
FILLEIGH 1A **164**
EX17 . . . . .2B **164**
EX32 . . . . .1A **164**
Fillham Moor La. PL21: Ivy 4H **145**
Filmer Way EX2: Mar B 2E **70**
Fincer Dr. PL21: Ivy 3E **144**
Finch Foundry 1G **49** (1A **170**)
Findon Gdns. PL6: Plym 6E **132**
Finewell St.
PL1: Plym 5E **8** (3J **141**)
Fingle Cl. EX4: Exe 4B **64**
Fingle Glen Golf Course 1C **171**
Finistere Av. EX7: Daw 2H **97**
Finnimore Ind. Est. EX11: Ott M . . .4B **80**
Fin St. PL1: Plym 7B **8** (4H **141**)
Firbank Rd. EX7: Daw 1J **97**
Fir Cl. EX14: Hon 4E **54**
EX15: Will 3D **44**
Fircroft Rd. TQ2: Torq 4G **135**
Firefly Wlk. PL6: Plym 5C **132**
Firestone Cl. PL6: Plym 2F **137**
Firestone La. TQ12: A'well 5D **108**
Firlands Rd. TQ14: Teignm 2H **107**
Firlands Rd. TQ2: Torq 3C **112**
Firleigh Rd. TQ12: Kingst 2G **105**
The Firs EX6: Kennf 1G **95**
EX8: Exmth 5F **77**
First Av. EX1: Heav 3K **7** (6J **65**)
EX2: Cou W 6B **72**
EX7: Daw 5F **97**
EX13: Axmin 2K **89**
PL1: Dev 2F **141**
PL9: Plyms 4G **143**
TQ1: Torq 5C **112**
TQ14: Teignm 4G **107**
First Dr. TQ14: Teignm 3K **107**
(The Rowdens)
TQ14: Teignm 4H **107**
(Second Dr.)
First Raleigh EX39: Bide 2D **22**
Fir Ter. EX36: S Mol 6D **26**
Fir Tree Cl. EX8: Exmth 2H **77**
Firtree Rd. PL21: Ivy 4H **145**
Firtree Rd. PL6: Plym 4F **133**
(off Glenfield Way)
Fir Wlk. TQ2: Torq 5J **111**
Fishacre Cl. TQ3: Paig 6E **114**
Fishchowter's La. TQ9: Tot 7E **102**
Fishcombe Cove Holiday Homes
. . . . .2D **122**
Fishcombe Rd. TQ5: Brixh 2D **122**
Fishermans Ct. EX8: Exmth 6A **76**
(off Victoria Rd.)
Fisher Rd. PL2: Plym 6F **135**
TQ14: New A 1E **108**
Fisher's Sq. EX4: Exe 7A **6** (1D **70**)
Fisher St. TQ4: Paig 2H **119**
Fishers Way EX16: Hal 6C **42**
Fishleigh Cl. EX31: Rou 7A **18**
Fishleigh Rd. EX31: Rou 7A **18**
FISHPOND BOTTOM 1D **173**
Fish Quay PL4: Plym 6H **9**
Fitness First
Exeter 5B **6**
Fitzford Cotts. PL19: Tavi 5G **59**
FITZHEAD 1B **166**
Fitzroy Rd. EX1: Sow 6D **66**
Fitzroy Ter. PL1: Plym 1F **141**
Five Acres TQ13: Bov T 7B **92**
Five Elms La. EX5: New C 7A **50**
Fivehead 1D **167**
FIVELANES 2A **168**
Five Lanes Rd. TQ3: Marl 4D **114**
Five Turnings EX34: C Mar 5B **12**
Flagstaff Rd. TQ6: Dartm 5E **124**
Flagstaff Wlk. PL1: Dev 3E **140**
Flamborough Rd. PL6: Plym 3B **132**
Flamborough Way PL6: Plym 4B **132**
Flamsted Cres. PL5: Plym 2D **134**
The Flats EX7: Daw 7B **96**
The Flavel Arts Cen. 1A **124**
(off Mayor's Av.)
Flavel Pl. TQ6: Dartm 1A **124**
Flavel St. TQ6: Dartm 1A **124**
Flax Meadow La. EX13: Axmin . . .3J **89**
Flayes Almshouses EX4: Whip 4B **66**
Fleet Cl. EX12: Seat 5F **87**
TQ1: Torq 2D **116**
Fleet St. PL2: Plym 5D **134**
TQ1: Torq 2D **116**
TQ2: Torq 2D **116**
Fleet Wlk. TQ2: Torq 2D **116**
(off Fleet St.)

Fleet Wlk. Shop. Cen. 2D **116**
Fleetwood Gdns. PL6: Plym 3B **132**
Fleming Av. EX10: Sidm 2D **84**
Fleming Way EX2: Exe 7J **7** (1H **71**)
Flemons Ct. TQ4: Paig 2G **119**
(off St Michael's Rd.)
Fletcher Cl. TQ2: Torq 6A **112**
Fletcher Cres. PL9: Plyms 6H **143**
Fletcher Ind. Est.
EX39: Bide 5D **22**
Fletcher Way PL9: Plyms 6H **143**
Flete Av. TQ12: New A 2J **109**
Flete Cl. TQ12: New A 2J **109**
Flete Rd. TQ12: New A 2C **134**
Flete Vw. Ter. PL21: Bitta 3C **146**
Flexa Pk. EX34: C Mar 6B **12**
FLEXBURY 3A **162**
The Flexton EX11: Ott M 3C **80**
(off Silver St.)
Flightway EX14: Dunk 4G **47**
Flint Fld. Way EX1: Pin 3F **67**
Floaters Rd. TQ6: Dartm 5F **125**
Flood's La. EX15: Cull 4G **45**
Flood St. TQ9: Sto G 3A **120**
Flora Cotts. PL1: Plym 5B **8** (3H **141**)
Flora Ct. PL1: Plym 4B **8** (2H **141**)
(not continuous)
Flora St. PL1: Plym 5B **8** (3H **141**)
Florence Pl. PL4: Plym 2B **142**
TQ12: New A 2G **109**
Florence St. PL5: Plym 2C **134**
Florence Way EX1: Sow 6C **66**
Florida Dr. EX4: Exe 2F **65**
Florida Gdns. PL3: Plym 5D **136**
Florida Rd. TQ1: Torq 1E **116**
Flowerpot La. EX4: Exe 5A **6** (7D **64**)
Flowers Mdw. TQ12: Live 4F **93**
(off Divett Dr.)
Flower St. EX5: W'bury 5C **78**
Flow La. TQ14: Bi'ton 4B **106**
(not continuous)
Floyd Cl. PL2: Plym 4E **134**
Floyers-Hay Ct. EX2: Exe 7D **6**
Fluder Cres. TQ12: Kingsk 2H **111**
Fluder Hill TQ12: Kingsk 1G **111**
Fluder Ri. TQ12: Kingsk 2H **111**
FLUXTON 7A **80** (1A **172**)
Foales Ct. TQ13: Ashb 4H **99**
(off North St.)
Foliot Av. PL2: Plym 5F **135**
Foliot Rd. PL2: Plym 4E **134**
Follafield Pk. TQ5: Brixh 6D **122**
Follaton TQ9: Darti 5A **102**
Follaton Bungs. TQ9: Tot 6B **102**
Follaton Ri. TQ9: Tot 6A **102**
Follett Rd. EX3: Top 5A **74**
EX16: Tive 5H **41**
The Folly PL9: Elb 5J **143**
Folly Cl. TQ13: Bov T 6C **92**
FOLLY CROSS 3C **163**
Folly Farm Cl. EX33: Brau 4H **15**
FOLLY GATE 1D **169**
Folly Hill TQ7: Bigb S 3C **154**
Folly La. TQ8: Salc 3D **158**
(off Fore St.)
Fonthill TQ1: Torq 2F **117**
Football La. TQ12: Kingst 3H **105**
Footland La. TQ12: Dacc 1A **112**
Footlands Rd. TQ4: Paig 3G **119**
Forbes Cl. TQ12: H'fld 2J **93**
Forcefield Rd. EX15: Cull 5G **45**
Forches Av. EX32: B'aple 5G **19**
FORCHES CROSS 4B **104**
Forches Cross TQ12: New A 7K **93**
Forches Gdns. EX32: B'aple 5G **19**
FORD
EX39 . . . . .1C **163**
PL2 . . . . .6F **135** (2A **174**)
PL8 . . . . .5C **150** (2C **175**)
TA4 . . . . .1A **166**
TA21 . . . . .3F **43**
TQ7 . . . . .3D **175**
Ford TQ6: Dartm 6E **124**
FORDA 6A **104** (3A **160**)
FORD BARTON 2D **165**
Ford Cl. PL21: Ivy 4E **144**
Ford Cres. EX22: Bradw 6C **28**
Ford Down La. EX36: S Mol 6A **26**
Forde Cl. TQ12: A'well 5D **108**
TQ12: New A 1G **109**
Fordens La. EX7: Holc 7F **97**
Forde Pk. TQ12: New A 2G **109**
FORDER GREEN 1D **175**
Forder Hgts. PL6: Plym 2C **136**
Forder La. PL21: Bitta, Ugb 3E **146**
TQ9: Darti 3A **102**
TQ10: S Bre 1C **100**
TQ13: Bov T 1A **92**
TQ14: Bi'ton 4A **106**
(not continuous)
Forder Mdw. TQ12: More 6H **61**
Forde Rd. TQ12: New A 1G **109**
Forder Valley
Local Nature Reserve 3E **136**
Forder Valley Rd. PL6: Plym 2C **136**
Forde Vs. TQ12: New A 2G **109**
Ford Farm Ct. EX6: Kenton 6H **95**

Ford Hill EX5: Thor 1B **50**
EX39: Hart 3J **27**
PL2: Plym 6F **135**
Fordishaies La. EX5: Bradn 1B **52**
Fordlands Cres. EX39: Bide 1E **22**
Fordlands Rd. TQ13: More 6H **61**
Ford La. EX11: W Hill 5H **79**
Ford Orchard EX16: Sam P 2B **42**
FORD PARK 6J **135**
Ford Pk. PL4: Plym 7K **135**
TQ13: Chud K 6B **94**
Ford Pk. La. PL4: Plym 7K **135**
Ford Pk. Rd. PL4: Plym 7J **135**
Ford Plain EX5: Thor 1A **50**
Ford Ri. EX39: Bide 5F **23**
Ford Rd. EX16: Bam 2J **33**
EX16: Tive 4F **41**
PL8: Torr 3C **150**
PL9: Wem 6A **148**
TQ9: Tot 5F **103**
TQ12: A'well 5E **108**
Fords Rd. EX2: Exe 7D **6** (1E **70**)
FORD STREET 2B **166**
Ford St. PL19: Tavi 4H **59**
TQ13: More 6H **61**
FORDTON 7K **39** (1C **171**)
Fordton Ind. Est. EX17: Cred 7K **39**
Fordton Plain EX17: Cred 7J **39**
Fordton Ter. EX17: Cred 7J **39**
Ford Valley TQ6: Dartm 6E **124**
Ford Way EX1: Pin 3G **67**
Foredown La. TQ12: Kingsk 1E **110**
Foreland Point Lighthouse 1D **161**
Foreland Vw. EX34: Ilfra 4H **11**
Forest Av. PL2: Plym 4H **135**
Foresters Rd. EX22: Hols 1C **34**
PL9: Plyms 5E **142**
Foresters Ter. TQ14: Teignm 5H **107**
Forest Hill EX39: Bide 6F **23**
Fore St. EX1: Heav 5K **7** (7J **65**)
EX2: Ide 3B **70**
EX3: Top 5B **74**
EX4: Exe 5C **6** (7E **64**)
EX5: Bradn 1C **52**
EX5: Silv 2H **51**
EX6: Kenton 6H **95**
EX8: Exmth 6C **76**
EX9: Bud S 7C **82**
EX9: Ott'n 6G **83**
EX10: Sidb 2H **85**
EX10: Sidm 7C **84**
EX12: Beer 7B **86**
EX12: Seat 5F **87**
EX15: Cull 4H **45**
EX15: Culm 2B **46**
EX15: Hemy 2G **47**
EX15: Kent 6B **46**
EX15: Uff 6H **43**
EX16: Bam 2H **33**
EX16: Tive 5C **40**
EX16: W'ridge 6J **33**
EX17: Morc 1B **38**
EX18: Chul 6C **32**
EX19: Dol 6G **31**
EX19: Wink 2C **36**
EX20: Brid 3H **57**
EX20: Exbo 5J **35**
EX20: N Taw 6A **36**
EX20: Oke 3B **48**
EX20: S Taw 1J **49**
EX22: Hols 2C **34**
EX34: Ilfra 2J **11**
EX36: N Mol 2B **26**
EX38: G Tor 2C **30**
EX39: Hart 3H **27**
EX39: Nort 6E **20**
PL1: Dev 2D **140**
PL5: Tam F 4G **131**
PL7: Plymp 5B **138**
PL8: Holb 7C **150**
PL8: Y'ton 2B **150**
PL11: Torp 1A **140**
PL12: Car 1A **130**
PL16: Lift 6A **56**
PL19: Mil A 2A **58**
PL20: Bere A 2C **128**
PL20: Bere F 6C **128**
PL21: Corn 6J **129**
PL21: Ivy 4G **145**
PL21: Ugb 6E **146**
TA21: Holc R 2G **43**
TQ1: Torq 5D **112**
TQ2: Torq 2B **112**
TQ5: Brixh 3E **122**
TQ6: Kingsw 6G **125**
TQ7: Ave G 7H **151**
TQ7: Kingsb 4F **157**
TQ7: Lodd 3E **153**
TQ8: Salc 3D **158**
TQ9: Tot 6E **102**
TQ10: S Bre 1B **100**
TQ11: B'leigh 4C **98**
TQ12: Ipp 6H **101**
TQ12: Kingsk 1F **111**
TQ12: Kingst 4H **105**
TQ13: Bov T 4C **92**
TQ13: Chud 2C **94**
TQ13: More 6H **61**

Fore St.—Geneva Cl.

Fore St. TQ14: Bi'ton .3B **106**
TQ14: Shal .6G **107**
TQ14: Teignm .4H **107**
(not continuous)
Fore St. Hill EX9: Bud S .6D **82**
EX18: Chul .6C **32**
Fore St. M. *EX4: Exe .5D 6*
(off Friernhay St.)
Forest Ridge Rd. TQ3: Pres .5F **115**
Forest Rd. TQ1: Torq .7C **112**
Forest Vw. PL6: Plym .3E **132**
Forge Cl. EX9: Bud S .5B **82**
PL6: Robo .1D **132**
Forge End EX19: Wink .3C **36**
Forge Pl. TQ13: Bov T .4B **92**
Forget Me Not La.
PL6: Plym .5G **133**
Forge Way EX15: Cull .4H **45**
Forgeway Cl. TQ2: Torq .2K **115**
Forresters Bus. Pk.
PL6: Plym .5G **133**
Forresters Dr. PL6: Plym .3E **132**
Forster Rd. TQ8: Salc .3C **158**
Fort Austin Av. PL6: Plym .1A **136**
Fort Bovisand .1A 148
FORTESCUE .3E 84
Fortescue Cl. EX33: Brau .5K **15**
Fortescue Pl. PL3: Plym .5B **136**
Fortescue Rd. EX2: Exe .2E **70**
EX10: Sidm .3E **84**
EX32: B'aple .7G **19**
EX34: Ilfra .2H **11**
TQ3: Pres .5J **115**
TQ8: Salc .4B **158**
Fortescue Ter. PL19: Tavi .3G **59**
Fortfield EX12: Seat .5F **87**
Fortfield Gdns. EX10: Sidm .7B **84**
Fortfield Lawn EX10: Sidm .7B **84**
Fortfield Pl. EX10: Sidm .7B **84**
Fortfield Ter. EX10: Sidm .7B **84**
Fort Flats EX10: Sidm .7B **84**
Forth Gdns. PL3: Plym .5E **136**
FORT HILL .4G 19
Fort Hill Dr. EX32: B'aple .4G **19**
Fortmead Cl. EX32: B'aple .4F **19**
FORTON .3D 167
Forton Rd. EX8: Exmth .3E **76**
Fort Stamford Health & Fitness Cen.
.6B **142**
Fort Stamford The Ramparts .6B **142**
Fort St. EX32: B'aple .4F **19**
Fort Ter. *EX32: B'aple .4F 19*
(off Alexandra Rd.)
EX39: Bide .4G **23**
PL6: Plym .7A **132**
Fortune Way TQ1: Torq .6D **112**
Fosbrooke Ct. PL3: Plym .5A **136**
Fosketh Hill EX39: W Ho .6B **20**
Fosketh Ter. EX39: W Ho .6B **20**
Fosse Rd. TQ7: Kingsb .3G **157**
Fosseway Cl. EX13: Axmin .4H **89**
Fosse Way Ct. EX12: Seat .6F **87**
Fosseway Pk. EX12: Seat .2E **86**
Foss Slip TQ6: Dartm .1A **124**
Foss St.
TQ6: Dartm .1A **124** (6F **125**)
Fosterlea EX15: Cull .4G **45**
Foulston Av. PL5: Plym .3A **134**
Foundry Ct. TQ13: Chud .2B **94**
Foundry La. PL8: Noss M .7H **149**
Foundry M. PL19: Tavi .3K **59**
Fountain Ct. EX4: Exe .3C **6**
TQ13: Bov T .4C 92
(off Fore St.)
TQ14: Teignm .5J 107
(off Triangle Pl.)
Fountain Flds. EX37: High B .2B **32**
Fountain Hill EX9: Bud S .7B **82**
Fountain Ho. EX1: Exe .2G **7**
Fountains Cres. PL2: Plym .3G **135**
Fouracre Cl. EX4: Whip .3K **65**
Four Acres EX39: Bide .3C **22**
Fouracre Way TQ12: Kingst .3J **105**
Four Cross Av. EX15: Will .3D **44**
Fourcross Hill EX13: Axmin .2F **89**
Fourcross Units TQ9: Sto G .7A **118**
Four Elms Hill EX10: Harp .5J **81**
Four Mills La. EX17: Cred .7J **39**
Four Oaks Cl. EX32: Land .1B **24**
Four Oaks Rd. EX6: Ted M .7J **49**
Four Seasons Village
EX19: Wink .1A **36**
Fourth Av. TQ14: Teignm .3G **107**
Fourview Cl. TQ5: Brixh .4G **123**
Four Ways Dr. EX18: Chul .5B **32**
Fowey Av. TQ2: Torq .5H **111**
Fowey Cl.
EX1: Heav .1K **7** (5J **65**)
Fowey Gdns. PL3: Plym .5E **136**
Fowey Rd. EX31: C'nor .1E **16**
Fowler Cl. EX6: Exmin .2C **74**
Fowlmere Cl. PL5: Plym .5D **130**
Foxbeare Rd. EX34: Ilfra .3K **11**
Fox Cl. EX20: Oke .2D **48**
Foxes Lair *EX20: Oke .3A 48*
(off Oaklands Pk.)
Fox Fld. Cl. PL3: Plym .6D **136**
Foxglove Chase EX15: Will .3D **44**
Foxglove Cl. EX14: Dunk .7H **47**
EX16: Tive .2F **41**
EX32: B'aple .5K **19**
TQ12: New A .6A **104**
Foxglove End PL20: C'stone .6B **126**
Foxglove Ri. EX4: Exe .4A **64**
Foxglove Rd. EX12: Seat .3F **87**
Foxglove Way TQ4: Paig .5E **118**
FOXHAYES .6B 64
Foxhayes Rd. EX4: Exe .6C **64**
Foxhill EX13: Axmin .4H **89**
EX39: Nort .6E **20**
Foxhole Hill EX6: Chri .2J **63**
Foxhole La. EX39: Nort .6E **20**
Foxhole Rd. TQ2: Torq .2K **115**
TQ3: Paig .1F **119**
Foxholes Hill EX8: Exmth .7E **76**
Foxhollows TQ12: New A .2K **109**
Foxlands TQ1: Torq .6E **112**
Foxlands Wlk. *TQ1: Torq .5E 112*
(off Fore St.)
Foxley Cres. TQ12: New A .1C **108**
Fox Rd. EX4: Whip .2A **66**
Fox Tor Cl. TQ4: Good .1H **121**
Foxtor Cl. PL5: Plym .7G **131**
Foxtor Rd. EX4: Exe .4B **64**
Foxwell La. TQ12: New A .7D **104**
Foxwood Gdns. PL6: Plym .5K **131**
PL9: Plyms .7F **143**
Foyle Cl. PL7: Plymp .4D **138**
Frances Gdns. EX1: Exe .3H **7**
Francis Cl. EX4: Exe .7A **6** (1C **70**)
Francis Ct. EX2: Exe .5K **7** (7H **65**)
EX17: Cred .6H 39
(off The Burrowe)
Francis Cres. EX16: Tive .5G **41**
Francis Dr. EX39: W Ho .6A **20**
Francis Pl. PL1: Plym .3A **8** (2G **141**)
Francis St. PL1: Plym .4A **8** (2G **141**)
Francis Way EX24: Colyf .1G **87**
Franeth Cl. TQ12: Kingst .3G **105**
Frankford La. EX6: Ted M .5J **49**
Frankfort Ga. PL1: Plym .4C **8** (2H **141**)
Franklea Cl. EX11: Ott M .4C **80**
Franklin St. EX2: Exe .6F **7** (7F **65**)
Franklyn Av. EX33: Brau .5K **15**
Franklyn Cl. EX2: Exe .2C **70**
Franklyn Dr. EX2: Exe .2C **70**
Franklyns PL6: Plym .6B **132**
Franklyns Cl. PL6: Plym .6B **132**
Frankmarsh Pk. EX32: B'aple .3G **19**
Frankmarsh Rd. EX32: B'aple .3G **19**
Fraser Ct. TQ3: Paig .2F **119**
Fraser Dr. TQ14: Teignm .3G **107**
Fraser Pl. PL5: Tam F .3H **131**
Fraser Rd. EX8: Exmth .2F **77**
PL5: Tam F .3H **131**
Fraser Sq. PL5: Tam F .2H **131**
FREATHY .2A 174
Frederick St. E.
PL1: Plym .4B **8** (2H **141**)
Frederick St. W.
PL1: Plym .4B **8** (2H **141**)
Frederick Ter. *EX7: Daw .4G 97*
(off Stockton Rd.)
Fredington Gro. PL2: Plym .5G **135**
Freedom Sq. PL4: Plym .1H **9** (1A **142**)
Freelands Cl. EX8: Exmth .4F **77**
Freeman's Wharf PL1: Plym .4F **141**
Freemantle Gdns. PL2: Plym .7E **134**
Freestone Rd. TQ12: Kingst .3G **105**
Fremantle Pl. PL2: Plym .7E **134**
FREMINGTON .6F 17 (3B 160)
Fremington Quay EX31: Frem .4G **17**
Fremington Quay Heritage Cen.
.4G **17** (3B **160**)
Fremington Rd. EX12: Seat .5D **86**
FRENCHBEER .2A 170
French Cl. EX5: Silv .1H **51**
French Furze Rd. TQ9: Blacka .2C **152**
French St. TQ14: Teignm .4J **107**
Frensham Av. PL6: Plym .4D **132**
Frensham Gdns. PL6: Plym .3D **132**
Freshford Cl. PL6: Plym .2D **136**
Freshford Wlk. PL6: Plym .2D **136**
Freshwater Dr. TQ4: Good .7G **119**
Frewin Gdns. PL6: Plym .4C **132**
Frewins EX9: Bud S .5B **82**
Friars Ga. EX2: Exe .6E **6** (7F **65**)
FRIARS GREEN .6D 6 (7E 64)
Friars Grn. *EX2: Exe .6E 6*
(off Southgate)
Friars La. PL1: Plym .6F **9**
Friars Wlk. PL19: Whit .5K **59**
Friars' Wlk. EX2: Exe .6E **6** (7F **65**)
Friary Ct. EX1: Exe .4E **6**
Friary Pk. PL4: Plym .4J **9** (2A **142**)
Friary St. PL4: Plym .5H **9** (3A **142**)
Friendship La. *EX34: Ilfra .2H 11*
(off High St.)
Friernhay Ct. EX4: Exe .5C **6**
Friernhay St. EX4: Exe .5C **6** (7E **64**)
FRITHELSTOCK .2C 163
Frithelstock Priory .2C **163**
FRITHELSTOCK STONE .2C 163
FRITTISCOMBE .3A 176
Frobisher App. PL5: Plym .1J **135**
Frobisher Cl. TQ14: Teignm .1G **107**
Frobisher Grn. TQ2: Torq .7J **111**
Frobisher La. TQ8: Salc .3B **158**
Frobisher Rd. EX8: Exmth .2E **76**
TQ12: New A .7J **105**
Frobisher Way PL19: Tavi .4H **59**
TQ4: Good .5H **119**
Frog La. EX5: Clyst M .2F **73**
EX33: Brau .4J **15**
EX36: S Mol .5B **26**
TA21: Holc R .2G **43**
FROGMORE .3D 175
Frogmore Av. PL6: Plym .3C **136**
(not continuous)
Frogmore Ct. PL6: Plym .4C **136**
Frogmore Rd. EX9: E Bud .2E **82**
Frogmore Ter. TQ7: Kingsb .5F **157**
Frog St. EX1: Exe .6C **6** (7E **64**)
EX4: Exe .6C **6** (7E **64**)
EX16: Bam .1H **33**
EX34: Wool .6A **10**
Frogstreet Hill
EX33: Forda, Geo .6A **14**
FROGWELL .3B 168
Frome Cl. PL7: Plymp .5D **138**
Frontfield Cres. PL6: Plym .5K **131**
FROST .3C 38
Froude Av. TQ2: Torq .1D **112**
Froude Rd. TQ8: Salc .6A **158**
Fry's La. EX10: Sidf .1D **84**
Fry St. EX22: Hols .2C **34**
Fulda Cres. EX17: Cred .7J **39**
FULFORD .1C 167
Fulford Cl. EX6: Ted M .7J **49**
EX39: Bide .5H **23**
Fulford Dr. EX15: Cull .5G **45**
Fulford La. EX6: Dunsf .4B **62**
Fulford Rd. EX1: Heav .5J **65**
Fulford Way EX5: W'bury .5C **78**
Fullaford Pk. TQ11: B'leigh .5B **98**
Fullers Ct. EX2: Exe .6D **6** (7E **64**)
Fullerton Rd. PL2: Plym .6F **135**
Fulmer Copse EX31: C'nor .1D **16**
Fulton Cl. TQ12: Ipp .6H **101**
FULWOOD .2C 167
Funder Zone .6J 19
Furland Cl. PL9: Hooe .7D **142**
FURLEY .3C 167
Furlong Cl. TQ11: Buck .2C **98**
Furneaux Av. PL2: Plym .6G **135**
Furneaux Rd. PL2: Plym .6G **135**
Furness Cl. TQ4: Paig .5G **119**
Furrough Ct. TQ1: Torq .5E **112**
Furrough Cross TQ1: Torq .5E **112**
Fursdon .3D 165
Fursdon Cl. PL9: Elb .6K **143**
Furse Pk. PL5: Plym .4B **134**
Furzeacre Cl. PL7: Plymp .2D **138**
Furzebeam Row EX38: G Tor .2A **30**
Furzebeam Ter. *EX39: Bide .4G 23*
(off Torrington La.)
Furzebrake Cl. TQ2: Torq .3J **111**
Furzebrook EX11: Ott M .3D **80**
Furze Cap TQ12: Kingst .1G **105**
Furze Cl. EX14: Gitt .5B **54**
Furze Ct. EX4: Exe .2B **70**
Furzedown Rd. TQ12: Kingsk .7K **109**
Furze Gdns. TQ9: Tot .6G **103**
Furzegood TQ3: Marl .4D **114**
Furzeham Ct. TQ5: Brixh .3D **122**
Furzeham Green .3E 122
Furzeham Pk. TQ5: Brixh .3E **122**
Furzehatt Av. PL9: Plyms .6H **143**
Furzehatt Pk. Rd. PL9: Plyms .6H **143**
Furzehatt Ri. PL9: Plyms .6H **143**
Furzehatt Rd. PL9: Plyms .6G **143**
Furzehatt Vs. PL9: Plyms .6G **143**
Furzehatt Way PL9: Plyms .6H **143**
FURZEHILL .2D 161
Furzehill EX10: Sidb .2H **85**
(not continuous)
Furze Hill Rd. EX34: Ilfra .3H **11**
Furzehill Rd. PL4: Plym .1H **9** (7A **136**)
PL9: Hey B .4B **148**
TQ1: Torq .7C **112**
Furze La. TQ5: Brixh .3F **123**
Furzeleigh La. TQ13: Bov T .3B **92**
Furze Pk. EX34: C Mar .6A **12**
Furzepark La. EX39: Hart .2K **27**
Furze Pk. Rd. EX31: Brat F .6H **13**
Furze Rd. EX5: W'bury .5C **78**
TQ9: Tot .6H **103**

G

Gabber La. PL9: Down T .2D **148**
The Gables EX8: Exmth .6F **77**
Gables Ct. *EX15: Will .4C 44*
(off Gables Lea)
Gables Lea EX15: Will .4C **44**
Gables Rd. EX15: Will .4C **44**
Gabriel Ct. EX2: Exe .6D **6**
Gabriels Wharf EX2: Exe .2F **71**
Gabwell Hill TQ12: S'head .1J **113**
Gabwell La. TQ12: S'head .1H **113**
Gainsborough Cl. TQ1: Torq .2F **117**
Gainsborough Dr. EX39: W Ho .6A **20**
Galahad Cl. EX4: Whip .3K **65**
Galbraith Rd. EX20: Oke .2E **48**
Gales Crest TQ13: Chud K .6A **94**
Galileo Cl. PL7: Plymp .3B **138**
Galleon Way EX39: W Ho .5D **20**
The Gallery *TQ2: Torq .2D 116*
(off Fleet St.)
Gallery Cl. EX14: Hon .3E **54**
Galloway Dr. TQ14: Teignm .2F **107**
GALMINGTON .1C 167
GALMPTON
TQ5 .3H 121 (2A 176)
TQ7 .2K 155 (3C 175)
Galmpton Ct. *TQ5: Galm .3H 121*
(off Galmpton Farm Cl.)
Galmpton Farm Cl. TQ5: Galm .3H **121**
Galmpton Glade TQ5: Galm .3H **121**
Galmpton Ri. EX4: Exe .3H **65**
Galmpton Touring Pk. .4H **121**
GALMPTON WARBOROUGH
.1H 121 (2A 176)
Galpin St. PL21: Modb .6G **147**
Galsworthy Cl. PL5: Plym .1H **135**
Galva Rd. PL7: Drak, Hem .1F **139**
Gamberlake EX13: Axmin .5G **89**
GAMMATON .1C 163
Gammaton Rd. EX39: Bide .4H **23**
Gammons Hill EX13: Kilm .2C **88**
Gammon Wlk. EX31: B'aple .4E **18**
Ganders Pk. TQ2: Torq .4G **111**
Gandy St. EX4: Exe .3D **6** (6F **65**)
GANG .2B 169
Ganges Rd. PL2: Plym .6F **135**
Ganna Pk. Rd. PL3: Plym .5J **135**
GAPPAH .5E 94 (3C 171)
Gara Cl. PL9: Elb .6J **143**
Gard Cl. TQ2: Torq .2C **112**
Garden Cl. EX2: Won .1B **72**
EX33: Brau .4G **15**
PL7: Plymp .4G **139**
PL8: Holb .7C **150**
TQ8: Salc .7C **158**
Garden Ct. EX9: Bud S .6C **82**
Garden Cres. PL1: Plym .7B **8** (4H **141**)
Gardeners La. PL8: Y'ton .2A **150**
The Garden Ho. .5B **126** (1A **174**)
Gardenia Dr. EX16: Tive .1E **40**
Garden La. PL19: Tavi .4H **59**
Garden Mill Ind. Est.
TQ7: Kingsb .5G **157**
Garden Pk. Cl. PL9: Elb .5J **143**
Garden Rd. TQ1: Torq .7D **112**
The Gardens EX10: New P .5G **81**
EX31: B'aple .2E 18
(off Higher Raleigh Rd.)
TQ13: Chud .1C **94**
Garden Spot La. TQ13: Chud .2D **94**
Garden St. PL2: Dev .7D **134**
Garden Ter. EX15: Cull .3H **45**
Gdn. Village PL9: Plyms .4G **143**
Gardiner Cl. EX5: Sto C .6K **51**
Gards La. PL5: Plym .1D **134**
Gareth Cres. EX4: Whip .2J **65**
Garfield Rd. TQ4: Paig .1J **119**
Garfield Ter. PL1: Plym .1E **140**
Garland Cl. EX4: Exe .4A **64**
Garlic Rea TQ5: Brixh .3F **123**
(not continuous)
Garners Cl. TQ12: E Ogw .3A **108**
Garners La. TQ12: E Ogw .3A **108**
Garratt Cl. EX8: Exmth .1E **76**
Garrett Cl. EX12: Seat .4F **87**
Garrett Rd. EX5: Clyst M .2G **73**
Garrick Cl. PL5: Plym .1H **135**
Garrison Cl. PL1: Dev .3D **140**
Garrison Grn. PL1: Plym .6F **9**
Garrow Cl. TQ5: Brixh .5E **122**
Garston Av. TQ12: New A .7E **104**
Garston Cl. PL9: Plyms .4H **143**
Garth Rd. TQ2: Torq .3C **112**
Gascon Cl. TQ12: E Ogw .4C **108**
Gascoyne Ct. PL4: Plym .4G **9**
Gascoyne Pl. PL4: Plym .4G **9** (2K **141**)
Gashouse La. PL4: Plym .6J **9** (3A **142**)
Gasking St. PL4: Plym .4G **9** (2K **141**)
Gas La. EX38: G Tor .2C **30**
Gatcombe La. EX12: Beer, Seat .3A **86**
Gate Fld. Rd. EX39: Bide .3C **22**
Gatehouse Barns EX7: Daw .2H **97**
Gatehouse Cl. EX7: Daw .3G **97**
EX15: Cull .4G **45**
Gatehouse Hill EX7: Daw .3H **97**
Gatehouse La. PL7: Plymp .4A **138**
Gatehouse Ri. EX7: Daw .3H **97**
Ga. Reach EX2: Exe .3G **71**
Gater La. EX1: Exe .5E **6** (7F **65**)
Gate Tree Cl. TQ12: Kingst .4J **105**
Gattery La. TQ5: Brixh .7B **122**
The Gavel EX36: S Mol .6D **26**
Gaydon St. EX32: B'aple .4F **19**
Gaze Hill TQ12: New A .6C **104**
Gdynia Way PL4: Plym .5K **9** (3B **142**)
Geasons La. PL7: Plymp .4B **138**
Gees La. PL21: Modb .6H **147**
Gemini Rd. PL9: Elb .7K **143**
Generals Cl. EX6: Star .2D **96**
Generals La. EX6: Star .2D **96**
Genesis La. EX34: C Mar .6B **12**
Geneva Cl. EX2: Exe .7K **7** (1H **71**)

Geneva Ct. EX2: Exe 7K 7
  EX39: Bide 4E 22
Geneva Pl. EX39: Bide 4E 22
Gentian Cl. TQ3: Marl 4D 114
Genting Casino
  Torquay 1C 116
George Arc. EX36: S Mol 6D 26
George Av. PL7: Plymp 3B 138
GEORGEHAM 5B 14 (3A 160)
Georgeham Rd.
  EX33: Croy, Forda 2D 14
  EX34: Wool 7D 10
George Hill EX17: Cred 5F 39
George Junction Park & Ride 4D 132
George La. EX13: Kilm 2B 88
  PL7: Plymp 4C 138
GEORGE NYMPTON 1B 164
George Nympton Rd.
  EX36: S Mol 7C 26
George Pl. PL1: Plym 5A 8 (3G 141)
George Rd. TQ3: Pres 5H 115
Georges Cl. EX1: Whip 6A 66
George Sq. PL1: Dev 3E 140
  (off Theatre Ope)
George's Sq. DT7: Lym R 5K 91
  (off Monmouth St.)
George St. EX1: Exe 5D 6 (7E 64)
  EX8: Exmth 5C 76
  EX13: Axmin 3H 89
  EX14: Hon 3F 55
  EX20: Oke 3B 48
  EX32: B'aple 3E 18
  PL1: Dev 3E 140
  TQ12: New A 1E 108
  TQ13: More 6H 61
  TQ14: Teignm 5J 107
George St. La. E. PL1: Dev 3E 140
Georgia Cres. PL3: Plym 5D 136
Georgian Ct. TQ1: Torq 7G 113
Gerald Dinnis Units EX2: Mar B 4G 71
Gerbera Way EX15: Cull 4J 45
GERMANSWEEK 1C 169
Gerston La. TQ7: Kingsb 7F 157
Gerston Pl. TQ3: Paig 1H 119
Gerston Rd. TQ4: Paig 1H 119
The Gerstons TQ3: Paig 1H 119
Gervase Av. EX2: Exe 7C 6 (7E 64)
Gerway Cl. EX11: Ott M 5C 80
Gerway La. EX11: Ott M 5D 80
Gestridge Rd. TQ12: Kingst 3G 105
Gibb PL8: Holb 6D 150
Gibb Hill PL21: Lutt 6F 129
Gibbon La. PL4: Plym 3F 9 (2K 141)
Gibbon St. PL4: Plym 3F 9 (2K 141)
Gibbs La. EX39: App 2H 21
  (off Market St.)
Giblands Pk. EX20: Oke 3D 48
Gibraltar Rd. EX8: Lymp 5G 75
Gibson Cl. EX8: Exmth 3G 77
Gibson Dr. TQ4: Good 6G 119
Gibson Gdns. TQ4: Good 6G 119
Gibson Rd. TQ4: Good 6G 119
GIDLEIGH 2A 170
Gidleys Mdw. TQ9: Darti 3A 102
Gifford Cl. EX33: Hart 3J 27
Gifford Pl. PL3: Plym 7J 135
Gifford Ter. Rd. PL3: Plym 6J 135
Gilbert Av. EX2: Won 1B 72
  TQ14: Teignm 2G 107
Gilbert Cl. TQ2: Torq 7K 111
Gilbert Cl. PL7: Plymp 3E 138
Gilbert Gro. EX34: Ilfra 2J 11
Gilbert La. PL2: Plym 6H 135
Gilbert Rd. TQ12: New A 1H 109
Gilbert Way TQ4: Good 5G 119
Gilbrook Cl. EX5: W'bury 6B 78
Gilchrist Way EX10: Sidm 5D 84
Gillard Rd. TQ5: Brixh 4G 123
Gillard Way PL21: L Mill 4C 144
Gilley Cl. TQ13: Bov T 4E 92
Gill Pk. PL3: Plym 6C 136
Gills Nursery TQ9: Tot 6E 102
  (off South St.)
Gilpin Cl. EX7: Daw 2J 97
Gilwell Av. PL9: Plyms 5H 143
Gilwell Hall PL4: Plym 3F 9
Gilwell Pl. PL4: Plym 3F 9 (2K 141)
Gilwell St. PL4: Plym 3G 9 (2K 141)
Gimbletts Ct. EX22: Hols 2C 34
Gipsy Hill La. EX1: Pin 4E 66
Gipsy Hill M. EX1: Pin 5E 66
Gipsy La. EX1: Pin 4E 66
  EX8: Exmth 4C 76
  EX34: Ilfra 3K 11
  PL21: Ivy 4D 144
  TQ11: B'leigh 6B 98
Girt La. EX34: C Mar 5E 12
Gissage Vw. EX14: Hon 3E 54
Gissons EX6: Exmin 2D 74
Gissons La. EX6: Kenn, Kennf 2G 95
GITTISHAM 7A 54 (1B 172)
Gittisham Cl. EX1: Sow 6C 66
The Glade PL20: C'stone 6C 128
Glade Cl. PL6: Plym 6B 132
The Glades EX16: Tive 4E 40
Glade Wlk. EX5: Clyst M 3K 73
Gladstone Pl. TQ12: New A 1F 109

Gladstone Rd. EX1: Exe 4J 7 (6H 65)
Gladstone Ter. TQ14: Teignm 4J 107
Glanville La. EX14: Offw 7K 55
  PL19: Tavi 4H 59
Glanvilles Mill PL21: Ivy 4G 145
Glanvilles Rd. PL21: Ivy 4H 145
Glanville St. PL4: Plym 3E 8 (2J 141)
Glanvill Way EX14: Hon 5D 54
Glascott Cl. EX20: Hath 3F 35
Glasshouse La. EX2: Cou W 5K 71
Glastonbury Cl. EX4: Whip 2K 65
Glave Saunders Av. EX2: Won 1B 72
Glazon Way EX3: Nort 4F 21
Gleanor Cl. PL5: Plym 2J 135
The Glebe EX5: Thor 3A 50
  EX31: Brat F 6H 13
  TQ12: Ipp 6G 101
Glebe Cl. EX8: Lit 5H 77
  EX8: Lymp 5G 75
  EX9: Ott'n 6H 83
  EX20: Hath 1H 35
  TQ12: New A 1C 108
Glebe Ct. EX39: Nort 5E 20
  TQ7: Thur 5C 154
Glebe Fld. EX33: Geo 5C 14
Glebefields EX39: Nort 6E 20
Glebe Land TQ7: Mar G 6H 151
Glebeland TQ7: Chur 1B 156
Glebelands DT7: Uply 3G 91
  EX6: Cher 2C 62
  EX6: Exmin 2C 74
  EX8: Lymp 5G 75
  EX10: New P 5H 81
  EX10: Sidm 6B 84
  EX22: Hols 2B 34
  EX33: Wraf 6K 15
  TQ11: B'leigh 3B 98
  TQ13: Chud 2C 94
The Glebelands TQ13: More 7H 61
Glebelands Rd. EX16: Tive 4G 41
Glebeland Way TQ2: Torq 5H 111
Glebe La. EX22: Hols 2C 34
Glebe Mdw. EX22: Hols 2B 34
Glebe Pk. 3J 57
Glebe Pk. TQ6: Sto F 2H 153
The Glen DT7: Uply 3G 91
  EX20: Oke 4B 48
  TQ12: New A 2J 109
  (off Castle La.)
Glenarm Ter. TQ9: Tot 5E 102
Glenavon Rd. PL3: Plym 6K 135
Glenburn Cl. PL3: Plym 4K 135
Glenburnie Rd. EX39: Bide 2F 23
Glencarnock Cl. TQ1: Torq 6A 112
Glen Cl. EX5: Clyst M 3K 73
Glencoe EX2: Exe 6J 7 (7H 65)
Glen Creedy Cl. EX17: Cred 6J 39
Glen Creedy Ter. EX17: Cred 6J 39
  (off Mill St.)
Glendale Rd. EX20: Oke 2A 48
Glendale Ter. EX39: Bide 2F 23
  TQ9: Tot 5E 102
  (off Castle St.)
Glendaragh Rd. TQ14: Teignm 4J 107
Glendower Rd. PL3: Plym 6J 135
Gleneagle Av. PL3: Plym 5A 136
Gleneagle Rd. PL3: Plym 5A 136
Gleneagle Vs. PL3: Plym 5A 136
  (off Gleneagle Av.)
Glen Farm Cres. EX14: Hon 4G 55
Glenfield Cl. PL6: Plym 4E 132
Glenfield Rd. EX39: Bide 1F 23
  PL6: Plym 5D 132
Glenfield Way PL6: Plym 4E 132
Glen Gdns. EX39: Bide 1E 22
Glengarth Ct. EX39: Nort 7F 21
Glenhaven Cl. PL7: Plymp 3E 139
GLENHOLT 4E 132
Glenholt Cl. PL6: Plym 4E 132
Glenholt Pk. PL6: Plym 4E 132
Glenholt Rd. PL6: Plym 4D 132
Glenhurst Rd. PL3: Plym 5K 135
Glenisla Ter. EX10: Sidm 7C 84
  (off Riverside Rd.)
Glen Lyn Gorge 2H 13
Glen Lyn Pk. TQ13: Bov T 6C 92
Glenmore Av. TQ2: Torq 6E 134
Glenmore Rd. EX2: Won 7K 65
  TQ5: Brixh 4E 122
Glenorchy Ct. EX8: Exmth 5C 76
  (off Exeter Rd.)
Glen Pk. Av. PL4: Plym 1E 8 (1J 141)
Glen Rd. EX10: Sidm 7B 84
  PL3: Plym 6A 136
  PL7: Plymp 3A 138
  TQ3: Paig 7H 115
Glenside PL5: Plym 1K 135
  (off Whitleigh Av.)
Glenside Cl. TQ14: Teignm 3H 107
Glenside Rd. PL7: Plymp 3B 138
Glenthorne Cl. TQ1: Torq 2F 117
Glenthorne Estate Walks 2D 161
Glenthorne Pinetum 2D 161
Glenthorne Rd. EX4: Exe 3D 64
Glentor Rd. PL3: Plym 4K 135
Glentorr Rd. EX39: Bide 2F 23
Glenview EX14: Hon 4G 55
Glen Wlk. EX4: Exe 2G 65

Glenwater Cl. EX12: Axmth 4H 87
Glenwood Dr. EX31: Bick 7K 17
Glenwood Ri. EX2: Exe 1G 71
Glenwood Rd. PL3: Plym 5K 135
Globefield EX3: Top 5B 74
Globe Hill EX5: W'bury 5B 78
Globe La. EX3: Top 5B 74
Globe Ley EX3: Top 5B 74
  (off Globefield)
Globe Theatre 3F 141
Gloster Rd. EX32: B'aple 5F 19
Gloucester Cl. EX14: Hon 4D 54
  TQ2: Torq 4B 112
Gloucester Ct. PL1: Plym 2D 8
Gloucester Cres. EX14: Hon 5C 54
Gloucester Pl. PL1: Plym 2D 8 (1J 141)
Gloucester Rd. EX4: Exe 1F 77
  EX8: Exmth 1F 77
  TQ12: New A 2F 109
  TQ14: Teignm 4H 107
Glove Cl. EX38: G Tor 2B 30
Glovers Cl. EX22: Hols 2C 34
Glynn Valley La. PL9: Plyms 3E 142
Gnome Reserve & Wild Flower Garden 2B 162
Goad Av. PL4: Plym 3B 142
Goaman Pk. EX39: Hart 3K 27
Goaman Rd. EX39: Bide 5H 23
Goats Hill Rd. EX39: Nort 6F 21
Goat Wlk. EX3: Top 7B 74
Goblin La. EX15: Cull 3F 45
Godborough Vw. EX39: Bide 3C 22
Godding Gdns. PL6: Plym 3K 131
GODFORD CROSS 3B 166
Godfrey Av. TQ3: Pres 4H 115
Godfrey Cl. EX11: Ott M 4B 80
Godfreys Gdns. EX17: Bow 5G 37
Godolphin Cl. EX5: New C 6D 50
Godwell La. PL21: Ivy 6H 145
Gogwell La. EX16: Tive 7F 41
GOLBERDON 3B 168
Golden Bay Ct. EX39: W Ho 5A 20
Golden Bay Holiday Village 5A 20
Golden Cap Holiday Pk. 1D 173
Golden Cl. TQ5: Brixh 6D 122
Golden Coast Holiday Village 7C 10
Golden Hind Museum Ship 3F 123
Golden Joy EX17: Cred 5J 39
Golden Lion Ct. TQ13: Ashb 4H 99
Golden Pk. EX15: Kent 6A 46
Golden Pk. Av. TQ2: Torq 2B 112
Golden Sands Holiday Pk. 7D 96
Golden Sq. PL7: Plymp 3B 138
Golden Ter. EX7: Daw 4G 97
Goldfinch Cl. TQ12: Kingst 3F 105
Goldfinch Gdns. PL19: Whit 7K 59
Goldfinch Gro. EX15: Cull 5F 45
Golds Cross Hill EX6: Ted M 7F 49
Golds La. EX6: Ted M 7F 49
Goldsmith Gdns. PL5: Plym 7J 131
Goldsmith St. EX1: Heav 4D 6 (6E 64)
  EX4: Exe 4D 6 (6E 64)
Gold St. EX11: Ott M 4C 80
  EX16: Tive 4D 40
GOLDWORTHY 1B 162
Golf Links Rd. EX39: Nort, W Ho 5B 20
  PL20: Yelv 7F 127
  TQ10: Wran 1D 146
Gollands TQ5: Brixh 3D 122
Gollands Cl. TQ5: Brixh 3C 122
Gollands La. EX17: Morc 4C 38
  (off Oldborough La.)
Golvers Hill Cl. TQ12: Kingst 4H 105
Golvers Hill Rd. TQ12: Kingst 4H 105
Goodeve Cl. PL9: Plyms 6F 143
Goodgates Cl. EX33: Brau 4H 15
Goodgates Cres. EX33: Brau 4G 15
Goodgates Gro. EX33: Brau 4G 15
Goodgates Pk. EX33: Brau 4G 15
Goodgates Rd. EX33: Brau 4G 15
Gooding Ri EX16: Tive 4B 40
GOODLEIGH 3C 161
Goodleigh La. EX19: Wink 2B 36
Goodleigh Rd. EX32: B'aple 4G 19
Goodleigh Vw. EX32: B'aple 4H 19
Goodridge Cl. EX7: Daw 2H 97
GOODRINGTON 6G 119 (2A 176)
Goodrington Orchard TQ4: Good 6G 119
  (off Hookhills Rd.)
Goodrington Rd. TQ4: Good 6G 119
Goodrington Station
  Dartmouth Steam Railway 3J 119 (2A 176)
Good Shepherd Dr. EX2: Exe 6E 6 (7F 65)
GOODSTONE 3B 170
Goodstone Way TQ4: Paig 4F 119
Goodwin Av. PL6: Plym 4B 132
Goodwin Cres. PL2: Plym 5F 135
Goodwood Pk. Rd. EX39: Nort 7F 21
Gooseberry La.
  PL1: Plym 6C 8 (3H 141)
Goose Grn. EX38: G Tor 2D 30
  (off Calf St.)
GOOSEHAM 2A 162
GOOSEWELL
  EX34 ....2A 12
  PL9 ....7G 143 (2B 174)
Goosewell Hill PL6: Plym 3C 136

Goosewell Pk. Rd. PL9: Plyms 6G 143
Goosewell Rd. PL9: Plyms 6G 143
Goosewell Ter. PL9: Plyms 6G 143
Gora La. EX34: Wool 6G 11
Gordon Rd. EX1: Exe 2J 7 (5H 65)
  EX3: Top 7D 72
Gordon's Pl. EX1: Heav 7J 65
Gordon Ter. EX12: Beer 7B 86
  PL4: Plym 1F 9 (7K 135)
Gordon Ter. La. E.
  PL4: Plym 1F 9 (7K 135)
Gore La. DT7: Uply 5F 91
  EX8: Exmth, San B 7G 77
  EX13: Kilm 3B 88
Gorfin Cl. EX8: Exmth 4G 77
Gornhay Orchard EX16: Tive 3G 41
Gorse Ho. EX4: Exe 4B 64
Gorse La. EX8: Exmth 1F 77
Gorse Way PL21: Ivy 5H 145
Gorseway EX10: Sidm 6A 84
Gorsey Cl. PL5: Plym 1K 135
Gorway TQ14: Teignm 3J 107
Gorwell Rd. EX32: B'aple 3G 19
Gorwood Rd. EX39: Buck B 4G 29
Gorwyn La. EX6: Cher 1E 62
Gosceline Wlk. EX14: Hon 5F 55
GOSFORD 1C 80
Gosford La. EX11: Tale 1B 80
Gosford Rd. EX11: Gos, Ott M 1C 80
Goshen Rd. TQ2: Torq 1A 116
The Goslings TQ7: Chil 6G 159
Goss Mdw. EX17: Bow 5H 37
Gostwyck Cl. EX20: N Taw 6B 36
Goswela Cl. PL9: Plyms 7G 143
Goswela Gdns. PL9: Plyms 7G 143
Gothic Rd. TQ12: New A 2E 108
Gould Cl. EX32: B'aple 5G 19
Gould Pl. TQ12: New A 7J 105
Gould Rd. EX32: B'aple 5G 19
  TQ8: Salc 3C 158
Gourders La. TQ12: Kingsk 3F 111
Govers Mdw. EX24: Colyt 5D 88
GOVETON 1K 157 (3D 175)
Gower Ridge Rd. PL9: Plyms 6E 142
Gowans Ter. EX20: N Taw 6A 36
Gowman's Ter. EX20: N Taw 6A 36
Grace Gdns. TQ14: Teignm 3G 107
Grace Rd. Central EX2: Mar B 3F 71
Grace Rd. Sth. EX2: Mar B 4G 71
Grace Rd. W. EX2: Mar B 3E 70
Grafton Cl. TQ1: Torq 2D 116
  (off Grafton Rd.)
Grafton Hgts. TQ1: Torq 1E 116
Grafton Rd. EX4: Exe 3D 64
  PL4: Plym 7K 135
  TQ1: Torq 2D 116
  TQ12: New A 1E 108
Grafton Ter. TQ1: Torq 2D 116
Graham La. EX16: Tive 3D 40
Graham Rd. TQ3: Pres 5G 115
Grainger Cl. EX2: Won 7B 66
Grainge Rd. PL6: Plym 2B 136
Grampian Cl. TQ4: Coll M 3D 118
Granary Cl. EX15: Cull 3K 45
Granary La. EX9: Bud S 5D 82
Granby Cl. PL1: Dev 2D 140
Granby Pl. PL1: Dev 2D 140
Granby St. PL1: Dev 1D 140
Granby Way PL1: Dev 2D 140
Grand Hotel Rd.
  PL1: Plym 7C 8 (4H 141)
Grandison Av. TQ14: Bi'ton 3C 106
Grandisson Ct. EX2: Cou W 3K 71
Grandisson Dr. EX11: Ott M 4E 80
Grand Pde. PL1: Plym 7C 8 (4H 141)
The Grand Pier
  Teignmouth 5J 107
Grand Prix Go Karts
  Paignton 4J 119
Grand Vw. Rd. TQ7: Hope 2G 155
Grand Western Canal Country Pk.
  Holcombe Rogus 2A 166
  Tiverton 4A 42 (2D 165)
Grand Western Canal Country Pk.
  Visitor Cen. 5E 40
Grand Western Canal Picnic Site 2A 166
The Grange EX2: Exe 7K 7 (1H 71)
  EX33: Brau 5K 15
Grange Av. EX8: Exmth 3D 76
  EX31: B'aple 7B 18
  TQ4: Good 5H 119
Grange Cl. EX8: Exmth 4D 76
  EX8: Lymp 6H 75
  EX32: Brat F 6J 13
  TQ12: New A 3G 109
Grange Cotts. EX5: Rock 3G 69
Grange Ct. EX32: B'aple 3F 19
  (off Yeo Vale Rd.)
Grange Dr. TQ14: Teignm 3H 107
Grange Hgts. TQ4: Good 5G 119
Grange Hgts. Cl. TQ4: Good 5G 119
Grange Hill EX31: Brat F 6J 13
Grange Hill Ind. Est.
  EX31: Brat F 5J 13
Grange La. EX20: Mert 5A 30
Grange Pk. TQ14: Bi'ton 3A 106
Grange Pk. Cvn. Pk. 6D 108

Grange Rd.—Hacker Cl.

Grange Rd. EX39: Bide 4G 23
PL7: Plymp 5C 138
PL20: Yelv 5F 127
TQ1: Torq 1E 116
TQ4: Good 6G 119
TQ11: Buck 2B 98
TQ12: A'well 6E 108
Grange Vw. TQ4: Good 5G 119
TQ12: A'well 6E 108
Gransmore Wlk. PL21: Erm 2H 147
Grantham Cl. PL7: Plymp 7J 137
Grantlands EX15: Uff 7G 43
Grantley Gdns. PL3: Plym 7B 136
Granville Av. EX32: B'aple 3E 18
Granville Pl. EX15: Will 3C 44
(off Station Rd.)
Granville Point EX34: Ilfra 2H 11
Granville Rd. EX34: Ilfra 2G 11
Grapple Cl. EX31: Frem 5F 17
Gras Lawn EX2: Exe 7J 7 (1H 71)
Grasmere Cl. PL6: Plym 5K 131
TQ2: Torq 3D 112
Grasmere Ct. EX4: Exe 7C 64
(off Lakelands Dr.)
Grassendale Av. PL2: Plym 4E 134
Grasslands Dr. EX1: Pin 4E 66
Grass La. PL2: Plym 5H 135
Grattans Way EX17: Bow 6H 37
GRATTON 2B 162
Gratton Cl. TQ6: Sto F 2H 153
Gratton Ct. EX31: Rou 7B 18
Gratton Dr. TQ7: Chil 6H 159
Gratton La. PL20: Yelv 7G 127
Gratton Pk. EX5: Cran 3C 68
Gratton Pl. PL6: Plym 2B 136
Grattons Dr. EX35: Lynt 2G 13
Grattons La. TQ9: L'ton 2F 103
Gratton Way EX31: Rou 7B 18
Gravel La. EX12: Seat 3F 87
Gravel Wlk. EX15: Cull 4H 45
Gravesend PL11: Torp 1A 140
Gravesend Gdns. PL11: Torp 1A 140
Gravesend Wlk. PL5: Plym 6C 130
Graybridge Rd. PL20: Horr 2E 126
Gray Cres. PL5: Plym 3B 134
Graynfylde Dr. EX39: Bide 3G 23
Gray's Hill EX15: Hemy 1J 47
Grays Mdw. TQ13: More 6H 61
Gt. Berry Rd. PL6: Plym 2A 136
Gt. Bridge TQ13: Ashb 3G 99
Gt. Burrow Ri. EX39: Nort 4E 20
Gt. Churchway PL9: Plyms 5H 143
Gt. Cliff EX7: Daw 5H 97
Great Cl. EX15: Culm 1B 46
Gt. Fellingfield PL19: Mary T 2B 60
Great Fld. Gdns. EX33: Brau 5H 15
Greatfield Rd. PL3: Plym 4C 136
Gt. Furlong TQ14: Bi'ton 3A 106
Great Gate La. TQ3: Paig 1H 119
(off Littlegate Rd.)
Gt. Headland Cres. TQ3: Pres 5J 115
Gt. Headland Rd. TQ3: Pres 5J 115
Gt. Hill TQ13: Chud 2C 94
Great Hill Rd. TQ2: Torq 1B 112
Great Hill Vw. EX4: Exe 2H 65
Greatlands Cres. PL2: Plym 5F 135
Greatlands Pl. PL2: Plym 5F 135
Great La. TQ7: Malb 6G 155
Gt. Links Tor Rd. EX20: Oke 3D 48
Gt. Mead EX6: Dunsf 7C 62
Gt. Meadow EX5: Cran 2C 68
Great Mis Tor 3D 169
Gt. Mis Tor Cl. PL20: Yelv 5F 127
Gt. Oak Mdw. EX22: Hols 1C 34
Gt. Orchard EX5: Cran 1E 68
Gt. Orchard Cl. PL9: Plyms 7F 143
Grea Tor Cl. TQ3: Pres 5F 115
Great Pk. TQ7: Malb 6G 155
Great Pk. Cl. PL7: Plymp 4F 139
TQ14: Bi'ton 4B 106
Greatpark La. TQ3: Paig 1D 118
Gt. Parks Rd. TQ3: Paig 2E 118
GREAT POTHERIDGE 2D 163
Gt. Rea Rd. TQ5: Brixh 3F 123
GREAT TORR 3C 175
GREAT TORRINGTON 2C 30 (2C 163)
Great Torrington Common 1A 30
Great Torrington Golf Course 1C 163
Great Torrington Tourist Information Centre
3C 30 (2C 163)
Gt. Tree Cl. TQ4: Good 6F 119
Gt. Tree Ct. TQ4: Good 7F 119
Gt. Tree Pl. TQ4: Paig 6F 119
Gt. Tree Vw. TQ4: Paig 6F 119
GREAT WEEKE 3K 61
Gt. Western Bus. Pk. EX14: Hon 5C 54
Gt. Western Cl. TQ4: Good 3H 119
Gt. Western Ind. Est.
EX32: B'aple 6G 19
Gt. Western Rd.
PL1: Plym 7B 8 (4H 141)
TQ4: Paig 1H 119
Gt. Western Way EX16: Tive 5D 40
Gt. Woodford Dr. PL7: Plymp 5J 137
Greatwood Ter. EX3: Top 5A 74
Grebe Cl. PL7: Plymp 4C 138
Grebe Way TQ12: Kingst 3F 105
Grecian Way EX2: Won 1B 72
The Greebys TQ3: Paig 1G 119
The Green EX2: Ide 4A 70
EX5: Whim 6G 53
EX8: Lit 5H 77
EX9: Ott'n 6H 83
EX15: Cull 4H 45
(off Fore St.)
EX17: Morc 1B 38
EX18: Chul 6C 32
EX31: Frem 6E 16
PL5: Plym 7D 130
PL8: New F 5J 149
PL9: Hooe 6C 142
PL20: Horr 2E 126
(off Jordan La.)
PL20: Meavy 7K 127
TQ13: Ashb 4H 99
(off St Andrews Cl.)
TQ14: Shal 6G 107
Grn. Acre EX16: Hal 6E 42
Greenacre EX5: Rock 3F 69
EX33: Brau 4H 15
Greenacre Cl. EX20: N Taw 6A 36
EX22: Bradw 6B 28
EX39: Nort 5F 21
Greenacres EX4: Exe 1D 64
PL9: Plyms 4G 143
Greenacres Cl. EX14: Fen 2G 53
Greenaway EX17: Morc 1B 38
Greenaway Rd. TQ12: New A 7D 104
Greenbank EX10: New P 5G 81
EX38: G Tor 1D 30
PL4: Plym 1H 9
TQ8: Bat 2C 158
Greenbank Av.
PL4: Plym 2J 9 (1A 142)
TQ12: Kingst 3G 105
Greenbank Cl. EX38: G Tor 1E 30
Greenbank Cotts. PL4: Plym 1H 9
PL7: Plymp 5A 138
(off Underwood Rd.)
Greenbank Ct. PL4: Plym 2H 9
Greenbank Rd. EX32: B'aple 5H 19
PL4: Plym 1G 9 (7K 135)
TQ5: Brixh 4D 122
Greenbanks Cl. TQ7: Slap 2H 159
Greenbank Ter.
PL4: Plym 2H 9 (1A 142)
PL20: Yelv 6G 127
TQ10: S Bre 1C 100
Green Cl. EX8: Exmth 4E 76
EX9: Ott'n 6H 83
(off Maunder's Hill)
TQ7: Kingsb 3G 157
Greenclose Ct. EX24: Colyt 6C 88
Greenclose Rd. EX34: Ilfra 2H 11
Greendale Bus. Pk. EX5: Wood S 1D 78
(not continuous)
Greendale La. EX5: Clyst M 1A 78
Greendale Rd. PL2: Plym 4F 135
Greenfield Cl. EX39: Bide 3D 22
Greenfield Cotts. PL19: Lam 6B 58
Greenfield Dr. PL21: Ivy 5H 145
TQ10: S Bre 3B 100
Greenfield Rd. TQ3: Pres 4G 115
Greenford Vs. EX2: Exe 7D 6 (1E 70)
Green Gdns. EX39: Nort 6D 20
GREENHAM
TA18 3D 167
TA21 1A 166
Greenhaven EX9: Bud S 5B 82
Greenhayes TQ9: Darti 3A 102
Greenhead EX10: Sidb 2F 85
Green Hill PL19: Tavi 3K 59
Greenhill PL19: Lam 6C 58
TQ9: E All 6C 152
TQ12: Kingst 5H 105
Greenhill Av. EX8: Exmth 5E 76
EX8: Lymp 6G 75
Greenhill Cl. PL9: Plyms 7G 143
Greenhill Gdns. TQ12: Kingsk 1F 111
Greenhill La. TQ12: Den 2H 101
Greenhill Rd. PL9: Spri 7H 143
TQ12: Kingsk 1F 111
TQ12: Kingst 5H 105
Greenhill Ter. TQ9: E All 6C 152
Greenhill Way TQ12: Kingst 5G 105
Greenhouse Gdns. EX15: Cull 4J 45
Greenings Rd. EX39: Buck B 2J 29
Greenlands Av. TQ3: Paig 1F 119
Greenlands Est. PL19: Tavi 4K 59
Green La. EX3: Ext 1F 75
EX4: Exe 7B 64
EX10: Sidb 2K 85
EX11: Ven O 1G 81
EX12: Axmth 3K 87
EX13: Ray H 2D 90
EX14: Fen 3G 53
EX19: Bea 3H 31
EX20: Hath 1K 35
EX24: Colyf 7C 88
EX31: B'aple 4E 18
(off High St.)
EX33: Brau 4K 15
EX39: App 2H 21
PL19: Tavi 4K 59
PL20: Yelv 7D 126
TQ5: Chur F 3A 122
Green La. TQ9: E All 5B 152
TQ9: Tot 7B 102
TQ10: Wran 1E 146
Green Lanes Shop. Cen. 4E 18
Green Lawn Way EX13: Axmin 2J 89
Greenlees Dr. PL7: Plymp 6E 138
Greenmeadow Dr. EX31: B'aple 3F 19
Green M. EX9: Bud S 6C 82
Green Mt. EX10: Sidm 5D 84
Greenover Cl. TQ5: Brixh 5D 122
Greenover Rd. TQ5: Brixh 5D 122
Green Pk. Av.
PL4: Plym 1E 8 (7J 135)
Greenpark Av. EX1: Pin 5C 66
Green Pk. Rd. PL9: Plyms 6E 142
TQ3: Pres 5F 115
Greenpark Rd. EX8: Exmth 2F 77
Green Pk. Wlk. TQ3: Pres 5F 115
Green Pk. Way TQ7: Chil 6G 159
Greenslade Rd. EX16: W'ridge 6H 33
TQ9: Blacka 3C 152
GREENSLINCH 1K 51
Greenslinch La. EX5: Silv 1K 51
Green St. PL4: Plym 4F 9 (2K 141)
Greensway Rd. PL19: Tavi 5G 59
Greenswood Cl. TQ5: Brixh 5E 122
Greenswood Rd. TQ5: Brixh 5E 122
Green Tree La. EX5: Broadc 6D 52
Greenville Way EX15: Cull 3H 45
Greenway 6E 120 (2A 176)
Greenway DT7: Lym R 5H 91
EX2: Exe 2B 70
EX5: W'bury 5B 78
EX12: Seat 5D 86
EX16: Hal 5D 42
EX17: Cred 6G 39
Greenway Av. PL7: Plymp 5J 137
Greenway Cl. PL20: Horr 1E 126
PL21: Ivy 4H 145
TQ2: Torq 4C 112
Greenway Gdns. EX9: Bud S 5C 82
EX16: Tive 4C 40
(off Wellbrook St.)
TQ2: Torq 3C 112
Greenway Halt
Dartmouth Steam Railway
5G 121 (2A 176)
Greenway La. EX9: Bud S 5B 82
EX10: Stow 2A 84
EX14: Awli 1A 54
TQ1: Torq 5D 112
Greenway Pk. TQ5: Galm 4H 121
Greenway Rd. TQ1: Torq 5D 112
TQ2: Torq 2K 115
TQ5: Galm 6E 120
Greenways EX34: Ilfra 3G 11
Greenways Valley Holiday Pk. 4D 30
Greenwood EX15: Will 3E 44
Greenwood Cl. PL21: Ivy 4G 145
TQ7: Ave G 6H 151
Greenwood Dr. EX2: Sow 7C 66
Greenwood Pk. Cl. PL7: Plymp 3E 138
Greenwood Pk. Rd.
PL7: Plymp 3E 138
The Greenwoods EX39: Hart 2J 27
Gregory Cl. EX16: Tive 4F 41
EX17: Bow 6H 37
Gregorys Ct. TQ13: Chag 2G 61
Gregory Ter. EX39: Hart 3J 27
Grenadier Rd. EX1: Sow 5D 66
Grenadine Cl. TQ2: Torq 2A 112
Grendon Almshouses
EX1: Exe 4J 7
Grendon Bldgs. EX1: Exe 5D 6
Grendon Ct. TQ14: Teignm 4G 107
Grendon Rd. EX1: Exe 4K 7 (6H 65)
GRENOFEN 3C 169
Grenville Av. EX4: Whip 4B 66
TQ2: Torq 7K 111
TQ14: Teignm 2G 107
Grenville Cl. EX36: S Mol 6C 26
TQ6: Dartm 6D 124
TQ7: Stoke 6K 159
TQ12: New A 1H 109
Grenville Ct. PL7: Plymp 3F 139
Grenville Dr. PL19: Tavi 6H 59
Grenville Est. EX39: Bide 5D 22
(off Clovelly Rd.)
Grenville Est. Cres. EX39: Bide 5D 22
Grenville Mdw. PL19: Tavi 6H 59
Grenville Pk. PL20: Yelv 6G 127
Grenville Rd. EX8: Exmth 2E 76
PL4: Plym 4J 9 (2A 142)
TQ8: Salc 4C 158
Grenville Rd. La. Sth.
PL4: Plym 2C 142
(off Grenville Rd.)
Grenville St. EX39: Bide 3F 23
Grenville Ter. EX39: Bide 4G 23
(off Torrington La.)
EX39: Nort 5F 21
Grenville Way EX31: Yell 7C 16
TQ4: Good 5H 119
Gresham Cl. PL5: Tam F 3H 131
Greycoat La. TQ12: New A 4B 104
Greyfriars Rd. EX4: Exe 4J 65
GREYLAKE 1D 167
Greysand Cres. EX39: App 2H 21
Greystoke Av. PL6: Plym 4D 136
Greystone Way TQ1: Torq 6D 112
Grey Wethers Stone Circles 2A 170
Gribble Cl. EX32: B'aple 5H 19
Gribble La. EX5: Rock 2G 69
Gribble Mead EX24: Colyt 6D 88
Grieg Dr. EX32: B'aple 4G 19
Griffin Way PL9: Elb 6K 143
Griggs Cl. EX39: Nort 6F 21
PL7: Plymp 5E 138
Griggs Gdn. EX31: Frem 6E 16
Grigg's La. EX10: Sidm 3E 84
GRIMSCOTT 3A 162
Grimspound 2B 170
Grimspound Cl. PL6: Plym 3F 137
Grimstone Ter. PL20: C'stone 6C 126
GRINACOMBE MOOR 1C 169
GRINDHILL 1C 169
Grindle Way EX5: Clyst M 3G 73
Grizedale Rd. PL6: Plym 4E 136
Gronau Cl. EX14: Hon 5F 55
The Grooms EX10: Sidm 7C 84
(off Russell St.)
Groper's La. TQ3: Comp 5A 110
TQ12: Ipp 5A 110
Grosvenor Av. TQ2: Torq 4J 111
Grosvenor Cl. TQ2: Torq 4J 111
Grosvenor Cotts. PL4: Plym 7A 136
(off Belgrave La.)
Grosvenor Ct. PL21: Ivy 4G 145
Grosvenor Mans. EX10: Sidm 7C 84
(off Church St.)
Grosvenor Pl. EX1: Exe 2H 7 (5G 65)
Grosvenor Rd. PL6: Plym 1A 136
TQ4: Paig 2H 119
Grosvenor St. EX32: B'aple 4F 19
Grosvenor Ter. EX32: B'aple 4F 19
(off Bear St.)
TQ4: Paig 2H 119
TQ14: Teignm 3H 107
The Grove EX4: Pin 2D 66
EX10: Sidm 6C 84
EX34: Wool 6A 10
PL3: Plym 7F 135
PL9: Plyms 4E 142
PL21: Moor 3C 146
TQ4: Paig 4E 118
TQ9: Blacka 3B 152
TQ9: Tot 6E 102
Grove Av. TQ14: Teignm 4H 107
Grove Cl. PL6: Plym 4J 131
TQ9: Tot 6E 102
Grove Ct. EX7: Daw 4J 97
TQ14: Teignm 3J 107
Grove Cres. TQ14: Teignm 4H 107
Grove Hill EX3: Top 5B 74
EX24: Colyt 6D 88
Grove Mdw. EX20: Stic 1F 49
Grove M. TQ9: Tot 6E 102
(off Grove Cl.)
Grove Pk. PL19: Tavi 4K 59
Grove Rd. EX5: Whim 6H 53
The Groves PL21: Ivy 3G 145
Grove Ter. TQ14: Teignm 4H 107
Growen La. EX15: Cull 2F 45
The Guardhouse Visitor Cen. 3J 123
Guardian Rd. EX1: Sow 6D 66
Gubbin's La. EX33: Brau 5J 15
Guelder Way PL6: Plym 4H 131
Guestland Rd. TQ1: Torq 6E 112
Guildford Cl. EX4: Exe 5B 64
PL5: Plym 7K 131
Guildford St. PL4: Plym 3G 9 (2K 141)
Guildhall
Exeter 4D 6 (1D 171)
Totnes 6E 102
Guildhall Shop. Cen.
Exeter 4D 6
Guildhall Sq. PL1: Plym 5E 8 (3J 141)
Guildhall Yd. TQ9: Tot 6E 102
GUINEAFORD 3B 160
Guinea St. EX1: Exe 5D 6 (7E 64)
Guinevere Way EX4: Whip 3K 65
Guinness La. EX4: Exe 4B 64
Gully Shoot EX24: Colyf 1E 86
GULWORTHY 3C 169
Gun La. PL1: Dev 2D 140
GUNN 3C 161
GUNNISLAKE 3C 169
Gunnislake Station (Rail) 3C 169
Gunswell La. EX36: S Mol 5A 26
Gurnard Wlk. PL3: Plym 5E 136
The Gurneys TQ3: Paig 2G 119
Gussiford La. EX8: Exmth 6C 76
Guy Miles Way PL5: Plym 7G 131
Guy's Quay PL4: Plym 6G 9 (3K 141)
Guys Rd. EX4: Exe 6C 64
Gwyn Rd. PL4: Plym 1K 9 (1B 142)
Gwythers EX36: S Mol 6D 26

H

Hacche La. EX36: S Mol 4C 26
Haccombe Cl. EX4: Exe 7B 64
Haccombe Path TQ12: New A 2J 109
Haccombe Way TQ12: Kingst 5J 105
Hacker Cl. EX10: New P 6H 81

Hackney La.—Hawthorn Rd.

Hackney La. TQ12: Kingst 5J 105
(not continuous)
TQ12: N'ton 6K 105
Hackney Marshes
Local Nature Reserve 6H 105
Hackworthy Cross La.
EX6: Ted M 6G 49
Hackworthy La. EX6: Ted M 7F 49
Haddeo Dr. EX2: Sow 1C 72
Haddington Rd. PL2: Dev 7D 134
Haddon Ct. TQ3: Paig 7H 115
(off Cecil Rd.)
Hadfield Ct. TQ13: Chud K 6A 94
Hadrian Dr. EX4: Exe 6B 64
Hadrians Way EX8: Exmth 3F 77
HAGGINTON HILL 3B 12
HALBERTON 6D 42 (2A 166)
Halberton Rd. EX15: Will 1A 44
Halcyon Ct. PL2: Plym 5F 135
Halcyon Rd. PL2: Plym 5F 135
TQ12: New A 1E 108
Haldene Ter. EX32: B'aple 3E 18
Haldon Av. TQ14: Teignm 3J 107
Haldon Belvedere 2C 171
Haldon Cl. EX3: Top 7D 72
TQ1: Torq 2G 117
TQ12: New A 2J 109
Haldon Ct. EX8: Exmth 2C 76
Haldon Forest (Colleywell Bottom)
Picnic Site 2D 171
Haldon Forest Park Picnic Site 2C 171
Haldon Forest Park Walks 2C 171
Haldon Ho. TQ1: Torq 4D 112
(off Teignmouth Rd.)
Haldon Pl. PL5: Plym 7F 131
Haldon Ridge Picnic Site 2D 171
Haldon Ri. TQ12: New A 2J 109
Haldon Rd. EX4: Exe 3B 6 (6D 64)
TQ1: Torq 2F 117
Haldon Ter. EX7: Daw 4G 97
(off High St.)
Haldon Vw. TQ13: Chud 2D 94
Haldon Vw. Ter.
EX2: Won 6K 7 (7J 65)
Halecombe Rd. PL9: Plyms 3E 142
Hale La. EX14: Hon 3H 55
Haley Cl. EX8: Exmth 2E 76
Halfmoon Ct. TQ11: B'leigh 6B 98
HALFORD 4F 93
Halfpenny Ct. PL1: Plym 3F 141
Hallamore La. PL21: Corn 5G 129
Hallerton Cl. PL6: Plym 2F 137
Hallett Ct. DT7: Lym R 4J 91
Halletts Way EX13: Axmin 3J 89
Halley Gdns. PL5: Plym 2D 134
Hall La. EX7: Holc 7F 97
EX17: Morc 2A 38
HALLSANDS 3A 176
HALLSANNERY 7G 23
Hallsannery Field Cen. 7G 23
Hall's La. TQ12: Kingsk 1F 111
Hall's Mill La. EX31: Cher 1D 18
HALLSPILL 1C 163
HALLWORTHY 2A 168
Halsbury Rd. EX16: Tive 4F 41
Halscombe La. EX2: Ide 4A 70
Halsdon Av. EX8: Exmth 3C 76
Halsdon La. EX8: Exmth 3C 76
Halsdon Nature Reserve 2D 163
Halsdon Nature Trails 2D 163
Halsdon Rd. EX8: Exmth 5C 76
Halsdon Ter. EX38: G Tor 2B 30
Halsdown Gdns. EX8: Exmth 2C 76
HALSE 1B 166
Halse Hill EX9: Bud S 6B 82
Halse La. EX20: N Taw 6D 36
Halses Cl. EX4: Exe 4A 64
Halse's La. EX10: N'town 3K 83
HALSINGER 3B 160
Halsteads Rd. TQ2: Torq 3C 112
The Halt EX2: Alph 4E 70
HALWELL 2D 175
HALWILL 1C 169
HALWILL JUNCTION 1C 169
Halwill Junction Nature Reserve 3C 163
Halyards EX3: Top 5A 74
EX8: Exmth 6A 76
HAM
EX13 ....3C 167
PL2 ....3F 135 (2A 174)
TA3 ....1C 167
TA20 ....2C 167
TA21 ....1B 166
Hambeer La. EX2: Exe 2B 70
Hamble Cl. PL3: Plym 4E 136
Hambleton Way TQ4: Paig 5G 119
HAMBRIDGE 1D 167
Ham Cl. PL2: Plym 3G 135
Ham Dr. PL2: Plym 4F 135
Hameldown Cl. TQ2: Torq 6H 111
Hameldown Rd. EX20: Oke 3E 48
Hameldown Way TQ12: New A 7G 105
Hamelin Way TQ2: Torq 6F 111
TQ3: Marl 6F 111
Ham Grn. PL2: Plym 4F 135
Ham Grn. Ct. PL2: Plym 4F 135
Ham Grn. La. PL2: Plym 4F 135
Hamilton Av. EX2: Won 3J 71
Hamilton Cl. EX10: Sidf 1E 84
EX39: Bide 5D 22
Hamilton Ct. EX8: Exmth 6D 76
Hamilton Dr. EX2: Sow 7C 66
TQ12: New A 7E 104
Hamilton Gdns.
PL4: Plym 1E 8 (7J 135)
Hamilton Gro. EX6: Star 2E 96
Hamilton La. EX8: Exmth 5D 76
Hamilton Rd. EX3: Top 7D 72
EX8: Exmth 5F 77
The Hamiltons TQ14: Shal 6G 107
Ham La. EX10: Sidm 7C 84
EX24: Colyt 6D 88
EX36: S Mol 6E 26
PL2: Plym 2E 134
PL5: Plym 2E 134
TQ6: Ditt 5C 120
TQ14: Shal 7F 107
HAMLET 5C 54
Hamlin Cl. EX16: Tive 5D 40
Hamlin Gdns. EX1: Heav 5K 65
Hamlin La. EX1: Heav 5K 65
Hamlyns La. EX4: Exe 3A 64
Hamlyns Way TQ11: B'leigh 4C 98
Hammett Rd. EX15: Cull 4G 45
Hammetts La. EX32: B Taw 4B 24
Hammett Sq. EX16: Tive 5D 40
(off Phoenix La.)
Hammond Cft. Way EX2: Alph 5E 70
Hamoaze Av. PL5: Plym 3C 134
Hamoaze Ct. PL1: Dev 3D 140
Hamoaze Pl. PL1: Dev 2C 140
Hamoaze Rd. PL11: Torp 2A 140
Hampden Pl. EX2: Exe 7C 6
Ham Pl. EX16: Tive 5C 40
PL2: Plym 3F 135
Hampshire Cl. EX4: Exe 1B 70
Hampson La. EX17: Bow 6F 37
HAMPTON 1C 173
Hampton Av. TQ1: Torq 5E 112
Hampton Bldgs.
EX4: Exe 1H 7 (5G 65)
Hampton Cl. TQ1: Torq 5E 112
Hampton Ct. EX13: Whit 5A 90
Hampton La. EX13: Shute, Whit 5A 90
TQ1: Torq 5E 112
Hampton Pk. EX39: Bide 1D 22
Hampton Rd. EX13: Shute, Whit 3B 88
TQ12: New A 1F 109
Hampton St. PL4: Plym 4F 9 (2K 141)
The Hams EX2: Ide 4A 70
Hams La. EX34: C Mar 5B 12
Hams Pl. EX34: C Mar 6B 12
Ham Woods Local Nature Reserve
.......2F 135
Hancock Cl. PL6: Plym 4J 131
HAND AND PEN 2K 69 (1A 172)
Hand & Pen Cotts. EX5: Whim 2K 69
Hand & Pen La. EX5: Whim 3K 69
Handley Ct. EX7: Holc 7G 97
Handsford Way EX11: Ott M 4B 80
Handy Cross EX39: Bide 5D 22
Hangar La. PL6: Plym 5C 132
Hangley Cleave Viewpoint 3D 161
Hangman Path EX34: C Mar 5A 12
HANNABOROUGH 3D 163
Hannaburrow La.
EX33: Forda, Saunt 7A 14
HANNAFORD 1A 164
Hannaford La. EX32: Swim 3F 25
Hannaford Rd. PL8: Noss M 7H 149
PL16: Lift 7B 56
Hanover Cl. EX1: Heav 6J 65
PL3: Plym 6D 136
TQ5: Brixh 5E 122
Hanover Ct. EX2: Matf 5F 71
Hanover Gdns. EX15: Cull 2H 45
Hanover Ho. TQ1: Torq 3F 117
Hanover Rd. EX1: Heav 6J 65
PL3: Plym 6C 136
Hansford Ct. EX14: Hon 4F 55
Hanson Pk. EX39: Bide 1E 22
Hantone Cl. EX31: C'nor 1D 16
Happaway Cl. TQ2: Torq 3C 112
Happaway Rd. TQ2: Torq 3B 112
HARBERTON 2D 175
Harberton Cl. TQ4: Paig 4E 118
HARBERTONFORD 6B 100 (2D 175)
The Harbour EX12: Seat 5G 87
Harbour Av. PL4: Plym 5G 9 (3K 141)
PL5: Plym 3D 134
Harbour Ct. EX8: Exmth 6B 76
EX12: Seat 5F 87
Harbourne Av. TQ4: Paig 4E 118
HARBOURNEFORD 1D 175
Harbour Rd. EX12: Seat 6F 87
Harbourside Ct. PL4: Plym 5G 9
Harbour St. PL11: Torp 1A 140
Harbour Vw. PL9: Hooe 5B 142
Harbour Vw. Cl. TQ5: Brixh 3E 122
Harbour Vw. Rd. PL5: Plym 3D 134
Harbour Way EX6: Cockw 3E 96
(off Cofton Hill)
HARCOMBE 1B 172
HARCOMBE BOTTOM 4D 90 (1D 173)
Harcombe Flds. EX10: Sidf 2E 84
Harcombe La. EX10: Sidf 2E 84
Harcombe Rd. DT7: Harc B 1H 91
EX13: Ray H 2C 90
Hardaway Head EX32: B'aple 4F 19
Harding Cres. EX16: Tive 2E 40
Hardwick Farm PL7: Plymp 1K 143
Hardy Cl. EX2: Cou W 5B 72
TQ1: Torq 4F 117
Hardy Cres. PL5: Plym 2K 135
Hardy Rd. EX2: Won 7C 66
Hardy's Ct. EX10: Col R 2H 83
HARE 2C 167
Harebell Copse EX4: Exe 4A 64
Harebell Dr. EX15: Will 3E 44
HAREFIELD 5J 75
Harefield Cl. EX4: Exe 4D 64
Harefield Cotts. EX8: Lymp 6F 75
Harefield Dr. EX8: Lymp 6H 75
TQ6: Sto F 2H 153
Harefield Rd. EX8: Lymp 5H 75
Harepath Hill EX12: Seat 2C 86
Harepath Rd. EX12: Seat 3E 86
Hares Grn. EX36: S Mol 6C 26
Hares La. TQ13: Ashb 4H 99
Hareston Cl. PL7: Plymp 6E 138
Hare Tor Cl. EX20: Oke 3E 48
Harewood TQ1: Torq 6E 112
(off Cary Pk.)
Harewood Cl. PL7: Plymp 4A 138
Harewood Cres. PL5: Plym 1F 135
HARFORD
EX32 ....1D 24
PL21 ....2C 175
Harford Rd. EX32: Land 1C 24
PL21: Harf, Ivy 4H 145
Harford Way EX32: Land 1C 24
Hargood Ter. PL2: Dev, Plym 7E 134
Hargreaves Cl. PL5: Plym 1E 134
Harlech Cl. PL3: Plym 4B 136
Harlequins Shop. Cen. 3D 6
HARLESTON 3D 175
Harlington Ct. TQ12: New A 7F 105
Harlseywood EX39: Bide 3D 22
Harlyn Dr. PL2: Plym 3J 135
Harman Wlk. EX32: B'aple 4H 19
Harnorlen Rd. PL2: Plym 4J 135
Harold Cl. EX11: Ott M 4A 80
Haroldsleigh Av. PL5: Plym 1K 135
Harper's Hill TQ9: Tot 7C 102
HARPFORD 4J 81 (1A 172)
Harpford Units EX8: Exmth 3H 77
Harpins Ct. TQ12: Kingsk 6K 109
Harpitt Cl. EX15: Will 5C 44
HARRACOTT 1D 163
Harrier Ct. EX5: Clyst H 7D 68
Harriers Cl. EX12: Seat 4E 86
Harrier Way EX2: Sow 1D 72
Harriet Gdns. PL7: Plymp 5J 137
Harringcourt Rd. EX4: Pin 2D 66
Harrington Dr. EX4: Pin 2D 66
Harrington Gdns. EX4: Pin 3D 66
Harrington La. EX4: Pin 2B 66
Harris Ct. PL9: Hooe 6C 142
Harrison St. PL2: Dev 7E 134
Harrisons Way EX5: Sto C 7J 51
Harris Pl. EX1: Pin 1E 66
Harris Way PL21: L Mill 5A 144
HARROWBARROW 3B 168
Harrowbeer La. PL20: Yelv 4F 127
Harrowbeer M. PL20: Yelv 6F 127
Harrowby Cl. EX16: Tive 4E 40
Harston Rd. PL21: Ivy 4E 144
HARTFORD 1D 165
HARTLAND 3J 27 (1A 162)
Hartland Abbey & Gardens 1A 162
Hartland Cl. PL6: Plym 3B 132
Hartland Forest Golf & Leisure Parc
.......2B 162
Hartland Point Lighthouse 1A 162
Hartland Pottery 3H 27
HARTLAND QUAY 1A 162
Hartland Quay Museum 1A 162
Hartland Tor Cl. TQ5: Brixh 6C 122
Hartland Vw. Rd. EX34: Wool 7C 10
HARTLEY 4K 135
Hartley Av. PL3: Plym 5A 136
Hartley Ct. PL3: Plym 5B 136
PL21: Ivy 4G 145
Hartley Pk. Gdns. PL3: Plym 5A 136
Hartley Rd. EX8: Exmth 6C 76
PL3: Plym 5K 135
TQ4: Paig 2G 119
HARTLEY VALE 3B 136
Hart Mnr. EX33: Wraf 7K 15
Harton Cross EX39: Hart 3J 27
Harton Way EX39: Hart 3K 27
Harton Way Ind. Est. EX39: Hart 3K 27
Hartopp Rd. EX8: Exmth 4C 76
Hartop Rd. TQ1: Torq 4D 112
Harts Cl. EX1: Pin 4D 66
TQ14: Teignm 3G 107
Hart's La. TQ7: Chur 2B 156
Harts La. EX1: Pin, Whip 4B 66
(not continuous)
Hart St. EX39: Bide 3F 23
HARTSWELL 1A 166
Hartwell Av. PL9: Elb 7K 143
Harvest La. EX39: Bide 2C 22
Harvey Av. PL4: Plym 3C 142
Harvey Cl. EX16: W'ridge 6H 33
Harveys Cl. TQ13: Chud K 6B 94
Harvey St. PL11: Torp 1A 140
Harveys Wlk. TQ7: Lodd 2H 151
Harwell Ct. PL1: Plym 4C 8 (2H 141)
Harwell La. TQ10: S Bre 1C 100
Harwell St. PL1: Plym 3C 8 (2H 141)
Harwin Apts. TQ4: Good 3J 119
Harwood Av. PL5: Tam F 3H 131
Harwood Cl. EX8: Exmth 3F 77
Haslam Ct. TQ1: Torq 6C 112
Haslam Rd. TQ1: Torq 6C 112
Hastings St. PL1: Plym 3C 8 (2H 141)
Hastings Ter. PL1: Plym 3C 8 (2H 141)
Haswell Cl. PL6: Plym 3B 136
HATCH BEAUCHAMP 1D 167
Hatchcombe La. TQ2: Torq 3B 112
Hatcher Cl. EX14: Hon 6F 55
Hatcher St. EX7: Daw 4G 97
Hatchett DT7: Lym R 4J 91
HATCH GREEN 2D 167
Hatchmoor Comn. La.
EX38: G Tor 1E 30
Hatchmoor Est. EX38: G Tor 2D 30
Hatchmoor Ind. Est. EX20: Hath 3G 35
EX38: G Tor 1E 30
Hatchmoor Rd. EX38: G Tor 2D 30
Hatfield TQ1: Torq 7D 112
Hatfield Rd. TQ1: Torq 7D 112
HATHERLEIGH 2H 35 (3D 163)
Hatherleigh La. TQ13: Bov T 7K 63
Hatherleigh Moor Viewpoint 3D 163
Hatherleigh Pl. EX16: Tive 4D 40
Hatherleigh Rd. EX2: Exe 3D 70
EX19: Wink 3A 36
EX20: Oke 2A 48
Hatshill Cl. PL6: Plym 7H 133
Hatshill Farm Cl. PL6: Bickl 1H 133
HATT 1A 174
Hatway Hill EX10: Sidb 2J 85
Hauley Rd. TQ6: Dartm 2B 124 (6F 125)
Havelock Rd. TQ1: Torq 4D 112
Havelock Ter. PL2: Dev 1E 140
PL21: Lutt 7F 129
The Haven TQ14: Bi'ton 3B 106
HAVEN BANKS 7E 6 (1F 71)
Haven Banks EX2: Exe 7D 6 (1E 70)
Haven Banks Outdoor Education Centre
.......7E 6 (1F 71)
Haven Banks Retail Pk. 7D 6 (1E 70)
Haven Cl. EX2: Exe 7D 6 (1E 70)
Haven Ct. EX12: Seat 6F 87
(off Harbour Rd.)
Haven Rd. EX2: Exe 7C 6 (1E 70)
Havenview Rd. EX12: Seat 5E 86
Hawarden Cotts. PL4: Plym 3C 142
(off Cavendish Rd.)
Haweswater Cl. PL6: Plym 6K 131
HAWKCHURCH 3D 167
HAWKERLAND 2A 172
Hawkerland Rd. EX10: Col R 2F 83
Hawkers Av. PL4: Plym 5G 9 (3K 141)
Hawkers La. PL3: Plym 6K 135
Hawkesdown Cl. EX12: Axmth 3H 87
Hawkes Way TQ9: Tot 6E 102
Hawkinge Gdns. PL5: Plym 6D 130
Hawkins Av. TQ2: Torq 6J 111
Hawkins Cl. PL6: Plym 5B 132
Hawkins Dr. TQ14: Teignm 3H 107
Hawkins La. EX11: W Hill 5H 79
Hawkins Pl. EX15: Cull 3H 45
(off Greenville Way)
Hawkins Rd. EX1: W Cly 1E 66
TQ12: New A 1J 109
Hawkins Wlk. EX20: Oke 3D 48
Hawkins Way EX17: Cred 6K 39
Hawkmoor Cl. PL7: Plymp 4A 138
HAWKRIDGE 1C 165
Hawkridge Rd. EX31: C'nor 1D 16
Hawksdown Vw. EX12: Seat 3E 86
Hawks Dr. EX16: Tive 3E 40
Hawksweed Cl. TQ12: New A 6A 104
Hawkswood Nature Reserve 1C 173
Hawley Cl. EX32: B'aple 4G 19
Hawley Mnr. EX32: B'aple 4G 19
Hawthorn Av. EX34: Ilfra 3K 11
Hawthorn Cl. EX14: Hon 4E 54
EX15: Cull 5G 45
PL6: Plym 3E 132
PL9: Hooe 7D 142
TQ7: Kingsb 5F 157
TQ12: New A 4J 109
Hawthorn Dr. EX10: Sidm 2A 84
PL9: Wem 7B 148
Hawthorne Cl. EX11: W Hill 4H 79
Hawthorne Rd. EX16: Tive 2F 41
Hawthorne Wlk. PL21: L Mill 5A 144
(off Holly Berry Rd.)
Hawthorn Gro. EX8: Exmth 3G 77
PL2: Plym 4H 135
Hawthorn Pk. EX20: Lyd 5H 57
EX39: Bide 4D 22
Hawthorn Pk. Cl. TQ2: Torq 3K 115
Hawthorn Pk. Rd. PL9: Wem 7B 148
Hawthorn Rd. EX2: Won 2J 71
EX17: Cred 6H 39
EX32: B'aple 5K 19
PL19: Tavi 7J 59

Hawthorn Row—Higher Barley Mt.

Hawthorn Row TQ9: Tot 7G 103
Hawthorn Way EX2: Alph 5D 70
PL3: Plym 4C 136
Haxter Cl. PL6: Robo 1C 132
Haxton Down La.
EX31: Brat F 7J 13
Haxton La. EX31: Brat F 6H 13
Haycock La. TQ5: Brixh 3G 123
Haycross Hill EX21: Sheb 6H 29
Haydn Cl. EX32: B'aple 4H 19
HAYDON .1C 167
Haydon Gro. PL5: Plym 2B 134
Haydon Rd. EX16: Tive 3B 40
Haydons Pk. EX14: Hon 4F 55
HAYE 3B 168
Haye Barton DT7: Lym R 4H 91
Haye Cl. DT7: Lym R 4H 91
Haye Gdns. DT7: Lym R 4H 91
Haye La. DT7: Lym R 3H 91
Haye Rd. PL9: Elb 2J 143
Haye Rd. Sth. PL9: Elb 5K 143
The Hayes TQ5: Chur F 3A 122
Hayes Barton Ct.
EX4: Exe 5B 6 (7D 64)
Hayes Cl. EX9: Bud S 5C 82
EX9: Ott'n 6H 83
TQ9: Tot 7G 103
Hayes Ct. DT7: Lym R 5J 91
TQ4: Paig 2F 119
Hayes End EX11: W Hill 4G 79
Hayes Gdns. TQ4: Paig 3G 119
Hayes La. EX9: E Bud 1A 82
Hayes Pl. PL6: Plym 3C 136
Hayes Rd. PL9: Plyms 5D 142
TQ4: Paig 3F 119
Hayes Sq. EX5: Cran 3B 68
Hayeswood La. EX9: E Bud 2A 82
Hayfield Rd. EX20: Exbo 5J 35
Hay La. TQ7: Malb 6G 155
Hayle Av. TQ4: Good 7H 119
Hayley Pk. TQ12: Kingsk 2F 111
Haymans Cl. EX15: Cull 5G 45
Haymans Grn. EX15: Cull 5G 45
Haymans Orchard EX5: W'bury 5C 78
HAYNE 3C 165
Hayne Cl. EX4: Exe 5K 65
EX10: Tip J 1J 81
Hayne Ct. EX16: Tive 1E 40
Hayne Hill EX10: Harp, Tip J 4J 81
Hayne La. EX5: Silv 3J 51
EX14: Gitt 5B 54
Hayne Pk. EX10: Tip J 1J 81
EX32: B'aple 5G 19
Hayridge M. EX14: Fen 2H 53
Haystone Pl. PL1: Plym 2B 8 (1H 141)
Haytor Av. TQ4: Paig 5F 119
Haytor Cl. PL5: Plym 7G 131
TQ14: Teignm 3F 107
Haytor Dr. EX4: Exe 5B 64
PL21: Ivy 5H 145
TQ12: New A 1J 109
Haytor Granite Tramway 3B 170
Haytor Gro. TQ12: New A 1K 109
Haytor Pk. TQ12: Kingst 4H 105
Haytor Rd. TQ1: Torq 6D 112
TQ13: Bov T 4A 92
Haytor Rocks 3B 170
Haytor Rocks Viewpoint 3B 170
Haytor Ter. TQ12: New A 1E 108
HAYTOR VALE 3B 170
Haytor Vw. TQ12: H'fld 1K 93
HAYTOWN 2B 162
Haywain Cl. TQ2: Torq 4H 111
Hay Webb Cl. EX1: W Cly 1E 66
Hazel Av. EX33: Brau 3K 15
Hazelbank Ct. PL5: Plym 2A 134
Hazel Cl. EX10: New P 5H 81
EX12: Seat 3E 86
PL6: Plym 4C 132
TQ7: Kingsb 5F 157
TQ12: New A 3K 109
TQ14: Teignm 1H 107
Hazeldene Gdns. EX8: Exmth 3C 76
Hazeldown Rd. TQ14: Teignm 2H 107
Hazel Dr. PL9: Elb 5K 143
Hazel Gro. EX5: Rock 4F 69
EX31: Rou 7B 18
PL9: Elb 4K 143
PL20: Yelv 5G 127
Hazelmead Rd. EX5: Clyst M 3J 73
Hazel M. EX36: S Mol 5D 26
Hazel Rd. EX2: Won 3J 71
PL19: Tavi 7J 59
Hazelwood TQ1: Torq 1F 117
(off Lwr. Warberry Rd.)
Hazelwood Cl. EX14: Hon 5F 55
TQ5: Brixh 4F 123
Hazelwood Cres. PL9: Elb 7K 143
Hazelwood Dr. EX7: Daw W 7D 96
PL6: Plym 2E 132
Hazelwood Holiday Pk. 7D 96
Headborough Rd. TQ13: Ashb 3F 99
Headingley Cl. EX2: Won 1B 72
Headland Cl. EX1: Whip 5B 66
Headland Cres. EX1: Whip 5B 66
Headland Gro. TQ3: Pres 5J 115
Headland Pk.
PL4: Plym 1G 9 (1K 141)
Headland Pk. Rd. TQ3: Pres 5J 115
Headland Rd. TQ2: Torq 4A 116
The Headlands TQ2: Torq 4A 116
Headlands Vw. Av.
EX34: Wool 5E 10
Headon Gdns. EX2: Cou W 4K 71
Headway Cl. TQ14: Teignm 4F 107
Headway Cross Rd.
TQ14: Teignm 3F 107
Headway Ri. TQ14: Teignm 3F 107
Head Weir Rd. EX15: Cull 2H 45
HEALE 2C 161
Heal Pk. Cres. EX31: Frem 6E 16
Heal's Fld. EX13: Axmin 2K 89
Healy Pl. PL2: Dev 1D 140
Heanton Hill La. EX31: C'nor 1D 16
Heanton Lea EX31: C'nor 1D 16
HEANTON PUNCHARDON 3B 160
Heanton St. EX33: Brau 5J 15
Heard Av. EX8: Exmth 4G 77
Heard Cl. EX39: Hart 3J 27
Hearts of Oak EX2: Sow 7D 66
HEASLEY MILL 3D 161
Heath Cl. EX14: Hon 5C 54
TQ12: H'fld 2K 93
Heathcoat Sq. EX16: Tive 4C 40
Heathcoat Way EX16: Tive 4E 40
Heath Ct. TQ5: Brixh 2G 123
TQ9: Tot 6E 102
HEATH CROSS 1B 170
Heather Cl. EX1: Whip 6A 66
EX12: Seat 3F 87
EX14: Hon 6C 54
EX16: Tive 2F 41
EX20: Oke 3B 48
PL19: Tavi 5K 59
TQ12: New A 7C 104
TQ14: Teignm 2H 107
Heatherdale EX8: Exmth 6E 76
Heatherdene TQ13: Bov T 4B 92
Heather Est. TQ12: H'fld 1J 93
Heather Grange EX11: W Hill 5H 79
Heather M. PL21: Ivy 4G 145
Heather Pk. TQ10: S Bre 1C 100
The Heathers EX8: Exmth 5F 77
EX20: Oke 2D 48
PL6: Plym 3E 132
Heather Ter. PL20: Prin 6C 60
Heather Wlk. PL21: Ivy 5H 145
Heather Way TQ5: Brixh 4C 122
HEATHFIELD
TA4, nr. Lydeard St Lawrence
. . . . .1B 166
TA4, nr. Norton Fitzwarren . . .1B 166
TQ12 . . . . .2J 93 (3C 171)
Heathfield Bus. Pk. TQ12: H'fld 1J 93
Heathfield Cl. TQ13: Bov T 6B 92
Heathfield Cotts. TQ12: H'fld 1K 93
Heathfield Ho. TQ13: Bov T 5B 92
(off Ashburton Rd.)
Heathfield Mdw. TQ13: Bov T 6B 92
Heathfield Pk. PL20: Dous 4H 127
Heathfield Rd. EX39: Bide 4H 23
PL4: Plym 1C 142
PL21: Corn 6H 129
TQ12: Den 2H 101
Heathfield Ter. TQ13: Bov T 5B 92
Heath Hill TQ12: H'fld 2K 93
Heathlands Ct. TQ14: Teignm 1G 107
(off Heathlands Ri.)
Heathlands Ri. TQ14: Teignm 1G 107
Heath Pk. TQ5: Brixh 3G 123
TQ12: New A 3K 109
Heathpark Ind. Est.
EX14: Hon 5C 54
Heathpark Way EX14: Hon 4C 54
Heath Ri. TQ5: Brixh 3G 123
Heath Rd. EX2: Won 1A 72
EX6: Bridf 7D 62
TQ5: Brixh 3F 123
HEATHSTOCK 3C 167
Heath Wlk. TQ13: Bov T 5E 92
Heath Way TQ9: Tot 6E 102
(not continuous)
Heaton Hill EX33: Wraf 6K 15
Heatree Cl. TQ14: Teignm 1H 107
Heaviside Cl. TQ2: Torq 2D 112
HEAVITREE 6K 65 (1D 171)
Heavitree Pk. EX1: Heav 7K 65
Heavitree Rd. EX1: Exe 3G 7 (6G 65)
Hebditch Cl. TQ13: Bov T 4D 92
Heberton Cl. EX5: Whim 6H 53
Hector Cl. EX19: Dol 6H 31
HEDDON .1A 164
Heddon Valley Nature Walk 2C 161
Heddon Valley Shop
Information Centre 2C 161
Hederman Cl. EX5: Silv 2H 51
Hedge Field Cl. EX14: Gitt 6C 54
Hedge Row Cl. EX17: Cop 6C 38
(off Wright Dr.)
Hedgerow Cl. EX17: Cred 5K 39
PL6: Plym 2F 133
HEDGING 1D 167
Hedingham Cl. PL7: Plymp 5F 139
Hedingham Gdns. PL6: Plym 3C 132
Heggadon Cl. EX5: Bradn 1D 52
The Heights PL19: Tavi 3G 59
HELE
EX5 .3D 165
EX34 . . . . .2B 160
PL15 . . . . .1B 168
TQ2 . . . . .4B 112 (1B 176)
TQ13 .3F 99
Hele Cl. EX31: Rou 6K 17
PL6: Bickl 1H 133
TQ2: Torq 4B 112
Hele Corn Mill 2B 160
Hele Cross TQ13: Ashb 3F 99
Hele Gdns. PL7: Plymp 5C 138
Hele La. EX31: Rou 6K 17
Helena Pl. EX8: Exmth 6C 76
Helens Mead Cl. TQ2: Torq 1C 112
Helens Mead Rd. TQ2: Torq 1C 112
Hele Pk. Development
TQ12: New A 6A 104
Hele Ri. EX31: Rou 6K 17
Hele Rd. EX4: Exe 2B 6 (5D 64)
EX5: Bradn 4B 52
TQ2: Torq 4A 112
TQ12: Kingst 2G 105
Heles Ter. PL4: Plym 2C 142
Helford Dr. TQ4: Good 7H 119
Helford Wlk. TQ4: Good 7H 119
Heligan Dr. TQ3: Paig 6E 114
HELLAND 1D 167
Hellevoetsluis Way TQ3: Marl 3E 114
Hellier Cl. EX14: Hon 5D 54
Hellings Gdns. EX5: Broadc 5C 52
Hellings Pk. La. EX5: Broadc 1K 67
Helmdon Ri. TQ2: Torq 5H 111
Helmers Way TQ7: Chil 6G 159
Helston Cl. TQ3: Paig 7F 115
Heltor Bus. Pk. TQ12: H'fld 7E 92
Hembury 3B 166
Hembury Castle 1D 175
Hembury Cock Hill TQ11: B'leigh 2B 98
Hembury Pk. TQ11: Buck 2C 98
HEMERDON 2F 139 (2B 174)
Hemerdon Hgts. PL7: Plymp 3D 138
Hemerdon La.
PL7: Hem, Plymp 1E 138
Hemerdon Vs. PL7: Plymp 3B 138
(off Colebrook Rd.)
Hemerdon Way PL7: Plymp 3A 138
Hems Brook Ct. TQ2: Torq 5H 111
HEMYOCK 2G 47 (2B 166)
Hemyock Castle 2B 166
Hemyock Rd. EX15: Culm 3B 46
Henacre La. TQ7: Kingsb 4H 157
Henacre Rd. TQ7: Kingsb 4G 157
Henbury Cl. TQ1: Torq 7D 112
Henderson Pl. PL2: Plym 5E 134
Hendwell Cl. PL6: Plym 4K 131
Heneaton Sq. EX2: Cou W 5A 72
HENFORD 1B 168
HENLADE 1C 167
Henlake Cl. PL21: Ivy 3F 145
HENLEY .1D 167
Henley Dr. PL5: Tam F 3H 131
Henley Rd. EX8: Exmth 5E 76
Hennapyn Rd. TQ2: Torq 3A 116
The Hennis EX4: Exe 2F 7
HENNOCK 2C 171
Hennock Ct. EX2: Mar B 4G 71
Hennock Rd. TQ4: Paig 5F 119
Hennock Rd. Central EX2: Mar B 4F 71
Hennock Rd. E. EX2: Mar B 4G 71
Hennock Rd. Nth. EX2: Mar B 3F 71
Henrietta Pl. EX4: Exe 3C 6
EX8: Exmth 5C 76
(off Clarence Rd.)
Henrietta Rd. EX8: Exmth 5C 76
Henry Avent Gdns. PL9: Elb 4K 143
Henry Cl. PL21: L Mill 5A 144
Henry Gdns. EX11: Ott M 4B 80
Henry Holland Dr. EX2: Cou W 4C 72
Henry Lewis Cl. EX5: Whim 6G 53
Henrys Run EX5: Cran 3B 68
Henry's Way DT7: Lym R 4K 91
Hensbury La. PL20: Bere F 6C 128
Hensford Rd. EX7: Daw 1F 97
Hensleigh Dr. EX2: Exe 5J 7 (7H 65)
Hensleigh Rd. EX16: Tive 4A 40
Hen St. EX5: Bradn 1C 52
Henty Av. EX7: Daw 3J 97
Henty Cl. EX7: Daw 2J 97
HENWOOD 3A 168
Heppenstall Rd. EX32: B'aple 3F 19
Heraldry Row EX2: Sow 1C 72
(off Heraldry Way)
Heraldry Wlk. EX2: Sow 1C 72
(off Heraldry Way)
Heraldry Way EX2: Sow 1C 72
Herbert Pl. PL2: Dev 7D 134
Herbert Rd. EX1: Heav 5J 65
TQ2: Torq 2K 115
TQ8: Salc 4B 158
Herbert St. PL2: Dev 7D 134
Hercules Rd. PL9: Elb 4K 143
Hereford Cl. EX8: Exmth 1F 77
Hereford Rd. EX4: Exe 6A 64
PL5: Plym 5G 131
Heritage Ct. EX14: Hon 3F 55
Heritage Grange EX8: Exmth 5E 76
Heritage Pk. PL19: Tavi 3K 59
Heritage Rd. EX1: Sow 5B 66
Heritage Way EX10: Sidm 2C 84
TQ5: Brixh 3G 123
Hermes Av. EX16: Tive 5E 40
The Hermitage EX34: Ilfra 3H 11
(off Hermitage Rd.)
Hermitage Ct. PL4: Plym 7K 135
Hermitage Rd. EX34: Ilfra 2H 11
PL3: Plym 6K 135
TQ6: Dartm 5D 124
Hermosa Gdns. TQ14: Teignm 4H 107
Hermosa Rd. TQ14: Teignm 4H 107
Hernaford Rd. TQ9: H'ford 7B 100
HERNER .1D 163
Hern La. PL8: Y'ton 2B 150
Heron Ct. EX8: Exmth 6E 76
EX32: B'aple 5K 19
Heron Pl. EX7: Daw 7C 96
Heron Rd. EX2: Exe 2A 70
EX2: Sow 7D 66
EX14: Hon 5E 54
Herons Brook EX20: Oke 2A 48
Herons Reach TQ7: W Cha 7K 157
Heron Way EX15: Cull 5G 45
(off Ploudal Rd.)
TQ2: Torq 2J 111
Herschel Gdns. PL5: Plym 2D 134
Herschell Rd. EX4: Exe 1J 7 (4H 65)
HERSHAM 3A 162
Hertland Wlk. PL2: Plym 4F 135
Hescane Pk. EX6: Cher 2C 62
Hesketh Cres. TQ1: Torq 3F 117
Hesketh M. TQ1: Torq 3F 117
Hesketh Rd. TQ1: Torq 3F 117
Hessary Dr. PL6: Robo 2D 132
Hessary Ter. PL20: Prin 6C 60
Hessary Vw. PL19: Tavi 3H 59
PL20: Prin 6C 60
Hestow Rd. TQ12: Kingst 1H 105
Hetling Cl. PL1: Plym 3B 8 (2H 141)
Hewers Row PL4: Plym 4G 9 (2K 141)
Hewett Cl. TQ12: New A 1K 109
HEWISH .3D 167
HEWOOD .3D 167
Hexham Pl. PL2: Plym 3F 135
HEXTON .6D 142
Hexton Hill Rd. PL9: Hooe 6C 142
Hexton Quay 6C 142
HEXWORTHY 3A 170
Hexworthy Av. EX4: Exe 4B 64
Heybrook Av. PL5: Plym 2C 134
HEYBROOK BAY 3B 148 (3A 174)
Heybrook Dr. PL9: Hey B 4B 148
Heydon's La. EX10: Sidm 6B 84
Heyridge Mdw. EX15: Cull 6G 45
Heyswood Av. EX32: B'aple 7H 19
Heywood Cl. EX39: Hart 3J 27
TQ2: Torq 6K 111
Heywood Dr. EX6: Star 1D 96
Heywood Est. TQ12: Kingst 6G 105
Heywood Forest Walk 2A 164
Heywood Rd. EX39: Bide, Nort 6E 20
Heywoods Cl. TQ14: Teignm 4J 107
(off Heywoods Rd.)
Heywoods Rd. TQ14: Teignm 4J 107
Hibernia Ter. PL5: Plym 3D 134
Hickory Cl. EX14: Hon 4H 55
Hickory Dr. PL7: Plymp 4E 138
Hicks La. PL4: Plym 5F 9 (3K 141)
Hides Rd. EX10: Sidm 2D 84
Hierns La. EX34: Ilfra 2J 11
High Acre Dr. PL21: Ivy 3E 144
HIGHAMPTON 3C 163
High Bank EX11: W Hill 5H 79
Highbank Cl. PL19: Tavi 5G 59
HIGH BICKINGTON 2C 32 (1A 164)
HIGH BRAY 3C 161
Highbridge Ct. PL7: Plymp 4B 138
(off Ridgeway)
HIGH BULLEN 1D 163
High Bullen EX5: Silv 1H 51
Highbullen Golf Course 1A 164
Highbury Cres. PL7: Plymp 2A 138
Highbury Hill EX39: Nort 4F 21
Highbury Pk. EX8: Exmth 3C 76
Highbury Rd. EX32: B'aple 6H 19
TQ1: Torq 7D 112
Highclere Gdns. PL6: Plym 2C 132
Highcliff Ct. EX7: Daw 4H 97
(off E. Cliff Rd.)
Highcliffe Cl. EX8: Lymp 7F 75
EX12: Seat 6D 86
Highcliffe Ct. EX8: Lymp 7F 75
Highcliffe Cres. EX12: Seat 6D 86
Highcliffe M. TQ4: Good 3J 119
Highcliff Rd. DT7: Lym R 5H 91
High Cl. TQ13: Bov T 4D 92
High Cft. EX4: Exe 3D 64
Highcroft Ct. EX4: Exe 3D 64
High Cross EX32: Swim 3H 25
(off High St.)
Highcross Rd. EX4: Exe 1E 6 (4F 65)
Higher Aboveway EX6: Exmin 3D 74
Higher Aller La. TQ13: Bov T 1A 92
HIGHER ASHTON 2C 171
Higher Audley Av. TQ2: Torq 5B 112
Higher Axmouth EX12: Axmth 4K 87
Higher Barley Mt. EX4: Exe 6B 64

Higher Bedlands EX9: Bud S 5B 82
Higher Bibbery TQ13: Bov T 4D 92
Higher Birch Dr. EX2: Sow 2D 72
Higher Brand La. EX14: Hon 6F 55
Higher Brimley TQ14: Teignm ...3H 107
Higher Brimley Rd.
  TQ14: Teignm 4H 107
HIGHER BRIXHAM 5E 122
Higher Broad Oak Rd.
  EX11: High M, W Hill 7G 79
Higher Broad Pk. TQ6: Dartm ...6D 124
Higher Brook Mdw. EX10: Sidf ...1D 84
Higher Brook Pk. PL21: Ivy 4E 144
Higher Brook St. TQ14: Teignm ...4H 107
Higher Buckeridge Rd.
  TQ14: Teignm 2H 107
Higher Budleigh Mdw.
  TQ12: New A 1C 108
Higher Buzzacott La.
  EX34: C Mar 7E 12
Higher Cadewell La. TQ2: Torq ...4H 111
HIGHER CHERITON 3B 166
Higher Church St. EX32: B'aple ...5F 19
Higher Churchway PL9: Plyms ...5H 143
Higher Clevelands EX39: Nort ...6E 20
  (off Churchill Way)
HIGHER CLOVELLY 6F 27 (1B 162)
HIGHER COMPTON ...5B 136 (2A 174)
Higher Compton Barton
  TQ3: Comp 7E 110
Higher Compton Rd. PL3: Plym ...5A 136
Higher Contour Rd. TQ6: Kingsw ...5H 125
Higher Coombe Dr.
  TQ14: Teignm 2G 107
Higher Copythorne TQ5: Brixh ...4C 122
Higher Cotteylands EX16: Tive ...5A 40
Higher Cross Mdw. EX16: Sam P ...2B 42
Higher Cross Orchard
  EX16: Sam P 2A 42
  (off Higher Cross Mdw.)
Higher Cross Rd. EX31: Bick ...5A 18
HIGHER DEAN 7A 98 (1D 175)
Higher Dean La. EX34: C Mar ...7D 12
Higher Doatshayne La.
  EX13: Mus 7D 90
Higher Down EX6: Kenton 6H 95
Higher Downs Rd. TQ1: Torq ...5E 112
Higher Dr. EX7: Daw 2J 97
HIGHER DUNSTONE 3B 170
Higher Duryard EX4: Exe 1F 65
Higher Edginswell La.
  TQ2: Torq 6G 111
Higher Efford Rd. PL3: Plym ...6C 136
Higher Elmwood EX31: Rou 6B 18
Higher Erith Rd. TQ1: Torq 2F 117
Higher Exeter Rd. TQ14: Teignm ...1G 107
Higher Exwick Hill EX4: Exe ...5B 64
Higher Fortescue EX10: Sidm ...3E 84
Higher French Pk. TQ12: New A ...1C 108
Higher Furlong Rd. EX5: Cran ...2F 69
Higher Furzeham Rd.
  TQ5: Brixh 2E 122
HIGHER GABWELL 1J 113 (1B 176)
Higher Gorse Rd. EX31: Bick ...7K 17
Higher Grn. TQ10: S Bre 2C 100
Higher Greenhead EX10: Sidb ...2G 85
Higher Grn. Pk. PL21: Modb ...6G 147
Higher Greenway La.
  EX10: Sidm, Stow 3A 84
Higher Gunstone EX39: Bide 3F 23
Higher Hill Vw. EX10: Sidm 5B 84
Higher Holcombe Cl.
  TQ14: Teignm 2J 107
Higher Holcombe Dr.
  TQ14: Teignm 1J 107
Higher Holcombe Rd.
  TQ14: Teignm 1J 107
Higher Hoopern La. EX4: Exe ...3F 65
  (not continuous)
Higher Island TQ9: Blacka 2C 152
HIGHER KEATON 7H 145
Higher King's Av. EX4: Exe 3G 65
Higher Kingsdown Rd.
  TQ14: Teignm 4F 107
Higher Kinsman's Dale
  TQ13: More 6H 61
Higher La. EX12: Axmth 3H 87
  PL1: Plym 5E 8
Higher La. CI. EX12: Axmth 3H 87
Higher Ley EX17: Nym R 2F 37
Higher Lincombe Rd. TQ1: Torq ...3F 117
Higher Loughborough EX16: Tive ...3B 40
Higher Maudlin St. EX32: B'aple ...3F 19
Higher Maunders Hill EX9: Ott'n ...7H 83
Higher Mead EX15: Hemy 2G 47
Higher Mdw. EX5: Cran 4B 68
  EX37: High B 2B 32
Higher Mdws. EX12: Beer 7B 86
HIGHER METCOMBE 7H 79
Higher Millhayes EX15: Hemy ...1G 47
Higher Mill La. EX15: Cull 4H 45
  TQ11: Buck 2C 98
  (not continuous)
Higher Moor Sq. EX16: Tive 2F 41
Higher Mowles PL3: Plym 5C 136

Higher New Cl. La. EX31: Ashf ...1K 17
Higher Orchard EX15: Cull 3G 45
Higher Pk. Cl. PL7: Plymp 6E 138
Higher Pk. Rd. EX33: Brau 4K 15
Higher Penn TQ5: Brixh 5F 123
Higher Polsham Rd. TQ3: Paig ...7H 115
Higher Queen's Ter. TQ1: Torq ...1D 116
Higher Raleigh Rd. EX31: B'aple ...2E 18
Higher Ramshill La.
  TQ3: Blag, Paig 6B 114
Higher Ranscombe Rd.
  TQ5: Brixh 4F 123
Higher Redgate EX16: Tive 3D 40
Higher Rews Ct. EX34: C Mar ...5A 12
Higher Ridgeway EX11: Ott M ...3D 80
Higher Ringmore Rd. TQ14: Shal ...6E 106
Higher Rd. EX5: Wood S 1A 78
  EX31: Frem 6F 17
Higher Roborough TQ13: Ashb ...3J 99
Higher Rydons TQ5: Brixh 4C 122
Higher Sackery TQ12: C'head ...7A 106
Higher Sandygate TQ12: Kingst ...1G 105
Higher Shapter Cl. EX3: Top ...6B 74
Higher Shapter St. EX3: Top 6B 74
Higherside TQ6: Dartm 2A 124
HIGHER SLADE 5F 11 (2B 160)
Higher Slade Rd. EX34: Ilfra ...5F 11
Higher Spring Gdns. EX11: Ott M ...4D 80
Higher Steps TQ5: Brixh 3E 122
  (off Higher St.)
Higher Stert Ter.
  PL4: Plym 4K 9 (2B 142)
Higher St. EX15: Cull 3H 45
  EX20: Hath 2H 35
  TQ5: Brixh 3E 122
  TQ6: Dartm 1B 124 (6F 125)
  TQ6: Ditt 6B 120
  TQ6: Kingsw 6G 125
Higher Summerlands
  EX1: Exe 3H 7 (6G 65)
HIGHER TALE 3A 166
Higher Ter. EX22: Bradw 5B 28
  (off North Rd.)
Higher Thorn Cl. EX33: Brau ...5J 15
HIGHER TOWN
  EX16 ....2A 42
  TQ11 ....4B 98
Higher Town EX16: Sam P 2A 42
  TQ1: Malb 6G 155
Hightertown PL20: Horr 1E 126
Higher Tuckers Pk. EX22: Bradw ...5B 28
Higher Union La. TQ2: Torq ...1C 116
Higher Union Rd. TQ7: Kingsb ...4F 157
Higher Warberry Rd. TQ1: Torq ...1E 116
Higher Warborough Rd.
  TQ5: Galm 2H 121
HIGHER WARCOMBE 2E 10
Higher Warren Rd. TQ7: Kingsb ...6H 157
Higher Way EX10: Harp 4J 81
HIGHER WEAR 4J 71
Higher Wear Rd. EX2: Cou W ...6B 72
Higher Weir TQ9: Darti 4D 102
Higher Wellbrook St. EX16: Tive ...4B 40
Higher Well Farm Holiday Pk. ...7B 118
Higher Westlake Rd. EX31: Rou ...7K 17
Higher Westonfields TQ9: Tot ...6G 103
HIGHER WHITELEIGH 1A 168
HIGHER WINSFORD 4B 22
Higher Woodfield Rd. TQ1: Torq ...3E 116
Higher Woodford La.
  PL7: Plymp 4K 137
Higher Woodway Cl.
  TQ14: Teignm 2J 107
Higher Woodway Rd.
  TQ14: Teignm 1H 107
HIGHER WOOLBROOK 3A 84
Higher Woolbrook Pk.
  EX10: Sidm 3A 84
HIGHER YALBERTON 4D 118 (2A 176)
Higher Yalberton Rd.
  TQ4: Paig 4D 118
Higher Yannon Dr.
  TQ14: Teignm 3G 107
Highfield EX3: Top 6E 72
  EX10: Sidm 5B 84
  (off Brewery La.)
  EX14: Hon 4E 54
  EX17: Lap 2K 37
  EX39: Nort 6H 21
Highfield Cl. EX32: B'aple 5G 19
  EX37: High B 2B 32
  PL3: Plym 6D 136
  TQ5: Brixh 5B 122
Highfield Cres. TQ3: Paig 1E 118
Highfield Dr. EX5: Cran 2F 69
  PL9: Wem 6B 148
  TQ7: Kingsb 5G 157
Highfield Gdns. EX34: C Mar ...6B 12
Highfield La. EX8: Exmth 6D 76
  EX34: Ilfra 3H 11
Highfield Ter. EX12: Beer 7B 86
  EX32: B Taw 5A 24
  EX34: Ilfra 3J 11
  PL21: Bitta 4C 146
Highfield Vineyards 4A 40
Highglen Dr. PL7: Plymp 2E 138
Highgrove EX31: B'aple 7B 18

Highgrove Pk. TQ14: Teignm ...2J 107
HIGH HAM 1D 167
High Ho. Cl. EX7: Daw 3H 97
High Ho. La. TQ7: Kingsb 5G 157
Highland Cl. TQ2: Torq 7J 111
Highland Pk. EX15: Uff 6G 43
Highland Rd. TQ2: Torq 7J 111
Highlands EX11: Ott M 4C 80
  PL8: Y'ton 2B 150
Highlands End Holiday Pk. 1D 173
Highlands Pk. TQ13: Chud 1C 94
Highland St. PL21: Ivy 4G 145
Highland Ter. EX15: Uff 6G 43
  EX16: Tive 4D 40
Highland Vw. EX20: Oke 5C 48
High Mdw. EX10: Sidm 3C 84
High Mdws. EX4: Exe 7B 64
Highmount Ct. EX15: Will 2D 44
High Pk. Cl. EX39: Bide 5C 22
High Rd. PL9: Wem 6A 148
High St. EX2: Ide 7D 72
  EX3: Top 7D 72
  EX4: Exe 4D 6 (6E 64)
  EX4: Exe 2C 52
  EX5: Bradn 2C 52
  EX5: Silv 1H 51
  EX5: Sto C 7J 51
  EX6: Kenton 6H 95
  EX7: Daw 4G 97
  EX8: Exmth 6C 76
  EX9: Bud S 7C 82
  EX9: E Bud 1D 82
  EX10: New P 5F 81
  EX10: Sidm 6C 84
  EX14: Hon 4E 54
  EX15: Cull 4H 45
  EX15: Hemy 2G 47
  EX15: Kent 6H 47
  EX15: Uff 6H 43
  EX16: Bam 5D 42
  EX16: Hal 5D 42
  EX17: Cred 6G 39
  EX19: Wink 2C 36
  EX20: Exbo 6J 35
  EX20: Hath 2H 35
  EX20: N Taw 6B 36
  EX20: Oke 4B 48
  EX22: Hols 2C 34
  EX31: B'aple 4E 18
  (not continuous)
  EX32: Swim 2C 20
  EX34: C Mar 6B 12
  EX34: Ilfra 3H 11
  EX37: High B 2C 32
  EX38: G Tor 2C 30
  EX39: Bide 5F 23
  EX39: Clov 5H 27
  PL1: Plym ....5F 9 (Buckwell St.)
  PL1: Plym ....3F 141 (Edgcumbe St.)
  TQ9: Tot 6D 102
  TQ13: Chag 6J 91
High Vw. EX14: Fen 1G 53
  EX39: Bide 4G 23
High Vw. Gdns. EX8: Exmth ...5D 76
High Vw. Ter. EX39: W Ho 4B 50
High Wall EX31: B'aple 5D 18
HIGHWEEK 6C 104 (3C 171)
Highweek Cl. TQ12: New A ...6C 104
Highweek Rd. TQ12: New A ...7D 104
  (not continuous)
Highweek St. TQ12: New A ...1E 108
Highweek Village TQ12: New A ...6C 104
Highweek Way TQ12: New A ...1E 108
Highwell Rd. EX12: Seat 5E 86
High Willhays 2D 169
Highwood Grange TQ12: New A ...2E 108
  (not continuous)
Hilary Cl. EX13: Axmin 3J 89
Hilary Gdns. EX13: Axmin 3J 89
The Hill EX13: Kilm 2B 88
Hill Barton Cl. EX1: Whip 5B 66
Hill Barton La. EX1: Whip 5B 66
Hill Barton Rd. EX1: Sow, Whip ...4C 66
  EX2: Sow 7C 66
Hillborough EX5: W'bury 5C 78
Hillbrook Ri. TQ9: Tot 6G 103
Hillbrook Rd. TQ9: Tot 6G 103
Hillcliff Ter. EX39: App 2H 21
  (off Irsha St.)
Hill Cl. EX4: Exe 3G 65
  PL7: Plymp 5A 138
HILLCOMMON 1B 166
Hill Cres. EX14: Hon 3G 55
Hill Crest EX6: Exmin 2C 74
  EX13: Kilm 2B 88
  EX16: Tive 3D 40
  PL3: Plym 6K 135
  PL21: Ferm 2H 147
Hillcrest EX11: Ott M 4C 80
  EX15: Cull 3H 45
  EX20: S Taw 1J 49
Hillcrest Cl. PL7: Plymp 4D 138
  PL9: Wem 7B 148
Hillcrest Dr. PL7: Plymp 5D 138
Hillcrest Gdns. EX8: Exmth ...3G 77
Hillcrest Pk. EX4: Exe 2F 65

Hillcrest Rd. EX5: Silv 1H 51
  EX32: B'aple 7G 19
  EX39: Bide 5J 23
Hillcroft Ter. EX39: Bide 3F 23
  (off Pitt La.)
Hilldale Rd. PL9: Plyms 6F 143
Hilldean Cl. PL5: Tam F 3H 131
Hilldown TQ9: Tot 6G 103
Hill Dr. EX8: Exmth 1D 76
Hilldrop Ter. TQ1: Torq 1D 116
Hiller La. TQ12: N'ton 2K 109
HILLERTON 1B 170
Hillesdon Rd. TQ1: Torq 1D 116
HILLFARRANCE 1B 166
Hillfield EX20: S Zeal 3H 49
  TQ9: Sto G 4B 120
Hill Gdn. Cl. EX39: Bide 3F 23
Hill Gdns. PL12: Car 1A 130
HILLHEAD 6K 123 (2B 176)
Hill Head EX16: Hal 6D 42
  (off Pond Hill)
Hillhead EX24: Colyt 7C 88
  PL8: Noss M 6H 149
Hillhead Holiday Pk. 7J 123
Hillhead Pk. TQ5: Hill 6J 123
Hillhead Ter. EX13: Axmin 4H 89
Hill House Gardens 1D 175
Hilliers EX19: Dol 6H 31
Hillington EX34: Ilfra 4G 11
Hill La. EX1: Whip 4A 66
  (not continuous)
  PL3: Plym 4A 136
Hillmans Rd. TQ12: New A 2F 109
HILLMOOR 3C 46
Hill Pk. PL21: Lutt 7G 129
Hillpark EX39: Buck B 2J 29
Hill Pk. Cl. TQ5: Brixh 4G 123
Hill Pk. Cotts. PL21: Lutt 6G 129
Hill Pk. Cres. PL4: Plym ...1G 9 (1K 141)
Hill Pk. M. PL4: Plym 1H 9 (1A 142)
Hill Pk. Rd. TQ1: Torq 6C 112
  TQ5: Brixh 4G 123
  TQ12: New A 7C 104
Hill Pk. Ter. TQ4: Paig 2J 119
Hill Path PL5: Plym 5E 130
Hillrise TQ5: Galm 3H 121
Hill Rise Rd. DT7: Lym R 5J 91
Hill Rd. DT7: Lym R 5J 91
  TQ12: New A 2E 108
HILLSBOROUGH 3K 11
Hillsborough PL4: Plym 7A 136
  TQ1: Torq 2D 116
  (off Hillesdon Rd.)
Hillsborough Av. EX4: Sow ...1F 7 (5F 65)
Hillsborough Pk. Rd. EX34: Ilfra ...3K 11
Hillsborough Rd. EX34: Ilfra ...2J 11
Hillsborough Ter. EX34: Ilfra ...2J 11
Hillsdunne Rd. PL3: Plym 5K 135
HILLSIDE 1C 100 (1D 175)
Hill Side EX10: Sidb 3H 85
Hillside EX10: New P 5F 81
  EX11: W Hill 3J 79
  EX12: Brans 5F 85
  EX24: Colyt 6C 88
  EX32: Land 2A 24
  PL21: Bitta 3C 146
  TQ10: S Bre 1B 100
Hillside Av. EX4: Exe 1E 6 (5F 65)
  PL4: Plym 7J 135
Hillside Cl. PL20: Buck M 5A 126
  TQ9: S Bre 1C 100
  TQ14: Teignm 2F 107
Hillside Cotts. PL8: Noss M ...7H 149
  PL21: Lutt 7G 129
  TQ12: A'well 6D 108
Hillside Ct. PL7: Plymp 3B 138
  PL20: Bere A 2C 128
  TQ6: Dartm 6E 124
Hillside Cres. PL9: Plyms 4G 143
Hillside Dr. PL8: Torr 3B 150
  TQ7: Kingsb 5G 157
Hillside Rd. EX10: Sidm 6C 84
  EX34: Ilfra 3K 11
  TQ3: Paig 7F 115
  TQ5: Brixh 4E 122
Hillside Ter. EX39: Bide 3F 23
  (off Pitt La.)
  TQ3: Paig 1J 119
  (off Colley End Pk.)
Hillside Vw. EX34: C Mar 6B 12
Hillside Way PL8: Torr 3C 150
Hill St. PL4: Plym 4G 9 (2K 141)
Hills Vw. EX32: B'aple 4F 19
  EX33: Brau 4J 15
Hill Top EX31: Frem 5F 17
Hill Top Crest PL5: Plym 1D 134
Hill Top Rd. EX1: Pin 4D 66
Hilltop Rd. EX39: Bide 1D 22
Hilltown Wood Forest Walks ...2A 164
Hilltown Wood Picnic Site 2B 164
Hill Vw. EX7: Holc 7F 97
  EX10: Sidm 5C 84
  EX11: Ott M 4C 80
  PL20: Buck M 5A 126

Hill Vw. Ter.—Howard Rd.

Hill Vw. Ter. TQ1: Torq 6C **112**
Hillway La. EX10: N'town 6J **81**
Hillyfield Rd. EX1: Whip 5B **66**
Hilly Gdns. Rd. TQ1: Torq 4D **112**
Hillymead EX12: Seat 4F **87**
Hilton Av. PL5: Plym 2H **135**
Hilton Cres. TQ3: Pres 4J **115**
Hilton Dr. TQ3: Pres 5J **115**
Hilton Pk. Homes EX33: Brau 5J **15**
Hilton Rd. TQ12: New A 2F **109**
Hindharton La. EX39: Hart 2J **27**
Hind St. EX11: Ott M 4C **80**
TQ13: Bov T 3C **92**
Hingston Ct. PL6: Plym 3B **136**
Hingston Rd. TQ1: Torq 6E **112**
Hinton Ct. PL6: Plym 2D **136**
HINTON ST GEORGE 2D **167**
Hirmandale Rd. PL5: Plym 7E **130**
Hirscombe La. EX17: Morc 1A **38**
HISCOTT .1D **163**
HITTISLEIGH 1B **170**
HITTISLEIGH BARTON 1B **170**
HM Dockyard PL1: Dev 2C **140**
HM Dockyard Nth. 5B **134**
HM Dockyard Sth. 3C **140**
HMP Channings Wood 1J **101**
HMP Dartmoor 5C **60**
HMP Exeter 2D **6** (5E **64**)
Hobart St. PL1: Plym 5A **8** (3G **141**)
Hobb's Hill EX33: Croy 3C **14**
Hobbs Way EX17: Bow 5G **37**
The Hobby Dr. EX39: Clov 5H **27**
Hoburne Holiday Pk. 4H **119**
Hockey Flds. TQ6: Sto F 2G **153**
Hockmoor Hill TQ11: B'leigh 1A **98**
Hockmore Dr. TQ12: New A 7J **105**
HOCKWORTHY 2A **166**
Hodder's La. DT7: Harc B 1H **91**
Hodders Way PL12: Car 1A **130**
Hodges Cl. EX14: Gitt 6C **54**
Hodges Wlk. EX38: G Tor 2D **30**
Hodson Cl. TQ3: Paig 7F **115**
THE HOE 7D **8** (4J **141**)
Hoe App. PL1: Plym 6E **8** (3J **141**)
Hoe Ct. PL1: Plym 6D **8**
Hoe Gdns. PL1: Plym 6E **8**
Hoegate Ct. PL1: Plym 6E **8**
Hoegate Pl. PL1: Plym 6E **8**
Hoegate St. PL1: Plym 6F **9** (3K **141**)
Hoe Park 6D **8** (4J **141**)
Hoe Rd. PL1: Plym 7C **8** (4H **141**)
Hoe St. PL1: Plym 6E **8** (3J **141**)
Hofheim Dr. EX16: Tive 2A **40**
Hogarth Cl. PL9: Elb 6J **143**
Hogarth Ho. *PL19: Tavi* *3J* ***59***
(off Taylor Sq.)
Hogarth Wlk. PL9: Elb 6J **143**
Hoile La. TQ9: Sto G 3A **120**
Hoker Rd. EX2: Won 7K **65**
Holbeam Cl. TQ12: New A 7B **104**
HOLBETON 6C **150** (2C **175**)
Holborn Pl. PL7: Plymp 3B **138**
Holborn Rd. TQ5: Brixh 2E **122**
Holborn St. PL4: Plym 5J **9** (3A **142**)
Holbrook Ter. TQ7: Stoke 6J **159**
HOLCOMBE 7F **97** (3D **171**)
Holcombe Court 1G **43**
Holcombe Down Rd. EX7: Holc 1H **107**
TQ14: Teignm 1H **107**
Holcombe Dr. EX7: Holc 7G **97**
PL9: Plyms 7G **143**
Holcombe La. EX11: Ott M 1E **80**
Holcombe Rd. EX7: Holc 7F **97**
TQ14: Teignm 2K **107**
HOLCOMBE ROGUS 2G **43** (2A **166**)
Holcombe Village EX7: Holc 7F **97**
HOLDITCH 3D **167**
Holdridge La. EX36: N Mol 2C **26**
Holdstone Way EX34: C Mar 7D **12**
Holdsworth Ho. TQ6: Dartm 2A **124**
Holdsworth St. PL4: Plym . . .1C **8** (1H **141**)
Holebay Cl. PL9: Plyms 7H **143**
Holebrook La. EX20: Exbo 5J **35**
Hole Cleave Rd. EX33: Forda, Lob . . .6A **14**
Hole Ct. EX20: Hath 1H **35**
Hole Hill EX16: W'ridge 4K **33**
EX20: Exbo 6K **35**
Hole La. EX33: Forda 7A **14**
HOLEMOOR 3C **163**
Holestone La. EX9: Ott'n 4K **83**
HOLLACOMBE 3B **162**
Hollacombe La. TQ3: Pres 5K **115**
Hollamoor Vw. EX31: Bick 6A **18**
Hollam Way TQ12: Kingst 3J **105**
Holland Cl. EX31: Bick 5K **17**
Holland Hall EX4: Exe 3D **64**
Holland Pk. EX2: Cou W 4C **72**
Holland Rd. EX2: Exe 1C **70**
EX8: Exmth 3F **77**
PL3: Plym 5K **135**
PL7: Plymp 4F **139**
PL9: Plyms 6G **143**
Hollands Pk. Av. EX34: C Mar 6C **12**
Hollands Rd. TQ14: Teignm 5J **107**
Holland St. EX31: B'aple 4E **18**
Holland Wlk. *EX31: B'aple* *4E* ***18***
(off Holland St.)
Hollerday Dr. EX35: Lynt 1G **13**
Holley Cl. EX6: Exmin 2C **74**
Holley Pk. EX20: Oke 2D **48**
HOLLICOMBE 4K **115**
The Hollies EX31: Rou 6A **18**
Hollingarth Way EX15: Hemy 1G **47**
Hollington Ho. TQ1: Torq 2F **117**
Hollis Cl. EX11: Ott M 3D **80**
HOLLOCOMBE 2A **164**
Holloway Gdns. PL9: Plyms 7H **143**
Holloway St.
EX2: Exe 6E **6** (7F **65**)
Hollow Hayes *PL6: Plym* *3C* ***136***
(off Goosewell Hill)
Hollow La. EX1: Pin 5C **66**
Hollowpits Ct. EX2: Alph 5E **70**
The Hollows EX8: Exmth 5D **76**
PL9: Elb 4J **143**
Hollowtree Ct. EX32: B'aple 6G **19**
Hollowtree Rd. EX32: B'aple 6G **19**
Holly Ball La. EX5: Whim 5J **53**
Holly Berry Rd. PL21: L Mill 5A **144**
Holly Cl. EX5: Broadc 5C **52**
EX14: Hon 5F **55**
EX16: Tive 3E **40**
TQ13: Chud 1D **94**
Holly Ct. PL6: Plym 4F **137**
Hollycroft Rd. PL3: Plym 4B **136**
Hollyhead Rd. EX12: Beer 4A **86**
Hollyhock Way PL6: Plym 1B **136**
TQ4: Paig 5E **118**
Holly La. EX5: Cran 2F **68**
Hollymount Cl. EX8: Exmth 1E **76**
Holly Pk. Cl. PL5: Plym 5F **131**
Holly Pk. Dr. PL5: Plym 5F **131**
Holly Rd. EX2: Won 2J **71**
EX16: Tive 3E **40**
Holly Wlk. EX8: Exmth 1F **77**
Hollywater Cl. TQ1: Torq 1F **117**
Holly Water Rd. EX17: Cher F 2F **39**
Holly Way EX15: Cull 2H **45**
Hollywood Ter. PL1: Plym 3A **8**
HOLMACOTT 1D **163**
Holman Cl. EX7: Daw 2J **97**
Holman Ct. PL2: Plym 3H **135**
Holman Hill TQ12: A'well 4A **110**
Holmans Bldgs. PL1: Dev 2C **140**
Holman Way EX3: Top 6B **74**
PL21: Ivy 3E **144**
Holmbush Way PL8: Brixt 3H **149**
Holmdale EX10: Sidm 6C **84**
Holme Ct. TQ1: Torq 1F **117**
Holmer Down PL6: Plym 3E **132**
Holmes Av. PL3: Plym 6C **136**
Holmes Fld. EX20: Stic 1G **49**
Holmes Rd. TQ12: H'fld 2J **93**
Holmwood Av. PL9: Plyms 7F **143**
HOLNE 1D **175**
Holne Chase PL6: Plym 3C **132**
Holne Ct. EX4: Exe 4B **64**
Holne Cross TQ13: Ashb 3F **99**
Holne Moor Cl. TQ3: Paig 7E **114**
Holne Ri. EX2: Won 7A **66**
Holne Rd. TQ11: B'leigh 2A **98**
HOLSWORTHY 2C **34** (3B **162**)
HOLSWORTHY BEACON 3B **162**
Holsworthy Information Centre 3B **162**
Holsworthy Leisure Cen. 1C **34**
Holsworthy Mus. 2C **34** (3B **162**)
Holsworthy Rd. EX20: Hath 3F **35**
Holsworthy Rural Life History Mus.
. . . . .2C **34**
Holsworthy Theatre 2C **34**
The Holt EX14: Hon 2H **55**
Holtwood Dr. PL21: Ivy 4E **144**
Holtwood Rd. PL6: Plym 4E **132**
Holwell Cl. PL9: Plyms 7H **143**
Holwell La. EX16: Colli 7C **40**
Holwell Rd. TQ5: Brixh 4D **122**
Holwill Dr. EX38: G Tor 2C **30**
Holwill Tor Wlk. TQ4: Paig 4F **119**
HOLY CITY 3D **167**
Holyford La. EX12: Seat 1D **86**
EX24: Colyf 1D **86**
(not continuous)
Holyford Woods
Local Nature Reserve 1B **86**
Holyrood La. PL1: Plym 6D **8**
Holyrood Pl.
PL1: Plym 7D **8** (4J **141**)
Holyshute Gdns. *EX14: Hon* *2G* ***55***
(off Monkton Rd.)
HOLYWELL LAKE 1B **166**
Homebaye Ho. *EX12: Seat* *6F* ***87***
(off Harbour Rd.)
Homebourne Ho. *TQ4: Paig* *2J* ***119***
(off Belle Vue Rd.)
Home Cl. TQ5: Brixh 5E **122**
TQ7: Chil 6H **159**
Homeclyst Ho. EX2: Exe 7C **6**
Homecombe Ho. *TQ1: Torq* *5E* ***112***
(off St Albans Rd.)
Homecourt Ho. EX4: Exe 5C **6**
Home Farm Cl. EX33: Croy 2D **14**
Home Farm Rd. EX31: Frem 6E **16**
PL9: Plyms 4F **143**
Home Fld. TQ7: W Alv 5E **156**
Homefield TQ7: Thur 6C **154**
Homefield Cl. EX11: Ott M 4D **80**
Homefield Rd. EX1: Heav 6J **65**
Homelace Ho. EX14: Hon 4F **55**
Homeland Cl. EX22: Bradw 5B **28**
Homelands Pl. TQ7: Kingsb 3F **157**
Homelands Rd. TQ7: Kingsb 3F **157**
Home Mdw. TQ9: Tot 6E **102**
Home Orchard EX16: Sam P 2B **42**
Homepalms Ho. *TQ1: Torq* *7B* ***112***
(off Teignmouth Rd.)
Home Park 6H **135**
Home Pk. PL2: Dev 7E **134**
TQ13: Ashb 3H **99**
Home Pk. Av. PL3: Plym 5K **135**
Homer Cl. EX31: Brat F 6H **13**
Homer Ct. EX33: Brau 3G **15**
Homer Cres. EX33: Brau 3G **15**
Homer Dr. EX33: Brau 3G **15**
Home Reach Rd. TQ9: Tot 7G **103**
Homer La. EX12: Seat 4D **86**
(not continuous)
Homer Pk. PL9: Hooe 7D **142**
Homer Pk. La. Sth. PL9: Hooe 7D **142**
Homer Ri. PL9: Elb 5J **143**
Homer Rd. EX33: Brau 3G **15**
Homers Cl. TQ12: Kingst 5G **105**
Homers Cres. TQ12: Kingst 5G **105**
Homers La. TQ12: Kingst 5G **105**
Homestead Rd. TQ1: Torq 5C **112**
Homestead Ter. TQ1: Torq 5C **112**
Home Sweet Home Ter.
PL4: Plym 6K **9** (3B **142**)
Hometeign Ho. *TQ12: New A* *7G* ***105***
(off Salisbury Rd.)
Hometor Ct. EX8: Exmth 4C **76**
The Homeyards *TQ14: Shal* *6G* ***107***
(off Commons Old Rd.)
Homeyards Botanical Gdns.
. . . . .6G **107** (3D **171**)
Honcray PL9: Plyms 4E **142**
Honestone St. EX39: Bide 4F **23**
HONEYCHURCH 3A **164**
Honey Cl. EX39: Bide 3J **23**
Honey Ditches Dr. EX12: Seat 4D **86**
Honeyford Cl. PL6: Plym 6B **132**
Honeylands Dr. EX4: Exe 5K **65**
Honeylands Way EX4: Exe 5K **65**
Honey La. EX1: Pin 2E **66**
EX5: Wood S 1C **78**
Honeymeadows EX22: Hols 2C **34**
Honey Pk. Rd. EX9: Bud S 5D **82**
Honey St. EX39: Nort 5F **21**
Honeysuckle Cl. EX16: Bam 3J **33**
EX16: Tive 2F **41**
EX31: Rou 6A **18**
PL6: Plym 3F **133**
TQ3: Paig 6E **114**
Honeysuckle Ct. EX4: Exe 4A **64**
Honeysuckle Dr. EX7: Daw 2G **97**
EX14: Hon 5C **54**
Honeywell TQ12: Kingst 5H **105**
Honeywell Cl. EX32: B'aple 7G **19**
Honeywell Rd. TQ12: Kingst 5H **105**
Honeywill Ct. EX2: Heav 7K **65**
HONICKNOWLE 1H **135**
Honicknowle Grn. PL5: Plym 7G **131**
Honicknowle La. PL2: Plym 2G **135**
PL5: Plym 2G **135**
HONITON 3F **55** (3B **166**)
Honiton Bottom Rd.
EX14: Hon 5F **55**
Honiton Bus. Pk. EX14: Hon 3E **54**
Honiton Cvn. & Camping Club 2H **55**
Honiton Cl. PL5: Plym 7G **131**
Honiton Golf Course 6H **55** (1B **172**)
Honiton Leisure Cen. 3F **55**
Honiton Rd. EX1: Heav, Sow 7A **66**
EX5: Clyst H 5F **67**
EX15: Cull 3J **45**
Honiton Road Park & Ride 6D **66**
Honiton Station (Rail) 4F **55** (3B **166**)
Honiton Swimming Pool 2F **55**
Honiton Wlk. PL5: Plym 6G **131**
Honors Farm EX5: Sto C 7J **51**
Hooda Cl. EX32: Swim 2H **25**
Hood Dr. EX2: Cou W 5B **72**
Hoodown La. TQ6: Kingsw 5G **125**
HOOE 6C **142** (2B **174**)
Hooe Hill PL9: Hooe 7D **142**
Hooe Lake PL10: Millb 7A **140**
Hooe Rd. PL9: Hooe 6C **142**
Hook Dr. EX2: Cou W 3C **72**
Hooker Cl. EX9: Bud S 5B **82**
Hook Farm Camping & Cvn. Pk. 3F **91**
Hookhills Dr. TQ4: Good 6J **119**
Hookhills Gdns. TQ4: Good 7H **119**
Hookhills Gro. TQ4: Good 6J **119**
Hookhills Rd. TQ4: Good 7H **119**
Hook La. TQ5: Galm 5G **121**
Hooksbury Av. PL7: Plymp 6E **138**
HOOKWAY 1C **171**
Hooper Cl. EX20: Hath 2G **35**
Hoopern Av. EX4: Exe 3F **65**
Hoopern La. EX4: Exe 1F **7** (4F **65**)
Hoopern M. EX4: Exe 1E **6** (4E **64**)
Hoopern St. EX4: Exe 1E **6** (5F **65**)
Hoopern Ter. *EX7: Daw* *4G* ***97***
(off Stockton Rd.)
Hoopers Ct. EX5: Rock 3E **68**
Hooper St. PL11: Torp 1B **140**
Hoopers Way EX38: G Tor 2E **30**
Hope Barton Barns
TQ7: Hope 4H **155**
Hope By-Pass TQ7: Hope 2G **155**
Hope Cl. PL2: Plym 2J **135**
TQ9: Tot 6H **103**
Hope Ct. *EX4: Exe* *4F* ***65***
(off Prince of Wales Rd.)
HOPE COVE 3G **155**
Hope Hall EX4: Exe 4F **65**
Hope Pl. EX2: Won 7K **65**
Hope Rd. EX2: Won 7K **65**
Hope's Cl. TQ14: Teignm 3G **107**
Hope Wlk. TQ9: Tot 6H **103**
Hopkins Ct. *TQ12: New A* *1F* ***109***
(off Hopkins La.)
Hopkins La. TQ12: New A 1F **109**
Hopperstyle EX31: Bick 6A **18**
Hopton Cl. PL6: Plym 3A **136**
Hopton Dr. EX38: G Tor 2E **30**
Horace Rd. TQ2: Torq 3B **112**
Horizon Vw. EX39: W Ho 5B **20**
Hornapark Cl. PL16: Lift 7B **56**
HORN ASH 3D **167**
Hornbeam Cl. EX14: Hon 5D **54**
EX16: Tive 3F **41**
Hornbeam Gdns. EX5: Bradn 1D **52**
Hornbeam Hollow EX31: Rou 6B **18**
Hornbrook Gdns. PL6: Plym 4J **131**
Hornby St. PL2: Plym 7E **131**
Hornchurch La. PL5: Plym 6D **130**
Hornchurch Rd. PL5: Plym 5D **130**
Horn Cross Rd. PL9: Plyms 5F **143**
HORNDON 1E **60** (2D **169**)
Hornebrook Av. *EX34: Ilfra* *3H* ***11***
(off Horne Rd.)
Horne Pk. Av. *EX34: Ilfra* *3H* ***11***
(off Horne Pk. Rd.)
Horne Pk. Rd. EX34: Ilfra 3H **11**
Horne Rd. EX34: Ilfra 3H **11**
Horn Hill TQ6: Dartm 1A **124**
Horn La. PL8: Brixt 2H **149**
PL9: Plyms 5F **143**
Horn La. Flats PL9: Plyms 5G **143**
HORNSBURY 2D **167**
HORNS CROSS 1B **162**
Horns Pk. TQ14: Bi'ton 3A **106**
HORRABRIDGE 2E **126** (1B **174**)
Horsdon Rd. EX16: Tive 4F **41**
Horsdon Ter. EX16: Tive 4F **41**
HORSEBRIDGE 3C **169**
Horseguards EX4: Exe 1E **6** (5F **65**)
Horse La. TQ14: Shal 6H **107**
Horsepond Mdw. EX36: S Mol 7C **26**
Horsepool St. TQ5: Brixh 5D **122**
Horseshoe Bend TQ4: Good 5J **119**
Horseshoe Cl. TQ13: Chud 2C **94**
Horseshoe Dr. PL7: Plymp 4A **138**
Horsham La. PL5: Plym 1H **135**
TQ5: Tam F 2G **131**
Horslears EX13: Axmin 5G **89**
Horswell Cl. PL7: Plymp 4E **138**
HORTON .2D **167**
HORTON CROSS 2D **167**
HORWOOD 1D **163**
Hosegood Way TQ12: Kingst 4G **105**
Hosford Cl. PL9: Plyms 7G **143**
Hoskings Ct. TQ11: B'leigh 4C **98**
Hospital Hill EX7: Daw 4G **97**
Hospital La. EX1: Whip 4B **66**
TQ13: Ashb 3J **99**
(not continuous)
Hospital Rd. PL4: Plym 2H **9** (1A **142**)
Hostle Pk. EX34: Ilfra 2J **11**
Hostle Pk. Gdns. *EX34: Ilfra* *2H* ***11***
(off Hostle Pk. Rd.)
Hostle Pk. Rd. EX34: Ilfra 2J **11**
Hotel Endsleigh Gardens 3B **168**
Hotham Pl.
PL1: Plym 2A **8** (1G **141**)
Houghton Gro. EX1: W Cly 1E **66**
Houghton La. EX10: N'town 1K **83**
Houldsworth Rd. PL9: Plyms 5D **142**
Houndbeare La.
EX5: Ayle, Mar G 7K **69**
Houndiscombe Rd.
PL4: Plym 1F **9** (1K **141**)
HOUNDSMOOR 1B **166**
Hound Tor Cl. TQ4: Good 1H **121**
Hound Tor Deserted Medieval Village
. . . . .3B **170**
House of Marbles 6C **92** (3C **171**)
Housman Cl. PL5: Plym 7J **131**
Howard Av. EX32: B'aple 5G **19**
Howard Cl. EX4: Exe 4B **64**
EX7: Daw *4F* ***97***
(off Penfield Gdns.)
EX7: Daw 4G **97**
(Brook St.)
EX20: Oke 2D **48**
PL5: Plym 1E **134**
PL19: Tavi 4G **59**
TQ2: Torq 7K **111**
TQ14: Teignm 2G **107**
Howard Ct. PL1: Plym 7B **8**
TQ14: Teignm 2G **107**
Howard Rd. PL9: Plyms 4F **143**

Howards Cl. EX36: S Mol 7C 26
Howards Way PL21: Ivy 3E 144
  TQ12: New A 7J 105
Howarth Cl. EX10: Sidm 2B 84
Howden Ind. Est. EX16: Tive 6B 40
Howden La. EX16: Tive 5B 40
Howden Rd. EX16: Tive 5B 40
Howell Rd. EX4: Exe 1B 6 (5D 64)
Howeson La. PL6: Plym 6B 132
HOWLEIGH 2C 167
HOWLEY 3C 167
How St. PL4: Plym 5F 9 (3K 141)
Howton Rd. TQ12: New A 5A 104
Hoxton Rd. TQ1: Torq 1D 116
Hoyles Ct. TQ3: Paig 6E 114
Hoyle's Rd. TQ3: Paig 6E 114
Hubbastone Rd. EX39: App 3H 21
Huccaby Cl. TQ5: Brixh 6B 122
Hughes Av. EX32: B'aple 6G 19
Hugh Squier Av. EX36: S Mol 5D 26
HUISH 7C 30 (2D 163)
HUISH CHAMPFLOWER 1A 166
HUISH EPISCOPI 1D 167
Huishlane End EX6: Ted M 6H 49
HULHAM 1D 76 (2A 172)
Hulham Rd. EX8: Exmth 3D 76
Hulham Va. EX8: Exmth 2E 76
Hulk La. EX5: Thor 4C 50
HUMBER 3D 171
Humber Cl. PL3: Plym 5E 136
Humber La. TQ12: Kingst 3J 105
  TQ14: Teignm 1A 106
Hume Av. EX3: Lynt 2F 13
Hummingbird Cl. EX1: Pin 3D 66
Humphries Pk. EX8: Exmth 3F 77
The Humpy EX7: Daw 3F 97
Hungerford Rd. PL2: Plym 5G 135
Hungry Fox Est. EX5: Broadc 1K 67
Huniver's La. EX17: Cred 7H 39
Hunivers Pl. EX17: Cred 7J 39
Hunsdon Rd. PL21: Ivy 6D 144
  TQ1: Torq 2E 116
Huntacott Way TQ2: Torq 5H 111
Hunter Cl. PL6: Plym 1A 136
Hunter La. EX34: Wool 6A 10
                    (off Mill La.)
Hunters Cl. PL21: Ivy 4F 145
Hunters Ct. TQ3: Blag 7A 114
Hunters Ga. EX20: Oke 2D 48
Hunters Hill EX15: Culm 1B 46
Hunter's Moon TQ1: Torq 2F 117
        (off Babbacombe Rd.)
Hunters Moon TQ9: Darti 4B 102
Hunters Tor Dr. TQ4: Good 1H 121
Hunters Way EX15: Culm 1B 46
            (not continuous)
Hunterswell Rd. TQ12: New A 1D 108
Hunterswood EX38: G Tor 2E 30
Hunter Wlk. EX32: B'aple 4H 19
           (off Martin Rd.)
HUNTHAM 1D 167
Hunthay La. EX13: Axmin 2E 88
Huntingdon Gdns. PL5: Plym 6J 131
Huntley Cl. EX13: Axmin 2K 89
Huntley Pl. PL3: Plym 7D 136
Huntley Vs. PL3: Plym 7D 136
Hunton Cl. EX8: Lymp 6G 75
HUNTSHAM 1A 166
Huntsham Rd. EX1: Sow 5C 66
HUNTSHAW 1D 163
HUNTSTILE 1C 167
HURCOTT 2D 167
Hurdwick Rd. PL19: Tavi 4G 59
Hurrabrook Cl. PL6: Plym 1F 137
Hurrabrook Gdns. PL6: Plym 1F 137
Hurrell Cl. PL6: Plym 4J 131
Hurrell Ct. PL3: Plym 6D 136
  TQ7: Kingsb 4F 157
Hurrell Rd. TQ7: Kingsb 4F 157
HURSEY 3D 167
Hursley Bus. Pk. PL6: Robo 1F 133
Hurst Av. EX2: Won 1A 72
Hurst Cl. PL9: Plyms 7G 143
Hurst's Almshouses
  EX2: Exe 5F 7
HUTCHERLEIGH 2D 175
Hutchings Cl. PL6: Plym 4J 131
Hutchings Mead EX1: Pin 4E 66
Hutchings Way TQ14: Teignm 3F 107
Hutgate Rd. EX14: Hon 3K 55
Hutton Rd. TQ3: Pres 5G 115
HUXHAM 7K 51 (1D 171)
Huxham Cl. PL6: Plym 3B 136
Huxhams Cross TQ9: Darti 1A 102
Huxley Cl. PL7: Plymp 2C 138
Huxley Va. TQ12: Kingsk 2F 111
Huxnor Rd. TQ12: Kingsk 2F 111
Huxtable Hill TQ2: Torq 2K 115
Hyde Pk. Rd. PL3: Plym 6K 135
Hyde Rd. TQ4: Paig 1H 119
Hyfield Gdns. TQ1: Torq 2D 116
           (off Grafton Rd.)
Hyfield Pl. EX39: Bide 4F 23
Hylands Cl. EX11: W Hill 5H 79
Hylton Gdns. EX4: Exe 6C 64
Hyne Town TQ6: Strete 5G 153
Hynetown Est. TQ6: Strete 5G 153

Hynetown Rd. TQ6: Strete 6G 153
Hyperion TQ2: Torq 4A 116

I

Ian Hay Cl. EX39: Bide 4H 23
Ibex Ct. EX39: App 2H 21
Icy Pk. TQ7: Ave G 6H 151
IDDESLEIGH 3D 163
Iddesleigh Rd. EX4: Exe 1H 7 (4H 65)
Iddesleigh Ter. EX3: Ext 2G 75
  EX7: Daw 5F 97
IDE 4A 70 (1C 171)
IDEFORD 3C 171
Ideford Common Viewpoint 3D 171
Ide La. EX2: Exe, Ide, Alph 2A 70
           (not continuous)
Idestone La. EX2: Ide 6A 70
Idewell Rd. TQ2: Torq 3D 112
Ikea Way EX2: Cou W 3C 72
Ilbert Rd. TQ7: Kingsb 4F 157
  TQ7: Thur 6A 154
Ilbert St. PL1: Plym 2C 8 (1H 141)
Ilex Cl. EX4: Whip 2A 66
ILFORD .2D 167
Ilford Pk. TQ12: New A 4J 93
ILFRACOMBE 2H 11 (2B 160)
Ilfracombe & Woolacombe Golf
  Driving Range 2A 160
Ilfracombe Aquarium 2K 11 (2B 160)
Ilfracombe Golf Course 2B 160
Ilfracombe Leisure Centre 3K 11
Ilfracombe Lifeboat Station 2J 11
Ilfracombe Mus. 2H 11 (2B 160)
Ilfracombe Rd. EX33: Brau 2J 15
Ilfracombe Tourist Information Centre
                    .2H 11 (2B 160)
Ilfracombe Yacht Club 2J 11
ILLAND .3A 168
ILMINSTER 2D 167
Ilsham Cl. TQ1: Torq 1H 117
Ilsham Cres. TQ1: Torq 2H 117
Ilsham Ho. TQ1: Torq 1G 117
Ilsham Marine Dr.
  TQ1: Torq 1H 117
Ilsham M. TQ1: Torq 1H 117
Ilsham Rd. TQ1: Torq 1G 117
ILSINGTON 3B 170
ILTON 2D 167
Ilton Way TQ7: Kingsb 4G 157
Imperial Cl. EX35: Lynt 2H 13
  TQ1: Torq 6E 112
Imperial M. TQ12: New A 1F 109
           (off Lemon Rd.)
Imperial Rd. EX8: Exmth 5B 76
Imperial Road Athletics Track 5B 76
Imperial St. EX4: Exe 7C 64
Inchcoulter Apts. EX8: Exmth 7E 76
Inchkeith Rd. PL6: Plym 4A 132
Incledon Hill EX33: Geo 4C 14
Independent St. EX39: Clov 5H 27
            (off High St.)
Indio Rd. TQ13: Bov T 5B 92
Ingleborough Hgts. EX39: W Ho 5D 20
INGLEIGH GREEN 3A 164
Ingleside Ct. EX9: Bud S 6C 82
Inglewood Ho. EX4: Exe 1G 7
Ingra Rd. PL3: Plym 5B 136
Ingra Tor PL20: Yelv 5F 127
Ingra Wlk. PL6: Robo 2C 132
Innerbrook Rd. TQ2: Torq 1A 116
INNER HOPE 3G 155 (3C 175)
Inner Ting Tong EX9: Know 1K 77
Inner Westland EX5: Cran 2C 68
INSTOW 3K 21 (3A 160)
Instow Signal Box 3K 21 (1C 163)
Instow Way PL5: Plym 7F 131
Inswell Ct. PL19: Tavi 3G 59
Inverdene PL3: Plym 6J 135
Inverteign Dr. TQ14: Teignm 4F 107
Inverteign Hgts.
  TQ14: Teignm 3F 107
INWARDLEIGH 1D 169
Iolanthe Dr. EX4: Whip 2K 65
Iona Av. EX8: Exmth 2C 76
IPPLEPEN 6H 101 (1A 176)
Ipplepen Cross TQ12: Den 2K 101
Ipplepen Rd. TQ3: Marl 7B 110
  TQ12: Ipp 7B 110
Ipswich Cl. PL5: Plym 6H 131
Irene Way EX16: Tive 2F 41
Iris Av. EX2: Exe 7C 6 (1E 70)
Iron Bri. EX4: Exe 3C 6 (6E 64)
Iron Mine La. PL20: Dous 5K 127
Irsha St. EX39: App 2H 21
Irsha St. EX39: App 2H 21
Irving Cl. EX33: Brau 4G 15
Isaac Cl. EX9: Ott'n 6H 83
Isaac Gro. TQ2: Torq 2B 112
Isaacs Rd. TQ2: Torq 2B 112
Isabel Ct. EX4: Exe 7A 6 (1D 70)
Isabella Rd. EX16: Tive 3D 40

Isambard Brunel Way
  PL1: Plym 6A 8 (3G 141)
Isambard Ct. TQ2: Torq 2D 112
Isambard Pde. EX4: Exe . . .1A 6 (5D 64)
Isca Cen. .3B 66
Isca Lofts EX4: Exe 2F 7
Isca Rd. EX2: Exe 7D 6 (1E 70)
  EX8: Exmth 7E 76
Isigny Rd. TQ7: Kingsb 4F 157
Isis Cl. EX14: Hon 2H 55
Island Av. EX5: Whim 2F 69
Island Quay TQ8: Salc 3D 158
Island St. TQ8: Salc 3D 158
Island Ter. TQ8: Salc 3D 158
Island Vw. TQ7: Thur 4A 154
ISLE ABBOTTS 1D 167
ISLE BREWERS 1D 167
Isleworth Rd. EX4: Exe 7B 64
Isley Marshes Bird Sanctuary 5A 16
Isley Marsh
  Nature Reserve 5A 16 (3A 160)
Iter Ct. EX17: Bow 5J 37
Iter Pk. EX17: Bow 5J 37
ITTON 1A 170
Ivanhoe Rd. PL5: Plym 1C 134
Ivatt Rd. TQ6: Dartm 6C 124
Iveagh Ct. EX4: Exe 4C 64
IVYBRIDGE 4H 145 (2C 175)
Ivybridge Information Centre
                    .4H 145 (2C 175)
Ivybridge La. PL20: Prin 7D 60
Ivybridge Leisure Centre & Outdoor Pool
                          .5H 145
Ivybridge Park & Ride 4K 145
Ivybridge Rd. PL21: Erm 1J 147
Ivybridge Station
  (Rail) 3K 145 (2C 175)
IVYBRIDGE VIADUCT 2H 145
Ivy Cl. EX2: Won 1K 71
  EX10: Sidm 3C 84
Ivy Ct. EX39: App 2H 21
Ivydale EX8: Exmth 1F 77
Ivydale Rd. PL4: Plym 7A 136
Ivydene Rd. PL21: Ivy 4F 145
Ivy Dr. PL6: Plym 4H 131
Ivy Ho. TQ14: Teignm 5H 107
            (off Ivy La.)
Ivy La. TQ6: Dartm 1A 124
  TQ14: Teignm 5H 107

J

Jackdaw Rd. PL6: Plym 1C 136
Jackets La. EX39: Nort 5E 20
Jacketts EX9: Ott'n 6H 83
JACK-IN-THE-GREEN 3D 68
Jackmans Cl. TQ2: Torq 5A 102
Jackman's La. TQ9: Harb 5A 102
Jack Sadler Way EX2: Cou W 4D 72
Jack's La. TQ2: Torq 2B 112
Jackson Cl. PL5: Plym 3D 134
Jackson Mdw. EX8: Lymp 6G 75
Jackson Pl. PL2: Dev 7E 134
Jacob's Pool EX20: Oke 3B 48
JACOBSTOW 1A 168
JACOBSTOWE 6F 35 (3D 163)
Jacolind Wlk. TQ5: Brixh 4F 123
Jacqueline Ho. TQ9: Tot 6E 102
          (off Ticklemore St.)
Jago Av. PL11: Torp 1A 140
James Av. TQ3: Paig 5E 114
James Cl. PL9: Elb 5J 143
James Ct. EX1: Exe 5E 6 (7F 65)
James Owen Ct. EX4: Exe 1G 7
James Rd. PL19: Whit 7K 59
James St. PL1: Dev 3D 140
  PL4: Plym 3E 8 (2J 141)
Janes Ct. EX16: Tive 4C 40
Jarvis Bungs. EX8: Exmth 5G 77
Jarvis Cl. EX8: Exmth 5G 77
Jasmine Cl. EX16: Tive 2F 41
Jasmine Gdns. PL6: Plym 4F 133
  PL7: Plymp 4E 138
Jasmine Gro. TQ3: Paig 6E 114
Jawbones Hill
  TQ6: Dartm 2A 124 (6F 125)
Jaycroft EX15: Will 4D 44
Jedburgh Cres. PL2: Plym 5F 135
Jefferson Wlk.
  PL3: Plym 1C 8 (1H 141)
Jeffery Cl. EX39: Hart 3J 27
Jefford Ho. EX4: Exe 3D 64
Jeffs Way EX13: Axmin 3J 89
Jellicoe Rd. PL5: Plym 2K 135
  TQ1: Torq 1J 109
Jellicoe Vs. TQ9: Tot 6D 102
Jenker's Hill EX33: Geo 6C 14
Jenkins Cl. PL9: Plyms 7H 143
Jennifer Cl. EX2: Exe 2H 71
  EX17: Cred 6G 39
Jennycliff La. PL9: Hooe 7B 142
Jennyscombe Cl. PL9: Plyms 7G 143
Jenwood Rd. EX14: Dunk 7G 47
Jephson Rd. PL4: Plym 1C 142
Jericho DT7: Lym R 4J 91

Jericho St. EX5: Thor 2B 50
Jerrard Cl. EX14: Hon 4F 55
Jerrard Cres. EX14: Hon 4F 55
Jesmond Rd. EX1: Exe 1J 7 (5H 65)
Jessops PL7: Plymp 2A 138
Jesu St. EX11: Ott M 4C 80
Jetsim Cen. 3E 70
Jetstream Way PL6: Plym 5C 132
Jetty Marsh Local Nature Reserve
                          .6F 105
Jetty Marsh Rd. TQ12: New A 6E 104
Jewell Cres. EX32: B'aple 3G 19
JH Taylor Dr. EX39: Nort 5F 21
Jingles La. EX32: B'aple 5F 19
Jinkin Av. PL4: Plym 1J 9 (1A 142)
Joan Spry Cl. EX16: W'ridge 6H 33
Jocelyn Mead EX17: Cred 5G 39
Jocelyn Rd. EX9: Bud S 5C 82
Jockey Hill EX17: Cred 5H 39
Jodel Cl. PL6: Plym 5C 132
John Fowler Holiday Pk. 4J 11
John Gay Cl. EX32: B'aple 5H 19
John Gaynor Homes 4G 9
John Gay Rd. EX32: B'aple 5G 19
John Greenway Cl. EX16: Tive 4D 40
            (off Gold St.)
John Hannam Ho. EX1: Exe 3G 7
John Howe Cl. EX38: G Tor 2C 30
John Hudson Way EX8: Exmth 5G 77
John Levers Way
  EX4: Exe 4A 6 (7C 64)
John Nash Dr. EX7: Daw 5F 97
John Penrose Rd. EX31: Rou 7A 18
John's Av. TQ2: Torq 5B 112
John Smale Rd. EX31: B'aple 5B 18
Johnson Cl. PL20: Bere A 2B 128
Johns Ter. EX16: Tive 4B 40
Johnstone Dr. EX16: Tive 3B 40
Johnston Ter. Ope PL2: Plym 5D 134
John St. EX1: Exe 5D 6 (7E 64)
  EX16: Tive 4B 40
Johns Way EX16: Tive 3C 40
Jones's Hill EX33: Croy 2C 14
Jonida Cl. TQ1: Torq 6C 112
Jordan DT7: Lym R 5K 91
Jordan Cl. EX32: B'aple 6H 19
Jordan Dr. TQ14: Teignm 3F 107
Jordan La. PL20: Horr 2E 126
Jordan Mdw. TQ13: Ashb 3J 99
Jordan Orchard TQ11: B'leigh 4B 98
           (off Jordan St.)
Jordan St. TQ11: B'leigh 4B 98
Jordons Brook TQ9: Tot 5A 102
Joseph Lock Way
  EX17: Cred 7K 39
Joslin Ct. TQ12: Kingst 3G 105
Joslin Rd. EX14: Hon 5D 54
Joy St. EX31: B'aple 4E 18
Jubilee Cl. EX6: Exmin 2D 74
  EX20: Oke 3B 48
  EX34: Ilfra 2H 11
  EX38: G Tor 1D 30
  PL21: Ivy 3K 145
  TQ1: Torq 1D 116
  TQ6: Dartm 6C 124
  TQ12: New A 2K 107
Jubilee Cotts. PL6: Plym 3C 136
          (off Church Hill)
Jubilee Ct. EX4: Exe 3C 6
  EX35: Lynt 2G 13
Jubilee Dr. EX8: Exmth 1E 76
  EX15: Hemy 2G 47
Jubilee Gdns. EX10: Sidm 2D 84
  EX15: Cull 5H 45
  EX36: N Mol 2C 26
Jubilee Gro. EX8: Lymp 6H 75
Jubilee Lodge EX12: Seat 5F 87
        (off The Underfleet)
Jubilee Path EX22: Hols 1C 34
Jubilee Pl. EX16: Tive 5C 40
         (off Orchard Leigh)
  PL3: Plym 7D 136
          (off Huntley Pl.)
Jubilee Rd. EX1: Heav 1K 7 (5H 65)
  EX5: Bradn 2C 52
  EX39: App 2G 21
  PL5: Plym 7E 130
  TQ7: Malb 6H 155
  TQ9: Tot 5G 103
  TQ12: New A 1E 108
Jubilee Sq. EX3: Top 6B 74
  EX39: Bide 3F 23
Jubilee St. TQ7: Ave G 6H 151
Jubilee Ter. EX17: Cop 6D 38
  PL4: Plym 2C 142
         (off Brentor Rd.)
  PL21: Bitta 4B 146
  TQ3: Paig 1G 119
Julian Rd. PL21: Ivy 4F 145
Julian St. PL4: Plym 6K 9 (3B 142)
Julian Wlk. PL6: Plym 4F 133
Julius Ho. EX4: Exe 2D 6
Jump Cl. PL6: Robo 1D 132
Junction Gdns. PL4: Plym 2B 142
Junction Rd. EX17: Bow 5J 37
Jungleland 6H 19 (3B 160)

Juniper Cl. EX4: Whip 2A 66
EX14: Hon 5D 54
EX16: Tive 2F 41
Juniper Ct. EX31: Rou 6B 18
Juniper Way PL7: Plymp 4E 138
Junket St. EX37: High B 3B 32
Jupes Cl. EX31: B'aple 3D 74
Juries La. EX38: G Tor 1C 30
Jury Pk. EX36: S Mol 6B 26
Jurys Cnr. Cl. TQ12: Kingsk 1G 111
Jutland Way EX2: Cou W 4C 72

K

Kabale Cl. EX16: Tive 2A 40
Kala Fair EX39: W Ho 5D 20
Kalendarhay La.
    EX1: Exe 4D 6 (6E 64)
Karageen Cvn. & Camping Pk. . .4J 155
Karen Cl. EX39: Bide 4J 23
Katherines La. EX11: Ott M 3D 80
Kathleaven St. TQ5: Plym 2C 134
Kay Cl. EX8: Exmth 4E 76
    PL7: Plymp 2C 138
Keals Cft. EX35: Lynt 2G 13
KEASON 3B 168
Keatings La. TQ14: Teignm 4G 107
Keaton La. PL21: Erm, Ivy 6H 145
Keaton Rd. PL21: Ivy 5G 145
    TQ14: Teignm 2F 107
Keats Cl. EX8: Exmth 7K 75
    TQ14: Teignm 2F 107
Keat St. PL2: Dev 7D 134
Kedlestone Av. PL5: Plym 7F 131
Keegan Cl. EX11: Ott M 4A 80
The Keep Gdns. TQ6: Dartm 6E 124
Keep La.
    TQ6: Dartm 1A 124 (5E 124)
KELLACOTT 2C 169
Kelland Cl. TQ3: Paig 1F 119
Kelland Hill EX17: Lap 4J 37
Kellands La. EX20: Oke 2D 48
KELLATON 3A 176
Kellett Cl. TQ13: Ashb 3J 99
Kellock Dr. TQ9: Tot 6D 102
KELLY 2B 168
KELLY BRAY 3B 168
Kelly Cl. PL5: Plym 4B 134
    TQ1: Torq 4E 116
Kelly Cross TQ13: Lust 5K 63
Kelvin Av. PL4: Plym 1K 9 (1B 142)
Kelvin Ct. TQ1: Torq 4E 112
    TQ5: Brixh 3F 123
Kemmings Cl. TQ4: Paig 6F 119
Kempe Cl. PL2: Plym 5E 134
Kempley Rd. EX20: Oke 3B 48
Kemp M. TQ13: Ashb 4H 99
    (off Bull Ring)
Kemps Fld. EX5: Cran 3B 68
Kemp's La. EX12: Axmth 3H 87
Kempton Ter. PL11: Torp 1A 140
Kemyell Pl. PL2: Dev 7D 134
Kenandy EX10: Sidm 7B 84
Kenbury Cres. EX6: Cockw 3E 96
Kenbury Dr. EX2: Alph 5F 71
Kendall Cl. EX4: Exe 1H 7 (5G 65)
Kendall Gro. TQ13: Bov T 4E 92
Kendal Pl. PL5: Plym 6K 131
Kendlewood Cl. TQ4: Paig 4F 119
Kenilworth TQ1: Torq 3F 117
Kenilworth Rd. PL2: Plym 4G 135
Kenley Gdns. PL5: Plym 6E 130
Kenmare Dr. PL7: Plymp 4E 138
KENN 3H 95 (2D 171)
Kennaway Rd. EX11: Ott M 3D 80
Kenn Cl. PL5: Plym 7G 131
Kennedy Way EX14: Dunk 6H 47
    EX16: Tive 3C 40
Kennel Hill PL7: Plymp 5A 138
Kennel Hill Cl. PL7: Plymp 7K 137
Kennel La. EX33: Geo 5C 14
    PL21: Ivy 4E 144
The Kennels PL21: Ivy 3F 145
Kennels Rd. TQ5: Chur F 5J 121
KENNERLEIGH 3C 165
Kennerley Av. EX4: Whip 4A 66
Kennet Cl. PL3: Plym 5C 136
Kenneth Cl. TQ2: Torq 5J 111
Kenneth Ter. TQ2: Torq 5J 111
    (off Kenneth Ct.)
KENNFORD 1H 95 (2D 171)
Kennford Rd. EX2: Mar B 2E 70
Kennford Intl. Holiday Pk. 2G 95
Kensey Cl. TQ1: Torq 7G 113
Kensham Av. EX5: Bradn 2D 52
Kensham Cl. EX5: Bradn 2C 52
Kensington Cl. EX31: B'aple 7B 18
Kensington Pl. PL4: Plym 7A 136
Kensington Rd.
    PL4: Plym 1H 9 (7A 136)
Kenson Hill EX5: Silv 4G 51
Kent Cl. EX2: Won 1K 71
KENTISBEARE 6B 46 (3A 166)
KENTISBURY 2C 161
KENTISBURY FORD 2C 161
KENTON 6H 95 (2D 171)
Kenton Brook Ct. TQ2: Torq 5H 111
Kenton Hill EX6: Kenton 6J 95

Kenton M. EX6: Kenton 6H 95
    (off Fore St.)
Kenton Pl. EX2: Mar B 3F 71
Kent Rd. PL2: Plym 6E 134
Kent's Cavern 1G 117 (1B 176)
Kent's Cavern Visitor Cen. 1G 117
Kents Cl. EX15: Uff 6H 43
Kent's La. TQ1: Torq 1G 117
Kent's Rd. TQ1: Torq 1G 117
Kenwith Dr. TQ7: Kingsb 4G 157
Kenwith Rd. EX39: Bide 1E 22
Kenwith Ter. EX39: Bide 2E 22
Kenwith Valley Nature Reserve
    . . . . .2E 22 (1C 163)
Kenwith Vw. EX39: Bide 3C 22
Kenwyn Rd. TQ1: Torq 7E 112
Keppel Pl. PL2: Dev 7E 134
Keppel St. PL2: Dev 7E 134
Keppel Ter. PL2: Dev 7E 134
    (off Keppel St.)
Kernou Rd. TQ4: Paig 1J 119
Kernow Ga. PL5: Plym 1B 134
Kerria Cl. TQ3: Paig 6E 114
Kerries Rd. TQ10: S Bre 2C 100
Kerrisdale Ct. EX14: Hon 3F 55
Kerse La. TQ7: Thur 5D 154
Kerslake's Cl. EX14: Hon 3F 55
Ker St. PL1: Dev 3D 140
Ker St. Ope PL1: Dev 2D 140
KERSWELL 3A 166
Kerswell Cl. PL21: Ivy 5J 145
Kerswell La. TQ12: Coff 7K 109
Kerswill Rd. EX4: Exe 1C 70
Kestell Rd. EX10: Sidm 6D 84
Kes Tor Cl. EX20: Oke 3D 48
Kestor Cl. PL2: Plym 4F 135
Kestor Dr. EX4: Exe 4B 64
    TQ3: Pres 5G 115
Kestral Pk. PL5: Plym 2F 135
Kestrel Bus. Pk. EX2: Sow 7E 66
Kestrel Cl. EX16: Tive 2E 40
    EX20: Oke 2B 48
Kestrel Ct. TQ1: Torq 5E 112
Kestrel Pk. PL19: Whit 7K 59
Kestrel Way EX2: Sow 7D 66
    EX7: Daw 7C 96
    EX32: B'aple 5K 19
    PL6: Plym 2E 132
Keswick Cres. PL6: Plym 1E 136
Keverel Rd. EX8: Exmth 3C 76
Keyberry Cl. TQ12: New A 3G 109
Keyberry Mill TQ12: New A 3G 109
Keyberry Pk. TQ12: New A 3G 109
Keyberry Rd. TQ12: New A 3G 109
Keyes Cl. PL1: Dev 2E 140
KEYHAM 5D 134
Keyham Rd. PL2: Dev 6D 134
Keyham St. PL5: Plym 3D 134
Keysfield Rd. TQ4: Paig 2J 119
Khartoum Pl. TQ7: Kingsb 4F 157
Kiln Orchard TQ12: New A 1C 108
Kiddicott EX17: Cred 6G 39
    (off Buller Rd.)
Kidwelly Cl. PL7: Plymp 5F 139
Kiel Pl. PL3: Plym 6E 136
Kiel Pl. La. PL3: Plym 6E 136
Kilbarran Ri. EX4: Exe 4D 64
Kilgannon Gdns. EX1: W Cly 1E 66
Kilkhampton 2A 162
Killerton 3D 165
Killerton Cl. TQ3: Paig 7H 115
Killerton La. PL9: Plyms 3E 142
Killerton Wlk. EX6: Exmin 1B 74
    (off Devington Pk.)
Killington Lane Station (Rail) 2C 161
Kilmar St. PL9: Plyms 3E 142
KILMINGTON 2B 88 (1C 173)
Kilmorie St. TQ1: Torq 3H 117
Kilmorie Cl. TQ1: Torq 3H 117
Kilmorie Hall EX4: Exe 4F 65
Kiln Cl. EX39: Ins 2K 21
    PL5: Plym 3B 134
    TQ13: Bov T 6B 92
Kiln Cl. La. EX39: Ins 2K 21
Kiln Cnr. EX1: Pin 4F 67
Kilnford Rd. TQ12: Kingst 4J 105
Kiln Forehead La. TQ12: Kingst 4J 105
Kiln Ho. TQ7: Kingsb 5G 157
Kiln La. EX12: Brans 6F 85
    EX32: B'aple 5F 19
    EX34: C Mar 7D 12
    TQ7: Stoke 6J 159
Kiln Rd. TQ3: Marl 3C 114
    TQ5: Galm 4G 121
    TQ13: Bov T 6B 92
Kilnwood Pk. EX31: Rou 6K 17
Kilworthy Hill PL19: Tavi 3J 59
Kilworthy Pk. PL19: Tavi 3J 59
Kilworthy Rd. PL19: Tavi 1J 59
Kimberley Pk. EX39: Nort 5F 21

Kimberley Rd. EX2: Exe 6F 7 (7F 65)
Kimberley Ter. EX39: Nort 4F 21
Kimberly Dr. PL6: Plym 2C 136
Kinevor Cl. EX34: Mort 3A 10
King Alfred Cres. EX4: Exe 6F 21
King Alfred Way EX10: New P 5G 81
King Arthur's Rd. EX4: Whip 2J 65
King Av. EX2: Cou W 5B 72
King Charles Bus. Pk.
    TQ12: H'fld 7E 92
King Charles Way EX10: Sidm 2C 84
Kingcome Ct. TQ11: B'leigh 4D 98
Kingdom M. EX4: Exe 2A 6 (5D 64)
Kingdom St. PL1: Plym 7B 8 (4H 141)
Kingdon Av. EX36: S Mol 5B 26
Kingdon Ent. Pk. EX39: Bide 5B 22
Kingdons Ct. EX36: S Mol 5D 26
Kingdon Way EX22: Hols 1B 34
King Edward Rd. EX13: Axmin 3H 89
    (Victoria Pl.)
    EX13: Axmin 4G 89
    (Widepost La.)
King Edward St. EX4: Exe 3D 64
    EX32: B'aple 3E 18
King Edward Studios EX4: Exe 3D 64
King Edwards Vw. EX16: Tive 4D 40
    (off Maple Gro.)
The Kingfisher EX1: Exe 2H 7
Kingfisher Av. EX2: Exe 1A 70
Kingfisher Cl. PL6: Plym 4F 133
    PL19: Whit 7J 59
    TQ2: Torq 3K 111
Kingfisher Ct. EX4: Pin 3C 66
Kingfisher Dr. EX4: Exe 2G 65
    EX20: Oke 2A 48
    EX32: B'aple 5K 19
Kingfisher Gallery & Watermill 3H 85
Kingfisher Way EX2: Sow 7D 66
    PL9: Plyms 5D 142
    TQ12: Kingst 3F 105
King Gdns. PL1: Plym 3C 8
King Henrys Rd. EX2: Exe 2H 71
King Point Marina 6A 8 (3G 141)
Kingsacre EX33: Brau 3A 16
Kingsale Rd. TQ8: Salc 4B 158
KINGSAND 2A 174
Kings Arms Pas. TQ7: Kingsb 4F 157
    (off Fore St.)
King's Ash Rd. TQ3: Paig 5E 114
Kings Av. EX11: Ott M 3F 80
    TQ3: Paig 7J 115
KINGSBRIDGE 4F 157 (3D 175)
Kingsbridge Bus Station 4F 157
Kingsbridge Cookworthy Mus.
    . . . . .3F 157 (3D 175)
Kingsbridge Hill TQ9: Tot 7E 102
Kingsbridge Information Centre
    . . . . .4G 157 (3D 175)
Kingsbridge La. TQ13: Ashb 4H 99
Kingsbridge La. M. TQ13: Ashb 4G 99
    (off Kingsbridge La.)
KINGSBURY EPISCOPI 1D 167
Kings Cinema 4F 157
King's Cl. EX32: B'aple 7H 19
Kings Cl. PL6: Plym 4F 133
Kings Coombe Dr.
    TQ12: Kingst 2H 105
KINGSCOTT 2D 163
Kings Cotts. TQ12: New A 1F 109
Kings Ct. EX12: Seat 5F 87
    EX14: Hon 3F 55
    (off King St.)
    EX14: Hon 3F 55
    (off New St.)
    PL1: Dev 1F 141
    TQ12: Kingsk 1F 111
    TQ12: Kingst 5H 105
King's Cres. EX16: Tive 4E 40
Kingsdale Ct. TQ2: Torq 2D 116
KINGSDON 5E 88
Kingsdon Hill EX24: Colyt 5E 88
Kingsdown Cl. EX7: Daw 3H 97
    TQ14: Teignm 4F 107
Kingsdown Cres. EX7: Daw 3H 97
Kingsdown Rd. TQ14: Teignm 4F 107
King's Dr. TQ5: Brixh 4F 123
The King's Dr. TQ2: Torq 2B 116
Kings Dwellings EX1: Exe 5D 6
    (off King St.)
Kings Farm La. EX19: Wink 2C 36
Kings Gdns. EX14: Hon 3F 55
    (off Kerslakes Ct.)
Kingsgate EX4: Exe 4F 65
Kingsgate Bus. Cen. EX14: Hon 5D 54
Kingsgate Cl. TQ2: Torq 1D 112
KINGSHEANTON 3B 160
Kingsholme EX24: Colyf 1G 87
Kingshurst Dr. TQ3: Paig 6H 115
KINGSKERSWELL 1F 111 (1A 176)
Kingskerswell By-Pass
    TQ12: Kingsk 7H 109
Kingskerswell Rd. TQ2: Torq 2A 112
    TQ12: Kingsk 1A 112
    TQ12: New A 3G 109
Kingslake Ct. EX8: Exmth 4C 76
Kingslake Ri. EX8: Exmth 4C 76
Kingsland Dr. TQ4: Paig 3E 118
Kingsland Gdn. Cl. PL3: Plym 5K 135

Kings La. EX10: Sidm 7C 84
Kingsleigh Mnr. TQ1: Torq 1E 116
    (off Lwr. Warberry Rd.)
Kingsley Av. EX4: Whip 4A 66
    EX32: B'aple 3E 18
    EX34: Ilfra 5H 11
    (not continuous)
    EX39: App 3H 21
    PL11: Torp 2A 140
    TQ2: Torq 2B 112
Kingsley Cl. PL21: L Mill 5C 144
Kingsley Cl. EX39: W Ho 6B 20
    TQ2: Torq 2B 112
    (off Kingsley Rd.)
Kingsley Mus. 5H 27
Kingsley Pk. EX39: W Ho 5D 20
Kingsley Rd. EX39: Bide 1E 22
    EX39: W Ho 6B 20
    PL4: Plym 7K 135
    TQ7: Kingsb 5F 157
Kingsley Sq. TQ2: Torq 2B 112
Kingsley St. EX39: Bide 3F 23
Kingsley Ter. EX34: C Mar 6B 12
    (off High St.)
    EX39: Bide 4F 23
King's Mkt. TQ7: Kingsb 4F 157
Kingsmead Dr. EX38: G Tor 1D 30
Kings Mdw. TQ12: Kingsk 1F 111
Kings Mdw. Dr. EX19: Wink 2C 36
Kings Mdw. EX14: Hon 4E 54
Kingsmill Ind. Est. EX15: Cull 2K 45
Kings Mill Rd. EX15: Cull 3J 45
KING'S NYMPTON 2A 164
King's Nympton Station (Rail) 2A 164
Kings Orchard TQ9: Tot 6G 103
Kings Pk. EX18: Chul 6C 32
Kings Quay
    TQ6: Dartm 1B 124 (5F 125)
King's Rd. EX4: Exe 1K 7 (4H 65)
    EX14: Hon 3G 55
Kings Rd. EX32: B'aple 3G 19
    PL1: Dev 2E 140
    PL5: Plym 7E 130
    TQ3: Paig 7J 115
Kings Row EX14: Hon 4F 55
Kings Rydon Cl. TQ9: Sto G 3B 120
KING'S TAMERTON 2E 134
King's Tamerton Rd.
    PL5: Plym 1D 134
KINGSTEIGNTON 4H 105 (3C 171)
Kingsteignton Retail Pk. 5G 105
Kingsteignton Rd. TQ12: New A 1F 109
    TQ13: Chud, Chud K 7C 94
Kingsteignton Swimming Pool 2G 105
King Stephen Cl. EX4: Exe 1E 6 (5F 65)
King's Ter. EX14: Hon 3F 55
KINGSTON 3C 175
Kingston Av. EX34: C Mar 6B 12
Kingston Cl. PL7: Plymp 4D 138
    TQ12: Kingsk 7K 109
Kingston Dr. PL7: Plymp 3D 138
KINGSTONE 2D 167
Kingston La. TQ6: Dartm 6D 124
Kingston Rd. EX8: Exmth 5E 76
KINGSTON ST MARY 1C 167
Kingston Tor PL20: Walk 2J 127
King St. EX1: Exe 5D 6 (7E 64)
    EX5: Silv 1G 51
    EX7: Daw 4G 97
    EX8: Exmth 6C 76
    EX14: Hon 4E 54
    EX16: Tive 4C 40
    EX24: Colyt 5C 88
    EX34: C Mar 5B 12
    EX36: S Mol 6C 26
    EX39: Bide 3F 23
    PL1: Plym 4A 8 (2G 141)
    PL11: Torp 1B 140
    PL19: Tavi 3H 59
    TQ5: Brixh 3F 123
    TQ12: New A 1F 109
King St. Bus. Cen. EX1: Exe 5D 6
King's Wlk. EX7: Daw 5H 97
Kingswater Ct. TQ5: Brixh 3E 122
Kings Way TQ7: Kingsb 5F 157
KINGSWEAR 6G 125 (2A 176)
Kingswear Cres. PL6: Plym 2C 136
Kingswear Rd. TQ5: Brixh, Hill 6J 123
Kingswear Station
    Dartmouth Steam Railway
    . . . . .6G 125 (2A 176)
King's Wharf EX2: Exe 6E 6
Kingswood Cl. EX4: Exe 4B 64
Kingswood Cl. TQ4: Paig 2J 119
    (off Cleveland Rd.)
Kingswood Ho. EX34: Ilfra 3G 11

Kingswood Mdw.—Larkstone La.

Kingswood Mdw. EX22: Hols 1D 34
Kingswood Pk. Av. PL3: Plym 5J 135
King William St.
EX4: Exe 2F 7 (6F 65)
Kiniver Ct. TQ14: Teignm 2J 107
Kinlacey Ct. TQ1: Torq 2E 116
Kinnaird Cres. PL6: Plym 3K 131
Kinnerton Ct. EX4: Exe 4C 64
Kinnerton Way EX4: Exe 4A 64
Kinross Av. PL4: Plym 1K 9 (7B 136)
Kinsale Rd. PL5: Plym 7E 130
Kinterbury Rd. PL5: Plym 3A 134
Kinterbury St.
PL1: Plym 5F 9 (3K 141)
Kinterbury Ter. PL5: Plym 3A 134
Kintyre Cl. TQ2: Torq 3A 112
Kinver Cl. PL6: Plym 6E 132
Kipling Cl. EX8: Exmth 1E 76
Kipling Ct. EX39: W Ho 6C 20
Kipling Dr. EX2: Won 1J 71
Kipling Gdns. PL5: Plym 1J 135
Kipling Ter. EX39: W Ho 6B 20
Kipling Tors 6A 20
Kirby Cl. EX13: Axmin 4H 89
Kirkby Pl. PL4: Plym 2E 8 (1J 141)
Kirkby Ter. PL4: Plym 2E 8
Kirkdale Gdns. PL2: Plym 4G 135
Kirkella Rd. PL20: Yelv 6G 127
Kirkham Ct. *TQ3: Paig 1G 119*
(off Colley End Rd.)
Kirkham St. TQ3: Paig 1H 119
Kirkland Cl. PL6: Plym 3D 132
Kirkstall Cl. PL2: Plym 4E 134
Kirkstead Cl. TQ2: Torq 5A 112
Kirkwall Rd. PL5: Plym 7K 131
(not continuous)
Kirton Dr. EX17: Cred 7J 39
Kirton Pl. PL3: Plym 6C 136
Kirtons Rd. TQ12: S'head 1H 113
Kistor Gdns. *TQ9: Tot 5E 102*
(off Castle St.)
Kit Hill Cres. PL5: Plym 3B 134
Kitley Vw. PL8: Brixt 2J 149
Kitley Wlk. *PL8: Y'ton 2A 150*
(off Tappers La.)
Kitley Way PL5: Plym 2D 134
Kits Cl. TQ13: Chud 2D 94
Kitter Dr. PL9: Plyms 7G 143
Kittersley Dr. TQ12: Live 4G 93
KITTISFORD 1A 166
Kittiwake Dr. TQ2: Torq 2J 111
Kitts La. EX10: N'town 6J 81
Kitwell St. EX15: Uff 6H 43
Kivell Cl. EX22: Hols 1B 34
Klondyke Rd. EX20: Oke 5C 48
Knackersknowle La. EX17: Morc 2C 38
Knap Down La. EX34: C Mar 5D 12
KNAPP 1D 167
Knapp Hill EX10: Sidm 5B 84
Knapp Pk. Rd. TQ4: Good 5J 119
Knapps Cl. PL9: Elb 6K 143
Knapp's La. EX10: Harp 4J 81
Knebworth Ct. TQ1: Torq 4E 112
Kneele Gdns. PL3: Plym 3K 135
Kneller Cl. EX34: Ilfra 4J 11
Knick Knack La. TQ5: Brixh 5E 122
KNIGHTACOTT 3C 161
Knighthayes Wlk. EX6: Exmin 2B 74
Knightley Rd. EX2: Exe 2H 71
KNIGHTON 5C 148 (3B 174)
Knighton Hill PL9: Wem 5D 148
Knighton Hill Bus. Cen.
PL9: Wem 5D 148
Knighton Rd. PL4: Plym 4J 9 (2A 142)
PL9: Wem 5C 148
Knightons Units PL20: Buck M 5B 126
Knighton Ter. PL20: Horr 1E 126
Knights Ct. EX20: Hath 2H 35
Knights Cres. EX2: Sow 2C 72
Knights Fld. Ri. EX39: Nort 4F 21
Knightshayes 2D 165
Knights Mead TQ13: Chud K 6B 94
Knights Pl. EX4: Whip 3J 65
Knightstone EX11: Ott M 6E 80
Knightstone La. EX11: Ott M 6E 80
Knightstone Rd. EX11: Ott M 6D 80
Knightswood EX15: Cull 6G 45
The Knoll PL7: Plymp 5J 137
Knowland Cl. PL1: Dev 2E 140
KNOWLE
EX9 ....5A 82 (2A 172)
EX17 ....3B 164
EX33 ....1K 15 (3A 160)
The Knowle TQ12: Kingst 5J 105
Knowle Av. PL2: Plym 5D 134
Knowle Bus. Units EX2: Mar B 4G 71
Knowle Cl. EX15: Cull 4F 45
EX32: Land 2B 24
TQ13: Ashb 5F 99
Knowle Cross La. EX5: Whim 5G 53
Knowle Dr. EX4: Exe 5B 64
EX10: Sidm 6A 84
Knowle Gdns. EX10: Sidm 6A 84
EX34: C Mar 7C 12
TQ7: Kingsb 3F 157
Knowle Hill EX9: Know 2K 77
Knowle Ho. Cl. TQ7: Kingsb 3G 157
Knowle M. EX9: Know 4A 82
Knowle Rd. EX9: Bud S, Know 5A 82
TQ8: Salc 3C 158
TQ13: Lust 6J 63
KNOWLE ST GILES 2D 167
Knowles Cl. EX14: Hon 3F 55
Knowles Dr. EX24: Colyt 7D 88
KNOWLES HILL 7E 104
Knowles Hill Rd. TQ12: New A 7E 104
Knowle Ter. PL20: Walk 2J 127
Knowle Vw. EX20: Oke 2D 48
Knowle Village EX9: Know 6A 82
Knowle Wlk. PL2: Plym 5E 134
KNOWSTONE 1C 165
Kola Dr. EX4: Pin 3C 66
Kynock Ind. Est. EX39: Bide 5G 23

L

Labatt Cl. PL6: Plym 7E 132
Laburnum PL19: Tavi 3J 59
Laburnum Cl. EX8: Exmth 1F 77
EX14: Hon 5C 54
Laburnum Ct. TQ12: A'well 6E 108
Laburnum Dr. EX32: B'aple 6K 19
PL9: Wem 6B 148
Laburnum Gro. *PL6: Plym 5E 132*
(off Beech Ct.)
TQ9: Darti 4C 102
Laburnum Rd. EX2: Won 2J 71
TQ12: New A 3H 109
Laburnum Row TQ2: Torq 7B 112
Laburnum St. TQ2: Torq 1B 116
Laburnum Ter. TQ12: A'well 5E 108
Laburnum Way EX20: Oke 3C 48
TQ9: E All 6D 152
Lace Wlk. EX14: Hon 3F 55
Lackaborough Ct. EX2: Alph 5D 70
Lacy Rd. TQ3: Pres 5G 115
Ladder La. EX34: C Mar 7D 12
Ladies Mile EX7: Daw 3K 97
Ladies' Mile EX32: B'aple 7F 19
LADRAM BAY 6K 83
Ladram Bay Holiday Cen. 5K 83
Ladram Rd. EX9: Ott'n 6J 83
LADYCROSS 2B 168
Lady Fern Rd. PL6: Robo 1D 132
Ladymead EX10: Sidm 2A 84
Lady Pk. Rd. TQ2: Torq 3K 115
Ladysmead 3C 40
Lady's Mile Holiday Pk. 1K 97
Ladysmith Ct. PL4: Plym 1K 9 (1B 142)
Ladysmith La. EX1: Heav 6J 65
Ladysmith Rd. EX1: Heav 2K 7 (5J 65)
PL4: Plym 1K 9 (1B 142)
Lady's Wood Nature Reserve 2C 175
Ladywell *EX31: B'aple 2E 18*
(off Under Minnow Rd.)
Ladywell Av. PL4: Plym 3G 9
Ladywell La. EX18: Chul 6B 32
Ladywell Mdws. EX18: Chul 6B 32
Ladywell Path EX35: Lynt 2F 13
Ladywell Pl. PL4: Plym 3G 9 (2A 142)
Lafrowda EX4: Exe 4F 65
Lag Hill EX17: Cher F 2J 39
Lagoon Vw. EX31: Yell 7B 16
LAIRA 7D 136
Laira Av. PL3: Plym 7E 136
Laira Bri. Rd. PL4: Plym 2C 142
Laira Gdns. PL3: Plym 7D 136
Laira Pk. Cres. PL4: Plym 7C 136
Laira Pk. Pl. PL4: Plym 7C 136
Laira Pk. Rd. PL4: Plym 7C 136
Laira Pl. PL4: Plym 4K 9 (2B 142)
Laira St. PL4: Plym 4K 9 (2B 142)
Laira Wharf PL4: Plym 3D 142
Laity Wlk. PL6: Plym 4J 131
LAKE
EX31 ....7D 18 (3B 160)
PL20 ....5J 127
Lake Av. TQ14: Teignm 2G 107
Lake Cl. EX14: Hon 4G 55
Lake Ind. Est. EX21: Sheb 6K 29
Lakeland TQ12: A'well 6E 108
Lakelands Cl. EX16: W'ridge 6J 33
Lakelands Dr. EX4: Exe 6C 64
Lake La. EX5: New C 4C 50
PL20: Dous 5H 127
Lakenham Hill EX39: Nort 5D 20
Lakerise EX7: Daw W 7D 96
Lake Rd. PL9: Hooe 6C 142
Lakes Cl. TQ5: Brixh 3C 122
Lakeside EX7: Daw W 7D 96
EX34: Wool 7C 10
PL19: Tavi 3H 59
TQ8: Salc 3C 158
Lakeside Av. EX2: Cou W 5A 72
Lakeside Cl. TQ13: Bov T 7B 92
Lakeside Dr. PL5: Plym 5C 130
Lakes Rd. TQ5: Brixh 4C 122
Lake St.
TQ6: Dartm 1A 124 (6F 125)
Lake Vw. EX17: Cred 5K 39
Lakeview EX7: Daw W 7D 96
Lake Vw. Cl. PL5: Plym 4G 131
Lake Vw. Dr. PL5: Plym 5F 131
Lalebrick Rd. PL9: Hooe 7B 142
Lamacraft Cl. EX7: Daw 2J 97
Lamacraft Dr. EX4: Exe 5K 65
Lamaton Pk. EX36: S Mol 7D 26
The Lamb TQ9: Tot 6D 102
Lamb All. EX1: Exe 4E 6
Lambert Cl. EX7: Daw 2J 97
Lambert Rd. *PL5: Tam F 4G 131*
(off Station Rd.)
Lambert's La. TQ14: Shal 7F 107
Lambhay Hill
PL1: Plym 6F 9 (3K 141)
Lambhay St.
PL1: Plym 7F 9 (4K 141)
Lamb Pk. EX34: Ilfra 4G 11
TQ13: Chag 2H 61
Lamb Pk. Cl. TQ12: Kingst 1H 105
Lambs Cl. TQ7: Thur 5C 154
Lame Johns Fld. EX17: Cred 5J 39
LAMERTON 6C 58 (3C 169)
Lamerton Cl. PL5: Plym 7G 131
LAMERTON GREEN 6B 58
Lamerton Vs. PL19: Lam 6B 58
Lammas La. TQ3: Pres 6F 115
Lamplough Rd. EX8: Exmth 1C 76
LANA
EX22, nr. Ashwater 1B 168
EX22, nr. Holsworthy 3B 162
Lancaster Cl. EX2: Won 7A 66
EX15: Cull 2H 45
Lancaster Ct. EX5: Clyst H 7B 68
Lancaster Dr. TQ4: Paig 5F 119
Lancaster Gdns. PL5: Plym 6J 131
Lancaster Ho. *TQ4: Paig 2J 119*
(off Belle Vue Rd.)
Lancelot Rd. EX4: Whip 2K 65
Landboat Vw. EX17: Cher F 2J 39
Landcombe La. TQ6: Strete 5J 153
LANDCROSS 1C 163
Landhayes Rd. EX4: Exe 7C 64
Landivisiau Wlk. EX39: Bide 3G 23
LANDKEY 2B 24 (3B 160)
LANDKEY NEWLAND 2C 24 (3B 160)
Landkey Rd. EX32: B'aple, Land 6G 19
Landmark Rd. TQ8: Salc 4A 158
Landmark Theatre 2H 11
Land Pk. EX18: Chul 5B 32
LAND PART 5B 84
Landpath TQ7: Thur 5C 154
Landrace Cl. TQ12: E Ogw 4C 108
LANDRAKE 1A 174
Landrake Cl. PL5: Plym 3B 134
Landreath Gdns. PL2: Plym 3J 135
Landscore EX17: Cred 6F 39
Landscore Cl. EX17: Cred 6G 39
TQ14: Teignm 4H 107
Landscore Rd. EX4: Exe 5A 6 (7C 64)
TQ14: Teignm 4G 107
LANDSCOVE 1D 175
Landscove Holiday Pk. 4H 123
Lands Pk. PL9: Plyms 5G 143
Lands Rd. EX4: Pin 3C 66
TQ5: Brixh 2H 123
LANDULPH 1A 174
Landulph Gdns. PL5: Plym 3B 134
Landunvez Pl. EX5: Bradn 3C 52
The Lane PL7: Plymp 3A 138
PL21: Lutt 7F 129
TQ6: Ditt 6C 120
LANEAST 2A 168
La. End EX39: Ins 2K 21
Lane End Cl. EX39: Ins 2K 21
TQ7: Slap 2H 159
Lane End Pk. EX32: B'aple 5J 19
Lane Fld. Rd. EX39: Bide 3C 22
LANE HEAD 3B 60
Lanehead EX12: Beer 7B 86
Lane Head Cl. EX33: Croy 2C 14
Lanehead Rd. EX12: Beer 7B 86
LANGAGE 5F 139
Langage Bus. Pk. PL7: Plymp 4G 139
Langage Energy Cen.
PL7: Plymp 4H 139
Langage Ind. Est. PL7: Plymp 4G 139
Langage Pk. PL7: Plymp 5G 139
Langage Pk. Office Campus
PL7: Plymp 5F 139
Langaller Cl. TQ13: Bov T 6A 92
Langaller La. TQ13: Bov T 7A 92
Langarron Pk. EX32: B'aple 4G 19
Langaton Gdns. EX1: Pin 3E 66
Langaton La. EX1: Pin 3E 66
Langdale Cl. PL6: Plym 2E 136
Langdale Gdns. PL6: Plym 2E 136
LANGDON 1A 168
Langdon Bus. Pk. EX5: Clyst M 3J 73
Langdon Ct. PL9: Elb 6J 143
LANGDON CROSS 2B 168
Langdon Flds. TQ5: Galm 2H 121
Langdon La. EX7: Daw 1F 97
TQ5: Galm 3H 121
Langdon Rd. EX7: Daw 1F 97
EX22: Bradw 5B 28
TQ3: Pres 5J 115
Langdon Vw. PL9: Wem 5D 148
Langdon Way EX5: Clyst M 2G 73
Langerwehe Way EX8: Exmth 6B 76
LANGFORD
EX15 ....3A 166
TA2 ....1C 167
Langford Av. EX14: Hon 3G 55
LANGFORD BUDVILLE 1B 166
Langford Cres. TQ2: Torq 2B 112
Langford Rd. EX14: Hon 2G 55
(not continuous)
Lang Gro. PL9: Elb 5J 143
PL19: Tavi 4K 59
Langham Levels PL21: Ivy 3F 145
Langham Pl. PL4: Plym 2B 142
Langham Way PL21: Ivy 4F 145
Langhill Rd. PL3: Plym 6J 135
Langlands Cl. TQ4: Paig 3E 118
Langlands Mdw. PL21: Ivy 5K 145
Langlands Rd. EX15: Cull 4F 45
Langleigh EX34: Ilfra 4G 11
Langleigh La. EX34: Ilfra 4F 11
Langleigh Pk. EX34: Ilfra 4F 11
Langleigh Rd. EX34: Ilfra 3G 11
Langleigh Ter. EX34: Ilfra 3G 11
LANGLEY 1A 166
Langley EX18: Chul 5C 32
Langley Av. TQ5: Brixh 4E 122
Langley Cl. PL6: Plym 3B 132
TQ5: Brixh 4E 122
Langley Cres. PL6: Plym 3A 132
Langley Gdns. EX18: Chul 6C 32
Langley La. EX18: Chul 5C 32
LANGLEY MARSH 1A 166
Langmead EX39: West 7K 21
Langmead Cl. PL6: Plym 3D 136
Langmead Rd. PL6: Plym 3D 136
Langmoor Cl. *DT7: Lym R 5J 91*
(off Pound St.)
Langmore Cl. PL6: Plym 3B 136
LANGORE 2A 168
LANGPORT 1D 167
LANGRIDGEFORD 1D 163
Langridge Rd. TQ3: Paig 6E 114
Langs Fld. EX33: Croy 3B 14
Langs Rd. TQ3: Pres 6J 115
Langstone Cl. TQ1: Torq 6F 113
TQ12: H'fld 2J 93
Langstone Dr. EX8: Exmth 2E 76
Langstone Rd. PL2: Plym 4H 135
Langstone Ter. PL2: Plym 4H 135
Langton Rd. PL20: Yelv 5F 127
LANGTREE 2C 163
Lang Way TQ12: Ipp 6J 101
Langwells Ct. TQ9: Blacka 3C 152
Langworthy Orchard EX5: Cran 2D 68
Lanherne EX7: Daw 4H 97
Lanhydrock Cl. TQ3: Paig 6D 114
Lanhydrock Rd.
PL4: Plym 3J 9 (2A 142)
(not continuous)
Lansdowne EX2: Won 1A 72
Lansdowne Ct. TQ2: Torq 1B 116
Lansdowne La. TQ2: Torq 7B 112
Lansdowne Pk. EX39: Nort 4E 20
TQ9: Tot 7G 103
Lansdowne Rd. EX9: Know 6A 82
PL6: Plym 1A 136
TQ2: Torq 7B 112
Lansdowne Ter. EX2: Exe 6F 7 (7F 65)
EX39: Bide 4E 22
Lansdown Ter. *EX32: B'aple 3F 19*
(off St George's Rd.)
Lansport La. EX7: Daw 6A 96
Lanteglos Cl. PL21: Bitta 4C 146
Lantern Ct. *EX34: Ilfra 2J 11*
(off Hillsborough Rd.)
Lanveoc Way PL21: Modb 6G 147
Lanyon Ho. PL4: Plym 4G 9
LAPFORD 2K 37 (3B 164)
LAPFORD CROSS 3J 37 (3B 164)
Lapford Mill 3J 37
Lapford Station (Rail) 3J 37 (3B 164)
Lapthorn Cl. PL9: Plyms 5D 142
Lapthorne Ind. Est.
TQ12: Ipp 5K 101
Lapwing Cl. EX7: Daw W 7C 96
EX15: Cull 5F 45
Larch Cl. EX8: Exmth 1F 77
EX12: Seat 2E 86
TQ14: Teignm 1H 107
Larch Dr. PL6: Plym 3F 133
Larch Rd. EX2: Exe 2C 70
Larch Wlk. TQ2: Torq 5J 111
LARKBEARE 7F 7 (1F 71)
Larkbeare Rd. EX2: Exe 7F 7 (1F 71)
Lark Cl. EX4: Exe 3G 65
Larkhall Ri. PL3: Plym 6C 136
Larkham Cl. PL7: Plymp 5K 137
Larkham La. PL7: Plymp 5J 137
Lark Hill PL2: Plym 5F 135
Larkin Cl. TQ13: Bov T 5E 92
Lark Ri. EX10: New P 5G 81
EX31: Rou 7K 17
Larks Cl. TQ14: Shal 7F 107
Larksmead Cl. TQ12: E Ogw 3D 108
Larksmead Way TQ12: E Ogw 3C 108
Larkspur Ct. TQ4: Paig 5E 118
Larkspur Dr. TQ12: New A 6A 104
Larkspur Gdns. EX32: B'aple 5K 19
Larks Ri. EX15: Cull 5F 45
Larkstone Cres. EX34: Ilfra 3K 11
Larkstone Gdns. EX34: Ilfra 3K 11
Larkstone La. EX34: Ilfra 2K 11

Larkstone Ter. EX34: Ilfra 2K 11
Laskeys Heath TQ12: Live 3F 93
Laskeys La. EX10: Sidm 6D 84
Latches Wlk. EX13: Axmin 3H 89
LATCHLEY 3C 169
Latchmount Gdns.
   EX13: Axmin 3H 89
Latham Cl. PL6: Plym 4B 136
Latimer Cl. PL7: Plymp 4E 138
Latimer Rd. EX4: Whip 4K 65
Latimer Wlk. PL6: Plym 3K 131
Lattitude 52 PL1: Dev 1D 140
Lauderdale Dr. EX32: B'aple 5G 19
Lauder La. EX31: Rou 7B 18
LAUNCELLS 3A 162
LAUNCESTON 2B 168
Launceston Cl. PL6: Plym 3C 132
Launceston Rd. EX20: Brid 4G 57
Launchycroft DT7: Uply 3G 91
Laundry La. EX10: Sidf 1D 84
Laura Av. TQ3: Paig 6H 115
Laura Gro. TQ3: Pres 6F 115
Laura Pl. TQ3: Paig 6H 115
            (off Well St.)
Laurel Av. EX39: Bide 4C 22
Laurel Cotts. PL5: Plym 2C 134
        (off Trelawney Pl.)
Laurel Ct. PL2: Plym 4F 135
Laurel Dene PL2: Plym 4F 135
Laurel Dr. PL6: Plym 5F 133
Laurel La. TQ14: Shal 6F 107
Laurel Ri. EX8: Exmth 4F 77
Laurel Rd. EX2: Won 2J 71
   EX14: Hon 5C 54
   PL2: Plym 4F 135
The Laurels EX10: Sidm 5B 84
   EX31: Rou 7A 18
Laureston Rd. TQ12: New A 2F 109
Laurie Av. TQ12: New A 7C 104
Lauriston Cl. TQ2: Torq 1B 116
Lavender Cl. TQ5: Brixh 4C 122
Lavender Rd. EX4: Exe 4B 64
Lavender Way EX32: B'aple 5H 19
        (off Willshere Rd.)
Lavington Cl. PL7: Plymp 4E 138
Lavinia Dr. PL7: Plymp 6K 137
LAWHITTON 2B 168
Law Memorial Ho's. EX32: B Taw . . .1F 25
     (off Bishop's Tawton Rd.)
The Lawn EX9: Bud S 7C 82
   PL19: Tavi 3J 59
Lawn Cl. PL7: Plymp 4F 139
   TQ2: Torq 2B 112
Lawn Dr. TQ13: Chud 2C 94
Lawn Gdns. TQ13: Chud 2C 94
Lawn Hill EX7: Daw 4H 97
Lawn Rd. EX8: Exmth 5C 76
The Lawns EX32: B'aple 7J 19
   PL5: Plym 2K 135
   PL11: Torp 7A 134
Lawns End TQ14: Bi'ton 3A 106
Lawn Ter. EX7: Daw 4H 97
Lawn Vista EX10: Sidm 5C 84
Lawrence Av.
   EX4: Exe 6A 6 (1D 70)
Lawrence Rd. PL9: Hooe 5A 142
Lawrence Wlk. EX6: Exmin 1B 74
Lawson Gro. PL9: Plyms 5D 142
Law Wlk. PL6: Plym 4J 131
Laxton Av. EX1: Heav 6B 66
LAYMORE 3D 167
Layne Cl. EX6: Chri 3J 63
Layne Flds. EX6: Chri 3J 63
Laywell Cl. TQ5: Brixh 6D 122
Laywell La. TQ5: Brixh 5C 122
Laywell Rd. TQ5: Brixh 5C 122
Lazenby Ct. EX4: Exe 4F 65
Lazenby Rd. EX16: Tive 5F 41
The Lea TQ14: Bi'ton, Teignm 3C 106
        (not continuous)
Lea Cliff Pk. EX7: Daw W 7E 96
Lea Combe EX13: Axmin 4H 89
Leacroft Touring Pk. 1A 86
Leadengate Cl. EX33: Croy 3B 14
Leadengate Flds. EX33: Croy 3B 14
Leader Cl. PL3: Plym 3G 123
Leader La. TQ3: Marl 4D 114
Leadstone Camping 1K 97
Leaholes Av. EX20: Oke 3C 48
Lealands TQ13: Bov T 5B 92
Lea La. EX9: Ott'n 6H 83
        (not continuous)
Lea Mt. TQ14: Bi'ton 3C 106
Lea Mt. Cl. EX7: Daw 5H 97
Lea Mt. Dr. EX7: Daw 5G 97
Lea Mt. Rd. EX7: Daw 5H 97
Leander Ct. TQ14: Teignm 5H 107
Leander Way PL5: Plym 1J 135
Lear La. EX13: Axmin 5G 89
Lea Rd. EX9: Ott'n 6H 83
   EX16: Tive 2D 40
   TQ2: Torq 2D 112
Lears La. TQ13: Chud 2D 94
The Leas EX34: Ilfra 5G 11
Leaside EX6: Dunsf 6B 62
Leas Rd. EX9: Bud S 6C 82
LEAT 7C 56
The Leat PL20: Walk 2J 127

Leat Cl. PL20: Dous 4K 127
   TQ12: Kingst 4H 105
Lea Ter. TQ39: App 3H 21
Leatfield Dr. PL6: Plym 5K 131
Leatherby Cl. PL6: Plym 3K 131
Leat Mdw. EX16: Tive 3B 40
   TQ12: Live 4G 93
Leat Rd. EX16: Tive 3B 40
   PL16: Lift 6B 56
Leatside EX1: Exe 6D 6
      (off Commercial Rd.)
   PL6: Robo 1D 132
Leat St. EX16: Tive 4B 40
Leat Ter. TQ12: Kingst 4H 105
Leat Wlk. PL3: Plym 5K 135
   PL6: Robo 1D 132
Leatway Gdns. EX15: Cull 4G 45
Lea Va. Rd. TQ12: New A 1D 108
Leaves Yd. PL3: Plym 5C 136
Lea Vw. EX15: Will 3D 44
Leaze Rd. TQ12: Kingst 3G 105
Lebanon Cl. EX4: Exe 3H 65
Ledgate La. PL7: Plymp, Spa 1J 139
Ledsgrove TQ12: Ipp 6J 101
LEDSTONE .3D 175
LEE
   EX34 .2A 160
   EX36 .1C 165
Leechwell Ct. TQ9: Tot 6E 102
       (off The Lamb)
Leechwell La. TQ9: Tot 6E 102
      (not continuous)
Leechwell St. TQ9: Tot 6E 102
      (not continuous)
Lee Cl. EX14: Hon 3E 54
Lee Ct. TQ5: Brixh 4G 123
Lee La. EX6: Dunsf 7B 62
LEE MILL 5A 144 (2B 174)
Lee Mill Ind. Est. PL21: L Mill 5B 144
LEE MOOR 1J 129 (1B 174)
Lee Moor Viewpoint 1B 174
Lee Pl. EX34: Ilfra 2J 11
        (off Ropery Rd.)
Lee Rd. EX35: Lynt 2G 13
Leeward Cl. EX8: Exmth 6A 76
Leeward La. TQ2: Torq 2A 112
Leeze Pk. EX20: Oke 5B 48
Legion La. PL8: Brixt 2H 149
Legion Way EX2: Alph 4E 70
Legis Wlk. PL6: Robo 2C 132
Leg o Mutton Cnr. PL20: Yelv 6F 127
Leicester Mead EX4: Exe 5B 64
LEIGHAM 2F 137 (2B 174)
Leigham Bus. Units EX2: Mar B 5G 71
Leigham Cl. EX7: Daw 4H 97
Leigham Mnr. Dr. PL6: Plym 4G 137
Leigham St. PL1: Plym 7C 8 (4H 141)
Leigham Ter. TQ7: Kingsb 4F 157
        (off Fore St.)
Leigham Ter. La.
   PL1: Plym 6C 8 (3H 141)
Leigham Ter. La. W.
   PL1: Plym 6C 8 (3H 141)
Leigh Cl. PL21: Bitta 3C 146
Leigh Ct. PL6: Plym 3B 136
Leigh Cross PL21: Bitta 3D 146
Leighdene Cl. EX2: Exe 7J 7 (1H 71)
Leigh La. PL6: Robo 1E 132
   PL21: Bitta 2C 146
Leighon Rd. TQ3: Paig 1J 119
Leigh Rd. EX18: Chul 6A 32
   EX39: Bide 4D 22
Leighton Rd. PL3: Plym 3K 135
Leighton Ter. EX4: Exe 2F 7 (5F 65)
Leigh Vs. EX18: Chul 6B 32
Leland Gro. PL21: Ivy 5H 145
Le Locle Cl. EX10: Sidm 2A 84
Le Marchant Cl. EX14: Dunk 7G 47
Lembury Rd. TQ9: Sto G 6A 118
Le Molay-Littry Way
   TQ13: Bov T 4C 92
Lemon Cl. TQ12: New A 1F 109
        (off Marsh Rd.)
Lemon M. TQ12: New A 1F 109
       (off The Avenue)
Lemon Pl. TQ12: New A 1F 109
Lemon Rd. TQ12: New A 1F 109
Lenards Rd. EX39: Nort 6E 20
Lendon Way EX19: Wink 3C 36
Lennard Rd. EX17: Cred 6H 39
Lennox Av. EX10: Sidm 6C 84
Lentney Cl. PL9: Hey B 3B 148
Lenwood Pk. EX39: Bide 1D 22
Lenwood Rd. EX39: Bide, Nort 1D 22
        (not continuous)
Leofric Rd. EX16: Tive 2D 40
LEONARD MOOR 3E 42
Leonard's Cl. TQ7: Thur 6C 154
Leonards Cove Holiday Pk. 3H 153
Leonards Rd. PL21: Ivy 4H 145
Leper's Well .5K 91
        (off Mill La.)
Leslie Rd. EX8: Exmth 4C 76
Lester Cl. PL3: Plym 5C 136
Lester Point EX34: C Mar 5A 12
Lestock Cl. EX8: Lit 5G 77
Lethaby Rd. EX32: B'aple 3F 19

Lethbridge Ct. TQ12: New A 1F 109
      (off Courtenay Pk. Rd.)
Lethbridge Rd. EX2: Won 7A 66
Letheren's La. EX20: N Taw 5B 36
Let's Go 3C 18
LETTAFORD .2B 170
LEUSDON 3B 170
The Level TQ6: Ditt 6C 120
Lever Cl. EX39: Nort 4E 20
Leverlake Cl. EX16: Tive 2F 41
Leverlake La.
   EX16: Chet, Tive 1F 41
LEWANNICK .2A 168
LEWDOWN 1A 56 (2C 169)
Lewesdon Ct. DT7: Lym R 5J 91
Lewes Gdns. PL5: Plym 6H 131
Lewhaven Cl. EX20: Lew 1A 56
Lewis Av. EX16: Tive 4E 40
Lewis Ct. EX34: Ilfra 3H 11
       (off Victoria Rd.)
Lewis Cres. EX2: Sow 2C 72
Lewis's Pas. EX34: Ilfra 3H 11
       (off Victoria Rd.)
LEWORTHY
   EX22 .3B 162
   EX31 .3C 161
Leworthy Dr. EX1: Pin 1D 66
LEWTHORN CROSS 3B 170
LEWTRENCHARD 2C 56 (2C 169)
LEY 3A 168
Leyburn Gro. TQ4: Paig 3G 119
Ley Cl. TQ12: Live 7G 93
Ley Cres. TQ12: Live 7G 93
Leyfield Wlk. EX7: Daw 3H 97
Leyford Cl. PL9: Wem 6C 148
Ley La. PL20: Bere F 5A 128
   TQ12: Kingst 3G 105
Ley Mdw. Dr. EX31: Rou 6K 17
Leypark Cl. EX1: Whip 5B 66
Leypark Cres. EX1: Whip 6B 66
Leypark Dr. PL6: Plym 1E 136
Leypark Rd. EX1: Whip 5B 66
Leypark Wlk. PL6: Plym 7F 133
Leys Rd. TQ2: Torq 1K 115
LEZANT 3B 168
Libbaton Golf Course 4B 32 (2A 164)
Liberator Way EX14: Dunk 7H 47
Liberty Cl. EX31: Rou 7A 18
Liberty Rd. EX31: Rou 7A 18
Liberty Way EX2: Sow 4C 72
Libra Gdns. EX34: C Mar 5A 12
Lichfield Av. TQ2: Torq 3C 112
Lichfield Cl. TQ5: Brixh 4C 122
Lichfield Dr. TQ5: Brixh 4C 122
Lichfield Rd. EX4: Exe 6A 64
Lichgate Rd. EX2: Alph 5E 70
Lickham Common Nature Reserve
   . . . . .2B 166
Lidburn Hill EX6: Ted M 5G 49
LIDDATON 2C 169
Liddle Way PL7: Plymp 3E 138
Lidford Tor Av. TQ4: Paig 4E 118
Lifeboat Station
   Appledore 2G 21
   Clovelly 5H 27
   Exmouth 7E 76
   Ilfracombe 2J 11
   Lyme Regis 6J 91
   Teignmouth 6H 107
   Torbay 2G 123
Liffey Ri. EX4: Exe 4B 64
LIFTON 6B 56 (2B 168)
LIFTONDOWN 2B 168
Lifton Rd. PL4: Plym 5J 9
Light La. TQ5: Galm 4H 121
Lilac Av. EX16: Tive 4A 40
Lilac Cl. PL9: Hooe 7D 142
Lilac Haven EX14: Hon 4F 55
Lilac Rd. EX2: Won 2J 71
   EX16: Tive 3F 41
Lilac Ter. PL4: Plym 4D 40
       (off Martins La.)
Lilac Way EX32: B'aple 5H 19
Lilford Gdns. PL5: Plym 1F 135
Lilian Cl. EX17: Bow 5G 37
Lillage La. EX9: E Bud 1C 82
LILLESDON 1D 167
Lilley Wlk. EX14: Hon 4G 55
LILLY 4K 19
Lillybrook La. EX6: Ted M 4K 49
Lilly La. EX5: New C 7D 50
Lillybridge EX39: Nort 5F 21
Lily Cl. EX39: Nort 4F 21
Lily Mt. EX4: Exe 4A 64
Lilypond La. EX5: Whim 6J 53
Limberland Av. TQ9: Darti 2A 102
Lime Av. TQ2: Torq 1B 116
Limeburners Rd. PL9: Hooe 6C 142
Lime Cl. EX5: Broadc 6C 52
   EX16: Tive 3E 40
Lime Cres. EX15: Will 4C 44
Lime Gro. EX6: Exmin 1C 74
   EX8: Exmth 1E 76
   EX39: Bide 3E 22
   EX39: Ins 4K 21
   TQ7: Kingsb 4F 157
Limegrove Rd. EX4: Exe 7C 64
Limehayes Rd. EX20: Oke 2C 48
Limekiln Cl. TQ4: Good 7F 119

Lime Kiln La. DT7: Uply 2F 91
   EX2: Cou W 4K 71
Limekiln La. EX8: Exmth 7E 76
   EX31: Ashf 1H 17
Lime Kiln Rd. EX16: Tive 5F 41
Limerick Pl.
   PL4: Plym 4K 9 (2B 142)
Lime Rd. EX16: Tive 3F 41
Limers Hill EX38: G Tor 2A 30
Limer's La. EX36: S Mol 7A 26
Limers La. EX20: Mert 4A 30
   EX39: Nort 7F 21
The Limes PL6: Plym 1A 136
Lime La. PL19: Tavi 3G 59
Lime St. TQ13: More 6H 61
Lime Tree Cl. EX2: Won 2B 72
Lime Tree Gro. TQ33: Brau 4H 15
Lime Tree Mead EX16: Tive 5G 41
Limetree Rd. PL3: Plym 4J 135
Lime Tree Wlk. TQ12: New A 3H 109
Lime Way EX12: Seat 3E 86
Linacre Rd. TQ2: Torq 2B 112
Lincoln Av. PL4: Plym 1K 9 (1B 142)
Lincoln Cl. EX8: Exmth 1G 77
   EX14: Fen 2G 53
Lincoln Grn. TQ2: Torq 4C 112
Lincoln Rd. EX4: Exe 6B 64
Lincombe Dr. TQ1: Torq 2G 117
Lincombe Hill Rd. TQ1: Torq 2G 117
Linda Cl. EX1: Heav 7A 66
Lindemann Cl. EX10: Sidm 2B 84
Linden Cl. EX8: Exmth 2F 77
   EX31: B'aple 6B 18
   EX33: Brau 4J 15
   EX38: G Tor 1B 30
Linden Gdns. EX31: B'aple 6B 18
Linden Rd. EX7: Daw 5F 97
   EX15: Cull 3H 45
Linden Ter. PL4: Plym 2B 142
   TQ12: New A 1D 108
Linden Va. EX4: Exe 1C 6 (5E 64)
Lindfield Cl. TQ2: Torq 5B 112
Lindisfarne Way TQ2: Torq 3A 112
Lindridge Cl. TQ12: Kingst 1G 105
Lindridge Hill TQ12: Kingst 1H 105
Lindridge La. TQ12: Kingst 1G 105
       (not continuous)
Lindridge Rd. TQ1: Torq 5E 112
   TQ14: Bi'ton, Teignm 2A 106
Lindsay Rd. TQ3: Pres 4G 115
Lindthorpe Way TQ5: Brixh 4D 122
Linfield Gdns. EX4: Exe 1C 70
Linhay Bus. Pk. TQ13: Ashb 2K 99
Linhay Cl. EX14: Hon 6E 54
   EX15: Culm 2B 46
   TQ5: Hill 6K 123
Linhay Dr. EX31: Frem 5G 17
   TQ12: Kingst 5J 105
Linhay La. PL9: Plyms 3E 142
Linhey Cl. TQ7: Kingsb 5G 157
Linkadells PL7: Plymp 3A 138
Linkadell Vs. PL7: Plymp 3A 138
Linketty La. PL7: Plymp 6K 137
Linketty La. E. PL6: Plym 2B 136
Linketty La. W. PL3: Plym 4K 135
   PL6: Plym 3A 136
Link Ho. Cl. EX39: W Ho 5B 20
LINKINHORNE 3B 168
Link Rd. EX20: Oke 2C 48
The Links EX39: Nort 5D 20
   TQ1: Torq 4E 112
Links Cl. EX8: Exmth 5E 76
   TQ5: Chur F 2A 122
Links Ct. TQ7: Thur 7C 154
Links Rd. EX9: Bud S 7A 82
Linnet Cl. EX4: Exe 2G 65
Linnet Dene EX15: Cull 5F 45
Linscott Cres. EX31: Yell 7B 16
Linseed Dr. EX13: Axmin 4J 89
Linton Cl. PL5: Tam F 2H 131
Linton Rd. EX1: Sow 6C 66
   PL5: Tam F 2H 131
Linton Sq. PL5: Tam F 2H 131
Linton Wlk. PL5: Tam F 2H 131
Lion Cl. TQ7: Kingsb 4F 157
Lion's Cl. Hill EX24: Colyt 4C 88
Lions Mill EX31: Cher 2D 18
Lippell Dr. PL9: Plyms 6E 142
LIPSON 1J 9 (7B 136)
Lipson Av. PL4: Plym 2K 9 (1B 142)
Lipson Ct. PL4: Plym 2H 9 (2A 142)
Lipson Hill PL4: Plym 1K 9 (7B 142)
Lipson Rd. PL4: Plym 4G 9 (2K 141)
       (Beaumont Pl.)
   PL4: Plym 1K 9 (7B 136)
       (Mostyn Av.)
Lipson Sports Cen. 7C 136
Lipson Ter. PL4: Plym 1K 9 (1B 142)
LIPSON VALE 7B 136
Lipson Va. PL4: Plym 7B 136
Lipstone Cres.
   PL4: Plym 1K 9 (1B 142)
Lisa Cl. EX2: Won 1K 71
Lisburne Cres. TQ1: Torq 2F 117
Lisburne Pl. TQ1: Torq 2F 117
       (off Lisburne Sq.)
Lisburne Sq. TQ1: Torq 2F 117
Liscawn Ter. PL11: Torp 1A 140

LISCOMBE 1C 165
Lisham's Drain EX24: Colyt 5D 88
Lisson Gro. PL4: Plym 7K 135
Lister Cl. EX2: Exe 7K 7 (1H 71)
  PL7: Plymp 3C 138
Lister Mill Bus. Pk. PL7: Plymp .3C 138
Lister Way TQ9: E All 6D 152
Litchaton Cres. PL7: Plymp 4J 137
Litchaton Way PL7: Plymp 4J 137
Litchdon La. EX32: B'aple 5E 18
Litchdon St. EX32: B'aple 5E 18
Litchfield Cl. PL7: Plymp 3E 138
Litelbury Rd. EX16: Tive 5H 41
Littabourne EX31: B'aple 2E 18
Little Ash Gdns. PL5: Plym 2A 134
Little Ash Rd. PL5: Plym 2A 134
Lit. Barley EX4: Exe 7C 64
Lit. Barton TQ12: Kingst 2H 105
Lit. Batten Rd. TQ9: Tot 7G 103
Lit. Bickington La.
  EX37: High B 3C 32
Lit. Bicton Ct. EX8: Exmth 6C 76
  (off Lit. Bicton Pl.)
Lit. Bicton Pl. EX8: Exmth 6C 76
LITTLEBOROUGH 2C 165
Lit. Bossell La. TQ11: B'leigh . . .5C 98
Littlebourne EX16: W'ridge 5H 33
Little Bradley Ponds Nature Reserve
  .5E 92
Little Bri. Bus. Pk. EX5: Clyst M .4J 73
Lit. Butts PL9: Plyms 6F 143
Lit. Castle St. EX4: Exe 5E 6 (6F 65)
Lit. Chockenhole La. EX9: Ott'n . .5K 83
Little Cl. EX11: Ott M 4C 80
  TQ12: Kingst 2H 105
Lit. Cotton Cvn. Pk. 7B 124
LITTLE DARTMOUTH 1K 153
Lit. Dock La. PL5: Plym 1F 135
Littledown Cl. EX8: Lit 5H 77
Lit. Down La. EX9: E Bud 2C 82
  PL6: Robo 1G 133
Littledown La. EX10: New P 6F 81
Lit. Down Orchard EX10: New P . .6F 81
Lit. Fancy Cl. PL6: Plym 3D 132
Little Fld. EX39: Bide 3C 22
Littlefield TQ14: Bi'ton 3A 106
Littlefield Cl. EX32: B'aple 5J 19
  TQ2: Torq 4K 111
Little Fld. Ct. PL19: Tavi 4K 59
Littlefields EX12: Seat 3E 86
Lit. Gate TQ7: Lodd 3H 151
Littlegate Rd. TQ3: Paig 1H 119
Lit. Gornhay La. EX16: Tive 2G 41
Little Haldon Picnic Site 3D 171
Little Haldon Viewpoint 3D 171
LITTLEHAM
  EX8 . . . . .5H 77 (2A 172)
  EX39 . . . . .1C 163
Littleham Chu. Path EX8: Lit 4K 77
Littleham Rd. EX8: Exmth, Lit 5F 77
  EX39: Bide 7F 23
Littleham Village EX8: Lit 5H 77
Lit. Hayes TQ12: Kingst 2H 105
LITTLEHEMPSTON 1F 103 (1A 176)
Lit. Hill TQ8: Salc 3B 158
Lit. John's Cross Hill EX2: Exe . . .2B 70
Lit. John's Wlk. TQ13: Bov T 1B 92
Littlejoy Rd. TQ12: New A 7A 104
LITTLE KNOWLE 6B 82
Lit. Knowle EX9: Bud S 6B 82
Lit. Knowle Ct. EX9: Bud S 6B 82
Little La. EX12: Beer 7B 86
Lit. Marsh Rd. EX20: Oke 2E 48
Lit. Mead EX5: Cran 1E 68
Lit. Mead Av. EX5: Cran 2F 69
Littlemead La. EX8: Exmth 1C 76
Lit. Meadow EX1: Pin 3F 67
  EX8: Exmth 1F 77
Lit. Meadow Campsite 1A 12
Lit. Meadow Way EX39: Bide 3D 22
Littlemoor La. EX31: Yell 7B 16
Lit. Orchard Cl. PL21: Modb 6G 147
Little Pk. PL20: Bere F 7C 128
Lit. Park Rd. TQ3: Paig 1G 119
LITTLE POTHERIDGE 2D 163
Lit. Queen St. EX4: Exe 4E 6 (6F 65)
Lit. Rack St. EX1: Exe 5D 6 (7E 64)
Lit. Roborough TQ13: Ashb 3H 99
Lit. Silver EX4: Exe 3C 6 (5E 64)
  EX16: Tive 5C 40
The Little Theatre 3F 117
Littleton Pl. PL2: Dev 7E 134
LITTLE TORRINGTON 2C 163
LITTLETOWN 5E 54
Littletown Rd. EX14: Hon 5E 54
Littletown Vs. EX14: Hon 5F 55
  (off Manor Cres.)
Lit. Triangle TQ14: Teignm 5J 107
  (off Triangle Pl.)
Littleway EX2: Exe 2C 70
Lit. Week Cl. EX7: Daw 1J 97
Lit. Week Gdns. EX7: Daw 1J 97
Lit. Week La. EX7: Daw 1J 97
Lit. Week Rd. EX7: Daw 1J 97
LITTLEWINDSOR 3D 167
Littlewood PL7: Plymp 5D 138
Livarot Wlk. EX36: S Mol 6B 26
LIVERMEAD 4A 116

Livermead Hill TQ2: Torq 4A 116
Livermore Rd. EX14: Hon 4F 55
Liverpool Hill EX4: Exe 5B 64
LIVERTON 7G 93 (3C 171)
Liverton Bus. Pk. EX8: Exmth 3H 77
Liverton Cl. EX8: Exmth 4G 77
Liverton Copse Nature Reserve . .3G 77
Liverton Dr. EX32: Swim 3G 25
Livery Dole Almshouses
  EX2: Exe 5K 7 (7H 65)
Living Coasts 3D 116 (1B 176)
Livingshayes Rd. EX5: Silv 1J 51
Livingstone Rd. TQ14: Teignm . . .3J 107
Livonia Rd. EX10: Sidm 4C 84
Livvy Dean Ct. TQ1: Torq 5D 112
Livvy Dean M. TQ1: Torq 5D 112
Lizard Cl. PL6: Plym 3A 132
Lizard Wlk. PL6: Plym 3B 132
Llantillio Dr. PL2: Plym 3G 135
Lloyd Av. TQ2: Torq 5K 111
Lloyd Maunder Rd. EX15: Will 4C 44
Lloyds Cl. EX1: Whip 4B 66
Lloyds Cres. EX1: Whip 5B 66
LOBB 2F 15 (3A 160)
Lobb Flds. Cvn. & Camping Pk. . . .3F 15
Locarno Av. TQ3: Pres 5K 115
Locarno Rd. EX4: Exe 1C 70
Lock Cl. EX10: Sidm 2B 84
Lockeridge Rd. PL20: Bere A 2A 128
Lockfield Ct. EX2: Alph 4E 70
Lockington Av. PL3: Plym 4A 136
Locks Cl. EX33: Brau 5J 15
  TQ1: Torq 6F 113
Locksey's La. EX12: Brans 4G 85
Locks Hill TQ1: Torq 6F 113
Locksley Cl. EX2: Cou W 5K 71
  TQ1: Torq 6D 112
Locksley Grange TQ1: Torq 6C 112
Locks Wlk. PL1: Dev 3D 140
Lockwood Ho. Camp Site 6B 96
Lockyear Pl. TQ13: Bov T 4E 92
Lockyer Av. EX10: Sidm 2D 84
Lockyer Ct. PL1: Plym 6D 8
Lockyer Cres. EX16: Tive 2A 40
Lockyer Rd. PL3: Plym 6K 135
Lockyers Quay
  PL4: Plym 6H 9 (3A 142)
Lockyer St. PL1: Plym 5D 8 (3J 141)
  (not continuous)
LODDISWELL 2G 151 (3D 175)
Loddiswell Bus. Pk. TQ7: Lodd . . .1G 151
Lodge Gdns. PL6: Plym 7K 131
Lodge Hill EX4: Exe 4D 64
  EX20: Oke 3A 48
Lodge La. EX13: Wey 1K 89
  EX18: Chul 6E 32
  PL8: Brixt 2G 149
Lodge Rd. EX16: Tive 4E 40
Lodge Trad. Est. EX5: Broadc 1K 67
Lofoten Cl. PL1: Dev 2D 140
Loftus Gdns. PL5: Plym 1B 134
Logan Rd. TQ3: Paig 7J 115
Logan Way EX15: Hemy 2F 47
Lombard La. EX39: Bide 5C 22
London Ct. PL21: Ivy 4H 145
London Inn Sq. EX4: Exe 3F 7 (6F 65)
London Rd. EX5: Rock, Whim 3G 53
Longacre PL7: Plymp 4J 137
Longacres EX2: Exe 6H 7 (7G 65)
Long Barton TQ12: Kingst 2H 105
Long Barton Av. EX20: Oke 2E 48
LONGBRIDGE 4F 137
LONG BRI. 5E 18
Longbridge Av. PL6: Plym 5G 137
Longbridge Mdw. EX15: Cull 4H 45
Longbridge Mdw. Trad. Est.
  EX15: Cull 4H 45
Longbridge Rd. PL6: Plym 4F 137
Longbrook TQ7: Chil 6H 159
Longbrook Barton PL7: Plymp 4A 138
Longbrook Cl. PL21: Ivy 4E 144
Longbrook La. EX8: Lymp 7G 75
Longbrook St. EX4: Exe 3F 7 (6F 65)
  PL7: Plymp 6C 138
Longbrook Ter. EX4: Exe 2E 6 (5F 65)
Longcause PL7: Plymp 5C 138
Long C'way. EX8: Exmth 6D 76
Long Copp EX9: Bud S 5C 82
Longcroft Av. TQ5: Brixh 5D 122
Longcroft Dr. TQ5: Brixh 5D 122
Long Culvering EX5: Rock 2C 68
Longdogs Cl. EX11: Ott M 4D 80
Longdogs La. EX11: Ott M 4D 80
LONGDOWN 1C 171
Long Down Gdns. PL6: Plym 7F 133
Long Drag EX15: Will 7E 44
Longdrag Hill EX16: Tive 4A 40
Long Entry DT7: Lym R 5K 91
Longfield EX39: App 3H 21
  PL21: Lutt 7F 129
Longfield Av. TQ12: Kingst 4J 105
Longfield Cl. EX33: Brau 5J 15
  PL21: Lutt 7F 129
Longfield Dr. TQ8: Salc 3B 158
Longfield Est. EX6: Star 1D 96

Longfield Pl. PL4: Plym 1H 9 (1A 142)
Longfield Rd. EX6: Star 1D 96
Longfields TQ7: W Alv 5D 156
Longfield Stables Cvn. & Camping Site
  . . . . .2J 105
Longfield Ter. EX34: Ilfra 3J 11
  (off Highfield Rd.)
Longfield Vs. PL9: Plyms 4E 142
Longford La. TQ12: Kingst 3H 105
Longford Pk. TQ12: Kingst 3H 105
Long Hill EX12: Beer 7B 86
Longland La. EX33: Geo 5C 14
Longlands EX7: Daw 4G 97
Longlands Dr. PL9: Hey B 3B 148
Longlands Rd. PL9: Plyms 4E 142
Long La. EX8: Exmth 6E 76
  EX16: Wash 1A 40
  EX31: Ashf 1K 17
  EX33: Forda, Lob 7A 14
  EX39: App, Nort 4F 21
  TQ12: Hacc 2K 109
  TQ14: Shal 7E 106
Long Ley PL3: Plym 5C 136
Longmead EX15: Hemy 1G 47
  EX35: Lynt 3H 13
Long Mdw. PL7: Plymp 2A 138
  TQ10: S Bre 2A 100
Longmeadow EX5: Clyst M 2F 73
  EX5: W'bury 5C 78
  EX16: Tive 3D 40
Long Mdw. Cl. PL7: Plymp 2B 138
Long Meadow Dr. EX32: B'aple 3G 19
Long Mdw. Rd. EX5: Cran 2F 69
Longmeadow Rd. EX8: Lymp 6H 75
Longmeadows EX17: Cred 5H 39
Longmead Rd. TQ3: Pres 5F 115
Longmead Wlk. TQ3: Pres 5F 115
Long Moor EX15: Cull, Will 2K 45
Long Orchard EX5: Cran 3B 68
  PL20: Bere A 2B 128
Long Pk. EX5: W'bury 5C 78
  PL21: Modb 5G 147
  TQ13: Ashb 2J 99
  TQ13: Chag 3H 61
Long Pk. Cl. PL9: Plyms 7G 143
Long Pk. Dr. PL6: Plym 3E 132
Longpark Hill TQ1: Maid 1J 113
Long Rd. TQ4: Paig 5B 116
Longroom PL1: Plym 7A 8 (4G 141)
Long Rowden PL3: Plym 5K 135
Long Rydon TQ9: Sto G 3B 120
Longstem Dr. TQ9: Darti 2A 102
Longstone Av. PL6: Plym 4B 132
Longstone Rd. TQ4: Paig 3E 118
Long Ter. Cl. PL7: Plymp 4F 139
Longtimber & Pithill Woods
  Woodland Walks 2H 145
Longview Ter. PL3: Plym 5C 136
Longwood Cl. PL7: Plymp 5D 138
Longwood La. EX16: Burl 4K 43
Long Wools TQ4: Broads 1K 121
Lonsdale Rd. EX1: Heav 7K 65
  TQ12: New A 2G 109
Lonsdale Vs. PL4: Plym 7A 136
  (off Pearson Av.)
Lonsee Gdns. TQ12: Kingsk 7J 109
Looe Rd. EX4: Exe 2B 6 (5D 64)
Looe St. PL4: Plym 5F 9 (3K 141)
Looseleigh Cl. PL6: Plym 6B 132
Looseleigh La. PL6: Plym 5K 131
Looseleigh Pk. PL6: Plym 5K 131
LOPEN 2D 167
Lopes Ct. EX20: Oke 3C 48
Lopes Dr. PL6: Robo 1D 132
Lopes Hall EX4: Exe 3F 65
Lopes Rd. PL2: Plym 5G 135
  PL20: Dous 4K 127
Lopwell Cl. PL6: Plym 5A 132
Loram Way EX2: Alph 5F 71
Lord Louis Cres. PL9: Hooe 6A 142
Lord Morley Way PL9: Plyms 5H 143
Lord Nelson Dr. TQ6: Dartm 6C 124
Lord Robarts Ct. PL4: Plym 4J 9
Lords Mdw. Ind. Est.
  EX17: Cred 6K 39
Lords Mdw. La. EX16: Bam 2H 33
Lords Meadow Leisure Cen. 6K 39
Lord's Pl. TQ1: Torq 7D 112
Lords Way EX2: Won 5E 71
Loretto Gdns. EX13: Axmin 4J 89
Loretto Rd. EX13: Axmin 4J 89
Loring Flds. EX32: Land 1B 24
Loring Rd. TQ8: Salc 4C 158
Lorn Haven Bus. Pk.
  TQ13: Ashb 3J 99
Lorrimore Av. PL2: Plym 6E 134
Lorris Dr. TQ14: Teignm 3G 107
Lotherton Cl. PL7: Plymp 6E 138
Loughboro Rd. PL5: Plym 2B 134
Loughwood Meeting House 1C 173
Louisa Pl. EX8: Exmth 6C 76
Louisa Ter. EX8: Exmth 7C 76
Louise Ter. EX38: G Tor 2B 30
Loup Ct. EX13: Axmin 4K 89
Louvigny EX14: Fen 2G 53
Louville Camp TQ5: Brixh 3H 123
Louville Cl. TQ4: Good 5J 119

Lovelace Cres. EX8: Exmth 4E 76
Lovelace Gdns. EX2: Alph 5E 70
Love La. EX24: Colyt 7C 88
  EX39: Bide 4D 22
  TQ3: Marl 2D 114
  (not continuous)
  TQ13: Ashb 4H 99
  TQ14: Teignm 2K 107
Love La. Cl. TQ3: Marl 2D 114
Lovelane Cotts. TQ3: Marl 2D 114
Lovell Cl. EX8: Exmth 1E 76
Lovell Rd. PL3: Plym 5A 136
Loventor Cres. TQ3: Marl 4D 114
Loventor La. TQ9: Berr P 4A 114
Lovering Cl. EX8: Exmth 1E 76
Loverings Ct. EX31: B'aple 4E 18
Lover's La. EX39: App 2G 21
Lovers' Wlk. EX32: B'aple 7F 19
Lowbrook EX5: Rock 4F 69
Lowena La. EX11: W Hill 3H 79
Lwr. Albert St. EX1: Exe 3H 7 (6G 65)
Lwr. Aller La. TQ13: Bov T 1A 92
Lwr. Anderton PL10: Millb 7B 140
Lwr. Argyll Pl. EX4: Exe 3D 64
LOWER ASHTON 2C 171
Lwr. Audley Av. TQ2: Torq 5B 112
Lower Av. EX1: Heav 3K 7 (6J 65)
Lwr. Barton EX5: Cran 3C 68
Lwr. Blagdon La. TQ3: Blag 1B 118
Lwr. Brand La. EX14: Hon 5F 55
Lwr. Brimley Cl. TQ14: Teignm 4J 107
Lwr. Brimley Rd. TQ14: Teignm 3J 107
Lwr. Broad Oak Rd.
  EX11: W Hill 4G 81
Lwr. Broad Pk. TQ6: Dartm 6D 124
Lwr. Broad Path TQ9: Sto G 1A 120
Lwr. Brookfield Ter. TQ13: Lust 6J 63
Lwr. Brook Mdw. EX10: Sidf 1D 84
Lwr. Brook Pk. PL21: Ivy 4E 144
Lwr. Brook St. TQ14: Teignm 5J 107
Lwr. Budleigh EX9: E Bud 2D 82
Lwr. Budleigh Mdw.
  TQ12: New A 1C 108
Lwr. Bull Ring EX15: Cull 4H 45
  (off Fore St.)
Lwr. Burwood Rd. EX38: G Tor 2D 30
Lwr. Cannon Rd. TQ12: H'fld 2J 93
LOWER CHERITON 3B 166
Lwr. Church St. EX24: Colyt 5D 88
  EX32: B'aple 5F 19
  (off Trinity St.)
Lwr. Clay Pk. EX39: Mort 4A 10
Lwr. Cleave EX39: Nort 7G 21
Lwr. Cleve EX33: Brau 3H 15
Lwr. Cloister Wlk. EX6: Exmin 1B 74
  (off Devington Pk.)
Lower Cl. EX16: Hal 6C 42
Lwr. Collapark TQ9: Tot 5D 102
Lwr. Collins Rd. TQ9: Tot 5D 102
LOWER COMPTON 6B 136
Lwr. Compton Rd. PL3: Plym 5A 136
Lwr. Congella Rd. TQ1: Torq 7E 112
Lwr. Contour Rd. TQ6: Kingsw 6H 125
Lwr. Coombe Rd. TQ12: Kingst 4J 105
Lwr. Coombe St.
  EX1: Exe 6D 6 (7E 64)
Lwr. Cotteylands EX16: Tive 5B 40
Lwr. Cot. Rd. PL8: New F 5F 149
Lwr. Crooked Mdw. EX20: Oke 3C 48
Lwr. Cross Rd. EX31: Bick 5K 17
LOWER DEAN 7B 98 (1D 175)
Lwr. Dean EX12: Brans 6F 85
Lwr. Dean La. EX34: C Mar 7D 12
LOWER DITTISHAM 6C 120
Lower Dr. EX7: Daw 2J 97
Lwr. Duck St. EX6: Exmin 3D 74
Lower East Lounston Nature Reserve
  . . . . .3B 170
Lwr. Ellacombe Chu. Rd.
  TQ1: Torq 7E 112
Lwr. Erith Rd. TQ1: Torq 2F 117
LOWER ERNESETTLE 5C 130
LOWER EYPE 1D 173
Lwr. Fairview Rd. TQ6: Dartm 6E 124
Lwr. Farm Rd. PL7: Plymp 5D 138
Lwr. Farthings EX10: New P 6G 81
Lwr. Fern Rd. TQ12: New A 4J 109
Lwr. Fore St. EX8: Exmth 6C 76
  PL12: Salt 1A 134
Lwr. Fowden TQ4: Broads 2K 121
Lwr. French Pk. TQ12: New A 1C 108
Lwr. Furlong Cl. EX5: Cran 2F 69
LOWER GABWELL 1B 176
Lwr. Gaydon St. EX32: B'aple 4F 19
  (off Richmond St.)
Lwr. Grn. TQ10: S Bre 2C 100
Lwr. Green Pk. PL21: Modb 6F 147
Lwr. Griggs EX10: Sidm 3E 84
Lwr. Gunstone EX39: Bide 3F 23
Lwr. Halsdon La. EX8: Exmth 3B 76
Lwr. Harrington La. EX4: Pin 3D 66
Lwr. Hill Barton Rd.
  EX1: Heav, Sow 6B 66
Lwr. Hill Head Rd. EX5: Clyst M 2G 73
LOWER HOLDITCH 3D 167
Lwr. King's Av. EX4: Exe 4G 65
Lwr. Kingsdown Rd.
  TQ14: Teignm 4F 107

Lwr. Kinsman's Dale—Mamhead Bus. Units

Lwr. Kinsman's Dale
TQ13: More 6H 61
Lwr. Knoll EX8: Exmth 6F 77
Lwr. Knowle Rd. TQ13: Lust 6J 63
Lwr. Ladram La. EX9: Ott'n 6K 83
Lower La. EX3: Ebf 6E 74
PL1: Plym 5E 8
Lwr. Long Cl. EX34: C Mar 3E 12
Lwr. Loughborough EX16: Tive 3B 40
LOWER LOVACOTT 1D 163
LOWER LOXHORE 3C 161
Lwr. Manor Rd. TQ5: Brixh 3E 122
Lwr. Marlpits Hill EX14: Hon 5G 55
Lwr. Mead EX13: Axmin 3J 89
Lwr. Meadow Ri. EX7: Daw 4F 97
Lwr. Meddon St. EX39: Bide 4F 23
Lwr. Millhayes EX15: Hemy 1G 47
Lwr. Mill La. EX15: Cull 4H 45
Lwr. Moor EX32: B'aple 5J 19
Lwr. Moor Way EX16: Tive 2G 41
Lwr. Northcote Rd. EX14: Hon 2H 55
Lwr. North St. EX4: Exe 3C 6 (6E 64)
Lower Pk. TQ3: Paig 7G 115
Lower Pk. Dr. PL9: Plyms 7G 143
Lower Pk. Rd. EX33: Brau 5K 15
Lwr. Penns Rd. TQ3: Pres 5J 115
Lwr. Polsham Rd. TQ3: Paig 7H 115
Lwr. Rackclose La. EX4: Exe 5C 6
Lwr. Raleigh Rd. EX31: B'aple 3F 19
Lwr. Ray EX5: Cran 2E 68
Lwr. Rea Rd. TQ5: Brixh 3F 123
Lwr. Redgate *EX16: Tive* *4D 40*
(off Bartows C'way.)
Lwr. Ridings PL7: Plymp 2E 138
Lower Rd. EX5: Wood S 1A 78
Lower St German's Rd.
EX4: Exe 4F 65
Lwr. Saltram PL9: Plyms 5D 142
LOWER SANDYGATE 1G 105
Lwr. Sandygate TQ12: Kingst 1G 105
Lwr. Shapter St. EX3: Top 6B 74
Lwr. Shillingford EX2: Shil A 7D 70
Lwr. Shirburn Rd. TQ1: Torq 6C 112
Lowerside PL2: Plym 3E 134
LOWER SLADE 5G 11 (2B 160)
Lwr. Sladesmoor Cres.
PL15: St G 6C 34
Lower St. PL4: Plym 5G 9 (3K 141)
TQ6: Dartm 2B 124 (6F 125)
TQ6: Ditt 5B 120
TQ7: W Alv 5D 156
TQ13: Chag 2H 61
Lwr. Summerlands
EX1: Exe 3H 7 (6G 65)
LOWER TALE 3A 166
Lower Ter. EX22: Bradw 5B 28
Lwr. Three Acres EX5: Whim 2F 69
Lwr. Thurlow Rd. TQ1: Torq 7C 112
LOWER TOWN
EX16, nr. Halberton 6C 42
EX16, nr. Sampford Peverell . . . 2B 42
TQ11 . . . . . 4D 98
Lwr. Town EX16: Hal 7C 42
EX16: Sam P 2B 42
EX19: Wink 3C 36
EX39: Wools 3B 28
TQ7: Malb 6G 155
Lwr. Trindle Cl. TQ13: Chud 2B 94
Lwr. Union La. TQ2: Torq 1C 116
Lwr. Union Rd. TQ7: Kingsb 4F 157
Lwr. Warberry Rd. TQ1: Torq 1D 116
Lwr. Warren Rd. TQ7: Kingsb 6G 157
Lwr. Way EX10: Harp 4J 81
LOWER WEAR 6A 72 (2D 171)
Lwr. Wear Rd. EX2: Cou W 5K 71
Lwr. Westlake Rd. EX31: Rou 7K 17
Lwr. Wheathill EX10: Sidm 2C 84
(not continuous)
Lwr. Winsham Rd. EX33: Win 1K 15
Lwr. Woodfield Rd. TQ1: Torq 3E 116
Lwr. Woodhayes Ct. EX5: Whim 7H 53
LOWER WOOLBROOK 4B 84
Lwr. Yalberton Holiday Pk. 6D 118
Lwr. Yalberton Rd. TQ4: Paig 5C 118
LOW HAM 1D 167
Lowley Brook Ct. TQ2: Torq 5H 111
Lowman Grn. *EX16: Tive* *4D 40*
(off Station Rd.)
Lowman Units EX16: Tive 3G 41
Lowman Way EX16: Tive 3F 41
Low Rd. PL9: Wem 6B 148
LOWTON
EX20 . . . . . 3A 164
TA3 . . . . . 2B 166
LOXBEARE 2D 165
Loxbury Ri. TQ2: Torq 2K 115
Loxbury Rd. TQ2: Torq 1K 115
LOXHORE 3C 161
Lucas Av. EX4: Exe 1H 7 (4G 65)
Lucas La. PL7: Plymp 3A 138
Lucas Ter. PL4: Plym 2C 142
Luccombe La. *EX2: Exe* *2D 70*
(off Alphington Rd.)
Luccombe Oak EX5: Cran 2E 68
Lucerne TQ1: Torq 2F 117
Lucius St. TQ2: Torq 1B 116
LUCKETT 3B 168
Luckhams La. TQ7: Malb 6G 155
Lucky La. EX2: Exe 6E 6 (7F 65)
Lucombe Ct. EX4: Exe 1H 7
Ludlow Rd. PL3: Plym 5K 135
Ludwell La. EX2: Won 1K 71
Ludwell Ri. EX2: Won 1A 72
LUFFINCOTT 1B 168
Lukesland Gdns. 1J 145 (2C 175)
Luke St. EX16: Bam 2H 33
Lulworth Cl. TQ4: Paig 5F 119
Lulworth Dr. PL6: Plym 3C 132
Lumley Cl. EX6: Kenton 6J 95
Lummaton Cross TQ2: Torq 3C 112
Lummaton Pl. TQ2: Torq 4D 112
Lundy Cl. EX32: B'aple 4H 19
PL6: Plym 3A 132
Lundy Flds. EX34: Wool 7C 10
Lundy Island 1A 160
Lundy Marine Conservation Zone
. . . . . 1A 160
Lundy North Light Lighthouse 1A 160
Lundy Old Light Lighthouse 1A 160
Lundy South Light Lighthouse 1A 160
Lundy Vw. EX39: Nort 5D 20
Lupin Way EX15: Will 3E 44
LUPPITT 3B 166
LUPRIDGE 2D 175
Lupton House 5A 122
LURLEY 2D 165
LUSCOMBE 4E 100 (2D 175)
Luscombe Cl. PL21: Ivy 4E 144
TQ12: Ipp 7H 101
Luscombe Cres. TQ3: Paig 1E 118
Luscombe La. TQ3: Paig 6D 114
Luscombe Rd. TQ3: Paig 7D 114
Luscombe Ter. EX7: Daw 4G 97
LUSON 6A 150 (3C 175)
LUSTLEIGH 6H 63 (2B 170)
Lustleigh Cleave 2B 170
Lustleigh Cl. EX2: Matf 5F 71
Lusways EX10: Sidm 6D 84
Lutehouse La. EX19: Wink 2A 36
LUTON
EX14 . . . . . 3A 166
TQ13 . . . . . 3D 171
Lutterburn St. PL21: Ugb 6E 146
LUTTON
PL21 . . . . . 7G 129 (2B 174)
TQ10 . . . . . 1C 175
LUTWORTHY 2B 164
Lutyens Dr. TQ3: Paig 7D 114
Lutyens Fold PL19: Mil A 2B 58
Luxmoore Way EX20: Oke 2D 48
Luxmore Cl. PL6: Plym 2F 137
Luxton Ct. EX15: Cull 4H 45
Luxton Rd. TQ12: E Ogw 4C 108
Luxtons Pk. EX11: Ott M 4B 80
Lych Cl. PL9: Hooe 6B 142
Lychgate Pk. EX17: Cop 6C 38
LYDCOTT 3C 161
Lydcot Wlk. PL6: Plym 3B 136
Lyddicleave EX31: Bick 6K 17
LYDEARD ST LAWRENCE 1B 166
LYDFORD 6H 57 (2D 169)
Lydford Castle & Saxon Town
. . . . . 6G 57 (2D 169)
Lydford Cl. PL21: Ivy 5H 145
Lydford Forest Trail 2C 169
Lydford Gorge 6G 57 (2D 169)
Lydford Ho. *TQ12: New A* *7G 105*
(off Hameldown Way)
Lydford Pk. Rd. PL3: Plym 6J 135
Lyd Gdns. PL19: Tavi 4K 59
Lydgates Rd. EX12: Seat 4D 86
Lydia Cl. EX10: New P 5F 81
Lydiate La. EX35: Lynt 3F 13
Lydia Way PL4: Plym 1H 9 (1A 142)
LYDMARSH 3D 167
Lydwell Pk. Rd. TQ1: Torq 7F 113
Lydwell Rd. TQ1: Torq 7F 113
Lym Cl. DT7: Lym R 5K 91
Lyme Bay Rd. TQ14: Teignm 2J 107
Lymeborne Av. EX1: Heav 6K 65
Lymebourne Av. EX10: Sidm 4C 84
Lymebourne La. EX10: Sidm 4C 84
Lymebourne Pk. EX10: Sidm 4C 84
Lyme Cl. EX13: Axmin 4H 89
Lyme M. EX12: Seat 6F 87
LYME REGIS 5K 91 (1D 173)
Lyme Regis Golf Course . . . 2K 91 (1D 173)
Lyme Regis Ind. Est.
DT7: Lym R 4H 91
Lyme Regis Lifeboat Station
. . . . . 6J 91 (1D 173)
Lyme Regis Marine Aquarium
. . . . . 6J 91 (1D 173)
Lyme Regis Mus. 5K 91 (1D 173)
Lyme Regis Sailing Club 6J 91
Lyme Regis Tourist Information Centre
. . . . . 5K 91 (1D 173)
Lyme Rd. DT7: Uply 2F 91
EX13: Axmin 4J 89
EX13: Ray H 4B 90
Lyme St. EX13: Axmin 3H 89
Lyme Vw. Cl. TQ1: Torq 6F 113
Lyme Vw. Rd. TQ1: Torq 6E 112
Lymington Rd. TQ1: Torq 6B 112
Lympne Av. PL5: Plym 5E 130
LYMPSTONE 6F 75 (2D 171)
Lympstone Commando Station
(Rail) 3G 75 (2D 171)
Lympstone Village Station
(Rail) 6F 75 (2D 171)
Lyn & Exmoor Mus. 2H 13 (2D 161)
LYNBRIDGE 3H 13 (2D 161)
Lynbridge Rd. EX35: Lynt 4G 13
Lynbro Rd. EX31: B'aple 2E 18
Lynch Cl. EX5: Thor 2A 50
EX13: Axmin 2H 89
Lynch Head EX11: S'ton, Ven O 2F 81
Lyncombe Cl. EX4: Exe 3H 65
Lyncombe Cres. TQ1: Torq 3G 117
Lyncourt TQ1: Torq 3F 117
Lyndale Rd. TQ12: Kingst 3G 105
Lyndhurst Av. TQ12: Kingsk 7K 109
Lyndhurst Cl. PL2: Plym 5H 135
TQ12: Kingsk 7K 109
Lyndhurst Rd. EX2: Exe 6J 7 (7H 65)
EX8: Exmth 4C 76
PL2: Plym 5H 135
Lyndrick Rd. PL3: Plym 4K 135
Lyn Gro. TQ12: Kingsk 6J 109
Lyngrove Ct. *TQ12: Kingsk* *6J 109*
(off Moor Pk. Rd.)
Lynhayes EX13: Kilm 2B 88
Lynher St. PL5: Plym 1C 134
Lyn Hill EX35: Lynt 3H 13
Lynhurst Av. EX31: B'aple 5A 18
LYNMOUTH 2H 13 (2D 161)
Lynmouth Av. TQ4: Paig 5F 119
Lynmouth Cl. PL7: Plymp 4K 137
Lynmouth Hill EX35: Lynm 2H 13
Lynmouth St. EX35: Lynm 1H 13
LYNSTONE 3A 162
LYNTON 2G 13 (2D 161)
Lynton & Barnstaple Railway 2C 161
Lynton & Lynmouth Cliff Railway
. . . . . 1G 13 (2D 161)
Lynton Cinema 1G 13
Lynton Rd. EX34: C Mar 7D 12
Lynton Tourist Information Centre
. . . . . 1G 13 (2D 161)
Lynway EX35: Lynt 2H 13
Lynway Ct. TQ1: Torq 7D 112
Lynwood TQ12: E Ogw 3C 108
Lynwood Av. EX4: Exe 5A 6 (7D 64)
PL7: Plymp 5H 137
Lynwood Ho. EX32: B'aple 7G 19
Lysander La. PL6: Plym 5C 132
Lyte Hill Ct. *TQ2: Torq* *2B 112*
(off Lyte Hill La.)
Lyte Hill La. TQ2: Torq 2B 112
Lyte La. TQ7: W Cha 7K 157
Lyte's Rd. TQ5: Brixh 4F 123
Lytton Ho. *TQ2: Torq* *2C 116*
(off St Luke's Rd. Sth.)

M

Mabel Pl. TQ4: Paig 2H 119
Mabry Way EX12: Seat 5F 87
Macadam Rd.
PL4: Plym 7K 9 (4B 142)
Macandrew Wlk. PL21: Ivy 3J 145
Macaulay Cres. PL5: Plym 2H 135
Macauley Cl. EX14: Hon 3H 55
McCaulay's Health Club
Ivybridge 2D 144
Plymouth 5C 8 (3H 141)
McCoys Arc. EX4: Exe 5C 6
Macey's Ter. EX20: Oke 2C 48
Macey St. PL11: Torp 1A 140
Mcilwraith Rd. TQ8: Salc 3B 158
McKay Av. TQ1: Torq 7B 112
Mackenzie Pl. PL5: Plym 1B 134
Mackenzie Way EX16: Tive 4F 41
Mackrells Ter. TQ12: New A 2D 108
Maclins Cl. EX36: S Mol 6C 26
Macwood Dr. EX12: Seat 4E 86
Madagascar Cl. EX8: Exmth 4G 77
Maddacombe Rd.
TQ12: Kingsk 2D 110
Maddacombe Ter.
TQ12: A'well 2C 110
Madden Rd. PL1: Dev 2E 140
Maddick Rd. EX1: Pin 1E 66
Maddicks Orchard TQ9: Sto G 4B 120
Maddock Cl. PL7: Plymp 6D 138
Maddock Dr. PL7: Plymp 5D 138
Maddocks Row EX4: Exe 3D 6 (6E 64)
Madeira Ct. EX8: Exmth 7D 76
Madeira Pl. TQ2: Torq 1C 116
Madeira Rd. PL1: Plym 7E 8 (4J 141)
Madeira Vs. EX8: Exmth 5C 76
Madeira Wlk. EX8: Exmth 7D 76
EX9: Bud S 7D 82
MADFORD 2B 166
Madge Ct. *PL19: Tavi* *3H 59*
(off King St.)
Madge La. PL19: Tavi 4H 59
Madison Av. EX1: Heav 6K 65
Madison Cl. EX5: Sto C 7J 51
Madison Wharf EX8: Exmth 6A 76
Madrepore Pl. *TQ1: Torq* *1D 116*
(off Pimlico)
Madrepore Rd. TQ1: Torq 2D 116
Maer Bay Ct. EX8: Exmth 7D 76
Maer La. EX8: Exmth, Lit 7E 76
Maer Rd. EX8: Exmth 7E 76
Maer Top Way EX31: B'aple 2F 19
Maer Va. EX8: Exmth 6E 76
Magdala Rd. EX31: Bick 6J 17
Magdalen Bri. Ct. EX2: Exe 5F 7
Magdalen Cotts.
EX1: Exe 5G 7 (7G 65)
Magdalene Cl. TQ9: Tot 6E 102
Magdalene Lawn EX32: B'aple 4F 19
Magdalene Rd. TQ1: Torq 7B 112
Magdalene Way EX36: S Mol 6B 26
Magdalen Gdns. EX2: Exe 5J 7 (7H 65)
PL7: Plymp 6C 138
Magdalen Pl. EX2: Exe 7H 65
Magdalen Rd. EX2: Exe 5G 7 (7G 65)
Magdalen St. EX2: Exe 5E 6 (7F 65)
Magistrates' Court
Barnstaple 4D 18
Exeter 4H 7 (6H 65)
Newton Abbot 1E 108
Plymouth 5E 8 (3J 141)
Torquay 1C 116
Magnolia Av. EX2: Won 2K 71
EX8: Exmth 4G 77
Magnolia Cen. *5C 76*
(off Chapel St.)
Magnolia Cl. EX32: B'aple 5K 19
PL7: Plymp 4E 138
Magnolia Ct. EX16: Tive 1E 40
PL9: Plyms *5G 143*
(off Horn Cross Rd.)
Magnolia Dr. TQ13: Chud 1D 94
Magnolia Wlk. EX8: Exmth 6C 76
Magnus Cl. PL6: Plym 4K 131
Magpie Cres. EX2: Exe 1A 70
Magpie La. EX14: Hon 6G 55
Magpie Leisure Pk. 1D 126
Maida Va. Ter.
PL4: Plym 1H 9 (7A 136)
MAIDENCOMBE 1J 113 (1B 176)
Maidencombe Ho.
TQ1: Torq 1E 112
Maidenfield TQ1: Maid 2H 113
MAIDENHAYNE 6C 90 (1C 173)
Maidenhayne La. EX13: Mus 6B 90
Maiden St. EX31: B'aple 4E 18
Maidenway La. TQ3: Paig 6F 115
Maidenway Rd. TQ3: Paig 6F 115
MAIDENWELL 3A 168
Maidenwell Rd. PL7: Plymp 6K 137
Maidstone Pl. PL5: Plym 6D 130
Main Av. TQ1: Torq 5C 112
Maine Cl. EX39: Bide 3C 22
Maine Gdns. PL2: Plym 4E 134
Main Rd. EX4: Pin 3D 66
EX5: Sto C 6K 51
EX6: Exmin 7K 71
(Sannerville Way)
EX6: Exmin 3E 74
(Station Rd.)
TQ8: Salc 4B 158
MAINSTONE 7G 133
Mainstone Av.
PL4: Plym 6K 9 (3B 142)
Main St. TQ9: Blacka 3C 152
Maitland Dr. PL3: Plym 3A 136
Majorfield Rd. EX3: Top 5B 74
Majors Mdw. EX20: Oke 3C 48
Major Ter. EX12: Seat 5E 86
Maker Rd. PL11: Torp 2A 140
Maker Vw. PL3: Plym 1A 8 (7G 135)
MALBOROUGH 6G 155 (3D 175)
Malborough Grn. TQ7: Malb 6F 155
Malborough Pk. TQ7: Malb 7H 155
Malden Cl. EX10: Sidm 3C 84
Malden La. EX10: Sidm 2C 84
Malden Rd. EX10: Sidm 2C 84
Malderek Av. TQ3: Pres 5J 115
Mallands Mdw. TQ12: A'well 5D 108
Mallard Cl. PL7: Plymp 4C 138
TQ2: Torq 2K 111
TQ12: Kingst 3F 105
Mallard Rd. EX2: Sow 7D 66
Mallet Rd. PL21: Ivy 3E 144
Malletts La. EX32: B'aple 4F 19
Mallison Cl. EX4: Exe 4C 64
Mallock Rd. TQ2: Torq 1A 116
Mallocks Cl. EX10: Tip J 1J 81
Mallow Ct. EX15: Will 3D 44
Malmesbury Cl. PL2: Plym 3G 135
MALMSMEAD 2D 161
Malory Cl. PL5: Plym 1J 135
Malt Fld. EX8: Lymp 6H 75
The Malt Ho. TQ9: Tot 6F 103
The Maltings EX2: Heav 7J 65
EX17: Cred 6J 39
Malt Mill La. TQ9: Tot 5D 102
Malvern Gdns. EX2: Won 1K 71
Malvernleigh *TQ1: Torq* *5D 112*
(off St Marychurch Rd.)
Malvern Rd. EX10: Sidm 4B 84
Malvern Way EX39: Bide 3C 22
Mambury Moor Nature Reserve
. . . . . 2B 162
Mamhead Bus. Units
EX2: Mar B 5G 71

Mamhead Forest Walk 2D 171
Mamhead Obelisk 2D 171
Mamhead Picnic Site 2D 171
Mamhead Rd. EX2: Won 1B 72
   EX6: Kenton 7G 95
Mamhead Vw. EX8: Exmth 6A 76
MANADON 2J 135
Manadon Cl. PL5: Plym 2K 135
Manadon Dr. PL5: Plym 2K 135
Manadon Football Development Cen.
   . . . . .1J 135
Manadon Sports Centre 1J 135
MANATON 2B 170
Manaton Cl. EX2: Matf 5F 71
Manaton Ct. EX2: Matf 5F 71
Manaton Tor Rd. TQ3: Pres 5F 115
Manby Gdns. PL5: Plym 6E 130
Manchester Rd. EX8: Exmth 6B 76
Manchester St. EX8: Exmth 5B 76
Mandrake Cl. EX2: Alph 4E 70
Mandrake Rd. EX2: Alph 4D 70
Manifold Gdns. PL3: Plym 6E 136
Manitoba Gdns. EX15: Cull 4G 45
Manleigh Holiday Pk. 7C 12
Manley Cl. EX5: Whim 6G 53
Manley La. EX16: Tive 6K 41
Manley Mdw. EX1: W Cly 1E 66
Manleys La. EX14: Dunk 5G 47
Manna Ash Ct. EX2: Exe 7H 7
MANNAMEAD 6A 136
Mannamead Av. PL3: Plym 6A 136
Mannamead Ct. PL3: Plym 5A 136
   (off Lwr. Compton Rd.)
Mannamead Rd. PL3: Plym 3K 135
   PL4: Plym 6K 135
Manning Av. EX15: Cull 5F 45
Mannings Mdw. TQ13: Bov T 4C 92
Mannings Way EX31: B'aple 2E 18
Manor Av. DT7: Lym R 4J 91
   TQ3: Pres 6J 115
Mnr. Bend TQ5: Galm 3J 121
MANOR BOURNE 2B 148
Mnr. Bourne Rd.
   PL9: Down T 2A 148
Manor Cl. EX7: Daw 4G 97
   EX10: Sidm 5B 84
   EX12: Seat 5E 86
   EX14: W'ton 4B 54
   EX15: Kent 6B 46
   EX15: Uff 5J 43
   EX31: B'aple 6B 18
   EX31: Frem 5F 17
   EX33: Wraf 6K 15
   PL19: Tavi 3G 59
   PL21: Ivy 4G 145
   TQ12: A'well 5D 108
   TQ12: Kingsk 2G 111
Manor Cotts. TQ12: New A 1E 108
   (off Wolborough St.)
Manor Ct. EX12: Seat 5E 86
   EX32: Land 2B 24
   PL3: Plym 5D 136
   TQ6: Sto F 3H 153
   TQ10: S Bre 1B 100
   TQ12: Kingsk 2G 111
   (off Torquay Rd.)
Manor Court Golf Course 2B 170
Manor Cres. EX14: Hon 5F 55
   TQ3: Pres 6J 115
Manor Dr. PL21: Ivy 4G 145
   TQ12: Kingsk 2G 111
   TQ13: Chag 3G 61
Manor Est. PL20: Horr 2D 126
Mnr. Farm PL20: Dous 4K 127
Mnr. Farm Camp Site 1A 142
Mnr. Farm Cvn. Site 3D 86
Manor Gdns. EX6: Kenton 5H 95
   (off Slittercombe La.)
   EX12: Seat 5F 87
   EX20: Exbo 2J 35
   PL1: Plym 5A 8 (3G 141)
   PL20: Horr 2D 126
   TQ1: Torq 3G 117
   TQ3: Pres 6J 115
   TQ7: Kingsb 3G 157
   TQ12: A'well 6E 108
   TQ12: Kingsk 2G 111
Manorglade Ct. TQ1: Torq 1F 117
The Mnr. Hall EX20: Hath 2H 35
Manor Ho. TQ1: Torq 3G 117
The Manor Ho. TQ9: Tot 5E 102
The Manor Ho. Apts.
   TQ2: Torq 3A 116
   (off Seaway La.)
Manor La. PL3: Plym 6E 136
The Manor Mill 2C 173
Mnr. Mill Rd. EX33: Know 1K 15
Mnr. Orchard TQ12: E Ogw 3A 108
   (off Garners La.)
Manor Pk. EX5: Clyst M 2F 73
   EX22: Bradw 6C 28
   EX31: B'aple 6B 18
   EX39: Wools 2B 28
   PL20: Dous 4K 127
   TQ7: Kingsb 3G 157
Manor Pk. Cl. PL7: Plymp 4C 138
Manor Pk. Dr. PL7: Plymp 5C 138
Manor Pavilion Theatre 7B 84

Manor Rd. EX4: Exe 6A 6 (7D 64)
   EX10: Sidm 7B 84
   EX12: Seat 5E 86
   EX32: Land 2B 24
   PL19: Tavi 3H 59
   TQ1: Torq 5D 112
   TQ3: Pres 6J 115
   TQ5: Brixh 3E 122
   TQ12: A'well 5D 108
   TQ12: New A 1C 108
   TQ13: Chag 3F 61
   TQ14: Bi'ton 3B 106
Mnr. Row EX7: Daw 4G 97
   (off Brook St.)
Mnr. Steps TQ5: Brixh 3E 122
Manor St. PL1: Plym 4A 8 (2G 141)
   TQ6: Ditt 6C 120
Manor Ter. EX12: Seat 5E 86
   (off Manor Rd.)
   TQ3: Paig 2G 119
   TQ5: Brixh 3E 122
Manor Va. Rd. TQ5: Galm 3J 121
Manor Vw. TQ12: New A 1D 108
Manor Way PL19: Tavi 3H 59
   PL21: Ivy 4G 145
   TQ6: Ditt 6E 102
Mansbridge Rd. TQ9: Tot 6G 103
Manscombe Cl. TQ2: Torq 3K 115
Manscombe Rd. TQ2: Torq 4K 115
Mansell Copse Wlk. EX2: Won . . .1J 71
Mansfield Rd. EX4: Exe 4H 65
Mansfield Ter. EX9: Bud S 5D 82
The Mansion PL21: Moor 3C 146
The Mansion Ho. EX6: Exmin 1B 74
Mansion Ho. St. TQ6: Dartm 2B 124
Manston Cl. PL5: Plym 5D 130
Manstone Av. EX10: Sidm 3B 84
   (not continuous)
Manstone Cl. EX10: Sidm 2C 84
   (not continuous)
Manstone La. EX10: Sidm 4C 84
Manstone Mead EX10: Sidm 2C 84
Manston Rd. EX1: Heav 1K 7 (5H 65)
Manston Ter. EX2: Exe 5K 7 (7H 65)
Manteo Way EX39: Bide 3H 23
Mantle Gdns. PL5: Plym 3C 134
Maple Av. TQ13: Bov T 7B 92
Maple Cl. EX12: Seat 3E 86
   EX14: Hon 6C 54
   EX15: Will 4C 44
   PL6: Plym 4F 133
   PL19: Tavi 6J 59
   TQ5: Brixh 6C 122
   TQ12: Kingst 5H 105
   TQ13: Chud K 6B 94
Maple Ct. EX6: Cher 3D 62
   PL9: Plyms 5G 143
Mapledene Cl. TQ9: Sto G 3B 120
Maple Dr. EX8: Exmth 1F 77
Maple Gro. EX16: Tive 4D 40
   EX31: Rou 6B 18
   PL4: Plym 1E 8 (7J 135)
   PL7: Plymp 6J 137
   TQ4: Good 5H 119
Maple M. EX9: Bud S 5D 82
   (off E. Buddleigh Rd.)
Maple Rd. EX4: Exe 6A 6 (7C 64)
   TQ5: Broadc 6D 52
   TQ5: Brixh 6C 122
   (not continuous)
Maple St. EX32: B'aple 5H 19
Mapleton Cl. EX4: Exe 7C 104
Mapleton Pl. TQ12: New A 1F 109
Maple Wlk. PL21: L Mill 5A 144
   TQ2: Torq 5J 111
Maple Way PL6: Plym 3F 133
Mapstone Hill TQ13: Lust 4G 63
Marazion Way PL2: Plym 3J 135
Marble Ct. TQ1: Torq 6B 112
Marcent Ho. TQ5: Brixh 5F 123
March Ct. EX20: Oke 3B 48
Marcombe Rd. TQ2: Torq 1A 116
Marcom Cl. EX8: Exmth 1F 77
Marcus Ho. EX4: Exe 2D 6
Marcus Rd. EX8: Exmth 3F 77
   EX14: Dunk 5G 47
Mardle Way TQ11: B'leigh 4C 98
Mardle Way Ind. Est.
   TQ11: B'leigh 4C 98
Mardon Cl. PL6: Plym 6E 132
Mardon Hall EX4: Exe 3E 64
Mardon Hill EX4: Exe 3E 64
Marett Rd. PL5: Plym 7E 130
Margaret Cl. TQ12: E Ogw 3C 108
   TQ12: Kingst 4H 105
Margaret Ct. EX4: Whip 3B 66
Margaret Gdns. TQ12: New A . . .2J 109
Margaret Pk. PL3: Plym 3K 135
Margaret Rd. EX4: Exe 3H 65
   TQ12: E Ogw 3C 108
   TQ12: Kingst 4H 105
Margaret St. EX8: Exmth 6C 76
   (off Chapel St.)
Margrove Ter. EX32: B'aple 3E 18
   (off Yeo Vale Rd.)
Marguerite Cl. TQ12: New A 7C 104

Marguerite Rd. EX16: Tive 2F 41
Marguerite Way TQ12: Kingsk 1G 111
MARHAMCHURCH 3A 162
MARIANSLEIGH 1B 164
Marina Cl. TQ5: Brixh 3G 123
Marina Ct. EX8: Exmth 7D 76
   TQ4: Paig 2J 119
   (off Roundham Rd.)
Marina Dr. TQ5: Brixh 3G 123
Marina Rd. PL5: Plym 7E 130
   TQ5: Brixh 4G 123
Marina Ter. PL4: Plym 1H 9 (7A 136)
Marina Way EX16: Tive 5G 41
Marine Academy Sports Complex
   . . . . .1D 134
Marine Cotts. PL4: Plym . . .7J 9 (4A 142)
Marine Ct. EX9: Bud S 7D 82
   EX39: Ins 3K 21
   PL11: Torp 2A 140
   TQ3: Pres 6J 115
Marine Cres. EX12: Seat 6E 86
   (off Marine Pl.)
Marine Dr. EX34: Wool 7A 10
   PL11: Torp 2A 140
   TQ3: Pres 7J 115
   TQ7: Bigb S 2B 154
Marine Gdns. EX39: Bide 4F 23
   (off New Rd.)
   TQ3: Pres 6J 115
Marine House at Beer Arts & Pottery
   . . . . .7C 86
Marine Mt. TQ1: Torq 3J 117
Marine Palms TQ2: Torq 2C 116
Marine Pde. DT7: Lym R 6J 91
   EX7: Daw 5H 97
   EX9: Bud S 7D 82
   EX39: App 3H 21
   EX39: Ins 3K 21
   TQ3: Pres 6K 115
   TQ14: Shal 6H 107
Marine Pk. TQ3: Pres 7J 115
Marine Pl. EX12: Seat 6E 86
   EX34: Ilfra 2H 11
   (off Wilder Rd.)
   PL4: Plym 7J 9 (4A 142)
Marine Rd. PL9: Plyms 5C 142
Mariners Cl. EX33: Brau 5J 15
Mariners Ct. PL1: Plym 3F 141
   PL4: Plym 5G 9
   TQ14: Shal 6G 107
   (off Commons Old Rd.)
Mariner's Way EX39: App 2H 21
Mariners Way TQ3: Pres 5F 115
Marine Ter. TQ14: Teignm 5H 107
   (off Foresters Ter.)
The Marine Theatre 5K 91
Marine Wlk. TQ5: Brixh 2E 122
Marine Way EX8: Exmth 5C 76
The Marino EX10: Sidm 7A 84
Marions Way EX8: Exmth 2F 77
Maristow Av. EX8: Exmth 2D 76
   PL2: Plym 6E 134
Maristow Cl. PL6: Plym 5A 132
Marist Way EX32: B'aple 7H 19
Maritime Ct. EX2: Exe 7E 6 (1F 71)
Marjon Hill PL6: Plym 6C 132
Marjon Sports & Leisure 6C 132
Marjorie Kelly Way PL21: Ivy 5G 145
Marjory Wlk. PL8: Y'ton 3A 150
Marker Cl. EX14: Gitt 7A 54
Markers EX15: Uff 6H 43
Marker's Cottage 5D 52 (1D 171)
Marker Way EX14: Hon 5F 55
The Market TQ6: Dartm 1A 124
   (off Market St.)
Market Av. PL1: Plym 4C 8 (2H 141)
Market Cl. EX16: Bam 2G 33
   PL1: Plym 3F 141
   TQ11: B'leigh 4B 98
   TQ13: Ashb 4H 99
The Market Forum 1D 116
Market M. EX2: Cou W 6C 72
Market Pl. EX10: Sidm 7C 84
   EX15: Will 3C 44
   EX24: Colyt 5D 88
   EX39: Bide 3F 23
The Market Pl. EX20: Lew 1B 56
Market Rd. PL7: Plymp 4A 138
   PL19: Tavi 4J 59
Market Sq. EX4: Exe 4D 6
   EX13: Axmin 3H 89
   EX34: Ilfra 2H 11
   PL1: Plym 4C 8 (2J 141)
   TQ6: Dartm 1A 124 (6F 125)
   TQ12: New A 1E 108
Mkt. Stalls PL1: Plym 4C 8 (2H 141)
Market St. EX1: Exe 5D 6 (7E 64)
   EX8: Exmth 6C 76
   EX17: Cred 6H 39
   EX20: Hath 1H 35
   EX20: N Taw 6B 36
   EX20: Oke 3B 48
   EX31: B'aple 4E 18
   EX34: Ilfra 2H 11
   EX35: Lynt 2H 13
   EX36: S Mol 6C 26
   EX39: App 3H 21

Market St. PL1: Plym 3F 141
   (not continuous)
   PL8: Y'ton 2B 150
   PL19: Tavi 3J 59
   TQ1: Torq 1D 116
   TQ5: Brixh 3E 122
   TQ6: Dartm 1A 124 (6F 125)
   TQ8: Salc 3D 158
   TQ11: B'leigh 4C 98
   TQ12: New A 1E 108
Market Ter. EX16: Tive 4D 40
Market Wlk. EX16: Tive 4D 40
   TQ12: New A 1E 108
Mkt. Way PL1: Plym 4C 8 (2H 141)
   TQ13: Chud 1C 94
Markham Ct. TQ4: Paig 2H 119
   (off Dartmouth Rd.)
Markham La. EX2: Alph 6E 70
   EX2: Ide, Shil A 6A 70
MARKWELL 2A 174
Marland Ter. EX39: Bide 4E 22
Marlborough Av. TQ1: Torq 1F 117
Marlborough Cl. EX8: Exmth 2G 77
   EX13: Mus 7C 90
   EX34: Ilfra 3H 11
Marlborough Ct. EX2: Matf 5F 71
   EX39: Bide 2F 23
Marlborough Dr. EX2: Won 7C 66
Marlborough Pk. EX34: Ilfra 3H 11
Marlborough Pl. TQ12: New A . . .7D 104
Marlborough Rd. EX2: Exe 6H 7 (7G 65)
   EX13: Mus 7C 90
   EX34: Ilfra 3H 11
   PL4: Plym 2F 9 (1K 141)
Marlborough Row PL1: Dev 2D 140
Marlborough St. PL1: Dev 2D 140
Marlborough Ter. TQ13: Bov T . . .4A 92
Marlborough Way EX34: Ilfra 4J 11
MARLDON 4D 114 (1A 176)
Marldon Av. TQ3: Paig 1G 119
Marldon Cl. PL5: Plym 7G 131
Marldon Cross Hill TQ3: Marl . . .3D 114
Marldon Gro. TQ3: Marl 3C 114
Marldon La. TQ3: Marl 2B 114
Marldon Rd. TQ2: Torq 6F 111
   TQ3: Paig 5E 114
   TQ12: Ipp 6K 101
Marldon Way TQ3: Marl 4E 114
Marlen Ct. EX39: Bide 5F 23
The Marles EX8: Exmth 2E 76
Marles Cl. EX14: Awli 2A 54
Marley Cl. EX16: Tive 2E 40
Marley Rd. EX8: Exmth 2D 76
Marlow Ct. EX39: W Ho 5C 20
Marlowe Cl. TQ2: Torq 6K 111
Marlow Gdns. PL9: Plyms 7G 143
Marl Pk. TQ9: H'ford 6C 100
Marlpit Cl. EX12: Seat 5D 86
Marlpit La. EX12: Seat 5D 86
Marlpits La. EX14: Hon 4F 55
Marmora Ter. EX12: Beer 7B 86
   (off Clapp's La.)
Marnham Rd. TQ1: Torq 6D 112
Marpool Cres. EX8: Exmth 4E 76
Marpool Hill EX8: Exmth 5D 76
Marrowbone Slip
   PL4: Plym 5H 9 (3A 142)
Marryat Gdns. PL5: Plym 2K 135
MARSH .2C 167
Marshall Cl. EX16: Tive 5F 41
   PL19: Whit 7K 59
Marshall Dr. PL21: Ivy 5G 145
Marshall Rd. PL7: Plymp 6H 137
   PL19: Whit 7K 59
Marshalls Mead EX19: Bea 3H 31
MARSHALSEA 3D 167
Marshals Fld. PL21: Ivy 4J 145
MARSH BARTON 3F 71
Marsh Barton Rd. EX2: Mar B . . .2E 70
Marsh Barton Trad. Est.
   EX2: Mar B 5H 71
   (Exeter Trade Cen.)
   EX2: Mar B 4H 71
   (Marsh Grn. Rd. E.)
Marsh Cl. PL6: Plym 5G 137
Marsh End EX17: Cred 6K 39
MARSHGATE 1A 168
MARSH GREEN 6K 69 (1A 172)
Marsh Grn. Hill EX5: Mar G 6K 69
Marsh Grn. La. EX5: Mar G 6K 69
Marsh Grn. Rd. E. EX2: Mar B . . .3F 71
Marsh Grn. Rd. Nth. EX2: Mar B . . .2F 71
Marsh Grn. Rd. W.
   EX2: Alph, Mar B 3E 70
Mars Hill Way EX35: Lynm 1H 13
Marsh La. EX3: Clyst G 7F 73
   EX5: New C 7C 50
   EX12: Seat 3F 87
   EX17: Bow 6C 39
   EX17: Cred 6K 39
   EX39: Ins 3K 21
   TQ7: Slap 2H 159
   TQ7: W Cha 7K 157
   TQ13: Bov T 5B 92
MARSH MILLS 5H 137
MARSH MILLS JUNC. 5G 137
Marsh Mills Pk. PL6: Plym 5G 137
Marsh Mills Retail Pk. 5G 137

Marsh Path TQ13: Bov T 4B **92**
Marsh Rd. EX12: Seat 5F **87**
EX17: Cred 6K **39**
TQ12: New A 1F **109**
MARSHWOOD 1D **173**
Marston Cl. EX7: Daw 3J **97**
The Mart EX20: Oke 3B **48**
MARTINHOE 2C **161**
MARTINHOE CROSS 2C **161**
Martinique Gro. TQ2: Torq 2B **112**
Martin La. PL1: Plym 5B **8**
PL4: Plym 5G **9**
Martin Rd. EX32: B'aple 4G **19**
Martins Cl. EX20: Hath 1H **35**
EX38: G Tor 2E **30**
Martins La. EX1: Exe 4E **6** (6F **65**)
EX16: Tive 4D **40**
Martins Rd. EX8: Exmth 2E **76**
Martin St. PL1: Plym 5A **8** (3H **141**)
Martin Way EX15: Cull 4F **45**
Martlesham Pl. PL5: Plym 6E **130**
Marven Cl. DT7: Uply 2G **91**
MARWOOD 3B **160**
Marwood Ct. EX38: G Tor 2C **30**
Marwood Hill Gardens 3B **160**
Marwood La. EX5: Ayle 7D **68**
Marwood Rd. *EX14: Hon 3G* **55**
(off Monkton Rd.)
Mary Arches St. EX4: Exe 4C **6** (6E **64**)
Mary Dean Av. PL5: Tam F 3H **131**
Mary Dean Cl. PL5: Tam F 3H **131**
MARYFIELD 2A **174**
Maryfield Av. EX4: Exe 4G **65**
Maryland Ct. EX1: Exe 4H **7**
Maryland Gdns. PL2: Plym 4E **134**
Mary La. EX16: Bam 2H **33**
Marypole Rd. EX4: Exe 3J **65**
Marypole Wlk. EX4: Exe 3J **65**
Mary Seacole Rd.
PL1: Plym 4A **8** (2G **141**)
MARYSTOW 2C **169**
Mary St. TQ13: Bov T 3B **92**
MARY TAVY 2B **60** (3D **169**)
Marythorne Rd. PL20: Bere A 2C **128**
Masefield Av. EX31: B'aple 2E **18**
Masefield Gdns. PL5: Plym 2G **135**
Masefield Rd. EX4: Whip 4B **66**
Masey Rd. EX8: Exmth 4F **77**
Mashford Av. TQ6: Dartm 5C **124**
Masons Yd. PL8: Holb 6C **150**
Massey Rd. EX16: Tive 2E **40**
Masterman Rd. PL2: Dev 7E **134**
Masterson St. EX2: Won 2J **71**
MATFORD 5F **71**
Matford Av. EX2: Exe 7H **7** (1G **71**)
Matford Bus. Pk. EX2: Mar B 5G **71**
The Matford Cen. 5G **71**
Matford La. EX2: Exe 7G **7** (1G **71**)
Matford M. EX2: Matf 6H **71**
Matford Park & Ride 6G **71**
Matford Pk. Rd. EX2: Matf 4F **71**
Matford Rd. EX2: Exe 7H **7** (1G **71**)
Matford Way EX2: Mar B 6G **71**
Mathews Cl. EX14: Hon 5E **54**
Mathill Cl. TQ5: Brixh 5D **122**
Mathill Rd. TQ5: Brixh 5D **122**
Matlock Lodge *TQ2: Torq 1C* **116**
(off St Luke's Rd.)
Maton Cl. PL21: Ivy 5H **145**
Matthew's Ct. EX15: Cull 4H **45**
Matthews Ct. EX4: Pin 2C **66**
Maudlin Dr. TQ14: Teignm 1H **107**
Maudlin Rd. TQ9: Tot 6E **102**
Maudlins La. PL19: Tavi 4G **59**
Maudlins Pk. PL19: Tavi 4G **59**
Maunder's Hill EX9: Ott'n 6H **83**
Maunders Pl. EX9: Ott'n 6H **83**
Maunsell Cl. PL2: Plym 4E **134**
Mavisdale PL2: Plym 5E **134**
Maxstoke Cl. TQ1: Torq 1F **117**
Maxwell Ct. *TQ1: Torq 7B* **112**
(off McKay Av.)
TQ12: New A 2G **109**
Maxwell Rd. PL4: Plym 4C **142**
MAXWORTHY 1A **168**
Maybank Rd. PL4: Plym . . .3K **9** (2B **142**)
Mayers Way PL9: Hooe 6E **142**
Mayfair EX16: Tive 3K **41**
Mayfair Cres. PL6: Plym 2C **136**
Mayfair Ho. PL4: Plym 3G **9**
Mayfair Rd. TQ12: Ipp 6H **101**
Mayfield PL21: Ivy 5E **144**
Mayfield Cres. TQ12: New A 1C **108**
Mayfield Dr. EX8: Exmth 6F **77**
Mayfield Rd. EX2: Won 7K **65**
EX4: Pin 3D **66**
Mayfield Way EX5: Cran 3B **68**
Mayflower Av. EX4: Exe 2G **65**
TQ12: New A 2J **109**
Mayflower Ct. EX7: Daw 4H **97**
EX37: C'ton 5H **25**
PL9: Plyms 5G **143**
PL20: Bere A 2B **128**
TQ6: Dartm 5C **124**
Mayflower Dr. PL2: Plym 6G **135**
TQ5: Brixh 5E **122**
Mayflower Int. Marina 4E **140**
Mayflower Mus. 6G **9** (3K **141**)

Mayflower Stone & Steps 7G **9** (4K **141**)
Mayflower St.
PL1: Plym 3D **8** (2J **141**)
May Hilder Way *EX39: W Ho 6B* **20**
(off Atlantic Way)
Maynarde Cl. PL7: Plymp 4E **138**
Maynard Pl. PL20: Bere A 2B **128**
Mayne Cl. EX20: Hath 2G **35**
Mayor's Av.
TQ6: Dartm 1B **124** (6F **125**)
May St. EX4: Exe 1H **7** (5G **65**)
May Ter. EX10: Sidm 6C **84**
PL4: Plym 3H **9** (2A **142**)
Mazzard Cl. EX32: Land 4H **11**
MEAD 2A **162**
The Mead EX5: Silv 1H **51**
PL7: Plymp 4K **137**
Mead Cl. EX15: Cull 5G **45**
PL21: Ivy 3E **144**
TQ12: Kingst 7H **115**
Meadcombe Rd. TQ7: Thur 6C **154**
Mead Cotts. EX8: Lit 5H **77**
Mead Cross EX5: Cran 3B **68**
Mead Dr. TQ7: Thur 6C **154**
Meadfoot TQ7: Thur 6C **154**
Meadfoot Cl. TQ1: Torq 2H **117**
TQ1: Torq 3E **116**
Meadfoot Cross *TQ1: Torq 3E* **116**
(off Parkhill Rd.)
Meadfoot Grange TQ1: Torq 3E **116**
Meadfoot La. TQ1: Torq 3E **116**
Meadfoot Rd. TQ1: Torq 3E **116**
Meadfoot Sea Rd. TQ1: Torq 3F **117**
Meadfoot Ter. PL4: Plym 6A **136**
Meadhurst Ct. EX10: Sidm 6B **84**
Mead La. TQ3: Paig 7H **115**
TQ7: Thur 6C **154**
Meadow Acre Rd. EX14: Gitt 6B **54**
Meadow Av. EX12: Seat 4E **86**
Mdw. Bank EX13: Kilm 2C **88**
Meadowbank TQ13: Chud K 6B **94**
Mdw. Brook EX31: Rou 6A **18**
PL19: Tavi 5G **59**
TQ9: Tot 6F **103**
Meadowbrook Cl. EX4: Exe 4B **64**
Meadow Bus. Pk. EX17: Cred 6K **39**
Meadow Cl. EX5: Clyst M 2K **73**
EX8: Lymp 6H **75**
EX9: Bud S 6B **82**
EX11: Ott M 3D **80**
EX31: Brat F 6H **13**
EX32: Land 3D **24**
EX34: Ilfra 4H **11**
PL7: Plymp 5G **139**
PL8: New F 4J **149**
TQ9: Tot 6H **103**
TQ12: Kingsk 6J **109**
Meadow Ct. EX39: Wools 3B **28**
Meadow Ct. Barns TQ7: Stoke 6K **159**
Meadow Cres. EX8: San B 6J **77**
Meadowcroft Dr. TQ12: Kingst 2G **105**
Meadow Dr. EX10: New P 5H **81**
PL8: Brixt 3H **149**
Meadowfield Pl. PL7: Plymp 6E **138**
Meadow Gdns. EX17: Cred 6J **39**
Mdw. Halt TQ12: E Ogw 2D **108**
Meadowland Rd. EX31: C'nor 1D **16**
Meadowlands EX5: New C 7C **50**
PL6: Plym 3E **132**
Meadowlands Leisure Pool 4H **59**
Meadow La. EX5: Cran 3B **68**
EX9: Bud S 6C **82**
EX15: Cull 5H **45**
EX33: Croy, Puts 1D **14**
EX39: Ins 3K **21**
Mdw. Lea EX5: Silv 1H **51**
Meadow Pk. EX7: Daw 3F **97**
EX15: Will 4C **44**
EX21: Sheb 6J **29**
EX31: Rou 7A **18**
EX36: S Mol 7C **26**
EX39: Bide 5C **22**
PL9: Hooe 7D **142**
TQ3: Marl 3D **114**
TQ5: Brixh 3D **122**
TQ11: B'leigh 3E **98**
TQ12: Ipp 6J **101**
Meadow Ri. EX7: Daw 3F **97**
PL7: Plymp 5D **138**
TQ12: New A 6A **104**
TQ14: Teignm 2F **107**
Meadow Rd. EX9: Bud S 6B **82**
EX12: Seat 5E **86**
EX31: B'aple 2C **18**
EX32: B'aple 5H **19**
TQ2: Torq 3A **116**
The Meadows EX12: Beer 7B **86**
TQ12: Kingst 5J **105**
Meadows Cres. EX14: Hon 4F **55**
Mdws. Edge EX6: Cher 2C **62**
Mdw. Side TQ12: New A 1D **108**
Meadowside EX31: Ashf 1K **17**
PL9: Plyms 5G **143**
TQ7: Chil 6G **159**
Meadowside Ct. EX17: Cop 6C **38**
Meadow St. EX8: Exmth 5C **76**
Meadowsweet La. EX31: Rou 6A **18**
TQ4: Paig 5E **118**

Meadow Va. EX20: Mert 5B **30**
Meadow Vw. EX8: Lymp 6H **43**
EX15: Uff 6H **43**
EX16: Bam 2G **33**
EX22: Hols 1C **34**
EX39: Hart 2J **27**
PL8: Brixt 3F **149**
TQ12: E Ogw 3C **108**
Meadow Vw. Cl. EX5: W'bury 5D **84**
Meadow Vw. Rd. EX8: Exmth 2G **77**
PL7: Plymp 6K **137**
Meadowville Rd. EX39: Bide 2F **23**
Mdw. Way EX2: Heav 7J **65**
EX10: Col R 3H **83**
PL7: Plymp 2A **138**
Mead Pk. EX31: Bick 5J **17**
Mead Pk. Cl. EX31: Bick 5J **17**
Mead Rd. TQ2: Torq 4K **115**
Meads Cl. EX14: Dunk 7G **47**
Mead Vw. Rd. EX14: Hon 4F **55**
Mead Way EX12: Seat 4E **86**
TQ12: New A 4G **109**
Meadway EX10: Sidm 4C **84**
MEADWELL 2C **169**
Meadwood TQ1: Torq 3F **117**
MEARE GREEN
TA3, nr. Curry Mallet 1C **167**
TA3, nr. Stoke St Gregory 1D **167**
Mear Top EX31: B'aple 2E **18**
Meatherel Cl. PL21: Ivy 5F **145**
MEAVY 7K **127** (1B **174**)
Meavy Av. PL5: Plym 1K **135**
TQ2: Torq 6H **111**
Meavy Bourne PL20: Yelv 6H **127**
Meavy La. PL20: Yelv 6G **127**
Meavy Vw. PL20: Prin 6C **60**
Meavy Vs. PL20: Yelv 6G **127**
Meavy Way PL5: Plym 1K **135**
PL19: Tavi 4K **59**
Mecca Bingo
Devonport 2D **140**
(off Fore St.)
Exeter 4D **6**
Medard Ho. EX32: B'aple 4F **19**
MEDDON 2A **162**
Meddon St. EX39: Bide 4E **22**
The Mede EX3: Top 5A **74**
EX4: Whip 4A **66**
Medland Cres. PL6: Plym 4J **131**
Medley Ct. EX4: Exe 4B **64**
Medway Pl. PL3: Plym 5E **136**
Medway Rd. TQ2: Torq 3D **112**
MEETH 3D **163**
Meeting La. EX8: Lymp 5G **75**
Meeting St. EX8: Exmth 5C **76**
EX39: App 2H **21**
Meetways La. EX8: Exmth 6F **77**
Melbourne Cotts.
PL1: Plym 3B **8** (2H **141**)
TQ6: Dartm 2A **124**
Melbourne Grn. PL1: Plym 3B **8**
Melbourne Ct. EX2: Exe 6F **7**
Melbourne Pl. EX2: Exe . . .6F **7** (7F **65**)
PL1: Plym 2B **8**
Melbourne St. EX2: Exe . . .7F **7** (1F **71**)
EX16: Tive 4B **40**
PL1: Plym 2B **8** (1H **141**)
Melcot Cl. TQ12: Kingst 4H **105**
MELDON 1D **169**
Meldon Ct. EX9: Bud S 6D **82**
Meldon Quarry Station (Rail) 1D **169**
Meldon Reservoir Picnic Site 1D **169**
Meldon Rd. TQ13: Chag 4H **61**
Meldrum Cl. EX7: Daw 4H **97**
Melhuish Cl. EX16: W'ridge 6H **33**
Mellons Cl. TQ12: New A 7A **104**
(off Mellons Cl.)
Mellons Wlk. TQ12: New A 7A **104**
(off Mellons Cl.)
Mellowes Ct. EX13: Axmin 3G **89**
Mellows Mdw. TQ12: New A 1C **108**
Melrose Av. EX1: Sow 6C **66**
PL2: Plym 3G **135**
Melville La. TQ2: Torq 2D **116**
Melville Pl. *PL2: Plym 6F* **135**
(off Melville Rd.)
TQ2: Torq 2D **116**
(off Melville St.)
Melville Rd. PL2: Plym 6F **135**
Melville St. TQ2: Torq 2D **116**
Melville Ter. La. PL2: Plym 6F **135**
MEMBLAND 5K **149**
MEMBURY .3C **167**
Membury Castle 3C **167**
Membury Cl. EX1: Sow 6C **66**
Membury Cres. EX1: Sow 5C **66**
Membury Rd. EX13: Axmin 1F **89**
Memory La. PL9: Plyms 5F **143**
Mena Pk. Cl. PL9: Elb 5J **143**
TQ4: Paig 5F **119**
Mena Pk. Rd. PL9: Elb 5J **143**
Mendip Rd. TQ2: Torq 3J **115**
Menors Pl. EX22: Hols 1C **34**
Merafield Cl. PL7: Plymp 6J **137**
Merafield Dr. PL7: Plymp 7K **137**
Merafield Farm Cotts.
PL7: Plymp 7J **137**
Merafield Ri. PL7: Plymp 7K **137**

Merafield Rd. PL7: Plymp 7H **137**
Mercer Ct. EX2: Cou W 3K **71**
Mercers Cl. EX16: Tive 2E **40**
Merchant Row EX2: Cou W 6B **72**
Merchants Cnr. *TQ12: New A 1G* **109**
(off Quay Rd.)
Merchant's House Mus. 5E **8**
Meredith Rd. PL2: Plym 4H **135**
Mere La. TQ14: Teignm 4J **107**
Meresyke EX8: Exmth 6E **76**
Meridian Pl. EX34: Ilfra 2H **11**
Merivale Cl. TQ14: Teignm 2J **107**
Merley Rd. EX39: W Ho 5A **20**
Merlin Bus. Pk. EX5: Clyst H 7C **68**
Merlin Cinemas
The Central Cinema 2D **116**
The New Carlton Cinema 3B **48**
The Tivoli Cinema 5D **40**
Merlin Cl. PL6: Plym 2E **132**
Merlin Cres. EX4: Whip 3K **65**
Merlin Way TQ2: Torq 3K **111**
Mermaid Ct. EX1: Exe 5D **6**
Mermaid Wlk. *EX31: B'aple 4E* **18**
(off Boutport St.)
Mermaid Yd. EX1: Exe 5D **6** (7E **64**)
Merrifield PL21: Fil 4K **145**
Merrifield Rd. TQ11: B'leigh 3A **98**
Merrion Av. EX8: Exmth 6F **77**
MERRIOTT .2D **167**
Merritt Flats *TQ3: Paig 2G* **119**
(off Merritt Rd.)
Merritt Rd. TQ3: Paig 2G **119**
MERRIVALE 3D **169**
Merrivale Cl. TQ2: Torq 1D **112**
Merrivale Prehistoric Settlement
. . . . .3D **169**
Merrivale Rd. EX4: Exe 1C **70**
EX20: Oke 2E **48**
PL2: Plym 4F **135**
PL5: Plym 7G **131**
Merrivale Vw. Rd. PL20: Dous 4K **127**
Merrow Down Dr. EX12: Seat 4D **86**
Merryfield Airfield 2D **167**
Merryfield Rd. EX39: Bide 4H **23**
Merryland Cl. TQ3: Pres 4H **115**
Merryland Gdns. TQ3: Pres 4H **115**
Merrylees Dr. EX32: B'aple 6H **19**
MERRYMEET 3A **168**
Merrythorn Rd. EX31: Frem 6D **16**
Merrywood TQ12: E Ogw 3C **108**
Mersey Cl. PL3: Plym 5E **136**
MERTON 5B **30** (2D **163**)
MESHAW 2B **164**
Meshaw Moor Nature Reserve 2B **164**
METCOMBE 1G **81** (1A **172**)
Metcombe Ri. EX11: Metc 1H **81**
Metcombe Va. EX11: Metc 1H **81**
Meteorological Office
Exeter 5C **66**
HPC Complex 4F **67**
Meteor Wlk. *EX32: B'aple 4G* **19**
(off Oliver Rd.)
METHERELL 1A **174**
Metherell Av. TQ5: Brixh 5E **122**
Metherell Av. Ind. Est.
TQ5: Brixh 5E **122**
Metherell Rd. EX39: Bide 4E **22**
The Mews EX7: Daw 4H **97**
PL1: Plym 1E **140**
PL21: Moor 3C **146**
Mews Gdns. TQ6: Dartm 1A **124**
Mewstone Av. PL9: Wem 7B **148**
Meyer Ct. EX2: Heav 7K **65**
Meyhew Gdns. PL7: Plymp 2B **138**
Meyrick Rd. TQ1: Torq 6E **112**
Michael Browning Way
EX2: Exe 7E **6** (1F **71**)
Michael Foot Av. PL1: Dev 3D **140**
Michael Rd. PL3: Plym 6B **136**
MICHELCOMBE 1C **175**
Michigan Way EX4: Exe 2F **65**
PL3: Plym 5D **136**
Mid Churchway PL9: Plyms 5H **143**
Middle Blagdon La. TQ3: Blag 1B **118**
Middleborough La. EX33: Croy 1A **14**
Middle Budleigh Mdw.
TQ12: New A 1C **108**
Middle Combe Dr. EX31: Rou 7K **17**
Middlecombe La. PL8: Noss M 7H **149**
MIDDLECOTT 2B **170**
Middlecott La. EX17: Morc 2A **38**
Middle Cross EX31: Bick 5A **18**
Middle Down Top TQ7: Tot 6B **102**
Middle Down Cl. PL9: Plyms 7H **143**
Middlefield Rd. PL6: Plym 4J **131**
Middle Grn. TQ10: S Bre 2C **100**
Middle Gunstone *EX39: Bide 3F* **23**
(off Lower Gunstone)
Middlehill La. EX33: Croy 1A **14**
Middle Leigh PL8: New F 5G **149**
Middle Lincombe Rd. TQ1: Torq 3F **117**
MIDDLE MARWOOD 3B **160**
Middlemead Rd. EX16: Tive 3D **40**
Middle Mill La. EX15: Cull 4H **45**
MIDDLE MOOR 1C **72**
MIDDLEMOOR 3C **169**
Middle Pk. Ter. TQ7: S Mil 6E **154**
Middle Ramshill La. TQ3: Paig 7C **114**

Middle Rd. PL9: Wem 6A 148
Middle St. EX9: E Bud 1D 82
  TQ5: Brixh 3E 122
  TQ14: Shal 6G 107
Middleton Rd. EX39: Bide 3E 22
Middleton Wlk. PL5: Plym 6C 130
Middletown La. EX9: E Bud 1D 82
Middle Warberry Rd. TQ1: Torq . .1E 116
MIDDLEWOOD
  EX6 . . . . .3D 96
  PL15 . . . . .3A 168
Middlewood Hill EX6: Cockw 4D 96
MIDDLE WOOLBROOK 3B 84
MIDDLEZOY 1D 167
Midella Rd. PL20: Yelv 6G 127
MIDELNEY 1D 167
Mid LAMBROOK 2D 167
Midvale Rd. TQ4: Paig 2H 119
Midway EX8: Exmth 4G 77
  TQ12: Kingsk 6J 109
Midway Cl. EX2: Alph 4D 70
Midway Ter. EX2: Alph 4D 70
Miers Cl. PL5: Plym 3B 134
Miglo Ind. Est. TQ4: Paig 4E 118
Mignonette Wlk. EX39: Bide 2F 23
                (off Northam Rd.)
MILBER 3H 109
Milber La. TQ12: Coff, New A . .5K 109
  TQ12: New A 2K 109
Milber Trad. Est. TQ12: New A . .3K 109
Milbury Cl. EX6: Exmin 1C 74
Milbury Farm Mdw. EX6: Exmin . .1C 74
Milbury La. EX6: Exmin 2D 74
Mildmay Cl. EX4: Exe 5C 64
Mildmay St. PL4: Plym . .2G 9 (1K 141)
Mildren Way PL1: Dev 2D 140
MILE END 6B 104
Mile End Rd. TQ12: New A 6B 104
Mile Gdns. EX4: Whip 2J 65
MILEHOUSE 6G 135
Milehouse Park & Ride 6H 135
Milehouse Rd. PL3: Plym 7F 135
Mile La. EX4: Whip 1J 65
Miles Mitchell Av. PL6: Plym 2B 136
MILFORD 1A 162
Milford Cl. TQ14: Teignm 4G 107
Milford La. EX5: Thor 2B 50
  PL5: Plym 5F 131
Military Rd. PL1: Dev 2E 140
                (off Raglan Rd.)
  PL3: Plym 5E 136
  PL6: Plym 4D 136
Milizac Cl. PL8: Y'ton 2A 150
Milkaway La. EX33: Croy 2D 14
The Milky Way Adventure Park 1B 162
The Mill EX2: Exe 7G 7 (1G 71)
  TQ12: New A 7F 105
Millards Hill EX39: Ins 2K 21
Mill Av. EX17: Cop 5C 38
MILLBAY 7B 8 (3G 141)
Millbay Docks PL1: Plym 4G 141
Millbay Marina Village
  PL1: Plym 7B 8 (4H 141)
Millbay Pk. 6B 8 (3H 141)
Millbay Rd. PL1: Plym 6A 8 (3G 141)
Mill Bottom La. TQ14: Shal 7C 106
Mill Bri. PL1: Plym 3A 8 (1G 141)
MILLBROOK 2A 174
Millbrook Dale EX13: Axmin 2J 89
Millbrook La. EX2: Exe 3H 71
Millbrook Pk. Rd. TQ2: Torq 1A 116
Millbrook Rd. TQ3: Paig 1H 119
Mill Cl. PL21: L Mill 5C 144
  TQ12: New A 7B 104
Millcombe Cnr. TQ9: Blacka 3B 152
Mill Ct. EX7: Daw 4F 97
  EX32: Swim 2H 25
Mill Cres. TQ6: Dartm 5D 124
Millcroft EX11: Ott M 4C 80
Milldale Cres. EX14: Hon 4E 54
Mill Dr. EX2: Cou W 4J 71
Mill End TQ12: Kingst 1H 105
Millennium Pl. EX16: Tive 3G 41
Millennium St. PL2: Plym 3H 135
Millennium Way EX15: Cull 2H 45
  EX39: W Ho 5D 20
Miller Cl. EX2: Won 1B 72
Miller Ct. PL1: Plym 5A 8 (3G 141)
Miller Cres. EX32: B'aple 4F 19
Miller Ho. EX2: Exe 3J 71
                (off Turnstone Rd.)
Millers Brook EX33: Croy 2D 14
Millers Cl. EX10: Sidm 6C 84
Millers La. TQ9: Sto G 4A 120
Millers Way EX6: Ted M 7J 49
  EX14: Hon 4E 54
Miller Way EX6: Exmin 1B 74
  PL6: Plym 6D 132
Milletts Cl. EX6: Exmin 2C 74
THE MILLFIELDS 2G 141
Millford Av. EX10: Sidm 6C 84
Millford Rd. EX10: Sidm 6C 84
Mill Grn. DT7: Lym R 5K 91
Millgreen Ct. DT7: Lym R 5K 91
Millgreen La. EX13: Kilm 1B 88
MILLHAYES
  EX14 . . . . .3C 167
  EX15 . . . . .1G 47 (2B 166)

Millhayes Farm EX15: Hemy 1G 47
Mill Head EX16: Bam 1H 33
  EX34: Ilfra 2J 11
Millhead Rd. EX14: Hon 4E 54
Mill Hill EX31: Frem 6F 17
  TQ9: Sto G 4B 120
Mill Hill Ct. TQ9: Sto G 4B 120
Mill Hill La. PL19: Tavi 3F 59
Millin Way EX7: Daw W 7D 96
Mill La. DT7: Lym R 5K 91
  DT7: Uply 3G 91
  EX2: Alph 4E 70
  EX2: Cou W 4J 71
              (not continuous)
  EX3: Ext 1G 75
  EX5: Broadc 3H 67
  EX10: New P 7G 81
  EX12: Brans 6H 85
  EX17: Bow 5G 37
  EX17: Cher F 1F 39
  EX20: N Taw 6A 36
  EX31: B'aple 3D 18
  EX31: Brat F 6F 13
  EX33: Croy 2D 14
  EX33: Wraf 3H 15
  EX34: Ber 3B 12
  EX34: Wool 3A 16
  TQ2: Torq 1B 116
  TQ3: Comp 5C 110
  TQ3: Paig 7H 115
  TQ5: Brixh 7C 122
  TQ5: Galm 4F 121
  TQ6: Sto F 3F 153
  TQ7: Ave G 7H 155
  TQ9: Tot 6F 103
  TQ12: E Ogw 3A 108
  TQ12: N Whil 4C 110
              (not continuous)
  TQ13: Ashb 3G 99
  TQ14: Teignm 3F 107
Mill Leat EX15: Hemy 1G 47
Mill Leat Cl. PL8: Y'ton 2C 150
Mill-Leat Gdns. EX32: Land 2B 24
Millmans Rd. TQ3: Marl 3D 114
Mill Mdw. EX34: C Mar 6B 12
  PL21: Ivy 4H 145
  TQ13: Ashb 3G 99
MILLMOOR 2B 46
Millmoor La. EX10: New P 5H 81
Millmoor Vw. EX10: New P 5H 81
Mill on the Mole Res. Pk.
  EX36: S Mol 6E 26
Mill Pk. Ind. Est. EX5: Wood S 1E 78
Mill Pk. Touring Cvn. & Camping Site
                   .2B 12
Mill Path TQ13: Ashb 4H 99
              (off St Andrews Cl.)
Mill Rd. EX2: Cou W 4J 71
  EX19: Bea 4F 31
  EX20: Oke 3B 48
  EX22: Bradw 5B 28
  EX31: B'aple 4D 18
  EX31: Frem 6F 17
  EX32: Land 3C 24
  EX37: High B 2A 32
  TQ9: Darti 3A 102
  TQ13: Lust 6H 63
  TQ13: Ashb 3G 99
Mill Row EX39: West 7K 21
Mills Rd. PL1: Dev 2E 140
Mill Stile EX33: Brau 5H 15
Millstream EX2: Exe 3J 71
Mill Stream Ct. EX11: Ott M 4B 80
Mill Stream Gdns. EX16: Hal 6D 42
Millstream Mdw. TQ13: Chud 1D 94
Mill St. EX10: Sidm 6C 84
  EX11: Ott M 4C 80
  EX14: Hon 4D 54
  EX15: Uff 6H 43
  EX17: Cred 6J 39
  EX36: S Mol 6C 26
  EX38: G Tor 3A 30
  EX39: Bide 4F 23
  PL1: Dev 2D 140
  TQ7: Kingsb 4F 157
  TQ13: Chag 2G 61
  EX3: Axmin 1K 89
Mills Way EX31: B'aple 3E 18
Mill Tail TQ9: Tot 6E 102
MILLTOWN 4D 66
Milltown La. EX10: Sidm 4D 84
Millway EX5: Bradn 2C 52
  TQ13: Chud 2C 94
Millway Gdns. EX5: Bradn 2C 52
Millway Pl. PL9: Plyms 4E 142
Millway Av. EX13: Axmin 3K 89
Millwey Ct. EX13: Axmin 4K 89
Millwey Ri. Ind. Est.
  EX13: Axmin 4K 89
Millwood TQ13: Bov T 7B 92
Millwood Bus. Pk. TQ12: New A . .7H 105
Millwood Dr. PL6: Plym 2F 137
Mill Yd. EX2: Cou W 4J 71
Milne Pl. PL1: Dev 1E 140
MILTON ABBOT 2B 58 (3C 169)
Milton Cl. EX8: Exmth 7K 75
  PL5: Plym 1H 135
  TQ5: Brixh 6D 122
MILTON COMBE 1A 174

Milton Ct. PL4: Plym 3B 142
              (not continuous)
Milton Cres. PL19: Tavi 4K 59
  TQ5: Brixh 6D 122
MILTON DAMEREL 2B 162
Milton Flds. TQ5: Brixh 6C 122
MILTON GREEN 3B 58
Milton Hill 3D 171
Milton Ho. TQ12: New A 2F 109
Milton La. TQ6: Dartm 7C 124
Milton Pk. TQ5: Brixh 6D 122
Milton Pl. EX39: Bide 4E 22
Milton Rd. EX2: Won 2J 71
  TQ12: New A 7E 104
Milton St. TQ5: Brixh 7C 122
Miltons Yd. EX13: Axmin 3H 89
Milton Ter. EX34: C Mar 6B 12
MILVERTON 1B 166
Mimosa Cl. EX16: Tive 2E 40
Mimosa Way TQ4: Paig 5E 118
Minacre La. TQ12: N Whil 5E 110
Mincent Cl. TQ2: Torq 2C 112
Mincent Hill TQ2: Torq 2C 112
Mincinglake Rd. EX4: Exe 3H 65
Minden Rd. TQ14: Teignm 4H 107
Miners Cl. TQ13: Ashb 3J 99
Minerva Bus. Pk. TQ12: New A . .1G 109
Minerva Cl. PL7: Plymp 3D 138
Minerva Way TQ12: New A 1H 109
Mines Rd. EX39: Bide 4H 23
              (not continuous)
Miniature Pony Centre 2B 170
Minifie Rd. EX14: Hon 3E 54
MINIONS 3A 168
Minnows Camping & Cvn. Site . . .1D 42
Minses Cl. PL9: Elb 5K 143
Minster Ct. EX13: Axmin 4G 89
Minster Rd. EX6: Exmin 1D 74
The Mint EX4: Exe 4C 6 (7E 64)
Mint Pk. Rd. EX33: Brau 3G 15
Mirador Pl. PL4: Plym 1C 142
Miranda Rd. TQ3: Pres 6F 115
Mirey La. EX5: W'bury 5C 78
Miry La. EX15: Kent 7C 46
Mission Ct. EX4: Exe 5F 65
Misterton Cl. PL9: Hooe, Plyms . . .7E 142
Mitchell Cl. PL9: Hooe, Plyms 7E 142
Mitchell Gdns. EX13: Axmin 4H 89
Mitchum's Beach Campsite 1A 14
Mitchum's Village Campsite 2C 14
Mitre Cl. PL19: Tavi 6G 59
  TQ14: Bi'ton 3A 106
              (not continuous)
Mitre Ct. PL1: Plym 6A 8
Mitre La. EX4: Exe 4C 6 (6E 64)
Mizzen Rd. PL1: Dev 3E 140
Moat Hill TQ9: Tot 7E 102
Moat Pk. PL6: Plym 2D 136
              (off Bircham Vw.)
MODBURY 6G 147 (2C 175)
Modbury Battle Site 2C 175
Modbury Cl. PL5: Plym 7G 131
Modbury Information Centre
            .6G 147 (2C 175)
Model Ter. EX39: Bide 4F 23
Modred Cl. EX4: Whip 3K 65
Modyford Wlk. PL20: Buck M 5A 126
Mogworthy 2C 165
Mohun's Cl. PL19: Tavi 5J 59
Mohun's Pk. PL19: Tavi 6J 59
Mole Bri. La. EX36: S Mol 6E 26
Mole Ridge Way EX36: S Mol 5C 26
Moles La. TQ3: Marl 5E 110
  TQ12: Kingst, N Whil 5E 110
Molesworth Cotts. PL3: Plym 7F 135
              (off Molesworth Rd.)
Molesworth Rd. PL1: Plym 7F 135
  PL3: Plym 7F 135
  PL7: Plymp 5J 137
Molesworth Way EX22: Hols 2A 34
MOLLAND 1C 165
Mollison Rd. PL5: Plym 1H 135
Molyneaux Pl. PL1: Dev 1E 140
Monastery Rd. TQ3: Paig 1G 119
Mondeville Way EX39: Nort 6E 20
The Moneycentre Precinct 3E 8
Monica Wlk. PL4: Plym . .1H 9 (1A 142)
Monitor Cl. EX2: Exe 7D 6 (1E 70)
MONKERTON 4D 66
Monkerton Cl. EX1: Pin 4D 66
Monkerton Ct. EX1: Pin 4D 66
Monkerton Dr. EX1: Pin 4D 66
Monkey La. EX10: New P 7F 81
Monkey Puzzle Dr. EX20: Oke 3E 48
MONKLEIGH 1C 163
Monkleigh Mill La. EX39: Buck B . . .1J 29
MONKOKEHAMPTON 3D 163
Monksbridge Rd. TQ5: Brixh 5D 122
Monks Cl. EX17: Cred 5G 39
  EX39: Bide 5J 23
Monksmead PL19: Tavi 5G 59
Monks Orchard TQ12: A'well 6D 108
Monk's Rd. EX4: Exe 1K 7 (5H 65)
Monkstone Gdns. EX13: Axmin 4J 89
              (off Cridlake)
Monks Way TQ13: Bov T 2A 92
Monkswell Rd. EX4: Exe 1K 7 (4H 65)
MONKTON 3B 166

MONKTON HEATHFIELD 1C 167
Monkton Rd. EX14: Hon, Monk'n 3G 55
              (not continuous)
MONKTON WYLD 1D 173
Monkton Wyld Camping Site 1D 90
MONKWOOD 1D 173
Monmouth Av. EX3: Top 6B 74
Monmouth Gdns. PL5: Plym 6G 131
Monmouth Hill EX3: Top 6B 74
Monmouth St. DT7: Lym R 5K 91
  EX3: Top 6B 74
Monmouth Way EX14: Hon 4G 55
Monroe Gdns. PL3: Plym 1C 8 (1H 141)
Monro Mead TQ12: Live 4F 93
Montacute Av. PL5: Plym 1F 135
Montagu Cl. EX2: Cou W 4C 72
  TQ7: Kingsb 3G 157
Montague Gdns. EX9: Bud S 6A 82
Montague Pl. EX39: Bide 4E 22
Montague Ri. EX4: Exe 1E 6 (5F 65)
Montague Ter. PL7: L Moor 1J 129
Montagu M. TQ7: Kingsb 3G 157
              (off Montagu Cl.)
Montagu Rd. TQ7: Kingsb 4F 157
Monterey EX8: Exmth 7E 76
  TQ4: Good 6J 119
             (off Hookhills Rd.)
Monterey Cl. TQ3: Paig 3A 116
Monterey Gdns. EX4: Exe 3H 65
Monterey Pk. TQ12: New A 3J 109
Montesson Cl. TQ3: Paig 7D 114
Montesson Rd. TQ3: Paig 7D 114
Montgomery Cl. PL21: Ivy 3J 145
Montgomery Dr. PL19: Tavi 3H 59
Montgomery Rd. EX2: Won 7C 66
              (off Sidmouth Rd.)
Mont Le Grand EX1: Heav 4K 7 (6H 65)
Montpelier Ct. EX4: Exe 2B 6 (5D 64)
  TQ3: Pres 5H 115
Montpelier La. EX34: Ilfra 2J 11
Montpelier M. EX34: Ilfra 2J 11
              (off Montpelier Rd.)
Montpelier Rd. EX34: Ilfra 2J 11
  PL2: Plym 4H 135
Montpelier Ter. EX34: Ilfra 2J 11
              (off Montpelier Rd.)
Montpellier Ct. EX8: Exmth 6D 76
              (off Montpellier Rd.)
Montpellier Rd. EX8: Exmth 6C 76
  TQ1: Torq 2D 116
Montpellier Ter. TQ1: Torq 2D 116
              (off Montpellier Rd.)
Montrose Way PL5: Plym 2J 135
Montserrat Ri. TQ2: Torq 2A 112
Monument St. PL1: Dev 3D 140
Moonhill Ct. EX2: Alph 5F 71
Moon La. PL21: Modb 6G 147
Moon Ridge EX2: Cou W 6B 72
Moon St. PL4: Plym 4G 9 (2K 141)
MOOR .2D 167
Moorashes TQ9: Tot 6E 102
              (off Grove Cl.)
MOORBATH 1D 173
Moor Cl. TQ14: Teignm 2J 107
Moorcourt Cl. EX10: Sidm 7A 84
Moor Cres. PL20: Prin 6C 60
Moorcroft Cl. EX20: Oke 3E 48
  PL9: Plyms 5H 143
Moorcroft Dr. EX20: Oke 3E 48
MOOR CROSS 2C 175
Moore Cl. TQ12: New A 4J 109
Moore Cres. EX22: Hols 2A 34
Moorfield EX24: Colyt 6D 88
  PL16: Lift 6B 56
Moorfield Av. PL6: Plym 4D 136
Moorfield Cl. EX8: Exmth 4E 76
Moorfield Rd. EX8: Exmth 4D 76
  PL15: St G 6C 34
Moorfields PL21: Moor 3D 146
Moorgate Viewpoint 2A 170
Moorhaven EX9: Bud S 5B 82
Moorhaven Cl. TQ1: Torq 6A 112
MOORHAVEN VILLAGE 3C 146
Moorhayes TQ13: Bov T 4C 92
Moorhen Cl. TQ12: Kingst 4F 105
The Moorings EX8: Exmth 6A 76
  EX33: Brau 4J 15
  TQ4: Paig 2J 119
              (off Belle Vue Rd.)
  TQ7: Kingsb 6G 157
Moorings Reach TQ5: Brixh 3F 123
MOORLAND 1D 167
Moorland Av. PL7: Plymp 3B 138
  TQ12: Den 1H 101
Moorland Cl. PL21: Bitta 3C 146
Moorland Ct. PL20: Yelv 7E 126
Moorland Gdns. PL7: Plymp 3C 138
Moorland Ga. TQ12: H'fld 2K 93
Moorland Pk. TQ10: S Bre 1B 100
Moorland Rd. PL7: Plymp 4B 138
Moorland Ri. EX36: S Mol 6C 26
Moorland Rd. PL7: Plymp 4B 138
Moorlands Cl. EX11: W Hill 3H 79
  EX16: Tive 2E 40
Moorlands Cl. TQ12: New A 2J 109
Moorlands Rd. EX9: Bud S 6A 82

Moorlands Vw. Ind. Est.—Newcause

Moorlands Vw. Ind. Est.
TQ4: Paig . . . 6F 119
Moorland Ter. EX38: G Tor . . . 2A 30
Moorland Vw. EX17: Lap . . . 2K 37
PL6: Plym . . . 5B 132
PL9: Elb . . . 5J 143
PL20: Prin . . . 6C 60
(not continuous)
TQ11: B'leigh . . . 4B 98
TQ12: New A . . . 2J 109
Moorland Vs. PL20: Yelv . . . 6G 127
Moorland Way EX4: Exe . . . 4B 64
Moor La. EX2: Sow . . . 6D 66
EX5: Clyst M, Wood S . . . 7K 73
EX9: Bud S . . . 5B 82
EX11: S'ton . . . 3G 81
EX20: Hath . . . 1J 35
EX33: Brau . . . 5F 15
EX33: Croy . . . 1A 14
PL5: Plym . . . 2D 134
TQ2: Torq . . . 2C 112
TQ13: Bov T . . . 6B 92
Moor La. Cl. TQ2: Torq . . . 2C 112
Moor Lea EX33: Brau . . . 5K 15
Moormead EX9: Bud S . . . 6B 82
Moor Pk. EX8: Exmth . . . 6E 76
EX14: Hon . . . 6E 54
PL21: Moor . . . 3C 146
TQ12: Kingsk . . . 6J 109
TQ13: Chag . . . 2H 61
Moor Pk. Cl. EX33: Croy . . . 1B 14
Moor Pk. La. EX10: Sidm . . . 4A 84
Moor Pk. Rd. TQ12: Kingsk . . . 6J 109
Moor Rd. TQ12: Ipp . . . 4F 101
Moors End TQ12: Kingst . . . 4G 105
Moorsend TQ12: New A . . . 7B 104
Moorside TQ7: Malb . . . 6G 155
Moors Pk. TQ14: Bi'ton . . . 4B 106
Moorstone Leat TQ4: Good . . . 6J 119
MOORTOWN . . . 1B 168
Moor Vw. EX20: Hath . . . 3G 35
EX20: N Taw . . . 7B 36
PL2: Plym . . . 6E 134
PL3: Plym . . . 7D 136
PL9: Plyms . . . 5E 142
PL11: Torp . . . 1A 140
PL19: Mary T . . . 2B 60
PL21: Bitta . . . 3C 146
TQ13: Bov T . . . 6B 92
(off Brimley Rd.)
TQ13: Chud . . . 2B 94
Moorview TQ3: Marl . . . 4D 114
Moor Vw. Cl. EX10: Sidm . . . 3A 84
Moorview Cl. EX4: Exe . . . 3G 65
Moorview Ct. PL6: Plym . . . 5G 133
Moorview Cres. TQ3: Marl . . . 4D 114
Moor Vw. Dr. TQ14: Teignm . . . 2F 107
Moorview End TQ3: Marl . . . 4D 114
Moor Vw. Ter. PL4: Plym . . . 1G 9 (7K 135)
PL20: Yelv . . . 6G 127
Moory Mdw. EX34: C Mar . . . 5A 12
MORCHARD BISHOP . . . 1B 38 (3B 164)
Morchard Road Station (Rail) . . . 3B 164
MORCOMBELAKE . . . 1D 173
MOREBATH . . . 1D 165
MORELEIGH . . . 2D 175
Moreleigh Rd. TQ9: H'ford . . . 7A 100
Moreton Av. EX39: Bide . . . 4D 22
PL6: Plym . . . 2A 136
Moreton Ct. EX39: Bide . . . 4C 22
Moreton Dr. EX39: Bide . . . 3D 22
MORETONHAMPSTEAD
. . . 6H 61 (2B 170)
Moretonhampstead Almshouses . . . 6J 61
Moretonhampstead Information Centre
. . . 6H 61 (2B 170)
Moretonhampstead Rd.
TQ13: Bov T . . . 2B 92
Moreton Pk. Rd. EX39: Bide . . . 5C 22
Moreton Ter. EX6: Bridf . . . 1F 63
Morgan Av. TQ2: Torq . . . 1C 116
Morgan Ct. *EX8: Exmth . . . 6C 76*
(off Rolle Rd.)
Morgan Rd. PL6: Plym . . . 4D 132
Morgans Quay TQ14: Teignm . . . 6H 107
Morgan Sweet EX5: Cran . . . 2D 68
Morice Sq. PL1: Dev . . . 2D 140
Morice St. PL1: Dev . . . 2D 140
MORICE TOWN . . . 7E 134
Morin Rd. TQ3: Pres . . . 6J 115
Morlaix Cl. EX7: Daw . . . 2H 97
Morlaix Dr. PL6: Plym . . . 6B 132
Morley Cl. PL7: Plymp . . . 6H 137
Morley Ct. PL1: Plym . . . 4C 8 (2H 141)
Morley Dr. PL20: C'stone . . . 6B 126
Morley Rd. EX4: Exe . . . 1K 7 (4H 65)
Morley Vw. Rd. PL7: Plymp . . . 5K 137
Morningside EX7: Daw . . . 6F 97
TQ1: Torq . . . 1G 117
(off Barrington Rd.)
Morris Cl. EX20: Hath . . . 2G 35
Morrish Pk. PL9: Plyms . . . 6G 143
Morshead Rd. PL6: Plym . . . 1A 136
MORTEHOE . . . 3A 10 (2A 160)
Mortehoe Mus. . . . 3A 10 (2A 160)
Mortehoe Sta. Rd.
EX34: Mort, Wool . . . 3A 10
Mortimer Av. TQ3: Pres . . . 6H 115
Mortimer Ct. EX2: Cou W . . . 3K 71
(not continuous)
Morton Cres. EX8: Exmth . . . 6B 76
Morton Cres. M. EX8: Exmth . . . 6B 76
Morton Dr. EX38: G Tor . . . 2C 30
Morton Rd. EX8: Exmth . . . 6B 76
Morton Way EX13: Axmin . . . 5H 89
Morven Dr. EX8: Exmth . . . 2C 76
Morville Pl. *EX16: Tive . . . 4D 40*
(off Water La.)
Morwell Gdns. PL2: Plym . . . 5F 135
Morwellham Cl. PL5: Plym . . . 3B 134
Morwellham Quay . . . 1A 174
Morwenna Pk. Rd. EX39: Nort . . . 5E 20
Morwenna Ter. *EX39: Nort . . . 5E 20*
(off Diddywell Rd.)
MORWENSTOW . . . 2A 162
Moses Cl. PL6: Plym . . . 3K 131
Moses Ct. *PL6: Plym . . . 3K 131*
(off Moses Cl.)
Mosshayne La. EX1: W Cly . . . 1F 67
EX5: Clyst H . . . 4H 67
Mossop Cl. EX11: Ott M . . . 4C 80
Mostyn Av. PL4: Plym . . . 1K 9 (7B 136)
Motehole Rd. TQ12: Ipp . . . 6H 101
MOTHECOMBE . . . 3C 175
Mothecombe Wlk. PL6: Plym . . . 2F 137
Motherhill Ct. TQ8: Salc . . . 3B 158
Moult Hill TQ8: Salc . . . 6A 158
Moulton Cl. PL7: Plymp . . . 4E 138
Moulton Wlk. PL7: Plymp . . . 5E 138
Moult Rd. TQ8: Salc . . . 6A 158
MOUNT . . . 3A 168
The Mount EX39: App . . . 2H 21
TQ2: Torq . . . 1B 112
TQ5: Brixh . . . 2E 122
TQ13: Chag . . . 3H 61
TQ14: Teignm . . . 3H 107
Mountain Cl. EX8: Exmth . . . 4H 77
The Mount Batten Cen. . . . 5A 142
Mt. Batten Cl. PL9: Plyms . . . 6E 142
Mountbatten Cl. EX8: Exmth . . . 2F 77
Mountbatten Dr. EX2: Cou W . . . 4B 72
Mountbatten Rd. EX16: Tive . . . 3C 40
Mt. Batten Way PL9: Plyms . . . 6E 142
Mt. Boone TQ6: Dartm . . . 1A 124 (5E 124)
Mt. Boone Hill
TQ6: Dartm . . . 1A 124 (5F 125)
Mt. Boone La.
TQ6: Dartm . . . 1A 124 (5F 125)
Mt. Boone Way TQ6: Dartm . . . 5E 124
Mt. Braddons M. TQ1: Torq . . . 2E 116
Mount Cl. EX14: Hon . . . 4E 54
MOUNT DINHAM . . . 4C 6 (6E 64)
Mt. Dinham Ct. EX4: Exe . . . 3C 6 (6E 64)
Mount Edgcumbe Country Pk.
. . . 6E 140 (2A 174)
Mount Edgcumbe Country Pk.
Formal Gdns. . . . 5D 140
Mount Edgcumbe House
. . . 6D 140 (2A 174)
Mt. Flagon Steps TQ6: Dartm . . . 1A 124
Mt. Ford PL19: Tavi . . . 4G 59
Mountford Dr. TQ13: Bov T . . . 4E 92
Mt. Galpine TQ6: Dartm . . . 1A 124
MOUNT GOULD . . . 1C 142
Mt. Gould Av. PL4: Plym . . . 2C 142
Mt. Gould Cres. PL4: Plym . . . 1C 142
Mt. Gould Rd. PL4: Plym . . . 1K 9 (1B 142)
Mt. Gould Way PL4: Plym . . . 1C 142
Mt. Hermon Rd. TQ1: Torq . . . 7D 112
Mt. Hill *EX12: Beer . . . 7B 86*
(off Long Hill)
Mounthill La. EX13: Mus . . . 7D 90
Mt. Howe EX3: Top . . . 6C 74
Mt. Pleasant EX13: Axmin . . . 4H 89
EX14: Offw . . . 4K 55
EX32: B Taw . . . 5B 24
EX39: Bide . . . 2H 23
PL5: Plym . . . 1G 135
TQ6: Kingsw . . . 6H 125
TQ13: Chud . . . 2D 94
TQ13: More . . . 7H 61
Mt. Pleasant Av. EX8: Exmth . . . 1D 76
Mt. Pleasant Cl. TQ7: Kingsb . . . 3G 157
TQ12: Kingsk . . . 2G 111
Mt. Pleasant Ct. EX8: Exmth . . . 2D 76
Mt. Pleasant La. TQ14: Shal . . . 6G 107
Mt. Pleasant M. TQ5: Brixh . . . 4E 122
Mt. Pleasant Rd. EX4: Exe . . . 1J 7 (4H 65)
EX7: Daw W . . . 1K 97
TQ1: Torq . . . 7D 112
TQ5: Brixh . . . 4E 122
TQ12: Kingsk . . . 2G 111
TQ12: New A . . . 2F 109
Mt. Pleasant Ter. *PL2: Dev . . . 7F 135*
(off Masterman Rd.)
MOUNT RADFORD . . . 5G 7 (7G 65)
Mt. Radford Cres.
EX2: Exe . . . 6G 7 (7G 65)
Mt. Radford Sq. EX2: Exe . . . 6G 7
Mt. Raleigh Av. EX39: Bide . . . 1D 22
Mt. Raleigh Dr. EX39: Bide . . . 2D 22
Mt. Ridley Rd. TQ6: Kingsw . . . 6H 125
Mount Ri. EX6: Kenn . . . 3J 95
Mount Rd. TQ5: Brixh . . . 4F 123
THE MOUNTS . . . 6A 152
The Mounts TQ9: E All . . . 5A 152
Mounts Farm Touring Pk. . . . 6A 152
Mt. Stone Rd. PL1: Plym . . . 4F 141
Mount St. PL1: Dev . . . 3D 140
PL4: Plym . . . 3G 9 (1K 141)
Mt. Tamar Cl. PL5: Plym . . . 1D 134
Mt. Tavy Rd. PL19: Tavi . . . 3K 59
Mount Vw. EX14: Fen . . . 1G 53
EX24: Colyt . . . 6D 88
EX34: Ilfra . . . 3J 11
Mountview Home Pk.
EX32: B'aple . . . 7K 19
Mount Vw. Ter. *TQ9: Tot . . . 6E 102*
(off Heath Way)
Mt. Wear Sq. EX2: Cou W . . . 5A 72
MOUNT WISE . . . 3E 140
Mt. Wise Cres. PL1: Dev . . . 3E 140
Mount Wise Outdoor Pools . . . 4D 140
Mowbray Av. EX4: Exe . . . 2F 7 (5F 65)
Mowbray Ct. EX2: Won . . . 7K 65
The Mowhay EX22: Hols . . . 2C 34
Mowhay Rd. PL5: Plym . . . 3E 134
(Coombe Way)
PL5: Plym . . . 2E 134
(Nth. Prospect Rd.)
Mowstead Pk. EX33: Brau . . . 3G 15
Mowstead Rd. EX33: Brau . . . 3G 15
Moxeys Cl. EX17: Cher F . . . 2H 39
Moyles Pk. PL21: Modb . . . 6F 147
Moyses La. EX20: Oke . . . 4A 48
Moyses Mdw. EX20: Oke . . . 4A 48
MUCHELNEY . . . 1D 167
MUCHELNEY HAM . . . 1D 167
Mucky La. EX19: Dol . . . 7F 31
Mudbank La. EX8: Exmth . . . 3B 76
MUDDIFORD . . . 3B 160
MUDDLEBRIDGE . . . 6H 17
Mudge Way PL7: Plymp . . . 4B 138
Mudstone La. TQ5: Brixh . . . 5F 123
Mulberry Cl. EX1: Whip . . . 6A 66
EX15: Will . . . 4D 44
PL6: Plym . . . 3F 133
TQ3: Paig . . . 7E 114
Mulberry Gro. PL19: Tavi . . . 7J 59
Mulberry Ri. EX12: Seat . . . 2E 86
Mulberry Rd. EX5: Cran . . . 2E 68
Mulberry St. TQ14: Teignm . . . 4H 107
Mulberry Way EX31: Rou . . . 7A 18
Mulgrave St.
PL1: Plym . . . 6D 8 (3J 141)
MULLACOTT . . . 7G 11 (2B 160)
Mullacott Farm EX34: Ilfra . . . 7G 11
Mullet Av. PL3: Plym . . . 7D 136
Mullet Cl. PL3: Plym . . . 7D 136
Mullet Rd. PL3: Plym . . . 7D 136
Mulligan Dr. EX2: Cou W . . . 3C 72
Muralto Ho. PL19: Tavi . . . 5G 59
MURCHINGTON . . . 2A 170
Murhill La. PL9: Plyms . . . 3E 142
Murley Cl. EX17: Cred . . . 5G 39
Murley Cres. TQ14: Bi'ton . . . 3A 106
Murley Grange TQ14: Bi'ton . . . 3A 106
Murrayfield Cl. PL2: Plym . . . 4H 135
MUSBURY . . . 7C 90 (1C 173)
Musbury Rd. EX13: Axmin . . . 6G 89
Museum Ct. TQ7: Kingsb . . . 3F 157
The Mus. of Barnstaple & North Devon
. . . 5E 18 (3B 160)
Mus. of British Surfing . . . 4J 15
Mus. of Dartmoor Life . . . 3B 48 (1D 169)
Museum Rd. TQ1: Torq . . . 2E 116
Mus. Way TQ1: Torq . . . 2E 116
Musgrave Ho. *EX4: Exe . . . 3E 6*
(off Musgrave Row)
Musgrave Row EX4: Exe . . . 3E 6 (6F 65)
Musket Rd. TQ12: H'fld . . . 2J 93
MUTLEY . . . 7K 135
Mutley Ct. PL4: Plym . . . 1G 9 (1K 141)
Mutley Plain PL4: Plym . . . 1G 9 (7K 135)
Mutley Plain La. PL4: Plym . . . 7K 135
Mutley Rd. PL3: Plym . . . 6K 135
Muttersmoor Rd. EX10: Sidm . . . 5A 84
MUTTERTON . . . 3A 166
Mutton La. EX2: Alph, Matf . . . 5F 71
EX38: Lit T . . . 4B 30
Muxey La. EX38: G Tor . . . 3B 30
Mylor Cl. PL2: Plym . . . 3J 135
Myra Ct. EX39: App . . . 2H 21
Myrtleberry La. EX35: Lynt . . . 4K 13
Myrtlebury Way EX1: Sow . . . 6C 66
Myrtle Cl. EX2: Alph . . . 4E 70
EX15: Will . . . 3E 44
PL20: Dous . . . 4K 127
Myrtle Cott. Rd. EX39: App . . . 4G 21
Myrtle Farm Vw. EX33: Croy . . . 2C 14
Myrtle Gdns. EX39: Bide . . . 3F 23
Myrtle Gro. EX39: Bide . . . 3F 23
Myrtle Hill TQ14: Teignm . . . 4J 107
Myrtle Rd. EX4: Exe . . . 1B 70
Myrtle Row EX8: Exmth . . . 6C 76
Myrtle St. EX39: App . . . 3H 21
Myrtleville PL2: Plym . . . 4F 135

N

Nadder La. EX36: S Mol . . . 6A 26
Nadder Mdw. EX36: S Mol . . . 6B 26
Nadder Pk. Rd. EX4: Exe . . . 7A 64
Nags Head Rd. EX14: Gitt . . . 6A 54
Naida Va. TQ6: Dartm . . . 4F 125
NAILSBOURNE . . . 1C 167
Napier St. PL1: Dev . . . 1E 140
Napier Ter. EX4: Exe . . . 4C 6 (6E 64)
PL4: Plym . . . 1F 9 (7K 135)
Napps Touring Holidays . . . 1C 12
Naps La. EX10: Col R . . . 1F 83
Nap Vw. EX14: Awli . . . 1A 54
Narracott La. EX36: S Mol . . . 7A 26
Narrow La. EX16: Tive . . . 5C 40
Naseby Dr. TQ12: H'fld . . . 2J 93
Nash Cl. PL7: Plymp . . . 4D 138
Nash Gdns. EX7: Daw . . . 6G 97
Nash Gro. EX4: Exe . . . 3D 64
Nasmith Cl. EX8: Exmth . . . 3F 77
Nassau Ct. EX39: W Ho . . . 5A 20
NATCOTT . . . 1A 162
Natcott La. EX39: Hart . . . 3K 27
National Marine Aquarium
. . . 6G 9 (3K 141)
Nats La. PL21: Corn, Ivy . . . 1B 144
Natson Mill La. EX17: Bow . . . 6G 37
Nattadon Rd. TQ13: Chag . . . 4H 61
Neadon La. EX6: Bridf . . . 1F 63
Neal Cl. PL7: Plymp . . . 5E 138
Neardale Ter. PL19: Lam . . . 7C 58
Neath Rd. PL4: Plym . . . 1B 142
Neath Rd. La. Sth. PL4: Plym . . . 1B 142
Needlewood Cl. EX11: W Hill . . . 5G 79
Needs Dr. EX39: Bide . . . 4D 22
Nellies Wood Vw. TQ9: Darti . . . 3D 102
Nelson Av. PL1: Plym . . . 1E 140
Nelson Cl. EX3: Top . . . 5A 74
TQ1: Torq . . . 4F 117
TQ14: Teignm . . . 3G 107
Nelson Dr. EX8: Exmth . . . 4G 77
EX39: W Ho . . . 5B 20
Nelson Gdns. PL1: Plym . . . 1E 140
Nelson M. EX39: W Ho . . . 5B 20
Nelson Pl. TQ12: New A . . . 6E 104
Nelson Rd. EX4: Exe . . . 7A 6 (1D 70)
EX39: W Ho . . . 5B 20
TQ5: Brixh . . . 3E 122
TQ6: Dartm . . . 7B 124
Nelson Rd. Ind. Est. *TQ6: Dartm . . . 5C 124*
(off Nelson Rd.)
Nelson St. PL4: Plym . . . 2G 9 (1K 141)
Nelson Ter. EX39: W Ho . . . 5B 20
PL6: Plym . . . 4F 133
Nelson Way EX2: Won . . . 7B 66
Nepean St. PL2: Plym . . . 6E 134
Neptune Pk. PL4: Plym . . . 4C 142
Ness Dr. TQ14: Shal . . . 6H 107
Ness Vw. Rd. TQ14: Teignm . . . 1J 107
Neswick St. PL1: Plym . . . 4A 8 (2G 141)
Neswick St. Ope
PL1: Plym . . . 4A 8 (2G 141)
Nether Cl. EX14: Gitt . . . 6B 54
NETHERCOTT . . . 3A 160
Nethercott Rd. EX33: Brau . . . 6E 14
NETHER EXE . . . 3D 165
Netherhams Hill EX33: Geo . . . 5B 14
Netherleigh Rd. TQ1: Torq . . . 6D 112
Nether Mdw. TQ3: Marl . . . 3D 114
NETHERTON . . . 3C 171
Netherton Est. PL20: Buck M . . . 4A 126
Netherton La. EX34: C Mar . . . 5C 12
Nethway Cross TQ6: Kingsw . . . 3K 125
Netley Rd. TQ12: New A . . . 7E 104
Nettlehayes PL9: Elb . . . 7K 143
NETTON . . . 3B 174
Netton Cl. PL9: Elb . . . 6J 143
Nevada Cl. PL3: Plym . . . 5E 136
Nevada Ct. EX12: Seat . . . 5E 86
Neville Rd. EX20: Oke . . . 3C 48
TQ12: New A . . . 7D 104
New Barn Hill PL7: Plymp . . . 6B 138
New Barnstaple Rd. EX34: Ilfra . . . 3K 11
Newberry Cl. EX34: Ber . . . 2D 12
Newberry Cotts. EX33: Geo . . . 5C 14
Newberry Hill EX34: Ber . . . 2E 12
Newberry La. EX34: C Mar . . . 2E 12
Newberry Rd. EX33: Geo . . . 5C 14
EX34: C Mar . . . 2E 12
Newberry Valley Touring & Camping Pk.
. . . 3E 12
Newbery Cl. EX13: Axmin . . . 3J 89
EX24: Colyt . . . 7D 88
Newbery Commercial Cen.
EX5: Clyst H . . . 7C 68
Newbridge Cl. EX39: Bide . . . 1F 23
New Bri. Gdns. *TQ7: Lodd . . . 3G 151*
(off Town's La.)
Newbridge Hill EX16: W'ridge . . . 5G 33
New Bri. St. EX4: Exe . . . 6C 6 (7E 64)
NEWBUILDINGS . . . 3B 164
New Bldgs. EX4: Exe . . . 1G 7
EX5: Broadc . . . 5C 52
EX16: Bam . . . 2H 33
EX31: Frem . . . 6F 17
EX32: B'aple . . . 4F 19
Newbury Cl. PL5: Plym . . . 6G 131
Newbury Dr. TQ13: Bov T . . . 4D 92
The New Carlton Cinema . . . 3B 48
Newcastle Gdns. PL5: Plym . . . 5G 131
Newcause *TQ11: B'leigh . . . 4C 98*
(off Jordan St.)

New C'way.—North St.

New C'way. *EX39: Nort 5E 20*
(off Diddywell Rd.)
Newcombe Cl. EX20: Oke 3D 48
Newcombes EX17: Cred 6H 39
Newcombe St. EX1: Heav 6J 65
Newcombe St. Gdns. EX1: Heav 6K 65
Newcombe Ter. *EX1: Heav 6J 65*
(off Newcombe St.)
Newcomen Engine House
1B 124 (6F 125)
Newcomen Rd.
TQ6: Dartm 2B 124 (6F 125)
NEWCOTT 3C 167
Newcourt Dr. EX2: Cou W 4C 72
Newcourt Rd. EX3: Top 5D 72
EX5: Silv 2H 51
Newcourt Station (Rail) 4D 72 (1D 171)
Newcourt Way EX2: Cou W 3C 72
NEW CROSS 2D 167
Newcross Pk. TQ12: Kingst 2F 105
New Cut EX12: Beer 7B 86
EX17: Cred 6G 39
(off High St.)
The New Cut EX15: Cull 4G 45
New England Hill PL7: Plymp 7A 144
New Esplanade Ct. TQ3: Paig 1J 119
New Est. EX5: New C 5D 50
New Exeter St. TQ13: Chud 1C 94
Newfoundland Cl. EX4: Exe 2H 65
Newfoundland Rd. TQ14: Teignm 4F 107
Newfoundland Way
TQ12: New A 1E 108
New George St.
PL1: Plym 4C 8 (2H 141)
New Grn. St. PL21: Ivy 5J 145
Newhaven EX5: Bradn 1C 52
The Newhay EX7: Daw 4F 97
Newhay Cl. EX7: Daw 4F 97
Newhayes TQ12: Ipp 7G 101
Newhayes Cl. EX2: Exe 3D 70
Newhouse Hill EX16: W'ridge 4H 33
New Inn Ct. EX15: Cull 4G 45
EX22: Hols 2C 34
NEWLAND 3D 161
Newland Cotts. EX32: Land 3D 24
Newland Pk. Rd. EX32: Land 3C 24
Newlands EX7: Daw 3H 97
EX14: Hon 3F 55
Newlands Av. EX8: Exmth 4F 77
Newlands Cl. EX2: Exe 3D 70
EX10: Sidm 2C 84
EX32: Land 2D 24
Newlands Dr. TQ13: Bov T 7B 92
Newlands Pk. EX12: Seat 4D 86
Newlands Rd. EX10: Sidm 2C 84
New La. EX11: Ott M 3D 80
EX33: Brau 1K 15
EX33: Croy 1B 14
New Launceston Rd. PL19: Tavi 3G 59
New London PL20: Prin 6D 60
Newman Ct. EX4: Exe 7B 64
Newman Cres. TQ9: Darti 3B 102
Newman Rd. EX4: Exe 1B 70
PL5: Plym 1D 134
Newmarket Ct. *PL19: Tavi 4J 59*
(off Duke St.)
New Mdw. PL21: Ivy 3E 144
New Mills Ind. Est. PL21: Modb 6F 147
Newnham Cl. PL7: Plymp 2D 138
Newnham Ind. Est. PL7: Plymp 2C 138
Newnham Rd. PL7: Plymp 3B 138
Newnham Way PL7: Plymp 3C 138
New Nth. Rd. EX4: Exe 1B 6 (4D 64)
EX8: Exmth 5C 76
New Orchard TQ10: S Bre 2B 100
New Pk. PL20: Horr 2F 127
(not continuous)
TQ13: Bov T 7B 92
New Pk. Cl. TQ5: Brixh 4F 123
New Pk. Cres. TQ12: Kingst 3G 105
New Pk. Est. EX6: Bridf 1F 63
New Pk. Rd. PL7: Plymp 5D 138
PL21: L Mill 5A 144
TQ3: Paig 7F 115
TQ12: Kingst 3G 105
New Pas. Hill PL1: Dev 1D 140
New Pl. EX16: Tive 4B 40
NEWPORT
EX32 6G 19 (3B 160)
PL15 2B 168
TA3 1D 167
Newport Pk. 6B 72
Newport Rd. EX2: Cou W 6B 72
EX32: B'aple 5F 19
Newport St. EX16: Tive 4C 40
PL1: Plym 3F 141
TQ6: Dartm 1A 124 (6F 125)
Newport Ter. EX32: B'aple 5F 19
EX39: Bide 4G 23
New Quay La. TQ5: Brixh 3F 123
New Quay St. EX39: App 3H 21
TQ14: Teignm 5H 107
New Rd. EX5: Rock 2F 79
EX6: Star 2D 96
EX12: Beer 6B 86
EX17: Morc 1D 38
EX20: Huish, Mert 6B 30
EX20: Oke 5A 48
New Rd. EX32: B Taw 6B 24
EX32: B'aple 5F 19
EX36: S Mol 6D 26
EX38: G Tor 2C 30
EX39: Bide 5F 23
EX39: Ins 3K 21
PL6: Bickl 1H 133
PL6: Robo 1D 132
PL8: Y'ton 2B 150
PL16: Lift, Tin 6B 56
PL20: Bere A 1B 128
PL21: Lutt 7G 129
PL21: Modb 6G 147
TQ5: Brixh 4D 122
TQ6: Sto F 4H 153
TQ7: Lodd 3H 151
TQ9: Sto G 4B 120
TQ9: Tot 5F 103
TQ11: B'leigh 4C 98
TQ14: Teignm 3H 107
(not continuous)
New Row EX39: Bide 3F 23
New Sidmouth Rd. EX24: Colyt 7A 88
New St. EX8: Exmth 5C 76
EX10: Sidm 7C 84
EX11: Ott M 3D 80
EX14: Hon 3F 55
EX15: Cull 4G 45
EX18: Chul 6C 32
EX38: G Tor 2A 30
(not continuous)
EX39: App 3H 21
EX39: Bide 3F 23
PL1: Plym 6F 9 (3K 141)
TQ3: Paig 1H 119
TQ13: Chag 3H 61
TQ13: More 6H 61
New St. Flats *EX39: Bide 3F 23*
(off New St.)
NEWTAKE 3J 109
Newtake Ho. TQ2: Torq 4B 112
Newtake Mt. TQ12: New A 2J 109
Newtake Ri. TQ12: New A 3J 109
Newtake Rd. PL19: Whit 7K 59
Newte's Hill EX16: Tive 6G 41
NEWTON ABBOT 1G 109 (3C 171)
Newton Abbot Leisure Cen. 7D 104
Newton Abbot Racecourse
6G 105 (3C 171)
Newton Abbot Rd. TQ9: Tot 6F 103
Newton Abbot Sailing Club 3F 109
Newton Abbot Station (Rail)
1G 109 (3C 171)
Newton Abbot Tourist Information Centre
1E 108 (3C 171)
Newton Abbot Town & GWR Mus.
1E 108
Newton Av. PL5: Plym 1D 134
Newton Cen. EX2: Mar B 5H 71
Newton Cl. PL8: New F 5J 149
Newton Ct. EX16: Bam 2H 33
NEWTON FERRERS 5J 149 (3B 174)
Newton Gdns. PL5: Plym 1E 134
Newton Hall TQ12: New A 2F 109
Newton Hill PL8: New F 5H 149
Newton Ho. EX5: New C 6C 50
NEWTON POPPLEFORD 5H 81 (2A 172)
Newton Rd. EX39: Bide 2F 23
TQ2: Torq 4J 111
TQ8: Salc 4C 158
TQ9: L'ton, Tot 5F 103
TQ12: H'fld 3H 93
TQ12: Kingsk 7K 109
TQ12: Kingst, New A 7F 105
TQ13: Bov T 4B 92
TQ14: Bi'ton 4A 106
Newton Rd. Retail Pk. 5G 105
NEWTON ST CYRES 6D 50 (1C 171)
Newton St Cyres Station (Rail)
5D 50 (1C 171)
NEWTON ST PETROCK 2C 163
Newtons Orchard EX13: Kilm 2B 88
Newton Sq. EX16: Bam 2H 33
NEWTON TRACEY 1D 163
NEW TOWN 6C 84
NEWTOWN
EX1 3J 7 (6H 65)
EX36 1B 164
PL15 3A 168
TA20 2C 167
Newtown EX10: Sidm 6C 84
PL21: Corn 6J 129
Newtown Cl. EX1: Exe 3H 7
New Valley Rd. EX4: Exe 5C 64
New Wlk. TQ9: Tot 6F 103
New Way EX5: Wood S 2C 78
New Way Bldgs. EX8: Exmth 5C 76
New Way Est. EX14: Dunk 5G 47
New Wood Cl. PL6: Plym 2G 133
New Zealand Ho.
PL3: Plym 1A 8 (7G 135)
NICHOLASHAYNE 2B 166
Nicholas Rd. EX1: Heav 6K 65
Nicholls Pl. TQ13: Bov T 4E 92
Nicholson Rd. PL5: Plym 1K 135
TQ2: Torq 3K 111
Nichols Way EX1: Exe 1J 7 (5H 65)
NIGHTCOTT 1C 165
Nightingale Cl. PL9: Elb 5K 143
TQ2: Torq 3A 112
Nightingale Lawns EX15: Cull 5F 45
Nightingale Wlk. EX2: Exe 2A 70
Nightjar Cl. TQ2: Torq 3A 112
Nile Rd. EX2: Cou W 5B 72
Nilgala Cl. EX39: Bide 1D 22
NIMMER 2D 167
Nine Oaks PL20: Dous 5K 127
Nineteen Steps *EX9: Bud S 7D 82*
(off Madeira Wlk.)
Nirvana Cl. PL21: Ivy 4G 145
Noelle Dr. TQ12: New A 7D 104
Noland Pk. TQ10: S Bre 2C 100
NOMANSLAND 2C 165
The Nook PL19: Tavi 3J 59
TQ7: Thur 5C 154
Norah Bellot Ct. *EX32: B'aple 4E 18*
(off Vicarage St.)
Norcombe Ct. *EX12: Seat 6F 87*
(off Harbour Rd.)
Norden La. TQ7: Kingsb 4E 156
Norfolk Cl. PL3: Plym 6D 136
Norfolk Rd. PL3: Plym 7D 136
Norfolk Ter. EX32: B'aple 5F 19
Norley Rd. EX33: Know 1K 15
Norman Cl. EX8: Exmth 2F 77
TQ12: New A 6B 104
Norman Ct. EX2: Matf 4F 71
Norman Cres. EX9: Bud S 5B 82
Norman Dr. EX15: Cull 2H 45
Normandy Cl. EX8: Exmth 3G 77
Normandy Hill PL5: Plym 1A 134
Normandy Ho. EX32: B'aple 5F 19
Normandy Pl. EX20: Hath 2H 35
Normandy Rd. EX1: Heav 6J 65
Normandy Way EX36: S Mol 6B 26
PL5: Plym 1B 134
TQ8: Salc 3D 158
Norman Lockyer Observatory 5E 84
Norman M. EX2: Sow 1C 72
Norman Pl. EX2: Sow 1C 72
Norman Rd. TQ3: Paig 7J 115
Normans Cleave EX35: Lynt 2G 13
NORMAN'S GREEN 3A 166
Norman Stevens Cl. EX8: Exmth 6E 76
Normans Way *EX34: Ilfra 3J 11*
(off Worth Rd.)
Norman Ter. EX39: Nort 5F 21
Norris Dr. PL6: Plym 4K 131
NORTHAM 5E 20 (1C 163)
Northam Burrows Country Pk.
2D 20 (3A 160)
Northampton Cl. PL5: Plym 5G 131
Northam Rd. EX39: Bide 2E 22
Northams Mdw. EX20: Oke 4A 48
North Av. DT7: Lym R 4J 91
EX1: Heav 3K 7 (6H 65)
EX39: Bide 4J 23
NORTHAY 2C 167
Nth. Boundary Rd. TQ5: Brixh 3C 122
NORTH BOVEY 2B 170
Nth. Bovey Rd. TQ13: More 7G 61
NORTH BOWOOD 1D 173
NORTH BRENTOR 2C 169
North Bri. Pl. EX4: Exe 3C 6 (6E 64)
Northbrook Approach Golf Course
3J 71 (1D 171)
Northbrook Cl. EX4: Whip 3K 65
NORTH BUCKLAND 4E 14 (2A 160)
NORTH CHIDEOCK 1D 173
Northcliffe *EX32: B Taw 7B 24*
(off New Rd.)
NORTH COOMBE 2C 165
NORTHCOTE 1J 55
Northcote Hill EX14: Hon 2H 55
Northcote La. EX14: Hon 3E 54
Northcote Rd. EX14: Hon 2H 55
NORTHCOTT
EX15 2A 166
PL15 1B 168
Northcott Gdns. EX39: Nort 5F 21
Northcott Ter. EX22: Hols 2C 34
Northcott Theatre 3E 64
NORTH CROSS 2D 8 (1J 141)
NORTH CURRY 1D 167
Northdene EX39: Bide 1D 22
Nth. Devon EX16: Tive 3B 40
North Devon Athletics Track 5K 15
Nth. Devon Crematorium 7C 18
North Devon Karting Cen. 2B 18
North Devon Leisure Cen. 5E 18
North Devon Maritime Mus.
3H 21 (3A 160)
North Devon Voluntary Marine Conservation Area 2B 160
North Devon Yacht Club 4K 21
Nth. Down Cres. PL2: Plym 5E 134
Northdown Dr. EX39: Bide 2E 22
Nth. Down Gdns. PL2: Plym 5E 134
Nth. Down Rd. EX33: Brau 4K 15
PL2: Plym 5G 135
Northdown Rd. EX39: Bide 3D 22
Nth. E. Quay PL4: Plym 5H 9 (3K 141)
North East St. EX39: Nort 5F 21
North Emb. TQ6: Dartm 1B 124 (5F 125)
North End Cl. TQ12: Ipp 6G 101
Northernhay TQ12: New A 2F 109
Northernhay Gdns. 2E 6 (5E 64)
Northernhay Ga. EX4: Exe 3D 6 (6E 64)
Northernhay Pl. EX4: Exe 3E 6 (6F 65)
Northernhay Sq. EX4: Exe 3D 6 (6E 64)
Northernhay St. EX4: Exe 4D 6 (6E 64)
Northern La. EX10: Brans 5F 85
Northesk St. PL2: Plym 7F 135
Northfield EX4: Exe 1B 6 (4D 64)
EX13: Mus 7D 90
Northfield La. EX31: B'aple 2E 18
Northfield Pk. EX31: B'aple 2E 18
Northfield Rd. EX20: Oke 3B 48
EX33: Geo 4D 14
EX34: Ilfra 2H 11
EX39: Bide 4H 23
Northfields Ind. Est. TQ5: Brixh 3D 122
Northfields La. TQ5: Brixh 3D 122
Northfield Ter. EX34: Ilfra 2H 11
NORTH FILHAM 4K 145
Northford Rd.
TQ6: Dartm 1A 124 (6E 124)
Nth. Furzeham Rd. TQ5: Brixh 2E 122
Northgate EX39: Hart 2H 27
TQ9: Tot 5E 102
(off Castle St.)
North Ga. Ho. EX4: Exe 3D 6
Northgate La. EX14: Hon 3K 55
Nth. Grange EX2: Sow 2C 72
North Grn. EX32: B'aple 5G 19
Northground La. EX10: Harc 4K 85
NORTH HEASLEY 3D 161
NORTH HILL 3A 168
Nth. Hill *EX39: Clov 5H 27*
(off High St.)
PL4: Plym 2F 9 (1K 141)
North Hill Cl. TQ5: Brixh 3D 122
NORTH HUISH 2D 175
Nth. Jaycroft EX15: Will 3D 44
North La. EX31: Bick 5K 17
Nth. Lawn Ct. EX1: Heav 6J 65
Northleat Av. TQ3: Paig 2E 118
NORTHLEIGH
EX24 1B 172
EX32 3C 161
Northleigh Hill Rd.
EX14: Hon, Offw 6H 55
NORTHLEW 1D 169
NORTH LOBB 1F 15
Nth. Lodge Cl. EX7: Daw 5F 97
NORTH MOLTON 2C 26 (1B 164)
NORTHMOOR GREEN 1D 167
NORTH MORTE 3B 10
Nth. Morte Farm Cvn. & Camping Pk.
2B 10
Nth. Morte Rd. EX34: Mort 3A 10
NORTHMOSTOWN 6J 81
NORTH NEWTON 1C 167
Northolt Av. PL5: Plym 6C 130
North Pk. EX20: N Taw 6A 36
North Pk. Almshouses EX1: Exe 5G 7
North Pk. Rd. EX4: Exe 3E 64
EX6: Ted M 7H 49
NORTH PETHERTON 1C 167
NORTH PETHERWIN 2A 168
NORTH PROSPECT 5F 135
Nth. Prospect Rd. PL2: Plym 3E 134
Nth. Quay PL4: Plym 5G 9 (3K 141)
NORTH RADWORTHY 3D 161
North Rd. EX20: Oke 2B 48
EX22: Bradw 4B 28
EX22: Hols 1C 34
EX31: B'aple 1F 19
EX36: S Mol 5C 26
EX37: High B 2B 32
EX39: Bide 3F 23
EX39: Hart 2H 27
PL11: Torp 2A 140
PL16: Lift 6B 56
PL20: Yelv 4E 126
PL21: L Mill 4B 144
North Rd. E. PL4: Plym 2D 8 (1J 141)
North Rd. Ind. Est. EX20: Oke 2C 48
North Rd. W.
PL1: Plym 3A 8 (2G 141)
Nth. Rocks Rd. TQ4: Broads 1H 121
North St. EX1: Heav 6J 65
EX3: Top 6B 74
EX4: Exe 4D 6 (6E 64)
EX8: Exmth 5C 76
EX11: Ott M 3D 80
EX13: Axmin 3H 89
EX16: W'ridge 6J 33
EX17: Cred 6H 39
EX19: Dol 6H 31
EX20: N Taw 6B 36
EX20: Oke 3B 48
EX33: Brau 4J 15
EX36: S Mol 6C 26
EX39: Hart 3H 27
EX39: Nort 5E 20
PL4: Plym 4G 9 (2K 141)
(not continuous)
PL19: Tavi 4J 59
TQ9: Tot 5E 102
TQ12: Den 1H 101
TQ12: Ipp 6G 101
TQ13: Ashb 3G 99
TQ13: Chag 2H 61

A-Z Devon Atlas 215

NORTH TAMERTON 1B 168
NORTH TAWTON 6B 36 (3A 164)
North Ter. EX31: Bick 5K 17
NORTH TOWN 3D 163
Northumberland Pl.
  TQ14: Teignm 5H 107
Northumberland St. PL5: Plym . . .3D 134
Northumberland Ter.
  PL1: Plym 7C 8
North Vw. EX21: Sheb 6J 29
  TQ14: Shal 6G 107
    (off Commons Old Rd.)
North Vw. Av. EX39: Bide 2E 22
North Vw. Hill EX39: Bide 2E 22
North Vw. Rd. TQ5: Brixh 3F 123
Northview Rd. EX9: Bud S 7B 82
Northville Pk. TQ7: Kingsb 3F 157
Northville Rd. TQ7: Kingsb 3F 157
North Wlk. EX31: B'aple 4E 18
  EX32: B'aple 4E 18
  EX35: Lynt 1F 13
North Wlk. Hill EX35: Lynt 1H 13
Northways La. PL21: Ugb 5C 146
Nth. Weald Gdns. PL5: Plym . . .5D 130
NORTH WHILBOROUGH
  . . . . .5E 110 (1A 176)
Northwood Acres EX5: Rock 3D 68
Northwood La. EX39: Buck B 2H 29
  TQ11: Buck 1C 98
Northwoods TQ13: Bov T 7B 92
NORTON 6A 124 (2A 176)
Norton Av. PL4: Plym 1K 9 (1B 142)
NORTON FITZWARREN 1C 167
Norton Pk. TQ6: Nort 6A 124
Norton Pl. EX8: Exmth 4G 77
Norton Vw. TQ6: Dartm 6C 124
Nortonwood La. EX5: New C 5E 50
Norwich Av. PL5: Plym 5F 131
Norwich Cl. EX8: Exmth 1F 77
Norwich Rd. EX4: Exe 6B 64
Norwood Av. EX2: Exe 1G 71
Norwood Ho. EX4: Exe 1F 7 (5F 65)
Norwood Rd. EX16: Tive 2D 40
NOSS MAYO 6H 149 (3B 174)
Notley Gdns. PL2: Plym 3F 135
Notre Dame Cl. PL6: Plym 5A 132
Notre Dame Ho. PL1: Plym 3B 8
Notte St. PL1: Plym 6D 8 (3J 141)
Nottingham Gdns. PL4: Plym 1G 9
Novorossiysk Rd. PL6: Plym 2E 136
Nuffield Health
  Plymouth 6K 9 (3B 142)
Nunnery Wlk. EX39: Bide 4F 23
    (off Lwr. Meddon St.)
Nurseries Cl. EX3: Ext 2G 75
  EX3: Top 7D 72
Nursery Cl. EX8: Exmth 4E 76
  PL5: Tam F 3G 131
  TQ3: Paig 2G 119
Nursery End EX31: B'aple 2E 18
Nursery M. EX8: Exmth 4E 76
Nursery Rd. TQ12: Kingst 4H 105
Nutaberry Hill EX39: Bide 4G 23
Nutaberry Works EX39: Bide 4G 23
Nutaberry Yd. EX39: Bide 4G 23
Nutbrook EX8: Exmth 3D 76
Nut Bush La. TQ2: Torq 6H 111
Nuthatch Dr. TQ2: Torq 3A 112
Nut Tree Ct. TQ5: Brixh 6D 122
Nut Tree Orchard TQ5: Brixh . . .6D 122
Nutwell Rd.
  EX8: Lymp 3J 75, 5G 76
Nymet Av. EX17: Bow 6H 37
Nymet Hayes EX17: Bow 5H 37
NYMET ROWLAND 2F 37 (3B 164)
NYMET TRACEY 7J 37 (3B 164)
NYNEHEAD 1B 166

O

Oakapple Cl. PL7: Plymp 4J 137
Oakbank TQ13: Bov T 7B 92
Oakbeer Orchard EX5: Cran 3B 68
Oak Bri. EX10: Sidb 2H 85
Oak Bus. Units EX2: Mar B 5H 71
Oakcliff Holiday Pk. 7E 96
    (not continuous)
Oak Cl. EX2: Shil A 7D 70
  EX4: Pin 3D 66
  EX5: Silv 1H 51
  EX6: Exmin 2C 74
  EX11: Ott M 5C 80
  EX16: Tive 3D 40
  TQ12: Kingst 5J 105
Oak Ct. EX22: Hols 1C 34
Oak Cres. EX15: Will 4C 44
Oakcroft Rd. PL2: Plym 5G 135
Oakdale Av. EX32: Swim 2H 25
Oakdene Rd. PL9: Plyms 6G 143
Oak Dr. EX15: Cull 1H 45
  PL6: Plym 7K 131
OAKE 1B 166
Oak End Ct. TQ3: Marl 4D 114
Oakery Cres. PL20: Prin 6D 60
Oakfield EX15: Will 3E 44
Oakfield Cl. PL7: Plymp 3F 139
Oakfield Pl. PL4: Plym 3C 142

Oakfield Rd. EX4: Exe 6A 6 (7D 64)
  EX20: Hath 1H 35
  PL7: Plymp 5K 137
Oakfields EX16: Tive 2D 40
Oakfield St. EX1: Heav 7J 65
Oakfield Ter. EX39: Nort 5F 21
    (off Diddywall Rd.)
Oakfield Ter. Rd. PL4: Plym 3B 142
OAKFORD 1D 165
Oakford TQ12: Kingst 4G 105
OAKFORDBRIDGE 1D 165
Oakford Cl. EX36: N Mol 2B 26
Oakford Vs. EX36: N Mol 2B 26
Oak Gdns. PL21: Ivy 4J 145
Oakham Rd. PL5: Plym 5G 131
Oakhay Ct. EX5: Sto C 6J 51
Oakhayes Rd. EX5: W'bury 5B 78
Oakhays EX36: S Mol 7D 26
Oak Hill EX7: Daw 6F 97
  E Bud 1E 82
Oakhill EX9: E Bud 1D 82
Oak Hill Cross Rd. EX7: Holc 6F 97
  TQ14: Teignm 2K 107
Oakhill Ri. EX31: Rou 6B 18
Oak Hill Rd. TQ1: Torq 7B 112
Oakland Av. EX31: B'aple 6B 18
Oakland Dr. EX7: Daw 6F 97
Oakland Rs. EX31: B'aple 6C 18
Oakland Pk. Sth. EX31: B'aple . . .5A 18
Oakland Rd. EX36: S Mol 6C 26
    (off South St.)
Oakland Rd. TQ12: New A 2H 109
OAKLANDS 2B 48
Oaklands EX39: Bide 5C 22
  PL19: Whit 7K 59
Oaklands Cl. EX12: Seat 2E 86
  EX18: Chul 6C 32
  PL6: Plym 3D 132
  TQ11: B'leigh 4B 98
Oaklands Cl. EX16: Tive 3F 41
Oaklands Dr. EX20: Oke 3B 48
    (not continuous)
Oaklands Gdns. EX31: B'aple 5C 18
Oaklands Pk. EX20: Oke 3A 48
  TQ11: B'leigh 3B 98
Oaklands Res. Pk. EX20: Oke 2B 48
Oaklands Rd. TQ11: B'leigh 2A 98
Oakland Wlk. EX7: Daw 5G 97
Oak Lawn TQ12: New A 2F 109
Oaklawn Ct. TQ1: Torq 6B 112
    (off Barton Rd.)
Oaklawn Ter. TQ1: Torq 6B 112
    (off St Vincent's Rd.)
Oaklea EX14: Hon 3E 54
  EX16: Tive 2D 40
Oaklea Cl. TQ7: Kingsb 5F 157
Oaklea Cres. EX31: Frem 6E 16
Oaklea Pk. TQ12: Live 4H 93
Oakleigh Rd. EX8: Exmth 5D 76
  EX32: B'aple 5F 19
Oakley Cl. EX1: Pin 3D 66
  TQ14: Teignm 2H 107
Oakley Wlk. EX5: Clyst M 2K 73
Oak Mdw. EX36: S Mol 6B 26
Oak Meadow Golf Course 2D 96
Oak Pk. Av. TQ2: Torq 5K 111
Oak Pk. Cl. TQ2: Torq 5K 111
Oak Pk. Rd. TQ12: New A 7C 104
Oak Pk. Vs. EX7: Daw 3H 97
Oak Pl. TQ12: New A 1F 109
    (not continuous)
Oak Ridge EX2: Alph 5D 70
  PL16: Lift 6A 56
Oak Rd. EX4: Exe 1C 70
  EX5: Ayle 6F 79
  EX11: High M 6F 79
  EX20: Oke 2C 48
  PL19: Tavi 6J 59
The Oaks EX15: Hemy 1G 47
  PL19: Mary T 2B 60
  TQ12: New A 4J 109
  TQ13: Bov T 4D 92
Oak Tree Cl. EX5: Broadc 6D 52
Oaktree Ct. EX8: Exmth 1D 76
  PL21: Ivy 4E 144
Oaktree Cr. PL6: Plym 2A 136
Oak Tree Dr. EX32: B'aple 5K 19
  TQ12: New A 4J 109
Oak Tree Gdns. EX11: W Hill 4H 79
Oak Tree Gro. TQ14: Shal 6G 107
Oak Tree La. PL19: Tavi 6J 59
Oak Tree Pk. PL6: Plym 4E 132
Oaktree Pk. EX20: Stic 1G 49
Oak Tree Pl. EX2: Matf 5F 71
Oaktree Rd. EX36: S Mol 6B 26
Oak Tree Sq. EX10: Sidm 3B 84
Oaktree Vs. EX10: New P 5H 81
Oak Vw. EX14: Hon 5D 54
  TQ9: Tot 5B 102
Oak Vw. Cl. TQ2: Torq 4H 111
Oakwell Cl. EX38: G Tor 2D 30
Oakwood Cl. EX31: Rou 7B 18
  PL6: Plym 3E 132
  TQ6: Dartm 6C 124
Oakwood Ct. EX36: S Mol 6D 26
Oakwood Dr. PL21: Modb 5G 147
Oakwood Pk. TQ7: Lodd 2G 151

Oakwood Ri. EX8: Exmth 1G 77
Oakymead Pk. TQ12: Kingst 5G 105
OARE 2D 161
OAREFORD 2D 161
Oates Rd. PL2: Plym 6G 135
OATH 1D 167
Oathills Cres. TQ4: Paig 6F 119
Oathills Pl. TQ4: Paig 6F 119
Oatlands Av. EX32: B Taw 7F 19
Oatlands Dr. TQ4: Paig 3G 119
Oberon Rd. EX1: Sow 5D 66
Occombe Farm 3E 114
Occombe Valley Rd. TQ3: Pres . . .4G 115
Ocean 7C 76
Ocean City Pl. PL1: Plym . . .3B 8 (2H 141)
Ocean Ct. PL1: Dev 4E 140
Ocean Pk. EX39: W Ho 5A 20
Ocean St. PL2: Plym 5D 134
Ocean Vw. Cres. TQ5: Brixh 7C 122
Ocean Vw. Dr. TQ5: Brixh 7C 122
Ochil Cl. EX39: Bide 5J 23
Ochre Ct. TQ5: Brixh 4F 123
Ockington Cl. EX20: Oke 3D 48
Ockment Ct. EX20: Oke 3B 48
THE OCTAGON 5B 8 (3H 141)
Octagon St. PL1: Plym 4B 8 (2H 141)
Octon Gro. TQ1: Torq 6A 112
Oddicombe Beach Hill
  TQ1: Torq 5E 112
Odeon Cinema 2G 7 (5G 65)
Odhams Wharf EX3: Ebf 5D 74
Odle Hill TQ12: A'well 5D 108
Odlehill Gro. TQ12: A'well 6D 108
Odun Pl. EX39: App 3H 21
Odun Rd. EX39: App 3H 21
Odun Ter. EX39: App 3H 21
Offields PL8: Holb 6C 150
OFFWELL 1B 172
Ogwell End Dr. TQ12: E Ogw 2C 108
Ogwell Grn. TQ12: E Ogw 3B 108
Ogwell Mill Rd. TQ12: New A 2B 108
Ogwell Rd. TQ12: E Ogw 3B 108
Oil Mill La. EX5: Clyst M 3H 73
Oil Mill Rd. EX5: Clyst M 3H 73
Okefield Av. EX17: Cred 5H 39
Okefield Ridge EX17: Cred 5G 39
Okefield Rd. EX17: Cred 5G 39
OKEHAMPTON 3B 48 (1D 169)
OKEHAMPTON CAMP 7B 48 (1D 169)
Okehampton Castle 5A 48 (1D 169)
Okehampton Cl. PL7: Plymp 5E 138
Okehampton Golf Course
  . . . . .6A 48 (1D 169)
Okehampton Pl. EX4: Exe . .6B 6 (7D 64)
Okehampton Rd. EX4: Exe . .5A 6 (7C 64)
Okehampton Station
  Dartmoor Railway 5C 48
Okehampton Station
  (Rail) 5C 48 (1D 169)
Okehampton Station Vis. Cen. 4C 48
Okehampton St. EX4: Exe . .6B 6 (7D 64)
Okehampton Tourist Information Centre
  . . . . .3B 48 (1D 169)
Okehampton Way PL21: Ivy 5H 145
Oke Tor Cl. EX20: Oke 3D 48
  TQ3: Pres 4G 115
Okewood Ct. EX8: Exmth 6D 76
Old Abbey Ct. EX2: Exe 2H 71
Old Bakery Cl. EX4: Exe . . .1A 6 (5C 64)
Old Barn Cl. EX5: Sto C 7J 51
Old Barn Dr. TQ13: More 6H 61
Old Barnstaple Rd.
  EX34: Ilfra, T Pot 4K 11
  EX39: Bide, West 3G 23
OLD BARTON 6D 148
Old Beer Rd. EX12: Seat 6C 86
Old Bideford Cl. EX31: Rou 7A 18
Old Bideford Rd.
  EX31: B'aple, Rou 7A 18
    (not continuous)
Old Blundell's EX16: Tive 4D 40
OLDBOROUGH 4C 38 (3B 164)
Oldborough La. EX17: Morc 4C 38
Old Bowling Green Picnic Site . . .2C 163
The Old Brewery TQ2: Torq 4D 112
    (off Lummaton Pl.)
Old Butterleigh Rd. EX5: Silv 1H 51
Old Bystock Dr. EX8: Exmth 1G 77
Old Chapel Gdns. EX19: Wink . . .2C 36
Old Chapel La. PL7: L Moor 1J 129
The Old Cider Press TQ4: Paig . . .2H 119
    (off Fisher St.)
Old Cider Works La.
  TQ12: A'well 5D 108
Old Coach La. EX1: Heav . . .4K 7 (6H 65)
Old Coach Rd. EX5: Broadc 6C 52
Old Coast Rd. EX34: Ber 2D 12
Old Cl. EX31: B'aple 5B 18
The Old Ct. Ho. EX5: W'bury 5B 78
Old Dawlish Rd. EX6: Kennf 1J 95
Old Ebford La. EX3: Ebf 6E 74
Old Elm Rd. EX14: Hon 5C 54
Oldenburg Pk. TQ3: Paig 7J 115
Old English Ind. Est. PL20: Dous . .5J 127
Old Exeter Rd. PL19: Tavi 3J 59
  TQ12: New A 7E 104
  TQ13: Ashb 2K 99

Old Exeter St. TQ13: Chud 1C 94
Old Farm Bungs. EX10: Sidm 3C 84
Old Farm Rd. PL5: Plym 3B 134
Old Farm Way EX7: Daw 6G 97
Oldfields EX7: Daw 6G 97
The Old Fire Station TQ13: Chag . .2G 61
Old Fore St. EX10: Sidm 7C 84
Old Gdn. Pasture EX5: Cran 3B 68
Old Gatehouse Rd. EX7: Daw 4H 97
Old George St. PL1: Plym . . .5D 8 (3J 141)
Oldham Rd. EX20: Hath 2G 35
Old Hill EX15: Cull 5J 45
Old Ide Cl. EX2: Ide 3B 70
Old Ide La. EX2: Ide 3B 70
Olditch Holiday Pk. 3G 49
Old Jaycroft EX15: Will 5D 44
Old Laira Rd. PL3: Plym 7C 136
Oldlands Cl. PL6: Plym 4C 132
Old Launceston Rd. PL19: Tavi . . .3G 59
The Old Laundry
  PL1: Plym 3A 8 (2G 141)
Old Liverton Rd. TQ12: Live 7G 93
Old Mnr. Cl. TQ13: Ashb 2F 99
Old Mnr. Gdns. EX24: Colyf 1G 87
The Old Market EX15: Hemy 2G 47
  TQ6: Dartm 1A 124
    (off Market St.)
Old Market Cl. EX2: Exe 2E 70
Old Market Dr. EX39: Wools 2A 28
Old Market Fld. Ind. Est.
  EX16: W'ridge 5G 33
Old Matford La. EX2: Matf 6G 71
OLD MILL 3B 168
The Old Mill EX15: Culm 2B 46
Old Mill Cl. EX2: Exe 7F 7 (1G 71)
  EX16: Tive 5C 40
Old Mill Ct. PL7: Plymp 4B 138
Old Mill Creek TQ6: Dartm 4C 124
Old Mill La. TQ6: Dartm 5C 124
Old Mill Rd. TQ2: Torq 4A 116
    (not continuous)
Old Newton Rd. TQ12: H'fld 6C 92
  TQ12: Kingsk 6H 109
  TQ13: Bov T 6C 92
Old Nursery Dr. EX4: Whip 4A 66
Old Okehampton Rd.
  EX4: Nad, White 5A 64
Old Orchard TQ13: Bov T 4C 92
Old Paignton Rd. TQ4: Paig 4K 115
    (Roundhill Rd.)
  TQ2: Torq 3K 115
    (Stoneleigh Dr.)
Old Park Av. EX1: Pin 1D 66
Old Pk. Rd. EX4: Exe 2F 7 (5F 65)
  PL3: Plym 5J 135
Old Pavilion Cl. EX2: Won 1B 72
Old Pinn La. EX1: Pin 3D 66
Old Plymouth Rd. TQ7: Kingsb . . .3F 157
Old Priory PL7: Plymp 4A 138
Old Quarry Dr. EX6: Exmin 1C 74
Old Quarry Rd. PL20: Buck M 5A 126
Old Quay TQ14: Teignm 5H 107
Old Quay La. EX39: Ins 3K 21
Old Quay St. TQ14: Teignm 5H 107
Old Rectory Cl. EX39: Ins 7A 16
Old Rectory Gdns. EX17: Morc . . .5C 154
  TQ7: Thur 5C 154
Old Rectory La. EX31: Brat F 6H 13
The Old Rice Mill PL16: Tin 6D 56
OLDRIDGE 1C 171
Oldridge Vw. EX6: Ted M 6J 49
Old Rd. EX16: Tive 4E 40
  EX20: Oke 4A 48
  PL8: Brixt 2H 149
  PL21: Lutt 7G 129
  TQ5: Galm 3H 121
  TQ6: Sto F 3G 153
  TQ9: H'ford 6B 100
Old Rydon Cl. EX2: Cou W 3D 72
Old Rydon La. EX2: Cou W 4B 72
Old Rydon Ley EX2: Cou W 3C 72
The Old Saddlery EX14: Hon 3F 55
    (off Queen St.)
The Old Sawmills EX10: Col R 2G 83
Old School Cl. EX16: Tive 4B 40
Old School Ct. EX3: Top 5B 74
    (off Majorfield Rd.)
  EX14: Hon 3F 55
  EX15: Hemy 2G 47
    (off Station Rd.)
Old School La. EX31: Frem 6F 17
Old School M. EX7: Daw 4G 97
    (off School Hill)
Old School Rd. EX32: B'aple 7H 19
  PL5: Plym 3B 134
Old Sidmouth Rd. EX24: Colyt . . .7A 88
Old Sludge Beds Nature Reserve
  . . . . .7B 72 (2D 171)
The Old Station PL20: Horr 3D 126
Old Station Rd. EX32: B'aple 5G 19
  PL20: Horr 3E 126
Old Station Yd. TQ7: Kingsb 4F 157
Old Sticklepath Hill EX31: B'aple . .6C 18
Old Stone Cl. EX39: W Ho 6A 20
Old's Vw. EX4: Exe 1A 6 (5D 64)
The Old Tannery Bus. Pk.
  PL4: Plym 2G 9 (1K 141)
Old Tannery M. TQ13: Chud 1C 94

Old Teignmouth Rd.—Palmerston Pk.

Old Teignmouth Rd. EX7: Daw 6G 97
Old Tinhay PL16: Tin 6C 56
Old Tiverton Rd. EX4: Exe 1H 7 (5G 65)
EX16: Bam 2J 33
EX17: Cred 6J 39
Old Torquay Rd. TQ3: Pres 6J 115
Old Torrington Rd. EX31: B'aple 7B 18
Old Torwood Rd. TQ1: Torq 2E 116
Old Totnes Rd. TQ11: B'leigh 4D 98
TQ12: New A 2D 108
(not continuous)
TQ13: Ashb 5G 99
Old Town EX39: Bide 4E 22
Old Town St. EX7: Daw 4F 97
PL1: Plym 4E 8 (2J 141)
Old Vicarage Cl. EX2: Ide 4A 70
Old Vicarage Gdn. DT7: Lym R 5J 91
Old Vicarage Rd.
EX2: Exe 7A 6 (1D 70)
Old Walls Hill
TQ14: Bi'ton, Teignm 2C 106
Old Warleigh La. PL5: Tam F 2E 130
(not continuous)
OLDWAY 7H 115
Oldway TQ13: Chud 3A 94
Oldway Mansion 6H 115 (1A 176)
Oldway Rd. TQ3: Paig, Pres 7H 115
OLDWAYS END 1C 165
The Old Wharf PL9: Plyms 5C 142
Old Widdicombe La. TQ3: Blag 6A 114
TQ3: Paig 7C 114
Old Woodlands Rd. PL5: Plym 7H 131
Old Woods Hill TQ2: Torq 6A 112
Old Woods Trad. Est.
TQ2: Torq 5A 112
Olga Ter. EX8: Lymp 6H 75
Olive Gdns. EX7: Daw W 7E 96
Olive Gro. EX7: Daw W 7E 96
Oliver Pl. TQ12: H'fld 2K 93
Oliver Rd. EX32: B'aple 3G 19
Olivia Ct. PL4: Plym 1H 9
Olympian Way EX15: Cull 3F 45
Olympic Way PL6: Plym 4D 132
Omaha Dr. EX2: Cou W 4C 72
Omaha Way EX31: Frem 5F 17
The Omega Cen. EX2: Sow 6D 66
One End St. EX39: App 3H 21
Onslow Rd. PL2: Plym 4H 135
TQ8: Salc 3B 158
Opie La. PL4: Plym 2H 9 (1A 142)
Ora Cl. EX33: Croy 2C 14
Ora La. EX33: Croy 2C 14
Orange Gro. TQ2: Torq 3C 112
The Orangery *EX6: Exmin 1B 74*
(off Devington Pk.)
Ora Stone Pk. EX33: Croy 3B 14
Orbec Av. TQ12: Kingst 4J 105
The Orchard EX6: Dunsf 7C 62
EX7: Holc 7F 97
EX10: Tip J 1J 81
EX12: Seat 5E 86
EX13: Kilm 2B 88
EX14: Hon 4E 54
(Mill St.)
EX14: Hon 2J 55
(Tunnel La.)
EX31: Bick 6K 17
EX34: Wool 7C 10
PL7: Spa 1J 139
PL8: Torr 3B 150
PL21: Modb 7H 147
TQ9: Tot 6F 103
(off Shute Rd.)
TQ11: B'leigh 4D 98
TQ12: A'well 6E 108
TQ14: Bi'ton 3B 106
Orchard Av. PL6: Plym 4C 136
Orchard Cl. EX1: Pin 3E 66
EX5: W'bury 5C 78
EX7: Daw 4G 97
EX8: Exmth 3D 76
EX8: Lymp 6G 75
EX8: San B 6J 77
(off Gore La.)
EX9: E Bud 1D 82
EX10: New P 5F 81
EX10: Sidf 2D 84
EX10: Sidm 7A 84
EX11: Ott M 4D 80
EX13: Whit 5A 90
EX15: Uff 6H 43
EX20: Oke 4B 48
EX24: Colyf 1G 87
EX31: B'aple 6B 18
EX33: Brau 4H 15
EX34: C Mar 6B 12
PL7: Plymp 4F 139
PL8: Torr 3B 150
PL15: St G 6C 34
PL19: Tavi 5F 59
TQ5: Brixh 5E 122
TQ5: Galm 3J 121
TQ9: Sto G 4B 120
(off Paignton Rd.)
TQ12: Den 2H 101
TQ12: E Ogw 3A 108
TQ12: Kingst 4J 105
(Ware Cl.)
Orchard Cl. TQ12: Kingst 1G 105
(Woodlands Copse)
TQ13: Chud 2D 94
TQ14: Shal 6F 107
Orchard Cotts. PL8: Holb 6D 150
PL19: Lam 7D 58
Orchard Ct. EX2: Sow 6D 66
EX5: Whim 6G 53
EX17: Cred 5H 39
EX20: N Taw 6B 36
PL19: Lam 5C 58
PL21: Ivy 4F 145
TQ8: Salc 3C 158
(off Island St.)
TQ12: New A 1E 108
(off Bradley La.)
Orchard Cres. PL9: Plyms 5D 142
Orchard Dr. EX9: Ott'n 6H 83
TQ8: Salc 3B 158
TQ12: Ipp 6H 101
TQ12: Kingsk 1F 111
Orchard Gdns. EX4: Exe 1C 70
EX5: Broadc 6D 52
EX7: Daw 4G 97
EX39: Bide 1F 23
TQ6: Dartm 6E 124
TQ12: Kingst 4H 105
(off Crossley Moor Rd.)
TQ14: Teignm 5J 107
Orchard Ga. EX19: Dol 6J 31
Orchard Gro. EX33: Croy 2C 14
TQ5: Brixh 6E 122
TQ12: New A 7A 104
ORCHARD HILL 2F 23 (1C 163)
Orchard Hill EX2: Exe 2B 70
EX39: Bide 1E 22
PL8: Wors 1E 150
Orchard Ho. TQ13: Chud 1C 94
Orchard Ind. Est. (North)
TQ7: Kingsb 4F 157
Orchard Ind. Est. (South)
TQ7: Kingsb 4F 157
Orchard La. EX5: Silv 1H 51
EX6: E'don 5D 96
PL7: Plymp 3A 138
Orchard Leigh EX16: Tive 5C 40
Orchard Mdw. EX17: Cop 6C 38
TQ13: Chag 2H 61
Orchardon La. EX33: Brau 7D 14
Orchard Pk. PL21: Ivy 5G 145
TQ6: Ditt 5C 120
TQ9: Darti 2B 102
Orchard Pl. EX32: B'aple 5J 19
TQ1: Torq 3F 117
ORCHARD PORTMAN 1C 167
Orchard Ri. EX39: Bide 1F 23
Orchard Rd. EX32: B'aple 5G 19
EX33: Know 1K 15
EX33: Wraf 7K 15
EX34: Ilfra 3J 11
(off Cambridge Gro.)
PL2: Plym 4F 135
PL8: Brixt 2H 149
TQ1: Torq 7D 112
TQ2: Torq 4B 112
TQ13: Ashb 4H 99
The Orchards EX32: Land 2C 24
EX32: Swim 3H 25
TQ5: Galm 3H 121
Orchardside EX10: Sidm 3C 84
Orchard Ter. EX6: Ted M 6H 49
EX32: B'aple 7G 19
EX35: Lynt 2G 13
(off Lydiate La.)
TQ9: Tot 6E 102
TQ11: B'leigh 4C 98
TQ12: A'well 5E 108
TQ12: Kingsk 7J 109
TQ13: Bov T 3C 92
TQ13: Chag 2H 61
Orchardton Ter. PL9: Plyms 7G 143
Orchard Vw. EX1: Heav 7J 65
EX16: Hal 6E 42
TQ7: Chil 6G 159
(off Helmers Way)
Orchard Way EX3: Top 5A 74
EX6: Kenton 6H 95
EX14: Hon 3G 55
(not continuous)
EX15: Cull 5G 45
EX15: Uff 6H 43
EX15: Will 4D 44
EX16: Tive 5B 40
EX17: Lap 2J 37
TQ2: Torq 4H 111
TQ7: Chil 6G 159
TQ9: Sto G 3B 120
TQ13: Bov T 3C 92
Orchard Waye TQ9: Tot 6D 102
Orchid Av. PL21: Ivy 3E 144
TQ12: Kingst 4H 105
Orchid Cl. EX16: Tive 2F 41
Orchid Paradise 4B 104 (3C 171)
Orchid Va. TQ12: Kingst 2H 105
Orchid Way TQ2: Torq 3B 112
Orcombe Ct. EX8: Exmth 4F 77
Ordnance St. PL1: Dev 2C 140
Ordulf Rd. PL19: Tavi 4G 59
Oregon Way PL3: Plym 5D 136
ORESTON 5D 142
Orestone Dr. TQ1: Maid 2J 113
Orestone La. TQ12: Dacc 2K 111
Oreston Quay PL9: Plyms 5C 142
Oreston Rd. PL9: Plyms 5D 142
Orient Rd. TQ3: Pres 5K 115
Oriole Dr. EX4: Exe 3G 65
Orkney Cl. TQ2: Torq 3A 112
Orkney M. EX16: Tive 2D 40
Orleigh Av. TQ12: New A 6E 104
Orleigh Cl. EX39: Buck B 2J 29
Orleigh Cross TQ12: New A 6E 104
Orleigh Mill Ct. EX31: B'aple 3E 18
Orleigh Pk. TQ12: New A 6E 104
Orley Common Viewpoint 1A 176
Ormidale Sq. EX16: Tive 2G 41
Ormond Lodge TQ4: Paig 2J 119
Orpington Ct. EX16: Hal 6E 42
Orwell Gth. EX4: Whip 4B 66
Osbern Rd. TQ3: Pres 4G 115
Osborn Cl. TQ12: Ipp 6H 101
Osborne Cl. EX39: Bide 3C 22
Osborne Ct. PL1: Plym 6D 8 (3J 141)
Osborne Gdns. EX31: B'aple 7B 18
EX32: B Taw 6A 24
Osborne La. EX39: Bide 3C 22
Osborne Pl. PL1: Plym 7D 8 (4J 141)
Osborne Rd. EX34: Ilfra 3G 11
PL3: Plym 1F 141
Osborne St. TQ12: New A 1G 109
Osbourne Ter. EX31: B'aple 5E 18
Osmand Gdns. PL7: Plymp 4A 138
Osmonds La. TQ14: Teignm 5H 107
Osney Av. TQ4: Good 3H 119
Osney Cres. TQ4: Good 2H 119
Osney Gdns. TQ4: Good 3H 119
Osprey Dr. TQ2: Torq 2K 111
Osprey Gdns. PL9: Elb 5K 143
Osprey Gro. EX7: Daw 7C 96
Osprey Ho. *TQ1: Torq 6F 113*
(off Babbacombe Rd.)
Osprey Rd. EX2: Sow 6E 66
OSSABOROUGH 7C 10
Ossaborough La. EX34: Wool 7C 10
Oswald Browning Way
EX31: B'aple 2F 19
Otago Cotts. EX2: Exe 2H 71
OTHERY 1D 167
Otterbourne Ct. *EX9: Bud S 7D 82*
(off Coastguard Rd.)
Otter Cl. EX10: Tip J 1J 81
EX11: W Hill 4H 79
EX20: Oke 2D 48
TQ2: Torq 6J 111
Otter Ct. EX2: Matf 5F 71
EX9: Bud S 6E 82
Otter Estuary Nature Reserve
6E 82 (2A 172)
OTTERFORD 2C 167
OTTERHAM 1A 168
Otter Mill EX11: Ott M 4B 80
Otter Reach EX10: New P 5H 81
Otter Rd. TQ2: Torq 6J 111
Otters Reach EX9: Bud S 5D 82
OTTERTON 6H 83 (2A 172)
Otterton Mill 6G 83 (2A 172)
Ottervale Rd. EX9: Bud S 6E 82
Otter Valley Pk. EX14: Hon 1J 55
Otter Vw. *EX11: Ott M 4C 80*
(off St Saviours Rd.)
Otter Wlk. *EX2: Exe 3J 71*
(off Turnstone Rd.)
Otter Way EX32: B'aple 5J 19
Ottery La.
EX10: Sidb, Sidm 1D 84, 3F 85
Ottery Moor EX14: Hon 3E 54
Ottery Moor La. EX14: Hon 3D 54
Ottery Rd. EX14: Fen 2G 53
OTTERY ST MARY 4C 80 (1A 172)
Ottery St Mary Leisure Cen. 4A 80
Ottery St. EX9: Ott'n 6H 83
Ouicks Fld. TQ10: S Bre 2B 100
Outcrop Rd. PL9: Hooe 5C 142
Outer Down PL19: Lam 6C 58
OUTER HOPE 2G 155 (3C 175)
Outer Ting Tong EX9: Know 1K 77
Outland Rd. PL2: Plym 6G 135
PL3: Plym 3K 135
Outlook Ct. *EX7: Daw 4H 97*
(off E. Cliff Rd.)
Oval Grn. *EX2: Won 2B 72*
(off Woodwater La.)
Overbeck's 7A 158 (3D 175)
Overbrook EX7: Daw 4F 97
Overcliff Ct. EX7: Daw 3H 97
Overclose TQ3: Paig 6E 114
Overdale EX6: Ted M 6J 49
Overdale Cl. TQ2: Torq 1B 112
Overdale Rd. PL2: Plym 4E 134
Overgang TQ5: Brixh 3F 123
Overgang Rd. TQ5: Brixh 2E 122
Overseas Est. TQ6: Sto F 4H 153
OVER STRATTON 2D 167
OVERTON 7C 24
Overton Cl. DT7: Lym R 3K 91
Overton Gdns. PL3: Plym 6A 136
Owen Dr. PL7: Plymp 4K 137
Oxenham Grn. TQ2: Torq 7K 111
Oxenpark Ga. EX6: Bridf 1F 63
Oxford Av. PL3: Plym 6K 135
Oxford Cl. EX8: Exmth 1G 77
Oxford Ct. TQ2: Torq 4B 112
Oxford Gdns. PL3: Plym 6K 135
Oxford Gro. EX34: Ilfra 2H 11
Oxford La. TQ5: Brixh 4C 122
Oxford Pk. EX34: Ilfra 3H 11
Oxford Pl. PL1: Plym 3D 8 (2J 141)
Oxford Rd. EX4: Exe 2G 7 (5G 65)
Oxford St. EX2: Exe 7B 6 (1D 70)
PL1: Plym 3C 8 (2J 141)
TQ6: Dartm 2B 124 (6F 125)
Oxford Ter. EX17: Cred 6J 39
PL1: Plym 3C 8
Ox Hill La. EX24: Colyt 6B 88
Oxlea Cl. TQ1: Torq 2G 117
Oxlea Rd. TQ1: Torq 2G 117
Oxmans La. EX39: Nort 5F 21
Oyster Bend TQ4: Good 5J 119
Oystercatcher Ct. TQ14: Shal 6F 107
Oyster Cl. TQ4: Good 5J 119
Ozone Ter. DT7: Lym R 6J 91

P

Packhall La. TQ5: Brixh 6C 122
(not continuous)
Packhorse Cl. EX10: Sidf 2E 84
Packington St. PL2: Plym 7F 135
Pack o' Cards 2B 160
Packs Cl. TQ9: H'ford 6B 100
Padacre Rd. TQ2: Torq 1C 112
Padbrook M. EX15: Cull 6G 45
Padbrook Pk. Golf Course
6G 45 (3A 166)
The Paddock EX7: Daw 3G 97
Paddock Cl. EX12: Seat 5D 86
PL9: Plyms 7F 143
Paddock Dr. PL21: Ivy 5H 145
The Paddocks EX14: Hon 7D 54
EX19: Dol 6H 31
TQ9: Tot 5F 103
TQ12: A'well 5E 108
Paddons Coombe
TQ12: Kingst 2H 105
Paddons La. TQ14: Teignm 2G 107
Paddons Row *PL19: Tavi 3J 59*
(off Brook St.)
Padshall Pk. EX39: Nort 1E 22
PADSON 1D 169
Pafford Av. TQ2: Torq 3D 112
Pafford Cl. TQ2: Torq 3C 112
Paige Adams Rd. TQ9: Tot 5D 102
Paiges Farm PL9: Down T 1C 148
Paiges La. EX31: B'aple 4E 18
PAIGNTON 1H 119 (1A 176)
Paignton Bus Station 1H 119
Paignton Fernacombe Towermill
5F 115
Paignton Holiday Pk. 2A 118
Paignton Pier 1K 119
Paignton Rd. TQ9: Sto G 3B 120
Paignton Sailing Club *2K 119*
(off South Quay)
Paignton Station
Dartmouth Steam Railway
2H 119 (1A 176)
Paignton Station
(Rail) 1H 119 (1A 176)
Paignton Tourist Info. Cen. 2H 119
Paignton Zoo 3F 119 (2A 176)
Pail Pk. EX33: Know 1K 15
Painters Ct. EX2: Exe 7D 6 (1E 70)
Paizen La. EX12: Beer 6A 86
Palace Av. TQ3: Paig 1H 119
Palace Cotts. *EX8: Exmth 5C 76*
(off Parade)
Palace Gdns. TQ13: Chud 2C 94
Palace Ga. EX1: Exe 4E 6 (7F 65)
Palace La. PL21: Fil 4K 145
Palace Mdw. TQ13: Chud 3C 94
Palace Pl. TQ3: Paig 1H 119
Palace St. PL1: Plym 5E 8 (3J 141)
PL4: Plym 5E 8 (3K 141)
Palace Theatre 1H 119
Palatine Cl. TQ1: Torq 1D 116
Pale Gate Cl. EX14: Hon 2G 55
Palermo TQ1: Torq 2F 117
Palermo Rd. TQ1: Torq 6E 112
Palk Cl. TQ14: Shal 6F 107
Palk Pl. *TQ1: Torq 4D 112*
(off Teignmouth Rd.)
Palk St. TQ2: Torq 2D 116
Palm Cl. EX8: Exmth 1F 77
Palm Ct. EX7: Daw W 7D 96
Palm Cross PL21: Modb 6G 147
Palmer Cl. EX1: W Cly 1F 67
Palmer Ct. EX9: Bud S 6C 82
Palmer M. *EX9: Bud S 7C 82*
(off Victoria Pl.)
Palmers Cl. EX33: Brau 5J 15
Palmers Ct. EX38: G Tor 2D 30
Palmer's La. EX5: Mar G 5K 69
Palmerston Dr. EX4: Exe 5B 64
Palmerston Pk. EX16: Tive 6B 40

Palmerston St.—Pennant Ho.

Palmerston St.
PL1: Plym 2A **8** (1G **141**)
Palm Rd. TQ2: Torq 1C **116**
The Palms TQ1: Torq 2F **117**
Palm Tree Vw. TQ4: Good 5H **119**
Palstone La. TQ10: S Bre 1C **100**
Palstone Lodges TQ10: S Bre 2D **100**
Pamela Rd. EX1: Heav 5J **65**
Pancheon Cl. EX31: Rou 7K **17**
Pancras Sq. EX4: Exe 4D **6**
PANCRASWEEK 3A **162**
Pankhurst Cl. EX8: Lit 5G **77**
The Panney EX4: Exe 5K **65**
Pannier Market *4J 59*
(off Market Rd.)
Pannier Mkt. EX38: G Tor 2C **30**
Pannier M. *EX39: Bide* *4F 23*
(off Silver St.)
Pannier St. EX17: Cred 6H **39**
Panorama *TQ2: Torq* *4A 116*
(off Livermead Hill)
Papaver Cl. EX31: Frem 5E **16**
Paper Makers La. PL21: Ivy 3J **145**
Parade EX8: Exmth 5C **76**
PL1: Plym 6F **9** (3K **141**)
TQ13: Chud 2C **94**
The Parade PL19: Mil A 2B **58**
Pde. Av. EX31: Frem 5F **17**
Parade Bus. Pk. PL19: Tavi 5J **59**
Parade Ope PL1: Plym 6F **9**
Parade Rd. PL5: Plym 7F **131**
Parade Ter. *EX34: Ilfra* *2J 11*
(off Capstone Rd.)
Paradise Glen TQ14: Teignm 3H **107**
Paradise Lawn EX36: S Mol 6D **26**
Paradise Pl. PL1: Dev 2F **141**
TQ5: Brixh 3E **122**
Paradise Rd. PL1: Dev 2E **140**
TQ14: Teignm 3H **107**
Paradise Wlk. TQ4: Good 3J **119**
TQ9: Tot 7G **103**
Paragon *EX34: Ilfra* *2H 11*
(off Granville Rd.)
Paramore Way EX36: S Mol 6C **26**
Parely Hill TQ13: Chag 2G **61**
Paris Rd. TQ3: Pres 6J **115**
Paris St. EX1: Exe 3F **7** (6F **65**)
The Park PL8: Brixt 2H **149**
Park & Ride
Barnstaple 7F **19**
Brixham 3K **121**
Coypool 5H **137**
Dartmouth 7C **124**
Digby 2C **72**
George Junction 4D **132**
Honiton Road 6D **66**
Ivybridge 4K **145**
Matford 6G **71**
Milehouse 6H **135**
Salcombe 3B **158**
Sowton 1D **72**
Park Av. EX31: B'aple 5B **18**
EX39: Bide 2F **23**
EX39: W Ho 5B **20**
PL1: Dev 1D **140**
PL9: Plyms 5E **142**
TQ5: Brixh 5D **122**
Parkbay Av. TQ4: Paig 5E **118**
Park Cl. EX5: Silv 2H **51**
EX5: W'bury 6C **78**
EX16: Tive 3D **40**
EX22: Hols 1C **34**
EX31: Frem 6F **17**
PL7: Plymp 4J **137**
PL21: Ivy 4G **145**
Park Ct. EX14: Hon 5C **54**
EX34: Ilfra 4H **11**
TQ5: Brixh 3G **123**
Park Cres. EX34: C Mar 7C **12**
PL9: Plyms 5D **142**
TQ1: Torq 4D **112**
Parkelands TQ13: Bov T 4B **92**
Parker Cl. PL7: Plymp 6J **137**
Parker Rd. PL2: Plym 5G **135**
TQ7: Bigb S 3B **154**
Parkers Cl. TQ9: Tot 7F **103**
Parkers Cross La. EX1: Pin 2E **66**
Parkers Hollow EX31: Rou 6A **18**
Parker's Rd. EX6: Star 2D **96**
Parkers Way TQ9: Tot 7F **103**
Parker Wlk. EX13: Axmin 2J **89**
Parkes Rd. EX38: G Tor 2D **30**
PARKFIELD 3B **168**
Parkfield .7J **115**
Parkfield TQ7: Thur 6B **154**
Parkfield Cl. TQ3: Marl 3D **114**
TQ9: Tot 6H **103**
Parkfield Dr. PL6: Plym 1G **137**
Parkfield Rd. EX3: Top 5B **74**
TQ1: Torq 6B **112**
Parkfield Ter. EX12: Brans 6H **85**
Parkfield Wlk. TQ7: Thur 6B **154**
Parkfield Way EX3: Top 5B **74**
Park Five Bus. Cen. EX2: Sow 1D **72**
Park Gdns. EX35: Lynt 2G **13**
Park Gro. EX22: Hols 1C **34**
Park Hall TQ1: Torq 3E **116**
PARKHAM 1B **162**
PARKHAM ASH 1B **162**
Parkham Field 4E **122**
Parkham Glade TQ5: Brixh 4E **122**
Parkham La. TQ5: Brixh 4E **122**
Parkham Rd. TQ5: Brixh 4E **122**
Parkham Towers *TQ5: Brixh* *4E 122*
(off Wren Hill)
Parkhayes EX5: Wood S 1C **78**
Park Hill EX16: Tive 3C **40**
TQ12: Ipp 6K **101**
TQ14: Teignm 5H **107**
Park Hill Rd. EX34: Ilfra 3H **11**
Parkhill Rd. TQ1: Torq 3D **116**
Park Hills Ind. Units
EX34: C Mar 7B **12**
Park Ho. PL4: Plym 2H **9** (1A **142**)
Parkhouse Rd. EX2: Exe 2C **70**
Parkhurst Rd. TQ1: Torq 6B **112**
Parkland Cvn. & Camping Site 1E **156**
Parkland Dr. EX2: Won 2B **72**
Parklands EX12: Seat 5E **86**
EX15: Hemy 2F **47**
EX20: Oke 5B **48**
EX31: Rou 6B **18**
EX36: S Mol 7B **26**
TQ9: Tot 5E **102**
Parklands Cl. EX36: S Mol 7B **26**
Parklands Leisure Cen.
Okehampton 4C **48**
Parklands Way TQ13: Bov T 7B **92**
Park La. EX4: Pin 1C **66**
EX8: Exmth 4C **76**
EX9: Bud S 6B **82**
EX9: Ott'n 7H **83**
EX13: Whit 5A **90**
EX17: Morc 1B **38**
EX32: B'aple 6F **19**
EX34: C Mar 6B **12**
EX39: Bide 2F **23**
PL9: Plyms 5D **142**
PL20: Bere A 1C **128**
TQ1: Torq 3D **116**
TQ9: Blacka 3B **152**
Park La. Steps *TQ1: Torq* *3E 116*
(off Park La.)
Park Mdw. Cl. EX17: Lap 1K **37**
Park M. TQ5: Brixh 3G **123**
Park Mill La. EX18: Chul 6C **32**
Park Pl. EX1: Heav 6J **65**
EX2: Exe 6H **7** (7G **65**)
EX19: Wink 2C **36**
Park Pl. La. PL3: Plym 7F **135**
Park Ri. EX7: Daw 5G **97**
TQ8: Salc 4B **158**
Park Rd. EX1: Heav 2K **7** (5H **65**)
EX5: Silv 2H **51**
EX7: Daw 4G **97**
EX8: Exmth 4C **76**
EX12: Beer 7A **86**
EX16: Tive 3D **40**
EX17: Cred 7J **39**
EX17: Lap 1K **37**
EX20: Hath 1H **35**
PL3: Plym 5B **136**
PL11: Torp 1A **140**
PL16: Lift 7B **56**
TQ1: Torq 4D **112**
TQ9: Darti 1D **102**
TQ12: Kingsk 7J **109**
Park Row EX20: Oke 3B **48**
Parks Dr. PL9: Spri 7H **143**
Parkside PL2: Plym 6D **134**
PL21: Ivy 4J **145**
TQ8: Salc 3C **158**
Parkside Ct. EX2: Exe 5F **7**
Parkside Cres. EX1: W Cly 1E **66**
Parkside Dr. EX8: Exmth 2F **77**
Parkside Rd. EX1: W Cly 1E **66**
TQ4: Paig 1J **119**
Parkside Vs. *TQ1: Torq* *6E 112*
(off Palermo Rd.)
Parks La. EX9: Bud S 7D **82**
Parkstone La. PL7: Plymp 3C **138**
Park St. EX15: Will 3C **44**
EX16: Tive 4D **40**
EX17: Cred 6J **39**
EX35: Lynt 2G **13**
PL3: Plym 7F **135**
PL21: Ivy 5G **145**
Park St. M. PL21: Ivy 5G **145**
Park St. Ope PL3: Plym 7F **135**
Park Ter. EX16: Tive 3D **40**
EX32: B'aple 5F **19**
PL4: Plym 4G **9**
PL21: Ivy *5G 145*
(off Park St.)
Park Vw. EX4: Exe 7A **6** (1D **70**)
EX6: Kenton 6K **95**
EX8: Lymp 6J **75**
EX19: Bea 3H **31**
EX24: Colyt 6C **88**
EX32: B'aple *3E 18*
(off Pilton C'way.)
PL4: Plym 4K **9** (2B **142**)
PL16: Lift 6B **56**
TQ12: New A 4J **109**
Park Vw. Cvn. Site 3F **19**
Park Vw. Cl. EX34: C Mar 7C **12**
Park Vw. Rd. EX32: B'aple 3F **19**
Park Vw. Ter. EX20: Oke 5C **48**
EX39: W Ho 5B **20**
Park Vw. Way EX32: B'aple 3F **19**
Park Vs. EX32: B Taw 7B **24**
Park Way EX8: Exmth 4E **76**
(not continuous)
Parkway EX2: Exe 2C **70**
EX5: W'bury 6C **78**
EX34: Ilfra 5H **11**
The Parkway PL5: Plym 1C **134**
PL6: Plym 3A **136**
Parkway Ct. PL6: Plym 4F **137**
The Parkway Ind. Estate
PL6: Plym 4F **137**
Parkway M. TQ13: Chud 2C **94**
Parkway Rd. TQ13: Chud 3C **94**
Parkwood Cl. PL6: Robo 1C **132**
Parkwood Ct. PL19: Tavi 3K **59**
Park Wood Ri. PL16: Lift 7A **56**
Parkwood Rd. PL19: Tavi 3J **59**
Parliament Ct. *EX34: Ilfra* *2J 11*
(off Hierns La.)
Parliament St. EX4: Exe 4D **6** (6E **64**)
EX17: Cred 6H **39**
Parlour Mead EX15: Cull 4F **45**
Parminter Cl. EX8: Exmth 5G **77**
Parnell Cl. PL6: Plym 3B **136**
PARRACOMBE 2C **161**
Parracombe Old St Petrock's Church
. . . . .2C **161**
Parracombe Picnic Site 2C **161**
Parr Cl. EX1: Exe 2H **7** (5G **65**)
Parr La. PL4: Plym 6J **9** (3A **142**)
Parrots Cl. *TQ7: Malb* *6G 155*
(off Higher Town)
Parr's La. TQ13: Chud 1B **94**
Parrs Pl. EX5: Clyst M 2G **73**
Parr St. EX1: Exe 2H **7** (5G **65**)
PL4: Plym 6J **9** (3A **142**)
Parrys Farm Cl. EX8: Exmth 2E **76**
Parsonage Ct. PL16: Lift 6B **56**
Parsonage La. EX5: Silv 1H **51**
EX14: Gitt 7A **54**
EX14: Hon 4G **55**
EX36: S Mol 5C **26**
PL21: Ugb 6E **146**
Parsonage Rd. PL8: New F 5J **149**
Parsonage St. EX5: Bradn 1D **52**
Parsonage Way EX5: W'bury 5C **78**
PL4: Plym 6H **9** (3A **142**)
Parson Cl. EX8: Exmth 2E **76**
Parson's Cl. EX15: Kent 6A **46**
Parsons Cl. EX10: New P 6F **81**
EX22: Hols 2C **34**
PL9: Plyms 7H **143**
Parsons La. EX5: Rock 4C **68**
EX12: Brans 6J **85**
Parsons Mdw. EX15: Kent 6A **46**
Parsons Path *EX3: Top* *5B 74*
(off Monmouth Av.)
Parson St. TQ14: Teignm 4H **107**
Parthia Pl. EX8: Exmth 3G **77**
Partridge Rd. EX8: Exmth 1E **76**
Partwayes PL19: Lam 6C **58**
Pasley St. PL2: Plym 7D **134**
Pasley St. E. PL2: Plym 7E **134**
Passaford La. EX10: N'town 2K **83**
EX20: Hath 3G **35**
Passage Rd. PL8: Noss M 6G **149**
Passmore Rd. EX5: Bradn 2B **52**
PATCHACOTT 1C **169**
Patches Rd. EX16: Tive 3B **40**
PATCHOLE 2C **161**
Paternoster La. TQ12: Ipp 6G **101**
Paternoster Row EX11: Ott M 3C **80**
EX31: B'aple *4E 18*
(off High St.)
The Path EX39: App 2H **21**
Pathdown La. EX33: Croy 3D **14**
(not continuous)
PATHE 1D **167**
Pathfield EX38: G Tor 2E **30**
Pathfield Cl. EX31: Rou 6K **17**
Pathfield Lawn EX31: B'aple 3D **18**
Pathfields EX15: Uff 6G **43**
EX16: Tive *5C 40*
(off King St.)
EX33: Croy 1C **14**
TQ9: Tot 6F **103**
Pathfields Cl. TQ9: Tot 6F **103**
PATHFINDER VILLAGE 1C **171**
Pathwhorlands EX10: Sidm 4B **84**
Patna Pl. PL1: Plym 2C **8** (1H **141**)
Paton Watson Quadrate PL1: Plym 7F **9**
Pato Point PL11: Wilc 5A **134**
Patricia Cl. EX4: Exe 2F **65**
Patterdale Cl. PL6: Plym 7E **132**
Patterdale Wlk. PL6: Plym 7E **132**
Patteson Dr. EX11: Ott M 3E **80**
Pattinson Cl. PL6: Plym 1F **137**
Pattinson Ct. PL6: Plym 1F **137**
Pattinson Dr. PL6: Plym 1F **137**
Paullet EX16: Sam P 2A **42**
Paul St. EX4: Exe 4D **6** (6E **64**)
Pauntley Gdns. EX10: Sidm 7A **84**
Pavey Run EX11: Ott M 4A **80**
Paviland Grange PL1: Plym 1F **141**
Pavilion Pl. EX2: Exe 5F **7** (7F **65**)
Pavilions **5J 107**
Pavilions Cl. TQ5: Brixh 3D **122**
Pavor Rd. TQ2: Torq 3D **112**
Paws Rd. EX37: High B 3A **32**
Paxford Ho. Sq. EX11: Ott M 3C **80**
PAYHEMBURY 3A **166**
Paynes Ct. EX4: Whip 4A **66**
Paynsford M. TQ12: New A 7E **104**
Paynsford Rd. TQ12: New A 7E **104**
Paynter Wlk. PL7: Plymp 4E **138**
PAYTON 1B **166**
Peacock Av. PL11: Torp 1A **140**
Peacock Cl. PL7: Plymp 2C **138**
Peacock La. PL4: Plym 5F **9**
Peacock Pl. EX6: Star 1E **96**
Peadhill La. EX16: Chev 1H **41**
Peak Hill Rd. EX10: Sidm 7A **84**
Peak Tor Av. TQ1: Torq 4E **116**
Pear Dr. EX15: Will 4D **44**
Peard Rd. EX16: Tive 5G **41**
Peards Down Cl. EX32: B'aple 5J **19**
Pear La. PL7: Plymp 4E **138**
Pearmain Cl. EX15: Will 4D **44**
Pearn Cotts. PL3: Plym 5A **136**
Pearn Gdns. PL3: Plym 4B **136**
Pearn Ridge PL3: Plym 4B **136**
Pearn Rd. PL3: Plym 4B **136**
Pearse Cl. EX20: Hath 2G **35**
Pearse Gdns. PL21: Modb 6G **147**
Pearson Av. PL4: Plym 7A **136**
Pearson Cl. EX22: Hols 1C **34**
Pearson Rd. PL4: Plym 7A **136**
Pear Tree Cl. EX6: Kenton 6J **95**
Pear Tree Way EX32: Land 2C **24**
Peasberry Pl. PL8: Y'ton 2A **150**
Peaseditch TQ5: Brixh 5F **123**
Peasland Rd. TQ2: Torq 1C **112**
Peaslands Rd. EX10: Sidm 5B **84**
PEASMARSH 2D **167**
Peazen Flats EX12: Beer 6A **86**
Pebblebed Cl. EX2: Cou W 6C **72**
Pebble Cl. EX39: W Ho 5C **20**
Pebble Ct. TQ4: Good 3H **119**
Pebble La. EX9: Bud S 7C **82**
Pebbleridge Rd. EX39: W Ho 5C **20**
Pecorama . . . .**7A 86 (2C 173)**
Pedlerspool La. EX17: Cred 4J **39**
Peek La. PL21: Bitta 3B **146**
Peeks Av. PL9: Plyms 5G **143**
Peel Row EX4: Whip 4B **66**
Peel St. PL1: Plym 3F **141**
Peel St. Flats PL1: Plym 2F **141**
Peep La. EX4: Exe 3B **6** (6D **64**)
EX17: Cred 6J **39**
Pegasus Ct. EX1: Heav 6J **65**
TQ3: Paig 6H **115**
Pegwell La. TQ14: Shal 7D **106**
Pelican Cl. EX39: W Ho 6A **20**
Pellew Arc. *TQ14: Teignm* *5H 107*
(off Teign St.)
Pellew Ho. *TQ14: Teignm* *5H 107*
(off Teign St.)
Pellew Pl. PL2: Dev 7E **134**
Pellew Way TQ14: Teignm 2G **107**
Pellinore Rd. EX4: Whip 3K **65**
Pembrey Wlk. PL5: Plym 6D **130**
Pembroke La. PL1: Dev 3D **140**
Pembroke Pk. TQ3: Marl 3E **114**
Pembroke Rd. TQ1: Torq 1D **116**
TQ3: Paig 7E **114**
Pembroke St. PL1: Dev 3D **140**
Pemros Rd. PL5: Plym 1A **134**
Pencarrow Rd. TQ3: Paig 7D **114**
Pencarwick Ho. EX8: Exmth 7C **76**
Pencorse Rd. TQ2: Torq 5B **112**
Pencreber Rd. PL20: Horr 2E **126**
Pencross Vw. EX15: Hemy 1G **47**
Pendeen Cl. PL6: Plym 4A **132**
Pendeen Ct. EX8: Exmth 5F **77**
Pendeen Cres. PL6: Plym 4A **132**
Pendeen Pk. TQ7: Chil 6G **159**
Pendennis Cl. PL3: Plym 3A **136**
Pendennis Rd. TQ2: Torq 5B **112**
Pendragon Rd. EX4: Whip 2J **65**
Penfield Gdns. EX7: Daw 4G **97**
Pengelly Cl. TQ12: Kingst 4J **105**
Pengelly Way TQ2: Torq 2A **112**
Pengilly Way EX39: Hart 3J **27**
Penhale Dr. EX22: Hols 1B **34**
Penhayes Cl. EX6: Kenton 6J **95**
Penhayes Rd. EX6: Kenton 6J **95**
PENHILL 4G **17**
Penhill Chalets TQ6: Sto F 3J **153**
Penhill La. TQ5: Hill 6J **123**
Peninsula Medical School
The John Bull Bldg. 7D **132**
Peninsula Pk. EX2: Won 1B **72**
Penitentiary Ct. EX2: Exe 6E **6** (7F **65**)
Penlee EX9: Bud S 7C **82**
Penlee Gdns. PL3: Plym 7F **135**
Penlee Pl. PL4: Plym 7A **136**
Penlee Rd. PL3: Plym 7F **135**
Penlee Way PL3: Plym 1A **8** (7F **135**)
Penleonard Cl. EX2: Exe 6J **7** (7H **65**)
PENN 1D **173**
Pennant Ho. *EX8: Exmth* *6A 76*
(off Shelly Rd.)

Pennant Way PL21: L Mill 5C **144**
Penn Ct. TQ5: Brixh 5F **123**
Pennine Dr. TQ4: Coll M 3D **118**
Pennington Cl. EX17: Cop 6C **38**
PENNINN 3G **109**
Penn Inn Cl. TQ12: New A 2H **109**
Penn La. TQ5: Brixh 5E **122**
Penn Mdws. TQ5: Brixh 5F **123**
Penn Mdws. Cl. TQ5: Brixh 5F **123**
Penns Way TQ12: Kingst 5J **105**
PENNSYLVANIA 3G **65** (1D **171**)
Pennsylvania Cl. EX4: Exe 4G **65**
Pennsylvania Ct. EX4: Exe 4G **65**
Pennsylvania Cres. EX4: Exe 4F **65**
Pennsylvania Pk. EX4: Exe 3G **65**
Pennsylvania Picnic Site 1D **171**
Pennsylvania Rd.
  EX4: Exe 1F **7** (1F **65**)
  TQ1: Torq 1D **116**
PENNTORR 1A **140**
Pennyacre Rd. TQ14: Teignm 3J **107**
PENNYCOMEQUICK 1C **8** (1H **141**)
Pennycomequick Vs. PL4: Plym 1C **8**
PENNYCROSS 3J **135** (2A **174**)
Pennycross Cl. PL2: Plym 3J **135**
Pennycross Pk. Rd. PL2: Plym 4H **135**
Penny Hill EX33: Croy 1C **14**
PENNYMOOR 2C **165**
Penny Pk. EX16: Tive 4B **40**
Penny Plot DT7: Lym R 4H **91**
Penny's Hill TQ1: Torq 6B **112**
Penny's La. TQ5: Brixh 6K **143**
Pennys Ter. EX13: Axmin 4H **89**
             (off Musbury Rd.)
Pennywell Farm 1D **175**
Penpethy Cl. TQ5: Brixh 4D **122**
Penpethy Ct. TQ5: Brixh 4D **122**
Penpethy Rd. TQ5: Brixh 3D **122**
Penpont Ct. EX39: Bide 3E **22**
PENQUIT 7K **145** (2C **175**)
Penrhyn Pl. TQ14: Shal 6G **107**
Penrith Cl. PL6: Plym 7E **132**
Penrith Gdns. PL6: Plym 7E **132**
Penrith Wlk. PL6: Plym 7E **132**
Penrose Gdns. EX22: Hols 2C **34**
Penrose Sq. EX32: B'aple 5F **19**
             (off Litchdon St.)
Penrose St. PL1: Plym 2C **8** (2H **141**)
Penrose St. W. PL1: Plym 3C **8**
Penrose Ter. EX22: Hols 2C **34**
Penrose Vs. PL4: Plym 7A **136**
Penshurst Rd. TQ12: New A 3E **108**
PENSILVA 3A **168**
Pensilva Pk. TQ5: Brixh 5E **122**
Pens La. EX15: Hemy 3G **47**
PENSTONE 3B **164**
Pentamar St. PL2: Dev 7D **134**
Pentgrove Ct. EX8: Exmth 5F **77**
Pentice La. EX34: C Mar 5C **12**
Pentillie Cl. PL20: Bere A 3C **128**
Pentillie Cres. PL4: Plym 7J **135**
Pentillie Rd. PL4: Plym 7K **135**
  PL20: Bere A 3C **128**
Pentillie Vw. PL20: Bere A 2C **128**
Pentland Cl. PL6: Plym 3A **132**
Penton Cl. EX17: Cred 5J **39**
Penton La. EX17: Cred 6J **39**
Penton Ri. EX17: Cred 5J **39**
Pentridge Av. TQ2: Torq 4J **115**
Pentyre Ct. PL4: Plym 2K **9**
Pentyre Ter. PL4: Plym . . .2J **9** (1A **142**)
Penwill Way TQ4: Good, Paig 3F **119**
Pen-y-Dre EX15: Cull 3H **45**
Peoples Pk. Rd. EX17: Cred 5G **39**
Peppercombe Av. EX41: Sow 5C **66**
Pepper La. PL9: Elb 7K **143**
Pepper St. PL19: Tavi 3J **59**
Peppery La. TQ14: Shal 6F **107**
Pepys Pl. PL5: Plym 2J **135**
Perceval Rd. EX4: Whip 3K **65**
Percy Rd. EX2: Exe 2E **70**
Percy St. PL5: Plym 2C **134**
Percy Ter. PL4: Plym 7B **136**
Peregrine Cl. TQ2: Torq 2K **111**
Peregrine Rd. PL6: Plym 1C **136**
Perinville Cl. TQ1: Torq 7G **113**
Perinville Rd. TQ1: Torq 6F **113**
Periwinkle Dr. EX31: Rou 6A **18**
  PL7: Plymp 4F **139**
Perranporth Cl. PL5: Plym 7D **130**
Perriam's Pl. EX9: Bud S 6C **82**
Perridge Ct. EX2: Sow 2B **70**
Perriman's Row EX8: Exmth 5C **76**
Perrin Way EX7: Kenn 3C **66**
Perros Cl. TQ14: Teignm 3F **107**
Perry Cl. PL19: Tavi 3H **59**
Perryfield Pl. PL9: Plyms 3E **142**
Perry Hill EX17: Cher F 4H **39**
Perry La. TQ12: New A 7K **93**
Perryman Cl. PL7: Plymp 2B **138**
Perry Rd. EX4: Exe 4E **64**
Perrys Gdns. EX11: W Hill 4H **79**
PERRY STREET 3D **167**
Perth Cl. EX4: Exe 2H **65**
Peryam Cres. EX2: Won 1K **71**
Peryn Pl. PL19: Tavi 4G **59**

Peterborough Rd. EX4: Exe 5B **64**
Peterclose Rd. EX16: Tive 5F **41**
Peter's Cl. PL9: Elb 5J **143**
Peters Cl. TQ4: Paig 6F **119**
Peters Cres. TQ3: Marl 3D **114**
Peters Fld. PL8: New F 4J **149**
Petersfield EX1: Pin 2E **66**
Petersfield Ct. PL3: Plym 5C **136**
PETERS MARLAND 3D **163**
Peters Pk. Cl. PL5: Plym 2D **134**
Peter's Pk. La. PL5: Plym 1C **134**
Peter St. EX5: Bradn 1C **52**
PETER TAVY 3D **169**
Pethertons EX16: Hal 6C **42**
PETHERWIN GATE 2A **168**
Pethick Cl. PL6: Plym 4J **131**
Pethill Cl. PL6: Plym 1G **137**
PETHYBRIDGE 6G **63**
Petitor M. TQ1: Torq 4D **112**
Petitor Rd. TQ1: Torq 4D **112**
Petitwell La. TQ1: Torq 4D **112**
Petrel Cl. TQ2: Torq 2J **111**
Petre St. EX13: Axmin 2J **89**
Petroc Dr. TQ12: New A 7F **105**
PETROCKSTOWE 3D **163**
Petticoat La. EX13: Axmin 1E **88**
PETTON 1A **166**
Peverall Pk. Rd. PL2: Plym 4J **135**
PEVERELL 4J **135**
Peverell Rd. PL2: Plym 4J **135**
Peverell Ter. PL3: Plym 6J **135**
Pew Tor Cl. PL19: Tavi 2G **59**
  PL20: Yelv 5F **127**
Phear Av. EX8: Exmth 5D **76**
Phear Park 4D **76**
Phelps Rd. PL1: Dev 2D **140**
PHILHAM 1A **162**
Philip Av. EX31: B'aple 7C **18**
Philip Cl. PL9: Plyms 6H **143**
Philip Gdns. PL9: Plyms 6G **143**
Philip Ho. EX2: Sow 6D **66**
Philip Rd. EX4: Exe 4J **65**
Philips La. EX33: Brau 5J **15**
Phillimore St. PL2: Plym 7E **134**
Phillipps Av. EX8: Exmth 3D **76**
Phillips Ct. EX13: Axmin 4H **89**
Phillips Path TQ7: Lodd 2G **151**
Phillips Sq. EX14: Hon 3E **54**
Philpott La. PL19: Tavi 7H **59**
Phoenix Cl. PL20: Horr 2E **126**
Phoenix La. EX16: Tive 5D **40**
Phoenix Pl. TQ7: W Alv 5D **156**
Phoenix St. PL1: Plym . . .5A **8** (3G **141**)
Piazza Terracina EX2: Exe 7E **6**
PIBSBURY 1D **167**
Piccadilly La. EX11: Ott M 4C **80**
             (off Mill St.)
Picket Head Hill TQ14: Shal 7G **107**
Picklecombe Dr. PL6: Plym 6K **131**
Pick Pie Dr. PL6: Plym 2F **133**
PICKWELL 2A **160**
Pickwick Arc. EX4: Exe 5D **6**
PICT'S HILL 1D **167**
Pidgeon's La. EX13: Ray H 1B **90**
Pidgley Rd. EX7: Daw 1J **97**
Pier Head EX8: Exmth 6A **76**
Piermont Pl. EX7: Daw 4H **97**
Pier St. PL1: Plym 7B **8** (4H **141**)
Piggy La. EX39: Nort 5E **20**
           (not continuous)
Pig La. EX13: Axmin 3H **89**
Pike Rd. PL3: Plym 6E **136**
Pikes Mead EX20: Oke 4B **48**
Pilgrim Cl. PL2: Plym 5G **135**
Pilgrim Dr. PL20: Bere A 2C **128**
Pilgrim Hall PL4: Plym 3F **9**
Pilgrim Ho. EX4: Exe 4J **65**
Pilland Way EX31: B'aple 3C **18**
Pillar Av. TQ5: Brixh 3D **122**
Pillar Cl. TQ5: Brixh 3D **122**
Pillar Cres. TQ5: Brixh 3D **122**
Pillar Wlk. PL6: Plym 4K **131**
PILLATON 1A **174**
Pill Gdns. EX33: Brau 6J **15**
Pill La. EX32: B'aple, B Taw 4A **24**
Pill Lawn EX32: B'aple 7F **19**
Pillman Dr. EX39: Hart 3K **27**
Pillory Hill PL8: Noss M 6H **149**
Pill Rd. EX39: Bide 3F **23**
Pilmuir Av. TQ2: Torq 1A **116**
Pilot Wharf EX8: Exmth 6A **76**
           (off Pier Head)
PILSDON 1D **173**
PILTON 2D **18**
Pilton C'way. EX32: B'aple 3E **18**
Pilton La. EX1: Pin 4C **66**
Pilton Lawn EX31: B'aple 3E **18**
Pilton Quay EX31: B'aple 3E **18**
Pilton St. EX31: B'aple 2E **18**
Pimlico TQ1: Torq 1D **116**
Pimm Rd. TQ3: Paig 7E **114**
Pinaster Cl. EX14: Hon 4H **55**
Pinbrook Ind. Est. EX4: Pin 3C **66**
Pinbrook M. EX4: Pin 2B **66**
Pinbrook Rd. EX4: Pin 3C **66**

Pinbrook Units EX4: Pin 3C **66**
Pinces Cotts. EX2: Exe 2D **70**
Pinces Gdns. EX2: Exe 2D **70**
Pinces Rd. EX2: Exe 2D **70**
Pincombe Ct. EX8: Exmth 5G **77**
Pinder Ct. PL19: Tavi 4F **59**
Pine Av. EX4: Exe 5C **64**
Pine Cl. EX16: Tive 4B **40**
  EX34: Ilfra 4K **11**
  TQ5: Brixh 6D **122**
  TQ14: Teignm 2K **107**
Pine Cones EX34: Wool 7C **10**
Pine Ct. TQ1: Torq 1F **117**
Pinefields Cl. EX11: W Hill 5J **79**
Pine Gdns. EX14: Hon 3G **55**
  PL3: Plym 5K **135**
Pine Gro. EX14: Hon 3G **55**
Pinehurst Way PL21: Ivy 3E **144**
Pine Pk. Rd. EX14: Hon 4G **55**
Pine Ridge DT7: Lym R 3K **91**
The Pines EX4: Exe 5C **64**
  EX14: Hon 5C **54**
Pines Cl. EX39: Hart 3J **27**
Pine Rd. EX8: Exmth 1E **76**
  TQ3: Paig 6E **114**
Pine Tree Cl. EX7: Daw W 7E **96**
Pine Vw. Av. TQ1: Torq 7E **112**
Pine Vw. Cl. EX8: Exmth 2H **77**
Pine Vw. Gdns. TQ1: Torq 7E **112**
Pine Vw. Rd. TQ1: Torq 7E **112**
Pine Wlk. DT7: Lym R 6J **91**
Pinewood Cl. EX7: Daw 2K **97**
  PL7: Plymp 3C **138**
Pinewood Dr. PL6: Plym 3F **133**
Pinewood Rd. TQ12: New A 2C **108**
PINHOE 2D **66** (1D **171**)
Pinhoe Rd.
  EX4: Exe, Pin, Whip 1K **7** (5H **65**)
Pinhoe Station (Rail) 3D **66** (1D **171**)
Pinhoe Trad. Est. EX4: Pin 3C **66**
Pink Ho. Cnr. EX8: Lymp 3J **75**
Pin La. PL1: Plym 6F **9** (3K **141**)
Pinnacle Quay PL4: Plym 4H **9**
          (off Harbour Av.)
Pinnbridge Ct. EX1: Pin 4D **66**
          (off Old Pinn La.)
Pinncourt La. EX1: Pin 2E **66**
Pinnex Moor Rd. EX16: Tive 2D **40**
Pinn Hill EX1: Pin 2E **66**
Pinn La. EX1: Pin 3D **66**
Pinn Valley Rd. EX1: Pin 3E **66**
Pinslow Cross PL15: St G 7B **34**
Pins Pk. EX22: Hols 1B **34**
Pintail Way PL6: Plym 1C **136**
Pinwill Cres. PL21: Erm 2J **147**
Pinwood La. EX4: Whip 2A **66**
         (not continuous)
Pinwood Mdw. Dr. EX4: Whip 2A **66**
Pioneer Cotts. EX12: Beer 7B **86**
          (off New Cut)
Pioneer Ter. TQ11: B'leigh 4B **98**
Pipehouse La. TQ13: Chud K 6B **94**
PIPERS POOL 2A **168**
Piper St. PL6: Plym 6C **132**
Pipistrelle Way TQ12: Kingst 3F **105**
PIPPACOTT 3B **160**
Pippen Share EX5: Rock 3D **68**
Pippin Cl. EX1: Heav 6B **66**
Pippin Cl. PL9: Elb 7K **143**
The Pippins PL21: Ivy 4E **144**
Pippins Ct. EX12: Beer 7B **86**
Pippins Fld. EX15: Uff 7G **43**
Pippins M. TQ13: Ashb 3J **99**
         (off Eastern Rd.)
Piscombe La. EX9: Ott'n 6J **83**
Pitcairn Cres. TQ2: Torq 2A **112**
Pitfield Cl. EX15: Will 5D **44**
Pitham La. EX11: Ott M 1D **80**
Pit Hill EX34: Ber 2A **12**
Pitley Rd. TQ13: Ashb 3K **99**
Pitman's La. PL21: Corn 7H **129**
PITMINSTER 2C **167**
PITNEY 1D **167**
PITSFORD HILL 1B **166**
Pitson La. EX10: N'town 7J **81**
Pitt Av. EX39: App 3H **21**
Pitt Ct. EX17: Nym R 2F **37**
  EX39: App 3H **21**
  TQ7: Lodd 2H **151**
Pitt Cres. TQ9: Berr P 4K **103**
PITT HILL 1G **145**
Pitt Hill EX6: Kenton 6H **29**
  EX21: Sheb 6H **29**
  EX39: App 4G **21**
Pitt Hill Rd. TQ12: New A 6C **104**
Pitt La. EX17: Bow 4F **37**
  EX39: Bide 3F **23**
Pitt Pk. EX5: Cran 3C **68**
Pitts Ct. EX2: Exe 7F **7** (1G **71**)
Pixie Dell EX33: Brau 3G **15**
Pixie La. EX33: Brau 3G **15**
Pixie Wlk. EX11: Ott M 4A **80**
Pixon La. PL19: Tavi 5H **59**
Pixon Trad. Cen. PL19: Tavi 5H **59**
Place La. TQ13: Ashb 2J **99**
PLAINMOOR 6D **112**
Plainmoor 6D **112**

Plainmoor Community Swimming Pool
  . . . . .6D **112**
Plainmoor Rd. TQ1: Torq 6D **112**
The Plains TQ9: Tot 6F **103**
Plaistow Cl. PL5: Plym 1D **134**
Plaistow Cres. PL5: Plym 1D **134**
Plantagenet Cl. EX15: Cull 1H **45**
Plantagenet Wlk. EX2: Sow 1C **72**
         (off Heraldry Way)
Plantation Cl. TQ12: New A 3J **109**
Plantation Ter. EX7: Daw 4G **97**
Plantation Way TQ2: Torq 4J **111**
  TQ9: Tot 5B **102**
Plant World Gardens 1A **176**
Plassey Cl. EX4: Exe 2G **65**
The Plat TQ6: Strete 6G **153**
Platt Cl. TQ8: Salc 4A **158**
Platway La. TQ14: Shal 6F **107**
The Play Hut 2H **11**
           (off Bath Pl.)
Playmoor Dr. EX1: Pin 3E **66**
Pleasant Ter. TQ3: Paig 1G **119**
The Pleasaunce PL8: New F 5J **149**
Pleasure Hill Cl. PL9: Plyms 4E **142**
Plintona Vw. PL7: Plymp 2B **138**
Ploudal Rd. EX15: Cull 5G **45**
The Plough Arts Cen. 2C **163**
Ploughman Way PL8: Torr 3C **150**
Plover Ri. PL21: Ivy 4F **145**
Plume of Feathers Cl.
  EX11: Ott M 3D **80**
The Plume of Feathers Inn
  PL20: Prin 7D **60**
Plumer Rd. PL6: Plym 1A **136**
Plumtree Dr. EX2: Won 1A **72**
Plumtree La. EX5: Whim 7H **53**
Plum Wlk. PL7: Plymp 4E **138**
Plum Way EX15: Will 4D **44**
PLUSHABRIDGE 3B **168**
Plymbridge Gdns. PL7: Plymp 4K **137**
Plymbridge La. PL6: Plym 6C **132**
Plym Bridge Riverside &
  Woodland Walks 1H **137**
Plymbridge Rd. PL6: Plym 2D **136**
         (Freshford Wlk.)
  PL6: Plym 4D **132**
         (Morgan Rd.)
  PL7: Plymp 1H **137**
Plym Cl. TQ2: Torq 6H **111**
Plym Cres. PL19: Tavi 4K **59**
PLYMOUTH 4F **9** (3K **141**)
Plymouth Albion RFC 2E **140**
Plymouth Argyle FC 6H **135**
Plymouth Arts Centre 3F **9**
Plymouth Arts Cinema 3F **9**
Plymouth City Market 4C **8** (2H **141**)
Plymouth Coach Station . . .3D **8** (2J **141**)
Plymouth Gin Distillery . . .6F **9** (3K **141**)
Plymouth Golf Cen. 3K **143**
Plymouth Hill PL20: Prin 7C **60**
Plymouth Intl. Bus. Pk.
  PL6: Plym 7A **132**
Plymouth Intl. Medical & Technical Pk.
  PL6: Plym 7B **132**
Plymouth Life Cen. 6H **135**
Plymouth Naval Memorial
  . . . . .7D **8** (4J **141**)
Plymouth Pavilions 5B **8** (3H **141**)
Plymouth RC Cathedral . . .3B **8** (2H **141**)
Plymouth Rd. PL3: Plym 6F **137**
  PL6: Plym 5G **137**
  PL7: Plymp 5H **137**
  PL19: Tavi, Whit 4H **59**
  PL20: Horr 2E **126**
  TQ7: Kingsb 1D **156**
  TQ9: Tot 5A **102**
  TQ10: S Bre 1B **100**
  TQ11: B'leigh, Lwr D 7B **98**
         (not continuous)
  TQ13: Chud K 6B **94**
Plymouth Rd. Ind. Est.
  PL19: Tavi 6J **59**
Plymouth Snowsports Centre 4F **137**
Plymouth Station (Rail) . . .1D **8** (1J **141**)
Plymouth Swallows School of Gymnastics
  . . . . .6D **132**
Plymouth Tourist Information Centre
  . . . . .6G **9** (3K **141**)
Plymouth Yacht Haven 2D **142**
PLYMPTON 4B **138** (8A **174**)
Plympton By-Pass PL7: Plymp 6H **137**
Plympton Castle 5B **138**
Plympton Hill PL7: Plymp 6C **138**
Plympton Pk. PL7: Plymp 3C **138**
PLYMPTON ST MAURICE 6C **138**
Plympton Swimming Pool 4A **138**
PLYMSTOCK 5F **143** (8A **174**)
Plymstock Rd. PL9: Plyms 5D **142**
Plymstock Sports Cen. 4G **143**
Plym St. PL4: Plym 3G **9** (2A **141**)
PLYMTREE 3A **166**
Plymtree Dr. PL7: Plymp 4K **137**
Plym Valley Mdws. PL6: Plym 3G **137**
Plym Valley Railway 4H **137** (2B **174**)
Plymview Cl. PL3: Plym 5E **136**
Poachers Paddock EX34: Wool 7C **10**
Pocklington Ri. PL7: Plymp 4B **138**
POCOMBE BRIDGE 2A **70**

Pocombe Hill. EX2: Exe 2A 70
Pode Dr. PL7: Plymp 5E 138
Poets Cnr. PL5: Plym 2H 135
Point Cotts. PL9: Hooe 5C 142
Point Exe EX4: Exe 2A 6 (5D 64)
Point Ter. EX8: Exmth 6A 76
POLBATHIC 2A 174
Polehouse La. EX2: Ide 5B 70
Poles Hill EX31: Cher 2D 18
Poleshill La. EX31: Cher 1C 18
Polhearne La. TQ5: Brixh 5D 122
Polhearne Way TQ5: Brixh 5D 122
Policeman's Hill EX32: B Taw 7B 24
(off Village St.)
Pollard Cl. PL9: Hooe 7C 142
The Pollards EX32: B'aple 6H 19
Pollard's Cl. EX4: Pin 3C 66
Pollards Pl. EX39: Bide 3H 23
Pollyblank Rd. TQ12: New A 1E 108
Polperro Cl. TQ3: Paig 7D 114
Polperro Pl. PL2: Plym 3J 135
Polruan Ter. PL1: Plym 3A 8 (2G 141)
Polsham Pk. TQ3: Paig 7H 115
POLSLOE BRIDGE 5K 65
Polsloe Bridge Station
(Rail) 5K 65 (1D 171)
POLSLOE PARK 2J 7 (5H 65)
POLSLOE PRIORY 1K 7 (4J 65)
Polsloe Rd. EX1: Exe 1J 7 (5H 65)
Polson Hill EX17: Morc 2B 38
Polston Pk. PL9: Spri 7H 143
POLTIMORE 1D 171
Poltimore Cl. EX36: S Mol 6D 26
Poltimore Ct. EX4: Polt 5A 52
Poltimore Dr. EX1: Pin 4D 66
Poltimore Lawn EX23: Appl 3G 19
Poltimore Rd. EX36: S Mol 6D 26
Poltimore Sq. EX4: Exe 2F 7 (5F 65)
Polwhele Rd. EX16: Tive 5H 41
POLYPHANT 2A 168
Polywell EX39: App 2G 21
Polzeath Gdns. PL2: Plym 3J 135
Pomeroy Av. TQ5: Brixh 3C 122
Pomeroy Pl. TQ12: Live 4F 93
Pomeroy Rd. EX16: Tive 3J 41
TQ12: New A 1E 108
Pomeroy Vs. TQ9: Tot 5F 103
POMPHLETT 4E 142
Pomphlett Cl. PL9: Plyms 4E 142
(not continuous)
Pomphlett Farm Ind. Est.
PL9: Plyms 3F 143
Pomphlett Gdns. PL9: Plyms 4E 142
Pomphlett Rd. PL9: Plyms 4E 142
Pond Cl. EX5: Whim 2F 69
Pond Hill EX16: Hal 6D 42
Ponsonby Rd. PL3: Plym 1A 8 (7G 135)
PONSWORTHY 3B 170
Pooh Cottage Holiday Pk. 4A 82
Pook La. TQ13: Ashb 3H 99
Pool Anthony Dr. EX16: Tive 3J 41
POOLE 1B 166
Poole La. EX34: Wool 5D 10
Poole Pk. Rd. PL5: Plym 3B 134
Poole's Ct. DT7: Lym R 5K 91
Pool Hill EX20: Brid 3H 57
Pool Pk. TQ10: S Bre 1C 100
Popes Cl. EX17: Cred 5H 39
Pope's La. EX17: Lap 2J 37
(not continuous)
Popes La. EX24: Colyt 1F 87
Popham Cl. EX16: Tive 4F 41
Poplar EX7: Daw W 7D 96
Poplar Cl. EX2: Exe 2D 70
EX8: Exmth 1F 77
PL7: Plymp 4E 138
TQ5: Brixh 7B 122
TQ12: New A 4K 109
Poplar Dr. TQ7: Kingsb 4F 157
Poplar Mt. EX13: Axmin 3H 89
Poplar Row EX9: Bud S 7D 82
The Poplars EX4: Pin 2D 66
TQ13: Chud K 5B 94
Poplars Dr. TQ3: Marl 4D 114
Poplars Wlk. EX5: Clyst M 3J 73
(off Hazelmead Rd.)
Poplar Ter. EX37: High B 3C 32
TQ12: Ipp 6H 101
Poplar Tree Dr. TQ2: Seat 3E 86
Poppin Ct. EX2: Cou W 5D 72
Popplestone Pk. PL8: Brixt 2G 149
Poppy Cl. EX4: Exe 4A 64
EX15: Will 4E 44
Porchester Hgts. EX4: Exe 2G 7
(off Acland St.)
Porlock Way TQ4: Paig 5F 119
Porsham Cl. PL6: Robo 1C 132
Porsham La. PL5: Tam F 3J 131
Portal Pl. PL21: Ivy 4F 145
PORT BRIDGE 7B 118
Porteous Cl. PL1: Dev 1E 140
Porter Gro. EX5: Cran 3C 68
Porter's La. EX8: Lymp 3J 75
PORTFIELD 1D 167
Portford La. TQ10: S Bre 2C 100
PORTGATE 2C 169
Portland Av. EX8: Exmth 6D 76
TQ14: Teignm 2J 107

Portland Bldgs. EX32: B'aple 3F 19
Portland Cl. EX15: Cull 4F 45
Portland Ct. DT7: Lym R 5H 91
EX32: B'aple 5F 19
(off Victoria Rd.)
PL1: Dev 1E 140
TQ1: Torq 6F 113
(off Portland Rd.)
Portland Head La. EX34: C Mar 6D 12
Portland M. PL4: Plym 2F 9
Portland Pk. EX34: Ilfra 2J 11
Portland Pl. E.
PL4: Plym 2F 9 (1K 141)
Portland Rd. PL1: Dev 1E 140
TQ1: Torq 6F 113
Portland Sq. PL4: Plym 3E 8 (1J 141)
(not continuous)
Portland Sq. La. Nth.
PL4: Plym 2E 8 (1J 141)
Portland St. EX1: Exe 2H 7 (6H 65)
EX32: B'aple 6G 19
EX34: Ilfra 2J 11
Portland Vs. PL4: Plym 2E 8 (1J 141)
Port La. TQ7: Chil 6F 159
Port La. Cl. TQ7: Chil 6F 159
Portlemore Cl. TQ7: Malb 6G 155
Portlemore Gdns. TQ7: Malb 6G 155
Portmarsh La. EX32: B'aple 5F 19
Port Mer Cl. EX8: Exmth 1G 77
Port Mill Cl. EX31: B'aple 3E 18
Portmore Golf Course 7K 19 (3B 160)
Portreath Gdns. PL2: Plym 3J 135
Port Rd. EX7: Daw 5A 96
Portsmouth Arms Station (Rail) 2A 164
Portugal Way EX20: Oke 3D 48
Portway EX15: A'hill 7K 43
Portway Cl. PL9: Elb 7K 143
PORTWRINKLE 2A 174
Posbury Pl. PL1: Sow 5C 66
Postal EX5: Pin 4F 67
POSTBRIDGE 3A 170
Postbridge Information Centre
Picnic Site 3A 170
Post Coach Way EX5: Cran 3C 68
Post Cross Bus. Pk. EX15: Kent 7A 46
Post Hill EX16: Tive 3J 41
Post Office La. EX17: Cher F 2J 39
Potacre St. EX38: G Tor 2C 30
(off Calf St.)
Potters Cl. EX11: W Hill 3H 79
Potters Hill TQ1: Torq 1D 116
Potters Lea Development
TQ12: Kingst 3F 105
Potters Stile EX14: Dunk 7H 47
Potters Way PL7: Plymp 4A 138
Potterswell EX31: Rou 6K 17
The Pottery TQ6: Dartm 7G 125
(off Warfleet Creek Rd.)
Pottery Cl. EX14: Hon 3G 55
TQ13: Bov T 6B 92
Pottery Cotts. TQ6: Dartm 7G 125
(off Warfleet Creek Rd.)
Pottery Ct. TQ6: Dartm 6D 124
Pottery La. EX31: Yell 6B 16
Pottery Rd. PL1: Dev 1C 140
TQ12: Kingst 5G 105
TQ13: Bov T 6B 92
Pottery Rd. Flats PL1: Dev 1C 140
Pottery Yd. TQ12: Live 7G 93
Pottington Bus. Pk. EX31: B'aple . . .3B 18
Pottington Dr. EX31: B'aple 3D 18
Pottington Ind. Est. EX31: B'aple . . .3C 18
Pottington Rd. EX31: B'aple 3D 18
Pottles Cl. EX6: Exmin 3C 74
POUGHILL
EX17 . . . . .3C 165
EX23 . . . . .3A 162
Poultney Cl. PL7: Plymp 4D 138
Pouncel La. EX5: Cran 3C 68
Pound Cl. EX3: Top 7D 72
EX8: Exmth 3E 76
EX10: Sidb 2H 85
Pound Fld. TQ9: Sto G 3B 120
Poundfield Cl. EX31: Frem 6G 17
Pound Hill EX12: Axmth 3H 87
TA21: Holc R 2G 43
Pound La. DT7: Uply 2F 91
EX3: Top 7D 72
EX5: W'bury 5C 78
EX6: Bridf 1F 63
EX8: Exmth 2D 76
EX10: Col R 1G 83
EX34: C Mar 7C 12
EX37: High B 2C 32
TQ12: Kingsk 1F 111
TQ14: Shal 6E 106
TQ14: Teignm 5J 107
Pound La. Cvn. & Camping Site . . .4C 78
Pound La. Trad. Est.
EX8: Exmth 3E 76
Pound Mdw. EX20: Hath 2H 35
Pound Pk. EX20: Oke 2D 48
Pound Pl. TQ12: New A 1E 108
(off Jubilee Rd.)
TQ13: Bov T 3C 92
Pound Rd. DT7: Lym R 5J 91
PL20: Buck M 5B 126
POUNDSGATE 3B 170

Poundsgate Cl. TQ5: Brixh 4G 123
Pounds Hill EX17: Cred 5J 39
Poundsland EX5: Broadc 6C 52
Pounds Pk. Rd. PL3: Plym 4J 135
PL20: Bere A 2B 128
Pound Sq. EX15: Cull 4H 45
(off Cockpit Hill)
POUNDSTOCK 1A 168
Poundstone Ct. TQ8: Salc 4C 158
Pound St. DT7: Lym R 5J 91
EX8: Exmth 6C 76
PL1: Plym 4F 141
TQ13: More 7H 61
Pound Wall EX5: Broadc 6C 52
Poundwell Mdw.
PL21: Modb 6G 147
Poundwell St. PL21: Modb 6G 147
POWDERHAM 2D 171
Powderham Castle 5K 95 (2D 171)
Powderham Cl. EX3: Top 7D 72
TQ12: New A 2E 108
Powderham Ct. TQ12: New A 1E 108
(off Powderham Rd.)
Powderham Cres. EX4: Exe . .1F 7 (4G 65)
Powderham Park 5K 95
Powderham Rd. EX2: Exe 7A 6 (1D 70)
PL3: Plym 4A 136
TQ2: Torq 4B 112
TQ12: New A 1E 108
Powderham Ter. TQ12: New A 2E 108
TQ14: Teignm 5J 107
Powderham Wlk. EX6: Exmin 1B 74
Powell La. EX12: Seat 4E 86
Powells Way EX14: Dunk 7H 47
Power of Water Exhibition 2H 13
Powhay Mills
EX4: Exe 5B 6 (7E 64)
Powis Gdns. PL5: Plym 1G 135
Powisland Dr. PL6: Plym 5A 132
Powlesland Rd. EX2: Alph 4E 70
Powys Ho. EX10: Sidm 6B 84
Poyers EX33: Wraf 6K 15
Prattshayes Farm Camp Site 6G 77
The Precinct TQ7: Kingsb 3G 157
Premier Pl. EX2: Exe 6H 7 (7G 65)
Presbytery M. PL6: Plym 4K 131
Prescot Rd. EX4: Exe 7B 64
PRESCOTT 2A 166
Prescott Pinetum 1D 173
Prescott Rd. EX15: Culm 1A 46
Prestbury Pk. TQ2: Torq 7B 112
(off Vansittart Rd.)
PRESTON
TQ3 . . . . .5J 115
TQ12 . . . . .1E 104 (3C 171)
PRESTON BOWYER 1B 166
Prestonbury Castle 1B 170
Prestonbury Cl. PL6: Plym 3C 132
Preston Down Av. TQ3: Pres 4H 115
Preston Down Rd. TQ3: Pres 3E 114
Preston Mnr. Clay Works
TQ12: Kingst 1E 104
Preston St. EX1: Exe 5D 6 (7E 64)
Prestor EX13: Axmin 4J 89
Pretoria Rd. EX1: Heav 2K 7 (5H 65)
Pretoria Ter. EX34: Ilfra 5G 11
Priddis Cl. EX8: Exmth 1E 76
Prideaux Cres. EX16: Tive 2D 40
Prideaux La. TQ6: Strete 5G 153
Prideaux Mdw. EX38: G Tor 2E 30
Prideaux Rd. PL21: Ivy 4J 145
Pridham La. PL2: Plym 4J 135
Pridhams Way EX6: Exmin 2C 74
Priest Hill EX15: Kent 6B 46
Priestley Av. EX4: Whip 4A 66
PL5: Plym 1D 134
Prigg Mdw. TQ13: Ashb 4H 99
Primley Ct. TQ3: Paig 2E 118
PRIMLEY CROSS 2F 119
Primley Gdns. EX10: Sidm 3D 84
Primley Mead EX10: Sidm 3D 84
Primley Paddock EX10: Sidm 3C 84
Primley Pk. TQ3: Paig 2F 119
Primley Pk. E. TQ3: Paig 2G 119
Primley Rd. EX10: Sidm 3C 84
(not continuous)
Primrose Av. EX32: B'aple 5K 19
Primrose Cl. EX16: Tive 2F 41
PL21: Ivy 4H 145
TQ7: Chil 6F 159
TQ12: Kingst 4H 105
Primrose Ct. EX16: Bam 3J 33
Primrose Dr. TQ12: New A 6A 104
Primrose Gdns. PL19: Tavi 5K 59
Primrose La. EX39: Nort 4G 21
Primrose Lawn EX4: Exe 4A 64
Primrose Mdw. PL21: Ivy 3E 144
Primrose Ter. TQ9: Tot 6G 103
Primrose Way EX12: Seat 2F 87
EX17: Cred 5K 39
TQ12: Kingsk 6J 109

Prince Maurice Ct.
PL4: Plym 4H 9 (2A 142)
Prince Maurice Rd.
PL4: Plym 1J 9 (1A 142)
Prince of Wales Dr. EX8: Exmth 4F 77
TQ6: Dartm 5F 125
Prince of Wales Rd.
EX4: Exe 1C 6 (4E 64)
EX17: Cred 5H 39
TQ7: Kingsb 4F 157
Prince Rupert Way TQ12: H'fld 2K 93
Prince's Point TQ1: Torq 3E 116
Princes Rd. PL6: Plym 4F 133
(off Sycamore Way)
TQ1: Torq 1D 116
Princes Rd. E. TQ1: Torq 1E 116
Princes Rd. W. TQ1: Torq 1D 116
Princess Av. EX34: Ilfra 3H 11
PL5: Plym 7F 131
PL9: Plyms 6F 143
Princess Cres. PL9: Plyms 6F 143
Princess Elizabeth Ter.
EX20: Brid 2J 57
Princess Gdns. 3D 116
(off Princess Pde.)
Princesshay EX1: Exe 4E 6 (6F 65)
Princesshay Garden Apts.
EX1: Exe 3F 7
(off Dix's Field)
Princesshay La. EX1: Exe 3F 7
Princesshay Sq. EX1: Exe 4E 6
Princess Pde. TQ2: Torq 3D 116
Prince's Sq. EX2: Exe 1D 70
Princess Rd. TQ12: Kingsk 1G 111
TQ12: Kingst 3G 105
Princess St. EX32: B'aple 3F 19
PL1: Plym 5D 8 (3J 141)
Princess St. Ope
PL1: Plym 5E 8 (3J 141)
Princess Theatre 3C 116
Princes St. EX7: Daw 4G 97
EX8: Exmth 6C 76
(off Union St.)
PL1: Dev 2D 140
TQ1: Torq 6F 113
TQ3: Paig 1H 119
Prince's St. E. EX2: Exe 2D 70
Prince's St. Nth. EX2: Exe 1D 70
Prince's St. Sth. EX2: Exe 2D 70
Prince's St. W. EX2: Exe 1D 70
Princess Way PL1: Plym 5D 8 (3J 141)
Prince St. TQ12: New A 1F 109
PRINCETOWN 6C 60 (3D 169)
Princetown Rd. PL20: Dous 5H 127
Prince William Ct. TQ5: Brixh 4E 122
Prings Ct. TQ5: Brixh 3E 122
(off Market St.)
The Printworks EX1: Exe 2G 7
Priors Pk. PL9: Plyms 3H 143
Priory TQ13: Bov T 3B 92
The Priory EX6: Exmin 1B 74
(off Devington Pk.)
PL21: Modb 6G 147
TQ12: A'well 5F 109
Priory Av. TQ9: Tot 5E 102
TQ12: Kingsk 7K 109
Priory Cl. EX9: E Bud 1D 82
EX31: B'aple 2E 18
PL19: Whit 6K 59
PL21: Ivy 4F 145
Priory Ct. TQ9: Tot 6E 102
Priory Dr. PL7: Plymp 4A 138
TQ9: Tot 5E 102
Priory Gdns. EX4: Exe 5C 6
EX7: Daw 4H 97
EX31: B'aple 2E 18
PL19: Whit 7K 59
TQ9: Tot 5E 102
Priory Ga. TQ9: Tot 5E 102
Priory Hill EX7: Daw 4H 97
TQ9: Tot 5E 102
Priory La. EX6: Chri 2J 63
Priory Lawn Ter. PL3: Plym 5B 136
Priory Mill PL7: Plymp 4A 138
Priory Pk. Rd. EX7: Daw 4G 97
Priory Ridge PL7: Plymp 4A 138
Priory Rd. EX4: Exe 1J 7 (4H 65)
EX7: Daw 4H 97
EX16: Tive 2F 41
EX31: B'aple 2E 18
PL3: Plym 5B 136
TQ1: Torq 5D 112
TQ12: A'well 5E 108
Priory St. TQ6: Kingsw 7G 125
Priory Ter. TQ9: Tot 5E 102
(off Priory Hill)
Priory Vw. EX4: Whip 4K 65
Priscott Way TQ12: Kingst 5H 105
Prison La. EX4: Exe 1E 6 (5F 65)
Prispen Dr. EX5: Silv 1H 51
Prispen Ho. EX5: Silv 1H 51
Prispen Vw. EX5: Silv 1H 51
PRIXFORD 3B 160
Promenade EX39: W Ho 5A 20
TQ3: Pres 6K 115
TQ4: Broads 1K 121
TQ4: Good 3J 119
(not continuous)

Promenade TQ7: Kingsb 4G **157**
TQ14: Teignm 5J **107**
The Promenade EX34: Ilfra 2H **11**
PL1: Plym 7C **8** (4H **141**)
TQ7: Kingsb 4G **157**
(off Bridge St.)
Prospect Cres. EX15: Uff 6H **43**
Prospect Gdns.
EX4: Exe 1J **7** (5H **65**)
Prospect Hill EX20: Oke 4B **48**
TQ7: Slap 1H **159**
Prospect Pk. EX4: Exe 4G **65**
Prospect Pl. EX4: Exe 7A **6** (1D **70**)
EX10: Sidm 7C **84**
(off Kings La.)
EX11: Ott M 4C **80**
EX15: Uff 6H **43**
EX16: Tive 4B **40**
(off Wellbrook St.)
EX32: B'aple 6G **19**
PL1: Plym 6B **8** (3H **141**)
TQ10: S Bre 1B **100**
Prospect Rd. TQ5: Brixh 3E **122**
Prospect Row PL1: Dev 3D **140**
Prospect Row Flats *PL1: Dev* . . .3D **140**
(off Prospect Row)
Prospect Steps *TQ5: Brixh* 3E **122**
(off Sth. Furzeham Rd.)
Prospect St. PL4: Plym 3G **9** (2K **141**)
Prospect Ter. EX24: Colyt 6C **88**
TQ12: New A 1F **109**
Prospect Way EX17: Lap 2J **37**
Protector Rd. PL5: Plym 1J **135**
Prouse Cres. PL2: Plym 3H **135**
Providence Pl. DT7: Lym R 5J **91**
PL1: Plym 1F **141**
Providence Row EX39: Bide 3F **23**
Providence St.
PL4: Plym 2G **9** (1K **141**)
Provident Cl. TQ5: Brixh 3G **123**
Prowse La. EX17: Lap 2K **37**
Prowses EX15: Hemy 2G **47**
Prynne Cl.
PL1: Plym 3C **8** (2H **141**)
Prysten House 5E **8**
PUCKINGTON 2D **167**
Puckridge Rd. EX4: Pin 2C **66**
Puddavine Ter. TQ9: Darti 3D **102**
PUDDINGTON 2C **165**
Pudleylake Rd. EX13: Abb G 7F **89**
Puffin Cl. TQ2: Torq 3J **111**
Puffin Way EX2: Exe 2A **70**
Pugsley Rd. EX16: Tive 4G **41**
Pulborough Farm Cvn. Pk. 5G **57**
Pulchrass St. EX32: B'aple 5F **19**
Pullen's Row EX16: W'ridge 6H **33**
Pulleys Cl. TQ7: Ave G 6H **151**
Pulling Rd. EX4: Pin 2C **66**
Pullins Ter. TQ13: Chud 1C **94**
Pulpit Wlk. EX23: Alph 6F **71**
Pump Field Cl. EX14: Dunk 7H **47**
Pump La. EX39: A'sham 3A **22**
Pump St. EX5: New C 7D **50**
TQ5: Brixh 3F **123**
Punchards Down TQ9: Tot 5A **102**
Purbeck Av. TQ2: Torq 4J **115**
Purcell Cl. EX2: Won 7B **66**
PURTINGTON 3D **167**
Purzebrook Cl. EX13: Axmin 4H **89**
PUSEHILL 7A **20**
Pusehill Rd. EX39: W Ho 6A **20**
PUTSBOROUGH 1D **14** (2A **160**)
Putsborough Cl. EX33: Geo 5B **14**
Putsborough Rd.
EX33: Geo, Puts 1D **14**
Pye Cnr. EX6: Kennf 1H **95**
EX15: Cull 4H **45**
Pykes Down PL21: Ivy 5K **145**
Pym St. PL1: Dev 1D **140**
PL19: Tavi 3J **59**
Pynes Cl. EX9: E Bud 1D **82**
EX17: Cher F 2H **39**
Pynes Hill EX2: Cou W 3A **72**
Pynes Hill Bus. Pk. EX2: Cou W . . .3B **72**
Pynes La. EX39: Bide 4D **22**
Pynes Wlk. EX39: Bide 4D **22**
Pyne Vs. PL9: Hooe 6C **142**
Pynsant Ct. TQ13: Chud 2C **94**
The Pyramids Swimming & Leisure Cen.
. . . . .3G **7** (6G **65**)
Pytte Gdns. EX3: Clyst G 6H **73**
PYWORTHY 3B **162**

Q

The Quadrangle EX4: Exe 1E **6** (5F **65**)
The Quadrant
EX2: Exe 6G **7** (7G **65**)
Quaker La. PL3: Plym 6K **135**
Quantocks EX33: Brau 4G **15**
Quantocks Rd. TQ2: Torq 3J **115**
Quant Pk. PL19: Tavi 3J **59**
The Quarries EX4: Exe 1A **70**
Quarries La. EX37: High B 3B **32**
Quarry Cl. EX39: Bide 3D **22**
TQ9: Tot 5B **102**
Quarry Cotts. PL5: Plym 1G **135**

Quarry Flds. EX20: Oke 2C **48**
Quarry Gdns. TQ3: Paig 7G **115**
Quarry La. EX2: Sow, Won 7A **66**
EX5: Silv 4F **51**
EX12: Beer 4K **85**, 7A **86**
EX17: Cop 5A **38**
Quarry Pk. Av. PL9: Plyms 5E **142**
Quarry Pk. Rd. TQ2: Won 1B **72**
PL3: Plym 6J **135**
PL9: Plyms 5E **142**
Quarry Rd. EX37: High B 3B **32**
Quarry St. PL11: Torp 1A **140**
Quarry Wood Cl. TQ4: Paig 6F **119**
Quarry Wood St. TQ4: Paig 6F **119**
The Quarterdeck PL1: Plym 4F **141**
Quarter Mile La. EX5: Mar G 7J **69**
The Quay EX2: Exe 6E **6** (7F **65**)
EX34: Ilfra 2J **11**
EX39: App 2J **21**
EX39: Bide 3F **23**
PL9: Plyms 4D **142**
PL19: Tavi 4H **59**
TQ5: Brixh 3E **123**
TQ6: Dartm 1B **124** (6F **125**)
TQ6: Ditt 6D **120**
TQ7: Kingsb 4F **157**
(off Prince of Wales Rd.)
TQ8: Bat 2B **158**
Quay Climbing Centre 7E **6**
Quayfield Path EX34: Ilfra 2J **11**
Quayfield Rd. EX34: Ilfra 2J **11**
Quay Hill EX2: Exe 6D **6** (7E **64**)
Quay La. EX2: Exe 6E **6** (7F **65**)
EX8: Lymp 7F **75**
EX39: Ins 3K **21**
Quay Rd. PL1: Plym 6F **9** (3K **141**)
TQ12: New A 1G **109**
(not continuous)
TQ14: Teignm 5H **107**
Quayside PL19: Tavi 4H **59**
TQ9: Tot 7F **103**
Quayside Leisure Cen. 5G **157**
Quay Steps EX2: Exe 6E **6**
Quay Ter. TQ12: New A 1G **109**
Quay Vw. EX31: Frem 5F **17**
Queen Alexandra Sq.
PL1: Plym 3A **8** (2G **141**)
Queen Anne Pl. PL4: Plym . . .7J **9** (4A **142**)
Queen Annes EX39: Bide 3F **23**
Queen Anne's Battery 7J **9** (4A **142**)
Queen Annes Copse TQ12: E Ogw . .3C **108**
Queen Anne's Ct. *EX31: B'aple* 4E **18**
(off Commercial Rd.)
Queen Anne's Wlk. *EX31: B'aple* 4E **18**
(off The Strand)
Queen Anne Ter. PL4: Plym 2F **9**
QUEEN DART 2C **165**
Queen Elizabeth Av. TQ6: Dartm . . .5E **124**
Queen Elizabeth Cl. EX39: W Ho . . .6B **20**
Queen Elizabeth Dr. EX17: Cred 5F **39**
TQ3: Paig 1E **118**
Queen La. EX7: Daw 4G **97**
Queen's Av. EX34: Ilfra 3J **11**
Queens Cl. PL6: Plym 4F **133**
TQ12: Kingst 3J **105**
Queen's Ct. *EX8: Exmth* 6C **76**
(off Queen Rd.)
Queens Ct. DT7: Lym R 4J **91**
EX24: Colyt 5C **88**
TQ5: Brixh 5F **123**
Queen's Dr. EX8: Exmth 7C **76**
The Queens Dr. EX4: Exe 3E **64**
Queen's Ga.
PL1: Plym 2A **8** (1G **141**)
PL4: Plym 1J **9** (1A **142**)
Queen's Ga. M.
PL4: Plym 1J **9** (1A **142**)
Queen's Gate Vs. PL4: Plym 1J **9**
Queen's Gate Vs. Rd.
PL4: Plym 1J **9** (1A **142**)
Queen's Ho. *EX32: B'aple* 4F **19**
(off Queen Rd.)
Queensland Dr. EX4: Exe 2H **65**
Queen's Pk. Rd. TQ4: Paig 1J **119**
Queen's Rd. EX2: Exe 7C **6** (2D **70**)
EX9: Bud S 5B **82**
PL4: Plym 1J **9** (1A **142**)
TQ4: Paig 1J **119**
TQ5: Brixh 2E **122**
TQ13: More 6H **61**
Queens Rd. PL5: Plym 7E **130**
Queen's Sq. EX24: Colyt 5C **88**
Queens Sq. EX5: Broadc 5C **52**
Queens Steps *TQ5: Brixh* 3F **123**
(off King St.)
Queen's Ter. EX4: Exe 2C **6** (5E **64**)
EX5: Sto C 6J **51**
TQ9: Tot 5E **102**
Queens Ter. EX38: G Tor 2A **30**
Queen's Theatre 4E **18**
Queen St. EX4: Exe 2D **6** (5E **64**)
EX7: Daw 4G **97**
EX8: Exmth 6C **76**
EX9: Bud S 7C **82**
EX12: Seat 5E **86**

Queen St. EX14: Hon 3F **55**
EX16: Tive 5C **40**
EX19: Wink 2C **36**
EX24: Colyt 6D **88**
EX32: B'aple 4E **18**
EX35: Lynt 2H **13**
EX36: S Mol 6C **26**
EX39: Bide 3F **23**
PL1: Dev 2C **140**
TQ1: Torq 1D **116**
TQ12: New A 1F **109**
TQ14: Teignm 5H **107**
Queens Wlk. DT7: Lym R 4J **91**
EX4: Exe 3D **6**
EX32: B'aple 4F **19**
Queensway EX16: Tive 3F **41**
TQ2: Torq 7K **111**
TQ12: New A 2H **109**
Queensway Cl. TQ2: Torq 6A **112**
Queensway Cres. TQ2: Torq 6A **112**
Queensway Ho. TQ12: New A 2H **109**
Quentin Av. TQ5: Brixh 6D **122**
Quern Ri. EX1: Pin 3G **67**
Questant La. EX10: Sidm 4D **84**
Quicks Wlk. EX38: G Tor 2E **30**
The Quilletts TQ7: Malb 6G **155**
Quince Honey Farm 5C **26** (1B **164**)
Quinnell Ho. *TQ14: Teignm* 4G **107**
(off Coombe Va. Rd.)
Quinta Cl. TQ1: Torq 7E **112**
Quinta Ct. TQ1: Torq 7E **112**
Quinta Rd. TQ1: Torq 7E **112**
Quintet Cl. EX1: Heav 7B **66**
QUODDITCH 1C **169**

R

Raceworld 1D **78**
Rackclose La. EX4: Exe 5C **6** (7E **64**)
RACKENFORD 2C **165**
Rackenford & Knowstone Moors
Nature Reserve 1C **165**
Rackenford Rd. EX16: Calv, Tive 2A **40**
EX16: W'ridge 5J **33**
EX31: B'aple 3E **18**
Rackfield EX16: Tive 5C **40**
EX31: B'aple 3E **18**
Rackfield Cotts. EX4: Exe 4C **64**
Rackfield Ct. *EX31: B'aple* 3E **18**
(off Rackfield)
Rackfield Dr. EX15: Hemy 1H **47**
Rackmead EX37: C'ton 5H **25**
Rackmead Ter. *EX37: C'ton* 6H **25**
(off South Vw.)
Rack Pk. EX38: G Tor 2A **30**
Rack Pk. Cl. EX38: G Tor 2B **30**
Rack Pk. Rd. TQ7: Kingsb 4F **9**
Rack St. EX1: Exe 5D **6** (7E **64**)
Radar Rd. PL6: Plym 5C **132**
Radcliffe Cl. PL6: Plym 4K **131**
Raddenstile Ct. EX8: Exmth 6D **76**
Raddenstile La. EX8: Exmth 6D **76**
Raddicombe Cl. TQ5: Hill 6K **123**
Raddicombe Dr. TQ5: Hill 6K **123**
Radford Av. PL4: Plym 3B **142**
Radford Pk. Dr. PL9: Plyms 6E **142**
Radford Pk. Rd. PL9: Plyms 6E **142**
Radford Rd. EX2: Exe 6F **7** (7F **65**)
PL1: Plym 7B **8** (4H **141**)
Radfords Turf EX5: Rock, Cran 2F **69**
Radford Vw. PL9: Plyms 6E **142**
Radford Way EX20: Oke 2E **48**
Radford Woods
Local Nature Reserve 7F **143**
Radnor Hall PL4: Plym 3G **9**
Radnor Pl. EX2: Exe 5G **7** (7G **65**)
PL4: Plym 3G **9** (2K **141**)
Radnor St. PL4: Plym 3G **9** (2K **141**)
Radnor Ter. TQ9: Tot 5E **102**
Radway EX10: Sidm 6C **84**
The Radway Cinema 6C **84**
Radway Ct. TQ14: Bi'ton 3C **106**
Radway Gdns. TQ14: Bi'ton 3C **106**
Radway Hill TQ14: Bi'ton 3C **106**
Radway La. EX9: Ott'n 4K **83**
Radway Pl. EX10: Sidm 6C **84**
Radway St. TQ14: Bi'ton 3C **106**
RAF Memorial 7E **8** (4J **141**)
Ragg La. EX9: Bud S 7C **82**
Raglan Ct. *PL1: Dev* 2E **140**
(off Damerel Cl.)
Rag La. EX5: Rock 7H **69**
Raglan Gdns. PL1: Dev 2E **140**
Raglan Rd. PL1: Dev 2E **140**
Raglans EX2: Alph 5F **71**
Railway Cotts. EX1: Whip 6B **66**
PL2: Plym 6E **134**
PL19: Tavi 3J **59**
Railway Ter. EX39: Bide 4G **23**
Railway Vw. PL8: Brixt 3F **149**
Rainbow Rd. TQ2: Torq 6A **112**
Raleigh Av. TQ2: Torq 7K **111**
Raleigh Cl. EX10: Sidm 3C **84**
EX36: S Mol 6B **26**
TQ2: Torq 7K **111**
TQ6: Dartm 6C **124**
Raleigh Cotts. EX31: B'aple 2F **19**

Raleigh Ct. EX9: Bud S 5D **82**
PL7: Plymp 3E **138**
Raleigh Dr. EX15: Cull 3H **45**
TQ4: Good 5H **119**
Raleigh Hgts. EX31: B'aple 2E **18**
Raleigh Hill EX39: Bide, Nort 7C **20**
(not continuous)
Raleigh Ho. EX2: Exe 5H **7**
EX10: Sidm 3C **84**
(off Raleigh Cl.)
Raleigh Lawn EX31: B'aple 2E **18**
Raleigh Mead EX36: S Mol 6C **26**
Raleigh Mdw. EX31: B'aple 3F **19**
EX36: S Mol 6B **26**
Raleigh Rd. EX1: Exe 4H **7** (7G **65**)
EX8: Exmth 6C **76**
EX9: Bud S 5D **82**
EX11: Ott M 3D **80**
EX31: B'aple 3E **18**
EX21: Ivy 3E **144**
TQ6: Dartm 5E **124**
TQ8: Salc 4B **158**
TQ12: New A 1J **109**
TQ14: Teignm 2G **107**
Raleigh St. PL1: Plym 4C **8** (2H **141**)
TQ6: Dartm 1B **124** (6F **125**)
Raleigh Vw. EX39: Bide 2F **23**
(off Kingsley Rd.)
Ralph Cl. EX33: Brau 4G **15**
Ralph Rd. EX33: Brau 4G **15**
Ralph's Ct. PL19: Tavi 4H **59**
Ramage Cl. PL6: Plym 7G **133**
RAME 3A **174**
Ramillies Av. PL5: Plym 6F **131**
Ramparts Wlk. *TQ9: Tot* 6E **102**
(off High St.)
Ramsey Gdns. PL5: Plym 2J **135**
Ramshill Rd. TQ3: Paig 6E **114**
Ramslade Cvn. Site 6A **118**
RAMSLEY 3H **49** (1A **170**)
Ramsley Common Viewpoint 1A **170**
Rance Dr. EX8: Exmth 1G **77**
Randell's Grn. EX8: Exmth 6G **77**
Randolph Cl. PL5: Plym 7K **131**
Randolph Ct. TQ12: New A 7D **104**
Randwick Pk. Rd. PL9: Plyms 5E **142**
Ranelagh Rd. EX20: Oke 3A **48**
Rangers Cl. TQ11: B'leigh 5C **98**
Ranscombe Cl. TQ5: Brixh 3G **123**
Ranscombe Rd. TQ5: Brixh 3F **123**
Ransom Pickard EX4: Exe 4F **65**
Ransum Way PL19: Tavi 5H **59**
Raphael Cl. PL9: Elb 6H **143**
Raphael Dr. PL9: Elb 6H **143**
RAPPS .2D **167**
Rashleigh Av. PL7: Plymp 2B **138**
Rathlin *TQ1: Torq* 6E **112**
(off Palermo Rd.)
Rathmore Rd. TQ2: Torq 2A **116**
(not continuous)
Ratsash La. EX15: Crad 6K **43**
RATTERY 1D **175**
Ravelin Gdns. EX32: B'aple 4G **19**
Ravelin Mnr. Rd. EX32: B'aple 4G **19**
Raven Cl. EX4: Exe 3F **65**
Ravenglass Cl. PL6: Plym 1F **136**
Ravensbourne La. TQ6: Sto F 2H **153**
Ravensbury Dr. TQ6: Dartm 7G **125**
Rawlin Cl. PL6: Plym 3D **136**
Rawlin Homes *PL4: Plym* 4G **9**
(off Green St.)
Rawlyn Rd. TQ2: Torq 2K **115**
Rawnsley La. EX34: Wool 6A **10**
RAWRIDGE 3C **167**
Rayer Rd. EX16: Tive 5H **41**
RAYMOND'S HILL 2B **90** (1D **173**)
Raymond Way PL7: Plymp 3A **138**
Rayners EX6: Kennf 1G **95**
Raynham Rd. PL3: Plym 1A **8** (1G **141**)
Rea Barn Cl. TQ5: Brixh 4F **123**
Rea Barn Rd. TQ5: Brixh 4F **123**
Read Cl. EX8: Exmth 3E **76**
Reading Wlk. PL5: Plym 6H **131**
Rear Dunmere Rd. *TQ1: Torq* 7D **112**
(off Dunmere Rd.)
Rear Hyde Pk. Rd. *PL3: Plym* 6K **135**
(off Gifford Ter. Rd.)
Recreation Rd. PL2: Plym 4H **135**
Recreation Way PL7: L Moor 1J **129**
Rectory Cl. EX5: Whim 6G **53**
EX15: Will 4D **44**
EX33: Wraf 6K **15**
(not continuous)
Rectory Dr. EX2: Alph 5E **70**
Rectory Gdns. EX3: Clyst G 7H **73**
Rectory Hill EX17: Cher F 2H **39**
EX34: Ber 3B **12**
Rectory La. EX34: C Mar 7B **12**
TQ6: Sto F 3H **153**
Rectory Pk. EX39: Bide 3E **22**
Rectory Rd. EX17: Morc 1B **38**
EX19: Dol 6H **31**
EX20: Brid 3H **57**
EX34: C Mar 7B **12**
PL1: Dev 2F **141**
TQ12: E Ogw 3B **108**

Redavon Ri. TQ2: Torq 5H 111
Red Brook Cl. TQ4: Good 6J 119
Redburn Cl. TQ3: Paig 7G 115
Redburn Rd. TQ3: Paig 7G 115
Redcliff Ct. EX9: Bud S 7C 82
Redcliffe Ct. TQ3: Pres 7K 115
Redcliffe Rd. TQ1: Torq 4E 112
Red Cow Village
   EX4: Exe 1A 6 (4D 64)
Reddaway Dr. EX6: Exmin 1B 74
Reddenhill Rd. TQ1: Torq 7E 112
Red Devon Ct. PL21: Modb 6G 147
   (off New Rd.)
Reddicliff Cl. PL9: Hooe 7E 142
Reddicliffe M. EX20: Lew 1A 56
Reddicliff Rd. PL9: Hooe 7D 142
Reddington Rd. PL3: Plym 4B 136
Redford Mdw. TQ7: Kingsb 4F 157
Redford Way TQ7: Kingsb 4F 157
REDGATE 3A 168
Redgate Cl. TQ1: Torq 7F 113
REDHILL 1A 38
Redhill Cl. PL5: Plym 6D 130
REDHILLS 6B 64
Redhills La. EX4: Exe 5A 64
   EX9: Bud S 7C 82
Redhills Cl. EX4: Exe 6B 64
Red Ho. Cl. TQ13: Chud K 6B 94
Redlake TQ9: Darti 3B 162
Redlake Trad. Est. PL21: Bitta 4A 146
Redlands EX10: Sidm 7B 84
The Redlands EX10: Sidm 7B 84
Redlands Cl. EX4: Whip 4K 65
Redlands Ct. TQ3: Paig 7F 115
Redlands Rd. EX31: Frem 6G 17
Redland Way EX15: Cull 4F 45
Red La. EX13: Ray H 3C 90
   EX20: Hath 1H 35
Redlap La. TQ6: Dartm, Sto T 2H 153
Redlap Rd. TQ6: Dartm 1J 153
Red Lion Hill PL8: Brixt 2H 149
Red Lion La. EX1: Exe 2G 7 (5G 65)
Red Lion Yd. EX20: Oke 3B 48
Redmoor Cl. PL19: Tavi 2G 59
Redoubt Hill TQ6: Kingsw 6G 125
RED POST 3A 162
Red Rock Rd. EX5: Bram S 4F 51
Redruth Cl. PL5: Plym 5F 131
Redstart Cl. TQ12: E Ogw 3C 108
Redvers Gro. PL7: Plymp 5B 138
Redvers Rd. EX4: Exe 6A 6 (7D 64)
Redvers Way EX16: Tive 2E 40
Redwalls Mdw. TQ6: Dartm 5E 124
Redwell La. TQ3: Paig 6F 115
Redwell Rd. TQ3: Paig 6F 115
Redwing Dr. PL6: Plym 2E 132
Redwood Cl. EX8: Exmth 1F 77
   EX14: Hon 5C 54
   EX15: Hemy 2G 47
   TQ13: Bov T 7B 92
Redwood Ct. EX7: Daw 4H 97
Redwood Dr. PL7: Plymp 4E 138
   TQ7: Lodd 3G 151
Redwood Rd. EX10: Sidm 5C 84
Redwoods TQ13: Bov T 6B 92
Redwood Way EX5: Cran 2E 68
Redworth Dr. TQ9: Tot 5D 102
   (off Station Rd.)
Redworth Ter. TQ9: Tot 5E 102
Reed Mdw. EX20: Hath 2H 35
Reeds Pl. EX15: Cull 4G 45
Reed Va. TQ14: Teignm 4G 107
Reed Wlk. EX2: Cou W 6B 72
REEDY 6E 62
Reedy Hill EX6: Dunsf 6D 62
Reel Cinema 5D 8
Reeves EX17: Bow 5G 37
Reeves Cl. TQ9: Tot 6F 103
   (off New Wlk.)
The Reeves Rd. TQ2: Torq 1K 155
Reeves Way TQ7: Chur 1B 156
Reflections Rd. PL9: Hooe 6C 142
Reform St. EX31: B'aple 3E 18
Regard Cl. TQ5: Brixh 3G 123
Regatta Ct. EX8: Exmth 6A 76
Regency Ct. EX34: Ilfra 3H 11
   (off Church St.)
Regency Cres. EX8: Exmth 6E 76
Regency Ga. EX10: Sidm 5D 84
Regent Cinema 5J 91
Regent Cl. EX31: B'aple 7B 18
   EX31: Frem 6G 17
   TQ2: Torq 5A 112
Regent Gdns. TQ14: Teignm 5J 107
   (off Regent St.)
Regent Pl. EX34: Ilfra 2H 11
Regents Ct. TQ4: Paig 2J 119
Regents Ga. EX8: Exmth 6D 76
Regent's Pk. EX1: Heav 3K 7 (6H 65)
   (not continuous)
Regent Sq. EX1: Heav 7J 65
Regent St. EX2: Exe 7B 6 (2D 70)
   EX7: Daw 4G 97
   PL4: Plym 3F 9 (2K 141)
   TQ14: Teignm 5J 107
Reigate Rd. PL9: Plyms 4F 143
Reme Dr. EX14: Hon 5C 54
Rena Hobson Ct. EX16: Tive 5F 41

Renaissance Gdns. PL2: Plym 4H 135
Rendells Mdw. TQ13: Bov T 4D 92
Rendlesham Gdns. PL6: Plym 7F 133
Rendlesham Rd. PL6: Plym 7F 133
Rendle St. PL1: Plym 4A 8 (2G 141)
Rennes Dr. EX4: Exe 3F 65
Rennie Av. EX1: Whip 5A 66
Renney Rd.
   PL9: Down T, Hey B 1C 148
Rennie Av. PL5: Plym 2B 134
Rennie Rd. EX16: Tive 5G 41
Renoir Cl. PL9: Elb 6H 143
Renown St. PL2: Plym 5D 134
Rensey La. EX17: Lap 1J 37
Renslade Ho. EX4: Exe 6C 6
Research Way PL6: Plym 6D 132
Reservoir Cres. PL9: Elb 5J 143
Reservoir La. PL3: Plym 5A 136
Reservoir Rd. PL3: Plym 5A 136
   PL9: Elb 6J 143
Reservoir Way PL9: Elb 5J 143
Resolution Ho. PL4: Plym 4H 9
Resolution Rd. EX2: Cou W 4C 72
Restarick Cl. EX39: Bide 5H 23
Restormel Rd.
   PL4: Plym 1E 8 (1J 141)
Restormel Ter. PL4: Plym 1E 8
Retail Pk. Cl. EX2: Mar B 2E 70
The Retreat EX8: Exmth 5F 77
   EX16: Tive 4D 40
   PL3: Plym 4C 136
Retreat Cl. TQ7: Kingsb 4F 157
The Retreat Drive EX3: Top 7C 72
Retreat Pl. EX39: App 2H 21
   (off Vernon's La.)
Retreat Rd. EX3: Top 7D 72
Revell Pk. Rd. PL7: Plymp 3A 138
Revel Rd. PL3: Plym 5B 136
Revelstoke Rd. PL8: Noss M 6H 149
REW
   TQ7 . . . . .3D 175
   TQ13 . . . . .2H 99
REWE .1D 171
Rewe La. EX5: Rock, Whim 3H 69
Rewlea Cotts. TQ13: Ashb 2H 99
Rew Rd. TQ13: Ashb 1H 99
Rew's Cl. EX34: C Mar 5A 12
Rews Mdw. EX1: Pin 3E 66
Rews Pk. Dr. EX1: Pin 3E 66
REXON 2C 169
Rexona Cl. EX2: Exe 3D 70
Reynell Av. TQ12: New A 1J 109
Reynell Rd. TQ12: E Ogw 4C 108
Reynolds Cl. EX4: Pin 3C 66
Reynolds Gro. PL5: Plym 3B 134
Reynolds Rd. PL7: Plymp 5K 137
REZARE 3B 168
Rheola Gdns. PL6: Plym 7E 132
Rhine Vs. TQ9: Tot 6F 103
Rhodanthe Rd. TQ3: Pres 5H 115
Rhode Island Dr. EX2: Cou W 4D 72
Rhode La. DT7: Uply 2G 91
Rhodes Cl. PL7: Plymp 2B 138
Rhododendron Av.
   EX14: Dunk 7G 47
   EX31: B'aple 6C 18
RHS Garden Rosemoor 2D 163
Ribble Gdns. PL3: Plym 4E 136
Ribston Av. EX1: Heav 6B 66
Ribston Cl. EX1: Heav 6B 66
Rice Bldgs. EX16: Tive 4C 40
Rices M. EX2: Exe 1D 70
Richard Cl. EX11: Ott M 4A 80
   EX39: Bide 5D 22
Richards Cl. EX7: Daw 5G 97
   EX8: Exmth 2F 77
   EX20: Oke 3D 48
Richardson Wlk. TQ1: Torq 7B 112
   (off Barton Rd.)
Richards Row PL3: Plym 4A 136
Richina Dr. EX20: N Taw 6A 36
Richmond Av. EX34: Ilfra 3G 11
Richmond Cl. EX16: Sam P 1B 42
   TQ1: Torq 4D 112
Richmond Ct. EX4: Exe 3C 6 (6E 64)
   EX7: Daw 4H 97
   (off Richmond Pl.)
   TQ3: Paig 7H 115
Richmond Gdns. EX24: Colyt 5C 88
Richmond Grn. EX39: App 3G 21
Richmond Hill TQ12: Kingsk 7K 109
Richmond Pk. EX39: Nort 5E 20
Richmond Pl. EX7: Daw 4H 97
   TQ14: Shal 6F 107
Richmond Rd. EX4: Exe 3C 6 (6E 64)
   EX8: Exmth 5F 77
   EX34: Ilfra 4G 11
   EX39: App 3H 21
   PL6: Plym 1B 136
Richmond St. EX32: B'aple 4F 19
Richmond Ter. EX12: Beer 7B 86
   (off Causeway)
   EX24: Colyt 5C 88
   EX32: B'aple 4F 19
   (off Bear St.)
   EX39: App 3H 21
   PL20: Buck M 5A 126
   (off The Village)

Richmond Vs. EX34: Ilfra 3G 11
   (off Station Rd.)
Richmond Wlk. EX32: B'aple 3F 19
   PL1: Dev 4D 140
RICKARD'S DOWN 2A 22
Rickards Grn. EX39: A'sham 3A 22
RICKHAM 6E 158 (3D 175)
Riddell Av. EX32: B'aple 3E 18
RIDDLECOMBE 2A 164
The Ride PL9: Plyms 3D 142
Rider's Rings Enclosures 1C 175
Ridge Hill EX34: Ber 3C 12
   EX34: C Mar 7A 12
Ridge Ho. PL4: Plym 1K 9 (7B 136)
Ridge La. EX16: Calv 2A 40
   TQ3: Marl 5F 111
Ridgemark Cl. TQ5: Brixh 3G 123
Ridgemonte EX24: Colyt 6C 88
   (off The Butts)
Ridge Pk. PL7: Plymp 4B 138
Ridge Pk. Av.
   PL4: Plym 1E 8 (7J 135)
Ridge Pk. Rd. PL7: Plymp 4B 138
Ridge Rd. PL7: Plymp 1K 143
   PL21: Ugb 6D 146
   TQ1: Maid 1H 113
The Ridges TQ6: Dartm 7D 124
Ridge Way EX6: Kenton 7J 95
Ridgeway EX4: Exe 1D 64
   EX10: Sidb 1H 85
   EX11: Ott M 3D 80
   EX14: Hon 5E 54
   PL7: Plymp 4A 138
Ridgeway Av. EX39: W Ho 5D 20
Ridgeway Cl. EX10: Sidb 2H 85
   EX39: W Ho 5C 20
   TQ12: New A 3J 109
Ridgeway Community Sports Cen.
   . . . . .4B 138
Ridgeway Ct. EX1: Exe 2J 7 (4H 65)
   EX39: W Ho 5C 20
Ridgeway Dr. EX39: W Ho 5C 20
Ridgeway Gdns. EX11: Ott M 3D 80
Ridgeway Grn. EX37: High B 3C 32
Ridgeway Hgts. TQ1: Torq 2F 117
Ridgeway Hill TQ3: Comp 7D 110
Ridgeway La. EX24: Colyt 6B 88
Ridgeway Mead EX10: Sidm 3A 84
Ridgeway Rd. TQ1: Torq 3F 117
   TQ12: New A 3J 109
Ridgeway Ter. EX39: Bide 1G 23
   (off Orchard Hill)
Ridgway Ct. EX13: Axmin 4H 89
The Ridings EX3: Ebf 6E 74
Ridley Hill TQ6: Kingsw 7G 125
Rifford Rd. EX2: Won 1K 71
Rifleman Wlk. PL6: Plym 3C 132
Riga Ter. PL3: Plym 7D 136
Rigdale Cl. PL6: Plym 4B 136
Rillage La. TQ2: Torq 7B 112
RILLA MILL 3A 168
RINGMORE
   TQ7 . . . . .3C 175
   TQ14 . . . . .6F 107 (3D 171)
Ringmore Cl. TQ7: Bigb S 2B 154
Ringmore Rd. TQ14: Shal 6E 106
Ringmore Way PL5: Plym 6F 131
Ringrone TQ8: Salc 6A 158
Ringslade Cl. TQ12: New A 6C 104
Ringslade Rd. TQ12: New A 5C 104
Ringswell Av. EX1: Heav 6B 66
Ringswell Pk. EX2: Won 7B 66
Ripon Cl. EX4: Exe 6B 64
Rippon Cl. EX16: Tive 5H 41
   TQ5: Brixh 6B 122
Riscombe Hill EX5: New C 7A 50
Risdon Av. PL4: Plym 3C 142
Risdon Dr. PL21: Ivy 4D 144
Riverbank Cotts. EX39: Bide 1G 23
River Cl. EX5: Sto C 7J 51
   TQ12: Kingst 6J 105
River Ct. EX10: Sidb 2J 85
   PL19: Tavi 3K 59
Riverdale EX12: Seat 3F 87
   TQ9: H'ford 6C 100
Riverdale Cl. EX12: Seat 3F 87
Riverdale Orchard
   EX12: Seat 3F 87
River Dart Adventures 1D 175
River Dart Country Park 3B 170
River Dr. EX15: Cull 4J 45
Riverford PL6: Plym 5G 133
Riverford Cl. PL6: Plym 3E 132
Riverford Organic Farm 1D 175
River Front EX3: Ext 1F 75
Rivermead EX15: Cull 5H 45
Rivermead Av. EX8: Exmth 2C 76
Rivermead Ct. EX8: Exmth 1C 76
Rivermead Rd. EX2: Exe 2G 71
River Pk. PL20: Horr 2F 127
   PL21: Erm 2J 147
River Plate Rd. EX2: Cou W 4C 72
Rivers Cl. PL21: Ivy 4J 145
Riversdale Av. EX34: Ilfra 2G 11
River's Edge Ct. EX20: Oke 2B 48
RIVERSIDE 1A 134

Riverside EX7: Daw W 7D 96
   EX10: Sidm 6C 84
   (off York St.)
   EX15: Hemy 1H 47
   EX36: N Mol 2D 26
   TQ9: Tot 4D 102
   TQ14: Shal 6G 107
Riverside 2 TQ12: New A 7G 105
Riverside Apts. EX36: S Mol 6E 26
Riverside Bus. Pk. PL1: Dev 1D 140
Riverside Cvn. Pk. 3G 137
Riverside Cl. EX14: Hon 3E 54
   EX39: Bide 1F 23
   PL20: Horr 2E 126
Riverside Ct. EX2: Exe 6E 6
   EX16: Tive 4D 40
   EX31: B'aple 4E 18
   (off Castle St.)
   EX39: Bide 1G 23
   (not continuous)
   TQ6: Dartm 1B 124
   (off South Embankment)
   TQ12: New A 7G 105
Riverside Leisure Cen.
   Exeter 7C 6 (1E 70)
Riverside Pl. PL1: Dev 2C 140
   (off Cannon St.)
Riverside Rd. EX3: Top 7D 72
   EX10: Sidm 6C 84
   EX31: B'aple 3B 18
   EX35: Lynm 1H 13
   TQ6: Ditt 5C 120
Riverside Rd. E. PL8: New F 6H 149
Riverside Rd. W. PL8: New F 6H 149
Riverside Ter. EX10: Sidm 6C 84
   (off York St.)
Riverside Units EX31: B'aple 3A 18
Riverside Valley Pk. 3G 71
Riverside Vw. EX11: Ott M 4C 80
Riverside Wlk. PL5: Tam F 4G 131
   PL8: Torr 2C 150
Riverside Way EX12: Seat 5G 87
Riverside Workshops
   EX12: Seat 5G 87
Riversleigh PL3: Plym 6F 137
Rivermeet EX3: Top 7C 74
   EX39: App 2H 21
Rivers Wlk. EX2: Cou W 6B 72
Rivervale Cl. TQ13: Chag 2G 61
River Valley Rd. TQ13: Chud K 6B 94
River Vw. EX32: B'aple 7H 19
   PL4: Plym 3C 142
Riverview TQ12: New A 2J 109
River Vw. Cl. EX24: Colyt 7D 88
   TQ13: Chud K 6B 94
River Vw. Commercial Cen.
   EX31: B'aple 3C 18
River Vw. Dr. EX24: Colyt 7D 88
River Vw. Dr. EX4: Exe 4C 64
River Vw. La. PL4: Plym 3B 142
Riverview Pl. TQ7: Kingsb 4F 157
   (off Fore St.)
River Vw. Ter. EX6: Exmin 3D 74
The Riviera TQ1: Torq 3D 116
   (off Parkhill Rd.)
   TQ4: Paig 2H 119
Riviera Bay Holiday Pk. 5G 123
Riviera Ct. TQ1: Torq 2E 116
Riviera International Cen. 2B 116
Riviera Ter. EX6: Exmin 3D 74
   EX7: Daw 3J 97
Riviera Way TQ2: Torq 4H 111
Rixey La. EX17: Morc 3C 38
Rixey Pk. TQ13: Chud 7C 94
RIXHILL 7H 59
RMB Chivenor 1C 16
ROACHILL 1C 165
Roach La. EX5: Silv 1H 51
Roadford Lake Country Park 1C 169
Roadford Lake Walks 1C 169
ROAD GREEN 5D 88
Robbins Hall PL4: Plym 3F 9
Robers Rd. TQ12: Kingst 3G 105
Robert Adams Cl. PL7: Plymp 6H 137
Robert Davy Rd. EX2: Cou W 4C 72
Roberts Av. PL11: Torp 1A 140
Roberts Cl. EX15: Cull 5G 45
   TQ2: Torq 3D 112
Roberts Fld. EX36: N Mol 2B 26
Roberts Rd. EX2: Exe 6F 7 (7F 65)
   PL5: Plym 3B 134
Roberts Way TQ12: New A 7C 104
Robert Way EX10: New P 5H 81
Robin Cl. EX15: Cull 5G 45
Robins Fld. TQ7: Chil 6F 159
Robins Hill EX39: Bide 1G 23
Robinsons Row TQ8: Salc 4D 158
   (off Fore St.)
Robins Pk. TQ7: Lodd 1G 151
Robins Way PL9: Plyms 4F 143
Robin Wlk. EX16: Tive 2E 40
Robin Way TQ12: Kingst 3F 105
ROBOROUGH
   EX19 . . . . .2D 163
   EX31 . . . . .1G 19
   PL6 . . . . .1D 132 (1B 174)
Roborough Av. PL6: Plym 5C 132
Roborough Cl. PL6: Plym 5C 132

Roborough Gdns. TQ13: Ashb 2J 99
Roborough La. PL5: Tam F 2H 131
(Allern La.)
PL5: Tam F 1A 132
(Soper's Hill)
PL6: Robo 1A 132
TQ13: Ashb 3H 99
Roborough Rd. EX31: B'aple, Shir . . .1F 19
Roborough Ter. TQ13: Ashb 3H 99
Robyns Cl. PL7: Plymp 4E 138
Roche Gdn. EX2: Cou W 5K 71
Rochester Rd. PL4: Plym 1G 9 (1K 141)
Rochford Cres. PL5: Plym 5E 130
The Rock EX31: B'aple 2E 18
Rock Av. EX32: B'aple 6F 19
EX35: Lynt 2F 13
ROCKBEARE 3F 69 (1A 172)
Rockbeare Hill EX5: Rock 3F 79
Rockcliffe Ct. EX34: Ilfra 2J 11
Rock Cl. TQ4: Broads 1J 121
Rockdale Rd. PL8: Torr 3C 150
Rock End Av. TQ1: Torq 4E 116
Rockfield Av. PL4: Plym 4A 132
Rockfield Cl. TQ14: Teignm 2K 107
Rockfield Ho. EX4: Exe 2F 7
Rockfield Rd. EX4: Wool 5A 10
Rock Gdns. EX32: B'aple 6F 19
PL9: Plyms 3E 142
Rock Hill EX18: Chul 7B 32
EX33: Brau 4J 15
EX33: Geo 5C 14
EX34: Ber 4B 12
PL5: Tam F 3H 131
TQ7: Ave G 7H 151
Rock Ho. La. TQ1: Maid 1E 112
Rockingham Rd. PL3: Plym 6B 136
Rocklands TQ13: Chud 3A 94
Rock La. EX34: C Mar 7C 12
(off Castle La.)
Rock Lodge Pk. EX35: Lynt 2G 13
Rockmount Ter. EX39: Bide 3F 23
(off Myrtle Gro.)
Rock Pk. TQ6: Dartm 5D 124
TQ13: Ashb 2J 99
Rock Pk. Ter. EX32: B'aple 5F 19
(off Park Ter.)
Rock Rd. TQ2: Torq 2D 116
TQ13: Chud 2C 94
Rockside EX4: Exe 4B 6 (6D 64)
Rockside Vs. EX4: Exe 3B 6 (6D 64)
The Rockstone EX7: Daw 3K 97
Rock Ter. PL7: Plymp 5A 138
Rock Vw. EX16: Hal 6E 42
Rockville Pk. PL9: Plyms 4F 143
Rock Wlk. TQ2: Torq 2C 116
ROCKWELL GREEN 2B 166
Rockwood Rd. PL6: Plym 2F 133
Rocky Hill PL19: Tavi 4H 59
Rocky La. EX34: C Mar 5B 12
TQ11: B'leigh 6B 98
TQ14: Teignm 3G 107
(not continuous)
Rocky Pk. Av. PL9: Plyms 4F 143
Rocky Pk. Rd. PL9: Plyms 5F 143
Rocombe Cl. TQ2: Torq 1B 112
Roddick Way PL7: Plymp 4F 139
Rodgemont's La. EX18: Chaw 7E 32
Rodgers Ind. Est. TQ4: Paig 4D 118
Rodney Cl. EX8: Lit 5J 77
TQ6: Dartm 6D 124
Rodney La. EX34: Ilfra 2J 11
(off Quayfield Rd.)
Rodney St. PL5: Plym 3C 134
TQ12: Kingsk 1F 111
Rods La. PL19: Mary T 1B 60
Roeselare Av. PL11: Torp 1A 140
Roeselare Cl. PL11: Torp 1A 140
Rogada TQ5: Brixh 6F 123
Rogate Dr. PL6: Plym 6E 132
Rogate Wlk. PL6: Plym 6E 132
Rogers Cl. EX16: Tive 2E 40
Rogers Cres. EX39: Bide 3J 23
Rohaise Cl. DT7: Uply 3G 91
Roland Bailey Gdns. PL19: Tavi 3G 59
Roland Matthews Ct. PL2: Dev 7D 134
(off Boscawen Pl.)
The Rolle EX9: Bud S 7C 82
Rolle Barton EX9: Ott'n 6G 83
Rolle Cotts. EX9: E Bud 2D 82
EX9: Know 5A 82
Rolle Ct. EX12: Seat 1E 86
EX38: G Tor 2B 30
(off New St.)
Rolle Quay EX31: B'aple 4D 18
Rolle Rd. EX8: Exmth 6C 76
EX9: Bud S 7C 82
EX38: G Tor 2A 30
Rolles Ter. EX39: Buck B 2H 29
Rollestone Cres. EX4: Exe 2H 65
Rolle St. EX8: Exmth 6C 76
EX31: B'aple 3D 18
Rolle Studios EX8: Exmth 6C 76
(off Rolle St.)
Rolle Ter. EX38: G Tor 2A 30
Rolle Vs. EX8: Exmth 6C 76
Rollis Pk. Cl. PL9: Plyms 4D 142
Rollis Pk. Rd. PL9: Plyms 4D 142
Roly Poly Hill EX2: Exe 3B 70

Romaleyn Gdns. TQ4: Good 3H 119
Roman Rd. DT7: Lym R 4H 91
EX13: Kilm 2B 88
PL5: Tam F 2D 134
Romans Way EX16: Tive 2F 41
Roman Wlk. EX1: Exe 4F 7
Roman Way EX5: Cran 4B 68
EX12: Seat 4D 86
EX14: Hon 2G 55
PL5: Plym 1D 134
Romilly Gdns. PL7: Plymp 6J 137
Romney Cl. PL5: Plym 2G 135
Romsey Dr. EX2: Exe 6J 7 (7H 65)
Ronald Ter. PL2: Plym 6E 134
Ronchetti Way EX2: Won 2J 71
Roncombe La. EX10: Sidb 1J 85
Ronsdale Cl. PL9: Plyms 4E 142
Rookbear Av. EX31: Bick 7K 17
Rookery Cotts. TQ3: Marl 2D 114
Rookery La. DT7: Harc B 1H 91
Rooklands Av. TQ1: Torq 6B 112
Rook La. PL21: Corn 4J 129
Rooksbridge Vw. EX31: Bick 7K 17
Rooks Cl. EX31: Rou 6A 18
Rooks Farm Rd. EX31: Yell 7B 16
Rooks Nest EX31: Frem 6F 17
Rooks Way EX16: Tive 2E 40
Rookswood Cl. EX31: Bick 7K 17
Rookswood La. EX5: Rock 4F 69
Rookwood Cl. EX14: Hon 3E 54
Roope Cl. PL5: Plym 4B 134
Roper Av. PL9: Plyms 4E 142
Ropers Ct. EX9: Ott'n 6H 83
Roper's La. EX9: Ott'n 6H 83
Ropery Rd. EX34: Ilfra 2J 11
Rope Wlk. EX39: Bide 3F 23
PL4: Plym 6G 9 (3A 142)
TQ14: Teignm 4H 107
Ropewalk TQ7: Kingsb 5F 157
The Rope Wlk. PL4: Plym . . .7K 9 (4B 142)
Ropewalk Hill TQ5: Brixh 3E 122
Ropewalk Ho. EX8: Exmth 4B 158
(off Shelly Rd.)
Rorkes Cl. PL5: Plym 1D 134
Rosalie Ter. EX34: Wool 6A 10
(off Arlington Rd.)
Roscoff Cl. EX38: G Tor 2D 30
Roscoff Ri. PL6: Plym 6C 132
Roscoff Rd. EX7: Daw 2H 97
Rosea Bri. La. EX34: C Mar 5A 12
Rose Acre Ter. TQ5: Brixh 4F 123
ROSE ASH 1B 164
Rose Av. EX1: Sow 6C 66
Rosebank Cres. EX4: Exe 3G 65
Rosebarn Av. EX4: Exe 3G 65
Rosebarn La. EX4: Exe 2G 65
Rosebery Av. PL4: Plym . . .2K 9 (1B 142)
PL4: Plym 1K 9 (1B 142)
Rosebery Rd. EX4: Exe 1J 7 (4H 65)
EX8: Exmth 4C 76
PL4: Plym 2K 9 (1B 142)
Roseclave Cl. PL7: Plymp 3F 139
Rose Cl. EX16: Tive 2F 41
Rose Cotts. PL6: Plym 3C 136
Rosedale Av. PL2: Plym 4J 135
Rosedale Ter. EX12: Seat 3F 87
Rose Dene TQ2: Torq 3B 112
Rosedown Av. PL2: Plym 4F 135
Rose Gdns. PL6: Plym 4E 132
TQ12: Ipp 6J 101
Rose Hill PL9: Wem 7B 148
TQ12: Kingsk 1F 111
Rose Hill Cl. TQ12: Kingsk 1F 111
Rosehill Ct. TQ1: Torq 1E 116
Rosehill Gdns. TQ12: Kingsk 1F 111
Rosehill Rd. TQ1: Torq 1D 116
Roseship Cl. PL6: Plym 3F 133
Roseland Av. EX1: Heav 6K 65
Roseland Cres. EX1: Heav 6K 65
Roseland Dr. EX1: Heav 7K 65
Roselands EX10: Sidm 6B 84
Roselands Dr. TQ4: Paig 4E 118
Roseland Sq. TQ12: Kingsk 4H 105
Roselands Rd. TQ4: Good, Paig 4F 119
TQ4: Paig 4E 118
Rose La. EX32: B'aple 6H 19
Rose Lawn EX32: Swim 3G 25
Rosemary Av. TQ12: New A 7C 104
Rosemary Cotts. TQ3: Pres 6H 115
Rosemary Gdns. TQ3: Paig 6F 115
Rose Mary Ho. EX15: Hemy 2G 47
(off Jubilee Dr.)
ROSEMARY LANE 2B 166
Rosemary La. EX13: Mus 7C 90
EX24: Colyt 5D 88
Rosemary St. EX4: Exe 7C 64
Rosemont Cl. TQ1: Torq 2F 117
Rosemont Ct. EX2: Alph 4E 70
Rosemoor Rd. EX38: G Tor 2D 30
Rosemount TQ4: Good 3J 119
(off Roundham Rd.)
Rosemount Cl. EX14: Hon 4E 54
Rosemount Ct. TQ8: Salc 3C 158
(off Church St.)

Rosemount La. EX14: Hon 4D 54
The Rosemullion EX9: Bud S 7C 82
Rosemullion Ct. EX9: Bud S 7C 82
Rosery Rd. TQ2: Torq 1A 116
Rosevale Ter. EX16: Tive 5C 40
(off Howden Rd.)
Rosevean Ct. PL3: Plym 5A 136
Rosevean Gdns. PL3: Plym 5A 136
Roseveare Cl. PL9: Plyms 4H 143
Rose Vs. PL21: Bitta 3B 146
Roseville St. . . . .
TQ6: Dartm 1A 124 (6F 125)
Rosewarne Av. TQ12: New A 2J 109
Roseway EX8: Exmth 4H 77
Rosewell Ct. EX14: Hon 2G 55
Rosewood Cl. PL9: Plyms 7G 143
Rosewood Cres. EX5: Clyst M 3K 73
Rosewood Gro. EX31: Rou 6B 18
Rosewood Ter. . . . .
EX4: Exe 1G 7 (4G 65)
Rospeath Cres. PL2: Plym 3J 135
Rosslyn Pk. Rd. PL3: Plym 6J 135
Ross Pk. Cvn. Pk. 5J 101
Ross St. PL2: Dev 7D 134
(not continuous)
Roswell Ct. EX8: Exmth 7D 76
Rosyl Av. EX7: Holc 7F 97
Rothbury Cl. PL6: Plym 6F 133
Rothbury Gdns. PL6: Plym 6E 132
Rotherfold TQ9: Tot 6D 102
Rothesay Gdns. PL5: Plym 7H 131
Rougemont Av. TQ2: Torq 4J 113
Rougemont Cl. PL3: Plym 4C 136
Rougemont Ct. EX6: Exmin 2B 74
Rougemont Pl. EX4: Exe 3E 6
Rougemont Ter. EX13: Axmin 5H 89
The Rough Nature Reserve 3B 166
Roundball Ct. EX14: Hon 5F 55
Roundball La. EX14: Hon 7E 54
Round Berry Dr. TQ8: Salc 4B 158
ROUNDHAM 3D 167
Roundham Av. TQ4: Good 3K 119
Roundham Cres. TQ4: Good 2K 119
Roundham Gdns. TQ4: Good 3J 119
Roundham Ho. TQ4: Paig 2J 119
(off Belle Vue Rd.)
Roundham Rd. TQ4: Paig 2J 119
Roundhead Rd. TQ12: H'fild 1J 93
ROUND HILL 4J 115 (1A 176)
Roundhill EX16: Tive 5B 40
Roundhill Cl. EX4: Exe 1D 64
Roundhill Rd. TQ2: Torq 4K 115
Roundhouse La. EX8: Exmth 2D 76
The Roundings TQ5: Galm 3H 121
Roundmoors Cl. TQ12: Kingsk 2G 111
Roundsleys La. PL19: Mary T 2C 60
Roundsnest PL8: Torr 3B 150
ROUNDSWELL 7A 18
Roundswell Bus. Pk. . . . .
EX31: Rou 7A 18
Roundtable Meet EX4: Whip 3A 66
The Roundway TQ12: Kingsk 6J 109
ROUSDON 1C 173
Rousdown Rd. TQ2: Torq 2A 116
Rowan Cl. EX14: Hon 5C 54
EX16: Tive 3F 41
PL7: Plymp 4E 138
PL19: Tavi 6J 59
TQ12: E Ogw 4C 104
Rowancroft EX1: Heav 4K 7 (6J 65)
Rowan Dr. EX12: Seat 2E 86
Rowan Pk. EX31: Rou 7B 18
Rowan Ter. EX6: Cher 3D 62
Rowantree Rd. TQ12: New A 3H 109
Rowan Way EX4: Exe 5C 64
PL6: Plym 3F 133
TQ5: Brixh 6B 122
Rowbrook Cl. TQ4: Paig 4E 118
Rowcroft Cl. EX14: Hon 4E 54
Rowcroft Rd. TQ3: Pres 6J 115
ROWDEN 1A 170
The Rowdens TQ2: Torq 1B 116
(off Belgrave Rd.)
TQ14: Teignm 3K 107
Rowdens Rd. TQ2: Torq 1B 116
Rowden St. PL3: Plym 6K 135
Row Down Cl. PL7: Plymp 5G 139
Rowe Cl. EX39: Bide 5E 22
Rowe Ho. EX4: Exe 4F 65
Rowells Mead TQ12: Live 4G 93
Rowes Farm Barns TQ9: Sto G 3B 120
Rowes Orchard EX15: Will 5C 44
Rowhorne Rd. EX4: Nad 5A 64
Rowland Cl. PL9: Hooe 7F 143
Row La. PL5: Plym 1D 134
Rowley Rd. TQ1: Torq 5E 112
Rowlstone Cl. EX8: Exmth 6F 103
Rowns La. EX34: C Mar 7C 12
Row Tor Cl. EX20: Oke 3D 48
ROYAL ALBERT BRIDGE . . . .
. . . . .1A 134 (2A 174)

Royal Albert Memorial Museum & . . . . . .
Art Gallery 3D 6 (6E 64)
Royal Av. EX8: Exmth 5B 76
Royal Charter Pk. EX18: Chul 6C 32
The Royal Citadel 7F 9 (4K 141)
Royal Clarence Apts. EX12: Seat 6F 87
(off Harbour Rd.)
EX34: Ilfra 2H 11
(off Regent Pl.)
Royal Cl. EX2: Alph 6E 70
Royal Ct. TQ1: Torq 6F 113
(off Bedford Rd.)
TQ12: New A 1F 109
TQ14: Teignm 5J 107
(off Den Cres.)
Royal Cres. EX2: Sow 2C 72
Royal Dart Yacht Club 7G 125
Royal Navy Av. PL2: Plym 6D 134
Royal North Devon Golf Course . . . .
. . . . .4D 20 (1C 163)
Royal Oak Cl. EX34: Dunk 5G 47
Royal Pde. PL1: Plym 5D 8 (3J 141)
Royal Pines TQ1: Torq 3F 117
Royal Plymouth Corinthian Yacht Club . . . .
. . . . .7F 9 (4K 141)
Royal Terrace Gdns. 2C 116
Royal Torbay Yacht Club 3D 116
Royal Way EX6: Star 1E 96
Royal William Rd. PL1: Plym 4F 141
Royal William Yard 5F 141
Royal William Yd. PL1: Plym 5F 141
Royston Ct. EX1: Whip 4B 66
Royston Rd. EX39: Bide 4E 22
ROYSTON WATER 2C 167
Rozel TQ1: Torq 3F 117
Ruckamore Rd. TQ2: Torq 1A 116
Ruda Holiday Pk. 1B 14
(not continuous)
Rudds Bldgs. EX16: Tive 4B 40
(off Melbourne St.)
Rudyard Way EX39: W Ho 6A 20
Rudyerd Wlk. PL3: Plym 5D 136
Rue St Pierre PL21: Ivy 4J 145
Rufford Cl. PL2: Plym 4F 135
Rugby Rd. EX4: Exe 7A 6 (1D 7b)
Ruggadon Middlepark Nature Reserve . . . .
. . . . .2C 171
Ruggaton La. EX34: Ber 4B 12
RUGWELL 4F 155
RUISHTON 1C 167
Rull La. EX15: Cull 1G 45
(not continuous)
Rumbelow Rd. EX16: Tive 2E 40
RUMSAM 7G 19
Rumsam Cl. EX32: B'aple 7G 19
Rumsam Gdns. EX32: B'aple 7G 19
Rumsam Mdws. EX32: B'aple 7G 19
Rumsam Rd. EX32: B'aple 7G 19
RUMWELL 1B 166
Rundle Rd. TQ12: New A 7F 105
RUNDLESTONE 3D 169
Runnacleave Cres. EX34: Ilfra 2H 11
(off Runnacleave Rd.)
Runnacleave Rd. EX34: Ilfra 2H 11
RUNNINGTON 1B 166
Runnymede Ct. PL6: Plym 1F 137
Runway Rd. PL6: Plym 5C 132
Rupertswood Ter. EX34: Ilfra 2J 11
(off Hillsborough Rd.)
Rushcott Cl. EX31: Yell 7B 16
RUSHFORD 7C 58 (3C 169)
Rushforth Pl. EX4: Exe 4B 64
Rushlade Cl. TQ4: Paig 5F 119
Rush Meadow Rd. EX5: Cran 2E 68
Ruskin Cres. PL5: Plym 1J 135
Russell Av. PL3: Plym 4A 136
Russell Cl. EX9: E Bud 1D 82
EX32: Land 2D 24
PL9: Plyms 5J 143
Russell Dr. PL19: Tavi 3H 59
TQ8: Salc 3D 158
(off Fore St.)
TQ9: Tot 6E 102
Russell Ct. Gdns. PL19: Tavi 3H 59
Russell Dr. EX9: E Bud 1D 82
Russell Pl. PL4: Plym 1D 8 (1J 141)
Russell St. EX1: Exe 3G 7 (6G 65)
EX10: Sidm 7C 84
PL19: Tavi 4J 59
Russell Ter. EX4: Exe 2C 6
(off Little Silver)
Russell Wlk. EX2: Sow 2B 72
Russell Way EX2: Cou W, Sow 2B 72
EX2: Sow 3C 72
Russell's Pk. La. EX5: Bradn 7F 45
Russet Av. EX1: Heav 6B 66
Russet Cl. EX1: Heav 6B 66
Russet Loop EX5: Rock 3D 68
Russets La. TQ11: B'leigh 4D 98
Russet Cl. EX15: Uff 7G 43
Russet Wood PL5: Plym 6E 130
Rutger Pl. PL1: Plym 1G 141
Ruthven Cl. EX2: Won 1K 71
Ruthven Cl. PL6: Plym 3A 136
Rutland Rd. PL4: Plym 7A 136

Rutt La. PL21: Ivy 3K 145
RYALL 1D 173
Ryalls Ct. EX12: Seat 5E 86
RYBHAY 5G 49
Rydal Cl. PL6: Plym 1E 136
Rydal M. EX4: Exe 7C 64
(off Windermere Cl.)
Ryde Cl. TQ2: Torq 3C 112
Ryder Cl. EX16: Tive 5H 41
Ryder Rd. PL2: Dev, Plym 6E 134
Ryders Bank TQ11: B'leigh 5B 98
RYDON 3H 105
Rydon Acres TQ9: Sto G 3B 120
TQ12: Kingst 3H 105
Rydon Av. TQ12: Kingst 3H 105
Rydon Est. TQ12: Kingst 3H 105
Rydon Ind. Est. TQ12: Kingst 5G 105
Rydon La. EX2: Cou W, Sow 4A 72
EX3: Ext 1H 75
EX5: W'bury 6A 78
EX9: Ott'n 5H 83
TQ12: A'well 6F 109
Rydon La. Retail Pk. 2B 72
Rydon Rd. EX2: Sow 1C 72
Rydon Path TQ12: Kingst 2H 105
TQ12: Kingst 2H 105
Rydons TQ5: Brixh 4C 122
Ryeland Cl. PL9: Wem 6C 148
Rye Pk. EX19: Bea 3H 31
Rye Pk. Cl. EX19: Bea 3H 31
Ryll Cl. EX8: Exmth 5D 76
Ryll Ct. Dr. EX8: Exmth 5D 76
Ryll Gro. EX8: Exmth 5D 76
Ryll La. EX9: Bud S 7D 82

S

Sabre Cl. TQ12: H'fld 1H 93
Sabre Wlk. EX32: B'aple 3G 19
(off Oliver Rd.)
Sackery TQ12: C'head 7A 106
Sackville Cl. PL9: Plyms 5G 143
The Saddle TQ4: Good 5J 119
Saddleback Cl. TQ12: E Ogw 4C 108
Saddlers La. EX11: Ott M 4C 80
Saddlers Way EX20: Oke 2D 48
Sadler Cl. EX8: Exmth 4G 77
Sadler Grn. TQ13: Bov T 5B 92
Saffron Ct. TQ7: Kingsb 4G 157
Saffron Pk. TQ7: Kingsb 4G 157
Sage Gro. EX16: Tive 4F 41
Sage Pk. Rd. EX33: Brau 3G 15
Sages Lea EX5: Wood S 2C 78
Sailmakers Ct. EX8: Exmth 6A 76
St Agnes La. TQ2: Torq 3A 116
St Aidan's Ct. PL5: Plym 5D 130
St Albans Cl. EX4: Exe 6B 64
St Albans La. TQ1: Torq 6E 112
St Albans Pk. PL20: Yelv 6G 127
St Albans Rd. TQ1: Torq 6E 112
St Andrew's Cl. EX14: Fen 2G 53
St Andrews Cl. EX6: Kenn 3J 95
EX15: Cull 4G 45
EX24: Colyt 5D 88
(off Dolphin St.)
PL20: Bere A 2C 128
TQ13: Ashb 4H 99
St Andrews Ct. EX16: Tive 2F 41
(off Rooks Way)
St Andrews Cross
PL1: Plym 5E 8 (3J 141)
St Andrews Dr. EX13: Axmin 2K 89
St Andrew's Est. EX15: Cull 3G 45
St Andrews Ho. EX8: Exmth 6B 76
(off St Andrew's Rd.)
St Andrews Mdw. DT7: Lym R 4J 91
St Andrews Orchard EX24: Colyt 5D 88
St Andrew's Rd. EX4: Exe 1C 64
EX5: Cowl 1B 64
EX8: Exmth 6B 76
St Andrews Rd. EX15: Cull 3G 45
EX31: Frem 5E 16
PL19: Whit 7K 59
TQ4: Paig 2J 119
St Andrews Sq. EX24: Colyt 5D 88
(off Rosemary La.)
St Andrews Ter. EX24: Colyt 5D 88
St Andrew St. EX16: Tive 5C 40
(not continuous)
PL1: Plym 5E 8 (3J 141)
St Annes EX6: Kenton 6H 95
St Anne's Chapel EX4: Exe 1H 7
St Anne's Ct. TQ12: New A 1D 108
St Annes Pl. EX5: Silv 2H 51
St Anne's Rd. PL6: Plym 4E 132
TQ1: Torq 6E 112
St Annes Rd. EX1: Heav 1K 7 (5H 65)
ST ANN'S CHAPEL
PL18 .3C 169
TQ7 .3C 175
St Anthony's Cl. EX11: Ott M 3D 80
St Aubyn Av. PL2: Plym 6E 134
St Aubyn Rd. PL1: Dev 2D 140
St Aubyn's Pk. EX16: Tive 5F 41
St Aubyn St. PL1: Dev 2D 140
St Aubyn's Vs. EX16: Tive 5F 41

St Aubyn Ter. PL7: L Moor 1J 129
St Augustine's Cl. TQ2: Torq 2C 112
St Austin Cl. PL21: Ivy 4G 145
St Barnabas Ct.
PL1: Plym 2B 8 (1H 141)
St Barnabas Ter.
PL1: Plym 2A 8 (1G 141)
St Bartholomews Rd.
TQ12: E Ogw 4C 108
St Bartholomew Way
TQ12: E Ogw 4A 108
St Bernard's Cl. EX2: Exe 1G 71
TQ11: Buck 2C 98
(not continuous)
St Boniface Cl. PL2: Plym 4H 135
St Boniface Dr. PL2: Plym 4H 135
St Boniface Rd. EX17: Cred 6F 39
St Brannock's Hill EX33: Brau 3J 15
St Brannock's Pk. Rd. EX34: Ilfra . . .3H 11
St Brannock's Rd. EX34: Ilfra 3H 11
St Brannock's Well Cl.
EX33: Brau 3J 15
St Briac Way EX8: Exmth 1G 77
St Bridget Av. PL6: Plym 2A 136
ST BUDEAUX 2C 134 (2A 174)
St Budeaux By-Pass
PL5: Plym 3D 134
St Budeaux Cl. EX11: Ott M 4D 80
St Budeaux Ferry Road Station
(Rail) 3C 134 (2A 174)
St Budeaux Orchard EX11: Ott M . . .4D 80
St Budeaux Victoria Road Station
(Rail) 2C 134 (2A 174)
St Catherine's Chapel & Almshouse
. . . . .4E 6
(off Bedford St.)
St Catherines Pk. PL8: New F 5J 149
St Catherine's Rd. TQ1: Torq 5D 112
St Chad Cl. PL5: Plym 6H 131
St Clares Cl. EX12: Seat 5E 86
ST CLEER 3A 168
St Clements Ct. TQ6: Dartm 5E 124
(off Church Rd.)
St Clements La. EX4: Exe 1B 6 (5D 64)
St Columba Cl. TQ12: Kingst 3H 105
St Cyres Rd. EX14: Hon 3E 54
ST DAVID'S 1B 6 (5D 64)
St David's Cl. EX13: Axmin 2K 89
St David's Dr. EX13: Axmin 2K 89
St David's Hill EX4: Exe 1B 6 (5D 64)
St David's Pk. TQ4: Coll M 3B 118
St Davids Pl. EX4: Exe 1A 6
St Davids Rd. PL19: Tavi 5K 59
St Davids Ter. EX4: Exe 3C 6 (6E 64)
ST DOMINICK 3B 168
St Dominics Cl. TQ1: Torq 5D 112
St Dunstans Rd. TQ8: Salc 4B 158
St Dunstan's Ter.
PL4: Plym 3K 9 (2B 142)
St Edmunds Ct. EX4: Exe 5C 6
St Edmunds TQ7: Kingsb 3F 157
St Edmund's Rd. TQ1: Torq 6D 112
(not continuous)
St Edmunds Wlk. TQ7: Kingsb 4F 157
St Edward Gdns. PL6: Plym 2C 136
St Efride's Rd. TQ2: Torq 1B 116
Sainte Honorine Du Fay Cl.
EX32: Swim 3H 25
St Elizabeth Cl. PL7: Plymp 5C 138
St Elmo Ct. TQ8: Salc 5A 158
ST ERNEY 2A 174
St Erth Rd. PL2: Plym 4J 135
St Eval Pl. PL5: Plym 6D 130
St Francis Ct. PL5: Plym 7F 131
St Gabriel's Av. PL3: Plym 6J 135
ST GENNYS 1A 168
St Georges EX13: Axmin 3H 89
(off Chard St.)
St Georges Av. PL2: Plym 4H 135
St Georges Av. EX13: Axmin 2K 89
St Georges Cl. PL21: Modb 7G 147
St George's Ct. TQ2: Torq 2D 112
St Georges Cres. TQ1: Torq 6E 112
St Georges Hill DT7: Lym R 4H 91
St George's Rd. EX32: B'aple 3E 18
TQ1: Torq 6E 112
St Georges Sq. TQ6: Dartm 2B 124
(off Fairfax Pl.)
St George's Ter. EX32: B'aple 3E 18
PL2: Plym 7E 134
St George's Vw. EX15: Cull 3G 45
St George's Way EX16: Tive 5C 40
St George's Well EX15: Cull 2G 45
(not continuous)
St George's Well Av. EX15: Cull 3G 45
ST GERMANS 2A 174
St German's EX4: Exe 4F 65
St Germans Rd. EX4: Exe 4F 65
St Germans Station (Rail) 2A 174
ST GILES IN THE WOOD 2D 163
ST GILES ON THE HEATH
. . . . .6C 34 (1B 168)
St Gregorys Ct. EX12: Seat 4E 86
St Helen's EX39: A'sham 3A 22
St Helen's Cl. EX33: Croy 2C 14
St Helens EX10: Sidm 7A 84

St Helen's Wlk. PL5: Plym 5H 131
St Hilarian EX8: Exmth 7D 76
St Hilary Ter. PL4: Plym 3K 9 (2B 142)
SAINT HILL 3A 166
St Hill Cl. EX2: Exe 3D 70
St Ida's Cl. EX2: Ide 4A 70
ST IVE 3B 168
St Ive's Ct. TQ1: Torq 7C 112
ST JAMES' 4G 65
St James Cl. EX4: Exe 1G 7 (5G 65)
EX32: Land 3D 24
St James Ct. EX20: Oke 3F 37
(off St James St.)
PL1: Plym 6C 8
PL11: Torp 1A 140
St James M. PL1: Plym 6C 8
St James' Park
Exeter 1G 7
St James' Park Station
(Rail) 1G 7 (5G 65)
St James Pl. EX34: Ilfra 2J 11
TQ1: Torq 6F 113
St James Pl. E.
PL1: Plym 6C 8 (3H 141)
St James Pl. W.
PL1: Plym 6C 8 (3H 141)
St James Rd. PL11: Torp 2A 140
TQ1: Torq 6C 112
St James' Rd. EX4: Exe 1G 7 (5G 65)
St James's Ho. TQ14: Teignm 4H 107
(off Fore St.)
St James's Pl. EX6: Chri 3J 63
St James's Pct. TQ14: Teignm 4H 107
(off Bitton Pk. Rd.)
St James St. EX20: Oke 3B 48
St James Ter. EX4: Exe 1G 7 (5G 65)
St James Way EX16: Tive 2E 40
ST JOHN .2A 174
St John Cl. EX14: Hon 3F 55
St Johns Av. PL19: Tavi 4J 59
St Johns Av. PL19: Tavi 4J 59
St John's Bri. Rd.
PL4: Plym 6J 9 (3A 142)
ST JOHN'S CHAPEL 1D 163
St Johns Cl. PL6: Plym 6E 132
PL21: Ivy 4F 145
TQ13: Bov T 5B 92
TQ14: Bi'ton 4B 106
St Johns Cl. EX16: Tive 2E 40
EX24: Colyt 6C 88
EX32: B'aple 6H 19
St John's Ct. TQ3: Paig 1H 119
(off Littlegate Rd.)
TQ9: Tot 6F 103
(off Weston Rd.)
St Johns Cl. PL19: Tavi 5H 59
St John's Dr. EX22: Bradw 6B 28
PL9: Hooe 6C 142
St John's Farm M. EX8: Exmth 1H 77
St John's La. EX32: B'aple 7H 19
St Johns La. TQ13: Bov T 4B 92
St Johns Pl. EX1: Exe 4E 6
TQ1: Torq 2D 116
(off Braddons Hill Rd. W.)
St John's Rd. EX1: Heav 1K 7 (5H 65)
EX8: Exmth 3F 77
(not continuous)
PL4: Plym 5J 9 (3A 142)
PL9: Hooe 6B 142
PL20: Horr 2E 126
PL21: Ivy 4F 145
St John's PL. PL4: Plym 5J 9 (3A 142)
St Johns St. TQ12: New A 7F 105
St John's Ter. TQ9: Tot 5D 102
St Johns Vs. EX2: Heav 7J 65
St Johns Yd. PL4: Plym 5H 9 (3A 142)
St Joseph's Cl. PL6: Plym 2A 136
St Josephs Cl. EX32: B'aple 7H 19
St Josephs Ct. TQ14: Teignm 5J 107
(off Carlton Pl.)
ST JUDE'S 2C 142
St Judes Rd. PL4: Plym 5J 9 (2A 142)
St Julian Cres. PL10: Crem 5D 140
St Katherine's Cl. EX31: Yell 6B 16
St Katherine's M. TQ9: Tot 6E 102
(off St Katherine's Way)
St Katherine's Rd. EX4: Whip 4K 65
TQ1: Torq 7A 112
St Katherine's Way TQ9: Tot 6E 102
St Keverne Pl. PL2: Plym 3J 135
St Keyes Cl. EX32: Land 2B 24
St Kitts Cl. TQ2: Torq 3B 112
St Lawrence Cl. EX16: Tive 5G 41
St Lawrence Cres. EX1: Heav 6C 66
St Lawrence Dr. EX17: Cred 5G 39
St Lawrence La. TQ13: Ashb 4H 99
St Lawrence M. PL4: Plym 1F 9
St Lawrence Rd.
PL4: Plym 1F 9 (1K 141)
St Lawrence's Grn. EX17: Cred 6G 39
ST LEONARD'S 6J 7 (7H 65)
St Leonard's Av. EX2: Exe 7F 7 (1F 71)
St Leonard's Cl. TQ12: New A 2E 108
St Leonard's Pl.
EX2: Exe 6G 7 (7G 65)
St Leonards Pl. EX5: Clyst M 2F 73
St Leonard's Rd. EX2: Exe 7G 7 (1G 71)
TQ12: New A 2E 108

St Leonards Rd. EX14: Hon 4D 54
PL4: Plym 5K 9 (3B 142)
St Leonard's Ter. EX24: Colyt 6C 88
(off The Butts)
St Leonard's Tower 1E 108
St Leo Pl. PL2: Dev 7D 134
St Levan Rd. PL2: Plym 6D 134
ST LOYE'S 1K 71
St Loyes Gdns. EX2: Won 7A 66
St Loyes Rd. EX2: Won 7K 65
St Loyes Ter. EX2: Won 1K 71
St Luke's Cl. TQ12: New A 3J 109
St Lukes Dr. TQ14: Teignm 3G 107
St Luke's Pk. TQ2: Torq 2C 116
St Luke's Rd. TQ2: Torq 1C 116
TQ12: New A 3H 109
St Luke's Rd. Nth. TQ2: Torq 2C 116
St Luke's Rd. Sth. TQ2: Torq 2C 116
St Luke's Sports Cen. 4J 7 (6H 65)
St Lukes Vw. EX2: Cou W 4J 71
St Malo Cl. EX8: Exmth 1G 77
St Marco Gdns. TQ7: Kingsb 3G 157
St Margaret's Av. TQ1: Torq 6D 112
St Margaret's Cl. TQ1: Torq 5D 112
St Margarets Cl. EX15: Hemy 1G 47
St Margaret's Ct. TQ1: Torq 5D 112
(off St Margaret's M.)
St Margarets Gdn. EX31: B'aple 3E 18
St Margaret's M. TQ1: Torq 5D 112
St Margaret's Rd. TQ1: Torq 5D 112
St Margarets Rd. PL7: Plymp 4J 137
St Margarets Ter. EX3: Top 5B 74
(off Exe St.)
St Margaret's Vw. EX8: Lit 5J 77
St Marks Av. EX1: Heav 1K 7 (5J 65)
St Mark's Dr. TQ1: Torq 3F 117
(off St Mark's Rd.)
St Mark's Rd. EX14: Hon 5D 54
TQ1: Torq 3F 117
St Marks Rd. PL6: Plym 5E 132
St Martin's Av. PL3: Plym 4J 135
St Martins Cl. EX10: Sidm 3C 84
EX17: Bow 5J 37
St Martins Cl. EX10: Sidm 4C 84
(off St Martins Cl.)
TQ2: Torq 4B 112
St Martins La. EX17: Cred 5G 39
St Martin's M. TQ1: Torq 5E 112
(off Fore St.)
ST MARYCHURCH 4E 112 (1B 176)
St Marychurch Rd. TQ1: Torq 4D 112
(not continuous)
. . . . .2H 109, 1B 112
St Maryhaye PL19: Tavi 4G 59
St Mary Magdalen Cl.
TQ14: Bi'ton 4B 106
St Marys EX13: Ray H 4A 90
St Mary's Arches
EX4: Exe 4D 6 (6E 64)
St Mary's Cl. EX6: Ted M 6J 49
EX13: Axmin 4K 89
EX38: G Tor 3A 30
PL7: Plymp 4A 138
TQ5: Brixh 6D 122
TQ13: Chud 2C 94
St Marys Cl. TQ12: A'well 6D 108
St Mary's Ct. PL7: Plymp 4A 138
TQ3: Paig 1G 119
St Marys Ct. TQ12: New A 1E 108
(off Highweek St.)
St Mary's Dr. TQ5: Brixh 5F 123
St Mary's Flats EX39: Bide 4F 23
(off Buttgarden St.)
St Mary's Hill TQ5: Brixh 5F 123
St Mary's La. DT7: Uply 4A 90
St Mary's Park 6E 122
St Mary's Pk. TQ4: Coll M 3C 118
St Marys Pk. EX11: Ott M 4D 80
St Mary's Pl. TQ12: Ipp 6H 101
(off Caunters Cl.)
St Mary's Rd. EX32: B'aple 3F 19
EX33: Croy 2D 14
PL7: Plymp 5K 137
TQ5: Brixh 6E 122
TQ12: New A 2E 108
TQ14: Teignm 2G 107
St Mary's Sq. TQ5: Brixh 5D 122
St Mary Steps Ter. EX1: Exe 5D 6
St Mary St. PL1: Plym 2G 141
St Marys Vw. EX5: Silv 2H 51
EX11: W Hill 3J 79
St Matthews Cl.
EX1: Exe 3H 7 (6G 65)
St Matthews Ct. EX1: Exe 3H 7
St Matthew's Rd. TQ2: Torq 2K 115
St Matthews Wlk.
EX1: Exe 3H 7 (6G 65)
St Matthias Chu. Rd. TQ1: Torq 1G 117
St Maurice M. PL7: Plymp 5B 138
St Maurice Rd. PL7: Plymp 6C 138
St Maurice Vw. PL7: Plymp 5E 138
St Mawes Dr. TQ4: Good 7H 119
St Mawes Ter. PL11: Torp 6E 122
ST MELLION 1A 174
St Michael Av. PL2: Plym 6E 134
ST MICHAELS 2H 119 (2A 176)
St Michaels DT7: Lym R 4K 91

St Michael's Cl.—Seaborough

St Michael's Cl. PL1: Dev . . . 3D 140
TQ1: Torq . . . 7A 112
St Michaels Cl. EX2: Alph . . . 4E 70
EX5: Clyst H . . . 4J 67
EX9: Ott'n . . . 6H 83
TQ10: S Bre . . . 2B 100
St Michael's Ct. *PL1: Dev* . . . *1E 140*
(off Stopford Pl.)
TQ4: Paig . . . *3G 119*
(off Derrell Rd.)
St Michaels Hill EX5: Clyst H . . . 4J 67
St Michael's M. EX4: Exe . . . 3C 6
St Michael's Rd. TQ1: Torq . . . 6A 112
TQ4: Paig . . . 2G 119
TQ12: Kingst . . . 5G 105
TQ12: New A . . . 3G 109
TQ14: Teignm . . . 2J 107
St Michael's Ter. PL1: Dev . . . 1E 140
TQ1: Torq . . . 1D 116
St Michaels Ter. TQ10: S Bre . . . 3B 100
St Michael's Ter. La.
PL4: Plym . . . 2D 8 (1J 141)
St Michaels Vw. EX21: Sheb . . . 6J 29
St Michaels Way EX5: Cran . . . 3C 68
St Modwen Rd. PL6: Plym . . . 4F 137
St Nazaire App. PL1: Dev . . . 2E 140
St Nazaire Cl. *PL1: Dev* . . . *2E 140*
(off St Nazaire App.)
ST NEOT . . . 3A 168
St Nicholas Cl. EX1: Pin . . . 4E 66
St Nicholas Priory . . . 5C 6
St Olans EX8: Exmth . . . 6D 76
St Olaves Cl. EX4: Exe . . . 5D 6 (6E 64)
St Olaves M. EX4: Exe . . . 4C 6
St Pancras Av. PL2: Plym . . . 2H 135
St Patricks Cl. TQ14: Teignm . . . 3G 107
St Paul's Cl. PL3: Plym . . . 6D 136
St Pauls Cl. EX2: Won . . . 2J 71
TQ13: Bov T . . . 4C 92
St Paul's Ct. *PL3: Plym* . . . *6D 136*
(off Torridge Way)
St Pauls Ct. *TQ1: Torq* . . . *6D 112*
(off St Edmunds Rd.)
St Paul's Cres. TQ1: Torq . . . 6D 112
St Pauls Dr. EX22: Hols . . . 1B 34
St Paul's Rd. EX14: Hon . . . 5D 54
TQ1: Torq . . . 6D 112
TQ3: Pres . . . 5K 115
TQ12: New A . . . 1F 109
St Paul's Sq. EX16: Tive . . . 5C 40
(not continuous)
St Paul St. EX16: Tive . . . 4C 40
PL1: Plym . . . 4F 141
St Peter's Cl. TQ13: Bov T . . . 3D 92
St Peters Cl. PL7: Plymp . . . 5C 138
TQ2: Torq . . . 7K 111
St Peter's Ct. EX16: Tive . . . 4C 40
St Peters Ct. *EX10: Sidm* . . . *7C 84*
(off Church St.)
PL1: Plym . . . 4A 8
St Peter's Hill TQ5: Brixh . . . 3F 123
St Peters Ho. EX2: Exe . . . 6E 6
St Peters Mt. EX4: Exe . . . 5A 64
St Peter's Quay TQ9: Tot . . . 7F 103
St Peter's Rd. EX14: Hon . . . 4D 54
St Peters Rd. EX22: Hols . . . 1B 34
EX31: Frem . . . 6E 16
PL5: Plym . . . 1H 135
St Peter's Ter. *EX31: B'aple* . . . *4E 18*
(off Butchers Row)
St Peters Ter. *EX34: Ilfra* . . . *3J 11*
(off Highfield Rd.)
TQ5: Brixh . . . *3F 123*
(off Elkins Hill)
St Peter St. EX16: Tive . . . 4C 40
St Peter's Way PL21: Ivy . . . 5J 145
St Peter's Well La. EX22: Bradw . . . 5C 28
St Petrock's Cl.
EX2: Exe . . . 6H 7 (7G 65)
St Pio La. EX2: Won . . . 2J 71
St Saviours Rd. EX11: Ott M . . . 4C 80
St Saviour's Way EX17: Cred . . . 6G 39
St Scholasticas TQ14: Teignm . . . 2K 107
St Sevan Way EX8: Exmth . . . 1G 77
St Sidwell's Av. EX4: Exe . . . 1G 7 (5F 65)
ST STEPHENS
PL12 . . . 2A 174
PL15 . . . 2B 168
St Stephen's Pl. PL7: Plymp . . . 4B 138
St Stephen's Rd. PL7: Plymp . . . 6C 138
St Stephen St. PL1: Dev . . . 3E 140
St Teresa Ho. PL4: Plym . . . 4G 9
St Teresa's Cl. EX39: Nort . . . 5E 20
St Teresa's Ct. *EX39: Nort* . . . *5E 20*
(off St Teresa's Cl.)
St Therese's Ct. *PL1: Dev* . . . *2E 140*
(off Raglan Rd.)
ST THOMAS . . . 7B 6 (1D 70)
St Thomas Cl. PL7: Plymp . . . 6C 138
TQ13: Bov T . . . 4D 92
St Thomas Ct. EX4: Exe . . . 7B 6 (1D 70)
EX16: Tive . . . 2E 40
PL4: Plym . . . 4G 9
St Thomas M. EX2: Exe . . . 1D 70
St Thomas Shop. Cen. . . . 6B 6 (1D 70)
St Thomas Station (Rail) . . . 7B 6 (1D 70)
St Vincent's Cl. TQ1: Torq . . . 7B 112
St Vincent's Rd. TQ1: Torq . . . 6B 112
St Vincent St. PL2: Plym . . . 7D 134
St Werburgh Cl. PL9: Wem . . . 7B 148
ST WINNOLLS . . . 2A 174
Salamanca St. PL11: Torp . . . 1A 140
SALCOMBE . . . 3D 158 (3D 175)
Salcombe Ct. EX10: Sidm . . . 6D 84
Salcombe Hgts. Cl. TQ8: Salc . . . 3B 158
Salcombe Hill EX10: Sidm . . . 6D 84
Salcombe Hill Cl. EX10: Sidm . . . 6C 84
Salcombe Hill Rd.
EX10: Sidm . . . 6C 84
Salcombe Lawn EX10: Sidm . . . 6C 84
Salcombe Lifeboat Station . . . 3D 175
Salcombe Maritime Mus. . . . 3D 158
Salcombe Park & Ride
Summer only . . . 3B 158
SALCOMBE REGIS . . . 2B 172
Salcombe RNLI Mus. . . . 3D 158
Salcombe Rd. EX10: Sidm . . . 6C 84
PL4: Plym . . . 1J 9 (7A 136)
TQ7: Malb . . . 6H 155
Salcombe Tourist Information Centre
. . . 3D 158 (3D 175)
Salcombe Yacht Club . . . 4C 158
Salem Chapel . . . 1D 82 (2A 172)
Salem Pl. EX4: Exe . . . 1H 7 (5G 65)
TQ12: New A . . . 1E 108
Salem Sq. *EX32: B'aple* . . . *5F 19*
(off Trinity St.)
Salem St. EX32: B'aple . . . 5F 19
Salisbury Av. EX14: Fen . . . 2G 53
TQ2: Torq . . . 3B 112
Salisbury Cl. EX14: Fen . . . 2G 53
Salisbury Ope PL3: Plym . . . 6G 135
Salisbury Rd. EX4: Exe . . . 1J 7 (4H 65)
EX8: Exmth . . . 5C 76
PL4: Plym . . . 3H 9 (2A 142)
TQ12: New A . . . 7G 105
Salisbury Rd. La. Nth.
PL4: Plym . . . 3J 9 (2A 142)
Salisbury Ter. EX13: Kilm . . . 2B 88
TQ14: Teignm . . . 4J 107
Salmon Leap Cl. TQ11: B'leigh . . . 4D 98
Salmon Pool La. EX2: Exe . . . 2H 71
Salmons Leap TQ9: Darti . . . 4D 102
Salston Barton EX11: Ott M . . . 5B 80
Salston Ride EX11: Ott M . . . 5A 80
SALTASH . . . 2A 174
Saltash Rd. PL2: Plym . . . 6C 134
PL3: Plym . . . 1C 8 (1J 141)
Saltash Sailing Club . . . 1A 134
SALTASH SERVICE AREA . . . 1A 174
Saltash Station (Rail) . . . 2A 174
Saltburn Rd. PL5: Plym . . . 1B 134
Salterne Mdws. EX9: Bud S . . . 5C 82
Saltern Rd. TQ4: Good . . . 6J 119
Salterns Ter. EX39: Bide . . . 3G 23
Salters Bldgs. *EX16: Tive* . . . *4D 40*
(off Barrington St.)
Salter's Ct. EX2: Won . . . 1K 71
Salter's La. EX24: Colyf . . . 7B 88
Salters Mdw. EX10: Sidm . . . 5C 84
Salter's Rd. EX2: Won . . . 1K 71
Salterton Ct. EX8: Exmth . . . 4H 77
Salterton Rd. EX8: Exmth . . . 6D 76
Salting Hill EX9: Bud S . . . 7E 82
The Saltings EX12: Seat . . . 3F 87
TQ14: Shal . . . 6F 107
Saltmer Cl. EX34: Ilfra . . . 6G 11
Saltpill Duck Pond . . . 4E 16
Salt Quay Moorings *TQ7: Kingsb* . . . *5G 157*
(off Embankment Rd.)
Saltram . . . 7G 137 (2B 174)
Saltram Ter. PL7: L Moor . . . 1J 129
PL7: Plymp . . . 4A 138
SALTRENS . . . 1C 163
Salt Wood La. EX34: C Mar . . . 3E 12
(not continuous)
Salty La. TQ14: Shal . . . 6F 107
Salutary Mt. EX1: Heav . . . 5K 7 (7J 65)
SALWAY ASH . . . 1D 173
Salway Cl. EX15: Cull . . . 4G 45
Salway Gdns. EX13: Axmin . . . 4K 89
Samara Bus. Pk. TQ12: H'fld . . . 1J 93
SAMPFORD ARUNDEL . . . 2B 166
SAMPFORD COURTENAY . . . 3A 164
Sampford Courtenay Station
(Rail) . . . 1A 170
Sampford Gdns. PL20: Horr . . . 1G 127
SAMPFORD PEVERELL . . . 2A 42 (2A 166)
SAMPFORD SPINEY . . . 3D 169
Sampford Ter. PL20: Horr . . . 1F 127
Sampson Cl. EX10: Sidm . . . 2B 84
Sampsons La. EX1: Heav . . . 2K 7 (5H 65)
Sampson's Plantation
EX31: Frem . . . 7D 16
Samuel Bassett Av. PL6: Plym . . . 3C 132
Sanctuary Cl. EX32: B Taw . . . 6B 24
PL2: Plym . . . 6E 134
Sanctuary La. EX20: Hath . . . 1H 35
Sanctuary Rd. EX22: Hols . . . 2C 34
Sand . . . 1K 85 (1B 172)
Sandalwood EX7: Daw W . . . 7E 96
Sandaway Beach Holiday Pk. . . . 2E 12
Sandaway La. EX34: Ber . . . 2E 12
Sand Down La. EX5: New C . . . 7D 50
Sanderling Ct. EX2: Sow . . . 6E 66
Sanders Cl. EX5: Broadc . . . 6D 52
Sanders La. EX22: Hols . . . 1C 34
EX32: B Taw . . . 6B 24
Sanderspool Cross TQ10: S Bre . . . 2C 100
Sanders Rd. EX4: Pin . . . 3C 66
EX17: Bow . . . 6H 37
TQ5: Brixh . . . 3C 122
SANDFORD . . . 3C 165
Sandford Cl. EX32: B'aple . . . 7J 19
Sandford Orleigh TQ12: New A . . . 6E 104
Sandford Rd. PL9: Plyms . . . 4G 143
Sandfords EX6: Kennf . . . 1H 95
Sandfords Gdns. EX38: G Tor . . . 3A 30
Sandford Vw. TQ12: New A . . . 7E 104
Sandford Wlk. EX1: Exe . . . 3H 7 (6G 65)
(not continuous)
Sandgate La. EX11: Wigg . . . 7B 80
Sand Gro. EX2: Cou W . . . 3C 72
Sandhills EX39: Ins . . . 1K 21
Sandhills Rd. TQ8: Salc . . . 5B 158
Sandhill St. EX11: Ott M . . . 3C 80
Sand La. TQ9: L'ton . . . 3H 103
The Sand Martins *TQ12: New A* . . . *2H 109*
(off St Marychurch Rd.)
Sandoe Way EX1: Pin . . . 1D 66
Sandon Wlk. PL6: Plym . . . 3B 136
Sandown Rd. TQ4: Paig . . . 5F 119
Sandpath Rd. TQ12: Kingst . . . 5H 105
Sandpiper EX7: Daw W . . . 7D 96
Sandpiper Ct. EX4: Pin . . . 3C 66
EX34: Wool . . . 6C 10
Sandpiper Dr. EX3: Ext . . . 2G 75
Sandpiper Grn. EX2: Exe . . . 1A 70
Sandpiper Rd. PL6: Plym . . . 1C 136
Sandpiper Way TQ2: Torq . . . 3J 111
Sand Pit Hill La. EX24: Colyt . . . 7A 88
Sandquay Rd. TQ6: Dartm . . . 4F 125
Sandquay Way TQ6: Dartm . . . 4F 125
Sandringham Dr. TQ3: Pres . . . 4G 115
Sandringham Gdns. EX31: B'aple . . . 7B 18
TQ3: Pres . . . 4H 115
Sandringham Rd. TQ12: New A . . . 1H 109
Sands Ct. EX12: Seat . . . 5D 86
TQ4: Paig . . . 2H 119
Sands Rd. TQ4: Paig . . . 2H 119
TQ7: Slap . . . 2J 159
Sandstone Cl. EX2: Sow . . . 2D 72
Sandy Bay . . . 3A 172
SANDYGATE
EX3 . . . 3E 72
TQ12 . . . 2G 105 (3C 171)
Sandygate TQ12: Kingst . . . 2F 105
Sandygate Bus. Pk.
TQ12: Kingst . . . 2F 105
Sandygate M. *TQ12: Kingst* . . . *1G 105*
(off Lower Sandygate)
Sandygate Mill TQ12: Kingst . . . 1G 105
Sandy La. EX5: Bram S . . . 6F 51
EX5: Broadc . . . 7D 52
EX5: Rewe . . . 4K 51
EX7: Daw . . . 2J 97
EX33: Croy . . . 2B 14
EX34: Wool . . . 6A 10
PL21: Ivy . . . 4H 145
TQ7: Gov, Kingsb . . . 1J 157
Sandymere Rd. EX39: Nort . . . 4D 20
Sandy Park . . . 3D 72
Sandy Pk. Way EX2: Cou W . . . 2D 72
Sandy Rd. PL7: Plymp . . . 5F 139
Sandy Vw. EX2: Sow . . . 2D 72
Sandy Way EX33: Croy . . . 3C 14
Sanford Pl. EX2: Exe . . . 7A 6 (1D 70)
Sanford Rd. TQ2: Torq . . . 1A 116
Sango Rd. PL11: Torp . . . 2A 140
Sannerville Way EX6: Exmin . . . 7K 71
San Remo Ter. EX7: Daw . . . 4J 97
San Sebastian Sq. PL1: Plym . . . 5D 8
Sanson Cl. EX5: Sto C . . . 7J 51
Sarah Cl. PL20: Bere A . . . 2B 128
Sargent Cl. EX1: Heav . . . 6B 66
Sarisdown Rd. EX8: Exmth . . . 5F 77
Sarum Cl. PL3: Plym . . . 4A 136
SATTERLEIGH . . . 1A 164
Saturday's La. TQ12: N Whil . . . 4F 111
Saundercroft Rd. EX5: Broadc . . . 1C 68
Saunders Wlk. PL6: Plym . . . 4J 131
Saunders Way EX15: Cull . . . 3J 45
TQ7: W Cha . . . 7K 157
SAUNTON . . . 3A 160
Saunton Cl. EX33: Brau . . . 4H 15
Saunton Down Viewpoint . . . 3A 160
Saunton Golf Course . . . 3A 160
Saunton Rd. EX33: Brau, Saunt . . . 3F 15
Savage Rd. PL5: Plym . . . 3B 134
Savery Cl. PL21: Ivy . . . 3J 145
Savery Ter. PL4: Plym . . . 7B 136
Savile Rd. EX4: Exe . . . 7C 64
The Savoy Cinema . . . *6C 76*
(off Rolle St.)
Savoy Hill EX4: Whip . . . 2K 65
The Savoy M. EX36: S Mol . . . 6D 26
Sawmill Cl. TQ9: Tot . . . 7F 103
Saw Mill Ct. *EX31: B'aple* . . . *3E 18*
(off Mills Way)
Sawmill La. EX9: E Bud . . . 1B 82
Sawmills Way EX14: Hon . . . 4F 55
Sawpit La. TQ9: Darti . . . 4B 102
Sawrey St. PL1: Plym . . . 5A 8 (3G 141)
Sawyer Dr. TQ14: Teignm . . . 2F 107
Sawyers Cl. TQ13: More . . . 6G 61
Saxon Av. EX4: Pin . . . 2D 66
Saxon Cl. EX17: Cred . . . 7J 39
Saxon Hgts. TQ5: Brixh . . . 4E 122
Saxon Mdw. TQ4: Coll M . . . 2C 118
Saxon Rd. EX1: Heav . . . 6J 65
PL19: Tavi . . . 3G 59
Saxons Cft. EX32: B'aple . . . 6H 19
Saxon Way EX15: Cull . . . 2H 45
TQ12: Kingst . . . 5J 105
Scalders La. PL21: Modb . . . 7G 147
Scalwell La. EX12: Seat . . . 3E 86
Scalwell Mead EX12: Seat . . . 3E 86
Scalwell Pk. EX12: Seat . . . 3E 86
Scanniclift Copse Nature Reserve
. . . 2K 63
Scarborough Pl. TQ2: Torq . . . 1B 116
Scarborough Rd. TQ2: Torq . . . 1B 116
Scarsdale EX8: Exmth . . . 7E 76
Scattor Vw. EX6: Bridf . . . 1F 63
Scholars Wlk. TQ7: Kingsb . . . 3G 157
School Cl. EX16: Bam . . . 2G 33
(not continuous)
EX31: Frem . . . 6F 17
PL7: Plymp . . . 2A 138
PL19: Tavi . . . 4K 59
School Cotts. TQ12: Teign . . . 3D 104
School Ct. TQ6: Dartm . . . 6D 124
School Dr. PL6: Plym . . . 3E 132
School Gdns. TQ10: S Bre . . . 1B 100
School Hill EX5: Whim . . . 6G 53
EX6: Cockw . . . 3E 96
EX7: Daw . . . 4G 97
EX8: Lymp . . . 6G 75
TQ9: Sto G . . . 4B 120
School Hill Cotts. *TQ9: Sto G* . . . *4B 120*
(off School Hill)
School Ho. Gdns. TQ7: Lodd . . . 2G 151
School La. EX2: Cou W . . . 4K 71
EX5: Broadc . . . 5C 52
EX5: Thor . . . 2B 50
EX6: Ted M . . . 6J 49
EX8: Exmth . . . 3D 76
EX10: New P . . . 5H 81
EX11: W Hill . . . 3H 79
EX14: Hon . . . 3F 55
EX24: Colyt . . . 6C 88
EX32: B Taw . . . 6B 24
EX38: G Tor . . . 1B 30
EX39: Hart . . . 3J 27
PL7: Plymp . . . 5B 138
PL21: Corn . . . 6J 129
TQ9: Blacka . . . 2B 152
TQ14: Shal . . . 6G 107
School Rd. EX2: Exe . . . 7B 6 (1D 70)
EX5: Silv . . . 2H 51
EX20: Lyd . . . 5H 57
PL19: Whit . . . 7K 59
PL21: Erm . . . 2H 147
TQ6: Sto F . . . 2F 153
TQ12: Kingsk . . . 7J 109
TQ12: New A . . . 1F 109
TQ12: Teign . . . 3C 104
School Steps TQ6: Dartm . . . 2A 124
School St. EX10: Sidf . . . 1D 84
School Ter. *EX7: Daw* . . . *4G 97*
(off School Hill)
School Way EX20: Oke . . . 3B 48
Schooner's Ct. EX8: Exmth . . . 6A 76
Scoldens Cl. PL21: Modb . . . 7G 147
Sconner Rd. PL11: Torp . . . 1A 140
Scoresby Cl. TQ2: Torq . . . 1D 112
Score Vw. EX34: Ilfra . . . 5J 11
Scorhill Stone Circle . . . 2A 170
SCORRITON . . . 1D 175
Scott Av. EX2: Won . . . 2J 71
EX39: App . . . 3H 21
PL5: Plym . . . 3B 134
Scott Bus. Pk. PL2: Plym . . . 5F 135
Scott Cinemas
The Alexandra Cinema . . . 1E 108
The Central Cinema . . . 4E 18
The Radway Cinema . . . 6C 84
The Regent Cinema . . . 5J 91
The Savoy Cinema . . . *6C 76*
(off Rolle St.)
Scott Cl. TQ12: New A . . . 1F 109
Scott Dr. EX8: Exmth . . . 2D 76
Scott Memorial . . . 3E 140
Scott Rd. PL2: Plym . . . 5F 135
(Beacon Pk. Rd.)
PL2: Plym . . . 6G 135
(Bowers Rd.)
Scotts EX16: Bam . . . 3G 33
Scotts Cl. TQ7: Chur . . . 1B 156
Scotts Cotts. *PL9: Plyms* . . . *4E 142*
(off Millway Pl.)
Scott's La. DT6: Monk W . . . 1D 90
Scratch Face La. EX2: Ide . . . 3A 70
Scratchface La. EX39: Bide . . . 6B 22
Scratton Path *TQ12: E Ogw* . . . *4C 108*
(off Reynell Rd.)
Screechers Hill TQ13: Ashb . . . 3G 99
Scurfield Cl. EX33: Brau . . . 3J 15
SEA . . . 2D 167
Seabee Pl. EX14: Dunk . . . 4G 47
Seabee Wlk. EX2: Cou W . . . 4D 72
SEABOROUGH . . . 3D 167

Seabourne Ct. TQ4: Good 3J **119**
(off Alta Vista Rd.)
Seabrook Av. EX2: Cou W 6B **72**
Seabrook M. EX2: Cou W 6B **72**
Seacliff TQ14: Teignm 3K **107**
Seacroft Rd. PL5: Plym 1B **134**
Seafield Av. EX8: Exmth 2C **76**
Seafield Gdns. 6E **86**
Seafield La. EX10: Sidm 7B **84**
Seafield Pk. 5A **20**
Seafield Rd. EX10: Sidm 6B **84**
EX12: Seat 6E **86**
Seafields TQ4: Good 5J **119**
Sea Front TQ2: Torq 4A **116**
Sea Haven EX12: Seat 6F **87**
(off Harbour Rd.)
Sea Hill EX12: Beer 7C **86**
EX12: Seat 5E **86**
Sea King Cl. EX31: Bick 5J **17**
Seaking Rd. EX31: Frem 5F **17**
Sea La. TQ5: Brixh 4G **123**
Sea Lawn Ter. EX7: Daw 3J **97**
Seale Cl. TQ6: Dartm 5D **124**
Seapoint TQ14: Teignm 5H **107**
(off Strand)
Searle St. EX17: Cred 5H **39**
Searle Ter. EX39: Nort 5F **21**
Seascape TQ2: Torq 3B **116**
Seaside EX34: C Mar 5A **12**
The Seasons EX4: Whip 4B **66**
(off Summerway)
SEATON 5E **86** (1C **173**)
Seaton Av. PL4: Plym 7K **135**
Seaton Bus. Pk. PL6: Plym 7C **132**
Seaton Cl. TQ1: Torq 6F **113**
Seaton Down Cl. EX12: Seat 4D **86**
Seaton Down Hill EX12: Seat 3C **86**
Seaton Down Rd. EX12: Seat 5D **86**
SEATON JUNCTION 1C **173**
Seaton La. PL4: Plym 7K **135**
Seaton Marshes
Local Nature Reserve 4F **87**
Seaton Mus. 5F **87** (2C **173**)
Seaton Orchard PL7: Spa 1K **139**
Seaton Pl. PL2: Plym 6E **134**
Seaton Rd. EX13: Mus 7C **90**
EX24: Colyf 2F **87**
Seaton Stop
Seaton Tramway 5F **87** (1C **173**)
Seaton Tourist Information Centre
. . . . .5F **87** (2C **173**)
Seaton Tramway
Colyford Stop 1G **87** (1C **173**)
Colyton Stop 5E **88** (1C **173**)
Seaton Stop 5F **87** (1C **173**)
Seaton Way PL20: C'stone 6B **126**
SEATOWN 1D **173**
Sea Vw. EX34: Ilfra 4K **11**
Seaview EX39: A'sham 4A **22**
Sea Vw. Av. PL4: Plym 1K **9** (1B **142**)
Sea Vw. Dr. PL9: Wem 6B **148**
Sea Vw. Gdns. TQ7: Hope 2G **155**
Sea Vw. Pl. EX39: App 3H **21**
(off New Quay St.)
Sea Vw. Rd. EX39: Nort 5E **20**
Seaview Rd. TQ7: Thur 5C **154**
Sea Vw. Ter. EX10: Sidm 5B **84**
EX12: Beer 7B **86**
PL4: Plym 2J **9** (1A **142**)
TQ5: Brixh 2E **122**
(off Overgang Rd.)
TQ7: Thur 5C **154**
SEAVINGTON ST MARY 2D **167**
SEAVINGTON ST MICHAEL 2D **167**
Seaward Cl. EX12: Brans 6J **85**
Seaward Pk. EX3: Clyst G 7H **73**
Seaway Cl. TQ2: Torq 3A **116**
Seaway Cl. TQ2: Torq 3B **116**
TQ5: Brixh 4D **122**
Seaway Cres. TQ3: Pres 6K **115**
Seaway Gdns. TQ3: Pres 6K **115**
Seaway Head EX24: Colyt 7C **88**
Seaway La. TQ2: Tip J 2J **81**
TQ2: Torq 2K **115**
Seaway Rd. TQ3: Pres 6J **115**
Seckington Hamlet 1A **36**
Secmaton La. EX7: Daw 2H **97**
Secmaton Ri. EX7: Daw 1H **97**
Second Av. EX1: Heav 3K **7** (6J **65**)
EX2: Cou W 6B **72**
EX7: Daw 5F **97**
EX13: Axmin 2K **89**
PL1: Dev 2F **141**
PL2: Plym 4D **134**
PL9: Plyms 3H **143**
TQ1: Torq 5C **112**
TQ14: Teignm 4G **107**
Second Dr. TQ14: Teignm 3K **107**
(Burwood Pl.)
TQ14: Teignm 4H **107**
(Third Dr.)
Second Fld. La. EX33: Brau 5H **15**
Sector La. EX13: Axmin 4J **89**
Sedemuda Cl. EX10: Sidm 2B **84**
Sedemuda Rd. EX10: Sidm 2A **84**
Sedgeclaire Cl. EX1: Pin 3E **66**
Sedge Cl. PL21: Ivy 5H **145**

Sedley Way PL5: Plym 7J **131**
Sefton Av. PL4: Plym 1K **9** (7B **136**)
Sefton Cl. PL4: Plym 1B **142**
EX7: Daw 4G **97**
TQ1: Torq 6F **113**
Segrave Rd. PL2: Plym 6G **135**
Selborne Cl. EX33: Brau 5J **15**
(off Barton La.)
Selborne M. PL2: Dev 7E **134**
Seldon Cres. EX1: Pin 1E **66**
Seldons Cl. PL21: Ugb 6E **146**
Selkirk Rd. PL4: Plym 1K **135**
Seller's Wood Hill EX12: Brans 4J **85**
Sellick Av. TQ5: Brixh 5F **123**
SELLICK'S GREEN 2C **167**
Sellon Cl. PL1: Plym 4C **8** (2H **141**)
Selsden Cl. PL9: Elb 6K **143**
Senate Cl. EX8: Exmth 3G **77**
(off Senate Way)
Senate Way EX8: Exmth 3F **77**
Sendall's Way PL6: Plym 7A **132**
Sennen Pl. PL2: Dev 7D **134**
Sentry Cnr. EX39: Bide 4H **23**
Sentry La. EX32: B Taw 6B **24**
Sentrys Orchard EX6: Exmin 3D **74**
Sercombes Gdns. EX6: Star 1E **96**
Serge Ct. EX2: Exe 6D **6**
Serpell Cl. PL6: Plym 4K **131**
Sett Cl. TQ13: Bov T 4C **92**
Seven Acre La. EX33: Brau 5K **15**
Seven Acres EX5: Cran 4B **68**
Seven Acres Pk. EX33: Brau 5K **15**
SEVEN ASH 1B **166**
Seven Brethren Bank
EX31: B'aple 5E **18**
Seven Crosses Rd. EX16: Tive 6A **40**
Seven Hills Ho. TQ2: Torq 1C **116**
(off Burridge La.)
Seven Stars La. PL5: Tam F 4G **131**
Seventh St. EX32: B'aple 3E **18**
(off King Edward St.)
Seven Trees Ct.
PL4: Plym 1G **9** (1A **142**)
Severn Brethren Ind. Est.
EX31: B'aple 6E **18**
Severn Pl. PL3: Plym 6D **136**
Severn Rd. TQ2: Torq 6H **111**
Seymour Av. PL4: Plym 2J **9** (1A **142**)
PL4: Plym 4H **93**
Seymour Cvn. Pk. 4H **93**
(off Old Liverton Rd.)
Seymour Ct. EX8: Exmth 2D **76**
TQ9: Tot 6F **103**
(off Seymour Rd.)
Seymour Dr. PL3: Plym 6A **136**
TQ2: Torq 1C **112**
TQ6: Dartm 6C **124**
Seymour Ho. PL1: Dev 3E **140**
Seymour M. PL4: Plym 2K **9** (1B **142**)
Seymour Pl. PL3: Plym 6B **136**
Seymour Pl. PL1: Plym 2A **8** (1G **141**)
TQ9: Tot 6F **103**
Seymour Rd. EX8: Exmth 2D **76**
PL3: Plym 6A **136**
PL7: Plymp 5J **137**
TQ9: Tot 6F **103**
TQ12: New A 7E **104**
Seymour St. PL4: Plym 3G **9** (2K **141**)
Seymour Ter. EX16: Tive 4C **40**
TQ9: Tot 6F **103**
(off Bridgetown)
Seymour Vs. EX34: Wool 5C **10**
Shackhayes EX34: C Mar 5B **12**
Shackleton Cl. EX8: Exmth 2D **76**
Shackleton Ct. PL5: Plym 2J **135**
Shackleton Wlk.
TQ14: Teignm 1G **107**
SHADYCOMBE 3C **158**
Shadycombe Ct. TQ8: Salc 3C **158**
Shadycombe Rd. TQ8: Salc 2B **158**
Shady La. TQ6: Sto F 3H **153**
Shady Nook Cvn. Site 4H **105**
Shaftesbury Cl. EX7: Daw 4H **97**
(off Plantation Ter.)
Shaftesbury Cotts.
PL4: Plym 1G **9** (1K **141**)
Shaftesbury Ct.
PL4: Plym 2G **9** (1K **141**)
Shaftesbury Pl. PL4: Plym 2G **9**
(off Shaftesbury Cotts.)
TQ9: Tot 6E **102**
(off Maudlin Rd.)
Shaftesbury Rd. EX2: Exe 1D **70**
EX34: Ilfra 3J **11**
Shaftesbury Theatre 4G **97**
Shakespeare Cl. EX16: Tive 2D **40**
TQ2: Torq 7K **111**
Shakespeare Rd. EX2: Won 2J **71**
PL5: Plym 1G **135**
Shakespeare Way EX8: Exmth 7K **75**
SHALDON 6G **107** (3D **171**)
Shaldon Approach Golf Course . .7H **107**
Shaldon Bri. TQ14: Shal 5G **107**
Shaldon Cres. PL5: Plym 7G **131**
Shaldon Rd. TQ2: C'head 7A **106**
TQ12: New A 2H **109**
TQ14: Shal 6B **106**
(not continuous)
Shaldon Tourist Information Centre
. . . . .7H **107** (3D **171**)
Shaldon Zoo 7H **107** (3D **171**)
Shale Row EX1: Pin 3F **67**
Shales Rd. EX4: Pin 3B **66**
Shalford Ter. EX13: Whit 5A **90**
SHALLOWFORD 2D **161**
Shallowford Cl. PL6: Plym 3D **136**
Shallowford Rd. PL6: Plym 4D **136**
Shambles Dr. EX17: Cop 5C **38**
Shamrock Cl. EX39: W Ho 5D **20**
Shamwickshire Cl. EX39: Bide 4H **23**
Shand Pk. EX13: Axmin 4G **89**
Shapland Pl. EX16: Tive 6B **40**
Shapleys Gdns. PL9: Plyms 7H **143**
Shapley Tor Cl. TQ5: Brixh 6C **122**
Shapley Way TQ12: Live 4F **93**
Shapter Ct. EX8: Lit 5H **77**
Shapters Rd. PL4: Plym 6K **9** (3B **142**)
Shaptor & Furzeleigh Woods
Nature Reserve 1B **92**
Shaptor Vw. TQ13: Bov T 6A **92**
Shareford Way EX5: Rock 3C **68**
Sharkham Cl. TQ5: Brixh 5F **123**
Sharkham Dr. TQ5: Brixh 5F **123**
Sharkham Ho. TQ5: Brixh 5F **123**
Sharland's Ct. EX16: Tive 4D **40**
(off Gold St.)
Sharland's La. EX33: Brau 4H **15**
Sharlands Vw. EX1: Pin 3F **67**
Sharon Way PL6: Plym 5B **132**
Sharper La. TQ4: Shal 7E **106**
Sharpham Dr. TQ9: Tot 7F **103**
Sharpham Wines & Cheeses 2A **176**
Sharp Hill EX20: Oke 4B **48**
Sharpitor TQ8: Salc 7A **158**
Sharpitor Cl. TQ3: Pres 5F **115**
Sharpitor Gdns. PL2: Plym 4F **135**
Sharpitor Row TQ2: Dous 3K **127**
Sharpland La. EX33: Puts 1D **14**
Sharp Rock EX34: Mort 4A **10**
Sharp's Cl. TQ12: H'fld 2K **93**
Sharps Ct. EX8: Exmth 6A **76**
Sharp's Crest TQ12: H'fld 2K **93**
Sharp Tor Viewpoint 3D **175**
Sharrose Rd. PL9: Hooe 7C **142**
Shatford La. EX31: B'aple 1B **174**
Shauls Ct. EX1: Exe 2G **7**
Shaw Way PL9: Hooe 5A **142**
Shearers Way TQ13: Chud 1D **94**
Shearford Cl. EX31: B'aple 1F **19**
Shearford La. EX31: B'aple 1E **18**
Shearman Ct. EX2: Exe 6D **6** (7E **64**)
SHEARSTON 1C **167**
Shearwater Dr. TQ2: Torq 2K **111**
Shearwater Way EX12: Seat 5F **87**
Shearwood Cl. PL7: Plymp 5A **137**
SHEBBEAR 6J **29** (3C **163**)
Shedden Hill TQ2: Torq 2C **116**
SHEEPSTOR 1B **174**
Sheepstor Rd. PL6: Plym 2E **136**
SHEEPWASH 3C **163**
SHELDON 3B **166**
Sheldon La. EX6: Dodd 1K **63**
Shell Cl. PL6: Plym 2F **137**
Shelley Av. PL19: Tavi 4K **59**
TQ1: Torq 5C **112**
Shelley Cl. EX2: Exe 3D **70**
Shelley Way PL5: Plym 2C **134**
Shells La. EX24: Colyf 7D **88**
Shelly Ct. EX8: Exmth 6A **76**
EX20: S Zeal 2J **49**
Shelly Reach EX8: Exmth 6B **76**
Shelly Rd. EX8: Exmth 6A **76**
EX20: S Zeal 3J **49**
Shelston Tor Dr. TQ4: Paig 4F **119**
Shelton Pl. EX1: Heav 6J **65**
Shepherd Cl. TQ8: Salc 2E **118**
Shepherds Cl. EX3: Ebf 6E **74**
Shepherds Hill EX2: Cou W 4K **71**
(off Countess Wear Rd.)
Shepherd's La. TQ14: Teignm 1E **106**
Shepherds La. EX10: Col R 1J **83**
PL4: Plym 5H **9** (3A **142**)
Shepherds Mdw. EX19: Bea 3J **31**
EX39: A'sham 3A **22**
Sheppard Rd. EX4: Exe 2G **65**
Sheppards Row EX8: Exmth 5C **76**
SHEPTON BEAUCHAMP 2D **167**
Sherborne Cl. PL9: Elb 6K **143**
Sherborne La. DT7: Lym R 5K **91**
Sherborne Rd. TQ12: New A 1E **108**
Sherbrook Cl. EX9: Bud S 7B **82**
Sherbrook Hill EX9: Bud S 7B **82**
Shercroft Cl. EX5: Broadc 2K **67**
SHERFORD 3D **175**
Sherford Cres. PL5: Plym 7F **131**
PL9: Elb 5K **143**
Sherford Proposed Development
PL7: Plymp 7C **138**
Sherford Rd. PL9: Elb 5K **143**
Sherford Wlk. PL9: Elb 7K **143**
Sheridan Rd. EX4: Whip 4B **66**
PL5: Plym 2H **135**
Sherman Tank Memorial 3A **176**
Sherratt's Oak EX31: B'aple 2G **19**
Sherrell Pk. PL20: Bere A 2B **128**
Sherril Cl. PL9: Plyms 7G **143**

Sherwell Arc. PL4: Plym 2F **9**
Sherwell Hill TQ2: Torq 1K **115**
Sherwell La. PL4: Plym 2F **9** (1K **141**)
TQ2: Torq 1K **115**
Sherwell Pk. Rd. TQ2: Torq 1K **115**
Sherwell Ri. Sth. TQ2: Torq 1K **115**
Sherwells Ct. EX7: Daw W 7D **96**
Sherwell Valley Rd. TQ2: Torq 7J **111**
Sherwill Cl. PL21: Ivy 3E **144**
Sherwood Cl. EX2: Won 7J **65**
Sherwood Dr. EX8: Exmth 1F **77**
SHERWOOD GREEN 1D **163**
Shetland Cl. TQ2: Torq 3A **112**
SHEVIOCK 2A **174**
The Shields EX34: Ilfra 4H **11**
(not continuous)
Shieling Rd. EX31: Bick 6J **17**
Shillands EX16: Tive 3B **40**
Shillingate Cl. EX7: Daw 6F **97**
SHILLINGFORD 1D **165**
SHILLINGFORD ABBOT 7D **70**
Shillingford Rd.
EX2: Alph, Shil A 6D **70**
SHILLINGFORD ST GEORGE 2D **171**
Shindle Pk. TQ7: Chil 6F **159**
SHINNER'S BRIDGE 2B **102** (1D **175**)
Shinners Bri. TQ9: Darti 2B **102**
Shinners Bri. Cen. TQ9: Darti 2B **102**
SHIPHAY 6J **111** (1A **176**)
Shiphay Av. TQ2: Torq 6J **111**
Shiphay La. TQ2: Torq 5J **111**
Shiphay Mnr. Dr. TQ2: Torq 6K **111**
Shiphay Pk. Rd. TQ2: Torq 6K **111**
Ship La. EX5: Clyst H 4J **67**
Shipley Cl. TQ10: S Bre 1C **100**
Shipley Rd. EX14: Hon 3G **55**
Shipley Wlk. PL6: Plym 2B **136**
Shirburn Rd. PL6: Plym 2C **136**
TQ1: Torq 6C **112**
Shire Cl. TQ4: Good 7G **119**
Shirehampton Ho. EX4: Exe 3B **6**
Shire La. DT7: Lym R 5G **91**
Shirley Cl. EX8: Exmth 1F **77**
Shirley Ct. TQ1: Torq 2F **117**
(off Torwood Gdns. Rd.)
Shirley Gdns. PL5: Plym 2H **135**
Shirley Towers TQ1: Torq 3D **116**
SHIRWELL 3B **160**
Shirwell Rd. EX31: B'aple, Shir 1F **19**
Shoalstone Pool 2H **123**
Shobbrook Rd. TQ12: New A 7B **104**
SHOBROOKE 3C **165**
Shooting Marsh Stile
EX2: Exe 7C **6** (1E **70**)
SHOP
EX22 . . . . .2B **162**
EX23 . . . . .2A **162**
The Shops at Dartington 2B **102**
SHOREDITCH 1C **167**
Shorelands Rd. EX31: B'aple 6C **18**
Shorelands Way EX31: B'aple 6C **18**
Sherwood Way EX39: W Ho 5D **20**
The Shore Line EX12: Seat 6G **87**
Shoreside TQ14: Shal 6G **107**
Shorland Cl. EX7: Daw 2J **97**
Shorneywell TQ7: Chil 6G **159**
SHORTACOMBE 2D **169**
Shortacombe Dr. EX33: Brau 3G **15**
Short Cl. EX39: Bide 3C **22**
Short Cotts. PL11: Torp 1A **140**
Shovel Down Stone Rows 2A **170**
Shoulsbury Castle 3D **161**
Shrewsbury Av. TQ2: Torq 4C **112**
Shrewsbury Rd. PL5: Plym 6G **131**
Shrinkhill La. EX16: Tive 5D **40**
The Shrubbery EX3: Top 5B **74**
EX13: Axmin 4H **89**
(off West St.)
EX20: Exbo 5J **35**
Shrubbery Cl. EX32: B'aple 6H **19**
SHUTE
EX13 . . . . .1C **173**
EX17 . . . . .3C **165**
Shute TQ7: Malb 6G **155**
Shute Barton 1C **173**
Shutecombe Ter. PL20: Bere F 6D **128**
Shute Hill TQ7: Malb 6G **155**
TQ14: Bi'ton 3C **106**
TQ14: Teignm 4J **107**
Shute Hill Cres. TQ14: Teignm 4J **107**

Shute La. EX19: Wink 3C **36**
   (not continuous)
   EX34: C Mar 6B **12**
   TQ12: Den 2H **101**
   TQ13: More 6J **61**
Shute Mdw. St. EX8: Exmth 5C **76**
   (off Meadow St.)
Shute Pk. TQ7: Malb 6G **155**
Shute Pk. Rd. PL9: Plyms 7G **143**
Shute Rd. EX13: Kilm 2A **88**
   EX13: Whit 5A **90**
   TQ7: Tot 6F **103**
Shutes Mead EX11: Ott M 3D **80**
Shuttern Cl. EX5: New C 7D **50**
Shutterton La. EX7: Daw, Daw W . . .7C **96**
Sicklemans Cl. TQ7: W Cha 7K **157**
SID 5D 84 (2B **172**)
Sidborough Hill EX17: Morc 4C **38**
SIDBURY 2H 85 (1B **172**)
Sidbury Cl. EX1: Sow 5C **66**
Sidcliffe EX10: Sidm 4D **84**
Siddalls Gdns. EX16: Tive 4E **40**
Sideling Flds. EX16: Tive 6F **41**
SIDFORD 1D 84 (1B **172**)
Sidford High St.
   EX10: Sidf, Stow 2A **84**
Sidford Rd. EX10: Sidm 4C **84**
Sidgard Rd. EX10: Sidm 4D **84**
Siding Rd. PL4: Plym 1D 8 (1J **141**)
Sidlands EX10: Sidm 6B **84**
Sidleigh EX10: Sidm 5D **84**
Sidmount Gdns. EX10: Sidm 5B **84**
SIDMOUTH 7C 84 (2B **172**)
Sidmouth Cotts. PL4: Plym 1J **9**
Sidmouth Golf Course 7A 84 (2B **172**)
Sidmouth Information Centre
   . . . . .7C 84 (2B **172**)
Sidmouth Leisure Cen. 3D **84**
Sidmouth Mus. 7C 84 (2B **172**)
Sidmouth Rd. DT7: Lym R 5G **91**
   EX2: Sow 1E **72**
   EX2: Sow, Won 7B **66**
   EX5: Clyst M 3G **73**
   (not continuous)
   EX11: Ott M, Wigg 4D **80**
   EX14: Hon 5D **54**
   EX24: Colyt 6C **88**
Sidmouth Swimming Pool 7C **84**
Sidney Ct. EX7: Daw 3F **7**
   (off Old Town St.)
Sidney Wlk. TQ4: Good 6H **119**
Sid Pk. Rd. EX10: Sidm 5C **84**
Sid Rd. EX10: Sidm 6C **84**
Sid Vale Cl. EX10: Sidf 1D **84**
Sid Vale M. EX10: Sidf 1D **84**
   (off Sid Vale Cl.)
Sidwell Ho. EX1: Exe 3F **7**
Sidwell St. EX4: Exe 3F 7 (6F **65**)
SIGFORD .3B **170**
Sigford Rd. EX2: Mar B 5G **71**
Signal Ct. EX33: Brau 5J **15**
The Signals EX14: Fen 2G **53**
Signal Ter. EX3: B'aple 5D **18**
Silbury Pl. EX17: Cred 6H **39**
Silford Cross EX39: W Ho 7B **20**
Silford Rd. EX39: Nort 7D **20**
Silvan Dr. EX33: Brau 3K **15**
Silverberry Cl. EX1: Whip 5B **66**
Silver Birch Cl. EX2: Won 2K **71**
   PL6: Plym 3D **132**
Silver Birch Ct. EX31: Rou 7B **18**
Silver Birch Vw. EX32: B'aple 3G **19**
Silver Bri. Cl. TQ4: Good 7J **119**
Silverdale EX5: Silv 1H **51**
   (not continuous)
   EX8: Exmth 1G **77**
Silverdown Office Pk.
   EX5: Clyst H 7C **68**
Silverhill TQ7: Malb 6G **155**
Silverhills Rd. TQ12: New A 4G **109**
Silveridge La. TQ7: Lodd 1K **151**
Silver La. EX4: Exe 1H 7 (5G **65**)
   EX5: Rock 4F **69**
Silver Lea EX13: Kilm 2B **88**
The Silvers EX3: Top 3E **72**
Silver Stream Way PL8: Brixt 2J **149**
Silver St. DT7: Lym R 5H **91**
   EX5: Thor 2B **50**
   EX11: Ott M 3C **80**
   EX13: Axmin 4H **89**
   EX13: Kilm 2B **88**
   EX14: Hon 3F **55**
   EX15: Culm 3A **46**
   EX15: Kent 6B **46**
   EX15: Will 4D **44**
   EX16: Bam 2H **33**
   EX16: Tive 4D **40**
   EX20: Lyd 6H **57**
   EX24: Colyt 5D **88**
   EX32: B'aple 4E **18**
   EX33: Brau 3J **15**
   EX34: Ber 3C **12**
   EX39: App 3H **21**
   EX39: Bide 4F **23**
   PL20: Bere F 7C **128**
   TQ11: B'leigh 4C **98**
   TQ12: Ipp 7G **101**

Silver Ter. EX4: Exe 3C 6 (6E **64**)
   PL10: Millb 6A **140**
SILVERTON 1H 51 (3D **165**)
Silverton Ri. EX14: Fen 2H **53**
Silverton Rd. EX2: Mar B 5G **71**
Silverwell Pk. PL21: Modb 6G **147**
Silverwood Av. TQ12: New A 3H **109**
Silverwood Hgts. EX32: B'aple 3G **19**
Simcoe Cl. EX15: Hemy 2F **47**
Simcoe Way EX14: Dunk 7G **47**
Simey Cl. EX4: Exe 5C **64**
Simmonds Pl. EX15: Cull 3K **45**
Simmons Cl. EX20: Oke 3C **48**
Simmons Park 4B **48**
Simmons Way EX20: Oke 4C **48**
Simmons Cl. PL9: Plyms 6F **143**
SIMONSBATH 3D **161**
Simpson Farm Nature Trail 3B **162**
Sinai Hill EX35: Lynt 2G **13**
Singer Cl. TQ3: Paig 2G **119**
Singmore Rd. TQ3: Marl 4E **114**
Sings La. EX33: Brau 5J **15**
Sir Alex Wlk. EX3: Top 7C **72**
Sir Christopher Ondaatje
   Indoor Cricket Cen. 3E **64**
Sir John Hawkins Sq. PL1: Plym 5F **9**
Sir John Hunt Sports Cen. 6J **131**
Sir Leonard Rogers Cl.
   PL3: Plym 5A **136**
Siskin Chase EX15: Cull 5F **45**
Sisna Pk. Rd. PL6: Plym 6F **133**
Sithney St. PL5: Plym 2B **134**
Sivell Ct. EX2: Heav 7J **65**
   (off Sivell Pl.)
Sivell M. EX2: Heav 7J **65**
   (off Sivell Pl.)
Sivell Pl. EX2: Heav 7J **65**
Six Mile Hill EX6: Dunsf 6E **62**
   EX6: Ted M 6J **49**
Six O'Clock La. PL7: Plymp 5B **138**
Skardale Gdns. PL6: Plym 3E **136**
Skelmersdale Cl. TQ7: Kingsb 4G **157**
Skern Cl. EX39: Nort 4E **20**
Skern Lodge Activity Cen. 2G **21**
Skern Way EX39: Nort 4E **20**
Skerries Rd. PL6: Plym 3A **132**
SKILGATE .1D **165**
Skinner Cl. EX16: Tive 4B **40**
   (off Shortridge Mead)
Skinners Cl. EX10: Sidm 2A **84**
Skirhead La. EX34: C Mar 7D **12**
Skye Cl. TQ2: Torq 3A **112**
Skylark EX7: Daw W 7D **96**
Skylark Ri. PL6: Plym 2F **133**
   PL19: Whit 7K **59**
Skylark Spinney EX31: Rou 7K **17**
Skyways Bus. Pk. EX5: Clyst H 7C **68**
Slade EX39: Bide 3D **22**
Sortridge Pk. PL20: Horr 1D **126**
Slade Cl. EX11: Ott M 3E **80**
   PL9: Plyms 7H **143**
Slade La. TQ5: Galm 3H **121**
   TQ12: A'well 6D **108**
   (not continuous)
Slade Rd. EX11: Ott M 4E **80**
   EX34: Ilfra 5G **11**
Slade Valley Rd. EX34: Ilfra 4G **11**
Sladnor Pk. Rd. TQ1: Maid 2H **113**
Slanns Mdw. TQ12: Kingst 5G **105**
Slapper's Hill TQ5: Hill 3K **125**
SLAPTON 2J 159 (3A **176**)
Slapton Ley Field Cen. 2J **159**
Slapton Ley National
   Nature Reserve 4J 159 (3A **176**)
Slapton Ley Nature Trail . . . . (3A **176**)
Slapton Monument 3K 159 (3A **176**)
Slatelands Cl. PL7: Plymp 6E **138**
Slate La. PL1: Plym 3G **141**
Sleap Hill EX9: E Bud 6F **83**
Sleepy Hollow EX2: Cou W 4D **72**
   (off Moon Ridge)
Sleepy La. TQ3: Pres 5G **115**
Slewton Cres. EX5: Whim 5G **53**
Slip Ct. EX31: Rou 7K **17**
Slipperstone Dr. PL21: Ivy 3E **144**
Slittercombe La. EX6: Kenton 5J **95**
Sloe La. EX32: Land 2C **24**
SLONCOMBE 2B **170**
SLOUGH GREEN 1C **167**
Sluggett Pl. EX1: Pin 1D **66**
Smallack Cl. PL6: Plym 1A **136**
Smallack Dr. PL6: Plym 1A **136**
Smallacombe Rd. EX16: Tive 4B **40**
SMALLBROOK 5A 50 (1C **171**)
Smallcombe Rd. TQ3: Paig 6E **114**
Smalldon La. TQ1: Torq 2D **112**
Small La. EX5: Broadc 5C **52**
SMALLRIDGE 3D **167**
Smallridge Cl. PL9: Plyms 7G **143**
Smallwell La. TQ3: Marl 3B **114**
Smardon Av. TQ5: Brixh 3C **122**
Smardon Cl. TQ5: Brixh 3C **122**
SMEATHARPE 2C **167**
Smeaton Sq. PL3: Plym 5E **136**
Smeaton's Tower 7D 8 (4J **141**)
Smithaleigh Cvn. & Camping Pk.
   . . . . .6K **139**
Smithay Mdws. EX6: Chri 3J **63**

Smith Ct. TQ1: Torq 7B **112**
Smith Fld. Rd. EX2: Alph 5D **70**
Smithfields TQ9: Tot 6C **102**
Smith Hill TQ14: Bi'ton 3B **106**
SMITHINCOTT 2A **166**
Smiths Ct. EX2: Exe 1E **70**
Smith St.
   TQ6: Dartm 1B 124 (6F **125**)
Smithys Way EX16: Sam P 2B **42**
Smockpark La. PL9: Wem 4C **148**
Smokey Ho. Caravans 4E **114**
Smoky Ho. La. EX31: B'aple 1G **19**
Smugglers Cl. EX12: Brans 6J **85**
Smugglers La. EX7: Holc 2G **97**
Smythen St. EX1: Exe 5D 6 (7E **64**)
SNAPPER .3B **160**
Snowberry Cl. TQ1: Torq 6B **112**
Snowdonia Cl. TQ4: Coll M 3D **118**
Snowdrop Cl. EX14: Hon 5D **54**
Snowdrop M. EX4: Exe 4A **64**
Soap St. PL1: Plym 6A 8 (3G **141**)
Soby M. TQ13: Bov T 6B **92**
Sog's La. EX11: Ven O 2H **81**
Solar Cres. EX4: Exe 1C **70**
SOLDON CROSS 2B **162**
Soloman Dr. EX39: Bide 4F **23**
Solsbro M. TQ2: Torq 2A **116**
Solsbro Rd. TQ2: Torq 2A **116**
Somer Flds. DT7: Lym R 5G **91**
Somerlea EX15: Will 3D **44**
Somerset Av. EX4: Exe 1B **70**
Somerset Cotts. PL3: Plym 7F **135**
Somerset Ct. TQ5: Brixh 3F **123**
   (off Mt. Pleasant Rd.)
Somerset Pl. EX31: B'aple 4E **18**
   (off Wells St.)
   PL3: Plym 7F **135**
   TQ9: Tot 6F **103**
   TQ14: Teignm 5H **107**
Somerset Pl. La. PL3: Plym 7F **135**
Somers Rd. DT7: Lym R 5H **91**
Somerville Cl. EX33: Croy 3C **14**
Somerville Cl. EX8: Exmth 3F **77**
   EX15: Will 3C **44**
Somerville Pk. EX15: Will 3C **44**
Somerville Rd. EX15: Will 4C **44**
Somerwell La. EX16: W'ridge 7G **33**
Sommers' Cres. EX34: Ilfra 2J **11**
Sonnet Cl. PL5: Plym 1H **135**
Soper Rd. TQ14: Teignm 2G **107**
Soper's Hill PL5: Tam F 1K **131**
Soper Wlk. TQ14: Teignm 2G **107**
Sophia Way TQ12: New A 2D **108**
Sorrell Ct. TQ12: Kingst 4G **105**
Sorrel Pl. TQ12: New A 6A **104**
Sorrento TQ1: Torq 1E **116**
Sourton Quarry
   (Conservation Area) 2K **57**
Sourton Sq. PL9: Plyms 3E **142**
SOUTH ALLINGTON 3D **175**
South Av. DT7: Lym R 4J **91**
   EX1: Heav 3K 7 (6H **65**)
   EX39: Bide 4J **23**
Sth. Bank Dr. EX39: Bide 3E **22**
Sth. Bay Holiday Pk. 6F **123**
SOUTH BOWOOD 1D **173**
Sth. Brent Rd. TQ7: Lodd 2G **151**
SOUTHBROOK 2A **92**
Southbrook Cl. TQ13: Bov T 3B **92**
Southbrook La. EX5: Whim 1F **69**
   TQ13: Bov T 3A **92**
   (not continuous)
Southbrook Mdw. EX5: Rock 2F **69**
Southbrook Rd. EX2: Cou W 3K **71**
   TQ13: Bov T 3B **92**
Sth. Burrow Rd. EX34: Ilfra 3H **11**
SOUTH CHARD 3D **167**
Sth. Church La. EX20: Oke 4A **48**
Southcliffe EX32: B Taw 7B **24**
South Cl. EX33: Brau 5J **15**
   (off South St.)
Southcombe St. TQ13: Chag 2H **61**
Southcombe Ter. EX12: Axmth 3J **87**
SOUTH COMMON 3D **167**
Southcote Orchard TQ9: Tot 6G **103**
SOUTHCOTT
   EX20 .1D **169**
   EX38 .2C **163**
   EX39 .1J **23**
Southcott Rd. EX39: Bide 1E **22**
Sth. Devon Coast Path
   TQ14: Shal 6H **107**
Sth. Devon M. TQ12: New A 1G **109**
South Devon Railway
   Buckfastleigh Station
   . . . . .4E 98 (1D **175**)
   Totnes Riverside Station
   . . . . .4E 102 (1A **176**)
South Devon Railway Mus. 4E **98**
South Devon Tennis Cen. 5G **145**
SOUTHDOWN 6A **140**
Southdown Av. TQ5: Brixh 6D **122**

Southdown Cl. EX12: Beer 7B **86**
   TQ5: Brixh 6D **122**
Southdown Hill TQ5: Brixh 6D **122**
Southdown Quay 6A **140**
Sth. Down Rd. PL2: Plym 5G **135**
Southdown Rd. EX12: Beer 7B **86**
   PL10: Millb 6A **140**
   TQ5: Brixh 7D **122**
South Dr. EX38: G Tor 2A **30**
Southella Rd. PL20: Yelv 6G **127**
South Emb.
   TQ6: Dartm 2B 124 (6F **125**)
End Cl. EX33: Brau 5J **15**
SOUTHERLY 2D **169**
Southern Cl. PL2: Plym 4E **134**
   TQ2: Torq 1C **112**
Southern Gdns. EX34: C Mar 6B **12**
   (off Valley La.)
Southernhay EX19: Wink 3C **36**
   TQ12: New A 2F **109**
Southernhay E. EX1: Exe 5E 6 (7F **65**)
   (not continuous)
Southernhay Gdns.
   EX1: Exe 4F 7 (6F **65**)
   (not continuous)
Southernhay W. EX1: Exe 5F 7 (7F **65**)
   (not continuous)
Southern Rd. EX8: Exmth 4C **76**
Southern Ter. PL4: Plym 1H 9 (7A **136**)
Southernway PL9: Plyms 5H **143**
Southern Wood EX8: Exmth 2G **77**
Southey Cres. TQ12: Kingsk 2G **111**
Southey Dr. TQ12: Kingsk 2G **111**
Southey La. TQ12: Kingsk 1G **111**
Sth. Farm Rd. EX9: Bud S 5D **82**
Southfield TQ7: W Alv 5D **156**
   (off Longfields)
   TQ9: Berr P 5K **103**
Southfield Av. TQ3: Pres 5F **115**
Southfield Cl. TQ3: Pres 6F **115**
Southfield Dr. EX17: Cred 5G **39**
Southfield Ri. TQ3: Paig 5G **115**
Southfield Rd. EX39: Bide 4H **23**
   TQ3: Paig 7G **115**
Southfield Way EX16: Tive 4A **40**
Sth. Ford Rd.
   TQ6: Dartm 1A 124 (6E **124**)
Southfork Caravan Park 2D **167**
Sth. Furzeham Rd. TQ5: Brixh 3E **122**
Southgate EX2: Exe 6E 6 (7F **65**)
Southgate Av. PL9: Plyms 7F **143**
Southgate Cl. PL9: Plyms 7F **143**
Southgate Ct. EX2: Exe 7F **65**
   (off Holloway St.)
Sth. Grange EX2: Sow 2C **72**
South Grn. EX32: B'aple 5G **19**
Sth. Hams Bus. Pk. TQ7: Chur 1C **156**
Sth. Hayes PL21: Modb 6G **147**
   (off Church St.)
Sth. Hayes Copse EX32: Land 2C **24**
Sth. Hayes Mdw. EX5: Cran 4B **68**
SOUTH HILL 3B **168**
Sth. Hill PL1: Plym 1F **141**
   PL9: Hooe 7D **142**
Sth. Hill Rd. TQ1: Torq 2E **116**
SOUTH HOLE 1A **162**
SOUTH HUISH 1K 155 (3C **175**)
SOUTH KNIGHTON 3C **171**
Southland Pk. Cres. PL9: Wem 6B **148**
Southland Pk. Rd. PL9: Wem 7B **148**
Southlands EX1: Heav 4K 7 (6H **65**)
   EX33: Brau 5J **15**
   (off Exeter Rd.)
   EX33: Wraf 6K **15**
Southlands Rd. TQ2: Torq 1B **116**
South La. EX39: Hart 3J **27**
Sth. Lawn EX2: Exe 5G **7**
   EX10: Sidm 2D **84**
Sth. Lawn Ter. EX1: Heav 6J **65**
Southlea EX39: Nort 6D **20**
South Lea Cl. EX33: Brau 5K **15**
SOUTHLEIGH 1C **173**
Southley Rd. EX36: S Mol 6C **26**
SOUTH MILTON 7A 156 (3D **175**)
Sth. Milton St. PL4: Plym . . .6K 9 (3B **142**)
SOUTH MOLTON 6C 26 (1B **164**)
South Molton & District Mus.
   . . . . .6C 26 (1B **164**)
Sth. Molton Rd. EX16: Bam 2F **33**
Sth. Molton St. EX18: Chul 5C **32**
South Molton Swimming Pool 6D **26**
South Molton Tourist Info. Cen. 6C **26**
Southolme Ter. EX39: Bide 3G **23**
South Pde. EX9: Bud S 7D **82**
South Pk. EX32: B'aple 6G **19**
   EX33: Brau 5K **15**
   EX39: Wools 3B **28**
South Parks Rd. TQ2: Torq 3B **112**
SOUTH PETHERTON 2D **167**
SOUTH PETHERWIN 2B **168**
South Pier TQ7: Kingsb 4G **157**
   (off Promenade)
SOUTH POOL 3D **175**
Southport Av. EX4: Exe 7B **64**
Sth. Quay TQ4: Paig 2J **119**
SOUTH RADWORTHY 3D **161**

South Rd. EX39: App 3H 21
  TQ12: New A 2E 108
SOUTH SANDS 6A 158
Sth. Sands TQ4: Good 5J 119
  TQ8: Salc 6A 158
South Sands Sailing 6A 158
Southside Ope PL1: Plym 6F 9
Southside St. PL1: Plym . . .6F 9 (3K 141)
South Sq. EX24: Colyt 7C 88
South St. EX1: Exe 4D 6 (6E 64)
  EX8: Exmth 6C 76
  EX13: Axmin 4H 89
  EX19: Dol 6H 31
  EX19: Wink 2C 36
  EX20: Hath 2H 35
  EX24: Colyt 6D 88
  EX32: B'aple 7G 19
  (not continuous)
  EX33: Brau 6J 15
  EX34: Wool 6A 10
  EX36: S Mol 6C 26
  EX38: G Tor 2B 30
  TA21: Holc R 2G 43
  TQ2: Torq 1B 116
  TQ9: Tot 6E 102
  TQ12: Den 2H 101
SOUTH TAWTON 1J 49 (1A 170)
South Ter. EX8: Lymp 6H 75
SOUTH TOWN 7K 95 (2D 171)
Sth. Town EX6: Kenton 6K 95
  TQ6: Dartm 7F 125
South Vw. EX15: Hemy 2G 47
  EX16: Tive 4D 40
  EX20: Lyd 6H 57
  EX31: B'aple 2C 18
  EX31: Brat F 6J 13
  EX32: B Taw 3A 24
  EX33: Brau 6J 15
  EX34: Ilfra 4F 11
  EX37: C'ton 6H 25
  PL5: Plym 1K 135
  PL7: Hem 2F 139
  PL8: Brixt 2H 149
  PL9: Elb 6J 143
  PL19: Mary T 2B 60
  PL20: Horr 2E 126
  PL21: Lutt 7G 129
  TQ12: A'well 6E 108
  TQ13: Bov T 4C 92
  (off Old Orchard)
  TQ14: Teignm 5H 107
Southview TA21: Holc R 1G 43
South Vw. Cl. EX15: Will 3D 44
  EX33: Brau 6J 15
  PL7: Plymp 2A 138
South Vw. Est. EX15: Will 3C 44
South Vw. Pk. PL7: Plymp 2A 138
South Vw. Pasture EX5: Cran 4B 68
South Vw. Rd. EX15: Will 3D 44
Southview Rd. TQ3: Paig 7G 115
South Vw. Ter. EX4: Exe . .1G 7 (4G 65)
  EX6: Exmin 2D 74
  EX15: Will 3D 44
  EX39: Bide 3E 22
  PL4: Plym 3K 9 (2B 142)
Southville Gdns. TQ7: Kingsb 6G 157
South Wlk. EX32: B'aple 5F 19
Southwater Ct. TQ7: Kingsb 5G 157
SOUTHWAY 3B 132
Southway EX6: Ted M 7J 49
  EX10: Sidm 6D 84
Southway Av. TQ2: Torq 4B 112
Southway Dr. PL6: Plym 5J 131
Southway La. PL6: Plym 4H 131
  (Coombe La.)
  PL6: Plym 3C 132
  (Lulworth Dr.)
Southway Valley Local Nature Reserve
  . . . . .4A 132
Southwell PL6: Plym 3K 135
SOUTH WHEATLEY 1A 168
Southwood Ct. TQ1: Torq 1E 116
Southwood Dr. EX39: Bide 2F 23
Southwood Mdws. EX39: Buck B 2A 20
Sth. Yd. Way PL1: Dev 2D 140
SOUTH ZEAL 2J 49 (1A 170)
Sovereign Cl. EX8: Exmth 3G 77
Sovereign Ct. EX2: Sow 2C 72
  PL7: Plymp 6K 137
Sovereign Ho. TQ1: Torq 2D 116
  (off The Terrace)
Sovereign M. TQ1: Torq 3D 112
Sowden La. EX8: Lymp 7F 75
  EX32: B'aple 4G 19
  (not continuous)
Sowden Pk. EX32: B'aple 5H 19
SOWTON 6G 67 (1D 171)
Sowton Ind. Est. EX2: Sow 7D 66
  (not continuous)
Sowton La. EX5: Sow 2J 73
Sowton Park & Ride 1D 72
Spa Ct. TQ1: Torq 2E 116
Sparkatown La. PL20: Dous 5K 127
Sparke Cl. PL7: Plymp 5E 138
Sparkhays Dr. TQ9: Tot 7F 103
Sparks Barn Rd. TQ4: Paig 3H 119
SPARKWELL 1J 139 (2B 174)
Sparkwell Golf Course . . .1K 139 (2B 174)

Sparrow Pk. TQ7: Malb 6H 155
Sparrow Rd. TQ9: Tot 6D 102
Sparrows Row EX20: Oke 3B 48
Speakers Rd. PL21: Ivy 4J 145
Spearfield Cl. EX36: S Mol 6D 26
Speculation Cotts. PL8: Y'ton 2A 150
  (off Underhay)
Speedwell Cl. EX32: B'aple 6K 19
  EX39: Bide 5E 22
  TQ5: Brixh 5E 122
  TQ12: New A 6A 104
Speedwell Cres. PL6: Plym 4B 136
Speedwell Units TQ6: Dartm 6C 124
Speedwell Wlk. PL6: Plym 4C 136
Spencer Cl. EX8: Exmth 2G 77
Spencer Ct. EX11: Ott M 4C 80
  (off St Saviours Rd.)
Spencer Dr. TQ12: New A 6F 41
Spencer Rd. PL9: Plyms 4F 143
  TQ3: Paig 1E 118
  TQ12: New A 2F 109
Spenser Av. EX2: Won 2J 71
Speranza Gro. TQ14: Teignm 4H 107
Spicer Cl. EX15: Cull 5G 45
Spicer Rd. EX1: Exe 5G 7 (7G 65)
Spider's La. EX8: Exmth 1E 76
Spindlebury EX15: Cull 5F 45
Spindle Cres. PL7: Plymp 4E 138
Spindlewood Cl. EX14: Hon 6F 55
Spinnaker Quay PL9: Hooe 5A 142
Spinnakers EX8: Exmth 6A 76
  (off Shelly Rd.)
The Spinney EX15: Uff 5H 43
  PL7: Plymp 5D 138
  PL21: Ivy 4E 144
Spinney Cl. EX2: Won 1B 72
  EX31: Bick 7K 17
Spinning Path EX4: Exe 1H 7
Spinning Path Gdns. EX17: Cred 7H 39
Spinster's Rock Burial Chamber . . .1B 170
Spion Kop Steps TQ8: Salc 4C 158
  (off Bennett Rd.)
Spire Ct. PL3: Plym 5C 136
Spitfire Av. EX5: Clyst H 4K 67
Spitfire Wlk. EX32: B'aple 6H 19
  (off Valley Cl.)
Spithead TQ6: Dartm 1B 124 (6F 125)
Spittis Pk. TQ6: Kingsw 6H 125
  (off Lwr. Contour Rd.)
Spittles La. DT7: Lym R 4K 91
Spitul La. EX10: Sidm 3A 84
Splashdown Quaywest Waterpark
  . . . . .4J 119
Splatford Dr. EX15: Cull 2H 45
SPLATT .2A 168
SPREYTON 1B 170
Spring Cl. EX39: Nort 6D 20
  TQ12: New A 7B 104
Spring Cotts. TQ9: Tot 5F 103
  (off Weston La.)
Springdale Cl. TQ5: Brixh 6E 122
Springfield 1A 36
Spring Fld. EX39: Hart 3H 27
Springfield EX14: Dunk 5H 47
  PL20: Horr 2F 127
  TQ12: Ipp 7H 101
Springfield Av. EX32: B'aple 6G 19
  PL9: Elb 6J 143
Springfield Cl. PL9: Elb 6J 143
Springfield Cres. EX31: Frem 5G 17
  EX39: Nort 5E 20
Springfield Dr. EX16: Tive 4B 40
  PL3: Plym 7F 135
  TQ7: Kingsb 5F 157
Springfield Gdns. EX7: Daw 1J 97
Springfield La. PL9: Elb 5J 143
Springfield Pk. EX20: Brid 3J 57
  TQ11: B'leigh 4E 98
Springfield Ri. PL9: Elb 5J 143
Springfield Rd. EX4: Exe 4G 65
  EX8: Exmth 3D 76
  EX14: Hon 4H 55
  EX31: Bick 6A 18
  EX34: Ilfra 3H 11
  EX34: Wool 6A 10
  PL9: Elb 6H 143
  TQ1: Torq 6D 112
  TQ10: S Bre 1B 100
Springfields EX24: Colyt 1F 87
Springfield Ter. EX34: C Mar 7B 12
  EX39: Bide 4G 23
  (off Grange Rd.)
  EX39: Nort 5B 20
  (off Diddywell Rd.)
  EX39: W Ho 5B 20
  TQ10: S Bre 1B 100
Spring Flower Av. EX32: B'aple 5H 19
Spring Gdns. EX11: Ott M 4D 80
Springhead DT7: Uply 3G 91
Springhead La. EX13: Kilm 2A 88
Spring Head Rd. DT7: Uply 1G 91
Spring Hill PL19: Tavi 4H 59
Springhill PL2: Plym 3H 135
Springhill Gdns. DT7: Lym R 4J 91
Springhill Grn. PL2: Plym 3H 135
Spring Hill Rd. TQ9: Tot 6G 103
Spring Pk. PL6: Plym 3F 133
Spring Rd. PL9: Down T, Wem 4D 148

Springwood Cl. PL7: Plymp 6D 138
  PL21: Ivy 4J 145
Spruce Cl. EX4: Whip 2A 66
  EX8: Exmth 1F 77
Spruce Pk. EX17: Cred 7H 39
Spruce Way TQ3: Paig 6E 114
Spry La. PL16: Lift 6D 56
Sprys Tenements PL20: Horr 1E 126
Spurge Rd. TQ12: New A 6A 104
Spurway Gdns. EX34: C Mar 7D 12
Spurway Hill EX6: Exmin 3B 74
Spurway Rd. EX16: Tive 5F 41
The Square EX4: Exe 4C 64
  EX5: Rock 4F 69
  EX5: Whim 6G 53
  EX10: Sidm 3A 84
  EX12: Beer 7B 86
  (off Fore St.)
  EX12: Seat 5E 86
  EX15: Uff 6H 43
  EX16: W'ridge 6H 33
  EX18: Chul 6C 32
  EX19: Dol 6G 31
  EX19: Wink 2C 36
  EX20: Mert 5B 30
  EX20: N Taw 6B 36
  EX21: Sheb 6H 29
  EX22: Bradw 5B 28
  EX22: Hols 2C 34
  EX31: Frem 6F 17
  EX32: B Taw 6B 24
  EX32: B'aple 4E 18
  EX32: Swim 2G 25
  EX33: Brau 4J 15
  EX36: N Mol 2C 26
  EX36: S Mol 6C 26
  (off Broad St.)
  EX37: C'ton 5J 25
  EX39: Hart 3H 27
  EX39: Nort 5E 20
  PL1: Plym 2F 141
  PL8: Holb 6C 150
  (off Brent Hill)
  PL20: Bere A 2C 128
  PL21: Erm 2H 147
  PL21: Lutt 7F 129
  PL21: Ugb 6E 146
  TQ6: Kingsw 6G 125
  TQ7: Hope 3G 155
  TQ13: Chag 2H 61
  TQ13: More 6H 61
Square's Quay TQ7: Kingsb 5G 157
Squires Cl. EX32: B'aple 7G 19
Squire's La. EX12: Axmth 5G 87
Squirrel Cl. PL6: Plym 6K 131
Stabb Cl. TQ4: Good 6G 119
Stabb Dr. TQ4: Good 6G 119
Stable Cotts. PL7: Plymp 4B 138
Stable La. TQ1: Torq 4D 112
  (off Havelock Rd.)
The Stables TQ9: Tot 5F 103
STADDISCOMBE 2B 174
Staddle Stone Rd. EX1: Pin 4E 66
STADDON 3B 162
Staddon Cl. EX4: Exe 5A 66
  EX33: Brau 4H 15
Staddon Ct. Cotts. PL9: Down T 2C 148
Staddon Cres. PL9: Plyms 6F 143
Staddon Gdns. TQ2: Torq 3D 112
Staddon Grn. PL9: Plyms 6E 142
Staddon Heights Golf Course
  . . . . .7B 142 (2A 174)
Staddon Pk. Rd. PL9: Plyms 7F 143
Staddon Rd. EX22: Hols 3E 34
  EX39: App 3G 21
Staddons Lea La. TQ2: Torq 7J 111
Staddons Vw. TQ13: Bov T 3B 92
Staddon Ter. La.
  PL1: Plym 2C 8 (1H 141)
Stadium Dr. TQ12: Kingsk 3G 111
Stadium Way EX4: Exe 1H 7 (5G 65)
Stadway Mdw. EX10: Sidm 5A 84
Staffick Cl. EX6: Kenton 6J 95
Stafford Cl. EX6: Chri 3J 63
Stafford Ct. TQ9: Tot 6G 103
Stafford La. EX24: Colyf 7C 88
Stafford Rd. EX4: Exe 7C 64
  EX19: Dol 6H 31
  TQ4: Paig 2J 119
Stafford Way EX19: Dol 6H 31
Staggers La. EX33: Wraf 7K 15
Stag La. PL9: Elb 4J 143
STAG'S HEAD 1A 164
Stallards EX33: Brau 3H 15
Stall Moor Stone Row 1C 175
Stamford Cl. PL9: Hooe 6B 142
Stamford Fort Cotts. PL9: Hooe 6B 142
  (off Stamford Rd.)
Stamford La. PL9: Hooe 7B 142
Stamford Rd. PL9: Hooe 6B 142
Stamps Hill PL8: Brixt 1H 149
STANBOROUGH CROSS 5K 143
Stanborough Rd.
  PL9: Elb, Plyms 5G 143
Stanbridge Pk. EX39: Bide 3C 22
Stanbury Av. PL6: Plym 2A 136
Stanbury Cl. PL15: St G 6C 34

Stanbury Copse EX34: Ilfra 4G 11
Stanbury Ct. EX17: Cred 6H 39
Stanbury Rd. EX33: Know 1K 15
  TQ2: Torq 6J 111
Standard Ct. PL19: Mary T 1B 60
Standarhay Cl. PL9: Elb 5K 143
Standarhay Vs. PL9: Elb 5K 143
Stanfield TQ1: Torq 1G 117
  (off Barrington Rd.)
Stanford Rd. EX2: Won 7B 66
Stangray Av. PL4: Plym 7J 135
Stanhope Cl. EX22: Hols 1C 34
Stanhope Dr. EX10: Sidm 4C 84
Stanhope Gdns. EX22: Hols 2C 34
Stanhope Rd. PL5: Plym 1B 134
Stanhope Sq. EX22: Hols 2C 34
Stanhope Ter. EX39: Bide 2F 23
Staniforth Dr. PL21: Ivy 5H 145
Stanley Ct. TQ1: Torq 5E 112
Stanley Gdns. TQ3: Paig 7F 115
Stanley M. EX9: Bud S 6C 82
Stanley Pl. PL4: Plym 2C 142
Stanley Rd. TQ1: Torq 5E 112
Stanley Sq. EX3: Top 6B 74
Stanley St. TQ14: Teignm 5H 107
Stanley Wlk. EX8: Exmth 1F 77
Stanmore Ri. EX7: Daw 3H 97
Stanmore Tor TQ3: Paig 2G 119
Stannary Bri. Rd. PL19: Tavi 3K 59
Stannary Cl. PL21: Ivy 4J 145
Stannary Ct. EX20: Oke 3D 48
  PL19: Tavi 4H 59
  (off Garden La.)
Stannary La. PL7: Plymp 4B 138
Stannary Pl. TQ13: Chag 3H 61
Stansfeld Av. TQ3: Paig 1G 119
Stantaway Hill TQ1: Torq 6B 112
  (off Stantaway Pk.)
Stantaway Pk. TQ1: Torq 6B 112
Stantor La. TQ3: Marl 7F 111
Stantyway Rd. EX9: Ott'n 7J 83
Stanwell Dr. EX39: W Ho 6B 20
Stanwell Hill EX39: W Ho 6A 20
Stanwey EX1: Heav 7K 65
Staplake La. PL6: Star 2C 96
Staplake Ri. EX6: Star 1D 96
Staplake Rd. EX6: Star 1E 96
Stapledon La. TQ13: Ashb 3H 99
STAPLE CROSS 1A 166
STAPLE FITZPAINE 2C 167
Stapleford Dr. TQ14: Teignm 2H 107
Stapleford Gdns. PL5: Plym 5E 130
STAPLEGROVE 1C 167
STAPLEHAY 1C 167
Staple Hill TQ9: Darti 3B 102
Staplehill Rd.
  TQ12: Live, New A 6F 93
Staple Orchard TQ9: Darti 3B 102
Staple's Bldgs. EX8: Exmth 5C 76
  (off Crudges La.)
Staples M. EX8: Exmth 5C 76
  (off Exeter Rd.)
Staples Ter. DT7: Lym R 4K 91
  (not continuous)
Stapleton Cl. TQ4: Paig 4E 118
Stapleton Mire Nature Reserve 2C 163
STAPLEY .2B 166
Star Barton La. EX5: Cowl 1A 64
STARCROSS 1E 96 (2D 171)
Starcross Fishing & Cruising Club
  . . . . .1E 96
Starcross Station (Rail) . .1E 96 (2D 171)
Starkey Cl. EX16: Tive 5G 41
Starling Dr. PL6: Plym 1B 136
Starlings Roost EX15: Cull 5F 45
Starpitten Gro. TQ2: Torq 2D 112
Starpitten La. W. TQ2: Torq 3C 112
Starre Cl. EX12: Seat 3F 87
START 1F 159 (3A 176)
Start Av. TQ7: Chil 6G 159
  TQ14: Teignm 2J 107
Start Bay Cvn. Pk. 5G 153
Start Bay Pk. TQ6: Strete 5G 153
Start Point Lighthouse 3A 176
STATHE .1D 167
Station App. EX17: Cred 7J 39
  TQ10: S Bre 1B 100
Station Bus. Pk. TQ14: Teignm 4J 107
  (off Lwr. Brimley Rd.)
Station Cl. EX22: Hols 2C 34
  EX33: Brau 5J 15
Station Ct. TQ13: Bov T 4B 92
Sta. Hill EX31: Brat F 4H 13
  EX32: Swim 2H 25
  EX35: Lynt 2G 13
  EX39: Bide 4G 23
  TQ5: Brixh 3E 122
  TQ13: Chud 3A 94
Station La. TQ4: Paig 2H 119
Station Rd. EX1: Pin 3D 66
  EX2: Ide 4A 70
  EX3: Ext 2G 75
  EX3: Top 5B 74
  EX4: Exe 1A 6 (4C 64)
  EX5: Broadc 7D 52, 2K 67
  EX5: New C 5D 50
  EX5: Whim 6H 53

Station Rd. EX6: Exmin	.3E 74	STICKLEPATH
EX7: Daw	.4H 97	EX20 . . . . .1G 49 (1A 170)
EX9: Bud S	.6C 82	EX31 . . . . .6C 18
EX10: Harp, New P	.5H 81	Sticklepath Ct. EX31: Taw 6D 18
EX10: Sidm	.5B 84	Sticklepath Hill EX31: B'aple 6C 18
EX14: Fen	.2G 53	Sticklepath Ter. EX31: B'aple 5E 18
EX15: Cull	.3H 45	Stidston La. TQ10: S Bre 1C 100
EX15: Hemy	.2G 47	Stile La. DT7: Lym R 5J 91
EX15: Will	.3C 44	Stile Orchard TQ7: Lodd 2H 151
EX16: Bam	.2H 33	Stillman Ct. PL4: Plym 5F 9
EX16: Tive	.4D 40	Stillman St. PL4: Plym 5F 9 (3K 141)
EX17: Bow	.7G 37	Stintway La. EX10: Sidm 5A 84
EX17: Cop	.5C 38	Stirling Ct. PL5: Plym 2B 134
EX17: Cred	.7J 39	Stirling Rd. PL5: Plym 2B 134
EX20: Brid	.4H 57	Stitchill Rd. TQ1: Torq 2E 116
EX20: Oke	.4B 48	Stoat Pk. EX32: B'aple 5J 19
EX22: Hols	.2C 34	Stoats Cl. EX36: S Mol 7C 26
EX24: Colyt	.5D 88	Stockbridge La. TQ10: S Bre 2B 100
EX31: B'aple	.5E 18	Stocker Rd. EX4: Exe 3E 64
EX31: Brat F	.6H 13	Stockham La. EX5: Cran 2E 68
EX33: Brau	.5J 15	STOCKLAND 3C 167
EX34: Ilfra	.3G 11	Stock La. EX12: Seat 5E 86
EX34: Wool	.6C 10	STOCKLEIGH ENGLISH 3C 165
EX36: S Mol	.5D 26	STOCKLEIGH POMEROY 3C 165
PL2: Plym	.6D 134	STOCKLINCH 2D 167
PL5: Tam F	.4D 130	Stockmeadow Gdns.
PL7: Plymp	.3B 138	TQ14: Bi'ton 4C 106
PL9: Elb	.5K 143	Stock Pk. EX20: Oke 2E 48
PL16: Lift, Tin	.6C 56	Stockton Av. EX7: Daw 4G 97
PL19: Mary T	.3A 60	Stockton Hill EX7: Daw 4G 97
PL20: Bere A	.1A 128	Stockton La. EX7: Daw 4G 97
PL20: Bere F	.6B 128	(off Stockton Rd.)
PL20: Horr	.2E 126	Stockton Rd. EX7: Daw 4G 97
PL20: Prin	.7C 60	Stoggy La. PL7: Plymp 3C 138
(not continuous)		(not continuous)
PL21: Ivy	.3H 145	STOKE
TQ7: Lodd	.2H 151	EX39 . . . . .1A 162
TQ9: Tot	.5E 102	PL3 . . . . .1A 8 (1G 141)
TQ10: S Bre	.1B 100	STOKE ABBOTT 3H 167
TQ11: B'leigh	.4D 98	STOKE CANON 7J 51 (1D 171)
TQ12: New A	.1G 109	STOKE CLIMSLAND 3B 168
TQ13: Bov T	.4B 92	STOKE FLEMING 2H 153 (3A 176)
TQ13: More	.7H 61	STOKE GABRIEL 4B 120 (2A 176)
TQ14: Teignm	.5J 107	Stoke Gabriel Rd.
Station Rd. Ind. Est. EX15: Hemy 1G 47		TQ5: Galm, Wadd 2E 120
Station Yd. EX4: Exe 2C 6 (5E 64)		STOKE HILL 3H 65
EX10: Sidm	.4B 84	Stoke Hill EX4: Exe 7C 126
EX13: Axmin	.4G 89	Stoke Hill Cres. EX4: Exe 3H 65
EX14: Hon	.4F 55	Stoke Hill La.
TQ13: Ashb	.4H 99	EX5: Sto C 7J 51, 2H 65
(off Prigg Mdw.)		TQ9: Sto G 4B 120
Station Yd. Ind. Est.		Stoke Ho. Gdns. TQ6: Sto F 3H 153
TQ7: Kingsb	.4F 157	(off Dartmouth Hill)
STAVERTON 1D 175		STOKEINTEIGNHEAD 3D 171
Staverton Station (Rail) 1D 175		Stokelake TQ13: Chud 4A 94
STAWLEY 1A 166		Stoke Lyne EX8: Exmth 3E 76
Steamer Quay Cvn. Club Site 6F 103		Stoke Mdw. Cl. EX4: Exe 2H 65
Steamer Quay Rd. TQ9: Tot 6F 103		STOKENHAM 6K 159 (3A 176)
Steam Gallery at Beer 7B 86		STOKE RIVERS 3C 161
(off Fore St.)		Stoke Rd. EX4: Exe 1C 6
Steartfield Rd. TQ3: Paig 7J 115		PL1: Plym 3A 8 (2G 141)
Steed Cl. TQ4: Good 7G 119		PL8: Noss M 6H 149
Steel Cl. EX14: Hon 3G 55		TQ1: Maid 1J 113
Steeperton Cl. EX20: Oke 3D 48		TQ4: Coll M, Paig 5B 118
Steep Hill TQ1: Maid 1J 113		STOKE ST GREGORY 1D 167
Steeple Cl. PL9: Plyms 7G 143		STOKE ST MARY 1C 167
Steeple Dr. EX2: Alph 6E 70		Stokesay Av. PL6: Plym 5A 132
Steer Pk. Rd. PL7: Plymp 4F 139		Stokes Cl. TQ13: Bov T 4E 92
Steer Point Rd. PL8: Brixt 3H 149		Stokes La. EX16: Tive 2J 33
Stefan Cl. PL9: Hooe 7C 142		(off Barrington St.)
Stella Maris Ct. EX39: Bide 2F 23		PL1: Plym 6F 9
Stella Rd. TQ3: Pres 5G 115		Stokes Mead EX5: W'bury 5C 78
STEMBRIDGE 1D 167		Stoke Valley Rd. EX4: Exe 1F 65
Stemson Av. EX4: Pin 3B 66		Stoke Woods Forest Walks 1D 171
STENHILL 2A 166		Stokingway Cl. PL9: Plyms 7F 143
Stenlake Pl. PL4: Plym 2C 142		Stokinteignhead Cl. TQ5: Brixh 5E 122
(off Stenlake Ter.)		Stone Ash La. EX17: Morc 1E 38
Stenlake Ter. PL4: Plym 2C 142		Stone Barton EX5: Cran 2D 68
Stentaway Cl. PL9: Plyms 4G 143		Stone Barton Rd. PL7: Plymp 5K 137
Stentaway Dr. PL9: Plyms 4G 143		Stone Barton Rd. EX1: Pin 4F 67
Stentaway La. EX33: Croy, Puts 1C 14		PL7: Plymp 5K 137
Stentaway Rd. PL9: Plyms 5G 143		Stoneborough Ct. EX9: Bud S 6D 82
Stentiford Hill TQ7: Kingsb 2F 157		Stoneborough La. EX9: Bud S 6D 82
Stentiford Hill Rd. TQ1: Torq 1D 116		Stone Cl. EX14: Hon 5E 54
Stepcote Hill EX1: Exe 5D 6 (7E 64)		Stone Ct. TQ2: Torq 4K 111
Stephenson Way PL5: Plym 1E 134		Stonehall Flats PL1: Plym 3F 141
Stephen St. EX4: Exe 4E 6 (6F 65)		Stonehedge Cl. PL21: Ivy 5H 145
Steppes Mdw. TQ12: New A 2D 108		STONEHOUSE 3F 141
Stepping Stone Gdns. EX20: Oke 2B 48		STONEHOUSE BRI. 3F 141
Stepps La. EX12: Axmth 4J 87		Stonehouse Creek Leisure Club 2F 141
Steps Bridge Nature Trail 2B 170		Stonehouse St. PL1: Plym 3F 141
Steps Cl. EX1: Pin 3E 66		Stoneland Cl. EX5: Cran 2D 68
Steps La. TQ2: Torq 2D 112		Stonelands M. EX7: Daw 4F 97
(not continuous)		Stonelands Pk. EX7: Daw 4F 97
Stepstone La. EX33: Know 1K 15		Stonelands Ter. EX7: Daw 4F 97
Sterlings Way EX20: Oke 2D 48		(off Stonelands Pk.)
Stevens La. EX10: Sidm 3B 84		Stone La. EX2: Exe 2D 70
STEVENSTONE 2D 163		EX8: Lymp 6G 75
Stevenstone Rd. EX8: Exmth 5F 77		Stone Lane Gardens 1B 170
Stewart Cl. EX8: Exmth 3G 77		Stone La. Retail Pk. 2E 70
Stewart Ct. EX13: Axmin 2J 89		Stoneleigh Dr. TQ2: Torq 3K 115
Stewart Gdns. EX7: Daw 3H 97		Stoneleigh Gdns. EX15: Cull 4G 45
Stewart Ho. EX7: Daw 3H 97		Stoneman's Hill TQ12: A'well 4E 108
(off Old Gatehouse Rd.)		Stoneman's La. EX38: G Tor 1B 30
STEWLEY 2D 167		Stone Pk. TQ4: Broads 2K 121
STIBB 2A 162		
STIBB CROSS 2C 163		
Stibb La. PL21: Ivy 3D 144		

Stonepark TQ13: Ashb	.5G 99	Strete Gate Nature Trail 3A 176
Stonepark Cres. TQ13: Ashb	.5G 99	Strete Gate Picnic Site 3A 176
Stonepark Ter. TQ13: Ashb	.5G 99	Stringland La. TQ3: Marl 1D 114
Stones Cl. PL21: Modb	.6H 147	Strode Rd. PL7: Plymp 2C 138
Stones Gallop EX5: Rock	.2F 69	TQ11: B'leigh 5C 98
Stone's Pl. EX15: Cull	.3H 45	Stroma Cl. PL6: Plym 3A 132
Stonewall La. EX17: Cred	.5H 39	Stroud Pk. Rd. PL2: Plym 4H 135
Stoneycliffe Pl. PL20: Prin	.6D 60	Stuart Ct. EX7: Daw 6G 97
STONEYCOMBE 3C 110		Stuart Cres. EX15: Cull 1H 45
STONEYFORD 3J 45 (3A 166)		Stuart Rd. EX1: Heav 6J 65
Stoneyford Pk. EX9: Bud S	.6D 82	PL1: Plym 1A 8 (1G 141)
Stoneyhill TQ12: A'well	.3A 110	PL3: Plym 1A 8 (1G 141)
Stoneylands EX5: Rock	.4E 68	Stuckey Farm Nature Reserve 2B 164
Stoney La. EX5: Bradn	.1C 52	Stucley Rd. EX39: Bide 4D 22
EX13: Axmin	.3J 89	Studhayes Rd. EX13: Kilm 1A 88
EX14: Hon	.7F 55	Studley Rd. TQ1: Torq 6C 112
Stoney Pk. La. EX20: Oke	.4A 48	Sturcombe Av. TQ4: Paig 4E 118
Stoneywell EX39: Ins	.2K 21	Sturdee Rd. PL2: Plym 6F 135
Stony Cl. La. EX12: Axmth	.5J 87	Sturges Rd. EX8: Exmth 4F 77
STONY CROSS 1D 163		Style Cl. EX32: B'aple 7G 19
Stony La. EX5: Wood S	.2C 78	Subway App. EX15: Will 3C 44
EX8: Lymp	.3K 75	Sugar Loaf Hill & Saltern Cove
EX16: Bam	.3J 33	Nature Reserve 6J 119 (2A 176)
EX39: App	.3G 21	Sugar Mill Bus. Pk. PL9: Plyms 3D 142
Stonypark La. EX17: Cred	.6G 39	Sullivan Rd. EX2: Won 7B 66
STOODLEIGH		Summer Cl. EX4: Whip 4A 66
EX16	.2D 165	EX8: Exmth 4G 77
EX32	.3C 161	EX15: Hemy 2F 47
Stooks Cl. EX5: Bram S	.6G 51	Summercourt Way TQ5: Brixh 6B 122
Stopford Pl. PL1: Dev	.1E 140	Summerfield EX5: W'bury 4C 78
Storrs Cl. TQ13: Bov T	.3B 92	EX10: Sidm 2C 84
Stott Cl. PL3: Plym	.6E 136	Summerfield Ct. PL21: Ivy 4E 144
Stour Cl. PL3: Plym	.5E 136	Summerfield Rd. TQ2: Torq 5A 112
Stovar Long La. EX12: Beer	.5A 86	Summerhayes EX7: Daw 6F 97
Stover Country Pk. 3K 93 (3C 171)		Summerhill TQ12: Live 4G 93
Stover Country Pk. Interpretation Cen.		Summerhill Cl. TQ12: Live 4G 93
. . . . .3K 93		Summerhill Dr. TQ12: Live 4G 93
Stover Ct. EX1: Exe 2G 7 (5G 65)		Summerhill Ho. DT7: Lym R 4K 91
TQ12: New A	.1F 109	(off Charmouth Rd.)
Stover Golf Course 4K 93 (3C 171)		Summerhill Rd. DT7: Lym R 4K 91
Stowbrook EX10: Sidm	.2A 84	TQ12: Live 4G 93
Stowe Gdns. PL5: Plym	.1G 135	Summerhill Ter. PL10: Millb 6A 140
Stowe La. EX20: Exbo	.6J 35	Summer Ho. Hill Path EX35: Lynt 4H 13
STOWFORD		Summerhouse Path EX35: Lynm 2H 13
EX10	.2A 172	Summering Cl. EX20: Oke 2E 48
EX20	.2C 169	Summerland EX14: Hon 4F 55
EX31	.2C 161	Summerland Av. EX7: Daw 3G 97
Stowford Bus. Pk. PL21: Ivy	.5H 145	Summerland Cl. EX7: Daw 4G 97
(off Blair Rd.)		Summerland Cotts. TQ12: New A 1F 109
Stowford Cl. PL20: Dous	.4K 127	(off Carlisle St.)
Stowford Hgts. EX12: Seat	.4D 86	Summerland Ct. TQ12: New A 1F 109
Stowford Moor Nature Reserve 2B 162		(off Summerland St.)
Stowford Ri. EX10: Sidm	.3A 84	EX36: S Mol 6C 26
STOWFORD WATER 6E 46		Summerlands Cl. PL7: Plymp 4F 139
Strand EX3: Top	.6B 74	TQ5: Brixh 6C 122
EX8: Exmth	.6C 76	Summerlands Ct. TQ5: Brixh 6C 122
TQ1: Torq	.2D 116	TQ12: Live 4H 93
TQ14: Shal	.6G 107	Summerlands Gdns. PL7: Plymp 4F 139
TQ14: Teignm	.6H 107	Summerland St. EX1: Exe 2G 7 (5G 65)
The Strand EX7: Daw	.4H 97	EX32: B'aple 4F 19
EX8: Lymp	.6F 75	Summerland Ter. EX32: B'aple 4F 19
EX15: Culm	.2B 46	(off Summerland St.)
EX31: B'aple	.4E 18	EX34: C Mar 6B 12
EX34: Ilfra	.2J 11	Summer La. EX4: Whip 3A 66
(off Hierns La.)		EX8: Exmth 1C 76
EX39: Bide	.3F 23	TQ5: Brixh 5C 122
TQ5: Brixh	.3F 123	TQ12: Teigng 1B 104
TQ14: Shal	.6E 106	Summer Mdw. EX5: Cran 3B 68
Strand Ct. EX31: Ashf	.1K 17	Summers Cl. PL6: Plym 4C 136
Strand Ct. EX3: Top	.6B 74	Summersby Cl. EX12: Seat 4E 86
EX39: Bide	.2F 23	Summersfield Cl. TQ4: Paig 2J 119
Strand Hill EX7: Daw	.4H 97	Summerway EX4: Whip 4A 66
Strand La. EX31: Ashf	.1J 17	Sumner Rd. PL21: Bitta 7C 112
Strand St. PL1: Plym	.4F 141	Sunbury Hill TQ1: Torq 7C 112
Strap La. TQ7: Kingst	.1G 105	Sun Ct. TQ4: Paig 2H 119
Strashleigh Vw. PL21: L Mill	.5C 144	Sun Ct. TQ12: New A 1E 108
Stratford Av. EX4: Whip	.4B 66	Suncrest Cvn. Site 2B 112
Stratheden Ct. TQ1: Torq	.1D 116	Suncrest Cl. TQ2: Torq 3B 112
(off Market St.)		Sunderland Cl. PL9: Hooe 6B 142
STRATTON 3A 162		Sunflower Rd. EX32: B'aple 4F 19
Stratton Wlk. PL2: Plym	.3J 135	Sunhill Av. EX3: Top 7E 72
Strawberry Av. EX2: Alph	.5F 71	Sunhill La. EX3: Top 7E 72
Strawberry Flds. EX20: N Taw	.7C 36	Sun La. TQ14: Teignm 5H 107
Strawberry Hill EX8: Lymp	.6G 75	(off Teign St.)
Strawberry La. EX5: Bradn	.1E 52	Sunningbrook Rd. EX16: Tive 3E 40
EX7: Holc	.7F 97	Sunningdale Ter. EX39: Bide 2F 23
EX11: Ott M	.5A 80	(off Northam Rd.)
Strawberry Ter. TQ12: Kingst	.3H 105	Sunny Bank EX32: B'aple 5G 19
Stray Pk. PL8: Y'ton	.2A 150	(not continuous)
Stream Ct. EX2: Exe 7D 6 (1E 70)		Sunnybank EX6: Kenton 6J 95
Streamers Mdws. EX14: Hon	.4F 55	TQ12: A'well 6E 108
Streatham Dr. EX4: Exe 1B 6 (4D 64)		TQ12: New A 6E 104
Streatham Ri. EX4: Exe 1B 6 (4D 64)		Sunny Cl. TQ12: New A 1J 109
Streatham Sports Pk.	.3E 64	Sunny Dene PL5: Plym 2C 134
STREET		Sunnyfield EX5: Broadc 5C 52
EX12	.6F 85	Sunnyhill EX11: Ott M 3D 80
EX22	.1A 168	Sunny Hollow TQ12: E Ogw 4A 108
TA20	.3D 167	Sunny Lands Way EX7: Holc 7G 97
The Street EX13: Kilm	.2B 88	Sunny Lyn Holiday Pk. 4G 13
EX13: Mus	.7C 90	Sunnymead EX17: Cop 6E 38
STREET ASH 2C 167		Sunnymead Ter. TQ9: Tot 6E 102
STRETCH DOWN 7K 33		(off Maudlin Rd.)
STRETE 6G 153 (3A 176)		Sunnymoor Cl. EX1: Pin 3E 66
		Sunny Side EX33: Brau 5J 15
		(off South St.)

Sunnyside EX10: New P 4H 81
  EX14: Awli 2B 54
  EX15: Cull 5H 45
  EX34: C Mar 7C 12
  EX34: Wool 7C 10
  EX39: Bide 4G 23
  PL8: Y'ton 2B 150
Sunnyside Cotts. PL9: Plyms 4E 142
  (off Roper Av.)
Sunnyside Rd. EX34: Wool 6A 10
  PL4: Plym 2C 142
  TQ12: Kingsk 2G 111
Sunnyside Ter. EX35: Lynt 2G 13
Sunny Vw. EX19: Wink 2C 36
Sunset Hgts. EX21: Sheb 6J 29
  EX32: B'aple 4F 19
Sunset Ho. EX12: Seat 6D 86
Sunshine Ter. PL19: Tavi 3K 59
Sun Ter. PL21: Modb 6G 147
Sun Valley Cl. TQ5: Brixh 3E 122
Sunway Cl. PL19: Tavi 3G 59
Sunwine Pl. EX8: Exmth 6D 76
Surbiton Cres. EX4: Exe 1C 70
Surf Bay Cvn. Pk. 4C 20
Sussex Cl. EX4: Exe 1B 70
  TQ2: Torq 2C 112
Sussex Pl. PL1: Plym 6E 8 (3J 141)
Sussex Rd. PL2: Plym 6E 134
Sussex St. PL1: Plym 6E 8 (3J 141)
Sussex Ter. PL2: Plym 6E 134
Sutcliffe Cl. TQ9: Darti 4B 102
SUTCOMBE 2B 162
Suter Dr. EX16: Tive 2E 40
Sutherlake Gdns. EX5: Broadc 6E 52
Sutherland Cl. TQ12: New A 4J 109
Sutherland Dr. TQ2: Torq 3D 112
Sutherland Pl. PL4: Plym . . .1E 8 (1J 141)
Sutherland Rd. PL4: Plym . . .1E 8 (1K 141)
  TQ1: Torq 1E 116
Sutton Cl. EX7: Daw 3G 97
  TQ2: Torq 1B 112
Sutton Ct. PL1: Dev 3E 140
Sutton Harbour 6G 9 (3K 141)
Sutton M. PL4: Plym 4G 9
Sutton Pl. PL4: Plym 6J 9 (3A 142)
Sutton Rd. PL4: Plym 5H 9 (3A 142)
Sutton Vw. EX17: Bow 5H 37
  PL4: Plym 4G 9
Sutton Wharf PL4: Plym . . .5G 9 (3K 141)
Swain Cl. EX13: Axmin 5H 89
Swaindale Rd. PL3: Plym 5K 135
Swains Ct. EX3: Top 5A 74
Swains Rd. EX9: Bud S 5D 82
Swale Cl. PL3: Plym 5C 136
  TQ2: Torq 2C 112
Swallow Cl. EX32: B'aple 5K 19
Swallow Ct. EX4: Exe 4C 64
  EX12: Seat 6G 87
  (off Harbour Rd.)
Swallow Dr. EX2: Exe 2A 70
Swallow Fld. EX31: Rou 7K 17
Swallowfield Ri. TQ2: Torq 3J 111
Swallowfield Rd. EX2: Cou W 3K 71
SWALLOWFIELDS 4D 102
Swallowfields TQ9: Tot 4D 102
Swallows Acre EX7: Daw 3H 97
Swallows End PL9: Plyms 4F 143
Swallow Way EX15: Cull 4F 45
Swanaford Rd. EX6: Bridf 7D 62
  (not continuous)
Swan Av. EX16: Tive 2E 40
Swanborough Rd. TQ12: New A 3J 109
Swan Ct. EX2: Exe 7G 7 (1G 71)
  TQ6: Dartm 6E 124
  (off Victoria Rd.)
Swan Gdns. PL7: Plymp 4C 138
Swan Hill Rd. EX24: Colyf 1F 87
Swannaton Rd. TQ6: Dartm 7F 125
Swanpool Marsh Nature Reserve
  . . . . .4F 15 (3A 160)
Swan Rd. EX6: Star 2D 96
  EX12: Seat 5F 87
Swan St. TQ2: Torq 2D 116
  (off Fleet St.)
Swanswood Gdns. EX39: W Ho 5C 20
Swan Units EX2: Sow 7D 66
Swan Yd. EX4: Exe 6B 6 (7D 64)
Swedwell La. TQ2: Torq 1C 112
Swedwell Rd. TQ2: Torq 1C 112
Sweetbriar Cl. EX7: Holc 7F 97
Sweetbriar La. EX7: Holc 7F 97
Sweetbriar La. EX1: Heav 6K 65
Sweet Chestnut EX5: Cran 2E 68
Sweet Coppin EX5: Rock 2C 68
SWEETHAM 4D 50 (1C 171)
SWEETS .1A 168
SWELL 1D 167
Swift Gdns. PL5: Plym 1H 135
Swift Ind. Est. TQ12: Kingst 5G 105
Swift Rd. EX7: Daw 7C 96
SWIMBRIDGE 3H 25 (1A 164)
Swimbridge Ct. EX32: Swim 1H 25
SWIMBRIDGE NEWLAND
  . . . . .3D 24 (3C 161)
Swim Torquay 6D 112
Swinburne Gdns. PL5: Plym 2G 135
Swincombe Dr. TQ4: Paig 1F 119

Swiss Cl. EX8: Exmth 1D 76
Sword Cl. EX31: Frem 5F 17
Swordfish Av. EX5: Clyst H 4K 67
Sybil Mead EX1: Pin 4E 66
Sycamore Av. EX7: Daw W 7C 96
  PL4: Plym 3B 142
  PL19: Tavi 7J 59
Sycamore Cl. EX1: Heav 7A 66
  EX5: Broadc 6D 52
  EX8: Exmth 2G 77
  EX14: Hon 5D 54
  EX15: Will 4C 44
  EX39: Ins 2K 21
  (off Marine Pde.)
  TQ4: Broads 1K 121
Sycamore Dr. EX36: S Mol 5C 26
  PL6: Plym 3D 132
Sycamore Rd. EX16: Tive 3E 40
Sycamore Wlk. PL21: L Mill 5A 144
Sycamore Way PL6: Plym 5F 133
  TQ5: Brixh 6C 122
  TQ13: Chud 1D 94
SYDENHAM DAMEREL 3C 169
Sydenham Ho. EX1: Exe 1J 7
Sydney Cl. PL7: Plymp 5B 138
Sydney Pl. EX2: Exe 7C 6
Sydney Rd. EX2: Exe 7B 6 (1D 70)
  PL11: Torp 1A 140
Sydney St. PL1: Plym 2C 8 (1H 141)
Sylvan Av. EX4: Exe 3G 65
Sylvan Cl. EX8: Exmth 2C 76
Sylvan Dr. EX8: Exmth 2C 76
  (off Exeter Rd.)
  PL1: Plym 1F 141
Sylvania Dr. EX4: Exe 2H 65
Sylvan Rd. EX4: Exe 3G 65
SYMONDSBURY 1D 173
Symons Cl. TQ13: Bov T 4E 92
Symons Pas. TQ9: Tot 6F 103
Synagogue Pl. EX4: Exe 4D 6 (6E 64)

T

Tabernacle Ct. EX1: Exe 6D 6
Tacket Ct. TQ7: Kingsb 5F 157
Tacketwood TQ7: Kingsb 5G 157
Taddiforde Rd.
  EX4: Exe 1B 6 (5D 64)
TADDIPORT 3A 30 (2C 163)
Taddyforde Ct. EX4: Exe 1A 6
Taddyforde Ct. Mans. EX4: Exe 4D 64
  (off Taddyforde Est.)
Taddyforde Est. EX4: Exe 1B 6 (4D 64)
Tadworthy Rd. EX39: Nort 5D 20
Tailyour Rd. PL6: Plym 1A 136
TALATON 1A 172
Talaton Rd. EX5: Whim 6H 53
Talbot Ct. TQ14: Teignm 4G 107
  (off Bitton Pk. Rd.)
Talbot Gdns. PL5: Plym 4C 134
Talbot Rd. DT7: Lym R 4J 91
TALEFORD 1A 80 (1A 172)
Taleford Cl. EX11: Tale 1B 80
Taleford Vs. EX11: Tale 1B 80
Tallow Wood Cl. TQ3: Paig 1E 118
Tamar Av. PL2: Plym 6D 134
  PL19: Tavi 4G 59
  TQ2: Torq 6H 111
Tamar Belle Heritage Centre 1A 174
TAMAR BRI. 1A 134
Tamar Bri. Rd. PL5: Plym 1B 134
Tamar Cl. PL20: Bere A 2D 128
Tamar Ho. PL1: Dev 3C 140
Tamarind EX15: Will 4C 44
Tamarisk Cl. EX4: Whip 2A 66
Tamar River Sailing Club 2A 134
Tamar Rd. EX31: C'nor 1E 16
Tamar Science Pk. PL6: Plym 6D 132
Tamar's Dr. EX15: Will 4C 44
Tamar St. PL1: Dev 1D 140
  PL11: Torp 1B 140
  PL12: Salt 1A 134
Tamar Valley Nature Trails 1A 174
Tamar Vw. PL19: Mil A 2B 58
Tamar Vs. PL9: Plyms 5E 142
Tamar Way PL5: Plym 1F 135
Tamar Wharf PL1: Dev 1C 140
Tamerton Av. PL5: Plym 2C 134
Tamerton Cl. PL5: Plym 4F 131
Tamerton Foliot Rd.
  PL5: Plym, Tam F 4H 131
  PL6: Plym 4H 131
Tamworth Cl. TQ12: E Ogw 4C 108
Tamwyn Cl. TQ3: Pres 6J 115
Tangmere Av. PL3: Plym 5D 130
Tan La. EX2: Exe 2E 70
Tanners Av. EX15: Cull 5G 45
Tanners M. EX15: Will 3E 44
Tanners Rd. EX32: Land 2D 24
  TQ4: Good 3J 119
Tannery Cl. EX36: S Mol 6B 26
Tanpits La. TQ7: Chil 6G 159
Tanpits Mdw. TQ7: Chil 6G 159
Tansy Cl. TQ12: New A 6A 104
TANTON'S PLAIN 1A 30
Tanyard La. EX7: Daw 7A 110

Tanyards Ct. EX12: Seat 5E 86
  (off Beer Rd.)
Tape La. EX14: Awli 3A 54
Tapeley Park 1C 163
Tapley Gdns. TQ14: Bi'ton 3C 106
Tappers Cl. EX3: Top 5B 74
Tappers Knapp DT7: Uply 3G 91
Tappers La. PL8: Y'ton 2A 150
Tappers Mdw. EX20: Oke 3D 48
Tapp's La. PL8: Brixt 2J 149
Taps Cl. EX6: Exmin 2D 74
Tapson Dr. PL9: Hooe 6B 142
Tarbet Av. EX1: Heav 5J 65
Tarka Cl. EX20: Oke 2D 48
Tarka Holiday Pk. 1K 17
Tarka La. EX34: Wool 7C 10
Tarka Tennis Cen. 6E 18
TARR 1B 166
Tarraway Rd. TQ3: Pres 5H 115
Tarr's Av. TQ12: Kingst 4H 105
Tarrs End TQ12: Kingst 4H 105
Tarr's La. TQ12: Kingst 4H 105
TARR STEPS 1C 165
Tarry La. EX34: Ilfra 3H 11
  (off Belvedere Rd.)
TATWORTH 3D 167
TAUNTON .1C 167
Taunton Av. PL5: Plym 5G 131
Taunton Cl. EX2: Exe 2D 70
Taunton Ct. TQ9: Tot 6F 103
  (off New Wlk.)
TAUNTON DEANE SERVICE AREA
  . . . . .1B 166
Taunton Pl. PL5: Plym 5G 131
Taunton Station (Rail) 1C 167
Tavern M. EX38: G Tor 2B 30
Tavis Rd. TQ3: Paig 6F 115
Tavistock College Sports Cen. 5G 59
Tavistock Golf Course 5K 59 (3C 169)
Tavistock Mus. 4J 59 (3C 169)
Tavistock Pl. PL4: Plym 3F 9 (2K 141)
  TQ4: Good 7H 119
Tavistock Rd. EX4: Exe 2A 6 (5D 64)
  PL2: Plym 3K 135
  PL5: Plym 3K 135
  PL6: Plym 6B 132
  PL6: Robo 1D 132
  PL20: Horr, Yelv 1D 126
  PL20: Prin 5B 60
Tavistock Tourist Information Centre
  . . . . .4J 59 (3C 169)
Tavy Av. TQ2: Torq 5H 111
Tavy Cleave 2D 169
Tavy Pl. PL4: Plym 7A 136
Tavy Rd. PL19: Tavi 4K 59
Taw Cl. PL3: Plym 5E 136
Taw Cres. EX31: C'nor 2E 16
Taw Grn. EX32: B'aple 5F 19
Taw Cres. EX31: C'nor 2E 16
TAW GREEN 1A 170
Taw Mdw. Cres. EX31: Frem 5G 17
Taw Rd. EX31: C'nor 1E 16
TAWSTOCK 7A 24 (1D 163)
Tawton La. EX20: S Zeal 2J 49
Taw Trade Pk. EX31: B'aple 3D 18
Taw Va. EX32: B'aple 5E 18
Taw Va. Av. EX20: N Taw 6A 36
Taw Va. Cl. EX20: N Taw 6A 36
Taw Vale Pde. EX32: B'aple 5E 18
  (off Taw Vale)
Taw Vw. EX31: Frem 5G 17
Taw Vw. Ter. EX32: B Taw 5A 24
Taw Wharf EX31: B'aple 5D 18
Tay Gdns. PL3: Plym 4E 136
Taylor Cl. EX7: Daw 5F 97
  EX11: Ott M 3A 80
Taylors Cl. EX16: Tive 1E 40
Taylors Fld. EX20: N Taw 6C 36
Taylors Newtake TQ12: Live 4F 93
Taylor Sq. PL19: Tavi 3K 59
Teachers Cl. PL9: Plyms 6G 143
Teal Cl. TQ2: Torq 3J 111
Teal Pl. EX7: Daw 7C 96
Teal Way EX2: Exe 3H 71
  (off Turnstone Rd.)
Teats Hill Flats PL4: Plym . . .7J 9 (4A 142)
Teats Hill Rd. PL4: Plym 6H 9 (3A 142)
Teazle Ct. EX2: Exe 6D 6
TEDBURN ST MARY 6H 49 (1C 171)
Tedders Cl. EX15: Hemy 1G 47
Tedstone La. EX8: Lymp 5J 75
Ted's Way EX20: Oke 3C 48
Tees Cl. PL3: Plym 4D 136
Teignbridge Bus. Cen. TQ12: H'fld . .1J 93
Teign Cl. TQ14: Bi'ton 3A 106
TEIGNCOMBE 2A 170
Teign Corinthian Yacht Club 4K 107
Teign Ct. TQ14: Bi'ton 3C 106
Teignfield Cvn. Site 6D 106
Teign Fort Dr. TQ12: Kingst 5J 105
TEIGNGRACE 3C 104 (3C 171)
Teigngrace Rd. TQ12: New A 4D 104
Teignharvey Rd. TQ14: Shal 6C 106
Teign Heritage Cen. 4J 107 (3D 171)
TEIGNMOUTH 5J 107 (3D 171)
Teignmouth Golf Course
  . . . . .1D 106 (3D 171)
Teignmouth Hill EX7: Daw 5H 97

Teignmouth Lido 4J 107
Teignmouth Lifeboat Station 6H 107
Teignmouth (Lucette) Lighthouse
  . . . . .3D 171
Teignmouth Rd. TQ1: Maid, Torq . . .4J 105
  TQ12: Kingst 4J 105
  TQ14: Bi'ton 4C 106
  TQ14: Teignm 2K 107
Teignmouth Station
  (Rail) 4J 107 (3D 171)
Teign Rd. PL3: Plym 5C 136
  TQ12: New A 1G 109
Teign St. TQ14: Teignm 5H 107
Teign Valley Golf Course 2C 171
Teign Valley Rd. EX6: Chri 1K 63
Teign Vw. TQ13: Chud K 5B 94
Teign Vw. Pl. TQ14: Teignm 5H 107
Teign Vw. Rd. TQ14: Bi'ton 2A 106
Telegraph La. EX5: Rock 2F 79
Telegraph Wharf PL1: Plym 4F 141
Telford Cres. PL5: Plym 1E 134
Telford Rd. EX4: Exe 1B 6 (5D 64)
Tembani Ct. TQ3: Pres 7J 115
Temeraire Rd. PL5: Plym 1J 135
Temperance Pl. TQ5: Brixh 3F 123
Temperance St. TQ2: Torq 1C 116
Templar Ter. TQ13: Bov T 6C 92
TEMPLE 3A 168
Temple Cres. EX16: Tive 4F 41
Temple Gdns. EX10: Sidm 5C 84
Temple Pl. EX2: Exe 6F 7 (7F 65)
Templer Pl. TQ13: Bov T 7C 92
Templer Rd. TQ3: Pres 3G 115
Templer's Way TQ12: New A 7G 105
Templer's Way TQ12: Kingst 2G 105
Templer Way TQ12: New A 7H 105
  (not continuous)
  TQ12: Teigng 1C 104
TEMPLETON 2C 165
Temple Wlk. PL2: Plym 4F 135
Tenby Rd. PL5: Plym 2B 134
Tencery Orchard EX14: Dunk 5H 47
Ten Commandments Stone 3B 170
Teneriffe TQ1: Torq 1E 116
  (off Middle Warberry Rd.)
Tennacott Hgts. EX39: Bide 5J 23
Tennacott La. EX39: Bide 5K 23
Tennyson Av. EX2: Won 2J 71
Tennyson Cl. TQ1: Torq 5C 112
Tennyson Gdns. PL5: Plym 2G 135
Tennyson Way EX8: Exmth 7K 75
Tenpin
  Plymouth 6J 9 (3B 142)
TERHILL 1B 166
Tern Gdns. PL7: Plymp 4C 138
The Terrace EX33: Brau 4J 15
  PL1: Dev 2C 140
  TQ1: Torq 2D 116
Terrace Wlk. TQ13: Ashb 3G 99
Terracina Ct. EX2: Exe 7E 6
Terra Nova Grn. PL2: Plym 6G 135
TETCOTT 1B 168
Tewkesbury Cl. PL2: Plym 3F 135
Tews La. EX31: Bick, Rou 6K 17
Tewsley Cl. EX31: Bick 6K 17
Thackeray Cl. EX11: Ott M 3D 80
Thackeray Gdns. PL5: Plym 2G 135
Thackeray Rd. EX4: Whip 4B 66
Thames Gdns. PL3: Plym 6E 136
Thanckes Cl. PL11: Torp 1A 140
Thanckes Dr. PL11: Torp 1A 140
Thatcher Av. TQ1: Torq 3H 117
Thatcher Dr. TQ14: Teignm 1J 107
Thatcher Hgts. TQ1: Torq 3H 117
Theatre La. EX31: B'aple 4E 18
  (off The Strand)
Theatre Ope PL1: Dev 3E 140
Theatre Royal 5D 8 (3J 141)
THELBRIDGE 2B 164
Thelma Hulbert Gallery 3E 54
Therlow Rd. PL3: Plym 5C 136
Thetford Gdns. PL6: Plym 3E 136
Third Av. EX1: Heav 3K 7 (6J 65)
  EX2: Cou W 6B 72
  EX2: Won 7C 66
  EX7: Daw 5G 97
  PL1: Dev 2F 141
  PL2: Plym 4D 134
  PL9: Plyms 3H 143
  TQ1: Torq 5C 112
  TQ14: Teignm 4G 107
Third Dr. TQ14: Teignm 4G 107
Thirlmere Gdns. PL6: Plym 6K 131
Thistle Bri. Rd. EX31: C'nor 1D 16
Thistle Cl. PL6: Plym 3F 133
  TQ12: New A 6A 104
Thomas Bassett Dr. EX24: Colyf 1F 87
Thomas Cl. EX8: Exmth 7K 75
Thomas La. EX4: Exe 4D 64
  (off Harefield Cl.)
  PL4: Plym 1A 142
Thomas Newcomen Ct.
  TQ6: Dartm 6C 124
  (off Ivatt Rd.)
Thompson Cl. EX7: Daw 3J 97
Thompson Rd. EX1: Heav 5K 65
  PL5: Plym 6G 131

Thornberry Av. EX1: Whip 6A **66**
THORNBURY 3C **163**
Thornbury Pk. Av. PL3: Plym 5J **135**
Thornbury Rd. PL6: Plym 6F **133**
Thorncliff Cl. TQ1: Torq 1G **117**
Thorn Cl. EX1: Whip 6A **66**
 TQ12: New A 7B **104**
THORNCOMBE 3D **167**
Thorn Cross TQ13: Bov T 6B **92**
Thorndale Courts EX1: Exe 4A **64**
THORNDON CROSS 1D **169**
Thorne Farm Nature Trail 3B **162**
Thorne Farm Way EX11: Ott M 3B **80**
Thorne La. EX17: Bow 7K **37**
Thorne Pk. EX17: Cred 6K **39**
Thorne Pk. Rd. TQ2: Torq 1K **115**
THORNE ST MARGARET 1A **166**
Thornes Ter. EX36: S Mol 6C **26**
THORNEY 1D **167**
Thorney Lakes Caravan Park 1D **167**
THORNFALCON 1C **167**
Thornfield Cl. EX8: Exmth 2C **76**
 EX12: Seat 3E **86**
THORNGROVE 1D **167**
THORNHILLHEAD 2C **163**
Thornhill Rd. PL3: Plym 5K **135**
Thornhill Way PL3: Plym 5K **135**
Thorning St. TQ8: Salc 3D **158**
Thornlea Av. EX5: Frem 6E **16**
Thornley Dr. TQ14: Teignm 4G **107**
Thornley Way EX39: Hart 3J **27**
Thorn Orchard TQ12: Ipp 6J **101**
Thorn Pk. PL3: Plym 6K **135**
Thornpark Ri. EX1: Whip 6A **66**
Thornton Av. PL4: Plym 2J **9** (1A **142**)
Thornton Cl. EX9: Bud S 7C **82**
 EX39: Bide 3D **22**
Thornton Hill EX4: Exe 1E **6** (4F **65**)
Thornton Pearn Ri. PL7: Lym R 4H **91**
Thorntree Bus. Units EX8: Exmth . . .3H **77**
Thornville Ter. PL9: Plyms 5D **142**
Thornyville Cl. PL9: Plyms 4D **142**
Thornyville Dr. PL9: Plyms 5D **142**
Thornyville Vs. PL9: Plyms 5D **142**
Thorpe Av. EX8: Exmth 1D **76**
THORVERTON 2B **50** (3D **165**)
Thorverton Rd. EX2: Mar B 5G **71**
Threadneedle St. EX15: Culm 2B **46**
 (off Hemyock Rd.)
Three Acre Cl. EX13: Axmin 3J **89**
Three Corner Fld. EX5: Cran 4B **68**
Three Corner Pl. EX2: Alph 5F **71**
Three Corners TQ12: Kingst 3J **105**
Three Ways EX31: Brat F 6H **13**
Threshers EX17: Cred 6F **39**
Threwstones Ct. EX16: Tive 3E **40**
Throgmorton Ho. TQ9: Tot 6F **103**
THROWLEIGH 1A **170**
Thrushel Cl. TQ5: Brixh 6C **122**
THRUSHELTON 2C **169**
THURDON 2A **162**
THURLBEAR 1C **167**
THURLESTONE 6C **154** (3C **175**)
Thurlestone Ct. TQ6: Dartm 6E **124**
 (off Victoria Rd.)
Thurlestone Gdns. TQ6: Dartm 6E **124**
Thurlestone Golf Course
 . . . . .7B **154** (3C **175**)
Thurlestone Rd. TQ12: New A 7E **104**
Thurlestone Wlk. PL6: Plym 2E **136**
 (not continuous)
Thurlow Cl. EX17: Cred 6F **39**
Thurlow Hill TQ1: Torq 7C **112**
Thurlow Pk. TQ1: Torq 7C **112**
Thurlow Rd. EX4: Exe 1J **7** (4H **65**)
 TQ1: Torq 7C **112**
THURLOXTON 1C **167**
Thursby Wlk. EX4: Pin 3C **66**
Ticklemore St. TQ9: Tot 6F **103**
Tidal Vw. Cl. TQ7: Ave G 7H **151**
Tidcombe Cl. EX16: Tive 5G **41**
Tidcombe La. EX16: Tive 4G **41**
Tidcombe Wlk. EX16: Tive 4G **41**
Tiddy Brook Rd. PL19: Whit 7K **59**
Tiddy Cl. PL19: Tavi 6H **59**
TIDEFORD 2A **174**
TIDEFORD CROSS 1A **174**
Tidwell Bus. Units EX8: Exmth 3H **77**
Tidwell Cl. EX9: Bud S 5C **82**
Tidwell La. EX9: Bud S 3C **82**
Tidwell Rd. EX9: Bud S 5C **82**
Tiger Moth Rd. EX5: Clyst H 4K **67**
Tigers Way EX13: Axmin 4J **89**
TIGLEY .1D **175**
Tillage Way EX5: Clyst M 2G **73**
Tillard Cl. PL7: Plymp 4F **139**
Tillhouse Rd. EX5: Cran 2C **68**
Tilly Cl. PL9: Plyms 7G **143**
Timber Hill DT7: Lym R 3K **91**
Timbers Cl. TQ11: B'leigh 6B **98**
Timbers Rd. TQ11: B'leigh 6B **98**
Timber Ter. TQ12: Kingsk 1F **111**
Timber Vale Cvn. Pk. 3K **91**
Times M. TQ9: Tot 6E **102**
Tinever Rd. EX31: C'nor 1C **16**
TINHAY 6C **56** (2B **168**)
Tinhay Ct. PL16: Tin 6C **56**
 (off Station Rd.)

Tinhay Mill Ind. Est. PL16: Tin 7C **56**
Tin La. EX2: Exe 7A **6** (1D **70**)
 PL4: Plym 5G **9** (3K **141**)
Tinside Lido 7D **8** (4J **141**)
Tintagel Cl. EX4: Whip 2K **65**
 TQ2: Torq 5B **112**
Tintagel Cres. PL2: Plym 3H **135**
Tintern Av. PL4: Plym 5K **9** (3B **142**)
Tip Hill EX11: Ott M 4C **80**
TIPPACOTT 2D **161**
TIPTON ST JOHN 1J **81** (1A **172**)
Tipton Va. EX11: Metc 1H **81**
TITCHBERRY 1A **162**
Titchfield Gdns. TQ3: Paig 7F **115**
Tithebarn Copse EX1: Pin 4E **66**
Tithebarn La. EX1: Pin 4E **66**
Tithebarn Way EX1: Pin 4D **66**
Tithe Hill TQ7: Chur 1B **156**
Tithe Rd. PL7: Plymp 4H **137**
TITSON .3A **162**
TIVERTON 4D **40** (2D **165**)
Tiverton Bus. Pk. EX16: Tive 2G **41**
Tiverton Castle 4C **40** (2D **165**)
Tiverton Cl. PL6: Plym 2C **132**
Tiverton Golf Course 3K **41** (2D **165**)
Tiverton Mus. of Mid Devon Life
 . . . . .5C **40** (2D **165**)
Tiverton Parkway Golf Driving Range
 . . . . .2C **42**
Tiverton Parkway Station
 (Rail) 3D **42** (2A **166**)
Tiverton Rd. EX5: Silv 1F **51**
 EX15: Cull 3F **45**
 EX16: Bam 4G **33**
TIVERTON SERVICES 2A **166**
Tiverton Tourist Information Centre
 . . . . .5D **40** (2D **165**)
Tiverton Town FC 3C **40**
Tiverton Way EX16: Tive 3F **41**
The Tivoli Cinema 5D **40**
Toadpit La. EX11: W Hill 1J **79**
Toby La. EX5: Wood S 3D **78**
Tokesen Dr. EX4: Pin 3B **66**
Tolchers TQ9: Darti 3B **102**
TOLLAND 1B **166**
Tollards Rd. EX2: Cou W 4K **71**
Tollbar Cl. PL21: Ivy 4K **145**
Tollit Gdns. TQ9: Tot 6F **103**
 (off Weston Rd.)
Tollox Pl. PL3: Plym 7C **136**
Tolman Cres. EX12: Seat 4F **87**
Tomouth Cres. EX39: App 3H **21**
Tomouth Rd. EX39: App 3H **21**
Tomouth Sq. EX39: App 3H **21**
Tomouth Ter. EX39: App 3H **21**
Tom Sanders Cl. EX34: C Mar 7C **12**
Tom's Fld. EX33: Croy 1C **14**
TONEDALE 1B **166**
Topcliff Rd. TQ14: Shal 4H **107**
 (not continuous)
TOPSHAM 5B **74** (2D **171**)
Topsham Mus. 6B **74** (2D **171**)
Topsham Pool 5B **74**
Topsham Rd.
 EX2: Cou W, Exe 7F **7** (1G **71**)
Topsham Station (Rail) . . .5B **74** (2D **171**)
Top Tor Viewpoint 3B **170**
TORBAY 6J **115** (3B **176**)
Torbay Bus. Pk. TQ4: Paig 6E **118**
Torbay Ct. TQ5: Brixh 3G **123**
Torbay Golf Cen. Driving Range . . .5H **119**
Torbay Holiday Chalets 2D **122**
Torbay Leisure Cen. 4H **119**
Torbay Lifeboat Station
 . . . . .2G **123** (2B **176**)
Torbay Olympic Gymnastic Club . . .4B **112**
Torbay Rd. TQ2: Torq 5K **115**
 TQ4: Paig 1J **119**
Torbay Trad. Est. TQ5: Brixh 4E **122**
Tor Bridge High Sports Cen. 1E **136**
Torbridge Rd. PL7: Plymp 3B **138**
 PL20: Horr 2E **126**
TORBRYAN 1A **176**
Torbryan Cl. PL6: Plym 3F **137**
Tor Chu. Rd. TQ2: Torq 1B **116**
Tor Cl. EX4: Whip 3K **65**
 PL3: Plym 4K **135**
 TQ4: Broads 1H **121**
Tor Cres. PL3: Plym 4K **135**
TORCROSS 3A **176**
Tor Dale TQ1: Torq 7C **112**
Tor Gdns. TQ12: E Ogw 3A **108**
Tor Haven TQ2: Torq 2D **116**
 (off Abbey Rd.)
Tor Hill Rd. TQ2: Torq 1C **116**
Toriana Pl. PL7: Plymp 3A **138**
 (off Boringdon Rd.)
Torland Rd. PL3: Plym 4K **135**
Toronto Ho. EX4: Exe 4G **65**
Toronto Rd. EX4: Exe 1H **7** (5G **65**)
Tor Pk. Rd. TQ2: Torq 7B **112**
 TQ4: Paig 4C **118**
TORPOINT 1A **140** (2A **174**)
Torpoint Mosquito Sailing Club 2B **140**
TORQUAY 1C **116** (1B **176**)
Torquay Coach Station 7C **112**

Torquay Crematorium 4A **112**
Torquay Golf Course 4E **112** (1B **176**)
Torquay Holiday Pk. 2A **112**
Torquay Mus. 2E **116** (1B **176**)
Torquay Rd. TQ2: Torq 1G **111**
 TQ3: Paig, Pres 1H **119**
 TQ12: Kingsk 1G **111**
 TQ12: Kingsk, New A 1F **109**
 TQ14: Shal 6G **107**
Torquay Station (Rail) . . .3B **116** (1B **176**)
Torquay United FC 6D **112**
TORRE 3C **150** (2B **174**)
Torr Bri. Pk. PL8: Y'ton 2C **150**
TORRE 1B **116** (1B **176**)
Torre Abbey 2B **116** (1B **176**)
Torre Cl. PL21: Ivy 4K **145**
Torre Station (Rail) 7A **112** (1B **176**)
Torr Hill PL8: Y'ton 2B **150**
Torridge Av. TQ2: Torq 6H **111**
TORRIDGE BRI. 1G **23**
Torridge Cl. EX39: Bide 4G **23**
 (off Torrington La.)
 PL7: Plymp 3D **138**
Torridge Hill EX39: Bide 4F **23**
Torridge Mt. EX39: Bide 4G **23**
Torridge Pl. EX39: Bide 4G **23**
Torridge Pool 5F **21**
Torridge Rd. EX31: C'nor 1E **16**
 EX39: App 2G **21**
 PL7: Plymp 3C **138**
Torridge St. EX39: Bide 4G **23**
Torridge Vw. EX38: G Tor 2A **30**
 EX39: Bide 4F **23**
Torridge Way PL3: Plym 6D **136**
Torrington 1646 . . . . .3C **30**
Torrington La. EX39: Bide 4G **23**
Torrington Mus. 2C **30** (2C **163**)
Torrington Pl. EX6: Kenton 6H **95**
 (off Chiverstone Rd.)
Torrington Pool 2C **30**
Torrington Rd. EX19: Wink 1B **36**
Torrington Sports Hall 2D **30**
Torrington St. EX39: Bide 4G **23**
Torr La. PL3: Plym 4J **135**
 PL8: Torr 3C **150**
Tor Rd. PL3: Plym 4K **135**
Tor Royal La. PL20: Prin 7D **60**
Torrs Pk. EX34: Ilfra 4G **11**
Torrs Wlk. Av. EX34: Ilfra 2G **11**
Torr Vw. Av. PL3: Plym 4J **135**
 TQ12: Kingsk 1F **111**
Tor Sands TQ4: Paig 2J **119**
 (off Sands Rd.)
Tors Pk. EX35: Lynm 2J **13**
Tor Sq. Ho. TQ2: Torq 7B **112**
 (off South St.)
Tors Rd. EX20: Oke 5B **48**
 EX35: Lynm 2J **13**
Tors Vw. EX39: W Ho 6A **20**
Tor Va. TQ1: Torq 7B **112**
Torver Cl. PL6: Plym 1E **136**
Tor Vw. EX20: Lew 1A **56**
 PL20: Horr 2E **126**
 PL20: Prin 5B **60**
 TQ11: B'leigh 5B **98**
Tor Vw. Av. TQ12: New A 2J **109**
Tor Vw. Gdns. TQ3: Paig 1G **119**
Torville Pk. EX39: W Ho 5C **20**
Torwood Cl. TQ1: Torq 3E **116**
Torwood Ct. TQ1: Torq 2F **117**
Torwood Gdns. Rd. TQ1: Torq 3E **116**
Torwood Rd. TQ1: Torq 3E **116**
Tory Brook Av. PL7: Plymp 3B **138**
Tory Brook Ct. PL7: Plymp 3B **138**
Tory Way PL7: Plymp 3A **138**
Tothill Av. PL4: Plym 3H **9** (2A **142**)
Tothill Ct. TQ14: Shal 6G **107**
Tothill Rd. PL4: Plym 4J **9** (2A **142**)
TOTNES 6E **102** (1A **176**)
Totnes Castle 5D **102** (1A **176**)
Totnes Cinema 6E **102**
Totnes Cl. PL7: Plymp 5E **138**
Totnes Down Hill TQ9: Tot 7E **102**
Totnes Elizabethan House Mus.
 . . . . .6E **102** (1A **176**)
Totnes Fashion & Textiles Museum
 . . . . .6E **102**
Totnes Image Bank & Rural Archive
 . . . . .6F **103**
 (within Tourist Info. Cen.)
Totnes Ind. Est. TQ9: Tot 5E **102**
Totnes Pavilion Leisure Cen. 5E **102**
Totnes Rare Breeds Farm 3E **102**
Totnes Riverside Station
 South Devon Railway
 . . . . .4E **102** (1A **176**)
Totnes Rd. PL21: Erm 3H **147**
 TQ2: Torq 3G **115**
 TQ3: Marl 7A **114**
 TQ3: Paig 3E **118**
 TQ4: Coll M, Paig 2A **118**
 TQ6: Strete 6H **153**
 TQ10: S Bre 1B **100**
 TQ11: B'leigh 4E **98**
Totnes Station (Rail) 5E **102** (1A **176**)

Totnes Town Mill 6F **103**
 (within Tourist Info. Cen.)
Tottons Ct. EX2: Alph 5D **70**
Touts Ct. EX36: S Mol 6D **26**
 (off East St.)
Tovey Cres. PL5: Plym 1J **135**
Tovey M. EX14: Hon 3F **55**
 (off King St.)
Towell La. EX19: Bea 2J **31**
Towerfield EX3: Top 6D **72**
Towerfield Dr. PL6: Plym 2D **132**
Tower Gdns. EX17: Cred 5H **39**
Twr. Hill EX17: Cher F 1H **39**
Tower Hill Rd. PL15: St G 5E **34**
Tower La. PL21: Moor 3C **146**
Tower Pk. EX36: S Mol 7C **26**
 TQ13: More 7H **61**
Tower Rd. EX14: Hon 6J **55**
 TQ3: Paig 1H **119**
Towers Cl. PL6: Plym 1G **137**
Tower St. EX8: Exmth 6C **76**
 EX39: Bide 4F **23**
 (off Buttgarden St.)
 EX39: Nort 5E **20**
Tower Vw. EX5: Broadc 7C **52**
Tower Wlk. EX2: Alph 5F **71**
Twr. Way EX14: Dunk 7G **47**
TOWN BARTON 6G **49**
Town Cl. TQ6: Dartm 1A **124** (6E **124**)
Town Cotts. TQ12: A'well 6E **108**
Town End EX5: Broadc 5D **52**
Town Farm Cl. EX14: Hon 3E **54**
 PL20: Horr 2E **126**
Town Farm Cotts. TQ9: Blacka 3C **152**
Townfield EX6: Exmin 2C **74**
Town Hall Pl. TQ13: Bov T 3C **92**
Town Hill EX5: Broadc 5C **52**
 EX15: Culm 2B **46**
 PL21: Erm 3H **147**
Townlands EX5: Bradn 2B **52**
 EX15: Will 5D **44**
Town La. EX5: W'bury 5C **78**
Town Mdw. EX20: Brid 3H **57**
Town Mdws. EX39: Wools 2A **28**
The Town Mill 5K **91**
Town Mill Ct. EX31: B'aple 3E **18**
 (off Mills Way)
Town Mill Gdns. PL19: Tavi 3J **59**
Town Pk. EX17: Cred 6G **39**
 EX38: G Tor 2A **30**
 TQ7: Lodd 3G **151**
 TQ7: W Alv 5E **156**
Town Quay TQ9: Tot 6F **103**
 (off The Plains)
TOWNSEND 6H **25**
Towns End EX33: Brau 4H **15**
Townsend EX12: Beer 6A **86**
 TQ12: Den 2H **101**
Townsend Av. EX12: Seat 4E **86**
Townsend Cl. TQ7: W Alv 5D **156**
Townsend Hill TQ12: Ipp 6G **101**
Townsend Rd. EX12: Seat 5E **86**
 TQ7: W Alv 5D **156**
Townsend Ter. TQ9: E All 6D **152**
Townshend Av. PL2: Plym 6D **134**
Town's La. TQ7: Lodd 3G **151**
TOWNSTAL 6D **124**
Townstal Cres. TQ6: Dartm 6D **124**
Townstal Hill
 TQ6: Dartm 1A **124** (6E **124**)
Townstal Pathfields TQ6: Dartm 6D **124**
Townstal Rd. TQ6: Dartm 6C **124**
Town Tree Hill EX7: Daw 4G **97**
Town Vw. EX17: Cred 6H **39**
Town Wlk. EX32: B'aple 5G **19**
Towsington La. EX6: Exmin 4B **74**
Tracey Ct. PL1: Plym 3C **8**
Tracey Grn. EX16: W'ridge 6H **33**
Tracey Rd. EX14: Hon 2D **54**
Traceys Av. EX12: Seat 4D **86**
Tracey Va. TQ13: Bov T 5B **92**
Tracey Vw. EX14: Hon 3E **54**
 (off Northcote La.)
Trafalgar Cl. PL5: Plym 3C **134**
 TQ12: New A 6E **104**
Trafalgar Ct. EX3: Top 5A **74**
 (off High St.)
 EX15: Uff 6H **43**
Trafalgar Gdns. EX32: B'aple 6F **19**
Trafalgar Lawn EX32: B'aple 6F **19**
Trafalgar Pl. EX4: Exe 1G **7** (5G **65**)
Trafalgar Pl. La. PL1: Dev 1E **140**
Trafalgar Rd. EX2: Cou W 5B **72**
 EX8: Lymp 5G **75**
Trafalgar St. PL4: Plym 4G **9** (2K **141**)
Trafalgar Ter. EX12: Brans 6H **85**
 TQ5: Brixh 2E **122**
 (off Higher Furzeham Rd.)
The Trafalgar Way
 EX13: Axmin, Kilm 2E **88**
Trafford M. EX2: Won 2B **72**
 (off Lords Way)
Trago Mills 5H **93** (3C **171**)
Traine Ter. PL21: Modb 7H **147**
Traine Vs. PL21: Modb 5H **147**
Tram Wlk. PL9: Hooe 5C **142**

Tramway Rd. PL6: Plym 3E 132
Tramways TQ1: Torq 6D 112
Transit Way PL5: Plym 7H 131
Travershes Cl. EX8: Exmth 3D 76
Trayes Ter. PL4: Plym 2C 142
Treacle Hill TQ12: Kingst 4H 105
(off Fore St.)
Treago Gdns. PL6: Plym 2D 132
TREBARTHA 3A 168
Trebblepark Rd. TQ7: Kingsb 3F 157
Trebblepark Wlk. TQ7: Kingsb 3F 157
TREBULLETT 3B 168
TREBURLEY 3B 168
Treby Rd. PL7: Plymp 5C 138
TRECOTT 3A 164
TREDAULE 2A 168
TREDINNICK 3A 168
Treefield EX32: Brat F 6J 13
Treefields TQ5: Brixh 4D 122
Treefield Wlk. EX32: B'aple 5J 19
(off Barton Rd.)
Treesdale Cl. TQ3: Paig 1F 119
Trefusis Gdns. PL3: Plym 7B 136
Trefusis Pl. EX8: Exmth 7C 76
Trefusis Ter. EX8: Exmth 7C 76
EX20: Mert 5B 30
(off Back La.)
Trefusis Way EX9: E Bud 1D 82
TREGADA 2B 168
TREGADILLETT 2A 168
TREGEARE 2A 168
Tregenna Cl. PL7: Plymp 5F 139
TREGOLE 1A 168
TREGONHAWKE 2A 174
TREHAN 2A 174
Trehill Cl. PL6: Plym 4K 131
Trehill Rd. PL21: Ivy 4H 145
TREKENNER 3B 168
TRELASH 1A 168
Trelawney Av. PL5: Plym 2C 134
Trelawney Ct. EX39: Nort 5F 21
(off Diddywell Rd.)
Trelawney La. PL3: Plym 6J 135
Trelawney Pl. PL5: Plym 2C 134
Trelawney Rd. PL3: Plym 6J 135
Trelawny Rd. PL7: Plymp 4K 137
PL19: Tavi 3J 59
Trelissick Cl. TQ3: Paig 7D 114
Trelissick Rd. TQ3: Paig 7D 114
Trelivan Cl. EX8: Exmth 1G 77
Trelorrin Gdns. PL3: Plym 6K 135
Treloweth Cl. PL3: Plym 3J 135
TREMAIL 2A 168
TREMAINE 2A 168
Tremaine Cl. EX14: Hon 3G 55
TREMAR 3A 168
TREMATON 2A 174
Trematon Av. TQ1: Torq 1C 116
Trematon Dr. PL21: Ivy 4J 145
Trematon Ter. PL4: Plym 7K 135
Tremayne Ri. PL19: Tavi 4H 59
Tremford Ct. EX9: Bud S 6B 82
Tremlet Mdw. EX5: Rock 3C 68
Tremlett Gro. TQ9: Darti 2A 102
TQ12: Ipp 6H 101
Tremletts Cl. EX6: Ted M 6H 49
Trenance Dr. PL19: Lam 6C 58
Trendlewood Rd. PL6: Plym 3E 132
TRENEGLOS 2A 168
TRENGUNE 1A 168
Trenode Av. EX34: C Mar 6A 12
Trentbridge Sq. EX2: Won 1B 72
Trent Cl. EX39: Bide 5J 23
PL3: Plym 5C 136
Trentham Cl. PL6: Plym 4C 132
TQ3: Paig 6E 114
TRENTISHOE 2C 161
Tresco Gdns. PL6: Plym 4A 132
Trescote Way EX20: Brid 1J 57
Tresillian Cotts. EX3: Top 7B 74
Tresillian Gdns. EX3: Top 6B 74
EX4: Exe 6K 9
Tresillian St. PL4: Plym 6K 9 (3B 142)
TRESKINNICK CROSS 1A 168
Tresluggan Rd. PL5: Plym 2C 134
TRESMEER 2A 168
TRESPARRETT 1A 168
TRESPARRETT POSTS 1A 168
Treston Cl. EX7: Daw 3H 97
Trethewey Gdns. PL7: Wot 1F 129
Tretower Cl. PL6: Plym 5A 132
TREVADLOCK 3A 168
Trevanna Rd. TQ7: Kingsb 5F 157
Trevannion Cl. PL6: Plym 3B 136
Trevelyan Rd. EX12: Seat 6G 87
Trevena Cl. EX5: Clyst M 2F 73
Treveneague Gdns. PL2: Plym 3J 135
Trevenn Dr. TQ12: Kingsk 2G 111
Treveor Gdns. PL21: Modb 5H 147
Treverbyn Cl. PL7: Plymp 3A 138
Treverbyn Rd. PL7: Plymp 3A 138
Trevessa Cl. PL2: Plym 3J 135
Trevethan Pk. PL20: Bere A 6C 128
TREVIGRO 3B 168
Trevisker Gdns. EX1: Pin 3G 67
Trevithick Rd. PL5: Plym 2D 134
TREVIVIAN 2A 168
Trevone Gdns. PL2: Plym 3J 135

Trevose Way PL3: Plym 5D 136
TREWARLETT 2B 168
TREWASSA 2A 168
TREWEEN 2A 168
TREWEN 2A 168
TREWINT 1A 168
Trewithy Ct. PL6: Plym 2A 136
Trewithy Dr. PL6: Plym 2A 136
Trews Weir Ct. EX2: Exe 1G 71
Trews Weir Reach
EX2: Exe 7G 7 (1G 71)
Trewyn Ct. PL21: Hols 1B 34
Trewyn Rd. EX22: Hols 1B 34
The Triangle EX6: Kenton 6H 95
(off Exeter Hill)
EX10: Sidm 7B 84
TQ14: Teignm 5J 107
Triangle Pl. TQ14: Teignm 5J 107
Trickey Cl. EX16: Tive 5D 6
Trickhay St. EX4: Exe 4D 6 (6E 64)
Trick's Ter. EX19: Bea 2H 31
Tricorn Cl. TQ2: Torq 4J 111
Trigger's Hill EX19: Bea, Robo 1G 31
Trigley La. EX36: S Mol 7C 26
Trill La. EX13: Abb G 7G 89
EX13: Mus 6E 90
TRIMSTONE 2B 160
Trimstone Cross Picnic Site 2B 160
Trinfield Av. EX8: Exmth 3D 76
Trinity Apts. EX1: Exe 4F 7
Trinity Cl. PL20: Bere A 2C 128
TQ14: Teignm 3H 107
Trinity Ct. EX1: Exe 5F 7 (7F 65)
EX10: Sidm 7C 84
EX39: W Ho 6A 20
(off Atlantic Way)
Trinity Gdns. EX34: Ilfra 3G 11
Trinity Hill TQ1: Torq 3E 116
Trinity Hill Local Nature Reserve . .3A 90
Trinity Hill Rd. EX13: Ray H 2A 90
Trinity M. TQ14: Teignm 3H 107
(off Maudlin Dr.)
Trinity Pl. EX32: B'aple 5F 19
PL1: Plym 7C 8 (4H 141)
Trinity Rd. EX8: Exmth 4A 76
Trinity Sq. EX13: Axmin 3H 89
Trinity St. EX32: B'aple 5F 19
PL1: Plym 7B 8 (4H 141)
Trinity Ter. EX13: Axmin 3H 89
(off Castle St.)
Trinity Way PL19: Tavi 5G 59
Trinnaman Cl. PL21: Ivy 5H 145
Trinnicks Orchard PL21: Ugb 6E 146
Tristan Cl. EX4: Whip 2K 65
Triumphal Cres. PL7: Plymp 4H 137
Triumph Pl. TQ14: Teignm 2J 107
Troarn Way TQ13: Chud 3C 94
Trojan Ind. Pk. TQ4: Paig 3E 118
Trood La. EX2: Matf 7G 71
Trott Cl. EX15: Cull 4F 45
Trough La. TQ13: Bov T 3C 92
Trouville EX32: B'aple 4F 19
(off Bevan Rd.)
Trowbridge Cl. PL5: Plym 6H 131
Trow Hill EX10: Sidf 2E 84
(not continuous)
truGym
Plymouth 4G 9
TRULL 1C 167
Trumans Ct. EX4: Exe 6C 6
Trumans Pl. EX7: Daw 4H 97
(off High St.)
Trumlands Rd. TQ1: Torq 4C 112
Trumpers Cl. PL21: Ivy 3E 144
Trumps Ct. EX10: Sidm 7C 84
(off East St.)
Trumps Orchard EX15: Cull 3F 45
Truro Av. TQ2: Torq 4C 112
Truro Dr. EX4: Exe 5B 64
EX8: Exmth 1F 77
PL5: Plym 5F 131
TRUSHAM 2C 171
Trusham Rd. EX2: Mar B 3F 71
TUCKENHAY 2A 176
Tucker Cl. PL5: Plym 3E 134
Tucker Ct. EX14: Hon 3F 55
TUCKERMARSH 1B 128
Tuckers Brook PL21: Modb 6G 147
Tuckers Ct. EX17: Cred 6F 39
PL8: Torr 2C 150
Tuckers Hall 5C 6 (7E 64)
Tucker's Hill EX21: Corn 7H 129
Tuckers Mdw. EX17: Cred 6F 39
Tuckers Pk. EX22: Bradw 5B 28
EX39: Buck B 2H 29
Tuckfield Cl. EX2: Won 1K 71
Tucking Mill La. EX36: S Mol 6D 26
Tuckwell Gro. EX1: W Cly 1F 67
Tudor Cl. EX39: Nort 6E 20
PL9: Plyms 7F 143
PL16: Lift 6E 60
(off Darkey La.)
TQ4: Paig 5G 119
TQ12: New A 1E 108
Tudor Ct. EX4: Exe 5C 6 (7E 64)
TQ13: Ashb 4H 99
(off North St.)
Tudor Dr. EX31: B'aple 7B 18

Tudor Gro. EX15: Cull 2H 45
Tudor Rd. TQ12: New A 1E 108
Tudor St. EX4: Exe 5C 6 (7E 64)
Tuffery Ct. EX4: Exe 1K 7 (4J 65)
Tugela Ter. EX5: Clyst M 2F 73
Tully St. EX31: B'aple 4E 18
Tully Gdns. EX10: Sidm 3C 84
The Tumbles EX20: Exbo 5J 35
Tumbling Fld. La. EX16: Tive 5D 40
Tumbling Flds. EX16: Tive 5D 40
Tumbling Weir 1A 172
Tumbling Weir Ct. EX11: Ott M 4B 80
Tumbling Weir Way
EX11: Ott M 4B 80
Tumbly Hill TQ7: Kingsb 5G 157
Tunnel La. EX14: Hon 2J 55
Tunnels Beaches 2G 11 (2B 160)
Tuns La. EX5: Silv 2G 51
Tuplins TQ12: Kingst 3H 105
Turbill Gdns. PL7: Plymp 4E 138
TURFMOOR 3C 167
Turkey La. EX5: Rock, Whim 3K 69
(not continuous)
Turk's Head La. EX14: Hon 4D 54
TURNCHAPEL 6B 142 (2A 174)
Turner Av. EX8: Exmth 5D 76
Turner Cl. EX10: New P 6H 81
Turners Cres. EX39: Hart 2H 27
Turnpike EX14: Hon 3G 55
EX16: Sam P 3A 42
Turnpike Cl. EX39: High C 6G 27
Turnpike Cres. PL21: Ivy 5K 145
Turnquay PL9: Plyms 5C 142
Turnstone Rd. EX2: Exe 3J 71
Turpins Plot EX20: Oke 3D 48
Turret Gro. PL4: Plym 7A 136
Tute's La. EX34: C Mar 5C 12
TUTWELL 3B 168
Tuxton Cl. PL7: Plymp 6E 138
Tweed Cl. EX14: Hon 5F 55
Tweenaway PL21: Ivy 5J 145
TWEENAWAYS 2E 118
Tweenaways TQ11: B'leigh 5B 98
Tweenways TQ12: Kingst 4G 105
Twelve Oaks Farm Cvn. Pk. 3D 104
Twickenham Rd. TQ12: New A 2J 109
Twickenham St. PL2: Plym 3G 135
Twindle Beer TQ13: Chud 2B 94
TWITCHEN
EX36 . . . . .3D 161
TA21 . . . . .3G 43
Twitchen Ho. Holiday Pk. 4C 10
Two Acre Cl. TQ3: Paig 1E 118
Two Acre Ct. EX2: Alph 5D 70
TWO BRIDGES 3A 170
Two Bridges Rd. EX10: Sidf 1D 84
PL20: Prin 6D 60
TWO MILE OAK 7B 108 (1A 176)
TWO POTTS 7K 11
Two Rivers Ind. Est. EX31: B'aple . . .3C 18
Two Trees Rd. EX31: Frem 6E 16
Twyford Pl. EX16: Tive 4D 40
Tylers Mdw. EX38: G Tor 2D 30
Tylney Cl. PL6: Plym 4C 132
Tyndale Cl. PL5: Plym 2G 135
Tyrell Mead EX10: Sidm 3C 84
Tyrrell Rd. EX16: Tive 4B 40
TYTHECOTT 2C 163
Tytheing Cl. EX5: New C 7D 50
TYTHERLEIGH 3D 167
Tything Wlk. PL3: Plym 5K 135

U

UFFCULME 6H 43 (2A 166)
Uffculme Ct. EX15: Uff 6H 43
(off Ashley Rd.)
Uffculme Rd. EX15: Culm 3A 44
EX15: Uff, Will 7F 43, 3E 44
UGBOROUGH 6E 146 (2C 175)
Ugborough Rd. PL21: Bitta 4C 146
Ugbrooke 3C 171
Ullswater Cl. EX4: Exe 7C 64
Ullswater Cres. PL6: Plym 5K 131
Ultimate Adventure Cen. 3A 22
Ulysses Pk. EX2: Sow 7D 66
Umber Cl. EX34: C Mar 5A 12
UMBERLEIGH 1A 164
Umberleigh Station (Rail) 1A 164
Undercliffe TQ6: Dartm 1B 124
Undercliff Rd. PL9: Hooe 5C 142
The Underfleet EX12: Seat 5F 87
Underfleet EX12: Seat 5F 87
(not continuous)
Underhay PL8: Y'ton 2A 150
Underhay Cl. EX7: Daw 2J 97
Underheath TQ1: Torq 1F 117
(off Middle Warberry Rd.)
Underhill EX8: Lymp 6F 75
Underhill Cl. EX8: Lymp 7G 75
Underhill Cres. EX8: Lymp 7G 75
Underhill Pk. EX16: Tive 3C 40
(off Johns Way)
Underhill Rd. PL3: Plym 7F 135
TQ2: Torq 3A 116
Underhill Ter. EX3: Top 5B 74

Underhill Vs. PL3: Plym 1F 141
Underidge Cl. TQ3: Paig 1E 118
Underidge Dr. TQ3: Paig 1E 118
Underidge La. TQ3: Paig 1E 118
Underidge Rd. TQ3: Paig 1E 118
Underlane EX22: Hols 3C 34
PL7: Plymp 6J 137
PL9: Plyms 6E 142
Underleat Cl. TQ13: Chud 1D 94
Underley Rd. TQ12: Kingsk 7A 86
Under Minnow Rd. EX31: B'aple 2D 18
Undertown PL21: Ugb 6E 146
Under Way TQ12: Coff 6K 109
Underwood PL20: Bere A 2C 128
UNDERWOOD 4A 138 (2B 174)
Underwood Cl. EX7: Daw 6G 97
Underwood Rd. PL7: Plymp 4A 138
Unicorn Cl. PL7: Plymp 5J 137
Unicorn St. EX2: Sow 1C 72
Union Cl. EX39: Bide 4E 22
Union La. TQ5: Brixh 3E 122
Union Pl. PL1: Plym 5A 8 (3G 141)
Union Rd. EX4: Exe 4G 65
EX17: Cred 6H 39
Union Sq. Shop. Cen. 1D 70
Union St. EX2: Exe 7B 6 (1D 70)
EX8: Exmth 6C 76
PL1: Plym 5A 8 (3G 141)
TQ1: Torq 1C 116
TQ2: Torq 7B 112
TQ6: Dartm 1A 124
TQ8: Salc 3D 158
TQ12: New A 1E 108
Union Ter. EX17: Cred 6H 39
EX31: Bick 5K 17
EX32: B'aple 5F 19
(off Litchdon St.)
Unity Cl. PL6: Plym 5E 132
Unity Pk. PL3: Plym 5C 136
University of Exeter
Knightley 4E 64
(off Streatham Dr.)
New North Rd. 1C 6 (5E 64)
Redcot 4E 64
(off Streatham Dr.)
St Lukes Campus 4H 7 (6G 65)
Streatham Campus 3E 64
University of Plymouth
Constantine St. 4G 9
Gibbon St. 3F 9
Marine Station 7H 9 (4A 142)
Peninsula Dental School 3H 71
Portland Sq. 3F 9 (1J 141)
UPCOTT
EX19 . . . . .3D 163
EX39 . . . . .6E 22
Upcott Av. EX31: B'aple 3B 18
Upcott Hill EX20: Oke 2A 48
EX39: Bide 6F 23
Upcottmead Rd. EX16: Tive 4B 40
Upcott Valley EX20: Oke 2A 48
UP EXE 2E 50 (3D 165)
Upexe La. EX5: Silv 2F 51
UPHAM 3C 165
Uphay La. EX13: Axmin 2F 89
Uphill Cl. PL21: Ivy 4J 145
Upland Chase EX14: Hon 6E 54
Upland Dr. PL6: Plym 5C 132
Upland Gdns. PL9: Wem 5C 148
Uplands PL19: Tavi 5G 59
Uplands Dr. EX4: Exe 3K 65
Uplands Rd. TQ3: Pres 4G 115
Uplands Ter. EX22: Hols 3C 34
UPLOWMAN 2A 166
Uplowman Rd. EX16: Tive, U'man . . .3J 41
UPLYME 2F 91 (1D 173)
Uplyme Rd. DT7: Lym R 4H 91
Uplyme Rd. Ind. Est. DT7: Lym R . . .4H 91
UPOTTERY 3C 167
Uppacott Wood Nature Reserve 1D 163
Uppaton La. PL21: Ivy 1C 144
Up. Barton EX5: Cran 3B 68
Up. Braddons Hill Rd. TQ1: Torq 2E 116
Up. Church St. EX8: Exmth 6C 76
Up. Churston Ri. EX12: Seat 4C 86
Up. Claypark EX34: Mort 4A 10
Up. Cloister Wlk. EX6: Exmin 1B 74
(off Devington Pk.)
Up. Cockington La. TQ2: Torq 7J 111
Up. Crooked Mdw. EX20: Oke 3C 48
Up. Headland Pk. Rd. TQ3: Pres 5J 115
Up. Hermosa Rd. TQ14: Teignm 4H 107
Up. Highfield EX10: Sidm 5B 84
Up. Knollys Ter. La.
PL3: Plym 1B 8 (7H 135)
Up. Longlands EX7: Daw 3F 97
Up. Manor Rd. TQ3: Pres 6H 115
Up. Mead EX13: Axmin 3J 89
Up. Morin Rd. TQ3: Pres 7J 115
Up. Paul St. EX4: Exe 3D 6 (6H 65)
Up. Penns Rd. TQ3: Pres 5J 115
Upper Plym Valley Prehistoric Sites
. . . . .1B 172
Up. Richardson St. EX5: Pin 4E 66
Up. Ridings PL7: Plymp 2E 138
Up. Stoneborough La. EX9: Bud S . . .6C 82
Upperton Rd. EX6: Dunsf 4A 62

Up. Torrs—Walcot Cl.

Up. Torrs EX34: Ilfra 3F 11
Up. Westhill Rd. DT7: Lym R 5H 91
Up. West Ter. EX9: Bud S 6C 82
Up. Wood La. TQ6: Kingsw 6H 125
UPPINCOTT 3C 165
UPTON
EX14 . . . . . 3A 166
EX23 . . . . . 3A 162
PL14 . . . . . 3A 168
TA4 . . . . . 1D 165
TQ1 . . . . . 7C 112
TQ7 . . . . . 3D 175
Upton Cl. PL3: Plym 4C 136
UPTON CROSS 3A 168
UPTON HELLIONS 3C 165
Upton Hill TQ1: Torq 7C 112
Upton Hill Rd. TQ5: Brixh 6E 122
Upton Mnr. Pk. TQ5: Brixh 6E 122
Upton Mnr. Rd. TQ5: Brixh 6D 122
UPTON PYNE 1D 171
Upton Rd. EX39: Bide 4G 23
(off Nutaberry Hill)
TQ1: Torq 7B 112
Usticke La. EX34: C Mar 7D 12
UTON 1C 171
Uxbridge Dr. PL5: Plym 6D 130

V

Vaagso Cl. PL1: Dev 2D 140
Vachell Cres. EX2: Sow 7C 66
(off Elliott Way)
Vale Cl. EX32: B'aple 3F 19
TQ5: Galm 3H 121
Vale La. EX13: Axmin 3H 89
Valenia Ter. TQ13: Ashb 4H 99
Valerian Pl. TQ12: New A 6A 104
Vale Rd. EX8: Exmth 5F 77
TQ12: Kingsk 7K 109
TQ12: New A 3G 109
Vales Rd. EX9: Bud S 6D 82
Valiant Av. PL5: Plym 6F 131
The Valiant Soldier Mus. & Heritage Cen. 4D 98 (1D 175)
Valletort Cotts. PL1: Plym 1F 141
Valletort Flats PL1: Plym 2F 141
(off Valletort Pl.)
Valletort Ho. PL1: Plym 3C 8
(Oxford St.)
PL1: Plym 5A 8 (3G 141)
(Union Pl.)
Valletort La. PL1: Plym 1F 141
Valletort Pk. TQ5: Brixh 4C 122
Valletort Pl. PL1: Plym 2F 141
Valletort Rd. PL1: Plym 1F 141
Valletort Ter. PL1: Plym 1G 141
(off Wilton Rd.)
Valley Cl. EX32: B'aple 4G 19
TQ14: Teignm 2F 107
Valley Dr. PL9: Wem 6B 148
Valley La. EX34: C Mar 6B 12
The Valley of Rocks 1F 13
Valley Pk. Cl. EX4: Exe 2G 65
Valley Path TQ12: New A 7B 104
Valley Rd. EX4: Exe 5C 64
EX5: Clyst M 2K 73
PL7: Plymp 6J 137
Valley Vw. EX5: Rock 3E 68
EX12: Seat 4E 86
EX13: Axmin 4J 89
EX21: Sheb 6J 29
EX32: Land 3D 24
EX39: Bide 3C 22
PL6: Plym 3E 132
TQ13: Chag 2H 61
Valley Vw. Cl. EX12: Seat 4F 87
PL3: Plym 4C 136
TQ1: Torq 6B 112
Valley Vw. Rd. EX12: Seat 4E 86
(off Valley Vw.)
PL3: Plym 4C 136
Valley Wlk. PL6: Plym 4E 132
Valley Way EX8: Exmth 1G 77
Van Buren Pl. EX2: Sow 2C 72
Vane Hill Rd. TQ1: Torq 3E 116
Vanguard Cl. PL5: Plym 2J 135
Vansittart Dr. EX8: Exmth 1E 76
Vansittart Rd. TQ2: Torq 7B 112
Vapron Rd. PL3: Plym 5K 135
Varco Sq. EX2: Won 1B 72
Varian Ct. TQ9: Tot 6G 103
Varley Ct. EX16: Tive 2E 40
Vauban Pl. PL2: Dev 7E 134
Vaughan Cl. PL2: Plym 4H 135
Vaughan Pde. TQ2: Torq 3D 116
Vaughan Ri. EX1: Whip 6A 66
Vaughan Rd. EX1: Whip 6A 66
TQ2: Torq 3D 116
Vauxhall Ct. PL4: Plym 5F 9
Vauxhall Quay PL4: Plym . . . 5G 9 (3K 141)
Vauxhall St. PL4: Plym 6F 9 (3K 141)
Vauxhall St. Flats PL4: Plym 5G 9
Vavasours Slip TQ6: Dartm 5F 125
Vealand Farm Nature Reserve 3A 162
Veale Cl. EX20: Hath 3G 35
Veale Dr. EX2: Won 2H 71
Veales Rd. TQ7: Kingsb 5F 157
Veasy Pk. PL9: Wem 6C 148
Veille La. TQ2: Torq 5J 111
(not continuous)
Veilstone Moor Nature Reserve 2C 163
Veitch Cl. EX2: Exe 7J 7 (1H 71)
Veitch Gdns. EX2: Alph 5E 70
VELATOR 6J 15
Velator Cl. EX33: Brau 6J 15
Velator Dr. EX33: Vel 6J 15
Velator Ind. Est. EX33: Vel 6J 15
Velator La. Av. EX33: Brau 5J 15
Velator Rd. EX33: Vel, Wraf 6J 15
Vellacott La. EX34: C Mar 6E 12
Velland Av. TQ2: Torq 1B 112
Vellator Way EX33: Brau 5J 15
VELLY 1A 162
Velwell Rd. EX4: Exe 1C 6 (5E 64)
Venborough Cl. EX12: Seat 4D 86
Venbridge Hill EX6: Cher 1C 62
Venford Cl. TQ4: Good 7H 119
VENHAY 2B 164
Venlake DT7: Uply 3F 91
Venlake Cl. DT7: Uply 3F 91
Venlake End DT7: Uply 3F 91
Venlake La. DT7: Uply 3G 91
Venlake Mdw. DT7: Uply 3F 91
Venlock Cl. EX32: B'aple 5J 19
VENN
EX32 . . . . . 5E 24
TQ7 . . . . . 7K 151 (3D 175)
Venn Cl. PL3: Plym 5K 135
TQ6: Sto F 2H 153
Venn Ct. PL3: Plym 5K 135
PL8: Brixt 3H 149
Venn Cres. PL3: Plym 5K 135
Venn Dr. PL8: Brixt 3H 149
Venn Gdns. PL3: Plym 4K 135
VENNGREEN 2B 162
Venn Gro. PL3: Plym 4K 135
Venn Hill PL19: Mil A 2B 58
Venn La. PL2: Plym 5H 135
TQ6: Dartm, Sto F 7A 124
Venn Orchard TQ12: Kingst 4G 105
VENN OTTERY 2F 81 (1A 172)
Venn Ottery Nature Reserve 7G 79 (1A 172)
Venn Ottery Rd. EX10: New P 5F 81
Venn Pk. TQ6: Sto F 1H 153
Venn Rd. EX32: B'aple, Land 7H 19
Venn Way PL3: Plym 4K 135
TQ6: Sto F 2H 153
Venny Bri. EX4: Pin 3C 66
VENNY TEDBURN 1C 171
VENTERDON 3B 168
Vention La. EX33: Puts 1D 14
Venton Dr. EX39: W Ho 5C 20
(not continuous)
Venture Cen. EX2: Mar B 6H 71
Venture Ct. TQ12: New A 1D 108
Verbena Ter. TQ14: Shal 6F 107
Verden Cl. PL3: Plym 6K 135
Vermont Gdns. PL2: Plym 4E 134
Verna Pl. PL5: Plym 1C 134
Verna Rd. PL5: Plym 1C 134
Verney St. EX1: Exe 2G 7 (5G 65)
Vernon Cl. TQ1: Torq 4E 116
Vernon Cres. EX2: Cou W 5B 72
Vernon Rd. EX8: Exmth 2F 77
Vernon's La. EX39: App 2H 21
Verona Ct. EX32: B'aple 3F 19
Veryan Cl. EX7: Daw 1H 97
Vestry Dr. EX2: Alph 5E 70
Vetch Pl. TQ12: New A 6A 104
Veysey Cl. EX2: Exe 2H 71
Viaduct Vw. EX22: Hols 2C 34
VICARAGE 6K 85 (2C 173)
Vicarage Cl. EX39: Hart 3H 27
TQ5: Brixh 3E 122
TQ9: Sto G 4B 120
Vicarage Gdns. EX2: Exe 1D 70
(off Old Vicarage Rd.)
EX7: Daw 4F 97
PL5: Plym 1A 134
PL19: Mil A 2B 58
Vicarage Gro. TQ9: Sto G 3B 120
Vicarage Hill PL8: Holb 6C 150
PL21: Corn 5K 129
TQ2: Torq 2J 115
TQ3: Marl 2D 114
(Church Hill)
TQ3: Marl 3D 114
(Nether Mdw.)
TQ5: Brixh 3E 122
TQ6: Dartm 1A 124 (6E 124)
TQ12: Kingst 4H 105
Vicarage La. EX4: Pin 2D 66
EX20: S Taw 1J 49
TQ6: Strete 6H 153
TQ13: Chud 2C 94
Vicarage Lawn EX32: B'aple 4E 18
Vicarage Rd. EX6: Cockw 3E 96
EX9: E Bud 1D 82
EX10: Sidm 6C 84
EX20: Oke 3A 48
EX32: Land 2B 24
PL7: Plymp 6K 137
PL11: Torp 2A 140
Vicarage Rd. TQ2: Torq 2K 115
TQ3: Marl 4E 114
TQ5: Brixh 5E 122
TQ9: Blacka 3B 152
TQ9: Sto G 3A 120
TQ10: S Bre 1B 100
TQ12: A'well 6E 108
Vicarage St. EX24: Colyt 5D 88
EX32: B'aple 4E 18
Vicary Cl. TQ12: New A 1D 108
Vickers Ground EX39: Nort 4E 20
Vickery Clo. EX1: W Cly 1E 66
Vickery Cl. EX15: Cull 4G 45
Vicks Mdw. EX20: Hath 2H 35
Victor Cl. EX1: Heav 7K 65
Victoria Av. PL1: Plym 2A 8 (1G 141)
Victoria Cl. EX1: Pin 4D 66
EX6: Kenton 6H 95
EX15: Will 4D 44
EX32: B'aple 5G 19
Victoria Cotts. PL6: Plym 3C 136
Victoria Ct. EX4: Exe 5B 6 (7D 64)
TQ1: Torq 1D 116
(off Victoria Rd.)
TQ9: Tot 6E 102
Victoria Cres. EX17: Cred 5J 39
EX39: App 2H 21
Victoria Gdns. EX8: Exmth 1C 76
EX39: Bide 4F 23
Victoria Gro. EX39: Bide 4F 23
Victoria Hgts. TQ6: Dartm 6E 124
Victoria Hill EX22: Hols 1C 34
Victoria Lawn EX32: B'aple 5G 19
Victoria Pde. TQ1: Torq 3D 116
Victoria Pk. 2A 8 (1G 141)
Victoria Pk. Rd. EX2: Exe 7J 7 (1H 71)
TQ1: Torq 6D 112
Victoria Pl. EX8: Exmth 6C 76
EX9: Bud S 7C 82
EX13: Axmin 3H 89
EX35: Lynt 2G 13
(off Lydiate La.)
EX36: S Mol 5C 26
PL1: Plym 6A 8
PL2: Dev 7E 134
TQ5: Brixh 2E 122
(off Higher Furzeham Rd.)
TQ6: Dartm 1A 124 (6F 125)
TQ8: Salc 3D 158
TQ12: New A 1F 109
Victoria Quay TQ8: Salc 3D 158
Victoria Rd. EX3: Top 5B 74
EX4: Exe 1G 7 (4G 65)
EX8: Exmth 6B 76
EX10: Sidm 6C 84
EX20: Hath 2H 35
EX32: B'aple 5F 19
(not continuous)
EX34: Ilfra 3H 11
PL5: Plym 2C 134
TQ1: Torq 7D 112
TQ5: Brixh 2H 123
TQ6: Dartm 1A 124 (6D 124)
Victoria Shop. Cen.
Paignton 1J 119
Victoria Sq. EX22: Hols 2C 34
(off Victoria Hill)
TQ4: Paig 1J 119
(off Parkside Rd.)
Victoria St. EX4: Exe 1G 7 (4G 65)
EX20: Oke 3C 48
EX22: Hols 2C 34
EX32: B'aple 5G 19
EX34: C Mar 7C 12
PL11: Torp 1A 140
TQ4: Paig 1H 119
TQ9: Tot 6E 102
Victoria Ter. EX6: Kennf 1H 95
(off Exeter Rd.)
EX11: Ott M 4B 80
EX14: Hon 3E 54
(off Dowell St.)
EX15: Cull 4H 45
(off Exeter Hill)
EX32: B'aple 5F 19
EX39: Bide 3F 23
(off Honestone St.)
EX39: Ins 3K 21
PL4: Plym 1E 8 (1K 141)
TQ5: Brixh 4E 122
(off Mt. Pleasant Rd.)
TQ12: Kingst 4H 105
(off Oakford)
TQ13: Bov T 3C 92
(off Mary St.)
TQ14: Shal 6G 107
(off Bridge Rd.)
Victoria Way EX8: Exmth 6B 76
Victoria Wharf PL4: Plym 7J 9
Victoria Yd. EX4: Exe 3D 6 (6E 64)
Victor La. EX1: Heav 7K 65
Victor St. EX1: Heav 7K 65
Victory Cl. TQ12: New A 6E 104
Victory Dr. EX2: Cou W 5B 72
Victory Ho. EX2: Exe 5F 7
TQ6: Dartm 2A 124
Victory Rd. TQ6: Dartm 6D 124
Victory St. PL2: Plym 5D 134
Victory Way EX38: G Tor 1B 30
Vieux Cl. EX9: Ott'n 6H 83
View Rd. DT7: Lym R 5J 91
Vigilance Av. TQ5: Brixh 3H 123
Vigo Bri. Rd. PL19: Tavi 3J 59
Vigo M. PL19: Tavi 3J 59
Villa Cl. EX32: B'aple 7G 19
The Village EX5: Clyst M 2F 73
EX5: Rock 4F 69
PL6: Bickl 1G 133
PL20: Buck M 5A 126
Village Cl. EX8: Lit 5H 77
Village Cross Rd. TQ7: Lodd 3G 151
Village Dr. PL6: Robo 1D 132
Village Rd. EX5: Wood S 1C 78
EX6: Chri 4J 63
TQ3: Marl 3D 114
Village St. EX32: B Taw 6B 24
Villa Rd. EX38: G Tor 2B 30
The Villas TQ12: Kingst 1G 105
Villiers Av. TQ12: New A 2J 109
Villiers Cl. PL9: Plyms 5E 142
Vincents Rd. TQ7: Kingsb 4G 157
Vine Cl. EX2: Exe 6G 7 (7G 65)
Vine Cres. PL2: Plym 5G 135
Vine Gdns. PL2: Plym 5G 135
Vinegar Hill EX39: Bide 3G 23
Vine Ho. EX9: Bud S 6D 82
Vine Pas. EX14: Hon 3F 55
(off Northcote La.)
Vine Rd. TQ2: Torq 7B 112
The Vinery TQ1: Torq 2D 116
(off Montpellier Rd.)
Vinery La. PL7: Plymp 7B 138
PL9: Elb 7K 143
Vine St. EX19: Wink 3C 36
Vine Ter. TQ7: Kingsb 3F 157
TQ7: Lodd 3G 151
Vineton Pl. EX14: Fen 2H 53
Vineyard Hill TQ9: Darti 3B 102
Vineyard La. EX13: Axmin 2G 89
The Vineyards EX22: Hols 1C 34
Vineyard Ter. TQ9: E All 6C 152
(off Addlehole)
Vinnicombes Rd. EX5: Sto C 6J 51
Vinstone Way PL5: Plym 2C 134
Violet Dr. PL6: Plym 2F 133
TQ12: New A 6A 104
Violet La. PL19: Tavi 4K 59
Virginia Cl. EX39: Bide 4F 23
Virginia Gdns. PL2: Plym 4E 134
Virginia Lodge TQ1: Torq 2F 117
(off Lwr. Erith Rd.)
VIRGINSTOW 1B 168
Vision Hill Rd. EX9: Bud S 5D 82
Vista Cl. DT7: Lym R 5H 91
Vittery Cl. TQ5: Brixh 3D 122
Vivid App. PL1: Dev 2D 140
Vixen Tor Cl. EX20: Oke 3E 48
PL20: Yelv 5F 127
Vixen Way PL2: Plym 4E 134
Voisey Cl. TQ13: Chud K 5B 94
Volehouse Moor Nature Reserve 2B 162
Voley Cl. EX1: Sow 5C 66
Vomero TQ1: Torq 2E 116
Voysey Hill EX17: Cher F 1J 39
Vue Cinema
Exeter 3G 7 (6G 65)
Paignton 1J 119
Plymouth 6J 9 (3A 142)
Vuefield Hill EX2: Exe 2B 70
Vyvyan Ct. EX1: Heav 7K 65
(off Fore St.)

W

WADBROOK 3D 167
WADDETON 2E 120 (2A 176)
Waddeton Cl. TQ4: Paig 6F 119
Waddeton Cotts. TQ5: Wadd 2E 120
Waddeton Dr. TQ4: Paig 6F 119
Waddeton Rd. TQ4: Paig 6F 119
(not continuous)
TQ5: Wadd 1E 120
TQ9: Sto G 7A 118
WADDON 3C 171
Waddon Cl. PL7: Plymp 2B 138
Wade Cl. EX8: Exmth 4G 77
WADEFORD 2D 167
Wadham Ho. EX4: Exe 3D 64
Wadham Ter. PL2: Plym 6F 135
Wadlands Mdw. EX20: Oke 3D 48
WADLEY HILL 3F 91
Waggoners Way EX4: Exe . . . 1A 6 (4D 64)
Waggon Hill PL7: Plymp 5D 138
Wagon Hill Way EX2: Won 1J 71
WAINHOUSE CORNER 1A 168
Wain La. TQ12: New A 7D 104
(not continuous)
Wain Pk. PL7: Plymp 5C 138
Wakefield Av. PL5: Plym 2D 134
Wakeham Ct. EX33: Brau 6K 15
(off Exeter Rd.)
Wakehams Cl. PL21: Modb 7H 147
Wake St. PL4: Plym 1C 8 (1H 141)
Walcot Cl. PL6: Plym 7F 133

Walcot Pl. TQ5: Brixh 3E **122**
Walcott Way EX14: Dunk 7H **47**
Walden Rd. EX14: Dunk 7H **47**
Waldland Gdns. PL6: Plym 4K **131**
Waldon Cl. PL7: Plymp 3E **138**
Waldon Ct. TQ2: Torq 2D **116**
   (off St Luke's Rd. Sth.)
Waldon Ho. TQ2: Torq 2D **116**
   (off St Luke's Rd. Sth.)
Waldon Point TQ2: Torq 2D **116**
   (off St Luke's Rd. Sth.)
Waldron's Almshouses
  EX16: Tive 4C **40**
   (off King St.)
Walkers Chocolate Emporium 2H **11**
Walker Ter.
  PL1: Plym 7B **8** (4H **141**)
Walkham Bus. Pk. PL5: Plym 2G **135**
Walkham Cl. TQ1: Tavi 4K **59**
Walkham Mdws. PL20: Horr 2F **127**
WALKHAMPTON 2J **127** (1B **174**)
Walkhampton Rd. PL20: Horr 2E **126**
Walkhampton Wlk. PL6: Plym 2F **137**
   (not continuous)
Walkham Ri. TQ2: Torq 5H **111**
Walkham Ter. PL20: Horr 1E **126**
Walkham Vw. PL20: Horr 2E **126**
Wallace Av. EX4: Whip 4A **66**
  EX7: Daw 3H **97**
  TQ2: Torq 5J **111**
Wallace Rd. PL7: Plymp 5D **138**
Wallaford Rd. TQ11: B'leigh 5A **98**
The Walled Gdn. EX2: Cou W 6B **72**
Wallfield Rd. TQ13: Bov T 6A **92**
Wallingford Rd. TQ7: Kingsb 3G **157**
Wallis Gro. TQ14: Bi'ton 3C **106**
Wall Pk. TQ9: Tot 5B **102**
Wall Pk. Cl. PL7: Plymp 2C **138**
  TQ5: Brixh 3G **123**
Wall Pk. Rd. TQ5: Brixh 3G **123**
Walls Cl. EX8: Exmth 2F **77**
Wallsend Ind. Est. PL4: Plym 4B **142**
Walls Hill Rd. TQ1: Torq 6F **113**
Wall St. PL1: Dev 2D **140**
Walnut Cl. EX6: Exmin 2C **74**
  PL7: Plymp 4E **138**
  TQ9: Tot 5D **102**
  TQ13: Chud 1C **94**
Walnut Ct. TQ5: Brixh 4F **123**
   (off Higher Ranscombe Rd.)
Walnut Dr. EX16: Tive 3F **41**
  EX17: Cred 5J **39**
  PL7: Plymp 4F **139**
Walnut Gdns. EX4: Exe 2B **6** (5D **64**)
  PL7: Plymp 4F **139**
Walnut Gro. EX8: Exmth 5E **76**
Walnut La. TQ2: Torq 2A **116**
Walnut Rd. EX2: Won 3J **71**
  EX14: Hon 5D **54**
  TQ2: Torq 2A **116**
Walnut Way EX32: B'aple 5J **19**
Walpole Cl. EX4: Whip 3B **66**
Walreddon Cl. PL19: Tavi 5H **59**
The Walronds EX16: Tive 6C **40**
Walsingham Ct. PL7: Plymp 3E **138**
Walsingham Pl. EX2: Sow 1C **72**
Walsingham Rd. EX2: Sow 1C **72**
Walson Rd. EX17: Bow 7J **37**
Waltacre PL8: Torr 3B **150**
Walters Fld. EX31: Bick 7K **17**
Walters Orchard EX15: Cull 4H **45**
Walters Rd. PL5: Plym 1B **134**
Waltham Pl. PL2: Plym 3F **135**
Waltham Rd. TQ12: New A 1D **108**
Waltham Way PL21: Ivy 5J **145**
Walton Cres. PL5: Plym 2H **135**
Walton Rd. EX2: Won 7B **66**
Walton Way EX32: B'aple 4G **19**
WAMBROOK 3C **167**
Wandle Pl. PL3: Plym 6E **136**
Wanstead Gro. PL5: Plym 7F **131**
Wantage Gdns.
  PL1: Plym 3A **8** (2G **141**)
Warberry Rd. W. TQ1: Torq 1D **116**
Warberry Va. TQ1: Torq 7D **112**
Warboro Ter. EX6: Star 1E **96**
Warborough Hill
  EX6: Kenton 6J **95**
Warborough Rd. TQ5: Chur F 2J **121**
Warbro Ct. TQ1: Torq 6D **112**
   (off St Marychurch Rd.)
Warbro Rd. TQ1: Torq 6D **112**
WARBSTOW 1A **168**
Warburton Gdns. PL5: Plym 2B **134**
Warcombe Farm Camping Pk. 4E **10**
Warcombe La. EX34: Mort 5E **10**
Wardens Cl. EX37: High B 2B **32**
Ward La. EX19: Wink 3E **36**
Wardlow Cl. PL6: Plym 3A **136**
Wardlow Gdns. PL6: Plym 3A **136**

Wardour Wlk. PL6: Plym 3C **132**
Ward Pl. PL3: Plym 6C **136**
Wardrew Rd. EX4: Exe 7A **6** (7C **64**)
WARE 6G **91**
Ware Barton Cvn. Site 5K **105**
Ware Cliff Chalets 6J **91**
Ware Cl. TQ12: Kingst 4J **105**
Ware Ct. EX14: Hon 5D **54**
Warecroft Rd. TQ12: Kingst 4J **105**
Ware Cross TQ12: Kingst 4J **105**
Ware Cross Gdns.
  TQ12: Kingst 4J **105**
Warefield Rd. TQ3: Paig 7J **115**
Ware Hill PL21: Ugb 6E **146**
Ware La. DT7: Lym R, Ware 6F **91**
Warelwast Cl. PL7: Plymp 4A **138**
Waresfoot Dr. EX17: Cred 5G **39**
Warfield Vs. EX34: Ilfra 3J **11**
WARFLEET 7G **125** (2A **176**)
Warfleet Creek Rd.
  TQ6: Dartm 7G **125**
Warfleet Rd. TQ6: Dartm 7G **125**
Waring Bowen Ct. EX2: Cou W 4J **71**
Waring Rd. PL6: Plym 3J **131**
Warkidons Way EX5: Wood S 2E **78**
WARKLEIGH 1A **164**
Warland TQ9: Tot 6E **102**
WARLEGGAN 3A **168**
Warleigh Av. PL2: Plym 6D **134**
Warleigh Cres. PL6: Plym 5A **132**
Warleigh La. PL2: Plym 6D **134**
Warleigh Point Nature Reserve
   . . . . .4C **130** (1A **174**)
Warleigh Rd. PL4: Plym 7K **135**
Warleigh Vw. PL20: Bere F 7B **128**
Warleigh Wood Nature Reserve . . .3D **130**
Warmwell Rd. PL5: Plym 6D **130**
Warneford Gdns. EX8: Exmth 2G **77**
Warne La. PL19: Mary T 2B **60**
Warnicombe La. EX16: Tive 6H **41**
Warran La. PL19: Tavi 6J **59**
The Warren TQ12: New A 1C **108**
Warren Cl. EX11: W Hill 4H **79**
  EX38: G Tor 2A **30**
  PL9: Wem 7B **148**
Warren Dr. EX9: Bud S 5D **82**
Warren Golf Course
  Dawlish Warren 7E **96** (3D **171**)
Warren Hill TQ2: Torq 2D **116**
Warren La. EX4: Exe 2F **7** (5F **65**)
  EX38: G Tor 2A **30**
  PL5: Tam F 2E **130**
  PL9: Wem 6D **148**
  PL21: Ivy 6B **144**
  TQ9: Darti 1D **102**
Warren Pk. EX11: W Hill 4H **79**
  PL6: Plym 3E **132**
Warren Rd. EX7: Daw 2K **97**
  PL19: Mary T 1B **60**
  TQ2: Torq 2C **116**
  TQ7: Bigb S 3B **154**
  TQ7: Kingsb 6H **157**
  TQ7: Thur 6B **154**
Warrens Mead EX10: Sidf 2E **84**
Warren St. PL2: Dev 7D **134**
Warren Vw. EX39: Bide 3D **22**
Warspite Gdns. PL5: Plym 1J **135**
Warton Cl. PL5: Plym 1J **135**
Warwick Av. EX1: Heav 7B **66**
  PL5: Plym 6J **131**
Warwick Cl. EX14: Fen 2H **53**
  TQ1: Torq 6G **113**
Warwick Orchard Cl.
  PL5: Plym 7G **131**
Warwick Rd. EX1: Heav 6B **66**
Warwick Ter. EX32: B'aple 3E **18**
Warwick Way EX4: Whip 4B **66**
Wasdale Cl. PL6: Plym 1E **136**
Wasdale Gdns. PL6: Plym 1E **136**
Washabrook La. TQ7: Kingsb 3H **157**
Washabrook Way TQ7: Kingsb 4H **157**
WASHBOURNE 2D **175**
Washbourne Cl. PL1: Dev 1D **140**
  TQ5: Brixh 3G **123**
Washbook Vw. EX11: Ott M 3D **80**
WASHFIELD 2D **165**
Washfield La.
  EX16: Tive, Wash 2A **40**
WASHFORD PYNE 2C **165**
Washington Cl. TQ3: Pres 5H **115**
WATCOMBE 2D **112** (1B **176**)
Watcombe Beach Rd.
  TQ1: Torq 2E **112**
Watcombe Hgts. Rd.
  TQ1: Torq 1D **112**
WATER .2B **170**
Waterbeer St. EX4: Exe 4D **6** (6E **64**)
Waterbridge Ct. EX2: Matf 5G **71**
Waterbridge Golf Course
   . . . . .4A **38** (3B **164**)
Watercolour Way PL9: Hooe 6C **142**

Waterdale Mobile Home Pk. 1G **111**
   (off Waterdale Rd.)
Waterdale Pk. TQ12: Kingsk 1G **111**
Waterford La. EX13: Mus 7B **90**
Watergate EX2: Exe 6E **6** (7F **65**)
Watergate Path EX2: Exe 6E **6**
   (off Watergate)
WATERHEAD 6G **151**
Waterhead Cl. TQ6: Kingsw 5H **125**
Waterhead Ter. TQ6: Kingsw 5H **125**
Watering Ct. EX9: Ott'n 6H **83**
Watering La. EX9: Ott'n 5J **83**
Waterlands EX34: Ilfra 2J **11**
   (off Quayfield Rd.)
Water La. EX1: Heav 7K **65**
   (off Victor La.)
  EX2: Exe 7D **6** (1E **70**)
  EX10: Sidm 5C **84**
  EX16: Tive 4D **40**
  EX17: Bow 5H **37**
  EX32: B'aple 6G **19**
  EX34: C Mar 6B **12**
  TQ2: Torq 5J **111**
  TQ12: Kingsk 1G **111**
  TQ12: New A 7C **104**
Water La. Cl. EX32: B'aple 6G **19**
   (off Water La.)
Waterleat Av. EX14: Hon 4G **55**
  TQ3: Paig 2E **118**
Waterleat Cl. TQ3: Paig 2F **119**
Waterleat Ct. TQ3: Paig 2F **119**
Waterleat Dr. TQ3: Paig 2F **119**
Waterleat Rd. TQ3: Paig 2E **118**
Waterloo Cl. PL1: Plym 2F **141**
Waterloo Rd. EX2: Exe 2D **70**
  EX22: Hols 1D **34**
  TQ1: Torq 7D **112**
  TQ7: Kingsb 3G **157**
Waterloo St. PL1: Plym 1E **140**
  PL4: Plym 2G **9** (1K **141**)
  TQ14: Teignm 5J **107**
Waterloo Ter. EX39: Bide 4E **22**
Waterloo Yd. Flats PL1: Plym 2F **141**
The Watermark 4H **145**
Water Mdw. EX15: Cull 5H **45**
Water Mdws. TQ2: Torq 3A **116**
   (off Underhill Rd.)
Water Mdw. Wlk. TQ9: Darti 4D **102**
Watermill Ct. TQ5: Brixh 4E **122**
   (off Bolton St.)
Watermore Ct. EX4: Exe 1K **7**
WATERMOUTH 1B **12**
Watermouth Castle 1B **12** (2B **160**)
Watermouth Cove Holiday Pk. 1B **12**
Watermouth Lodges EX34: Ber 1B **12**
Watermouth Valley Camping Pk. . . .1B **12**
Watermouth Yacht Club 1B **12**
Water Pk. Rd. EX39: Bide 3C **22**
Waterpool Rd.
  TQ6: Dartm 2A **124** (7D **124**)
WATERROW 1A **166**
Waters Edge TQ9: Tavi 3K **59**
Waterside EX2: Exe 7D **6** (1E **70**)
  TQ7: Kingsb 5G **157**
  TQ9: Tot 6F **103**
  TQ13: Bov T 4C **92**
Waterside Holiday Pk. 6J **119**
Waterside Ho. PL21: Ivy 5G **145**
  TQ9: Tot 6F **103**
   (off The Plains)
Waterside M. PL1: Dev 1C **140**
Waterside Rd. TQ4: Broads 6J **119**
Waterside Row PL21: Ivy 5G **145**
   (off Keaton Rd.)
Waterside Vw. TQ4: Broads 6J **119**
Waterslade Dr. PL21: Ivy 5J **145**
Waterslade La. EX5: Clyst H 4J **67**
Waterslade Way EX5: Clyst H 4K **67**
Watersmeet 2D **161**
Watersmeet Rd. EX35: Lynm 2J **13**
Waterstream Sq. TQ13: Chud 1D **94**
Water Ter. EX34: C Mar 6B **12**
WATERTOWN 3F **21**
Waterwell La. EX6: Chri 4K **63**
Waterworks La. TQ14: Shal 7F **107**
Watery La. EX5: W'bury 4B **78**
  EX13: Smal 1J **89**
  EX16: Tive 3E **40**
  EX33: Croy 2D **14**
  EX34: C Mar 6C **12**
  EX38: G Tor 2D **30**
   (Roscoff Cl.)
  EX38: G Tor 3A **30**
   (St Mary's Cl.)
Watkins Way EX39: Bide 3H **23**
  TQ3: Paig 7D **114**
Watson Gdns. PL4: Plym . . .4J **9** (2A **142**)
Watson Pl. EX2: Exe 7K **7** (1H **71**)
  PL4: Plym 4K **9** (2B **142**)
WATTON 1D **173**
Watts Pk. Rd. PL2: Plym 4H **135**

Watts Rd.
  PL4: Plym 3K **9** (2B **142**)
  PL19: Tavi 4H **59**
Waveney Gdns. PL5: Plym 7H **131**
Waverley Av. EX4: Exe 1E **6** (5F **65**)
Waverley Rd. EX8: Exmth 4C **76**
  PL5: Plym 1C **134**
  TQ7: Kingsb 5F **157**
  TQ12: New A 7E **104**
Waverley Ter. EX35: Lynt 2G **13**
   (off Lydiate La.)
Waves Leisure Pool 2B **116**
Waybrook Cotts. EX2: Matf 6E **70**
Waybrook Cres. EX2: Alph 5E **70**
Waybrook La. EX2: Shil A 7D **70**
Waycott Wlk. PL6: Plym 4H **131**
Wayfaring EX32: B'aple 6J **19**
WAYFORD 3D **167**
Wayland Av. EX2: Exe 7H **7** (1G **71**)
Waylands Cnr. EX16: Torq 1D **40**
Waylands Rd. EX16: Tive 2D **40**
Wayside PL21: Ivy 4G **145**
  TQ5: Brixh 4C **122**
Wayside Cl. TQ5: Brixh 4C **122**
Wayside Cres. EX1: Whip 5A **66**
Way's La. EX15: Cull 5H **45**
WAY VILLAGE 2C **165**
Wear Barton Rd. EX2: Cou W 5A **72**
Wear Cl. EX2: Cou W 6B **72**
WEARE GIFFARD 1C **163**
WEARNE 1D **167**
Weatherdon Dr. PL21: Ivy 4K **145**
Weatherill Rd. EX14: Hon 6F **55**
Weaver Ct. TQ2: Torq 5H **111**
Weavers Ct. EX2: Exe 6D **6**
Weavers Wlk. EX15: Cull 5G **45**
Weavers Way TQ9: Darti 3A **102**
  TQ12: Kingsk 1F **111**
Webber Cl. TQ12: E Ogw 4C **108**
Webbers Cvn. & Camping Pk. 5D **78**
Webbers Cl. EX5: Whim 6G **53**
Webbers Est. TQ9: Darti 3B **102**
Webbers Mdw. EX5: W'bury 5D **78**
Webbers Way EX15: Will 4D **44**
  EX16: Tive 2E **40**
  TQ9: Darti 3A **102**
Webbs Orchard EX20: N Taw 6C **36**
Webland Farm Holiday Pk. 3E **100**
Webley Rd. EX2: Exe 2C **70**
Webster Cl. TQ12: New A 1F **109**
Wedgwood Ct. TQ14: Teignm 5H **107**
   (off Somerset Pl.)
Wedlake M. EX7: Daw 4G **97**
   (off Brook St.)
Weech Cl. EX7: Daw 4F **97**
Weech Rd. EX7: Daw 4F **97**
WEEK
  EX18 . . . . .2B **164**
  EX20 . . . . .6A **36** (3A **164**)
  EX31 . . . . .1D **163**
  TA22 . . . . .1D **165**
  TQ9 . . . . .2A **102** (1D **175**)
Weekaborough Dr. TQ3: Marl 4D **114**
WEEKE .3B **164**
Weeke Hill TQ6: Dartm, Sto F 1J **153**
WEEK GREEN 1A **168**
Week La. EX7: Daw, Daw W 1J **97**
WEEK ST MARY 1A **168**
Weeksland Rd. TQ2: Torq 7J **111**
Weir Cl. PL6: Plym 1G **137**
Weirfield Ho. EX2: Exe 7F **7**
Weirfield Path EX2: Exe 2G **71**
Weirfield Rd. EX2: Exe 7F **7** (1F **71**)
Weirfields TQ9: Tot 5E **102**
Weir Gdns. PL6: Plym 1G **137**
Weir Rd. PL6: Plym 7F **133**
Weirside Pl. EX2: Exe 7F **7** (1F **71**)
Weirside Way EX32: B'aple 3G **19**
Welbeck Av.
  PL4: Plym 1E **8** (1J **141**)
Welch's La. EX31: Yell 7A **16**
WELCOMBE 2A **162**
Welcome Family Holiday Pk. 7E **96**
Welcome St. EX2: Exe 1E **70**
Weld Pk. Av. EX34: Ilfra 3K **11**
Welland Gdns. PL3: Plym 6D **136**
Wellands Cl. EX15: Uff 7J **43**
Wellbrook Grn. EX16: Tive 4B **40**
Wellbrook St. EX16: Tive 4B **40**
Wellbrook Ter. EX16: Tive 4B **40**
   (off Wellbrook St.)
  EX39: Bide 4F **23**
Well Cl. TQ12: Kingst 4H **105**
Wellclose Rd. EX33: Brau 5J **15**
Welle Ho. Gdns. TQ7: Kingsb 3G **157**
Weller Rd. EX13: Axmin 5H **89**
Wellesley Rd. TQ1: Torq 7D **112**
Wellfield Cl. PL7: Plymp 4F **139**
Well Gdns.
  PL1: Plym 3C **8** (2H **141**)
Wellhay Cl. PL9: Elb 6K **143**

Well Hill TQ7: Malb 6G 155
Well Hill Cl. TQ7: Malb 6G 155
WELLINGTON 1B 166
Wellington Cl. EX2: Won 7C 66
Wellington Pl. TQ1: Torq 7D 112
Wellington Rd. EX2: Exe 2D 70
  TQ1: Torq 1D 116
Wellington Sq. TQ10: S Bre 1B 100
Wellington St. PL1: Plym 1F 141
  PL4: Plym 2G 9 (1K 141)
  PL11: Torp 1A 140
  TQ14: Teignm 5J 107
Well La. EX39: Hart 3H 27
Well Mead EX13: Kilm 2B 88
Well Oak Pk. EX2: Won 1J 71
Well Pk. EX22: Hols 1C 34
Wellpark Cl. EX4: Exe 7C 64
Well Pk. Pl. TQ6: Sto F 3H 153
Well Pk. Rd. EX38: G Tor 2C 30
  PL11: Torp 1A 140
Wells Av. EX14: Fen 2G 53
Wellsbourne Pk. PL3: Plym 5B 136
Wells Cl. EX8: Exmth 1G 77
Wellspring Pl. PL9: Elb 4K 143
Wells St. EX32: B'aple 4E 18
Wells Ter. EX17: Cher F 2H 39
Wellstones Cl. PL21: Ivy 5J 145
Well St. EX4: Exe 2G 7 (5G 65)
  EX6: Star 1E 96
  EX38: G Tor 2C 30
  TQ3: Paig 1G 119
WELLSWOOD 1F 117 (1B 176)
  (not continuous)
Wellswood Av. TQ1: Torq 1F 117
  TQ1: Torq 1G 117
Wellswood Mnr. TQ1: Torq 1F 117
Wellswood Pk. TQ1: Torq 1F 117
Wellswood Path TQ1: Torq 1F 117
WELLTOWN 1K 127
WELSFORD 1A 162
Welsford Av. PL2: Plym 6E 134
Welsury Rd. TQ2: Torq 3J 111
WEMBURY 6C 148 (3B 174)
Wembury Dr. TQ2: Torq 3D 112
Wembury Marine Cen.
  . . . . .7A 148 (3B 174)
Wembury Mdw. PL9: Wem 5C 148
Wembury Pk. Rd. PL3: Plym 5J 135
Wembury Rd.
  PL9: Elb, Spri, Wem 7H 143
Wembury Voluntary Marine
  Conservation Area 3B 174
WEMBWORTHY 3A 164
Wendover Way EX2: Cou W 3A 72
Wenlock Gdns. PL7: Plym 3G 135
Wensum Cl. PL7: Plym 5D 138
Wentwood Gdns. PL6: Plym 7F 133
Wentwood Pl. PL6: Plym 7F 133
Wentworth Gdns. EX4: Exe 1B 70
Wentworth Pl. PL4: Plym 2C 142
Wentworth Rd. TQ12: H'fld 2J 93
WERRINGTON 2B 168
Wesley Av. PL3: Plym 6K 135
Wesley Cl. EX2: Exe 2D 70
  EX16: Tive 5G 41
  TQ2: Torq 2C 112
Wesley Ct. PL1: Plym 6C 8
  PL11: Torp 1B 140
  (off Tamar St.)
  TQ2: Torq 2C 112
  TQ6: Dartm 1A 124
Wesley M. TQ2: Torq 3C 112
  (off Starpitten La. W.)
Wesley Pl. PL2: Dev 7F 135
  PL3: Plym 6K 135
Wesley Rd. EX22: Hols 1B 34
Wesley Ter. EX39: Hart 3H 27
Wesley Vw. TQ12: Ipp 6H 101
  (off Croft Rd.)
Wesley Way EX2: Alph 5E 70
Wessex Cl. EX3: Top 7C 72
Wessex Est. EX4: Exe 1A 6 (4D 64)
Wessex Way TQ6: Dartm 7C 124
Wessiters EX12: Seat 5D 86
Westabrook Av. TQ13: Ashb 3G 99
Westabrook Cl. TQ13: Ashb 3G 99
Westabrook Dr. TQ13: Ashb 3G 99
WESTACOTT 5K 19
Westacott Mdw. EX32: B'aple 6K 19
Westacott Rd. EX32: B'aple 6J 19
W. Acres EX12: Seat 5D 86
WEST ALVINGTON 5D 156 (3D 175)
W. Alvington Hill
  TQ7: Kingsb 5E 156
WEST ANSTEY 1C 165
WEST APPLEDORE 2H 21
West Av. EX4: Exe 1F 7 (4F 65)
  EX31: B'aple 6C 18
  PL19: Tavi 4H 59

Westaway EX31: Frem 6F 17
Westaway Cl. EX31: B'aple 2F 19
Westaway Hgts. EX31: B'aple 1F 19
Westaway Plain EX31: B'aple 2E 18
Westaway Rd. EX24: Colyt 6C 88
WEST BAGBOROUGH 1B 166
W. Ball Hill EX39: Hart 2H 27
Westbeach Apts. EX34: Wool 6A 10
  (off Beach Rd.)
Westbourne Gro. EX34: Ilfra 3G 11
Westbourne Rd. PL3: Plym 6J 135
  TQ1: Torq 6C 112
Westbourne Ter. EX9: Bud S 7B 82
  EX34: C Mar 6C 12
  EX39: W Ho 5B 20
Westbridge Cl. EX20: Oke 3B 48
Westbridge Cotts. PL19: Tavi 5H 59
Westbridge Ind. Est.
  PL19: Tavi 5H 59
Westbrook Av. TQ14: Teignm 4G 107
Westbrook Cl. EX4: Whip 4A 66
Westbrook Cl. EX4: Whip 4A 66
Westbrook Pl. EX16: Tive 4E 40
  (off Chapel St.)
W. Buckeridge TQ14: Teignm 3H 107
WEST BUCKLAND
  EX32 . . . . .3C 161
  TA21 . . . . .1B 166
  TQ7 . . . . .4B 154 (3C 175)
Westbury Cl. PL5: Plym 6G 131
W. Challacombe La.
  EX34: C Mar 5B 12
WEST CHARLETON 7K 157 (3D 175)
W. Charleton Ct.
  TQ7: W Cha 7K 157
W. Cliff EX7: Daw 4H 97
  (off The Mews)
Westcliff TQ14: Teignm 5H 107
  (off Mulberry St.)
West Cliff Cl. EX7: Daw 5G 97
Westcliffe EX32: B Taw 7B 24
Westcliffe Ter. EX12: Seat 6E 86
  TQ5: Brixh 3F 123
  (off Nth. Furzeham Rd.)
West Cliff Pk. Dr. EX7: Daw 5G 97
W. Cliff Rd. EX7: Daw 4F 97
West Cl. EX13: Axmin 4G 89
WEST CLYST 1F 67
W. Clyst Barnyard EX1: W Cly 1G 67
Westcombe Cl. EX2: Alph 5E 70
Westcombe Cres. PL9: Hooe 7E 142
Westcombe La. EX39: Bide 3E 22
Westcombe Pk. TQ12: Kingsk 6K 109
Westcots Dr. EX19: Wink 3C 36
WESTCOTT 3A 166
Westcott Cl. PL6: Plym 3B 136
Westcott La.
  EX5: Mar G, Rock 7H 69
Westcott Rd. EX16: Tive 5H 41
Westcott Way EX14: Hon 3G 55
Westcountry Cl. PL2: Plym 4E 134
Westcroft Cl. EX39: Bide 4F 23
Westcroft Rd. EX22: Hols 2B 34
  PL5: Plym 2C 134
Westcroft Ter. EX39: App 2H 21
W. Cross EX33: Brau 4J 15
  (off Caen St.)
W. Croyde EX33: Croy 3B 14
WEST CURRY 1A 168
W. Devon Bus. Pk. PL19: Tavi 6H 59
WEST DOWN 2B 160
W. Down Cl. EX5: Cran 3C 68
W. Down La. EX8: Lit, San B 5H 77
W. Down Rd. PL2: Plym 5G 135
Westella Rd. PL20: Yelv 6G 127
W. End EX31: B'aple 3D 18
W. End Rd. EX5: Bradn 3B 52
  TQ11: B'leigh 5B 98
W. End Ter. EX36: S Mol 6C 26
  TQ12: Den 2H 101
  TQ13: Ashb 5G 99
Westeria Ter. PL7: Plym 4H 135
Westerland TQ6: Kingsw 3A 118
Westerland La. TQ3: Marl 4D 114
Wester-Moor Cl. EX31: Rou 7K 17
  (off Wester-Moor Way)
Western Av. EX2: Cou W 6C 72
  (off Central Av.)
  EX39: App 2H 21
Western Backway TQ7: Kingsb 4F 157
  (off Fore St.)
Western Bus. Pk. TQ4: Paig 5F 119
Western By-Pass TQ9: Tot 7D 102
Western College Rd.
  PL4: Plym 6A 136
Western Ct. EX10: Sidm 7B 84
  (off Bedford Sq.)

Western Dr. EX6: Star 1E 96
  PL3: Plym 7C 136
  TQ12: New A 7C 104
Western Gdns. EX34: C Mar 6B 12
Western Pl. EX24: Colyt 6C 88
Western Ri. EX34: Wool 6C 10
Western Rd. EX4: Exe 5A 6 (7D 64)
  EX17: Cred 5F 39
  EX22: Hols 2C 34
  PL21: Ivy 5G 145
  TQ1: Torq 4D 112
  TQ12: New A 2F 109
  TQ13: Ashb 5G 99
Western Ter. EX31: B'aple 4D 18
  EX34: Ilfra 4G 11
  TQ9: Tot 6D 102
  (off Lwr. Collins Rd.)
WESTERN TOWN 7B 84
Western Vs. TQ9: Tot 6D 102
  (off Lwr. Collins Rd.)
Western Way EX1: Exe 6C 6 (7E 64)
  (Edmund St.)
  EX1: Exe 5F 7 (7F 65)
  (Pavilion Pl.)
Western Wood Way PL7: Plym 4G 139
Wester Way EX35: Lynm 1H 13
West Exe Nth. EX16: Tive 4C 40
West Exe Sth. EX16: Tive 5C 40
Westfield EX5: Bradn 3B 52
  EX6: Exmin 3D 74
  PL7: Plym 3C 138
Westfield Av. EX31: B'aple 5C 18
  PL9: Hooe 6D 142
Westfield Bus. Pk. TQ4: Paig 6D 118
Westfield Cl. EX9: Bud S 6C 82
  TQ5: Brixh 5D 122
Westfield Gdns. EX9: Bud S 6C 82
Westfield Rd. EX9: Bud S 6C 82
  EX16: Tive 5C 40
Westfield Ter. EX16: Tive 5C 40
  (off Exeter Rd.)
WESTFORD 1B 166
West Gth. Ct. EX4: Exe 2C 64
West Gth. Rd. EX4: Exe 2D 64
Westgate EX17: Lap 2K 37
W. Golds Rd. TQ12: New A 6E 104
W. Golds Way TQ12: New A 6E 104
West Gro. Rd.
  EX2: Exe 7G 7 (7G 65)
Westhampnett Pl.
  PL5: Plym 5E 130
W. Hartley TQ9: Blacka 1B 152
WEST HATCH 1C 167
Westhays Cl. PL9: Plyms 7G 143
WEST HILL 4H 79 (1A 176)
W. Hill EX9: Bud S 6B 82
  PL9: Hey B 4B 148
Westhill Av. TQ1: Torq 5D 112
  TQ1: Torq 6D 112
W. Hill Ct. EX9: Bud S 7B 82
Westhill Cres. TQ3: Paig 7H 115
West Hill Gdns.
  EX9: Bud S 7B 82
West Hill La. EX9: Bud S 6B 82
  EX33: Brau 4J 15
W. Hill Rd. DT7: Lym R 5J 91
  EX11: Ott M, W Hill 5G 79, 5A 80
  PL4: Plym 1J 9 (7A 136)
Westhill Rd. TQ1: Torq 5C 112
  TQ3: Paig 7G 115
Westhill Ter. TQ12: Kingsk 1G 109
West Hoe Park 7C 8 (4H 141)
W. Hoe Rd. PL1: Plym 6B 8 (3H 141)
Westholme TQ1: Torq 1E 116
  (off Middle Warberry Rd.)
WESTLAKE 2C 175
Westlake Ri. PL9: Hey B 3B 148
Westlake Rd. PL9: Down T 3A 148
WEST LAMBROOK 2D 167
Westlands EX8: Exmth 6E 76
  EX33: Wraf 6H 15
Westlands La. TQ1: Torq 6D 112
Westland Way EX5: Cran 2D 68
West La. EX17: Lap 1J 37
  EX19: Dol 7F 31
  TQ3: Blag 7A 114
  TQ3: Marl 1C 114
Westleat Av. TQ3: Paig 1E 118
WEST LEIGH 3A 164
WESTLEIGH
  EX16 . . . . .2A 166
  EX39 . . . . .6K 21 (1C 163)
Westleigh Way PL9: Plyms 3E 142
WEST LYN .4J 13
WEST LYNG 1D 167
W. Malling Av. PL5: Plym 5D 130
W. Manley La. EX16: Tive 3H 41
Westmead Cl. EX33: Brau 4H 15
West Mdw. EX33: Brau 3G 15
West Mdw. Rd. EX33: Brau 4F 15

Westminster Cl. EX8: Exmth 1F 77
  EX14: Fen 2G 53
Westminster Rd. EX4: Exe 6A 64
WEST MONKTON 1C 167
West Newton 4E 20
Westmoor Cl. PL7: Plymp 3F 139
W. Moor Way EX39: Nort 4E 20
West Mt. TQ12: New A 3G 109
WEST NEWTON 1C 167
WEST OGWELL 1A 176
WESTON
  EX10 . . . . .2B 172
  EX14 . . . . .4B 54 (3B 166)
Weston Cl. TQ5: Brixh 5E 122
Westonfields TQ9: Tot 6G 103
Weston Ho. TQ9: Berr P 6J 103
Weston La. EX14: Awli 2A 54
  TQ9: Tot 6G 103
WESTON MILL 4E 134
Weston Mill Crematorium 4E 134
Weston Mill Dr. PL5: Plym 4D 134
Weston Mill Hill PL5: Plym 2D 134
Weston Mill La. PL5: Plym 2F 135
Weston Mill Rd. PL5: Plym 2D 134
Weston Pk. Rd. PL3: Plym 4J 135
  TQ1: Torq 6F 103
Weston Ter. EX11: Ott M 3D 80
  (off Sandhill St.)
Westover Cl. PL21: Ivy 4F 145
  TQ5: Brixh 4F 123
Westover Ind. Est.
  PL21: Ivy 5F 145
Westover La. PL21: Ivy 5F 145
WESTOWN 3E 46
Westown Rd. EX2: Ide 4A 70
W. Pafford Av. TQ2: Torq 3C 112
WEST PANSON 1B 168
WEST PARK 7F 131
West Pk. EX33: Brau 4H 15
  EX36: S Mol 5B 26
  TQ6: Sto F 1H 153
West Pk. Dr. PL7: Plymp 4F 139
West Pk. Hill PL7: Plymp 2E 138
West Pk. M. TQ7: Hope 2H 155
West Pk. Rd. EX10: Sidm 5B 84
Westpark Vs. PL20: Horr 1E 126
Westpoint Arena 2H 73
WESTPORT 2D 167
WEST PUTFORD 2B 162
West Rd. EX34: Wool 6A 10
WEST SANDFORD 3C 165
West St. EX1: Exe 5C 6 (7E 64)
  EX13: Axmin 4G 89
  EX16: Bam 2G 33
  EX16: W'ridge 6H 33
  EX20: Oke 3B 48
  EX36: S Mol 6C 26
  EX39: Hart 3H 27
  PL19: Tavi 4H 59
  TQ12: Den 2H 101
  TQ13: Ashb 4G 99
  TQ14: Bi'ton 3B 106
West St. M. EX1: Exe 5C 6
West Ter. EX1: Heav 6J 65
  EX9: Bud S 6C 82
  EX38: G Tor 2A 30
WEST TOWN
  EX5 . . . . .7C 50
  EX17 . . . . .6G 39
  EX39 . . . . .2A 28
W. Town TQ14: Bi'ton 3A 106
W. Town Mdw. TQ14: Bi'ton 3A 106
W. Town Rd. EX5: New C 7C 50
W. Underleys EX12: Beer 7B 86
West Vw. EX12: Beer 7B 86
  EX22: Hols 1C 34
  EX24: Colyf 1F 87
  EX31: B'aple 5D 18
  PL19: Whit 7K 59
West Vw. Av. EX39: Bide 3G 23
  W. Vw. Cl. TQ12: E Ogw 3C 108
Westview Cl. EX5: Whim 6H 53
West Vw. Rd. EX20: Oke 3C 48
  PL20: Bere A 1C 128
  TQ3: Marl 3D 114
West Vw. Ter. EX4: Exe 5C 6 (7E 64)
  EX14: Hon 3E 54
  (off Dowell St.)
  TQ8: Salc 4B 158
Westville Hill TQ7: Kingsb 5F 157
  (off Frogmore Ter.)
West Wlk. EX12: Seat 6E 86
Westward Cl. TQ9: Tot 6E 102
Westward Dr. EX8: Exmth 5D 76
WESTWARD HO! 5B 20 (1C 163)
Westward Ho! 1C 163
Westward Vw. TQ12: New A 2K 109
Westwater Hill EX6: Ted M 6G 49
Westway PL9: Hooe 7C 142
WEST WEMBURY 5C 148

WESTWOOD
  EX5 . . . . .1A 172
  EX6 . . . . .3D 96
  EX17 . . . . .6F 39
Westwood Av. PL6: Plym 4D 132
Westwood Cleave TQ12: E Ogw . .4C 108
Westwood Cl. EX17: Cred 6F 39
Westwood Hill EX6: Cockw 3D 96
Westwood La. EX6: Long 2A 70
Westwood Rd. EX17: Cred 6F 39
  TQ12: E Ogw 4D 108
Westwood Way EX12: Seat 3F 87
WEST WORLINGTON 2B 164
WEST YELLAND 7A 16
W. Yelland EX31: Yell 7A 16
WEST YOULSTONE 2A 162
Wethered Cl. EX16: Tive 5C 40
Wet La. EX6: Chri 3J 63
  EX34: C Mar 7C 12
WEYCROFT 1K 89 (1D 173)
Weycroft Av. EX13: Axmin 1K 89
Weycroft Cl. EX1: Sow 6C 66
Weymouth Pk. TQ7: Hope 2G 155
Whalley La. DT7: Uply 4F 91
The Wharf PL19: Tavi 4J 59
Wharf Rd. TQ12: New A 7G 105
WHATLEY 3D 167
Whatley M. PL9: Plyms 3E 142
Wheal Betsy 2D 169
Wheal Rd. PL19: Mary T 1C 60
Wheatfield Cl. EX15: Cull 5G 45
Wheat Field La. EX5: Cran 3B 68
Wheatlands Rd. TQ4: Good 3G 119
WHEATLEY 2A 70 (1C 171)
Wheatley Cl. EX4: Exe 7B 64
Wheatley Ct. EX1: Exe 5D 6
Wheatridge PL7: Plymp 4J 137
Wheatridge La. TQ2: Torq 4A 116
Wheatsheaf EX5: Cran 3C 68
Wheatsheaf Way EX2: Alph 4D 70
Wheelbarrow La.
  EX15: Hemy 1J 47
Wheel Cl. EX31: Rou 7K 17
Wheelwright Ct. PL20: Walk 2J 127
Whickham Lodge EX7: Daw 3H 97
Whidborne Av. TQ1: Torq 2H 117
Whidborne Cl. TQ1: Torq 2H 117
Whidborne M. TQ14: Bi'ton 2C 106
WHIDDON
  EX21 . . . . .3C 163
  EX32 . . . . .7J 19
WHIDDON DOWN 1A 170
Whiddon Dr. EX32: B'aple 6J 19
Whiddon Rd.
  TQ12: A'well, Two O 7C 108
Whiddon Valley EX32: B'aple 6J 19
Whiddon Valley Ind. Est.
  EX32: B'aple 6J 19
Whidley La. EX6: Dunsf 7A 62
Whilborough Rd.
  TQ12: Kingst, N Whil 5D 110
WHIMBLE 3E 34 (3B 162)
Whimble Hill EX22: Hols 3D 34
Whimbrels Edge TQ7: Thur 6C 154
Whimbrel Way PL9: Elb 4K 143
WHIMPLE 6G 53 (1A 172)
Whimple Heritage Cen. 6G 53
Whimple Station (Rail) . .6H 53 (1A 172)
Whimple St. PL1: Plym 5E 8 (3K 141)
Whin Bank Rd. PL5: Plym 1J 135
WHIPCOTT 2J 43
WHIPTON 4A 66 (1D 171)
Whipton Barton Rd. EX1: Whip . . .5A 66
Whipton La. EX1: Heav 7K 65
Whipton Rd. EX4: Whip 4K 65
Whipton Village Rd. EX4: Whip . . .4A 66
Whistley Down PL20: Yelv 6D 126
Whistley Hill TQ13: Ashb 4H 99
Whitaker Cl. EX1: Pin 1E 66
Whitby Cres. PL6: Plym 2B 136
Whitby Rd. PL6: Plym 2B 136
WHITCHURCH 7K 59 (3C 169)
Whitchurch Av. EX2: Won 1A 72
WHITCHURCH CANONICORUM . .1D 173
Whitchurch Rd. PL19: Tavi, Whit . .4J 59
  PL20: Horr 1E 126
Whitear Cl. TQ14: Teignm 2F 107
Whitears Way TQ12: Kingst 4H 105
Whitebeam Cl. EX4: Whip 2A 66
  TQ3: Paig 7E 114
Whitebeam Gro. EX14: Dunk 7G 47
Whitebridges EX14: Hon 5E 54
Whitebrook Ter. TA21: Holc R 3F 43
White Cl. TQ3: Pres 4H 115
White Cross Ct. PL4: Plym 3G 9
Whitecross Gdns. EX12: Seat 3F 87
White Cross Hill EX17: Cher F 1K 39
White Cross Rd. EX5: Wood S 2D 78
White Farm La. EX11: W Hill 5H 79
WHITEFIELD 1A 166
Whitefield Ter. PL4: Plym . .2H 9 (1A 142)

Whiteford Rd. PL3: Plym 5K 135
Whiteford Rd. La. Sth.
  PL3: Plym 6K 135
White Friars La.
  PL4: Plym 4H 9 (2A 142)
Whitefriars Wlk. EX4: Exe 4J 65
White Gables TQ2: Torq 2A 116
Whitegates EX34: C Mar 6A 12
WHITEHALL 2B 166
Whitehall Cl. EX36: S Mol 7C 26
Whitehall Dr. PL9: Elb 5J 143
  PL20: Bere A 1C 128
Whitehall Mnr. TQ7: Chur 1B 156
Whitehaven Way PL6: Plym 3B 132
Whitehayes Cl. EX13: Kilm 2B 88
White Heather Ter. TQ13: Bov T . . .3C 92
Whitehill Cl. TQ12: New A 6E 104
Whitehill Cotts. TQ12: New A 6C 104
Whitehill Country Pk. 5B 118
Whitehill Gdns. PL7: L Moor 1J 129
Whitehill La. EX3: Top 5D 72
  TQ4: Paig 7B 118
  TQ9: Sto G 7B 118
Whitehill Rd. TQ12: New A 6C 104
Whitehorse La. EX39: App 3F 21
White Ho. Cl. EX39: Ins 2K 21
WHITELACKINGTON 2D 167
White Lady Rd.
  PL9: Hooe, Plyms 7E 142
Whitelake Pl. TQ12: New A 6E 104
White Lake La. PL1: Plym 6G 9
Whiteley Av. TQ9: Tot 5A 102
White Lodge EX9: Bud S 7D 82
    (off Coastguard Rd.)
Whitemoor Hill EX32: B Taw 6B 24
White Rock Cl. TQ4: Good 6F 119
White Rock Ct. TQ4: Good 7F 119
White Rock Development
  TQ4: Paig 6E 118
White Rock Rd. TQ4: Good 7F 119
White Rock Sports Cen. 6E 118
White Rock Way TQ4: Paig 6F 119
Whiteside Cl. EX2: Won 1B 72
White's La. EX38: G Tor 2B 30
Whites La. EX31: B'aple 2E 18
Whitethorn Cl. EX10: Sidm 2A 84
  EX14: Hon 5F 55
White Tor Cl. EX20: Oke 3D 48
Whitewater Ct. PL7: Plymp 3A 138
Whiteway Cl. EX5: Whim 6H 53
Whiteway Dr. EX1: Heav 6K 65
Whiteway Rd. TQ12: Kingst 4G 105
Whiteways EX5: Cran 2D 68
WHITEWORKS 3A 170
WHITFORD 5A 90 (1C 173)
Whitford Rd. EX13: Mus, Whit 6A 90
Witham Pk. PL19: Tavi 5J 59
Whiting Cl. EX39: Bide 5F 23
WHITLEIGH 6H 131 (2A 174)
Whitleigh Av. PL5: Plym 1K 135
Whitleigh Cotts. PL5: Plym 1K 135
    (off Whitleigh Av.)
Whitleigh Ct. PL5: Plym 6J 131
Whitleigh Grn. PL5: Plym 6H 131
Whitleigh Vs. PL5: Plym 1K 135
Whitleigh Way PL5: Plym 7H 131
Whitleigh Wood
  Local Nature Reserve 5J 131
Whitley Rd. TQ4: Paig 3G 119
Whitlow Copse EX2: Won 1B 72
Whitman Cl. EX8: Exmth 7K 75
Whitmore Way EX14: Hon 5D 54
WHITNAGE 2A 166
Whitsoncross La. PL5: Tam F 3H 131
WHITSTONE
  EX22 . . . . .1A 168
  TQ13 . . . . .2B 92
Whitstone La. TQ13: Bov T 2B 92
Whitstone Rd. TQ4: Paig 2H 119
Whittingham Rd. EX34: Ilfra 3J 11
Whittington St.
  PL3: Plym 1A 8 (1G 141)
  EX34: Ilfra 3K 11
Whitton Ct. EX10: Sidm 3A 84
Whitton Way EX15: Cull 3H 45
Whitwell La. EX24: Colyf 7B 88
Whitycombe Way EX4: Exe 4A 64
WICK
  EX14 . . . . .3B 166
  TA10 . . . . .1D 167
Wickham Cl. EX39: Bide 4H 23
Widdicombe Dr. PL21: Ivy 5H 145
Widdicombe Farm Touring Pk. . . .1E 114
WIDDICOMBE IN THE MOOR 3B 170

Widecombe Way EX4: Exe 3H 65
Widemoor La. TQ5: Chur F 4J 121
WIDEMOUTH BAY 3A 162
Widend Touring Pk. 6A 114
Widepost La. EX13: Axmin 4G 89
WIDEWELL 3C 132
Widewell La. PL6: Plym 3D 132
Widewell Rd. PL6: Plym 4C 132
Widey Ct. PL6: Plym 2A 136
Widey Hill PL8: New F 5K 149
Widey La. PL6: Plym 2A 136
Widey Vw. PL3: Plym 5A 136
Widgery Dr. EX36: S Mol 6C 26
Widgery Rd. EX4: Whip 4K 65
WIDWORTHY 1C 173
WIGBOROUGH 2D 167
WIGGATON 7D 80 (1B 172)
Wilbarn Rd. TQ3: Paig 7J 115
Wilbraham Ct. TQ14: Teignm 2J 107
    (off Higher Woodway Rd.)
Wilbury Way EX7: Daw 3H 97
Wilcocks Rd. EX4: Pin 3C 66
WILCOVE 2A 174
Wilcove Cl. PL5: Plym 3D 134
Wilderness Rd. PL3: Plym 6K 135
Wilder Pk. EX34: Ilfra 3H 11
Wilder Rd. EX34: Ilfra 2G 11
Wildersmouth Ct. EX34: Ilfra 2H 11
Wildwood Escot 1A 172
Wildwoods Cres. TQ12: New A . . .7J 105
Wildwoods La. TQ3: Marl 5A 114
Wildworthy EX2: Won 7A 66
Wilkey Cl. EX32: B'aple 5G 19
Wilkins Dr. TQ4: Paig 5E 118
Willake Rd. TQ12: Kingsk 7K 109
Willand Ind. Est. EX15: Will 3C 44
Willand Moor M. EX15: Will 3E 44
    (off Willand Moor Rd.)
Willand Moor Rd. EX15: Will 3D 44
Willand Old Village EX15: Will 5C 44
Willand Rd. EX15: Cull 3H 45
  EX15: Will 1A 44
  EX16: Hal 6E 42
  EX33: Brau 4H 15
Willas Rd. PL16: Lift 6A 56
Willet St. EX39: Bide 3F 23
WILLETT 1B 166
Willey La. EX20: Stic 1A 50
Willey's Av. EX2: Exe 7C 6 (1E 70)
Willeys Ct. EX2: Exe 1E 70
Willhayes Pk. EX13: Axmin 3H 89
Willhay La. EX13: Axmin 2H 89
Willhayne La. EX24: Colyt 4B 88
Willhays Cl. TQ12: Kingst 2H 105
William Crossing Memorial 1C 175
William Evans Cl. PL6: Plym 5J 131
William Morris Monument 3D 163
William of Orange Statue 3F 123
William Prance Rd.
  PL6: Plym 7B 132
Williams Av. EX2: Exe 7C 6 (1E 70)
  PL4: Plym 3C 142
  TQ5: Brixh 4F 123
Williams Ct. EX31: Rou 7B 18
  TQ11: B'leigh 4C 98
Williamson Cl. EX33: Geo 5B 14
Williamson Way EX36: S Mol 6C 26
William St. EX16: Tive 4D 40
Willicombe Rd. TQ3: Paig 2G 119
Willis Ct. TQ1: Torq 6C 112
Willis La. EX1: Pin 2F 67
Willmott Cl. EX8: Exmth 3G 77
Willoughby Cl. EX8: Exmth 1E 76
Willoughby Rd. TQ1: Torq 7E 112
Willoughby Way
  PL1: Plym 6B 8 (3H 141)
Willow Av. EX8: Exmth 1D 76
  TQ2: Torq 2C 112
Willoway Cl. EX33: Brau 4H 15
Willoway Gro. EX33: Brau 4H 15
Willoway La. EX33: Brau 2G 15
Willowbrook Av. EX4: Whip 4B 66
Willowby Gdns. PL20: Yelv 6G 127
Willowby Pk. PL20: Yelv 6G 127
Willow Cl. EX5: Sto C 7J 51
  EX12: Seat 2E 86
  EX34: Ilfra 3K 11
  PL3: Plym 6F 137
  TQ12: New A 4J 109
Willow Cotts. PL7: Plymp 4A 138
Willow Ct. EX2: Won 1K 71
  PL6: Plym 4F 137
Willowdale Cl. EX14: Hon 3E 54
Willowfield EX33: Brau 3H 15
Willowfield Rd. TQ2: Torq 3B 112
Willow Gdns. EX5: Broadc 6C 52
Willow Gro. EX39: Bide 3E 22
Willowpark La. TQ12: Coff 1J 111

Willow Rd. PL19: Tavi 6J 59
The Willows EX31: Frem 6D 16
  TQ2: Torq 3K 111
Willow St. TQ14: Teignm 4H 107
Willow Tree Cl. EX20: Oke 3C 48
Willow Tree Ct. EX31: Rou 7A 18
Willow Tree Rd. EX32: B'aple 7G 19
Willow Wlk.
  EX4: Exe 1G 7 (4G 65)
  EX14: Hon 5E 54
  EX17: Cred 5K 39
  PL6: Plym 5E 132
Willow Way EX4: Whip 4B 66
  EX7: Daw W 7D 96
Wills Av. TQ3: Pres 5J 115
Wills Cl. PL6: Plym 3K 131
Willsdown Rd. EX2: Alph 5F 71
Willshere Rd. EX32: B'aple 5H 19
Wills Rd. TQ9: Tot 5F 103
WILMINGTON 1C 173
WILMINSTONE 1K 59
Wilminstone Ind. Est.
  PL19: Tavi 2K 59
Wilmot Gdns. PL5: Plym 1J 135
Wilnecote Lodge TQ1: Torq 7C 112
    (off Furzehill Rd.)
Wilson Cres. PL2: Plym 6G 135
Wilson Ter. TQ1: Torq 7B 112
Wilton Cl. TQ12: A'well 6E 108
Wilton Rd. PL1: Plym 1F 141
  TQ3: Pres 4H 115
Wilton St. PL1: Plym 2A 8 (1G 141)
Wilton Way EX1: Sow 6C 66
  TQ12: A'well 6D 108
Wiltshier Cl. EX5: Broadc 5C 52
Wiltshire Cl. EX4: Exe 1B 70
  PL4: Plym 7A 136
Wimborne Ter. EX32: B'aple 3F 19
    (off Yeo Vale Rd.)
Winchester Av. EX4: Exe 5B 64
  TQ2: Torq 4B 112
Winchester Cl. EX14: Fen 2G 53
Winchester Dr. EX8: Exmth 1F 77
Winchester Gdns. PL5: Plym 5F 131
Windeatt Sq. TQ9: Tot 6F 103
    (off Warland)
Windermere Cl. EX4: Exe 6C 64
Windermere Cres. PL6: Plym 6A 132
Windermere Rd. TQ1: Torq 7E 112
Winding Wlk. TQ6: Dartm 5F 125
Windjammer Ct. EX8: Exmth 6A 76
Windmill Av. TQ3: Pres 5G 115
Windmill Cl. TQ5: Brixh 4F 123
Windmill Ct. TQ5: Brixh 4F 123
Windmill Gdns. TQ3: Pres 5G 115
WINDMILL HILL 2D 167
Windmill Hill TQ5: Brixh 4E 122
Windmill La. EX11: W Hill 3H 79
  EX39: Nort 5F 21
  TQ3: Pres 5F 115
  TQ12: N Whil 5D 110
Windmill Rd. EX22: Hols 3D 34
  TQ3: Pres 5G 115
  TQ5: Brixh 4F 123
Windrush Ri. EX11: Ott M 4C 80
Windsbatch La. PL9: Plyms 3E 142
Windsor Av. TQ12: New A 1J 109
Windsor Cl. EX4: Exe 1B 6 (5D 64)
  EX15: Cull 1H 45
  PL21: Ivy 5H 145
  TQ1: Torq 7D 112
  TQ12: New A 2F 109
Windsor Ct. EX34: Ilfra 3H 11
  TQ7: Kingsb 4G 157
Windsor Dr. EX7: Daw 7B 96
Windsor Gdns. EX31: Rou 7B 18
Windsor Mead EX10: Sidf 1C 84
Windsor Pl.
  PL1: Plym 6D 8 (3J 141)
Windsor Rd. EX31: B'aple 2D 18
  EX39: Nort 5E 20
  PL3: Plym 5C 136
  TQ1: Torq 7D 112
  TQ6: Dartm 6C 124
  TQ7: Kingsb 4G 157
Windsor Sq. EX8: Exmth 5C 76
Windsor Ter. DT7: Lym R 4J 91
  EX6: Kennf 1H 95
    (off Exeter Rd.)
  PL11: Torp 1B 140
Windsor Vs. PL1: Plym 6D 8
Windthorn La. TQ3: Comp 6B 110
  TQ12: Ipp 6B 110
Windward Cl. EX8: Exmth 6A 76
Windward La. EX7: Holc 7G 97
Windward Ri. EX7: Holc 7G 97
Windward Rd. TQ2: Torq 2A 112
Windwhistle La. EX16: Bam 4G 33
Windy Ash Hill EX32: B'aple 7H 19
Windys Way EX8: Exmth 5F 77

Wingate La. EX20: Hath 1J 35
Wingfield TQ7: Thur 6C 154
Wingfield Cl. EX16: Tive 5C 40
Wingfield Rd.
 PL3: Plym 1A 8 (1F 141)
Wingfield Way
 PL3: Plym 1A 8 (1G 141)
Winifred Baker Ct. PL4: Plym 7F 9
Winifred Cliff Ct. EX16: Bam 2G 33
 (off School Cl.)
WINKLEIGH 2C 36 (3A 164)
Winkleigh Cl. EX2: Exe 3D 70
Winneford La.
 EX14: Awli, W'ton 4B 54
Winner Hill Rd. TQ3: Paig 1G 119
Winners 2000 Fitness Ltd. 6H 105
Winner St. TQ3: Paig 1G 119
Winner St. (Rear) TQ3: Paig 1G 119
 (off Winner St.)
Winnicott Cl. PL6: Plym 3K 131
Winnings Way TQ1: Torq 6F 113
 (off Princes St.)
Winnow Cl. PL9: Plyms 7G 143
Winsbury Ct. PL6: Plym 2B 136
Winsford Rd. TQ2: Torq 3J 115
Winsford Walled Garden 3C 163
WINSHAM
 EX33 . . . . .3A 160
 TA20 .3D 167
Winsham Rd. EX33: Know, Win 1K 15
Winslade M. EX10: Sidm 4C 84
Winslade Pk. 4G 73
Winslade Pk. Av. EX5: Clyst M 3F 73
Winslade Rd. EX10: Sidm 4B 84
Winsland Av. TQ9: Tot 5A 102
Winstanley Wlk. PL3: Plym 5E 136
Winston Av.
 PL4: Plym 1E 8 (1J 141)
Winston Cl. TQ12: Kingst 4H 105
Winston Ct. TQ14: Teignm 3J 107
Winstone Av. TQ2: Torq 4C 112
Winstone La. PL8: Brixt 2J 149
Winston Pk. EX36: S Mol 5C 26
Winston Rd. EX8: Exmth 1G 77
Winsu Av. TQ3: Pres 6G 115
WINSWELL 2C 163
Winswood EX17: Cred 7J 39
Winsworthy EX39: High C 6G 27
Winterbourne Rd.
 TQ14: Teignm 4H 107
Winter Gdn. TQ2: Torq 2D 116
WINTERHAY GREEN 2D 167
Winterland La. EX22: Hols 4C 34
Winter's La. EX11: Ott M 4C 80
Wiriga Way EX16: W'ridge 6H 33
Wishcroft Ter. EX15: Cull 3H 45
Wishings Rd. TQ5: Brixh 5F 123
Wish Mdw. La. EX5: Broadc 1J 67
Wisteria Cl. TQ7: Kingsb 4G 157
 (off Windsor Rd.)
Wistlandpound Reservoir Nature Reserve
 . . . . .2C 161
Wistlandpound Reservoir Nature Trail
 . . . . .2C 161
Wistman's Wood National Nature Reserve
 . . . . .3A 170
Witcombe La. EX6: Kenton 6H 95
Withalls Gdns. EX8: Lymp 6G 75
Witham Gdns. PL3: Plym 6D 136
Witheby EX10: Sidm 7A 84
WITHERIDGE 6H 33 (2C 165)
The Withey EX5: Whim 6H 53
WITHIEL FLOREY 1D 165
Withies St. PL9: Plyms 3E 142
WITHLEIGH 2D 165
Withy Bed La. EX5: Mar G 7J 69
Withy Cl. EX16: Tive 5E 40
Withycombe Pk. Dr.
 EX8: Exmth 2G 77
WITHYCOMBE RALEIGH
 . . . . .3F 77 (2A 172)
Withycombe Pk. EX8: Exmth 4C 76
Withycombe Village Rd.
 EX8: Exmth 4D 76
Withy La. EX15: Hemy 1F 47
WITHYPOOL 3D 161
Withywell La. EX33: Croy 3B 14
Witten Gdns. EX39: Nort 7F 21
WIVELISCOMBE 1A 166
Wixenford Cl. PL9: Plyms 4G 143
Wixenford Farm Ind. Est.
 PL9: Plyms 3H 143
Wizz-Kidz 3D 122
Woburn Cl. TQ3: Paig 7D 114
Woburn Ter. PL9: Plyms 5D 142
WOLBOROUGH 3C 108 (3C 171)
Wolborough Chu. Path
 TQ12: New A 2D 108
Wolborough Cl. TQ12: New A 2F 109
Wolborough Gdns. TQ5: Brixh 2G 123
 TQ12: New A 2F 109

Wolborough Ga. TQ12: New A 2F 109
 (off Wolborough Cl.)
Wolborough St. TQ12: New A 2D 108
Wolford Chapel 3B 166
Wollaton Gro. PL5: Plym 7E 130
Wolrige Av. PL7: Plymp 4D 138
Wolrige Way PL7: Plymp 4D 138
Wolsdon Pl. PL1: Plym 3A 8
Wolsdon St. PL1: Plym 3A 8 (2G 141)
Wolseley Bus. Pk.
 PL2: Plym 6F 135
Wolseley Cl. PL2: Plym 6F 135
Wolseley Rd. PL2: Plym 4D 134
 (not continuous)
 PL5: Plym 6F 135
 (Normandy Hill)
 PL5: Plym 2C 134
 (Trelawney Av.)
Wolseley Rd. Flats PL2: Plym 5E 134
Wolston Cl. TQ5: Brixh 2D 122
Wolverton Dr. TQ12: Kingst 4G 105
Wolverwood Cl. PL7: Plymp 6F 139
Wolverwood La. PL7: Plymp 6C 138
Wombwell Cres. PL2: Plym 4D 134
WONFORD 1K 71
Wonford Rd. EX2: Exe 6G 7 (7G 65)
Wonford Sports Cen. 2K 71
Wonford St. EX2: Won 1K 71
Wonnacott's Rd. EX20: Oke 3C 48
WONSON 2A 170
WOODACOTT 3B 162
Woodah Rd. EX4: Exe 7C 64
Wooda Rd. EX39: Nort 4G 21
Woodbine Pl. EX12: Seat 5E 86
Woodbine Ter.
 EX4: Exe 2C 6 (5E 64)
WOODBRIDGE 1B 172
Woodbrook Rd. TQ9: Tot 6G 103
Woodburn Cl. PL21: Ivy 4F 145
WOODBURY 5C 78 (2A 172)
Woodbury Castle 2A 172
Woodbury Ct. EX8: Exmth 6E 76
Woodbury Gdns. PL5: Plym 7F 131
Woodbury La. EX13: Axmin 5H 89
Woodbury Pk. EX13: Axmin 5G 89
Woodbury Park Golf Course 2A 172
Woodbury Rd. EX3: Clyst G 6H 73
 EX5: W'bury 4A 78
WOODBURY SALTERTON
 . . . . .1C 78 (2A 172)
Woodbury Vw. EX2: Exe 3D 70
 EX5: Broadc 6C 52
Woodbury Wlk. EX6: Exmin 1B 74
 (off Devington Pk.)
Woodbury Way EX13: Axmin 5H 89
Woodchurch PL20: C'stone 5C 126
Wood Cl. EX6: Chri 3K 63
Woodcote Ct. EX5: W'bury 5C 78
 (off Culvery Cl.)
Woodcourt Rd. TQ9: H'ford 7A 100
Woodcroft PL20: C'stone 6C 126
Woodend Rd. PL6: Plym 3E 132
 TQ1: Torq 2F 117
Wood Fld. Av. EX31: Bick 7K 17
Woodfield Cl. EX8: Exmth 2G 77
Woodfield Ct. TQ1: Torq 3F 117
Woodfield Cres. PL21: Ivy 5J 145
Woodfields EX12: Seat 3E 86
WOODFORD
 EX23 . . . . .2A 162
 PL7 . . . . .5J 137 (2B 174)
 TQ9 . . . . .3A 152 (2D 175)
Woodford Av. PL7: Plymp 5H 137
Woodford Cl. PL7: Plymp 4H 137
Woodford Cres. PL7: Plymp 5H 137
Woodford Gdns. EX32: B'aple 7H 19
Woodford Grn. PL7: Plymp 5J 137
Woodford Rd. PL6: Plym 4E 132
Woodhaye Cl. TQ10: S Bre 2B 100
Woodhayes Cl. EX7: Daw 2J 97
Woodhayes Dr. EX14: Dunk 6H 47
Woodhayes La. EX5: Whim 7H 53
Woodhaye Ter. TQ10: S Bre 2B 100
WOODHILL 1D 167
Woodhill Vw. EX14: Hon 6E 54
Woodhouse Cl. TQ7: Kingsb 5F 157
Woodhouse La. DT7: Uply 3F 91
WOODHUISH 2B 176
WOODLAND 1D 175
Woodland Av. PL9: Plyms 4H 143
 TQ12: Kingsk 7J 109
 TQ14: Teignm 2K 107
Woodland Bus. Pk. TQ2: Torq 5A 112
Woodland Cl. EX16: Bam 3G 33
 EX32: B'aple 5K 19
 PL21: Ivy 4F 145
 TQ2: Torq 5A 112
 TQ12: Den 2G 101
Woodland Ct. EX32: B'aple 5F 19
 (off Summerland St.)
 PL21: Ivy 4E 144

Woodland Dr. EX2: Sow 2D 72
 PL7: Plymp 7J 137
 PL8: Brixt 2J 149
Woodland Gdns. TQ14: Teignm 4J 107
 (off Lwr. Brimley Rd.)
WOODLAND HEAD 1B 170
Woodland M. EX5: Broadc 6D 52
 (off Woodland Rd.)
Woodland Pk. EX39: Nort 1F 23
 TQ3: Paig 7H 115
Woodland Rd. EX1: Pin 5C 66
 EX5: Broadc 6C 52
 PL7: Plymp 5K 137
 PL21: Ivy 4D 144
 (not continuous)
 TQ2: Torq 5A 112
 TQ9: H'ford 6B 100
 TQ12: Den 2G 101
 TQ13: Ashb 4H 99
Woodlands 2A 176
Woodlands EX5: New C 7C 50
 EX9: Bud S 7A 82
 EX10: Sidm 6B 84
 EX34: C Mar 2E 12
 PL9: Plyms 6G 143
 PL20: Dous 4K 127
 TQ7: Chur 1B 156
 TQ12: Kingst 1G 105
Woodlands Cvn. Pk. 1D 152
Woodlands Cl. EX33: Know 1K 15
 TQ7: Chur 1B 156
 TQ14: Teignm 4J 107
Woodlands Copse
 TQ12: Kingst 1G 105
Woodlands Ct. EX8: Exmth 1D 76
 PL5: Plym 7F 131
Woodlands Dr. EX8: Exmth 1D 76
Woodlands End PL6: Plym 5E 132
Woodlands Gdns.
 TQ12: New A 2J 109
Woodlands La. PL6: Plym 2G 137
Woodlands Leisure Pk. 1D 152
Woodlands Rd. TQ12: New A 2J 109
Woodlands Wlk. TQ13: Bov T 7B 92
Woodlands Way EX5: Clyst M 2J 73
Woodland Ter. EX39: Bide 3F 23
 (off North Rd.)
 PL4: Plym 2H 9 (1A 142)
 PL21: Ivy 5F 145
 TQ6: Kingsw 6G 125
Woodland Ter. La.
 PL4: Plym 2H 9 (1A 142)
Woodland Vw. EX22: Hols 3C 34
 EX35: Lynt 3H 13
Woodland Wood Local Nature Reserve
 . . . . .6G 131
Wood La. EX5: Chri 3J 63
 EX8: Exmth 3F 77
 EX17: Morc 1B 38
 EX34: C Mar 7D 12
 TQ6: Kingsw 6G 125
 TQ7: Slap 2J 159
 TQ12: A'well, Two O 6D 108
Woodlark La. EX31: Rou 7K 17
WOODLEIGH 3D 175
Woodleigh Cl. EX4: Exe 1D 64
Woodleigh Pk. TQ14: Shal 7H 107
Woodleigh Rd. TQ12: New A 1C 108
Woodley La. EX5: New C 7A 50
Woodleys Dr. EX10: New P 5F 81
Woodleys Mdw. TQ2: Torq 4A 116
Woodmans Cres.
 EX14: Hon 4F 55
WOODMANTON 7C 78 (2A 172)
Woodmead Rd. DT7: Lym R 5J 91
 EX13: Axmin 4G 89
Woodmere Way TQ12: Kingst 5H 105
Wood Pk. PL6: Plym 2E 132
 PL21: Ivy 3H 145
Wood Pk. La. EX34: Ber 4B 12
Woodpark La. TQ3: Marl 5E 110
Woodpecker Way EX6: Cher 2C 62
 PL19: Whit 7K 59
Woodroffe Mdw. DT7: Lym R 4H 91
Woodroffe Vs. DT7: Lym R 4H 91
The Woods TQ1: Torq 2G 117
Woodside
 PL4: Plym 2J 9 (1A 142)
Woodside Av. PL9: Hooe 6D 142
Woodside Cl. EX13: Ray H 1D 90
 PL21: Ivy 5H 145
Woodside Ct. EX31: Rou 7A 18
 EX35: Lynm 2J 13
 PL7: Plymp 5A 138
Woodside Dr. TQ1: Torq 2E 116
Woodside La. PL4: Plym . . .2J 9 (1A 142)
Woodside Ter. PL20: C'stone 6C 126
Woodside Wlk. EX14: Hon 3G 55
 (off Langford Av.)
Woods La. EX5: Up E 1E 50
Woods Pasture EX5: Cran 3C 68

Woodstock Gdns. PL5: Plym 2C 134
Woodstock Rd. EX2: Won 7K 65
WOODTOWN
 EX39, nr. Bideford 1C 163
 EX39, nr. Littleham 1C 163
Woodvale Ct. TQ12: New A 1E 108
 (off East St.)
Wood Vw. TQ12: New A 1D 108
Woodview Pk. PL9: Elb 6H 143
Wood Vw. Rd. TQ4: Paig 7E 118
Wood Vw. Ter. PL21: Erm 3H 147
Woodville EX31: B'aple 5B 18
Woodville Av. PL20: Prin 6C 60
Woodville Cl. EX31: B'aple 5B 18
Woodville Rd. EX2: Exe 2E 70
 EX8: Exmth 4C 76
 PL2: Plym 4E 134
 TQ1: Torq 7D 112
Woodward Rd. EX16: Tive 6B 40
Woodwater La. EX2: Won 1K 71
 (not continuous)
Woodway PL9: Plyms 5H 143
Woodway Cl. TQ14: Teignm 2J 107
Woodway Dr. TQ14: Teignm 3J 107
Woodway Rd. TQ14: Teignm 2J 107
Woodway St. TQ13: Chud 1C 94
WOODY BAY 2C 161
Woody Bay Station (Rail) 2C 161
Woody La. EX35: Lynt 4J 13
WOOLACOMBE 6A 10 (2A 160)
Woolacombe & Mortehoe Golf Course
 . . . . .3C 10 (2A 160)
Woolacombe Bay Holiday Village
 . . . . .5C 10
Woolacombe Ct. EX34: Wool 6B 10
Woolacombe Ri. EX34: Wool 6D 10
Woolacombe Rd. PL20: Bere A 2D 128
Woolacombe Sands Holiday Pk. 6C 10
Woolacombe Sta. Rd.
 EX34: Wool 6D 10
Woolacombe Tourist Information Centre
 . . . . .6A 10 (2A 160)
Woolaway Av. EX6: Exmin 2D 74
Woolbarn Lawn EX32: B'aple 5J 19
Woolbrook Cl. EX10: Sidm 4B 84
Woolbrook Mead EX10: Sidm 3A 84
Woolbrook Mdws. EX10: Sidm 3B 84
Woolbrook Pk. EX10: Sidm 3B 84
Woolbrook Ri. EX10: Sidm 3B 84
Woolbrook Rd.
 EX10: Sidm, Stow 2A 84
Wool Cl. EX15: Cull 3F 45
Woolcombe La. EX10: Sidm 5C 84
 PL21: Ivy 5H 145
WOOLCOTTS 1D 165
Woolcott Way EX15: Cull 5G 45
WOOLFARDISWORTHY
 EX17 . . . . .3C 165
 EX39 . . . . .2B 28 (1B 162)
Woolhanger's La. EX34: Ber 4D 12
Woollcombe Av. PL7: Plymp 5C 138
WOOLLEY 2A 162
WOOLMINSTONE 3D 167
Woolms Mdw. PL21: Ivy 5E 144
WOOLSERY 2B 28 (1B 162)
Woolsery Av. EX4: Whip 4A 66
Woolsery Cl. EX4: Whip 4A 66
Woolsery Gro. EX4: Whip 4K 65
Woolster Ct. PL4: Plym 5F 9
WOOLSTON 3D 175
WOOLSTON GREEN 1D 175
WOOLWELL 2E 132 (1B 174)
Woolwell Cres. PL6: Plym 2D 132
Woolwell Dr. PL6: Plym 3D 132
Woolwell Rd. PL6: Plym 2D 132
Woolwell Shop. Cen. 2E 132
WOOTTON FITZPAINE 1D 173
Worcester Cres. EX15: Will 4D 44
Wordland Cross
 EX17: Cher F 3J 39
Wordsworth Av. EX31: B'aple 2E 18
Wordsworth Cl. EX8: Exmth 7K 75
 TQ2: Torq 7A 112
Wordsworth Cres. PL2: Plym 4E 134
Wordsworth Rd. PL2: Plym 4E 134
The Works EX16: Tive 4C 40
The World of Country Life
 . . . . .6J 77 (2A 172)
Worthele Cl. PL21: Ivy 4E 144
Worth Rd. EX34: Ilfra 3J 11
WOTTER 1F 129 (1B 174)
Wotton Cotts. EX4: Pin 2B 66
Wotton La. EX8: Lymp 6J 75
WRAFTON 6K 15 (3A 160)
Wrafton Rd. EX33: Brau, Wraf 5J 15
WRANGATON 1E 146
Wrangaton Golf Course
 . . . . .1D 146 (2C 175)
Wrangaton La. TQ10: Wran 2D 146
Wrangaton Rd. PL21: Bitta 3C 146
WRANGWAY 2B 166

WRANTAGE 1D 167
Wreford's Cl. EX4: Exe 1C 64
Wreford's Dr. EX4: Exe 1D 64
Wreford's La. EX4: Exe 1D 64
Wreford's Link EX4: Exe 1D 64
   (not continuous)
Wren Cl. EX14: Hon 5E 54
  EX39: Nort 6F 21
Wren Ct. TQ5: Brixh 4E 122
Wren Gdns. PL7: Plymp 5K 137
Wren Hill TQ5: Brixh 4E 122
Wren Pk. 3K 111
Wrens Ga. PL9: Plyms 4F 143
Wrentham Est. EX4: Exe 4G 65
Wressing Vw. EX15: Kent 6A 46
Wrey Av. EX31: B'aple 5C 18
WREYLAND 6J 63 (2B 170)
Wright Cl. PL1: Dev 1D 140
Wright Dr. EX17: Cop 6C 38
Wright's La. TQ1: Torq 6C 112
Wrights La. PL8: New F 5H 149
Wrigwell La. TQ12: Ipp 7J 101
Wrinkleberry La.
  EX39: High C 6G 27
Wroxall Grange TQ1: Torq 2E 116
   (off Grafton Rd.)
Wulphere Cl. EX14: Dunk 7G 47
Wyatt Av. PL2: Plym 4E 134
Wyatt Cl. TQ13: Bov T 4E 92
Wyatts La. PL19: Tavi 3H 59
Wychall Orchard
  EX12: Seat 4E 86
Wychall Pk. EX12: Seat 3D 86
Wychwood Cl. EX7: Daw 3H 97
Wycliffe Rd. PL3: Plym 7C 136
WYKE .1C 171
WYKE GREEN 7H 89
Wykeham Dr. PL2: Plym 4E 134
Wyke La. EX13: Wy G 7H 89
Wyke Rd.
  EX13: Axmin, Wy G 6H 89
Wykes Rd. EX1: Heav 5J 65
Wymering Ct. TQ14: Teignm 2J 107
Wynards Cl. EX2: Exe 5F 7
Wynards Cl. EX9: E Bud 1D 82
Wynards La.
  EX2: Exe 5F 7 (7F 65)
Wynards Rd. EX9: E Bud 1D 82
Wyndham Av. EX1: Heav 6J 65
Wyndham La.
  PL1: Plym 3A 8 (2G 141)
Wyndham M. PL1: Plym 3A 8
Wyndham Pl. PL1: Plym 3A 8
Wyndham Rd. EX5: Silv 2H 51

Wyndham Sq.
  PL1: Plym 3A 8 (2G 141)
Wyndham St. E.
  PL1: Plym 3B 8 (2H 141)
Wyndham St. W.
  PL1: Plym 3A 8 (2G 141)
Wyndthorpe Gdns. EX34: Ilfra 2J 11
   (off Castle Hill)
Wynford Rd. EX4: Exe 3J 65
Wyoming Cl. PL3: Plym 5D 136
Wyre Cl. TQ4: Paig 5G 119
Wythburn Gdns. PL6: Plym 7E 132

Y

Yacht Haven Quay PL9: Plyms 4D 142
Yalberton Ind. Est. TQ4: Paig 4D 118
   (not continuous)
Yalberton Rd. TQ4: Paig 4C 118
Yalberton Tor Ind. Est.
  TQ4: Paig 4D 118
Yallop Way EX14: Hon 5E 54
Yannon Dr. TQ14: Teignm 3G 107
Yannon La. TQ12: Kingsk 7H 109
   (not continuous)
The Yannons TQ14: Teignm 3H 107
Yannons Rd. TQ4: Paig 5E 118
Yannon Ter. TQ14: Teignm 3H 107
YARCOMBE 3C 167
Yarda Wlk. PL8: Brixt 3H 149
   (off Holmbush Way)
Yarde Cl. EX10: Sidm 3C 84
Yarde Hill Orchard
  EX10: Sidm 3C 84
Yardelands EX10: Sidm 3C 84
Yardelands Cl. EX10: Sidm 3C 84
Yarde Mead EX10: Sidm 3C 84
Yardley Gdns. PL6: Plym 7F 133
Yards La. TQ5: Brixh 7D 122
Yarlington Mill EX5: Cran 2C 68
YARNACOTT 1H 25
Yarner Wood Nature Trails 3B 170
YARNSCOMBE 1D 163
Yarrow Mead PL9: Elb 7K 143
YAWL 1D 173
YEALMBRIDGE 1D 150
Yealmbury Hill PL8: Y'ton 2B 150
Yealmbury Vs. PL8: Y'ton 2B 150
Yealm Gro. TQ5: Brixh 6J 111
Yealm Pk. PL8: Y'ton 2A 150
Yealmpstone Cl.
  PL7: Plymp 5D 138
Yealmpstone Dr.
  PL7: Plymp 5E 138

YEALMPTON 2B 150 (2B 174)
Yealm Rd. PL8: New F 5G 149
Yealm Vw. Rd.
  PL8: New F 6J 149
Yeats Cl. PL5: Plym 1H 135
Yellaford Way
  EX31: Bick 6A 18
YELLAND 7B 16 (3A 160)
Yelland Rd.
  EX31: Frem, Yell 6B 16
Yellowmead Rd. PL2: Plym 4F 135
YELVERTON 6G 127 (1B 174)
Yelverton Bus. Pk.
  PL20: C'stone 6D 126
Yelverton Cl. PL5: Plym 7D 130
Yelverton Golf Course 1B 174
Yelverton Golf Driving Range
  . . . . .7C 126
Yelverton Ter. PL19: Tavi 3K 59
  PL20: Yelv 6G 127
   (off Meavy La.)
Yeo Cl. PL3: Plym 6D 136
Yeo Dr. EX39: App 3H 21
YEOFORD 1B 170
Yeoford Station (Rail) 1B 170
Yeoford Way EX2: Mar B 5G 71
Yeoland La. EX32: Swim 2H 25
The Yeolands TQ9: Sto G 3B 120
Yeo La. EX20: N Taw 4A 36
Yeolland La. PL21: Ivy 4H 145
Yeolland Pk. PL21: Ivy 4H 145
YEOLMBRIDGE 2B 168
Yeomans Way
  PL7: Plymp 5D 138
YEO MILL 1C 165
Yeo Pk. PL8: Y'ton 1D 150
Yeo Rd. EX31: C'nor 1E 16
Yeo Vale Cross Ind. Est.
  EX17: Lap 3J 37
Yeo Vale Rd. EX32: B'aple 3E 18
Yerris Rd. EX15: Kent 7A 46
Yes Tor .1D 169
Yettington Rd. EX9: E Bud 1C 82
Yew Cl. EX14: Hon 5C 54
  TQ5: Brixh 6B 122
Yewdale Gdns. PL6: Plym 1E 136
The Yews PL6: Robo 1D 132
Yew Tree Cl. EX4: Exe 3H 65
  EX8: Exmth 1E 76
Yew Tree Dr. TQ12: Kingst 5H 105
Yolhey La. TQ12: A'well 7F 109
Yonder Acre Way
  EX5: Cran 2E 68
Yonder Cl. EX11: Ott M 4D 80

Yonder Cnr. EX11: Ott M 4D 80
   (off Chapel La.)
Yonder Mdw. TQ9: Sto G 3B 120
Yonder Mt. EX13: Mus 7D 90
Yonder St. EX11: Ott M 4D 80
  PL9: Hooe 6C 142
YONDERTOWN 7F 129
Yon St. TQ12: Kingsk 1F 111
York Cl. EX8: Exmth 2G 77
  EX13: Axmin 3J 89
  EX14: Fen 2G 53
York Cres. EX14: Fen 2G 53
  TQ1: Torq 5E 112
Yorke Rd. TQ6: Dartm 7D 124
York Gdns. TQ4: Paig 3H 119
York Ho. EX4: Exe 1F 7 (5F 65)
York Pl. EX15: Cull 2H 45
  EX39: Bide 2F 23
  PL2: Dev 7E 134
York Ri. EX39: Bide 3E 22
York Rd. EX4: Exe 1F 7 (5F 65)
  EX12: Seat 5E 86
  PL5: Plym 3D 134
  PL11: Torp 1A 140
  TQ1: Torq 5E 112
  TQ4: Paig 3G 119
York St. EX10: Sidm 7C 84
   (not continuous)
  PL1: Dev 2D 140
York Ter. EX4: Exe 1G 7 (5G 65)
  PL2: Plym 6E 134
York Vs. TQ1: Torq 5E 112
   (off Babbacombe Rd.)
Youings Dr. EX31: B'aple 1F 19
Youldons Cl. TQ9: H'ford 6C 100
Youldon Way PL20: Horr 3E 126
Youngaton Rd. EX39: W Ho 5B 20
Younghayes Rd. EX5: Cran 4B 68
Young's Pk. La. TQ4: Good 3J 119
Young's Pk. Rd. TQ4: Good 3J 119

Z

ZEAL MONACHORUM 3B 164
Zeal Rd. EX6: Dunsf 5C 62
Zephyr Cres. EX32: B'aple 4G 19
Zeth Hill La. PL21: Ivy 2D 144
Zig Zag Path EX9: Bud S 7B 82
Zion Pl. PL21: Ivy 4G 145
  TQ6: Dartm 1A 124 (5F 125)
Zion Rd. TQ2: Torq 1B 116
Zion's Pl. EX32: B'aple 5E 18
   (off Litchdon St.)
Zion St. PL1: Plym 6E 8 (3J 141)

HOSPITALS, HOSPICES and selected HEALTHCARE FACILITIES covered by this atlas.

N.B. Where it is not possible to name these facilities on the map, the reference given is for the road in which they are situated.

AXMINSTER HOSPITAL 3H **89**
Chard Road
AXMINSTER
EX13 5DU
Tel: 01297 630400

BIDEFORD HOSPITAL 3E **22**
Abbotsham Road
BIDEFORD
EX39 3AG
Tel: 01271 322577

BRIXHAM COMMUNITY HOSPITAL 5E **122**
Greenswood Road
BRIXHAM
TQ5 9HW
Tel: 01803 881399

BUDLEIGH SALTERTON HOSPITAL 6D **82**
East Budleigh Road
BUDLEIGH SALTERTON
EX9 6HF
Tel: 01395 442020

**CHILDREN'S HOSPICE SOUTH WEST
LITTLE BRIDGE HOUSE** 6G **17**
Redlands Road
Fremington
BARNSTAPLE
EX31 2PZ
Tel: 01271 325270

CREDITON HOSPITAL 6F **39**
Western Road
CREDITON
EX17 3NH
Tel: 01363 775588

DAWLISH COMMUNITY HOSPITAL 4G **97**
Barton Terrace
DAWLISH
EX7 9DH
Tel: 01626 868500

DERRIFORD HOSPITAL 6C **132**
Derriford Road
PLYMOUTH
PL6 8DH
Tel: 0845 155 8155

**EXETER COMMUNITY HOSPITAL
(WHIPTON)** 5B **66**
Hospital Lane
EXETER
EX1 3RB
Tel: 01392 208333

EXETER NUFFIELD HEALTH HOSPITAL 1H **71**
Wonford Road
EXETER
EX2 4UG
Tel: 01392 262110

EXMOUTH HOSPITAL 5D **76**
Claremont Grove
EXMOUTH
EX8 2JN
Tel: 01395 279684

FRANKLYN HOSPITAL 2C **70**
Franklyn Drive
EXETER
EX2 9HS
Tel: 01392 208400

GLENBOURNE UNIT 7C **132**
Morlaix Drive
Derriford
PLYMOUTH
PL6 5AF
Tel: 01752 763103

HOLSWORTHY HOSPITAL 1D **34**
Dobles Lane
HOLSWORTHY
EX22 6JQ
Tel: 01409 253424

HONITON HOSPITAL 4F **55**
Marlpits Lane
HONITON
EX14 2DE
Tel: 01404 540540

HOSPISCARE 7K **7** (1J **71**)
Dryden Road
EXETER
EX2 5JJ
Tel: 01392 688000

ILFRACOMBE TYRRELL HOSPITAL 3H **11**
St Brannock's Park Road
ILFRACOMBE
EX34 8JF
Tel: 01271 863448

LANGDON HOSPITAL 7B **96**
Exeter Road
DAWLISH
EX7 0NR
Tel: 01626 888372

LEE MILL UNIT 4B **144**
Beech Road
IVYBRIDGE
PL21 9HL
Tel: 01752 314800

LYNTON RESOURCE CENTRE 2G **13**
Lee Road
LYNTON
EX35 6BP
Tel: 01598 753226

**MINOR INJURIES UNIT
(BIDEFORD HOSPITAL)** 3E **22**
Abbotsham Road
BIDEFORD
EX39 3AG
Tel: 01271 322577

**MINOR INJURIES UNIT
(CUMBERLAND CENTRE)** 3E **140**
Damerel Close
PLYMOUTH
PL1 4JZ
Tel: 0845 155 8003

MINOR INJURIES UNIT (DAWLISH) 4G **97**
Dawlish Community Hospital
Barton Terrace
DAWLISH
EX7 9DH
Tel: 01626 868500

**MINOR INJURIES UNIT
(ILFRACOMBE TYRRELL HOSPITAL)** 3H **11**
St Brannock's Park Road
ILFRACOMBE
EX34 8JF
Tel: 01271 863448

MINOR INJURIES UNIT (KINGSBRIDGE) 3F **157**
Plymouth Road
KINGSBRIDGE
TQ7 1AT
Tel: 01548 852349

**MINOR INJURIES UNIT
(LYNTON RESOURCE CENTRE)** 2G **13**
Lee Road
LYNTON
EX35 6BP
Tel: 01598 753226

**MINOR INJURIES UNIT
(NEWTON ABBOT)** 6E **104**
West Golds Road
NEWTON ABBOT
TQ12 2TS
Tel: 01626 324500

**MINOR INJURIES UNIT
(NORTH DEVON DISTRICT HOSPITAL)** 1F **19**
Raleigh Park
BARNSTAPLE
EX31 4JB
Tel: 01271 322577

**MINOR INJURIES UNIT
(SOUTH MOLTON HOSPITAL)** 6C **26**
Widgery Drive
SOUTH MOLTON
EX36 4DP
Tel: 01769 573811

**MINOR INJURIES UNIT
(TORRINGTON HOSPITAL)** 2C **30**
Calf Street
TORRINGTON
EX38 7BJ
Tel: 01805 623222

MORETONHAMPSTEAD HOSPITAL 6H **61**
Ford Street
Moretonhampstead
NEWTON ABBOT
TQ13 8LN
Tel: 01647 440217

MOUNT GOULD HOSPITAL 1C **142**
Mount Gould Road
PLYMOUTH
PL4 7QD
Tel: 01752 268011

MOUNT STUART PRIVATE HOSPITAL 6B **112**
St Vincent's Road
TORQUAY
TQ1 4UP
Tel: 01803 313881

NEWTON ABBOT COMMUNITY HOSPITAL 6E **104**
West Golds Road
NEWTON ABBOT
TQ12 2TS
Tel: 01626 324500

**NHS WALK-IN CENTRE
(EXETER- SIDWELL STREET)** 3F **7**
Unit 4
31 Sidwell Street
EXETER
EX4 6NN
Tel: 01392 276892

Hospitals, Hospices and selected Healthcare Facilities

NHS WALK-IN CENTRE
(EXETER- WONFORD) 1J **71**
Barrack Road
EXETER
EX2 5DW
Tel: 01392 406304

NORTH DEVON DISTRICT HOSPITAL 2G **19**
Raleigh Park
BARNSTAPLE
EX31 4JB
Tel: 01271 322577

NORTH DEVON HOSPICE 7G **19**
Deer Park Road
BARNSTAPLE
EX32 0HU
Tel: 01271 344248

OKEHAMPTON COMMUNITY HOSPITAL 3C **48**
Cavell Way
OKEHAMPTON
EX20 1PN
Tel: 01837 658000

OTTERY ST MARY HOSPITAL 4A **80**
Keegan Close
OTTERY ST. MARY
EX11 1DN
Tel: 01404 816000

PAIGNTON HOSPITAL 1H **119**
Church Street
PAIGNTON
TQ3 3AG
Tel: 01803 557425

PLYMOUTH NUFFIELD HEALTH HOSPITAL
. . . . .6C **132**
Derriford Road
PLYMOUTH
PL6 8BG
Tel: 01752 547451

THE REI 6C **132**
Derriford Road
Crownhill
PLYMOUTH
PL6 8DH
Tel: 0845 155 8094

ROWCROFT HOSPICE 7A **112**
Avenue Road
TORQUAY
TQ2 5LS
Tel: 01803 210800

ROYAL DEVON & EXETER HOSPITAL
(HEAVITREE) 4J **7** (6H **65**)
Gladstone Road
EXETER
EX1 2ED
Tel: 01392 411611

ROYAL DEVON & EXETER HOSPITAL
(WONFORD) 7K **7** (1J **71**)
Barrack Road
EXETER
EX2 5DW
Tel: 01392 411611

ST LUKE'S HOSPICE 6B **142**
Stamford Road
PLYMOUTH
PL9 9XA
Tel: 01752 401172

SCOTT HOSPITAL, PLYMOUTH
CHILD DEVELOPMENT CENTRE 5F **135**
Scott Business Park
Beacon Park Road
PLYMOUTH
PL2 2PQ
Tel: 0845 155 8174

SEATON & DISTRICT
COMMUNITY HOSPITAL 4E **86**
Valley View
SEATON
EX12 2UU
Tel: 01297 23901

SIDMOUTH VICTORIA HOSPITAL 6B **84**
All Saint's Road
SIDMOUTH
EX10 8EW
Tel: 01395 512482

SOUTH HAMS HOSPITAL 3F **157**
Plymouth Road
KINGSBRIDGE
TQ7 1AT
Tel: 01548 852349

SOUTH MOLTON HOSPITAL 6C **26**
Widgery Drive
SOUTH MOLTON
EX36 4DP
Tel: 01769 572164

TAVISTOCK HOSPITAL 4H **59**
Spring Hill
TAVISTOCK
PL19 8LD
Tel: 01822 612233

TIVERTON & DISTRICT HOSPITAL 3C **40**
Kennedy Way
TIVERTON
EX16 6NT
Tel: 01884 235400

TORBAY HOSPITAL .5K **111**
Newton Road
TORQUAY
TQ2 7AA
Tel: 01803 614567

TORBAY HOSPITAL (ANNEXE) 4K **111**
Newton Road
TORQUAY
TQ2 7BA
Tel: 01803 614567

TORRINGTON HOSPITAL 2C **30**
Calf Street
TORRINGTON
EX38 7BJ
Tel: 01805 622208

TOTNES COMMUNITY HOSPITAL 5E **102**
Coronation Road
TOTNES
TQ9 5GH
Tel: 01803 862622

WONFORD HOUSE HOSPITAL 1J **71**
Dryden Road
EXETER
EX2 5AF
Tel: 01392 208866

SAFETY CAMERA INFORMATION

PocketGPSWorld.com's CamerAlert is a self-contained speed and red light camera warning system for
SatNavs and Android or Apple iOS smartphones/tablets. Visit www.cameralert.com to download.

Safety camera locations are publicised by the Safer Roads Partnership which operates them in order to encourage drivers to comply
with speed limits at these sites. It is the driver's absolute responsibility to be aware of and to adhere to speed limits at all times.

By showing this safety camera information it is the intention of Geographers' A-Z Map Company Ltd., to encourage
safe driving and greater awareness of speed limits and vehicle speed. Data accurate at time of printing.